Building Applied Models for Problem Solving

Shalin Hai-Jew
https://orcid.org/0000-0002-8863-0175
Hutchinson Community College, USA

IGI Global
Scientific Publishing
Publishing Tomorrow's Research Today

Vice President of Editorial	Melissa Wagner
Director of Acquisitions	Mikaela Felty
Director of Book Development	Jocelynn Hessler
Production Manager	Mike Brehm
Cover Design	Jose Rosado

Published in the United States of America by
IGI Global Scientific Publishing
701 East Chocolate Avenue
Hershey, PA, 17033, USA
Tel: 717-533-8845 | Fax: 717-533-7115
Website: https://www.igi-global.com E-mail: cust@igi-global.com

Library of Congress Cataloging-in-Publication Data

Names: Hai-Jew, Shalin editor
Title: Building applied models for problem solving / edited by Shalin Hai-Jew.
Description: Hershey, PA : IGI Global Scientific Publishing, [2026] | Includes bibliographical references and index. | Summary: "This book presents various research works and case studies related to the building and use of applied models for problem solving"-- Provided by publisher.
Identifiers: LCCN 2025025990 (print) | LCCN 2025025991 (ebook) | ISBN 9798337333014 h/c | ISBN 9798337333021 s/c | ISBN 9798337333038 ebook
Subjects: LCSH: Computer simulation | Mathematical models | Problem solving--Methodology | Decision making--Methodology
Classification: LCC QA76.9.C65 B835 2026 (print) | LCC QA76.9.C65 (ebook)
LC record available at https://lccn.loc.gov/2025025990
LC ebook record available at https://lccn.loc.gov/2025025991

British Cataloguing in Publication Data
A Cataloguing in Publication record for this book is available from the British Library.

Table of Contents

Research into Applied Models

Section 4
Case Studies in Applied Modeling

Detailed Table of Contents

The creation of applied models is anchored in a rich tapestry of theories and guiding principles that shape their structure, function, and impact. This chapter explores the conceptual foundations underpinning model development, drawing on insights from diverse disciplines to highlight the interplay between theory and practice. It examines the principles that ensure models are both methodologically sound and contextually adaptable, addressing the tension between generalizable frameworks and problem-specific customization. By tracing the journey from abstract concepts to operational tools, the discussion reveals how successful models synthesize analytical rigor with creative adaptability. Ultimately, the chapter underscores the importance of grounding applied models in solid theoretical underpinnings while maintaining the flexibility to evolve alongside the dynamic challenges they are designed to address.

In the age of big data, constructing applied models from multiple data sources is crucial for solving complex problems in various sectors, including business, healthcare, finance, and smart city management. This chapter discusses methodologies, challenges, and best practices in building robust models by integrating diverse data types, such as structured, unstructured, real-time, and historical data. Key steps, including data preprocessing, feature engineering, and selecting the appropriate modeling approach, are outlined. The chapter also examines the importance of frameworks like CRISP-DM and DIKW in guiding model development. Real-world applications demonstrate the power of multi-source models, though challenges in data security, complexity, and model interpretability remain. Future advancements, including AI, edge computing, and federated learning, promise to enhance the effectiveness of these models.

Applied models are indispensable tools for understanding complex phenomena, enabling predictions, decision-making, and problem-solving in various contexts. Building applied models from data is one of the most powerful methodologies in today's data-driven world, where organizations and researchers across fields increasingly rely on large datasets to inform their models. This chapter will explore the process of building applied models using data, emphasizing the methods, challenges, and considerations that come with this approach. By discussing how data-driven models are constructed, tested, and refined, the chapter will provide a comprehensive overview for administrators, faculty, staff, and researchers working with data to create accurate, generalizable, and actionable models. The chapter will focus on methods for ensuring the robustness, sensitivity, and adaptability of these models to both local and global contexts.

Crisis events—from natural disasters to health emergencies—require rapid, accurate, responsible communication. In digital media's fast-paced landscape, structured approaches are essential to maintain credibility, relevance, and engagement. This chapter presents an applied communication model for crisis reporting that integrates case studies of real-time coverage during pandemics, floods, and unrest. The model comprises modular components: source verification, message framing, multimodal dissemination, audience feedback loops, and platform-specific calibration. Emphasizing adaptability in newsrooms, government, and humanitarian settings, it supports future reuse. Development combines field observation, social media analytics, and simulation (in vitro/in vivo) testing. Cultural sensitivity and regional language integration enhance effectiveness. By systematizing communication, this research advances public trust, counters misinformation, and equips practitioners with practical tools for high-stakes reporting.

experimental research, randomization is reinterpreted as an instructional instrument aimed at cultivating adaptability, metacognitive awareness, and creative reasoning. The chapter draws on constructivist and sociocultural theories to present a university-level intervention in a course on English morphosyntax in which grammar instruction was randomized. The students participated in a series of syntactic tasks that were not anticipated and that prompted them to adopt a flexible mindset and engage in reflective practice. The findings indicate that pedagogical randomization has the potential to enhance conceptual understanding and instructional creativity. The chapter presents a replicable model for integrating structured unpredictability into teacher education, demonstrating how randomness can support dynamic, context-aware, and learner-centered instruction.

Agile methodologies have transformed software development by promoting flexibility, collaboration, and user-focused design. This paper compares major Agile frameworks—Scrum, Kanban, XP, Lean, FDD, Crystal, and SAFe—highlighting their impacts on productivity, adaptability, and teamwork. Case studies like Spotify and Toyota show that while all adhere to Agile principles, each framework differs in execution and results. Scrum offers structured planning, Kanban emphasizes visual flow, XP focuses on engineering rigor, and Lean aims to eliminate waste. SAFe and Crystal address scalability and adaptability. Though Agile boosts communication and responsiveness, it also presents challenges like cultural resistance and scaling issues. The study concludes that successful Agile adoption requires organizational readiness, leadership support, and continuous learning, emphasizing that Agile works best when tailored to specific contexts.

This chapter elucidates the construction of applied models from observational research in education as a transdisciplinary, praxis-oriented methodology for capturing and transforming complex pedagogical ecologies. Integrating theories from constructivism, experiential learning, systems thinking, and situated cognition,

academics and practitioners in supply chain management with the latest developments and encourage the exploration of new research avenues.

Section 4
Case Studies in Applied Modeling

Bibliometric analysis is a powerful tool for evaluating research trends, identifying key contributors, and mapping the intellectual structure of a scientific field. With the increasing volume of academic publications, systematic approaches are essential for deriving meaningful insights from scholarly data. This paper presents a stepwise approach to conducting bibliometric analysis using the Biblioshiny app in Bibliometrix package in R software. Bibliometrix provides a comprehensive framework for importing, processing, and visualizing bibliographic data from databases such as Web of Science, Scopus and Dimensions.ai.The paper outlines key stages of bibliometric analysis, including data collection, preprocessing, descriptive statistics, network analysis, and thematic mapping. It also explores citation analysis, co-authorship networks, and keyword co-occurrence patterns to uncover research trends and collaboration dynamics. By leveraging R's powerful statistical capabilities, this approach ensures reproducibility and flexibility in bibliometric studies.

In Colombia, small and medium-sized enterprises (SMEs) are the backbone of the national economy, representing 99.5% of the formal business fabric and generating approximately 79% of the country's employment (BBVA Research, 2023). However, SMEs face structural challenges, such as the scarcity of financial resources, the low adoption of sustainable technologies, and the limited capacity to implement efficient management models that balance sustainability with business competitiveness (Rizos et al., 2021; Lieder & Rashid, 2020). To address these problems, the Comprehensive Optimization Model in Sustainability (MOIS) is proposed, a methodological tool designed to strengthen the business processes of SMEs in Colombia based on a comprehensive approach that combines sustainability, logistics efficiency and

Preface

In academia, research, and IT, the editor's main career areas, applied models have always played a role. Then, most recently, during a multi-year stint in full-time grant-funded work (until the federal funds for academia were clawed back across the board in the U.S.), several grant NOFOs (notices of funding opportunities) had mentioned the desire for the grant recipients to create models from their programs and projects and research and learning.

That sparked an interest in this edited collection, *Building Applied Models for Problem Solving*.

WHAT ARE APPLIED MODELS?

An applied model may seem like something esoteric and intellectual, when in fact, such practical models are all around. An applied model is an abstraction of some in-world phenomena or dynamic. These applied models are used to help people understand complexity, arrive at certain conclusions, predict an outcome, make certain decisions, and otherwise engage the world with heightened knowledge, skills, and abilities / attitudes. Some models are generalist and apply to the wider word.

Other models are designed for particular contexts and purposes. Applied models may be expressed in different ways. They may be expressed as text, symbols, maths, diagrams and visuals, and mixed modalities. Some are emplaced in software programs. Some inform digital simulations on background. Applied models are built in various ways...abstracting from projects, data, observations, research, theorizing, and other approaches, in stand-alone ways and in combinatorial ones. The abstracting of in-world phenomena is an important way of understanding the world by isolating particular elements and over-simplifying selectively. Ideally, applied models map well to reality and add value for those who will adopt them. After all, the models may illuminate a context, a system, a procedure, or a decision.

For many, applied models are heritable. Those who use inherited models may assess them for validity and for applicability to local conditions. Those that function with insight and elegance may be kept on into near-perpetuity. Modular pieces may be added to those models for extended capabilities, heightened efficiencies, local adaptability, and new functions. Infused adaptations may be introduced for a better fit to the local (cultural, organizational, or other) context.

WHERE DO APPLIED MODELS COME FROM?

Applied models can be abstractions from stand-alone and mixed sources: data and data patterns (such as from statistical analyses), in-world and professional observations, experimentation, fieldwork, interviews, focus groups, surveys, case studies, theories, hypothesizing, and others. Applied models may be prompted from Generative AI as well. Depending on the model creator, all available information may be exploited.

SOME EXPRESSIONS OF APPLIED MODELS

A model may be expressed in text, symbols, mathematics, spatial depictions (maps, diagrams), and other modalities. A model may be instantiated in code and programs. It may be manifested in codebooks (whether manual or computational, the latter in CAQDAS tools).

Applied models, by definition, are practical. They are to be applied in real-world contexts to benefit awareness, decision-making, design, and other work. As with paper prototyping, models introduce efficiencies and lowered costs.

Models are designed with non-obvious insights in mind. They are informed by professional values and ethics. They are informed by thinkers. They are informed by real-world practices in the field.

Some models are designed for particular contexts…but may be picked up, adapted (revised), and adopted for uses in other contexts. How well an applied model generalizes in part based on the model's design…but also on the inheritor's capabilities with abstraction and adoption.

Models may be built into various systems: techniques (processes, procedures) and technologies (simulations, software, programs). They may be overlaid with strategy and tactics.

Years ago, a colleague and I were discussing research. We discussed how much effort it may take just to get to one assertable sentence. That observation seems to apply to the making of applied models as well.

ORGANIZATION OF THE BOOK

Part 1: Building Applied Models

Chapter 1: Theories and Principles Governing the Development of Applied Models

The creation of applied models is anchored in a rich tapestry of theories and guiding principles that shape their structure, function, and impact. This chapter explores the conceptual foundations underpinning model development, drawing on insights from diverse disciplines to highlight the interplay between theory and practice. It examines the principles that ensure models are both methodologically sound and contextually adaptable, addressing the tension between generalizable frameworks and problem-specific customization. By tracing the journey from abstract concepts to operational tools, the discussion reveals how successful models synthesize analytical rigor with creative adaptability. Ultimately, the chapter underscores the importance of grounding applied models in solid theoretical underpinnings while maintaining the flexibility to evolve alongside the dynamic challenges they are designed to address.

Chapter 2: Building Applied Models from Multiple Sources

In the age of big data, constructing applied models from multiple data sources is crucial for solving complex problems in various sectors, including business, healthcare, finance, and smart city management. This chapter discusses methodologies, challenges, and best practices in building robust models by integrating diverse data types, such as structured, unstructured, real-time, and historical data. Key steps, including data preprocessing, feature engineering, and selecting the appropriate modeling approach, are outlined. The chapter also examines the importance of frameworks like CRISP-DM and DIKW in guiding model development. Real-world applications demonstrate the power of multi-source models, though challenges in data security, complexity, and model interpretability remain. Future advancements, including AI, edge computing, and federated learning, promise to enhance the effectiveness of these models.

Chapter 3: Building Applied Models from Data: Approaches, Methods, and Challenges

Applied models are indispensable tools for understanding complex phenomena, enabling predictions, decision-making, and problem-solving in various contexts. Building applied models from data is one of the most powerful methodologies in today's data-driven world, where organizations and researchers across fields increasingly rely on large datasets to inform their models. This chapter will explore the process of building applied models using data, emphasizing the methods, challenges, and considerations that come with this approach. By discussing how data-driven models are constructed, tested, and refined, the chapter will provide a comprehensive overview for administrators, faculty, staff, and researchers working with data to create accurate, generalizable, and actionable models. The chapter will focus on methods for ensuring the robustness, sensitivity, and adaptability of these models to both local and global contexts.

Chapter 4: Developing an Applied Communication Model for Crisis Reporting in Digital Media Ecosystems

Crisis events—from natural disasters to health emergencies—require rapid, accurate, responsible communication. In digital media's fast-paced landscape, structured approaches are essential to maintain credibility, relevance, and engagement. This chapter presents an applied communication model for crisis reporting that integrates case studies of real-time coverage during pandemics, floods, and unrest. The model comprises modular components: source verification, message framing, multimodal dissemination, audience feedback loops, and platform-specific calibration. Emphasizing adaptability in newsrooms, government, and humanitarian settings, it supports future reuse. Development combines field observation, social media analytics, and simulation (in vitro/in vivo) testing. Cultural sensitivity and regional language integration enhance effectiveness. By systematizing communication, this research advances public trust, counters misinformation, and equips practitioners with practical tools for high-stakes reporting.

Part 2: Inheriting, Modifying, and Evolving Applied Models

Chapter 5: The Rationales Behind the Creation of Applied Models for Problem Solving

Applied models for problem solving are not merely technical frameworks; they are deliberate constructs designed to navigate the intricate terrain between theory and practice. This chapter explores the underlying rationales that drive their creation, revealing how real-world complexities demand approaches that extend beyond abstract logic. By examining the influence of context, stakeholder needs, and the dynamic nature of problems, the discussion highlights how models become living tools—capable of adaptation and refinement over time. It also addresses the tension between model simplicity and the messy realities they aim to address, offering insights into how practitioners can balance clarity with flexibility. Ultimately, the chapter invites readers to see applied models not as static templates, but as evolving companions in the continuous journey of problem solving.

Chapter 6: Work-Based Models: Bridging Theory and Practice in Problem Solving

Work-based models offer a dynamic bridge between academic theory and real-world application, enabling professionals to address complex challenges through experiential engagement. This chapter examines how such models harness workplace environments as living laboratories, where theory is not merely applied but adapted, tested, and refined. By drawing on established frameworks and embedding them in authentic contexts, work-based approaches foster both immediate problem-solving capacity and long-term professional growth. The discussion explores key mechanisms—such as reflective practice, collaborative inquiry, and iterative learning—that enhance the integration of conceptual knowledge into daily operations. Case examples and evaluative perspectives illustrate the tangible benefits and limitations of these models, while also identifying pathways for innovation. Ultimately, the chapter positions work-based models as essential tools for cultivating adaptable, critically minded professionals capable of navigating evolving professional landscapes.

Part 3: Research into Applied Models

Chapter 7: Randomization as a Problem-Solving Tool in 21st-Century Learning

This chapter explores the pedagogical potential of randomization as a problem-solving strategy in 21st-century education. Departing from its conventional application in experimental research, randomization is reinterpreted as an instructional instrument aimed at cultivating adaptability, metacognitive awareness, and creative reasoning. The chapter draws on constructivist and sociocultural theories to present a university-level intervention in a course on English morphosyntax in which grammar instruction was randomized. The students participated in a series of syntactic tasks that were not anticipated and that prompted them to adopt a flexible mindset and engage in reflective practice. The findings indicate that pedagogical randomization has the potential to enhance conceptual understanding and instructional creativity. The chapter presents a replicable model for integrating structured unpredictability into teacher education, demonstrating how randomness can support dynamic, context-aware, and learner-centered instruction.

Chapter 8: Optimizing Software Development through Agile Framework Diversity

Agile methodologies have transformed software development by promoting flexibility, collaboration, and user-focused design. This paper compares major Agile frameworks—Scrum, Kanban, XP, Lean, FDD, Crystal, and SAFe—highlighting their impacts on productivity, adaptability, and teamwork. Case studies like Spotify and Toyota show that while all adhere to Agile principles, each framework differs in execution and results. Scrum offers structured planning, Kanban emphasizes visual flow, XP focuses on engineering rigor, and Lean aims to eliminate waste. SAFe and Crystal address scalability and adaptability. Though Agile boosts communication and responsiveness, it also presents challenges like cultural resistance and scaling issues. The study concludes that successful Agile adoption requires organizational readiness, leadership support, and continuous learning, emphasizing that Agile works best when tailored to specific contexts.

Chapter 9: Building Applied Models from Observational Research and Fieldwork in Educational Settings

This chapter elucidates the construction of applied models from observational research in education as a transdisciplinary, praxis-oriented methodology for capturing and transforming complex pedagogical ecologies. Integrating theories from constructivism, experiential learning, systems thinking, and situated cognition, it outlines the methodological arc from data collection to model abstraction and validation. Through diverse case illustrations, the chapter demonstrates how applied models function as diagnostic, design, and governance tools across classroom, institutional, and policy levels. Emphasizing ethical reflexivity, epistemic justice, and methodological transparency, it positions applied models as dynamic epistemic instruments for educational transformation in volatile, diverse, and inequitable learning systems.

Chapter 10: The Efficiency of Freemium Business Models: The Duolingo Case Study

This study aims to explore and assess the efficiency of freemium business models, using Duolingo as a compelling case study. By delving into the intricacies of its strategies, and gaining valuable insights into the factors driving the consumer's decision-making process and the conversion from free to paying users, as well as highlight the aspects that differentiate Duolingo from its competitors and other businesses with similar models. Through a quantitative research methodology, an online questionnaire was implemented and answered by 80 participants in total, both current and past users of the app, with the goal to shed light on the nuances of freemium dynamics and their impact on user acquisition, retention, and revenue generation. The findings show that the even though most people are not familiar with the concept of freemium businesses, it is a part of their daily lives. These models can be extremely efficient and profitable, depending on the customer retention strategies and the value given away in the basic, free versions of the product.

Chapter 11: The Evolution, Integration and Implementation of Supply Chain Modeling

This chapter highlights the role of models in advancing scientific knowledge, reviewing existing research on scientific modeling and the process of building models. It delves into the philosophical underpinnings of modeling, bridging this theoretical foundation to practical applications in supply chain management (SCM). Through presenting modeling applications in supply chain performance measurement, collaboration and coordination, and sustainability, the chapter provides a holistic view of the field's modeling landscape. By consolidating recent research, this chapter aims to equip academics and practitioners in supply chain management with the latest developments and encourage the exploration of new research avenues.

Part 4: Case Studies in Applied Modeling

Chapter 12: Navigating Bibliometric Analysis: A Stepwise Approach Using Bibliometrix Library in R Software

Bibliometric analysis is a powerful tool for evaluating research trends, identifying key contributors, and mapping the intellectual structure of a scientific field. With the increasing volume of academic publications, systematic approaches are essential for deriving meaningful insights from scholarly data. This paper presents a stepwise approach to conducting bibliometric analysis using the Biblioshiny app in Bibliometrix package in R software. Bibliometrix provides a comprehensive framework for importing, processing, and visualizing bibliographic data from databases such as Web of Science, Scopus and Dimensions.ai.The paper outlines key stages of bibliometric analysis, including data collection, preprocessing, descriptive statistics, network analysis, and thematic mapping. It also explores citation analysis, co-authorship networks, and keyword co-occurrence patterns to uncover research trends and collaboration dynamics. By leveraging R's powerful statistical capabilities, this approach ensures reproducibility and flexibility in bibliometric studies.

Chapter 13: Integrated Optimization Model in Sustainability (MOIS): An Integrative Approach for Business Management in Colombian SMEs

In Colombia, small and medium-sized enterprises (SMEs) are the backbone of the national economy, representing 99.5% of the formal business fabric and generating approximately 79% of the country's employment (BBVA Research, 2023). However, SMEs face structural challenges, such as the scarcity of financial resources, the low adoption of sustainable technologies, and the limited capacity to implement efficient management models that balance sustainability with business competitiveness (Rizos et al., 2021; Lieder & Rashid, 2020). To address these problems, the Comprehensive Optimization Model in Sustainability (MOIS) is proposed, a methodological tool designed to strengthen the business processes of SMEs in Colombia based on a comprehensive approach that combines sustainability, logistics efficiency and internal control. This model is based on the articulation of three strategic axes: the Analytical Model of Sustainable Business Performance (MADES), the Logistics Evaluation and Analysis Model (MEAL) and the Comprehensive Diagnosis Model of the Internal Control System (DISCI).

Chapter 14: StructVis A Tool For Visual Operation Of Data Structures

The exclusive use of static theoretical study methods makes the learning process for Data Structures and Algorithms (DSA) highly complicated for students. Through an interactive system development users obtain real-time visual displays of running algorithm codes using step-by-step execution. The platform offers a user interface which functions through React.js and receives its aesthetic appearance from Tailwind CSS. Concepts related to sorting and searching and basic DSA principles achieve their dynamic visualization capabilities from D3.js. All backend functions on this platform work effectively through REST API structures. Code execution security occurs through Docker implementations that operate submitted user programs within designated containers. Through the interface users can adjust animation speeds and they can both reset steps alongside viewing the entire algorithm sequence. The visual interface of the tool delivers teaching experiences for DSA through simultaneous explanatory guidance together with dynamic visual representation and interactivity.

Chapter 15: An Observational Applied Model of an Academic Grants Marketplace

Many come at academic grants with rose-colored glasses. Viewing academic grants as part of a larger "marketplace" (analogically) can benefit understandings for newcomers to the space and improve the grant applications submitted for consideration. This chapter proposes an applied model based on experiences and observations in the space that span decades in higher education in multiple states in the U.S. This model includes main stakeholders in the space: grant applicants, grant funders, and third-party beneficiaries, among others. This applied model is designed to benefit grant applicant awareness and strategic and tactical decision-making in the academic grants space. The applied model is dubbed "Observational Applied Model of an Academic Grants Marketplace" (OAMAGM).

CONCLUSION

The making of abstract applied models stand to benefit people if more of these were made and shared to enhance performance in different contexts. When they are inherited and applied, there are various localisms that will apply, to either strengthen or dilute a model beyond the model's own enablements and constraints. This would suggest that more oversight in terms of model efficacy may enhance the work in the origination, development, and testing of such models.

Even if these models are not applied to work in the real, they can enhance understandings and insights across a range of topics.

Section 1
Building Applied Models

Chapter 1
Theories and Principles Governing the Development of Applied Models

Mustafa Kayyali
https://orcid.org/0000-0003-3300-262X
Maaref University of Applied Sciences, Syria

ABSTRACT

The creation of applied models is anchored in a rich tapestry of theories and guiding principles that shape their structure, function, and impact. This chapter explores the conceptual foundations underpinning model development, drawing on insights from diverse disciplines to highlight the interplay between theory and practice. It examines the principles that ensure models are both methodologically sound and contextually adaptable, addressing the tension between generalizable frameworks and problem-specific customization. By tracing the journey from abstract concepts to operational tools, the discussion reveals how successful models synthesize analytical rigor with creative adaptability. Ultimately, the chapter underscores the importance of grounding applied models in solid theoretical underpinnings while maintaining the flexibility to evolve alongside the dynamic challenges they are designed to address.

INTRODUCTION

The development of applied models is not merely a technical exercise; it is a deeply intellectual endeavor that sits at the intersection of theory, methodology, and real-world necessity. At its core, an applied model is a structured representa-

DOI: 10.4018/979-8-3373-3301-4.ch001

tion of reality—an intentional simplification designed to illuminate the dynamics of a problem, clarify relationships between variables, and guide decision-making toward effective solutions. Yet, beneath the visible structure of any model lies an intricate web of theories and principles that inform its creation. These foundational elements provide both the conceptual scaffolding and the philosophical orientation necessary for transforming an abstract problem into a workable solution pathway.

In the realm of problem-solving, applied models serve as bridges between the abstract universes of academic knowledge and the tangible challenges encountered in practical contexts (Qadhi, 2023). They are the translation devices that turn theoretical insights into operational strategies, allowing practitioners to act with both confidence and clarity. However, this translation is never automatic. It requires deliberate selection of theoretical frameworks, careful alignment with guiding principles, and an acute awareness of the socio-cultural and technological contexts in which the model will operate. Without such alignment, models risk becoming either too rigid—detached from the dynamic realities they aim to address—or too fluid, lacking the methodological discipline necessary for reliability and replication.

Theories provide the "why" behind a model's design. They define the conceptual territory, articulate the assumptions that frame the scope of inquiry, and offer predictive insights into the behavior of systems. Principles, on the other hand, provide the "how." They determine the rules of construction, the logic of operation, and the ethical boundaries within which the model must function. Together, theories and principles form the intellectual DNA of an applied model, ensuring it is not just an ad hoc construction but a coherent, purposeful, and accountable instrument for problem-solving (Wu & Or, 2025).

The importance of grounding model development in robust theoretical and principled foundations has only grown in the current era, where complexity, uncertainty, and rapid change dominate the problem-solving landscape. Issues such as climate change, global health crises, technological disruption, and socio-political instability demand models that can accommodate multifaceted realities without losing conceptual clarity (Tähtinen, 2025). In such contexts, theoretical pluralism—drawing insights from multiple disciplines—and principled adaptability—balancing methodological rigor with situational responsiveness—become essential.

This chapter positions the development of applied models as a disciplined yet creative process. It begins by unpacking the foundational theories that have historically informed model construction, from systems theory and behavioral science to design thinking and computational modeling. It then explores the principles that give these models coherence, reliability, and ethical legitimacy. Throughout, the discussion emphasizes the interplay between structure and flexibility, predictability and adaptability, and the enduring challenge of ensuring that models remain relevant in a rapidly evolving world.

By weaving together theoretical depth and practical sensibility, this chapter invites readers to see applied models not as static tools, but as living frameworks—capable of evolving, adapting, and refining themselves in response to the ever-changing contours of the problems they are designed to solve. In doing so, it sets the stage for a deeper understanding of how rigorous intellectual foundations and principled approaches can elevate model development from a procedural task to a form of creative, impactful problem-solving.

FOUNDATIONS OF APPLIED MODEL DEVELOPMENT: A THEORETICAL OVERVIEW

The roots of any applied model run far deeper than the lines on a diagram or the logic embedded in a formula. Beneath its surface lies a dense sediment of thought—layers of philosophical assumptions, methodological preferences, and quiet, often unspoken convictions about how the world works and how it ought to be understood. A model, after all, is never neutral. Even when draped in the garb of objectivity, it carries the fingerprints of the intellectual traditions that shaped it (Mandavilli, 2023). To examine the foundations of applied model development is to peel back the polished surface and wander into that understructure, tracing the hidden beams and joints that hold the whole thing together.

In its essence, an applied model is a deliberate act of selection. It accepts that the world is far too unruly, too brimming with interdependencies, to be captured in its entirety. So, it draws boundaries. It asks: Which elements are indispensable? Which can be omitted without distorting the truth beyond recognition? The answers to these questions are never dictated by data alone. They are guided by theory—by the deep, sometimes ancient frameworks that offer a vantage point from which complexity can be glimpsed in outline. Without theory, the process becomes guesswork, an unanchored tinkering with variables that may produce something superficially convincing but ultimately fragile.

Theories are not cages; they are lenses. They frame what is visible and, just as importantly, what is ignored. A developer steeped in systems theory will see interlocking feedback loops and emergent properties where another, guided by behavioral economics, might see incentives, biases, and decision heuristics. Neither is necessarily wrong; each is attuned to a different pattern of signals. The choice of theoretical lens is thus the first act of creation in model development, shaping not just the structure of the model but the very nature of the problem it is meant to solve.

There is a quiet irony here. Theory promises stability, a fixed foundation on which to build, yet the history of knowledge is one of shifting ground (Mackintosh, 2021). What seemed immutable in one era—the certainty of linear cause and effect, for instance—may unravel under the scrutiny of another. The applied model developer works, therefore, in a space of negotiated certainty. Theories must be embraced with conviction but held lightly enough to adapt when the world refuses to fit their prescriptions. This is not weakness; it is survival.

The philosophical underpinnings of modeling also carry their own tensions. There is the realist's belief that models can mirror an external reality with faithful accuracy, and there is the constructivist's counterpoint that models are, in the end, human artifacts—useful fictions built to serve particular ends. Most practitioners, whether consciously or not, work somewhere in between. They aim for truth, or something close to it, but acknowledge the scaffolding of interpretation that inevitably shapes the result.

Foundations also draw from the intellectual soil of multiple disciplines (Huber & Morreale, 2023). Engineering contributes its precision and tolerances, economics its attention to scarcity and trade-offs, sociology its appreciation of social systems and collective behavior. Each discipline offers not just methods but worldviews—a sense of what counts as evidence, what is worth measuring, what can be safely abstracted away. When building an applied model, the developer becomes something of a polyglot, borrowing conceptual tools from one field, methodological rigour from another, interpretive frameworks from yet another. This interdisciplinarity is not a decorative feature; it is the very condition of robustness. A model that can only breathe within the narrow confines of a single discipline rarely survives contact with the complexities of real-world application.

Yet, even as theories provide a map, they can seduce the builder into oversimplification. The temptation is always there: to stretch the model over the entirety of reality like a single skin, ignoring the wrinkles and bulges where the fabric doesn't quite fit. This is where the craft of modeling—distinct from its science—becomes evident. The skilled practitioner resists the pull toward elegance at the cost of truth. They know when to let the model grow a little ungainly, when to preserve the messiness of the thing it represents rather than ironing it flat for the sake of aesthetic symmetry.

At its best, theory does more than justify the model's architecture; it provokes the imagination (Myers, 2021). It suggests hidden relationships, counterintuitive outcomes, and potential levers for change. Systems thinking, for instance, invites the developer to look for reinforcing or balancing loops that may turn small interventions into large impacts—or swallow them without a trace. Game theory prompts consideration of strategic behavior, of how actors might anticipate and respond to one another's moves. Network theory highlights the invisible webs of connection that can amplify or dampen the spread of influence, information, or contagion. Each of these theories offers not just explanatory power but a repertoire of metaphors, images, and narratives that seep into the model's design.

Figure 1. Theoretical lenses influencing applied models

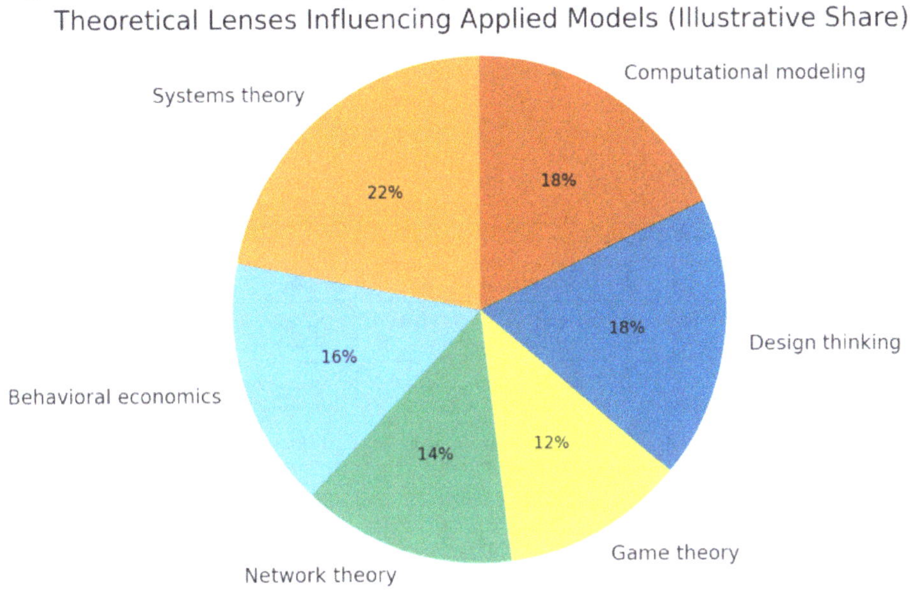

It would be naïve to pretend that these foundations are purely intellectual. Every theoretical choice carries with it a set of values, whether acknowledged or not (Shaturaev, 2022). A model rooted in neoclassical economics may privilege efficiency and equilibrium; one built on ecological theory may elevate resilience and balance. These values shape what the model treats as a problem worth solving and what it regards as an acceptable solution. Theories, in this way, are moral as well as cognitive instruments, and the responsible model developer must remain alert to their normative implications.

Then there is the matter of scale. Some theories lend themselves to the grand sweep—to models that attempt to encompass entire systems or predict long-term trajectories. Others are more comfortable at the micro level, capturing the fine-grained behaviors of individuals, firms, or cells. Choosing the appropriate theoretical foundation requires a sensitivity to scale: building a macro-level model on a micro-level theory can lead to dangerous distortions, while applying a broad, systemic theory to a tightly defined local problem risks drowning in abstraction.

Foundations are also temporal. A model is not built in a vacuum; it emerges at a particular moment in history, under the influence of prevailing scientific paradigms, technological capabilities, and cultural expectations. A model designed in the computational scarcity of the 1970s, constrained by limited processing power, would inevitably differ from one conceived today, when machine learning algorithms can churn through vast datasets in seconds. Theoretical frameworks, too, are shaped by their time—what counts as a persuasive theory in one era may seem quaint or even misguided in another. This temporal contingency is not a flaw; it is a reminder that models, like the problems they address, are living things, subject to the currents of change.

Table 1. Theory modeling implications matrix

Theory/Lens	Core idea	Modeling implications	Common pitfalls	When to prefer
Systems theory	Interdependence & feedback loops	Causal loop diagrams; stock flow models; sensitivity tests	Over-aggregation; ignoring delays	Multi-actor, dynamic problems
Behavioral economics	Bounded rationality & biases	Choice architecture; error-pattern-aware features	Overgeneralizing lab effects	User/decision-centric interventions
Network theory	Structure of relations matters	Centrality analysis; contagion models	Static networks; missing ties	Diffusion, supply chains, ecosystems
Game theory	Strategic interaction & payoffs	Equilibrium scenarios; incentive-compatible designs	Overly rigid assumptions	Markets, negotiations, policy design
Design thinking	Human-centered iteration	Rapid prototyping; qualitative insight loops	Anecdote-driven drift	Ambiguous, novel problem spaces
Computational modeling	Data-driven generalization	Simulation; ML + hybrid symbolic layers	Opacities; overfitting	Large, complex data with patterns

In this light, the foundation of applied model development is less like a rigid concrete slab and more like a flexible but resilient lattice—firm enough to hold its shape, elastic enough to absorb new insights and withstand external shocks. Theories provide the struts and beams, principles supply the joinery, and the builder's judgment determines how these elements are arranged, reinforced, and, when necessary, replaced (Arya, 2022).

Perhaps what distinguishes a truly enduring model is its ability to contain within its structure a recognition of its own provisional nature. It does not cling to the illusion of finality. Instead, it builds into itself the possibility of revision—what some might call "designing for doubt." This humility, paradoxically, strengthens rather than weakens the model's authority. Users can trust a model that knows its limits, that signals not just where it is strong but where the fog thickens.

In the end, the theoretical foundations of applied model development are less about providing a fixed answer and more about cultivating a disciplined way of seeing. They teach the developer to ask sharper questions, to listen for the quiet signals that might otherwise be drowned out, to recognize patterns that are not immediately obvious. Theories are the scaffolding, but also the compass; they shape the terrain as much as they map it. And in the unpredictable, often chaotic landscapes where applied models are deployed, such a compass can make the difference between a tool that illuminates and one that misleads.

CORE PRINCIPLES SHAPING EFFECTIVE PROBLEM-SOLVING MODELS

When one strips away the technical jargon and ornate diagrams, what remains at the heart of any effective problem-solving model is a handful of principles—quiet but unyielding anchors that keep the whole construct from drifting into irrelevance. These principles are not mere methodological checklists; they are habits of thought, commitments almost philosophical in nature, that shape the way a model is conceived, refined, and deployed. Without them, even the most dazzlingly complex model risks becoming a hollow contraption, impressive in appearance but empty of real utility.

At the top of this invisible scaffolding sits clarity of purpose. A model that does not know precisely what it is for will spend its life wandering. Purpose is not just a mission statement scribbled in the introduction; it's a deep and sometimes stubborn sense of the problem's true core (Kayyali, 2025). In practice, this clarity often emerges through friction—by resisting the urge to please every stakeholder at once, by refusing to dilute the model's focus in the name of universality. The sharper the purpose, the more surgical the model's ability to cut through noise and address the signal. And yet, clarity is not rigidity. It must coexist with a willingness to evolve the purpose itself when the original question proves to be the wrong one or when the world shifts underfoot.

Coupled with clarity is the principle of fidelity to reality. All models simplify—this is their nature—but simplification is a dangerous slope (Jin et al, 2023). Pare away too much and the model collapses into caricature; carry too much and it becomes an unwieldy replica of the very complexity it was meant to tame. Fidelity, then, is not about slavish completeness but about preserving the dynamics that truly matter. It's about knowing which relationships, thresholds, and constraints are non-negotiable, and which can be left to the margins without sabotaging the insight the model is meant to produce. Achieving this balance is less science and more craft, requiring not only empirical grounding but a feel for the living texture of the system in question (Rivard, 2021).

Figure 2. Complexity vs performance during iterative refinement

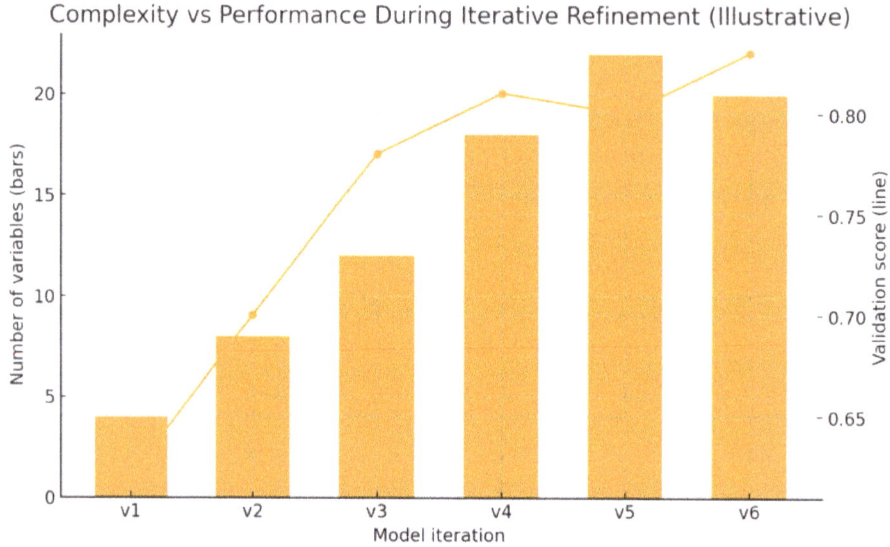

Another principle, often underestimated, is coherence. A model must be internally consistent—not just mathematically, but conceptually. The assumptions it makes in one corner cannot silently contradict the rules it follows in another. Coherence demands that the narrative of the model holds together, that there is a discernible thread connecting inputs to outputs without abrupt leaps of logic (Mani, 2022). Incoherence is a subtle killer; it may not be obvious until the model's recommendations are tested in the real world and collapse under their own contradictions. This is why coherence is often safeguarded not in the glamorous stages of development but in the slow, meticulous work of aligning definitions, units of analysis, and causal assumptions.

Transparency follows closely behind. It is tempting to hide the inner workings of a model behind a wall of complexity, especially when the mechanics are proprietary or politically sensitive. But opacity corrodes trust. An effective model invites inspection—not because it has nothing to hide, but because it understands that scrutiny strengthens legitimacy. Transparency means that those who use or are affected by the model can see, at least in outline, how it reaches its conclusions, what data it rests on, and where its blind spots lie. This does not require that every user becomes an expert, but it does require that the path from premise to conclusion is traceable. A model that cannot survive being looked at closely has already failed.

Adaptability is another cornerstone. The most elegantly designed model will wither if it cannot adapt to new conditions (Fernandez, 2023). The world is not static; data streams shift, human behavior mutates, and unexpected events throw carefully calibrated assumptions into disarray. An adaptable model is built with this inevitability in mind—it has joints that can flex without breaking, mechanisms for incorporating new information without tearing out the foundations. Adaptability is not the same as endless malleability; a model that changes shape with every breeze loses its identity. Rather, it is a measured responsiveness, an ability to recalibrate while holding fast to the principles that define its core logic.

An often-overlooked principle is relevance to stakeholders. Models do not live in laboratories; they live in boardrooms, clinics, classrooms, city councils—places where decisions are made by people who often care less about the elegance of the equations and more about whether the tool helps them decide wisely. Relevance means that the model speaks to the actual needs, constraints, and language of those who will use it. It means resisting the temptation to build for one's peers alone and instead listening—really listening—to the rhythms of the environment where the model will land. An irrelevant model, no matter how rigorous, will sit on a shelf gathering dust.

Ethical integrity, though sometimes treated as an afterthought, must be woven into the fabric from the beginning (Mahajan, 2025). Every model makes choices—about what to measure, whose interests to prioritize, what risks are acceptable—and these choices have ethical consequences. A principle-driven model acknowledges these consequences openly, rather than hiding behind the shield of technical neutrality. It asks uncomfortable questions: Does this model privilege certain groups over others? Could its recommendations cause harm if misused? Who benefits, and who bears the cost? Such questions are not distractions; they are safeguards against the quiet drift of modeling into complicity with inequity or harm.

Another thread in this fabric is parsimony—the principle of achieving the necessary explanatory power with the fewest possible elements. This is not about stripping a model to its bones for the sake of elegance; it is about discipline. Every added variable, every extra layer of complexity, demands justification in terms of the insight it delivers. Parsimony protects against bloat, which can make models not only harder to maintain but more prone to overfitting—performing brilliantly on past data and failing miserably on the future it was meant to predict (Ting, 2024). Yet parsimony must also be tempered by the earlier principle of fidelity; a model that is too lean may omit vital dynamics and thus mislead.

Finally, there is the principle of iterative refinement. A model is not born fully formed. It emerges, awkward and imperfect, from an initial attempt, and is shaped through cycles of testing, feedback, and revision. Iteration acknowledges that understanding deepens through use, that weaknesses reveal themselves only in the friction of application. The best models evolve over time, their rough edges smoothed not by theoretical speculation alone but by the stubborn, unpredictable realities they encounter. Iteration requires humility—the willingness to admit that the first version will almost certainly be wrong in some important way—and a commitment to keep learning from both successes and failures.

Taken together, these principles do more than guide the construction of problem-solving models; they shape the mindset of those who build and use them (Gale et al, 2022). They foster a way of thinking that values clarity without rigidity, simplicity without distortion, transparency without oversimplification, and adaptability without loss of identity. And while they may seem abstract, they leave tangible fingerprints on every stage of the process—from the first scribbled sketch on a whiteboard to the final decision taken in a high-stakes room.

It is tempting to see these principles as a checklist to be ticked off in turn, but they are less like a sequence and more like a set of tensions to be balanced. Parsimony pulls against fidelity. Adaptability tugs at coherence. Ethical integrity sometimes complicates relevance to certain stakeholders (Alibašić, 2025). Navigating these tensions is where the real artistry lies. There is no formula that will tell you exactly how much complexity to retain or exactly when to loosen the model's structure in response to new data. These judgments are made in the messy, ambiguous spaces where technical knowledge meets human judgment.

An effective problem-solving model, then, is not simply the outcome of correct technical choices—it is the expression of a principled stance toward the act of modeling itself. The builder's respect for reality, openness to scrutiny, responsiveness to change, and willingness to pare away the inessential all leave their mark. And in a world increasingly crowded with models of every kind—from crude heuristics to sprawling AI-driven simulations—the ones that endure are those whose principles are not bolted on afterward but are fused into the structure from the first moment of conception.

INTEGRATING INTERDISCIPLINARY PERSPECTIVES IN MODEL DESIGN

The act of designing a model—any model worth its salt—has always been a little like standing at the mouth of a wide river where several tributaries meet. Streams of thought from different disciplines converge, sometimes clashing in their currents, sometimes slipping past each other in quiet harmony, but always changing the flow. The temptation to build a model from the comfort of a single disciplinary vantage point is strong; it promises coherence, familiar methods, and a sense of control (Miller, 2022). But in the messy terrain of real-world problem-solving, single-discipline purity rarely survives first contact with reality. Problems do not arrive neatly wrapped in the categories our academic departments favor. They sprawl, spilling across boundaries—part economic, part psychological, part environmental, part political. To address them with any seriousness, the modeler must learn to speak in more than one tongue.

This is where the work becomes both exhilarating and treacherous. Integrating interdisciplinary perspectives is not a matter of collecting a few buzzwords from various fields and sprinkling them like garnish over an otherwise unchanged recipe. It requires letting the logic of other disciplines seep deep into the bones of the model, altering its assumptions, its vocabulary, even its sense of what counts as evidence (Kayyali, 2024). It's the difference between inviting someone into your home for a polite visit and moving in together, sharing the same kitchen, negotiating whose taste in furniture will prevail. The integration has to be lived, not just performed.

Of course, each discipline brings with it a way of seeing—a lens polished over decades, even centuries, of focused attention. Economists look for trade-offs, marginal returns, and equilibrium points. Psychologists attend to cognition, emotion, and bias (Enke, 2024). Engineers think in terms of constraints, tolerances, and failure modes. Anthropologists probe cultural patterns, rituals, and power relations. To integrate these perspectives is to invite multiple, sometimes contradictory realities into the same space, and then to resist the urge to smooth over their differences too quickly. The friction is where the insight often hides.

There's an art to knowing when to let a disciplinary frame dominate and when to loosen its grip. If you're modeling public health interventions, epidemiology might be the anchor discipline, but without the behavioral sciences you risk designing an intervention that is technically flawless and socially inert. Likewise, a climate resilience model grounded in ecological theory may falter without the political science needed to understand governance structures, or the economics needed to map incentives (Kayyali, 2022). Integration is not about parity for its own sake; it's about recognizing the specific constellations of knowledge that the problem demands.

And yet, the act of blending disciplines is rarely symmetrical. Some speak more loudly than others. Quantitative fields can overshadow qualitative ones simply because their outputs look more authoritative in the language of numbers. Cultural or ethical considerations can be treated as decorative appendages, tacked on after the "real" work is done. True integration pushes back against this hierarchy, refusing to relegate certain types of knowledge to the footnotes (Vogel et al, 2024). A model that fails to give serious weight to all its constituent perspectives risks a kind of epistemic tunnel vision—it sees with one eye closed.

One of the subtler challenges lies in the fact that disciplines disagree not only on methods but on the very nature of truth. A physicist's notion of validity, grounded in repeatable experiments and measurable constants, is not the same as a historian's, who may value the richness of narrative and the irreducibility of context. When these worldviews meet inside a model, something has to give—or better yet, something has to stretch. The modeler's job is less about forcing consensus and more about creating a structure in which different kinds of truth can coexist without collapsing into incoherence. This may mean building modular components—each faithful to its own disciplinary rigor—while ensuring they can talk to each other in a shared dialect.

Language itself becomes a battleground in interdisciplinary work. Terms that seem solid in one field turn slippery in another. "Resilience" means something different to an ecologist than it does to an engineer or a social worker. Without deliberate effort to define, translate, and sometimes invent shared terminology, the integration will be little more than parallel monologues. Crafting a model that genuinely integrates perspectives often requires building this linguistic bridge first, lest the structure be erected on a foundation of misunderstandings (Fatihi, 2024).

The rewards of true integration are worth the struggle. When it works, the model gains a kind of depth and texture that no single discipline could have produced alone. An urban planning model enriched by sociology can predict not just traffic flows but community displacement; a supply chain model informed by environmental science can account for biodiversity impacts alongside cost efficiency. These richer models are not necessarily more complex in the sense of having more variables—they are more complex in the sense of inhabiting a broader conceptual space, one that is better aligned with the tangled reality they aim to illuminate (Kendall & Oprea, 2024).

And yet, integration is not without risk. Bringing multiple perspectives into a single model can lead to an unwieldy behemoth—too many moving parts, too many competing logics, the whole thing groaning under its own weight. There is a delicate line between integration and overload. The key is discernment: knowing which perspectives are essential for the problem at hand, and which, while interesting, might dilute focus or introduce contradictions that weaken the whole. It's a lesson in humility—accepting that no model can hold everything, and that choosing what to leave out is as important as deciding what to bring in.

What often goes unsaid is that interdisciplinary integration changes the modeler, too (Clark & Terway, 2022). To work meaningfully across boundaries, one has to let go of the comfort of being an expert in all aspects of the work. There will be moments of fumbling in unfamiliar terrain, of feeling like an amateur in someone else's workshop. This vulnerability is not a weakness—it's the price of admission to the deeper, more generative conversations that integration demands. Over time, the modeler becomes a kind of intellectual nomad, comfortable crossing borders, carrying tools from one domain to another, adapting them to new terrains.

It's also worth noting that integration happens in a social and political context. Disciplines are not abstract entities; they are communities with histories, rivalries, and status hierarchies. Bringing their perspectives together means navigating not just ideas but egos, institutional loyalties, and sometimes deeply entrenched suspicions. A model design process that ignores this human dimension will stumble, no matter how sound its technical architecture (Bernstein, 2022). Building trust across disciplinary lines—showing respect for different ways of knowing, creating space for voices that might otherwise be marginalized—is as critical to integration as the computational algorithms or statistical methods involved.

In practice, successful interdisciplinary integration often emerges from iteration rather than grand design. Initial attempts may be awkward—components don't align, assumptions clash—but through cycles of testing and revision, the model begins to develop a grammar of its own, one that can accommodate the accents of its constituent disciplines without forcing them into uniformity. This is less like engineering a machine and more like cultivating a garden, where different species grow together, sometimes competing, sometimes cooperating, but all contributing to the vitality of the whole.

Perhaps the most profound aspect of interdisciplinary integration in model design is that it invites a certain intellectual humility. No matter how sophisticated the mathematics, how elegant the simulations, the model is a human construct, and its view of the world is partial. Bringing in perspectives from multiple disciplines is not a guarantee of truth—it is an acknowledgment of complexity, a way of resisting the seductive illusion that any single lens can capture the whole. It is, at its best, an act of respect for the richness of the world and the diversity of the minds trying to make sense of it.

BALANCING RIGOR AND FLEXIBILITY IN APPLIED FRAMEWORKS

There is a quiet, persistent tension that threads through the life of every applied framework, whether it is shaping a business strategy, guiding a policy intervention, or structuring a complex engineering solution. On one side, the pull toward rigor—the desire for precise definitions, consistent rules, airtight logic, and a repeatable method that can withstand scrutiny from even the most unforgiving critic. On the other, the call for flexibility—the willingness to bend when reality refuses to cooperate, to accommodate local nuance, to adjust on the fly without feeling that the integrity of the whole has been compromised. Both impulses are necessary, yet they do not always coexist peacefully. In fact, if one listens closely, the hum of tension between them is often the sound of the framework breathing.

Rigor has its own seductions. There is a comfort in knowing that a model, method, or process is meticulously documented, tested against edge cases, and defended with data (Savaglio & Fortino, 2021). It gives the creator the reassurance that their work won't collapse under the weight of a pointed question. It also offers the user a sense of stability—if the rules are clear and consistently applied, the results feel less like guesswork and more like dependable insight. In academic and technical circles, rigor becomes a kind of currency; the more exacting the standards, the more weight a framework carries. But rigor, left unchecked, can ossify. It can turn into a fortress whose walls are so thick that nothing new can enter without being reshaped beyond recognition—or rejected outright.

Flexibility, by contrast, thrives in movement. It's the quality that allows a framework to survive contact with contexts it was never explicitly designed for. It lets a set of principles adjust to shifting cultural expectations, unexpected data, or disruptive events that rewrite the rules of the game overnight. Flexibility feels alive—reactive, intuitive, open to improvisation. Yet it can also slide into shapelessness (Cedercreutz, 2024). Without some measure of constraint, flexibility risks becoming an excuse for inconsistency, a way to avoid the hard work of defining boundaries and making difficult trade-offs.

What complicates the balance further is that the right mix of rigor and flexibility is not fixed. It shifts with the life stage of the framework, the volatility of the environment, and the nature of the problem itself. A new framework, still finding its footing, may benefit from greater flexibility, allowing for rapid learning and adaptation. As it matures, the emphasis might swing toward rigor, cementing the practices that have proven effective. Then, in times of disruption—technological upheaval, political shifts, ecological crises—the pendulum may swing back again, loosening the rules to absorb new realities. A rigid devotion to either extreme ignores the simple fact that contexts evolve, and so must the balance.

In practice, maintaining this equilibrium is less about mathematical proportion and more about a kind of listening. Rigor speaks in the voice of structure—it demands consistency in definitions, replicability in methods, and accountability in interpretation. Flexibility speaks in the voice of the unexpected—it reminds the framework's custodians that the world will not stand still for their convenience. A modeler or strategist attuned to both voices will know when to tighten the rules and when to allow them to stretch, even if doing so invites a measure of uncertainty.

The temptation, of course, is to treat rigor and flexibility as opposites on a single spectrum, to imagine that more of one automatically means less of the other (Geuss, 2022). But this is a false choice. The most resilient frameworks are not those that occupy a middling compromise, but those that find ways to embed both qualities at once. Think of a bridge: its structure must be strong enough to bear weight, yet elastic enough to sway in high winds without cracking. The strength is not despite the flexibility; it is because of it. Likewise, a truly effective applied framework can maintain rigorous internal logic while still allowing its components to adapt, swap out, or reconfigure in response to fresh demands.

There's also an emotional undercurrent to this balancing act. Rigor often feels like discipline—hard edges, rules, the safety of knowing exactly what is expected. Flexibility feels like trust—a willingness to let go of control, to allow the system to find its own solutions within broad guardrails. The discomfort comes when one is forced to lean into the opposite instinct. The rigor-minded developer may balk at the ambiguity of adaptive processes, fearing it will erode the credibility of the work. The flexibility-driven innovator may bristle at the formalities of documentation and verification, seeing them as a brake on creativity. Yet the act of integrating both perspectives—holding space for the comfort of structure and the vitality of adaptability—creates a richer, more durable result.

Figure 3. Principle compliance score for an applied model

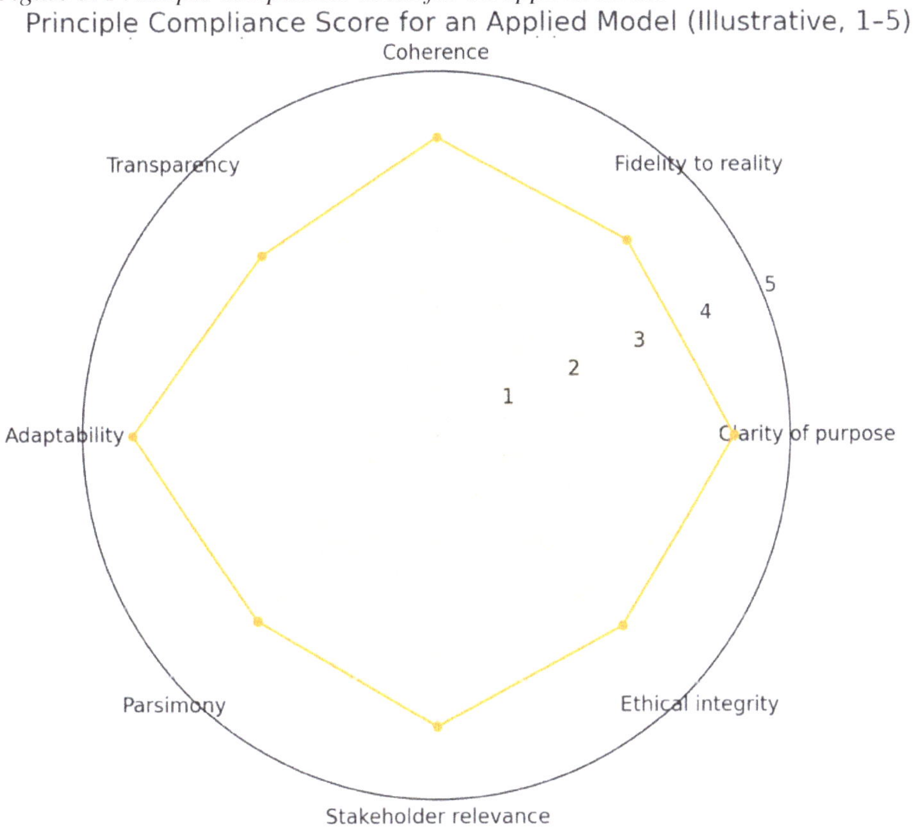

One way to think about this integration is to distinguish between the framework's core and its periphery (Klimczuk & Klimczuk-Kochańska, 2023). The core—its fundamental principles, its non-negotiable constraints—should be rigorously defined and preserved. These are the parts that give the framework its identity and ensure that, no matter how far it stretches, it remains recognizably itself. The periphery—the implementation details, the local adaptations, the contextual adjustments—can be more fluid, responding to the particularities of the setting without undermining the integrity of the whole. In this sense, flexibility is not the absence of rigor but its strategic deployment, allowing the framework to live in multiple worlds without fracturing.

But the challenge deepens when the boundary between core and periphery blurs. In some fields, what counts as "core" is itself contested. Consider a public policy framework designed to improve urban housing. Is the core the principle of equitable access? The specific metrics for affordability? The methods of community consultation? Different stakeholders will answer differently, and the balance between rigor and flexibility will tilt depending on which answer prevails. Negotiating these definitions becomes as much a political exercise as a technical one, and the outcome will shape how the framework behaves in practice.

Time also exerts its own pressure on the balance. In the early, exploratory phase of applying a framework to a new problem, flexibility is often the default posture—testing, iterating, refining. Over time, as patterns emerge and confidence in the framework's logic grows, the scaffolding of rigor is strengthened. But time can also breed complacency. A framework that has been in use for years may become so rigid that it resists necessary change, clinging to methods that no longer match the environment it serves. Periodic stress tests—deliberate attempts to apply the framework in unfamiliar conditions—can help prevent this calcification, forcing it to stretch just enough to stay alive.

The interplay of rigor and flexibility is also visible in the tools and technologies we choose to embed in frameworks. Data-driven components, for instance, can anchor rigor through quantifiable evidence and statistical validation, yet they must be paired with flexible mechanisms that allow for qualitative insights, expert judgment, and contextual nuance (Tripathi et al, 2021). A purely algorithmic decision-support model might excel at processing vast datasets but falter in situations where human values, cultural norms, or ethical dilemmas outweigh numeric optimization. The reverse is also true: a model built entirely on qualitative input may adapt gracefully to subtle shifts in context but struggle to maintain consistency or defend its recommendations against quantitative scrutiny. Bridging the two—letting data and narrative, measurement and meaning, coexist—can transform the framework from brittle to resilient.

And then there's the matter of failure. Rigor tries to design it out; flexibility assumes it will happen and plans for recovery. A framework that tilts too heavily toward rigor may treat failure as a sign that the entire system is flawed, prompting defensive retrenchment rather than learning. A framework that overindulges in flexibility may treat failure too lightly, adapting endlessly without addressing deeper structural issues (Adobor & Kudonoo, 2025). The healthiest balance treats failure as feedback—sometimes calling for tighter controls, sometimes for looser ones, but always as a prompt to reassess the current equilibrium.

What makes this balancing act especially human is that it cannot be reduced to a formula. It is not a problem to be solved once and for all, but a dynamic posture to be maintained, adjusted, and sometimes renegotiated altogether. It requires sensitivity to the subtleties of context, an openness to signals that may at first appear contradictory, and the patience to sit in the discomfort of ambiguity. Rigor without flexibility is brittle; flexibility without rigor is mush. Between them lies a living tension that, if tended well, becomes a source of strength rather than a site of conflict.

FROM THEORY TO PRACTICE: TRANSLATING PRINCIPLES INTO REAL-WORLD SOLUTIONS

There's a peculiar restlessness in theory. No matter how elegant the framework, how symmetrical the logic, there's an itch—almost an impatience—to see it collide with reality. On paper, principles line up like disciplined soldiers, every step accounted for, every assumption declared. Out there, beyond the safety of the desk, the world is a little less orderly. Variables refuse to behave. People improvise. Contexts shift midstream. And this is precisely where the act of translation begins—not as a mechanical transposition, but as a messy, living negotiation between the purity of an idea and the stubborn, often contradictory texture of the real.

Moving from theory to practice is not a simple descent from the abstract to the concrete (Tian & Ha, 2022). It's more like stepping from a blueprint into a half-built structure while the weather changes overhead. The designer carries the plan in one hand, a pencil behind the ear, and a willingness—perhaps even an obligation—to redraw as they go. This is where principles stop being inert statements and start behaving like organisms: adapting, bending, holding their shape where they must, mutating where they mustn't, and revealing, in their application, what they are truly made of.

A principle on its own is a promise, but a promise in need of proof. Consider something as foundational as "ensure stakeholder engagement." In theory, it's self-evident and noble. In practice, it's a tangle of invitations, scheduling conflicts, competing agendas, and the unspoken hierarchies that decide whose voice actually counts. To translate that principle into action is to navigate personalities as much as processes. It means designing not just a meeting, but an environment in which people feel safe to contribute, where input isn't merely collected but visibly shapes the outcome. It's the difference between announcing a value and embodying it.

The translation also exposes the limits of theory. Principles are often crafted in a space of relative calm, insulated from the immediate heat of decision-making.

They assume time for deliberation, data to fill the gaps, and a willingness among all parties to engage in good faith. Reality laughs at such assumptions. Time runs short. Data arrives incomplete, or not at all (McStay, 2023). Key actors walk into the room with agendas already set. In those moments, the translator's task is to hold on to the spirit of the principle while letting go of its letter when the letter becomes a cage. This requires a particular kind of judgment—one that cannot be learned from the principle itself, but only from living through the friction of its application.

And then there's the question of sequencing. Theories tend to speak as if all their principles can be enacted in harmony, a kind of symphonic implementation. Practice often demands triage. Faced with limited resources, competing urgencies, and imperfect information, some principles will have to wait their turn. This is not betrayal; it's realism. The skill lies in sequencing without eroding the credibility of the framework—making clear that a principle deferred is not a principle abandoned, and ensuring that when its moment comes, the ground has been prepared for its arrival.

One of the quiet truths of translating theory into practice is that fidelity and improvisation are not opposites; they are companions (Kennedy, 2023). A principle is a compass, not a GPS. It points toward a direction, but the terrain may force detours. A public health model might dictate "prioritize high-risk populations" as a guiding principle. On the ground, that could mean recalculating risk based on emerging epidemiological patterns, or recognizing that the "high-risk" group identified in the abstract is not the same as the one actually bearing the brunt of the crisis in a particular location. To remain faithful to the principle is to accept that its real-world expression may look nothing like its original, abstract formulation—and to be at peace with that.

The act of translation also has an emotional dimension. Principles, in their theoretical form, are often clean and unburdened by the compromises that practical application demands (Jackson, 2024). Bringing them into practice can feel like sullying something pure. But purity is an illusion; the principle's worth is not in its untouched state, but in its capacity to survive contact with imperfection. If a principle can't withstand adjustment, it wasn't as robust as it appeared in the comfort of theory. The tension is not a flaw in the process—it is the process.

An effective translator also understands that practice has a way of teaching theory things it didn't know about itself. Feedback loops matter here. When a principle fails in practice, the reflex may be to blame the application, to insist that the theory was sound and the implementation flawed. Sometimes that's true. Other times, the flaw lies in the principle's own blind spots—assumptions smuggled in without scrutiny, cultural contexts ignored, unintended consequences left unimagined. The passage from theory to practice should not be one-way traffic; it should be a corridor wide enough for experience to carry lessons back to the drawing board (DiSalvo, 2022).

It's worth noting that principles rarely travel alone. They jostle against each other, sometimes pulling in different directions. One may urge caution, another speed; one may demand inclusivity, another efficiency. In the abstract, these tensions can be acknowledged and set aside for "further study." In practice, they require choices. A disaster response team, guided by principles of both rapid deployment and community consultation, may find the two in direct conflict when lives hang in the balance. Translation, in this sense, is as much about adjudication as it is about execution—about deciding which principle to privilege in the moment, and carrying the weight of that choice.

In translating principles into solutions, there's also a choreography between the universal and the local. Theories often aspire to generality—principles that apply across cases, contexts, and cultures. Practice is relentlessly specific (Scaratti & Ivaldi, 2021). A solution that honors the principle of "environmental sustainability" will look very different in a Scandinavian fishing village than in a desert mining community. The translation requires sensitivity to these differences, not as deviations from the "real" principle, but as its legitimate manifestations. The universal lives through the local, not in spite of it.

Table 2. Principles practices indicators

Principle	Operational practice	Metric/indicator
Clarity of purpose	Problem framing canvas; scope boundaries	Decision relevance score; change requests avoided
Fidelity to reality	Retention of key constraints/thresholds	Out-of-sample error; face-validity checks passed
Coherence	Assumption registry; unit/definition alignment	Contradiction count; peer review flags
Transparency	Model cards; data lineage; explainers	Docs completeness; stakeholder comprehension
Adaptability	Modular components; update playbooks	Time-to-update; performance drift caught
Parsimony	Feature pruning; information criteria	AIC/BIC; maintenance hours per release
Stakeholder relevance	Co-design sessions; decision theatre	Adoption rate; decision turnaround
Ethical integrity	Bias audits; privacy-by-design; redress	Gap (Î") reduced; incidents per year

And yet, the act of translation is not merely reactive—it can be creative. The principle sets boundaries, yes, but within those boundaries there is room for invention. Constraints often sharpen imagination. A principle like "ensure transparency" might inspire a technical solution in one context—a publicly accessible dashboard—and a narrative one in another, such as regular storytelling sessions where data is shared alongside personal accounts. The principle is the spine; the practice can still dance.

There's an unglamorous side to all of this: the mundane mechanics of implementation. Theories rarely concern themselves with scheduling, procurement, or the politics of budget allocation. Practice lives in these details. Translating a principle into a solution means knowing which levers to pull, which allies to court, which procedural hurdles to anticipate. The principle without this scaffolding remains aspirational; the scaffolding without the principle is machinery without purpose. It is their meeting that produces something that works.

In the end, translation is an act of stewardship. The translator—whether a policymaker, engineer, community organizer, or teacher—carries the principle across the threshold into the world, aware that it will be changed in the process (Coenye et al, 2024). The task is not to prevent change, but to ensure that the change deepens rather than dilutes the principle's intent. This requires a strange blend of stubbornness and adaptability, of holding fast to the core while letting the edges shift with the winds. It's a craft as much as it is a discipline.

And perhaps that is the hidden beauty of it: theory is not diminished by its journey into practice. It becomes more layered, more human, more aware of its own fragility and resilience. Principles that survive this journey emerge not as museum pieces but as living tools, carrying the marks of their encounters, the dents and polish of real use. They are no longer just ideas—they are ideas that have learned how to walk in the world.

CONCLUSION

The journey through the theories and principles governing the development of applied models reveals that effective problem-solving is neither a matter of blind application nor of pure abstraction—it is the careful orchestration of conceptual insight, methodological rigor, and contextual sensitivity. Applied models are most powerful when they are rooted in solid theoretical foundations, guided by clear principles, and attuned to the realities of the environments in which they are deployed. Without this triad, models risk degenerating into either rigid formulas that ignore human and environmental complexity or vague frameworks that inspire little confidence in their reliability.

One of the central takeaways from this exploration is that theories do more than provide an intellectual backdrop; they actively shape the boundaries, logic, and predictive capacity of a model. They offer a map of possibilities and constraints, allowing the model's designer to see beyond immediate appearances and anticipate underlying dynamics. Principles, in turn, ensure that these theoretical insights are implemented with consistency, transparency, and ethical responsibility. They serve as the guardrails that keep the development process aligned with both scientific integrity and societal values.

Yet, the world in which applied models operate is rarely stable. Global challenges are increasingly interconnected and volatile, requiring models that can pivot without losing their conceptual grounding. This necessity points to a vital conclusion: adaptability is not the opposite of rigor—it is its companion. The most effective models are those that are built on theories resilient enough to accommodate new evidence and principles flexible enough to guide adjustments without undermining the model's core integrity.

Furthermore, the development of applied models is as much an art as it is a science. It requires the ability to synthesize insights from multiple disciplines, translate abstract concepts into practical terms, and engage with stakeholders who bring diverse perspectives and priorities. This collaborative and iterative process transforms model development into a living dialogue—between theory and practice, between ideal frameworks and imperfect realities, and between the aspirations of problem-solvers and the limitations of the systems they seek to improve.

Looking ahead, the challenge will be to design models that can thrive in the face of accelerating change while remaining anchored in enduring principles. This demands a culture of continuous learning, where model developers remain open to revising assumptions, incorporating emerging knowledge, and embracing innovation without sacrificing foundational rigor. It also calls for a heightened awareness of the ethical dimensions of modeling, particularly in contexts where decisions based on models carry significant consequences for individuals, communities, and ecosystems.

In conclusion, the development of applied models should be understood not as a linear process leading to a fixed endpoint, but as an evolving practice—one that must be informed by theory, guided by principles, and responsive to the shifting landscapes of the problems it seeks to address. By honoring this triadic foundation, we can build models that are not only technically robust but also intellectually honest, ethically grounded, and practically transformative. Such models do more than solve problems—they expand our capacity to think critically, act responsibly, and shape a more adaptable and equitable future.

REFERENCES

Adobor, H., & Kudonoo, E. C. (2025). Antifragility and organizations: An organizational design perspective. *Leadership and Organization Development Journal, 46*(2), 351–375. DOI: 10.1108/LODJ-03-2024-0185

Alibašić, H. (2025). Advancing disaster resilience: The ethical dimensions of adaptability and adaptive leadership in public service organizations. *Public Integrity, 27*(3), 209–221. DOI: 10.1080/10999922.2024.2388285

Arya, C. (2022). *Design of structural elements: concrete, steelwork, masonry and timber designs to eurocodes*. CRC Press. DOI: 10.1201/9781003208037

Bernstein, P. (2022). *Machine learning: Architecture in the age of artificial intelligence*. Riba Publishing. DOI: 10.4324/9781003297192

Cedercreutz, I. (2024). What is improvisation in leadership?.

Clark, S. G., & Terway, T. M. (2022). A Model Integrated-Interdisciplinary Foundational Course for Environmental Science and Management Programs. Journal of Multidisciplinary Research (1947-2900), 14(2).

Coenye, T., Ahonen, M., Anderson, S., Cámara, M., Chundi, P., Fields, M., Foidl, I., Gnimpieba, E. Z., Griffin, K., Hinks, J., Loka, A. R., Lushbough, C., MacPhee, C., Nater, N., Raval, R., Slater-Jefferies, J., Teo, P., Wilks, S., Yung, M., & Webb, J. S. (2024). Global challenges and microbial biofilms: Identification of priority questions in biofilm research, innovation and policy. *Biofilm, 8*, 100210. DOI: 10.1016/j.bioflm.2024.100210 PMID: 39221168

DiSalvo, C. (2022). *Design as democratic inquiry: Putting experimental civics into practice*. MIT Press. DOI: 10.7551/mitpress/13372.001.0001

Enke, B. (2024). The cognitive turn in behavioral economics. Unpublished manuscript. https://benjamin-enke. com

Fatihi, A. R. (2024). *Bridging Worlds through Translatology: A Linguistic Approach to Translation*. Cambridge Scholars Publishing.

Fernandez, L. J. (2023). *The art of business Origami: folding your way to success*. Lloyd Jose Fernandez.

Gale, A. P., Chapman, J. O., White, D. E., Ahluwalia, P., Williamson, A. K. J., Peacock, K. R., Akagbosu, R., Lepine, T. M., Arizor, I., Bone, L. A., Brown, J., Fahrngruber, A. M., Goldberg-Flood, A., Kovirineni, S., Lamb-Laurin, S. J., Zia, N., Innocent, S., Lee, W., Moran, G., & Cooke, S. J. (2022). On embracing the concept of bccoming environmental problem solvers: The trainee perspective on key elements of success, essential skills, and mindset. *Environmental Reviews*, *30*(1), 1–9. DOI: 10.1139/er-2021-0040

Geuss, R. (2022). *Not thinking like a liberal*. Harvard University Press.

Huber, M. T., & Morreale, S. P. (Eds.). (2023). *Disciplinary styles in the scholarship of teaching and learning: Exploring common ground*. Taylor & Francis. DOI: 10.4324/9781003444268

Jackson, T. (2024). Principles of clean production—Developing an operational approach to the preventive paradigm. In *Clean Production Strategies Developing Preventive Environmental Management in the Industrial Economy* (pp. 143–164). CRC Press. DOI: 10.1201/9781003575535-10

Jin, L., Wei, J., Luo, C., & Qin, T. (2023). Slope stability analysis based on improved radial movement optimization considering seepage effect. *Alexandria Engineering Journal*, *79*, 591–607. DOI: 10.1016/j.aej.2023.08.029

Kayyali, M. (2022). *Management of Higher Education Institutions: The Impact of ICT Based Good Governance*. Entrepreneurship, and Quality Assurance on the Operation of Academic Institutions.

Kayyali, M. (2024). Design thinking and creativity in entrepreneurial innovation. In *Applying Business Intelligence and Innovation to Entrepreneurship* (pp. 155–170). IGI Global Scientific Publishing. DOI: 10.4018/979-8-3693-1846-1.ch008

Kayyali, M. (2025). The evolution of quality assurance in higher education: Models, systems, and frameworks. In *Navigating Quality Assurance and Accreditation in Global Higher Education* (pp. 1–26). IGI Global Scientific Publishing.

Kendall, C., & Oprea, R. (2024). On the complexity of forming mental models. *Quantitative Economics*, *15*(1), 175–211. DOI: 10.3982/QE2264

Kennedy, P. C. (2023). Libertas regimine crescit–developing a working theory of improvising in the course of composing music for improvised performance (Doctoral dissertation, University of Oxford).

Klimczuk, A., & Klimczuk-Kochańska, M. (2023). Core-periphery model. In *The Palgrave encyclopedia of global security studies* (pp. 239–245). Springer International Publishing. DOI: 10.1007/978-3-319-74319-6_320

Mackintosh, L. (2021). *Shifting grounds: deep histories of Tāmaki Makaurau Auckland*. Bridget Williams Books. DOI: 10.7810/9781988587332

Mahajan, P. (2025). *The Soul of the AI: Governance*. Ethics, and the Future of Human–AI Integration.

Mandavilli, S. R. (2023). Elucidating the Certainty uncertainty principle for the Social Sciences: Guidelines for hypothesis formulation in the Social Sciences for enhanced objectivity and intellectual multi-polarity. Available at *SSRN* 4531179. DOI: 10.2139/ssrn.4531179

Mani, I. (2022). *Computational modeling of narrative*. Springer Nature.

McStay, A. (2023). *Automating empathy: Decoding technologies that gauge intimate life*. Oxford University Press. DOI: 10.1093/oso/9780197615546.001.0001

Miller, B. (2022). *Distant readings of disciplinarity: Knowing and doing in composition/rhetoric dissertations*. University Press of Colorado.

Myers, J. (2021). Reasoning with imagination. In *Epistemic uses of imagination* (pp. 103–121). Routledge. DOI: 10.4324/9781003041979-8

Qadhi, S. (2023). Knowledge Dynamics: Educational Pathways from Theories to Tangible Outcomes. In From Theory of Knowledge Management to Practice. IntechOpen.

Rivard, S. (2021). Theory building is neither an art nor a science. It is a craft. *Journal of Information Technology*, *36*(3), 316–328. DOI: 10.1177/0268396220911938

Savaglio, C., & Fortino, G. (2021). A simulation-driven methodology for IoT data mining based on edge computing. *ACM Transactions on Internet Technology*, *21*(2), 1–22. DOI: 10.1145/3402444

Scaratti, G., & Ivaldi, S. (2021). Uniqueness and generalization in organizational psychology: Research as a relational practice. *Frontiers in Psychology*, *12*, 638240. DOI: 10.3389/fpsyg.2021.638240 PMID: 33613408

Shaturaev, J. (2022). Bad management hypotheses are demolishing management practices. Архив научных исследований, 2(1).

Tähtinen, L. (2025). Navigating adverse futures for resilience: Expanding understanding of future crises and their impacts in the built environment.

Tian, Y., & Ha, D. (2022, April). Modern evolution strategies for creativity: Fitting concrete images and abstract concepts. In International conference on computational intelligence in music, sound, art and design (part of evostar) (pp. 275-291). Cham: Springer International Publishing.

Ting, L. (2024). Prognosticating Parsimony: An Ebullient Ensemble Approach to Predictive Modeling in Artificial Intelligence.

Tripathi, S., Muhr, D., Brunner, M., Jodlbauer, H., Dehmer, M., & Emmert-Streib, F. (2021). Ensuring the robustness and reliability of data-driven knowledge discovery models in production and manufacturing. *Frontiers in Artificial Intelligence*, *4*, 576892. DOI: 10.3389/frai.2021.576892 PMID: 34195608

Vogel, B., Džuverović, N., Tripathi, S., Kušić, K., Zapata, M. L., Ramachandran, S., Dhungana, N., & Taithe, B. (2024). Upholding Hierarchies of Knowledge Production: Mundane Obstacles to Global International Relations. *International Studies Perspectives*, •••, ekae025. DOI: 10.1093/isp/ekae025

Wu, J., & Or, C. K. (2025). Position Paper: Towards Open Complex Human-AI Agents Collaboration System for Problem-Solving and Knowledge Management. arXiv preprint arXiv:2505.00018.

KEY TERMS AND DEFINITIONS

Adaptability: Designed-in capacity to update structure/parameters as contexts and data shift without breaking the core.

Applied Model: A structured, simplified representation of reality used to illuminate relationships and guide decisions in practical contexts.

Coherence: Internal consistency of assumptions, definitions, and causal logic across the model's components.

Fidelity to Reality: Preserving the system's key dynamics and constraints while simplifying enough to remain useful.

Parsimony: Achieving necessary explanatory power with the fewest moving parts to avoid bloat and overfitting.

Theoretical Lens: The conceptual viewpoint (e.g., systems, behavioral, network) that frames assumptions, boundaries, and what counts as signal.

Translation to Practice: Turning principles into workable interventions via iteration, stakeholder fit, and ethical guardrails.

Chapter 2
Building Applied Models From Multiple Sources

Satya Subrahmanyam
https://orcid.org/0000-0003-0441-2742
Holy Spirit University of Kaslik, Lebanon

ABSTRACT

In the age of big data, constructing applied models from multiple data sources is crucial for solving complex problems in various sectors, including business, healthcare, finance, and smart city management. This chapter discusses methodologies, challenges, and best practices in building robust models by integrating diverse data types, such as structured, unstructured, real-time, and historical data. Key steps, including data preprocessing, feature engineering, and selecting the appropriate modeling approach, are outlined. The chapter also examines the importance of frameworks like CRISP-DM and DIKW in guiding model development. Real-world applications demonstrate the power of multi-source models, though challenges in data security, complexity, and model interpretability remain. Future advancements, including AI, edge computing, and federated learning, promise to enhance the effectiveness of these models.

I. INTRODUCTION

1.1 Purpose of the Chapter

In an increasingly data-driven world, the complexity of real-world problems necessitates sophisticated solutions that draw upon diverse data and knowledge sources. The purpose of this chapter is to explore the methodologies and best practices involved in building applied models by integrating information from multiple

DOI: 10.4018/979-8-3373-3301-4.ch002

origins. This involves understanding the conceptual foundations of applied modeling, identifying and acquiring relevant data, and developing frameworks that synthesize heterogeneous sources into coherent, actionable models. Rather than relying on a single dataset or knowledge domain, this chapter emphasizes a holistic approach to model construction, one that recognizes the value of multiple perspectives, formats, and disciplines. The ability to construct such integrated models is critical not only for academic research but also for practical decision-making across industries such as healthcare, finance, urban planning, and logistics.

1.2 Relevance to Problem Solving

The relevance of building applied models from multiple sources becomes evident when considering the multifaceted nature of contemporary challenges. Complex problems rarely reside within the boundaries of a single discipline or dataset. Designing effective public health intervention may require epidemiological statistics, behavioral data from social media, and insights from medical professionals. Financial risk analysis might depend on structured historical transaction data, real-time market trends, and unstructured news sentiment analysis. Integrating these sources allows for a more nuanced understanding of the problem and leads to more accurate, robust, and actionable models (Provost & Fawcett, 2013).

Relying solely on one data source can result in biased or incomplete models, which may overlook key variables or relationships critical to decision-making. By leveraging multiple sources, practitioners can better account for data sparsity, reduce the risk of overfitting, and improve generalizability. Cross-source modeling enables organizations to combine internal knowledge - such as proprietary operational data - with external insights, such as market intelligence, for a competitive edge (Kitchin, 2014). In essence, the integration of diverse data enhances both the breadth and depth of problem-solving capabilities.

1.3 Overview of the Chapter

This chapter unfolds in a structured manner to guide readers through the journey of building applied models from multiple sources. Following this introduction, the next section provides a foundational understanding of applied models, distinguishing between descriptive, predictive, prescriptive, and diagnostic models, and emphasizing their roles in various problem-solving contexts.

Subsequently, the chapter explores the need for multi-source integration. This includes a discussion of the limitations of single-source models, the benefits of incorporating diverse perspectives, and real-world examples of the kinds of data sources that can be integrated, including quantitative datasets, qualitative inputs, domain expertise, and unstructured data like images or text.

The chapter then discusses data gathering and preparation techniques. Readers will learn how to find and acquire appropriate data, solve data quality issues, and harmonise and integrate datasets here. A solid modelling foundation requires data cleansing, normalisation, and inconsistency management.

Frameworks and techniques for integrating varied sources are then discussed in model design. Topics include feature engineering across sources, using machine learning or statistical modelling approaches, and using hybrid models. Discussing case-based modelling will show how comparative assessments may improve model robustness. The chapter discusses multi-source modelling issues for balancing. Technical problems like data incompatibility and processing complexity and conceptual problems like contradictory information are examples. Integrating data raises ethical and legal issues including privacy, consent, and intellectual property.

Following obstacles, the chapter discusses data integration and model creation methods and technology. Cloud platforms, ETL tools, and sophisticated analytics environments like Python and R are examples. We will also quickly examine model interpretation and communication visualisation and reporting tools.

The chapter uses case studies from public health, economics, and urban planning to demonstrate how integrated models may address complicated issues. These examples demonstrate multi-source modeling's practical uses and advantages.

The chapter concludes with the integrated applied model best practices and standards. Early planning, data quality, cross-disciplinary cooperation, and iterative model building are recommended. Future trends include using AI to automate data integration and creating interoperable data sharing platforms. The chapter stresses the necessity of multi-source integration in applied modelling. By summarising the essential ideas and calling for action, readers are urged to use integrative modelling in academic research, industry, and public policy.

2. UNDERSTANDING APPLIED MODELS

Applied models serve as practical frameworks that translate theoretical concepts into real-world solutions. They integrate data, methods, and contextual insights to address complex problems effectively. Understanding applied models involves exploring their design principles, data integration techniques, and adaptability across diverse domains, forming the foundation for constructing models from multiple, interconnected sources.

2.1 Definition and Scope

Applied models are structured representations of real-world systems, processes, or phenomena, designed specifically to assist in solving practical problems. In contrast to purely theoretical models, applied models are rooted in empirical data and are developed with the primary goal of informing decisions, optimizing performance, or explaining observed behaviors. These models often serve as simplified yet functional abstractions of reality, capable of simulating scenarios, predicting outcomes, or guiding action within specific contexts (Subrahmanyam, 2025).

In the context of problem-solving, applied models offer a framework for understanding the variables involved in a particular situation, identifying relationships among them, and quantifying potential outcomes of various interventions or decisions. Whether employed in business, public policy, healthcare, engineering, or environmental management, applied models are crucial tools for translating complex real-world issues into manageable, actionable insights. Their utility is not confined to academic exercises; rather, they provide decision-makers with evidence-based instruments for responding to dynamic and uncertain environments.

The scope of applied modeling spans multiple disciplines and applications. In public health, models might simulate the spread of infectious diseases to inform vaccination strategies. In supply chain logistics, models may optimize inventory levels and transportation routes. What unifies these diverse applications is the model's operational purpose, each is tailored to address a specific challenge, using relevant data, assumptions, and methodologies suited to the context in which it operates (Pidd, 2004).

2.2 Types of Applied Models

To choose the right tool for the job, you need to know what kinds of applied models are out there. There are four basic kinds of applied models: diagnostic, descriptive, predictive, and prescriptive.

Descriptive models focus on summarizing and organizing data to provide a clear picture of the current or historical state of a system. These models do not attempt to predict the future or recommend specific actions; instead, they aim to enhance understanding. Demographic analyses or business dashboards that illustrate key performance indicators (KPIs) fall into this category. Descriptive models serve as the foundation for more advanced modeling efforts, offering insights into trends, patterns, and anomalies (Shmueli & Koppius, 2011).

To foretell what's to come from past data, predictive models use statistical and machine learning approaches. Demand forecasting, credit scoring, and risk assessment are just a few of the many applications that make extensive use of these models. By seeing trends in historical data and projecting those trends into the future, they help stakeholders prepare for potential outcomes. Neural networks, decision trees, and linear regression are common approaches (Kuhn & Johnson, 2013).

Prescriptive models go a step further by not only predicting what might happen but also suggesting optimal courses of action. These models integrate data, constraints, and objectives to support decision-making in complex environments. Operations research techniques such as linear programming, simulation modeling, and optimization algorithms are frequently used in prescriptive modeling. An example includes recommending pricing strategies based on customer behavior predictions and business objectives (Delen & Demirkan, 2013).

Diagnostic models are designed to identify the causes of observed phenomena. These models explore why something happened, rather than what will happen or what should be done. In fields such as healthcare or industrial engineering, diagnostic models help trace system failures or inefficiencies to their root causes. They often employ causal inference techniques, sensitivity analysis, or systems thinking approaches (Pearl, 2009).

Each type of model serves a distinct purpose, and in practice, they are often used in combination. A diagnostic model may be used to understand a past failure, followed by a predictive model to assess the likelihood of recurrence, and a prescriptive model to recommend preventive measures.

2.3 Role of Data in Applied Modeling

Data plays a foundational role in applied modeling, serving as both the input that informs model structure and the benchmark against which model performance is evaluated. High-quality, relevant, and representative data are essential for building models that are accurate, reliable, and generalizable. The effectiveness of any applied model is largely determined by the extent to which the underlying data captures the realities of the system being modeled (Provost & Fawcett, 2013).

Data influences every stage of the modeling process, from initial hypothesis formulation and variable selection to model training, validation, and deployment. For descriptive models, data provides the narrative. For predictive models, historical data is mined for patterns that can forecast future events. In prescriptive modeling, data defines constraints and informs optimization objectives. For diagnostic models, data provides clues that help trace causality.

The nature of the data - whether structured (e.g., numerical databases), semi-structured (e.g., JSON or XML formats), or unstructured (e.g., text, images, videos) - dictates the modeling techniques and tools that can be employed. Increasingly, applied modeling involves integrating data from multiple sources, such as internal enterprise systems, external public datasets, sensor networks, and user-generated content. This diversity requires robust data processing and fusion methods, but it also significantly enhances the model's ability to reflect complex realities (Kitchin, 2014).

Take data limits into account. An inadequate, biassed, or outdated dataset may compromise model fidelity. Modelling requires data preparation, validation, and monitoring. Data governance—accuracy, consistency, security, and ethics—is becoming increasingly crucial as models influence high-stakes decisions. Use models to solve cross-domain problems. They handle complex system understanding, prediction, prescription, and diagnosis. Data literacy and governance are crucial for modern modellers since data quality and integration affect model accuracy and value.

3. THE NEED FOR MULTIPLE SOURCES

Relying on a single data source often limits the depth and accuracy of analysis. Multiple sources enrich applied models by providing diverse perspectives, reducing bias, and enhancing reliability. Integrating varied datasets - quantitative, qualitative, and contextual - ensures comprehensive understanding, enabling more robust, adaptive, and evidence-based decision-making in complex and dynamic environments.

3.1 Limitations of Single-Source Models

Relying on a single source of data for applied modeling presents several fundamental limitations that can adversely affect the reliability, accuracy, and generalizability of the model. One of the most critical issues with single-source models is bias. When a model is built from a single dataset, it is inherently influenced by the assumptions, limitations, and structure of that dataset. This can lead to systematic errors that are not representative of broader contexts. A model developed solely using data from a particular geographic region or demographic group may not apply effectively to other regions or populations (Friedman et al., 2001).

Another significant limitation is incompleteness. No single data source is likely to capture all the dimensions of a complex problem. Consider healthcare decision-making: patient records may provide rich clinical information but lack behavioral, social, or economic data that significantly influence outcomes. Financial models developed solely using historical transaction data may overlook sentiment, regulatory changes, or geopolitical factors that are crucial to predictive accuracy (Provost & Fawcett, 2013). This lack of a holistic view results in models that can miss critical variables and relationships.

Single-source models often suffer from poor generalizability. They may perform well within the context of their origin but struggle to adapt to new, unseen situations. This is particularly problematic in dynamic environments where data distributions shift over time or between domains, a phenomenon known as "dataset shift" (Quionero-Candela et al., 2009). When models are not trained on diverse data reflecting the variability in the real world, they are more susceptible to overfitting and less effective when deployed in practice.

Table 1. Limitations of single-source models

Aspect	Description	Illustrative Example
Bias	Single-source models are inherently influenced by the assumptions and limitations of one dataset, leading to skewed or unrepresentative results.	A predictive model trained only on data from one geographic region may fail to generalize to other regions with different socio-economic conditions.
Incompleteness	A single data source rarely captures all relevant dimensions of a problem, omitting critical contextual variables.	Healthcare models based only on patient records may overlook behavioral or social factors influencing outcomes.
Poor Generalizability	Models perform well within the context of origin but fail in new or dynamic environments due to lack of diversity in training data.	Financial forecasting models based on past data may underperform when market dynamics shift.
Overfitting Risk	Limited data diversity increases the chance of overfitting, reducing predictive power in unseen scenarios.	Machine learning models trained solely on one dataset can memorize noise rather than learn true patterns.
Lack of Contextual Relevance	Narrow data perspectives hinder holistic understanding of multi-dimensional phenomena.	Models built from clinical data alone ignore socio-economic and cultural determinants of health.

3.2 Advantages of Multi-Source Integration

In contrast, integrating data from multiple sources can greatly enhance the robustness and applicability of applied models. Enhanced reliability is one of the most immediate benefits. When data from different origins converge on similar findings or predictions, model developers gain confidence in the validity of their outputs. Cross-verifying information helps reduce the impact of errors or anomalies that may be present in individual datasets (Kitchin, 2014).

Multi-source integration also provides a broader context for understanding complex systems. Diverse data types and perspectives allow models to account for the multifaceted nature of real-world problems. In urban planning, combining satellite imagery, traffic data, public surveys, and economic indicators can provide a 360-degree view of development challenges and inform more balanced decision-making. This holistic approach is particularly valuable in interdisciplinary domains where the problem cannot be encapsulated by a single type of data (Subrahmanyam, 2025).

Multi-source models yield better insights by uncovering relationships and patterns that may not be visible when using one data stream. Integrating structured and unstructured data, for example, allows for the modeling of both quantitative trends and qualitative nuances. In customer behavior analysis, numerical sales data may reveal buying patterns, while textual data from reviews and feedback may expose motivations and sentiments driving those behaviors. Such richer insights can lead to more targeted and effective interventions (Shmueli & Koppius, 2011).

Another key advantage is increased adaptability and generalizability. By training on data that represents diverse scenarios, multi-source models are better equipped to handle variability and perform well in a range of contexts. This capacity is critical in domains like disaster response or public health, where unpredictable and rapidly changing conditions demand flexible modeling approaches.

Finally, redundancy and resilience are additional benefits. In cases where one source becomes unavailable, outdated, or corrupted, other sources can serve as backups or substitutes. This improves the sustainability and reliability of applied models in the long run.

Table 2. Advantages of multi-source integration

Benefit	Description	Application Example
Enhanced Reliability	Integrating multiple data sources improves consistency and minimizes the influence of anomalies or errors in individual datasets.	Cross-verification of clinical, behavioral, and genetic data enhances diagnostic accuracy.
Broader Contextual Understanding	Combining heterogeneous data types offers a holistic view of complex systems.	Urban planning models integrating satellite, traffic, and survey data provide comprehensive insights into development dynamics.
Richer Insights	Multi-source data uncovers relationships and patterns not visible in isolated datasets.	Combining sales data with customer reviews reveals both behavioral trends and emotional drivers of purchase decisions.
Improved Adaptability and Generalizability	Models trained on diverse datasets adapt more effectively to new conditions or domains.	Disaster response systems using real-time social media and environmental data improve situational awareness.
Redundancy and Resilience	When one data source becomes obsolete or unavailable, others can act as substitutes, ensuring model sustainability.	In epidemiological modeling, if hospital data is delayed, public health reports can temporarily fill the gap.

3.3 Examples of Diverse Sources

The richness of applied modeling is significantly enhanced by the strategic inclusion of diverse data types. These sources can be broadly categorized into quantitative data, qualitative data, domain expertise, academic literature, and simulations.

Quantitative data includes numerical and structured data collected through databases, sensors, and digital transactions. These are often used for statistical and machine learning models. Environmental models might utilize sensor data on temperature, humidity, and pollution levels to forecast climate trends. Financial models might depend on transaction records, stock prices, and economic indicators. Such data is often voluminous, timely, and suitable for algorithmic processing (Kuhn & Johnson, 2013).

Qualitative data offers context and depth that quantitative data may lack. This includes information obtained through interviews, focus groups, open-ended survey responses, ethnographic observations, or case studies. Qualitative data is particularly useful in capturing user experiences, organizational culture, and subjective motivations. In healthcare, for instance, patient interviews can provide insights into treatment adherence and satisfaction that numbers alone cannot capture. Qualitative coding, thematic analysis, and narrative methods help incorporate these rich insights into applied models (Subrahmanyam, 2025).

Domain expertise is another invaluable source, especially in areas where tacit knowledge plays a critical role. Experts often possess nuanced understandings that may not be documented or quantifiable. Their input can guide variable selection, model design, and the interpretation of outputs. For example, in cybersecurity, ethical hackers' experiential knowledge can help frame attack simulations and anticipate system vulnerabilities.

Literature reviews and scientific publications offer access to validated theories, empirical findings, and established methodologies. Reviewing existing research ensures that models are grounded in proven concepts and avoid redundancy. Incorporating literature-based parameters or assumptions helps align models with the current state of knowledge in the field.

Simulations and synthetic data represent another category, especially useful when real data is scarce, sensitive, or costly to obtain. Agent-based modeling can simulate the behavior of individuals within a system to predict emergent outcomes. Synthetic datasets generated using statistical techniques or AI can help train models when real-world data is inadequate, allowing for experimentation without ethical or practical constraints (Epstein, 2006).

The integration of these diverse sources requires thoughtful preprocessing, alignment, and calibration. Challenges such as differing scales, formats, and terminologies must be addressed through standardization and transformation processes. The synergistic value of diverse data far outweighs the complexity of integration.

Multiple sources are needed in applied modelling because real-world issues are complicated, diverse, and dynamic. Single-source models are handy yet biassed, incomplete, and unadaptable. Multi-source integration improves applied models' dependability, contextual depth, and generalisability. By using quantitative, qualitative, expert, and simulated data, modellers may create powerful, intelligent, and practical problem-solving solutions. In an increasingly complex environment, careful integration of different sources is essential for producing scientifically sound and practically usable models.

4. DATA ACQUISITION AND PREPROCESSING

Data collecting and preprocessing are essential to building strong applied models from numerous sources. These actions are crucial to model quality, dependability, and relevance. Data from internal and external, structured and unstructured sources must be carefully planned and preprocessed to be clean, harmonised, and ready for integration and analysis. This section discusses how to find good sources, acquire data efficiently, clean and standardise it, and use it meaningfully for applied modelling.

4.1 Identifying Relevant Sources

The first step in building applied models is to identify the data sources that are most relevant to the problem at hand. Broadly, these sources fall into two categories: internal and external.

Internal sources refer to data generated within an organization or project environment. These can include enterprise databases, transaction records, CRM logs, ERP systems, employee surveys, or operational reports. Such data is often easily accessible, relatively clean, and aligned with the specific objectives of the modeling effort (Provost & Fawcett, 2013). A retail company might use sales logs, customer feedback forms, and inventory data for modeling product demand.

External sources, on the other hand, come from outside the organization and can complement internal data by offering broader context or filling in missing gaps. Examples include government databases (e.g., census data), social media content, academic datasets, satellite imagery, market research reports, and third-party APIs. While external data can be valuable, it may also pose challenges in terms of access rights, reliability, and compatibility with internal systems (Kitchin, 2014).

An additional way to categorise data is by its structure or lack thereof. Conventional data management solutions make short work of structured data because of its established forms, which might be anything from relational tables to spreadsheets. According to Witten et al. (2016), extracting valuable information from unstructured data, which includes things like written documents, audio recordings, videos, and photographs, necessitates the use of sophisticated methods such as natural language processing (NLP) or image recognition.

A hybrid approach that combines structured and unstructured data across internal and external sources often yields the richest modeling outcomes, enabling the model to capture both quantifiable metrics and qualitative context.

4.2 Data Collection Strategies

It is necessary to implement suitable data gathering procedures after identifying relevant sources. Data characteristics, study aims, and accessible resources all play a role in approach selection.

One of the most common methods for collecting primary data is surveys. Surveys can be administered via online forms, phone interviews, or in-person meetings to gather quantitative metrics and qualitative insights. When designed properly, surveys can capture a broad range of variables, such as attitudes, preferences, and behaviors (Subrahmanyam, 2025).

Web scraping is a technique used to automatically extract information from websites. This is particularly useful for collecting real-time or large-scale data from e-commerce platforms, news sites, or public forums. Tools like BeautifulSoup, Scrapy, or Selenium in Python are widely used for this purpose. However, ethical considerations and website terms of service must be observed when using scraping tools (Mitchell, 2015).

APIs (Application Programming Interfaces) offer structured access to real-time or static data provided by third parties. Many platforms, such as Twitter, Google, and World Bank, provide APIs to facilitate secure data exchange. API-based collection is more structured and reliable than scraping and allows seamless integration into automated pipelines (Kuhn & Johnson, 2013).

Data repositories, including government portals, academic archives, and open data platforms like Kaggle or UCI Machine Learning Repository, offer pre-collected and cleaned datasets suitable for benchmarking or model training.

In domains where tacit knowledge is essential, expert interviews serve as a valuable qualitative data collection method. These interviews can provide insights not captured by formal data systems and help contextualize the variables and assumptions used in modeling (Yin, 2017).

4.3 Data Cleaning and Harmonization

Once data is collected, it rarely arrives in a form ready for immediate analysis. The next critical phase - data cleaning and harmonization - ensures consistency, accuracy, and completeness. This process involves several steps:

Handling missing data: Missing values are a common issue and must be addressed using techniques such as deletion, imputation, or substitution. Depending on the situation, methods like mean substitution, regression imputation, or more advanced machine learning techniques like k-nearest neighbors (KNN) can be applied (Allison, 2002).

Resolving inconsistencies: Datasets collected from different sources may contain contradictory information or inconsistencies in naming conventions, units of measurement, or coding schemes. One dataset might label gender as "M/F" while another uses "Male/Female." Standardizing such attributes is essential for accurate modeling.

Standardizing formats: Data values must be transformed into a uniform format. This includes ensuring date-time formats are consistent (e.g., ISO 8601), normalizing text (e.g., converting to lowercase, removing punctuation), and encoding categorical variables properly (e.g., one-hot encoding or label encoding).

Detecting and handling outliers: Outliers can skew model results and must be identified using techniques like z-scores, IQR (interquartile range), or visual inspection through box plots. Depending on context, outliers may be corrected, removed, or flagged for further investigation (Friedman et al., 2001).

The goal of cleaning is to produce a harmonized dataset that reflects a coherent view of the variables involved, reducing noise and error while preserving signal.

Figure 1. Data acquisition and preprocessing

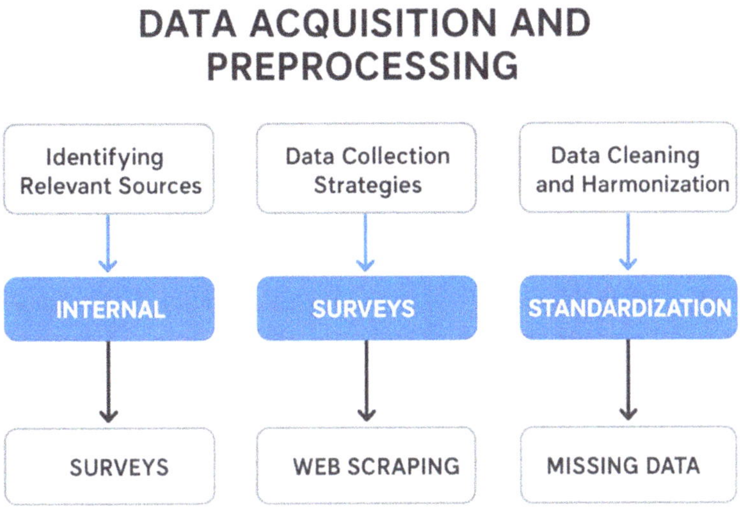

4.4 Data Integration Techniques

After data cleaning, integration is the final step in preprocessing, where disparate datasets are merged to form a comprehensive dataset for modeling. Effective integration enhances the model's contextual richness and predictive power.

Merging is the most straightforward technique, where datasets are combined using shared keys such as IDs, timestamps, or geographical codes. This requires careful alignment to avoid duplications or misalignment errors. Techniques such as inner joins, outer joins, and left/right joins are used based on the nature of the relationship between datasets.

Linking involves establishing connections between entities across datasets, often where common identifiers are not available. This can involve probabilistic record linkage or fuzzy matching techniques that compare strings for similarity, useful in cases where names or addresses may be spelled differently across sources (Christen, 2012).

Matching goes a step further by aligning variables or records across datasets based on rules or machine learning algorithms. Entity resolution methods, for example, identify which records refer to the same entity (person, place, product) across sources. This is crucial in fraud detection, customer 360 modeling, and social network analysis.

Integration also includes temporal alignment when datasets are collected at different timescales or intervals. Resampling techniques help align time-series data, while interpolation may be used to estimate missing intervals.

In complex scenarios, data warehousing or data lakes may be employed as infrastructure solutions to store and manage large volumes of integrated data, ensuring scalability, traceability, and security (Kimball & Ross, 2013).

Building applied models needs data collection and preparation from several sources. Complete problem-solving requires the right mix of internal, external, structured, and unstructured data. Smart data collection techniques like surveys and APIs provide diverse perspectives and insights. Integration makes data coherent and useable; while cleansing and harmonisation eliminate errors. These approaches transform raw, fragmented data into a sophisticated modelling tool that replicates real-world complexity and improves decision-making.

5. MODEL DESIGN USING INTEGRATED SOURCES

Theory, technique, and implementation must be balanced when designing applied models employing integrated sources. Building successful models requires a thorough, adaptive integrative strategy such as data origin, format, and granularity diversify. A framework for integration, feature engineering across sources, modelling method selection, and case-based modelling are covered in this chapter. These components enable the creation of strong, contextually rich applied models that handle complicated real-world situations.

5.1 Framework for Integration

Effective model design begins with a solid framework for integrating data from multiple sources. Integration can be conceptual, methodological, or operational, and these three layers must align to ensure coherent modeling outcomes.

Conceptual integration involves aligning the various data sources under a unified theoretical or conceptual model. This ensures that all data contributes meaningfully to a shared understanding of the problem. In a public health model predicting disease spread, epidemiological data, behavioral surveys, and geographic information systems (GIS) data must all adhere to a common conceptual structure that defines the relationships among variables (Bardach & Patashnik, 2019).

Methodological integration refers to the alignment of analytic methods and assumptions. Different datasets may have different units of analysis (e.g., individuals, regions, time points), distributions, or levels of precision. Methodological integration may involve normalization, data transformation, or using statistical techniques like multilevel modeling to reconcile these differences (Gelman & Hill, 2007).

Operational integration deals with the technical aspects of merging and processing data, including data warehousing, ETL (Extract, Transform, Load) pipelines, and real-time data handling. It requires the use of software tools and platforms that can process and synchronize diverse data types (Kimball & Ross, 2013). Integration frameworks such as data lakes or federated databases often serve as the infrastructure for operational alignment.

A comprehensive integration framework ensures consistency, reduces the risk of bias, and enhances the scalability of the applied model.

5.2 Feature Engineering Across Sources

Feature engineering - the process of selecting, modifying, or creating input variables for a model - is especially important when dealing with heterogeneous sources. This step transforms raw data into features that enhance model learning and predictive accuracy.

From structured data (e.g., spreadsheets, databases), common techniques include aggregation (e.g., total sales per region), normalization (e.g., min-max scaling), and encoding (e.g., one-hot encoding of categorical variables). In financial modeling, time-based features such as rolling averages and volatility measures are derived from raw price data (Zheng et al., 2018).

From unstructured sources like text, audio, or images, techniques such as natural language processing (NLP) and computer vision are used to extract features. NLP allows models to extract sentiment, topics, or keyword frequencies from textual data, while convolutional neural networks (CNNs) help in deriving spatial features from images (Jurafsky & Martin, 2020).

Cross-source feature engineering is particularly powerful. For instance, in a healthcare model, linking biometric sensor data with patient surveys and electronic health records (EHR) allows the creation of composite features such as "activity-adjusted stress levels" or "symptom frequency by medication adherence."

Feature selection methods, including mutual information scores, recursive feature elimination, and principal component analysis (PCA), help in reducing dimensionality and selecting the most informative features (Guyon & Elisseeff, 2003). Feature engineering serves as the creative and technical bridge between raw data and model learning.

5.3 Selecting Modeling Techniques

Once the features are defined, the appropriate modeling technique must be selected based on the nature of the problem, the structure of the data, and the modeling goals. A range of techniques can be employed, often in combination:

Regression Models: Useful for problems with a clear dependent variable and continuous outputs. Linear regression, logistic regression, and multivariate regression models are well-suited for forecasting, risk estimation, and scoring problems (Montgomery et al., 2012).
Machine Learning Models: For high-dimensional data, methods like decision trees, support vector machines (SVMs), random forests, and gradient boosting models work well for discovering intricate patterns. In order to model things from text, images, and other forms of unstructured data, more and more people are turning to neural networks and deep learning (Goodfellow et al., 2016).
Simulation Models: In systems where stochastic behavior and interaction over time are important, simulation modeling (e.g., agent-based models, system dynamics) allows for scenario analysis and policy evaluation. These are frequently used in public health, logistics, and environmental modeling (Sterman, 2000).
Optimization Models: When the goal is to determine the best decision under constraints, optimization techniques such as linear programming, integer programming, or heuristic methods are employed. These models are critical in operations research, supply chain management, and scheduling tasks (Hillier & Lieberman, 2020).
Hybrid Models: Often, no single technique is sufficient. Hybrid models combine the strengths of multiple approaches, such as integrating machine learning with optimization for intelligent decision-making systems. An example is using predictive models to estimate demand and optimization models to allocate resources accordingly (Bertsimas & Kallus, 2019).

Model selection is often iterative, involving model validation techniques like cross-validation, bootstrapping, and A/B testing to determine performance and generalizability.

5.4 Case-Based Modeling Approaches

In addition to purely data-driven models, case-based modeling approaches emphasize the use of real-world examples, comparative analysis, and domain knowledge. This is particularly valuable in applied settings where contextual nuance is essential.

Case studies provide rich, detailed examples from which models can be abstracted. In organizational behavior, a model for employee attrition might be developed by studying several firms across industries to understand the interplay between culture, incentives, and job satisfaction (Yin, 2017).

Comparative case analysis allows for the identification of common patterns or conditions that lead to desired outcomes. This approach is useful in policy evaluation and social science modeling, where controlled experiments may not be feasible.

Exemplar modeling involves selecting representative cases from clusters within the data to inform model parameters or structure. In public administration, for instance, models of successful municipal governance might be built on data from high-performing cities and compared against those with lower performance.

Case-based approaches support triangulation, the validation of model assumptions and results using multiple perspectives and sources. They also promote interpretability, especially in stakeholder-driven contexts where model transparency is as important as accuracy.

Figure 2. Model design using integrated sources

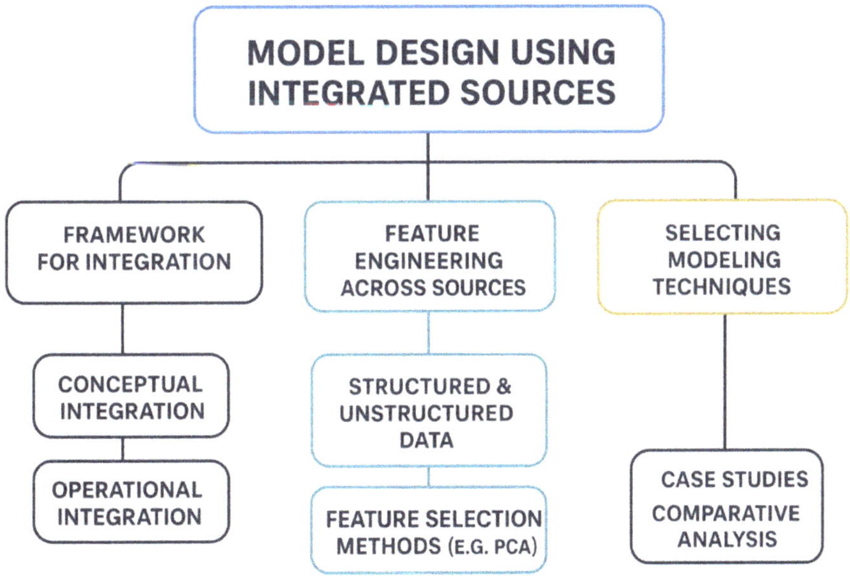

Applied models using integrated sources need data alignment, feature derivation, strategy selection, and real-world cases. Integration of ideas, techniques, and processes supports coherent modelling. Inputs become actionable variables via feature engineering. Nature and data characteristics must dictate the modelling technique, with hybrid approaches offering flexibility and power. Case-based modelling contextualises and interprets abstract analysis for real-world application. These strategies are essential for building technically sound and practically relevant models as data diversifies and grows more sophisticated.

6. CHALLENGES IN MULTI-SOURCE MODELING

Developing applied models from multiple data sources offers significant advantages in terms of comprehensiveness, robustness, and contextual relevance. It also introduces a host of complex challenges that must be systematically addressed. These challenges range from technical issues related to data compatibility and scalability to strategic concerns involving conflicting information and ethical-legal obligations. This section explores the key obstacles encountered in multi-source modeling and provides an overview of the methods used to navigate these difficulties.

6.1 Data Incompatibility

One of the foremost technical challenges in multi-source modeling is data incompatibility, which manifests in structural, semantic, and syntactic mismatches. Structural incompatibility arises when datasets are organized differently, for example, one dataset may use a flat-file structure while another employs a relational database schema. Integrating such data requires mapping and transformation processes that align formats and hierarchies (Batini & Scannapieco, 2006).

Semantic mismatches involve differences in meaning, labeling, or interpretation of data. One dataset might record "income" as gross earnings, while another may refer to net income after tax deductions. Such discrepancies, if unrecognized, can introduce serious biases into the resulting model (Doan et al., 2012). Syntactic differences, such as date formats, units of measurement, or naming conventions, can also lead to integration errors if not standardized during preprocessing.

To resolve incompatibility, data harmonization techniques, including schema matching, ontology mapping, and unit normalization, are employed. Data lakes and federated database systems can further assist in reconciling format discrepancies and ensuring a seamless modeling pipeline (Chebotko et al., 2008).

6.2 Conflicting Information

Another major challenge in multi-source modeling is dealing with conflicting information. This occurs when different sources provide contradictory data or conclusions about the same phenomenon. A social media dataset might suggest high customer satisfaction, while survey data indicates discontent among users. Without a principled strategy to resolve these conflicts, models may produce misleading or ambiguous outputs.

Approaches to resolving conflicting information include source weighting, where more reliable or contextually appropriate sources are given higher importance in the model. Consensus modeling, another common method, involves aggregating insights from multiple sources to produce a balanced outcome, often using techniques such as Bayesian inference or ensemble learning (Dietterich, 2000).

Conflict resolution protocols also include truth discovery algorithms that identify the most trustworthy source among conflicting datasets based on past accuracy or expert validation (Zhao et al., 2012). Integrating domain knowledge or expert feedback can further assist in resolving discrepancies and improving model credibility.

6.3 Scalability and Computational Constraints

The importance of scalability and computing limits grows in direct correlation with the complexity and quantity of sources. Managing massive amounts of structured, semi-structured, and unstructured data may be computationally costly when dealing with multi-source modelling.

Challenges include data volume, which affects memory and storage; data velocity, in cases involving real-time or streaming data; and variety, which complicates processing logic. Combining satellite images, IoT sensor readings, and demographic data in a disaster response model requires substantial computational power and robust data architecture (Katal et al., 2013).

Distributed computing frameworks like Spark and Hadoop are extensively used to manage large data workloads in order to tackle these difficulties. Scalable infrastructure for data intake, transformation, and model training is also offered by cloud computing platforms like AWS, Azure, and Google Cloud. Pruning, quantisation, and knowledge distillation are model compression strategies that may assist decrease training time and model size without losing performance (Cheng et al., 2018).

Modular model design allows for decomposition of complex modeling tasks into smaller, manageable components, facilitating parallel processing and model updating. Scalability is thus not only a technical concern but also a matter of thoughtful model architecture and resource planning.

6.4 Ethical and Legal Considerations

When dealing with sensitive or individually identifiable data, multi-source modelling also brings up substantial ethical and legal considerations. Using data responsibly, protecting people from harm, being fair, and protecting their privacy are all issues with ethical implications. In the US, the California Consumer Privacy Act (CCPA) and the EU's General Data Protection Regulation (GDPR) are two examples of data protection legislation that must be considered.

Key concerns include:

- Informed Consent: Ensuring that data subjects are aware of how their data will be used, especially when data is drawn from diverse, possibly non-consenting sources like public forums.
- Data Privacy and Anonymization: De-identifying personal data to prevent re-identification while preserving data utility for modeling (Sweeney, 2002).
- Intellectual Property (IP): Respecting the ownership rights of data providers, especially in cases where proprietary datasets are used or combined with open-source data.
- Bias and Discrimination: Multi-source models may unintentionally amplify biases present in one or more sources, leading to discriminatory outcomes. Algorithmic fairness techniques and bias auditing tools are critical to mitigate this risk (Barocas et al., 2023).

A strong governance framework is essential to ensure that data integration and modeling practices align with ethical norms and legal statutes. This includes establishing data stewardship roles, conducting regular privacy impact assessments, and maintaining transparent documentation of data lineage and model assumptions.

Multi-source modelling enhances practical problem-solving but presents technological, strategic, and ethical obstacles. Incompatible data needs thorough format, semantic, and structural harmonisation. Intelligent weighing and consensus-building must reconcile conflicting information. Scalability challenges need modern computer systems and model optimisation. Ethical and legal issues need proactive privacy, fairness, and compliance. Addressing these difficulties is essential to the integrity, effectiveness, and social acceptability of applied models in today's complex data context.

7. TOOLS AND TECHNOLOGIES FOR INTEGRATION

An efficient technical environment for data collection, integration, modelling, visualisation, and insight sharing is needed to generate applied models from numerous sources. With data amount, diversity, and velocity rising, tools and technologies are crucial to multi-source modelling efficiency and effectiveness. This section discusses data integration platforms, modelling environments, and visualisation tools that enable end-to-end model construction for complicated problem-solving.

7.1 Data Integration Platforms

Integrating data from multiple sources is a foundational step in applied modeling. Data integration platforms are designed to extract, transform, and load (ETL) data from diverse systems into a unified repository for analysis.

ETL tools such as Talend, Apache NiFi, and Informatica are widely used to manage the workflows associated with data cleansing, transformation, and migration. These tools support both batch and real-time data processing and are often equipped with built-in connectors for databases, cloud platforms, and software applications (Vassiliadis, 2009). They offer user-friendly graphical interfaces that allow non-technical users to design integration pipelines, monitor jobs, and manage errors.

Cloud-based data lakes, such as Amazon S3, Google Cloud Storage, and Azure Data Lake, provide scalable and flexible storage for structured and unstructured data. Unlike traditional data warehouses, which require predefined schemas, data lakes support schema-on-read models, making them ideal for heterogeneous data integration (Giebler et al., 2019). They facilitate the consolidation of raw data from various sources - IoT sensors, social media, enterprise systems - into a single repository, thus enhancing the comprehensiveness of applied models.

Application Programming Interfaces (APIs) also play a critical role in real-time data integration. RESTful APIs enables dynamic interaction between software systems and allows for automated data retrieval from third-party services, including financial markets, weather data providers, and social media platforms. Tools like Postman and Swagger help developers design, test, and manage APIs efficiently (Fielding, 2000).

7.2 Modeling Tools and Environments

Once data is integrated and preprocessed, the next step involves using appropriate tools and environments to build and refine models. Depending on the complexity and nature of the problem, analysts and data scientists can choose from a range of programming languages, statistical software, and simulation environments.

When it comes to statistical modelling and machine learning, two of the most well-known open-source programming languages are R and Python. From classification and regression to deep learning and NLP, Python's libraries like Pandas, Scikit-learn, TensorFlow, and PyTorch make it suitable for a broad variety of modelling jobs (Van Rossum & Drake, 2009). R is perfect for sophisticated econometric modelling and exploratory data analysis due to its strong statistical capabilities and data visualisation capabilities (R Core Team, 2023).

MATLAB and SAS are proprietary environments that offer extensive toolboxes for modeling, simulation, and optimization. MATLAB is particularly useful in engineering and scientific domains, while SAS is widely used in healthcare, banking, and government for its robust data handling and statistical capabilities (MathWorks, 2023; SAS Institute, 2022). Both platforms provide user interfaces that allow for low-code or no-code model development, thereby broadening accessibility to non-programmers.

Simulation software such as AnyLogic, Simul8, and Arena are essential when modeling dynamic systems or agent-based environments. These tools enable users to simulate real-world systems under varying conditions, allowing decision-makers to test different scenarios and evaluate potential outcomes before implementation (Borshchev, 2013). In applied modeling, simulation is especially useful in logistics, healthcare, and manufacturing domains where predictive accuracy and operational efficiency are critical.

7.3 Visualization and Reporting Tools

Effective communication of modeling results is just as important as the model itself. Visualization and reporting tools translate complex data and model outputs into intuitive visual formats, enhancing understanding and supporting decision-making.

Tableau and Power BI are leading business intelligence platforms that enable users to create interactive dashboards, charts, and maps from integrated datasets. These tools support real-time data updates, drill-down capabilities, and integration with numerous data sources, including SQL databases, Excel files, and cloud services (Few, 2009). Their drag-and-drop interfaces make them accessible to non-technical users while retaining advanced functionalities for experienced analysts.

Dashboards built using programming frameworks like Dash (Python) or Shiny (R) offer more customization and interactivity. These frameworks are ideal for deploying web-based visualizations that accompany applied models, allowing stakeholders to explore various scenarios or input values dynamically.

Data storytelling tools, such as Flourish and Adobe Express, go beyond traditional dashboards by integrating narrative elements - text, annotations, and multimedia - with visuals. This approach is particularly effective when communicating insights to non-technical stakeholders or broader audiences, as it places data in a relatable and persuasive context (Segel & Heer, 2010).

Many modeling platforms include built-in reporting functionalities that allow for automated generation of technical summaries, performance metrics, and model documentation. Jupyter Notebooks and R Markdown support the creation of dynamic documents that combine code, analysis, and visualizations in a single narrative structure—ideal for reproducible research and transparent reporting (Kluyver et al., 2016).

Figure 3. Tools and technologies for integration

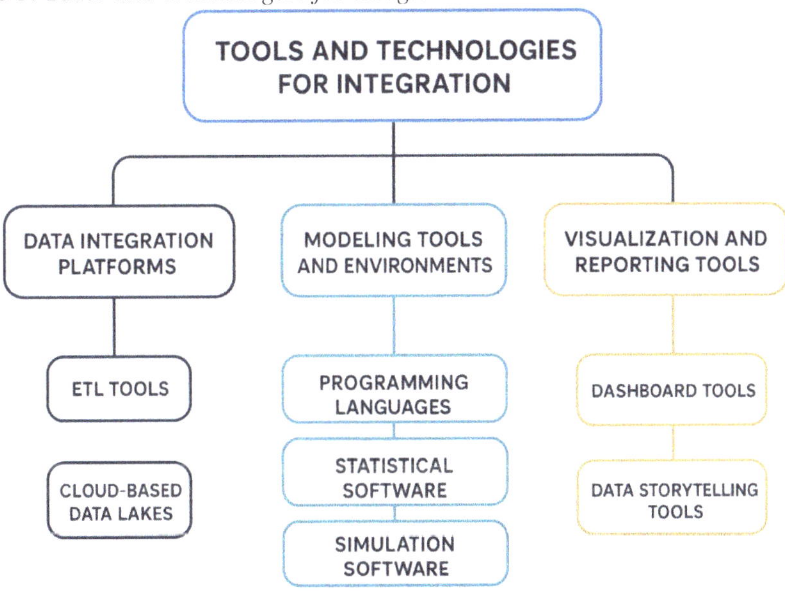

Selecting and integrating applicable tools and technologies is key to multi-source applied modelling. Data integration solutions streamline dataset collecting and preparation, while modelling environments enable analysis. Visualisation and reporting aid outcomes communication and action. These technologies facilitate applied modelling from data collection and preparation to model deployment and insight sharing. Data-driven decision-making will need strategic use of these tools as problems grow more complex and vaster.

8. CASE STUDIES

Case studies offer valuable insight into how applied models built from multiple sources are utilized across different sectors to solve complex, real-world problems. They showcase the practical utility of multi-source data integration and the diverse ways it can enhance decision-making, efficiency, and responsiveness. This section examines three illustrative cases in public health, financial risk modeling, and urban planning, demonstrating the power of synthesizing data from heterogeneous origins for robust applied modeling.

Case 1: Public Health Decision Support

In the realm of public health, applied models that are drawn from multiple data sources are vital for disease surveillance, outbreak prediction, and policy formulation. A compelling example emerged during the COVID-19 pandemic, where integrating traditional epidemiological data with social media trends and expert input significantly enhanced public health responses.

Epidemiological data, such as case counts, hospitalizations, and mortality rates, were collected from public health departments and hospitals. These structured datasets provided a foundational understanding of disease transmission and burden. They often came with reporting delays and limitations in granularity.

To address these gaps, social media platforms like Twitter and Facebook were mined for real-time public sentiment, symptom self-reports, and behavioral patterns. Natural language processing (NLP) techniques were used to analyze trends, detect early warning signs, and evaluate public compliance with health guidelines (Paul & Dredze, 2011).

Expert input, including forecasts and scenario analyses from epidemiologists and infectious disease modelers, was incorporated using Bayesian modeling approaches. These expert judgments helped contextualize data anomalies and validate model assumptions.

A well-documented implementation of such a multi-source approach was the COVID-19 Mobility Network (CMN), which integrated Google and Facebook mobility data with epidemiological trends to forecast disease spread and guide lockdown decisions (Chang et al., 2021). The combined use of structured surveillance data, social signals, and expert knowledge enabled a more comprehensive, timely, and adaptive decision-support system.

Case 2: Financial Risk Modeling

Financial institutions increasingly rely on multi-source data integration to construct sophisticated risk models that account for market volatility, credit risk, and systemic threats. The limitations of models based solely on historical market data became especially evident during the 2008 global financial crisis, prompting a shift toward broader, more dynamic data integration strategies.

Historical financial data - such as balance sheets, loan performance records, and interest rate trends - remains essential for baseline risk assessments. Reliance on these alone can lead to models that are overly backward-looking and fail to capture emerging threats.

To enhance foresight, market trend data such as real-time stock prices, commodity indices, and derivatives trading are integrated. These data offer high-frequency signals about investor sentiment and liquidity risk, allowing models to adjust dynamically (Allen et al., 2012).

News analytics—using NLP tools to parse financial news articles, analyst reports, and regulatory announcements—add an additional predictive layer. For instance, sentiment analysis tools evaluate the tone and content of financial journalism to anticipate market movements or identify reputational risk.

One illustrative case is the integration approach used by hedge funds and trading firms employing quantitative risk models. These firms combine structured financial data with unstructured text data from news feeds and even alternative data such as satellite imagery (e.g., tracking the number of cars in retailer parking lots to predict earnings). The use of such diverse data enables more responsive and accurate risk assessments and investment strategies (Kolanovic & Krishnamachari, 2017).

Case 3: Urban Planning and Smart Cities

In the context of urban planning, smart city initiatives exemplify how multi-source modeling can transform urban governance and infrastructure optimization. Applied models in this domain often leverage real-time data to monitor traffic, air quality, energy use, and citizen needs.

Sensor data, such as inputs from traffic cameras, GPS systems, and environmental monitors, provide granular, real-time information about city dynamics. These structured, high-frequency datasets allow for continuous monitoring and anomaly detection in urban systems (Batty et al., 2012).

To complement these technical inputs, citizen feedback from mobile apps, online forums, and participatory platforms is integrated. These qualitative data sources provide insights into resident satisfaction, safety concerns, and service needs. NLP and crowdsourcing tools help analyze and synthesize this feedback at scale.

Administrative records - including zoning maps, utility usage logs, and public transportation schedules - add a layer of institutional knowledge. These data are essential for validating predictive models and ensuring regulatory compliance.

A notable example is Barcelona's smart city initiative, which combines sensor data with citizen feedback and municipal databases to optimize traffic flow, reduce pollution, and allocate public services more efficiently (Bakıcı et al., 2013). Integrated dashboards enable real-time decision-making by city administrators, while predictive models help plan infrastructure investments and emergency responses.

Multi-source data integration changes applied modelling across disciplines, as seen in these case studies. Real-time public health monitoring and informed interventions, dynamic risk management and strategic finance investments, and responsive and participatory urban planning governance are possible. Using organised, unstructured, quantitative, and qualitative data, these models provide deeper insights and stronger solutions to complex situations. As data availability and variety increase, model quality and problem-solving effectiveness will rely on data source diversity.

9. FUTURE TRENDS

As the scope and complexity of problem-solving continue to expand across industries, the future of building applied models from multiple sources will be shaped by several key trends. The rapid advancement in artificial intelligence (AI), the push for interoperable data ecosystems, and a growing focus on ethical AI and model transparency are poised to redefine how models are developed, integrated, and trusted. This section explores these emerging trends and their implications for the next generation of applied modeling.

9.1 AI and Automated Data Integration

One of the most transformative developments in the future of multi-source modeling is the increasing reliance on AI and machine learning to automate data integration tasks. Traditional data preprocessing activities such as cleaning, transformation, and fusion have been labor-intensive and time-consuming. AI-driven automation is significantly improving the efficiency and accuracy of these processes.

Machine learning algorithms, particularly those utilizing natural language processing (NLP) and pattern recognition, can now detect data anomalies, fill missing values, harmonize data formats, and reconcile semantic mismatches with minimal human intervention. Unsupervised learning techniques can identify outliers or suggest plausible imputations for incomplete datasets (Kandel et al., 2011). AI can automate schema mapping across heterogeneous databases, enabling more scalable and flexible data integration pipelines (Stonebraker & Ilyas, 2018).

Tools like Google's Cloud AutoML, Microsoft Azure ML Studio, and Amazon SageMaker provide automated machine learning (AutoML) functionalities that support the preprocessing of disparate data sources before model training. These tools increase leverage reinforcement learning and generative AI models to improve decision-making in real time. The convergence of AutoML and data integration is expected to reduce technical barriers, democratizing the use of complex models in business and science.

9.2 Interoperable Data Ecosystems

As organizations and researchers work to integrate diverse datasets, the movement toward interoperable data ecosystems is gaining momentum. Interoperability refers to the ability of different data systems and formats to work together seamlessly. This requires not only technical compatibility but also shared semantics and governance frameworks.

One promising development in this area is the rise of open data standards, such as the FAIR principles - Findable, Accessible, Interoperable, and Reusable. These principles are being adopted widely in scientific research, healthcare, and government data initiatives to ensure that data can be easily shared and integrated across platforms (Wilkinson et al., 2016).

Global Open Data for Agriculture and Nutrition (GODAN), the Open Data Institute (ODI), and the European Open Science Cloud (EOSC) are among the collaborative platforms that are leading the charge to establish standards and infrastructure that will facilitate data sharing and integration across many sources. Richer modelling and improved decision-making are fostered by these ecosystems, which allow stakeholders to contribute and access varied resources, often in real-time (Attwood et al., 2017).

This movement is being aided by developments in semantic web technologies and linked data as well. Intelligent model building is made possible by the use of ontologies and metadata formats such as RDF (Resource Description Framework) and OWL (Web Ontology Language), which allow for the meaningful integration of data from many domains.

Looking forward, interoperable data ecosystems will be essential for tackling global challenges - such as climate change, public health crises, and financial stability - where collaborative, cross-domain data integration is necessary.

9.3 Ethical AI and Trustworthy Modeling

As multi-source modeling becomes more powerful and pervasive, the call for ethical AI and trustworthy modeling is becoming more urgent. The integration of data from varied origins, especially personal or sensitive information, raises significant concerns regarding privacy, bias, and accountability.

Model transparency and explainability are one of the big future prospects in this subject. Decisions made by models are under increased scrutiny from end users and authorities who want to know the reason behind them. This is especially true in high-stakes areas like healthcare diagnosis, credit scoring, and criminal justice. In order to deconstruct the roles played by certain characteristics in multi-source models, explainable AI (XAI) techniques like SHAP and LIME are being used (Ribeiro et al., 2016; Lundberg & Lee, 2017).

Ethical frameworks such as those proposed by the European Commission's "Ethics Guidelines for Trustworthy AI" stress the importance of fairness, accountability, and robustness in AI systems. These guidelines highlight the need to mitigate bias that can emerge when merging datasets with different demographic, temporal, or geographic characteristics (Floridi et al., 2018). In response, researchers and practitioners are investing in bias detection algorithms, algorithmic auditing, and participatory model design.

Data governance also plays a crucial role. In the future, we can expect increased regulation and standardized protocols for obtaining informed consent, anonymizing data, and maintaining data provenance. Technologies such as differential privacy, federated learning, and blockchain-based data auditing are gaining traction as mechanisms to uphold data integrity while enabling effective multi-source modeling (Kairouz et al., 2021).

Multi-source applied model development will be shaped by AI, data interoperability, and ethics. AI-driven automation will improve data integration and consumption. Integrating data ecosystems boosts knowledge synthesis and cooperation. As ethical, transparent, and trustworthy modelling approaches gain popularity, data collection, processing, and use will change. These patterns indicate stronger, scalable, inclusive, and responsible applied models. Improved capacity, infrastructure, and stakeholder interdisciplinary cooperation are needed. Doing so may keep multi-source modelling essential for complex problem-solving.

10. CONCLUSION

To improve problem-solving, this chapter stressed the necessity of constructing applicable models from diverse sources. Single-source data is biassed, partial, and limited in generalisability, hence multi-source modelling is justified. Integrating quantitative, qualitative, expert information, and simulation outputs improves model robustness, accuracy, and contextual relevance. This entails carefully identifying suitable sources, using rigorous data gathering and preparation methods, and using heterogeneous data-friendly modelling frameworks. Artificial intelligence-driven data integration systems and visualisation tools help practitioners manage complexity and scale analyses.

The value of multi-source modeling is evident across numerous application domains, such as public health, finance, and urban planning, where combining diverse inputs leads to richer insights and better-informed decisions. However, challenges such as data incompatibility, conflicting information, computational constraints, and ethical considerations require careful management to maintain model integrity and trustworthiness.

Looking ahead, the integration of artificial intelligence for automated data fusion, the emergence of interoperable data ecosystems, and a focus on ethical and explainable AI promise to make multi-source modeling more accessible and reliable. These advancements will be essential as problem-solving increasingly involves complex, interconnected systems where single data sources cannot capture the full picture.

Practitioners and researchers are encouraged to embrace the complexity inherent in integrating multiple data sources rather than simplifying problems at the cost of insight. By doing so, they can unlock deeper understanding and more effective solutions to real-world challenges. The ongoing evolution of multi-source applied modeling calls for continuous learning, collaboration, and innovation, positioning integration as a foundational approach in the future of problem-solving.

REFERENCES

Allen, L., Bali, T. G., & Tang, Y. (2012). Does Systemic Risk in the Financial Sector Predict Future Economic Downturns? *Review of Financial Studies*, *25*(10), 3000–3036. DOI: 10.1093/rfs/hhs094

Allison, P. D. (2002). *Missing data*. SAGE Publications. DOI: 10.4135/9781412985079

Attwood, T. K., Blackford, S., Brazas, M. D., Davies, A., & Schneider, M. V. (2017). A global perspective on evolving bioinformatics and data science training needs. *Briefings in Bioinformatics*, *20*(2), 398–404. DOI: 10.1093/bib/bbx100 PMID: 28968751

Bakıcı, T., Almirall, E., & Wareham, J. (2013). A Smart City Initiative: The Case of Barcelona. *Journal of the Knowledge Economy*, *4*(2), 135–148. DOI: 10.1007/s13132-012-0084-9

Bardach, E., & Patashnik, E. M. (2019). *A practical guide for policy analysis: The eightfold path to more effective problem solving* (6th ed.). CQ Press.

Barocas, S., Hardt, M., & Narayanan, A. (2023). *Fairness and machine learning: Limitations and opportunities*. The MIT Press.

Batini, C., & Scannapieco, M. (2006). *Data quality: Concepts, methodologies and techniques*. Springer.

Batty, M., Axhausen, K. W., Giannotti, F., Pozdnoukhov, A., Bazzani, A., Wachowicz, M., Ouzounis, G., & Portugali, Y. (2012). Smart cities of the future. *The European Physical Journal. Special Topics*, *214*(1), 481–518. DOI: 10.1140/epjst/e2012-01703-3

Bertsimas, D., & Kallus, N. (2019). From predictive to prescriptive analytics. *Management Science*, *66*(3), 1025–1044. DOI: 10.1287/mnsc.2018.3253

Borshchev, A. (2013). *The Big Book of Simulation Modeling: Multimethod Modeling with AnyLogic 6*. AnyLogic North America.

Chang, S., Pierson, E., Koh, P. W., Gerardin, J., Redbird, B., Grusky, D., & Leskovec, J. (2021). Mobility network models of COVID-19 explain inequities and inform reopening. *Nature*, *589*(7840), 82–87. DOI: 10.1038/s41586-020-2923-3 PMID: 33171481

Chebotko, A., Lu, S., Fotouhi, F., Arpinar, I. B., & Sheth, A. (2008). Semantics-enabled data integration. [JDM]. *Journal of Database Management*, *19*(4), 1–27. DOI: 10.4018/jdm.2008100101

Cheng, Y., Wang, D., Zhou, P., & Zhang, T. (2018). Model compression and acceleration for deep neural networks: The principles, progress, and challenges. *IEEE Signal Processing Magazine*, *35*(1), 126–136. DOI: 10.1109/MSP.2017.2765695

Christen, P. (2012). *Data matching: Concepts and techniques for record linkage, entity resolution, and duplicate detection*. Springer. DOI: 10.1007/978-3-642-31164-2

Delen, D., & Demirkan, H. (2013). Data, information and analytics as services. *Decision Support Systems*, *55*(1), 359–363. DOI: 10.1016/j.dss.2012.05.044

Dietterich, T. G. (2000). Ensemble methods in machine learning. In J. Kittler & F. Roli (Eds.), *Multiple classifier systems: First international workshop, MCS 2000, Cagliari, Italy, June 21–23, 2000* (Vol. 1857, pp. 1–15). Springer. https://doi.org/ DOI: 10.1007/3-540-45014-9_1

Doan, A., Halevy, A. Y., & Ives, Z. G. (2012). *Principles of data integration*. Morgan Kaufmann.

Epstein, J. M. (2006). *Generative social science: Studies in agent-based computational modeling*. Princeton University Press.

Few, S. (2009). *Now You See It: Simple Visualization Techniques for Quantitative Analysis*. Analytics Press.

Fielding, R. T. (2000). *Architectural styles and the design of network-based software architectures* (Doctoral dissertation, University of California, Irvine). UMI Dissertation Publishing.

Floridi, L., Cowls, J., Beltrametti, M., Chatila, R., Chazerand, P., Dignum, V., Luetge, C., Madelin, R., Pagallo, U., Rossi, F., Schafer, B., Valcke, P., & Vayena, E. (2018). AI4People—An ethical framework for a good AI society: Opportunities, risks, principles, and recommendations. *Minds and Machines*, *28*(4), 689–707. DOI: 10.1007/s11023-018-9482-5 PMID: 30930541

Friedman, J., Hastie, T., & Tibshirani, R. (2001). *The elements of statistical learning: Data mining, inference, and prediction*. Springer.

Gelman, A., & Hill, J. (2007). *Data analysis using regression and multilevel/hierarchical models*. Cambridge University Press.

Giebler, C., Gröger, C., Hoos, E., Schwarz, H., & Mitschang, B. (2019). Leveraging the data lake: Current state and challenges. In *Big Data Analytics and Knowledge Discovery* (pp. 179–188). Lecture Notes in Computer Science. Springer., DOI: 10.1007/978-3-030-27520-4_13

Goodfellow, I., Bengio, Y., & Courville, A. (2016). *Deep learning*. MIT Press.

Guyon, I., & Elisseeff, A. (2003). An introduction to variable and feature selection. *Journal of Machine Learning Research, 3*, 1157–1182. https://www.jmlr.org/papers/volume3/guyon03a/guyon03a.pdf

Hillier, F. S., & Lieberman, G. J. (2020). *Introduction to operations research* (10th ed.). McGraw-Hill.

Jurafsky, D., & Martin, J. H. (2020). *Speech and language processing* (3rd ed.). Pearson.

Kairouz, P., McMahan, H. B., Avent, B., Bellet, A., Bennis, M., Bhagoji, A. N., ... & Zhao, S. (2021). Advances and open problems in federated learning. *Foundations and Trends® in Machine Learning*, 14(1–2), 1–210. http://dx.doi.org/DOI: 10.1561/2200000083

Kandel, S., Paepcke, A., Hellerstein, J. M., & Heer, J. (2011). Wrangler: Interactive visual specification of data transformation scripts. In *Proceedings of the SIGCHI Conference on Human Factors in Computing Systems* (pp. 3363–3372). Association for Computing Machinery. https://doi.org/DOI: 10.1145/1978942.1979444

Katal, A., Wazid, M., & Goudar, R. H. (2013). Big data: Issues, challenges, tools and good practices. In *2013 Sixth International Conference on Contemporary Computing (IC3)* (pp. 404–409). IEEE. https://doi.org/DOI: 10.1109/IC3.2013.6612229

Kimball, R., & Ross, M. (2013). *The data warehouse toolkit: The definitive guide to dimensional modeling* (3rd ed.). Wiley.

Kitchin, R. (2014). *The data revolution: Big data, open data, data infrastructures and their consequences*. SAGE Publications.

Kluyver, T., Ragan-Kelley, B., Pérez, F., Granger, B., Bussonnier, M., Frederic, J., Kelley, K., Hamrick, J., Grout, J., Corlay, S., Ivanov, P., Avila, D., Abdalla, S., Willing, C., & Jupyter Development Team. (2016). Jupyter Notebooks – a publishing format for reproducible computational workflows. In F. Loizides & B. Schmidt (Eds.), *Positioning and power in academic publishing: Players, agents and agendas* (pp. 87–90). IOS Press. https://doi.org/DOI: 10.3233/978-1-61499-649-1-87

Kolanovic, M., & Krishnamachari, R. T. (2017). Big data and AI strategies: Machine learning and alternative data approach to investing. *J.P. Morgan Global Quantitative and Derivatives Strategy*. Big Data & AI Investing Strategies: Machine Learning & Alternative Data

Kuhn, M., & Johnson, K. (2013). *Applied predictive modeling*. Springer. DOI: 10.1007/978-1-4614-6849-3

Lundberg, S. M., & Lee, S. I. (2017). A unified approach to interpreting model predictions. In Guyon, I., Luxburg, U. V., Bengio, S., Wallach, H., Fergus, R., Vishwanathan, S., & Garnett, R. (Eds.), Vol. 30, pp. 4765–4774). Advances in neural information processing systems. Curran Associates, Inc., https://proceedings.neurips.cc/paper/2017/file/8a20a8621978632d76c43dfd28b67767-Paper.pdf

MathWorks. (2023). *MATLAB* (Version R2023a) [Software]. MathWorks. https://www.mathworks.com/products/matlab.html

Mitchell, R. (2015). *Web scraping with Python: Collecting data from the modern web*. O'Reilly Media.

Montgomery, D. C., Peck, E. A., & Vining, G. G. (2012). *Introduction to linear regression analysis* (5th ed.). Wiley.

Paul, M. J., & Dredze, M. (2011). You are what you Tweet: Analyzing Twitter for public health. In *Proceedings of the Fifth International AAAI Conference on Weblogs and Social Media* (pp. 265–272). Association for the Advancement of Artificial Intelligence., https://ojs.aaai.org/index.php/ICWSM/article/view/14137

Pearl, J. (2009). *Causality: Models, reasoning and inference* (2nd ed.). Cambridge University Press. DOI: 10.1017/CBO9780511803161

Pidd, M. (2004). *Computer simulation in management science* (5th ed.). Wiley.

Provost, F., & Fawcett, T. (2013). *Data science for business: What you need to know about data mining and data-analytic thinking*. O'Reilly Media.

Quionero-Candela, J., Sugiyama, M., Schwaighofer, A., & Lawrence, N. D. (Eds.). (2009). *Dataset shift in machine learning*. The MIT Press.

R Core Team. (2023). *R: A language and environment for statistical computing*. R Foundation for Statistical Computing. https://www.r-project.org/

Ribeiro, M. T., Singh, S., & Guestrin, C. (2016). "Why should I trust you?": Explaining the predictions of any classifier. In *Proceedings of the 22nd ACM SIGKDD International Conference on Knowledge Discovery and Data Mining* (pp. 1135–1144). Association for Computing Machinery. https://doi.org/DOI: 10.1145/2939672.2939778

SAS Institute. (2022). *SAS software* (Version 9.4) [Software]. SAS Institute Inc. https://www.sas.com/en_us/software.html

Shmueli, G., & Koppius, O. R. (2011). Predictive analytics in information systems research. *Management Information Systems Quarterly*, *35*(3), 553–572. DOI: 10.2307/23042796

Sterman, J. D. (2000). *Business dynamics: Systems thinking and modeling for a complex world.* Irwin/McGraw-Hill.

Stonebraker, M., & Ilyas, I. F. (2018). Data integration: The current status and the way forward. *A Quarterly Bulletin of the Computer Society of the IEEE Technical Committee on Data Engineering, 41*(2), 3–9. https://cs.uwaterloo.ca/~ilyas/papers/StonebrakerIEEE2018.pdf

Subrahmanyam, S. (2025). Data Governance and Privacy in Smart Cities. In Sharma, A., Mansotra, V., & Singh, P. (Eds.), *Citizen-Centric Artificial Intelligence for Smart Cities* (pp. 433–456). IGI Global Scientific Publishing., DOI: 10.4018/979-8-3693-7832-8.ch017

Subrahmanyam, S. (2025). Experimental and Simulation-Based Research: Designing Controlled Experiments for Maritime Training and Safety. In Mobo, F. (Ed.), *Research Methods for Advancing the Maritime Industry* (pp. 145–170). IGI Global Scientific Publishing., DOI: 10.4018/979-8-3373-1052-7.ch006

Subrahmanyam, S. (2025). Introduction and Fundamentals of Qualitative Research in Business. In Segura, L., Vasconcelos, A., & Slomski, V. (Eds.), *Exploring Qualitative Research in Business: Approaches, Strategies, And Methods* (pp. 1–28). IGI Global Scientific Publishing., DOI: 10.4018/979-8-3693-7698-0.ch001

Sweeney, L. (2002). k-anonymity: A model for protecting privacy. *International Journal of Uncertainty, Fuzziness and Knowledge-based Systems, 10*(5), 557–570. DOI: 10.1142/S0218488502001648

Van Rossum, G., & Drake, F. L. (2009). *Python 3 reference manual.* CreateSpace. https://docs.python.org/3/reference/

Wilkinson, M. D., Dumontier, M., Aalbersberg, I. J., Appleton, G., Axton, M., Baak, A., Blomberg, N., Boiten, J.-W., da Silva Santos, L. B., Bourne, P. E., Bouwman, J., Brookes, A. J., Clark, T., Crosas, M., Dillo, I., Dumon, O., Edmunds, S., Evelo, C. T., Finkers, R., & Mons, B. (2016). The FAIR Guiding Principles for scientific data management and stewardship. *Scientific Data, 3*(1), 160018. DOI: 10.1038/sdata.2016.18 PMID: 26978244

Witten, I. H., Frank, E., & Hall, M. A. (2016). *Data mining: Practical machine learning tools and techniques* (4th ed.). Morgan Kaufmann.

Yin, R. K. (2017). *Case study research and applications: Design and methods* (6th ed.). SAGE Publications.

Zhao, B., Rubinstein, B. I., Gemmell, J., & Han, J. (2012). A Bayesian approach to discovering truth from conflicting sources for data integration. *Proceedings of the VLDB Endowment International Conference on Very Large Data Bases*, *5*(6), 550–561. DOI: 10.14778/2168651.2168656

Zheng, A., Casari, A., & Fawcett, T. (2018). *Feature engineering for machine learning: Principles and techniques for data scientists*. O'Reilly Media.

KEY TERMS AND DEFINITIONS

Applied Model: A structured representation used to understand, predict, or prescribe solutions to real-world problems by applying theoretical concepts and data. Applied models translate insights into actionable outcomes in decision-making contexts.

Case-Based Modeling: An approach that builds models using insights from specific instances or case studies, facilitating comparative analysis and knowledge transfer from prior experiences.

Data Harmonization: The process of standardizing and reconciling data from diverse sources to ensure consistency, resolve conflicts, and enable effective integration for modeling purposes.

Descriptive Model: A model that summarizes or characterizes historical data to provide insights into patterns, trends, or relationships without making predictions about the future.

Ethical AI and Trustworthy Modeling: Principles and practices ensuring that models built from multiple sources adhere to ethical standards, including transparency, explainability, privacy protection, and fairness.

Feature Engineering: The practice of transforming raw data into meaningful variables (features) that enhance the predictive power or explanatory capability of a model.

Interoperable Data Ecosystems: Collaborative platforms or frameworks that allow seamless sharing, access, and integration of data across different systems and organizations, supporting large-scale multi-source modeling.

Multi-Source Data Integration: The process of combining data from heterogeneous sources - quantitative, qualitative, expert knowledge, literature, or simulations - to improve model robustness, reliability, and comprehensiveness.

Predictive Model: A model that uses historical or current data to forecast future outcomes, often relying on statistical or machine learning techniques.

Prescriptive Model: A model designed to recommend actions or strategies based on data-driven insights, optimizing decision-making to achieve specific objectives.

Chapter 3
Building Applied Models From Data: Approaches, Methods, and Challenges

Mohit Sharma
https://orcid.org/0009-0007-2280-8077
Maharshi Dayanand University, India

Nitika Malik
https://orcid.org/0009-0006-3991-9526
Maharshi Dayanand University, India

Rishi Chaudhry
Maharshi Dayanand University, India

Raj Kumar
Maharshi Dayanand University, India

ABSTRACT

Applied models are indispensable tools for understanding complex phenomena, enabling predictions, decision-making, and problem-solving in various contexts. Building applied models from data is one of the most powerful methodologies in today's data-driven world, where organizations and researchers across fields increasingly rely on large datasets to inform their models. This chapter will explore the process of building applied models using data, emphasizing the methods, challenges, and considerations that come with this approach. By discussing how data-driven models are constructed, tested, and refined, the chapter will provide a comprehensive overview for administrators, faculty, staff, and researchers working

DOI: 10.4018/979-8-3373-3301-4.ch003

with data to create accurate, generalizable, and actionable models. The chapter will focus on methods for ensuring the robustness, sensitivity, and adaptability of these models to both local and global contexts.

INTRODUCTION

In today's data-driven world, the process of building applied models from data is a crucial practice across various sectors, ranging from business and healthcare to government and environmental studies. The exponential growth in data availability and the advancement of analytical techniques have made it possible to gain insights into complex systems and to create predictive models that aid decision-making. Applied models, by definition, aim to address specific real-world problems by utilizing data to generate forecasts, identify patterns, and offer solutions. These models provide a structured approach to interpreting and acting upon large datasets, making them indispensable tools in modern problem-solving. Building applied models from data is an iterative and multifaceted process. While the core idea behind modeling is relatively simple—use data to make predictions or understand phenomena—its execution is far from straightforward. Creating accurate, robust, and interpretable models requires careful planning, data collection, methodology selection, model development, and validation. Researchers, analysts, and practitioners must navigate a variety of challenges at each stage of the process, such as data quality issues, bias, overfitting, and ethical concerns. Moreover, ensuring that the resulting models are both applicable to local contexts and adaptable to larger or global scenarios adds another layer of complexity. This chapter provides a comprehensive overview of the process of building applied models using data. It emphasizes the methods, challenges, and considerations that practitioners must be aware of in order to create models that are both accurate and actionable. The chapter is structured to guide administrators, faculty, staff, and researchers through the necessary steps involved in model building, while also offering insights on how to overcome common pitfalls, such as overfitting and bias, and address critical ethical considerations.

THE IMPORTANCE OF DATA-DRIVEN MODELS IN DECISION-MAKING

In the contemporary world, decision-making is increasingly driven by data. As the volume of available data continues to grow, organizations, governments, and researchers are finding new ways to leverage these resources for competitive advantage, improved service delivery, and innovation. Data-driven decision-making

(DDDM) is an emerging practice in which data serves as the foundation for decision-making processes, ensuring that decisions are based on objective evidence rather than intuition or anecdotal information. The key strength of data-driven models lies in their ability to transform raw data into actionable insights, which can guide decision-making at every level of an organization (Brynjolfsson & McAfee, 2014). The use of data in decision-making spans multiple fields. In business, for example, organizations rely on predictive models to forecast sales, optimize inventory management, and design personalized marketing campaigns. In healthcare, models built from patient data can predict disease outcomes, improve treatment protocols, and streamline operations. In the public sector, predictive models are used for policy analysis, crime prediction, and resource allocation. The key to success in these areas lies in the ability to build accurate, reliable, and generalizable models that reflect real-world phenomena.

STEPS IN BUILDING APPLIED MODELS FROM DATA

The process of building applied models from data is typically broken down into several stages. Each stage presents its own set of challenges and requires specific methodologies to ensure that the resulting model is effective, reliable, and scalable.

1. Defining the Problem:

The first step in building an applied model is to clearly define the problem or research question. This stage involves collaborating with subject matter experts (SMEs) and stakeholders to understand the scope and objectives of the modeling process. The problem should be framed in such a way that it is both specific and measurable. For example, in a marketing context, a company may seek to predict customer churn based on certain demographic and behavioral characteristics. In healthcare, a hospital might want to develop a model to predict patient readmission rates based on historical medical records. The problem definition phase also includes selecting the appropriate methodology for the problem at hand. Different types of models are suited to different types of problems. For example, if the goal is to classify data into categories, classification models such as logistic regression or decision trees may be suitable. On the other hand, if the goal is to predict a continuous outcome, regression models or time series analysis techniques might be more appropriate.

2. Data Collection and Preparation:

Once the problem is defined, the next step is to gather the relevant data. This can be a time-consuming and resource-intensive process. Data can come from a variety of sources, including internal systems (e.g., customer databases, transaction logs), external sources (e.g., public datasets, third-party vendors), or sensors and other real-time data streams.

Data collection is followed by data preparation, which involves cleaning, transforming, and structuring the data in a way that makes it suitable for modeling. Raw data is often messy—containing missing values, outliers, and inconsistencies—that must be addressed before it can be used in a model. Data cleaning is critical because the quality of the data directly influences the accuracy of the model. Methods such as imputation for missing values, outlier detection, and data normalization are common in this stage (Kelleher et al., 2015).

3. Model Selection and Development:

With prepared data in hand, the next step is to select the appropriate model. Model selection is often guided by the problem definition. For instance, if the problem is to classify email messages as spam or non-spam, a classification model like Naive Bayes or a support vector machine (SVM) may be appropriate. For predicting a continuous variable, linear regression or more advanced techniques such as decision trees or random forests may be used. The choice of model depends on various factors, including the type of data, the complexity of the problem, the need for interpretability, and the computational resources available. Over the years, machine learning models, particularly those in the family of supervised learning algorithms, have gained significant attention due to their ability to learn patterns from data without explicit programming (Bishop, 2006). These models can be particularly powerful when dealing with large, complex datasets, but they also require careful management to avoid issues like overfitting and model interpretability.

4. Model Evaluation and Validation:

Once the model is built, it is essential to evaluate its performance. The model is typically tested using data that was not involved in the training process to assess how well it generalizes to new, unseen data. Common evaluation metrics include accuracy, precision, recall, F1 score, and mean squared error (MSE), among others (Kohavi, 1995).

In addition to traditional evaluation, model validation often involves checking for robustness and adaptability. Cross-validation, where the data is split into multiple subsets, is a common technique for assessing model performance. This technique helps to identify whether the model is overfitting (i.e., too closely tied to the training data) or underfitting (i.e., not capturing the underlying patterns in the data).

5. Model Deployment and Monitoring:

After a model has been validated, it is deployed for practical use. In business applications, this may involve integrating the model into decision-making systems, where it will provide real-time predictions or insights. In healthcare, a model might be used to inform clinical decisions or resource allocation. Deployment is followed by ongoing monitoring and maintenance. Models can degrade over time as new data becomes available or as the underlying environment changes. Continuous monitoring helps ensure that the model continues to perform well and that any drift in predictions is detected early (Lai & Xie, 2013). In some cases, retraining the model with updated data may be necessary to maintain its accuracy.

CHALLENGES IN BUILDING APPLIED MODELS

While the process of building applied models is powerful, it is not without its challenges. Several key issues can complicate the process, including overfitting, bias, data quality problems, and ethical concerns.

1. Bias and Fairness:

Bias in models is a significant concern, particularly in sensitive areas like hiring, lending, or law enforcement. A model that learns from biased data can perpetuate or even exacerbate societal inequalities. For example, if a hiring algorithm is trained on historical data where certain demographic groups were underrepresented, it may unintentionally favor candidates from those groups, perpetuating bias. Ensuring fairness in applied models requires careful consideration of the data used, as well as the methods employed to develop the model. It is crucial to test the model for disparate impacts on different demographic groups and to adopt strategies that minimize bias (Barocas et al., 2019).

2. Ethical and Privacy Concerns:

Ethical considerations are central to the responsible use of data in model building. In particular, issues such as data privacy, consent, and transparency are vital in ensuring that models are developed and used ethically. With increasing concerns over surveillance and privacy violations, it is crucial to establish clear ethical guidelines for the collection, use, and dissemination of data. The process of building applied models from data is a complex but essential practice that underpins much of modern decision-making. From defining the problem to collecting and preparing data, selecting the appropriate model, evaluating performance, and deploying it for real-world use, each step requires careful thought, expertise, and validation. The challenges of overfitting, bias, data quality, and ethical considerations highlight the importance of rigorous and thoughtful approaches to model building. In the coming years, as the volume and complexity of data continue to increase, the ability to build effective and ethical applied models will remain a key skill for researchers, businesses, and policymakers alike.

BACKGROUND OF THE STUDY

In the context of modern data-driven decision-making, the creation of applied models has become essential across various disciplines and industries. These models are fundamental tools for organizations seeking to improve their operational efficiency, develop innovative products, and predict future trends. Applied models, which use historical data to build representations of systems, play a crucial role in solving complex problems, enhancing strategic planning, and driving data-centric decision-making processes. However, building effective and robust applied models presents a range of challenges, especially as the volume, complexity, and diversity of data continue to increase. The process of constructing applied models is not only about data analysis; it involves a rigorous and methodological approach that integrates theory, data collection, model selection, validation, and implementation. The need for sophisticated models is growing due to the increasing availability of big data, which presents both opportunities and challenges in generating insights that can lead to better decision-making. Organizations today, across sectors such as healthcare, marketing, finance, and environmental management, are looking to leverage data to build models that inform operational strategies, mitigate risks, predict customer behaviors, optimize processes, and solve a myriad of complex issues. This chapter explores the development of applied models from data, outlining the methods used, the challenges encountered, and the factors that researchers and practitioners must consider to ensure the success of their modeling efforts. It examines the historical context of applied modeling, its evolution, and its relevance in the context of contemporary data analysis. By understanding the background and evolution of applied modeling, we can appreciate how these models have become an indispensable part of modern analytical practices.

THE HISTORICAL DEVELOPMENT OF APPLIED MODELS

Applied modeling is deeply rooted in the history of statistics and data analysis, which began in earnest during the early 20th century. However, the modern approach to applied models has evolved significantly, especially in the last few decades, as computational power, access to large datasets, and machine learning techniques have made modeling more accessible and impactful. The early roots of applied models can be traced back to classical statistics. Sir Francis Galton's work in regression analysis in the late 19th century, which examined the relationship between two variables, laid the foundation for predictive modeling (Galton, 1886). The emergence of linear regression as a core modeling tool allowed researchers to understand the relationship between variables and make forecasts. Over the decades, statistical methods expanded into more sophisticated models, including multiple regression, time series analysis, and Bayesian methods, which offered new ways to account for complexity and uncertainty in data. The introduction of computational technology in the 1950s and 1960s enabled a major shift in the capacity to apply models to data. The development of early computers allowed for more efficient and extensive analysis of large datasets, marking the beginning of data-driven decision-making. However, it was not until the 1990s and early 2000s, with the advent of powerful personal computers and the internet, that data analysis began to expand dramatically. The digital revolution led to the explosive growth of data, and new fields such as big data analytics and machine learning emerged, allowing for the development of more complex, non-linear models. Today, the field of applied modeling is characterized by a synergy between traditional statistical methods and advanced machine learning techniques, such as deep learning and artificial intelligence (AI). These models go beyond simple predictions to encompass adaptive, real-time analytics capable of handling vast amounts of data from multiple sources. Whether in predicting market trends, diagnosing diseases, or optimizing supply chains, applied models have become central to the decision-making process across industries (Bishop, 2006).

THE ROLE OF DATA IN BUILDING APPLIED MODELS

The explosion of data availability over the past two decades has had a profound impact on the development of applied models. Traditionally, data for modeling purposes was scarce and expensive to collect. Researchers and organizations had to rely on small datasets and often spent significant time on data collection and preparation. The digital age, however, has changed this paradigm. With the advent of the internet, social media, sensor technologies, and large-scale data storage solutions, vast quantities of data are now available for analysis, enabling researchers and organizations to build more accurate and robust models. Data is the cornerstone of applied models, as the accuracy and effectiveness of a model depend on the quality and relevance of the data used. In recent years, the concept of "big data" has gained prominence, referring to datasets that are so large, complex, and varied that they cannot be processed using traditional data-processing tools. Big data technologies, such as Hadoop and Spark, have made it possible to store, manage, and analyze these large datasets, paving the way for the creation of more advanced models that can capture hidden patterns, identify trends, and make predictions. One of the key challenges in building applied models from data is ensuring the data used is clean and relevant. Data collection and preparation are often the most time-consuming parts of the modeling process, as raw data is typically messy, containing missing values, duplicates, outliers, and inconsistencies. Effective data preprocessing techniques, such as normalization, imputation, and feature selection, are essential to ensure that the data is usable for modeling purposes (Kelleher et al., 2015). The reliability of the data is critical because even small errors in data can lead to biased or inaccurate models that produce unreliable predictions. The diversity of data sources is another factor influencing the construction of applied models. Data can come from various structured and unstructured sources, including transactional data from databases, textual data from social media, images, video, and sensor data. The challenge of integrating these heterogeneous data sources into a unified model has led to the development of advanced techniques in data fusion, multi-source learning, and natural language processing (NLP). These techniques have enabled more robust models capable of handling diverse forms of data, but they also present additional challenges in terms of computational complexity and model interpretability.

THE METHODS USED IN BUILDING APPLIED MODELS

The methods used to build applied models have evolved significantly with advances in statistics, machine learning, and artificial intelligence. In the past, applied modeling typically relied on statistical techniques such as linear regression, logistic regression, and time series analysis, all of which were designed to model simple relationships between variables. While these methods are still widely used in many fields, the rise of machine learning and AI has led to the development of more advanced techniques capable of handling complex, high-dimensional data.

Machine Learning:

Machine learning, a subset of AI, has become the dominant approach for building applied models in recent years. Machine learning algorithms learn patterns from data without being explicitly programmed. The most common types of machine learning include supervised learning, unsupervised learning, and reinforcement learning. Supervised learning, which is used for both regression and classification problems, involves training a model on labeled data, where the correct output is already known. Examples of supervised learning algorithms include decision trees, support vector machines (SVMs), and neural networks. These models learn to make predictions by identifying relationships between the input variables and the target variable (Goodfellow et al., 2016). Unsupervised learning, on the other hand, is used to identify patterns or structure in unlabeled data. Techniques such as clustering and dimensionality reduction are common in unsupervised learning. For example, clustering algorithms like k-means can be used to group customers based on purchasing behavior, while principal component analysis (PCA) can reduce the dimensionality of data to make it more manageable and interpretable. Reinforcement learning, a more advanced form of machine learning, focuses on decision-making over time. It is used in applications such as robotics, game playing, and autonomous vehicles, where an agent learns to make a sequence of decisions that maximize a reward function (Sutton & Barto, 2018).

Deep Learning:

A subset of machine learning, deep learning has become an essential technique for building applied models, especially in fields such as image and speech recognition, natural language processing, and autonomous driving. Deep learning models, particularly neural networks, are capable of learning hierarchical representations of data, making them highly effective for tasks that involve large amounts of unstructured data. However, deep learning models often require large datasets and significant computational resources, making them both powerful and resource-intensive (LeCun et al., 2015).

Statistical Methods:

Despite the rise of machine learning and deep learning, traditional statistical methods remain integral to applied modeling. For instance, regression analysis continues to be a widely used method for modeling relationships between variables. Generalized linear models (GLMs), such as logistic regression, are commonly used for binary classification problems, while time series analysis methods like ARIMA are used for forecasting. Bayesian methods, which provide a probabilistic framework for modeling uncertainty, are also gaining popularity in applied modeling. These methods allow researchers to incorporate prior knowledge into the modeling process, which can be particularly useful when dealing with small datasets or uncertain information (Gelman et al., 2013).

CHALLENGES IN BUILDING APPLIED MODELS

While the methods used to build applied models have advanced significantly, the process of constructing effective and accurate models is not without challenges. Several factors complicate the modeling process, including data quality issues, overfitting, bias, and ethical considerations.

Data Quality:

The quality of the data is one of the most significant challenges in building applied models. Data is often noisy, incomplete, and inconsistent, which can significantly impact the model's performance. Data cleaning and preprocessing are essential steps to ensure that the data is of high quality, but even with these techniques, some level of uncertainty remains in the data, which can lead to errors in predictions (Kelleher et al., 2015).

Bias and Fairness:

Another major challenge in building applied models is ensuring that the models are fair and unbiased. Bias in data can arise from various sources, such as historical inequities, sampling biases, and human prejudices, which can lead to discriminatory outcomes when applied to real-world problems. For example, algorithms used in hiring, lending, or criminal justice may inadvertently perpetuate existing biases, leading to unfair treatment of certain groups. Addressing these issues requires thoughtful consideration of fairness, transparency, and accountability in the modeling process.

Ethical Considerations:

Ethics plays an increasingly important role in applied modeling. As data-driven models become more integrated into decision-making, concerns about privacy, accountability, and transparency have come to the forefront. Researchers and organizations must be mindful of ethical issues related to the use of personal data, informed consent, and the potential for harm caused by biased or inaccurate models. The growing awareness of these issues has led to the development of ethical guidelines and frameworks to ensure that models are used responsibly and in ways that benefit society as a whole (O'Neil et al., 2016). Building applied models from data has become an essential methodology for addressing complex problems across various fields. The availability of big data, coupled with advancements in machine learning, deep learning, and statistical modeling techniques, has transformed the way organizations approach decision-making. However, constructing effective and robust models is fraught with challenges, including data quality issues, model complexity, bias, and ethical considerations. As the field continues to evolve, the ability to build accurate, generalizable, and actionable models will remain crucial for researchers, organizations, and policymakers seeking to navigate an increasingly data-driven world.

RESEARCH METHODOLOGY

For this study, secondary data has been used to build applied models. Secondary data refers to data that has already been collected and processed by other researchers, organizations, or institutions for purposes different from the current research objective. This data is typically available through public or private repositories, government databases, academic journals, market reports, and other published sources. In the context of applied modeling, secondary data serves as a valuable resource for understanding complex phenomena and generating insights that inform decision-making. One of the main advantages of using secondary data in this study is the availability of large, high-quality datasets. These datasets often come from reputable sources such as government agencies, research institutions, and international organizations, making them reliable for use in model development. For example, datasets from national surveys, financial markets, or healthcare systems can provide a comprehensive view of the phenomena being studied. This allows researchers to focus on model construction and validation rather than data collection, thereby saving time and resources. Secondary data also enables the study to leverage existing research, which can enhance the model's relevance and contextual understanding. By utilizing data that has already been curated, researchers can ensure that the models are grounded in real-world data, offering a practical and actionable approach to problem-solving. Moreover, the use of secondary data provides a broader scope for analysis, allowing for the inclusion of diverse variables that might not have been easily accessible through primary data collection methods. However, there are certain challenges associated with the use of secondary data, which this study acknowledges. One of the main concerns is the potential lack of data consistency or completeness. Since secondary data was not originally collected for the current study's specific needs, it may contain gaps, inaccuracies, or irrelevant information. For example, missing data, outliers, or inconsistencies in measurement can affect the quality of the models. To address this, extensive data cleaning and preprocessing are necessary to ensure that the secondary data is suitable for model building. This includes handling missing values, correcting data discrepancies, and transforming the data into a format that aligns with the modeling requirements. Another challenge is ensuring that the secondary data aligns with the research questions and objectives. Since secondary data often comes from various sources with different methodologies and contexts, it is crucial to assess its relevance and applicability to the study's specific focus. For instance, if the study aims to model consumer behavior in a particular industry, it is important that the data used accurately reflects the behaviors and trends of interest. Despite these challenges, secondary data remains an essential tool in applied model building. It allows researchers to focus on analyzing patterns and building predictive models without the burden of data collection, while still utilizing rich datasets that reflect real-world conditions. By combining secondary data with robust data preparation and modeling techniques, this study aims to create accurate, generalizable, and actionable models for decision-making and problem-solving in various contexts.

FINDINGS OF THE STUDY

In this study, we explored the process of building applied models from data, focusing on the methods, challenges, and ethical considerations that are essential for constructing accurate and generalizable models. Through a combination of theoretical insights and practical case studies, this research underscores the importance of data-driven decision-making in various sectors, including business, healthcare, and public policy. The findings provide valuable insights into how secondary data, in particular, is leveraged for building applied models, along with the obstacles and best practices for overcoming them. Below are the detailed findings derived from the study, organized by key themes.

1. Significance of Data-Driven Models in Real-World Applications

The study highlights that data-driven models have become indispensable tools in addressing complex problems across numerous domains. From predicting customer behavior in business to improving medical diagnoses in healthcare, applied models based on secondary data allow organizations to make informed decisions and drive innovation. The increasing reliance on large datasets has transformed decision-making from intuition-based approaches to evidence-based strategies. The key strength of these models lies in their ability to provide actionable insights that can guide decisions in a way that improves efficiency, accuracy, and outcomes. In healthcare, secondary data, such as patient histories and medical records, plays a vital role in developing predictive models that can forecast patient outcomes, optimize treatment plans, and enhance operational efficiency. Similarly, businesses are increasingly utilizing secondary data to predict sales trends, optimize supply chain operations, and personalize marketing efforts. Governments and non-profit organizations also benefit from applied models by using them to predict policy outcomes, allocate resources efficiently, and improve public services. These findings emphasize that, in today's data-driven world, the use of secondary data to construct applied models is not only effective but also essential for staying competitive and responsive in an increasingly complex global environment.

2. The Process of Data Collection and Preparation

A significant finding from this study was the critical role of data collection and preparation in ensuring the effectiveness of applied models. Secondary data, while highly valuable, often requires extensive preprocessing to be usable for model building. Raw secondary datasets are frequently incomplete, noisy, and inconsistent, presenting challenges that must be addressed before meaningful models can be built. Data preparation steps such as data cleaning, transformation, and normalization are necessary to ensure that the data is ready for use in modeling. The study found that common issues in secondary data, such as missing values, outliers, and inconsistencies in data formats, required careful handling. For example, imputation techniques were used to address missing values, while data normalization ensured that features were on comparable scales, improving the efficiency of model training. Additionally, categorical variables often needed to be encoded into numerical values for compatibility with many machine learning algorithms. The importance of data quality cannot be overstated, as the study found that poorly prepared data could lead to inaccurate models that failed to generalize to new data. Proper preprocessing, therefore, is crucial to ensure that the models developed are both reliable and valid.

3. Overfitting and Underfitting: Striking the Right Balance

One of the most significant challenges identified in this study was the issue of overfitting, particularly when using secondary data. Overfitting occurs when a model becomes too tailored to the training data, memorizing patterns that do not generalize well to unseen data. This study found that models trained on secondary data often performed exceptionally well on training data but exhibited poor performance when tested on new, unseen datasets. Overfitting can lead to models that are not useful in real-world applications, as they fail to make accurate predictions on data that was not included in the training process. To mitigate overfitting, the study employed several techniques, including cross-validation, regularization, and model pruning. Cross-validation, particularly k-fold cross-validation, was used to ensure that the models were not overfitting to a particular subset of the data. Regularization techniques, such as Lasso and Ridge regression, were used to penalize overly complex models, thus promoting simplicity and generalizability. Pruning, especially in decision trees, was employed to remove unnecessary branches that may contribute to overfitting. The study also explored the issue of underfitting, which occurs when a model is too simplistic and fails to capture the underlying patterns in the data. Underfitting can be equally problematic, as it leads to models that cannot make accurate predictions, even on the training data. To address underfitting, the study found that using more sophisticated models, such as ensemble methods (e.g., random forests and boosting algorithms), helped capture more complex relationships in the data without leading to overfitting. Striking the right balance between overfitting and underfitting is a critical aspect of model development, and this study emphasizes the importance of model evaluation techniques in achieving this balance.

4. Addressing Bias and Fairness in Applied Models

A key finding of this study is the importance of addressing bias and fairness when building applied models, particularly when working with secondary data. Secondary datasets often reflect historical biases, which can perpetuate or exacerbate inequalities when used to build predictive models. The study found that, in sensitive areas such as hiring, lending, and criminal justice, biases in secondary data could lead to discriminatory outcomes. For example, if a model used to assess loan eligibility was trained on historical lending data where certain demographic groups were underserved, the resulting model could reinforce these disparities. To mitigate bias, the study employed techniques to detect and correct for biases in the data. These included fairness algorithms that adjust the model's predictions to ensure equitable outcomes across different demographic groups. Additionally, the study explored the use of oversampling or undersampling methods to address imbalances in the representation of various groups in the data. The study's findings underscore that ensuring fairness in applied models is not just about technical adjustments but also involves careful consideration of the societal implications of model outcomes. Bias detection and fairness auditing should be integral parts of the model development process, particularly when dealing with sensitive and high-stakes applications.

5. Ethical Considerations and Data Privacy

Another crucial finding from the study was the importance of ethical considerations and data privacy when using secondary data to build applied models. The study highlighted that secondary data often contains sensitive information, which necessitates stringent data privacy and security measures. Protecting the privacy of individuals whose data is used in model building is paramount, especially in sectors like healthcare, where data may include personal medical histories, treatment plans, and other sensitive information. The study adhered to ethical guidelines in the collection and use of secondary data, ensuring that all data was anonymized or pseudonymized before being used for modeling purposes. In addition, the study emphasized the need for transparency and accountability in the use of data. Stakeholders involved in the model development process should be fully informed about how data will be used, and individuals should have the option to consent to the use of their data.

Furthermore, the study explored the ethical implications of using secondary data for decision-making in high-stakes areas like law enforcement and criminal justice. Here, the use of data to predict outcomes such as recidivism or the risk of future crimes must be approached with caution, as biased data can have significant consequences for individuals and communities.

6. Model Testing, Evaluation, and Validation

The study found that the evaluation and validation of applied models are essential steps in ensuring their accuracy and reliability. After developing a model, it is critical to assess its performance on a test dataset that was not involved in the training process. Common evaluation metrics, such as accuracy, precision, recall, F1 score, and mean squared error (MSE), were used in this study to measure the performance of the models.

In addition to traditional evaluation, the study emphasized the importance of model validation to check for robustness and adaptability. Cross-validation techniques were frequently used to ensure that models were not overly dependent on specific subsets of data. The study found that cross-validation helped to identify whether models were overfitting or underfitting, which allowed for better generalization.

The study also explored the concept of model drift, where the performance of a model degrades over time due to changes in the underlying data distribution. This is a common issue when working with real-world data, and the study emphasized the need for continuous monitoring and retraining of models to ensure they remain accurate and relevant.

7. Deployment and Monitoring of Models

Once a model has been validated, it is deployed for real-world use. The study found that model deployment often involves integrating the model into decision-making systems, where it can provide real-time predictions or insights. In business, this might involve embedding the model into customer relationship management (CRM) systems, while in healthcare, the model could be used to inform clinical decisions or predict patient outcomes.

Deployment is followed by ongoing monitoring and maintenance to ensure that the model continues to perform effectively. The study found that as new data becomes available, models can drift or become outdated, requiring retraining with fresh data to maintain their predictive power. Continuous monitoring is essential to detect any decline in model performance and address any issues promptly.

8. Key Challenges and Future Directions

The study highlighted several challenges in building applied models using secondary data, including data quality issues, overfitting, bias, and ethical concerns. It also noted the importance of staying abreast of emerging trends and technologies in data science and machine learning. As data collection methods evolve and new machine learning techniques are developed, the ability to build effective, ethical models will remain a crucial skill for researchers, businesses, and policymakers.

Future research should explore methods for integrating secondary data with primary data to overcome some of the limitations of relying solely on secondary sources. Furthermore, the study suggests that as machine learning techniques become more advanced, there will be increasing opportunities for automating parts of the model development process, improving efficiency, and enabling faster decision-making. The findings of this study highlight the importance of data-driven models in solving complex real-world problems. While secondary data provides valuable insights, building accurate, fair, and ethical models requires careful attention to data preparation, model selection, and validation. Addressing challenges such as overfitting, bias, and ethical concerns is crucial for ensuring that models are both reliable and just. As data science continues to evolve, the principles and practices discussed in this study will remain essential for creating applied models that drive effective decision-making and problem-solving across various sectors.

IMPLICATIONS OF THE STUDY

The study on building applied models from data has significant implications for various stakeholders, ranging from researchers and practitioners to policymakers and industry leaders. As we continue to experience a surge in the availability of large datasets, the ability to create accurate, generalizable, and actionable models will play a crucial role in driving informed decision-making and addressing complex real-world challenges. This section discusses the key implications of the study in detail, emphasizing the impact on academic research, business practices, healthcare, public policy, and ethical considerations in model development.

1. Implications for Academic Research and Knowledge Advancement

The study emphasizes the critical role of data-driven models in academic research, particularly in disciplines such as social sciences, economics, healthcare, environmental studies, and business. The insights gained from this study have several implications for academic scholars and researchers working with large datasets and complex systems.

- **Enhancing Methodological Rigor**: One of the key implications of this study is the need for researchers to adhere to rigorous methodological practices when building applied models. The study outlines the stages of data collection, preparation, model selection, evaluation, and deployment, highlighting the importance of each step. Researchers must prioritize data quality, proper handling of missing values, outliers, and imbalances, and choose appropriate models for the task at hand. This approach will lead to more robust and reliable findings in academic research.
- **Integration of Advanced Techniques**: As machine learning and artificial intelligence (AI) techniques continue to evolve, researchers must be prepared to integrate new technologies into their modeling practices. The study identifies that supervised learning algorithms, ensemble methods, and regularization techniques offer valuable tools for improving model performance and addressing challenges like overfitting and bias. Academic researchers in data science, statistics, and related fields can benefit from staying up-to-date with the latest advancements in machine learning to refine their models and improve their predictive accuracy.
- **Cross-disciplinary Collaboration**: Building effective applied models often requires collaboration between data scientists, domain experts, and subject matter specialists. The study highlights the importance of involving domain experts at every stage of model development, from problem definition to interpretation of results. This implies that interdisciplinary collaboration will be crucial for advancing applied research, particularly in fields where complex phenomena need to be modeled (e.g., healthcare, climate science, economics). Researchers in academia must therefore foster partnerships with professionals from other fields to improve the relevance and accuracy of their models.

- **Ethical Research Practices**: The ethical considerations discussed in the study have far-reaching implications for academic researchers. Ensuring that data is used responsibly, with due consideration of privacy, consent, and bias, is fundamental for maintaining the integrity of academic research. The study's emphasis on fairness in model development encourages researchers to actively address ethical concerns in their work, ensuring that research findings contribute positively to society without perpetuating harmful stereotypes or inequalities.

2. Implications for Business and Industry

Data-driven decision-making has become a cornerstone of modern business practice. The study's findings are highly relevant to business leaders, marketers, data scientists, and operational managers who rely on applied models to enhance organizational performance, optimize processes, and drive innovation. Below are the key implications for business and industry:

- **Improved Decision-Making and Strategic Planning**: The study reinforces the importance of using data-driven models for informed decision-making in businesses. Whether it is predicting customer behavior, optimizing supply chains, or forecasting sales, organizations can leverage data models to make more accurate and strategic decisions. By focusing on the process of model development—ranging from problem definition to model deployment—businesses can enhance their decision-making processes, minimize risks, and identify new opportunities for growth. For instance, predictive models can help companies anticipate market trends, enabling them to adapt their strategies proactively.
- **Enhancing Personalization and Customer Experience**: In marketing and customer relationship management, applied models based on data can be used to create personalized experiences for customers. By utilizing customer data, businesses can develop models that predict individual preferences, behaviors, and purchasing patterns. This enables businesses to target customers with tailored content, products, and services that align with their needs. The study's findings on model evaluation and bias also suggest that businesses need to ensure that personalization efforts do not inadvertently exclude or disadvantage certain demographic groups, thus fostering inclusivity and fairness.
- **Operational Efficiency and Cost Optimization**: The use of applied models can significantly improve operational efficiency across various industries. In logistics and supply chain management, for example, predictive models can optimize inventory management, reduce operational costs, and streamline

production processes (Malik et al., 2025a; Malik et al., 2025b; Selvakumar et al., 2025a; Selvakumar et al., 2025b; Selvakumar et al., 2025c). Similarly, in human resources, models can be employed to optimize recruitment processes, identify skill gaps, and predict employee retention. The study underscores the importance of model validation and continuous monitoring to ensure that models remain effective over time and adapt to changing business conditions.

- **Innovation in Product Development**: Data-driven models can also play a vital role in innovation (Aradhya et al., 2025; Madaan et al., 2025; Mishra et al., 2025; Charan et al., 2025). By analyzing secondary data from customer feedback, market research, and competitive analysis, businesses can identify unmet needs and gaps in the market, thereby guiding the development of new products or services. The study's emphasis on robust model development and validation provides a framework for businesses to use data to drive innovation with confidence.
- **Challenges in Data Privacy and Ethics**: As businesses increasingly rely on consumer data to build applied models, ethical concerns related to privacy and data security must be prioritized (Samal et al., 2025; Selvakumar et al., 2025d; Selvakumar et al., 2025e; Kaur et al., 2025; Kunnathully et al., 2025). The study's discussion of ethical considerations highlights the need for businesses to implement stringent data protection measures and ensure that they comply with privacy regulations such as the GDPR. Failure to address ethical concerns can result in reputational damage, legal repercussions, and loss of consumer trust. Businesses must therefore adopt responsible data practices and be transparent with customers about how their data will be used.

3. Implications for Healthcare

The healthcare sector is one of the areas where the application of data-driven models has the potential to bring about significant improvements in outcomes. From disease diagnosis to treatment optimization and resource allocation, the findings of this study have important implications for healthcare organizations, practitioners, and policymakers.

- **Improved Patient Outcomes**: The study emphasizes that applied models can be used to predict disease outcomes, enhance treatment protocols, and streamline clinical operations. Predictive models based on secondary data, such as patient histories and medical records, can enable healthcare providers to identify high-risk patients early, thereby improving the chances of successful interventions. For example, machine learning models that predict patient readmission rates can help hospitals allocate resources more effectively, ensuring that high-risk patients receive appropriate care and attention.

- **Precision Medicine and Personalization**: Applied models have the potential to revolutionize personalized medicine by providing healthcare professionals with insights tailored to individual patients. By analyzing data from clinical trials, electronic health records, and genomic databases, predictive models can identify which treatments are most likely to be effective for specific patient populations. This approach promotes more personalized care, reducing the trial-and-error nature of traditional treatment methods. The study's emphasis on model evaluation and validation ensures that such models are reliable and clinically actionable.
- **Resource Allocation and Operational Efficiency**: Healthcare organizations are under constant pressure to optimize resource utilization while maintaining high standards of care. The study's findings suggest that data-driven models can be used to forecast patient demand, optimize scheduling, and reduce waiting times. By deploying predictive models to forecast patient volumes, hospitals can adjust staffing levels, improve patient flow, and minimize bottlenecks in the system. This leads to more efficient healthcare delivery and better patient experiences.
- **Ethical and Privacy Concerns**: In healthcare, the ethical use of secondary data is especially critical due to the sensitive nature of patient information. The study highlights the need for strong ethical guidelines and data privacy practices when using medical records and other healthcare-related data for model building. Ensuring that patients' personal information is anonymized and used with consent is essential to maintaining trust in healthcare systems. Furthermore, healthcare organizations must address issues such as bias and fairness in their predictive models to avoid exacerbating health disparities.

4. Implications for Public Policy and Governance

The findings of this study are also highly relevant for public policymakers and government agencies that rely on data to shape policies, allocate resources, and evaluate the effectiveness of public programs.

- **Data-Driven Policy Making**: The study demonstrates that data-driven models can play a crucial role in informing public policy decisions. Predictive models based on secondary data can be used to forecast economic trends, predict the impact of policies, and optimize resource allocation. For example, governments can use data models to forecast the effects of changes in tax policy, healthcare reform, or climate change regulations. By incorporating empirical data into policy decisions, governments can make more informed and effective choices that better serve the needs of the population.

- **Improving Social Programs and Resource Distribution**: Public programs aimed at addressing social issues, such as poverty, education, and healthcare, can benefit from data-driven models. The study emphasizes the importance of ensuring fairness and addressing bias when developing models for public policy. By using secondary data to identify communities or demographic groups in need of assistance, governments can allocate resources more effectively and ensure that support is directed to those who need it most.
- **Transparency and Accountability**: The ethical implications of using secondary data for public policy highlight the need for transparency and accountability in government decision-making. Public policymakers must ensure that the data used to develop models is representative, unbiased, and ethically sourced. Furthermore, they should be transparent about the methodologies used to build and validate models, as well as the potential impacts of their decisions on different groups in society.

5. Ethical Implications and Social Responsibility

Finally, the study's focus on ethical considerations and bias in model development carries important social and ethical implications. As applied models are increasingly used in high-stakes areas such as hiring, law enforcement, healthcare, and finance, it is crucial to ensure that these models are developed and deployed in a responsible and ethical manner.

- **Bias and Fairness**: The study emphasizes the need to address bias in data and model predictions. This is particularly important in sensitive applications where biased models can exacerbate social inequalities and lead to unfair outcomes. The implications of bias and fairness are significant, as discriminatory models can have far-reaching consequences for individuals and communities, especially when they are used in critical areas like hiring, criminal justice, or lending.
- **Data Privacy and Consent**: Ethical use of data, especially in sectors like healthcare and finance, requires strict adherence to privacy standards and informed consent. The study highlights the importance of protecting individuals' privacy rights and ensuring that data is used responsibly and transparently.

The findings of this study have profound implications across a range of sectors, from academia and business to healthcare, public policy, and ethics. The study reinforces the importance of building applied models that are accurate, fair, and ethical, highlighting both the potential benefits and the challenges involved. By ensuring methodological rigor, addressing bias, and adhering to ethical standards, stakeholders can harness the power of data to drive innovation and solve complex real-world problems while promoting fairness, transparency, and social responsibility.

CONCLUSION

In the contemporary world, where data is often considered the new oil, the process of building applied models from data has emerged as one of the most transformative methodologies across multiple disciplines (Mayer-Schönberger & Cukier, 2013). From business to healthcare, public policy to education, and environmental studies to finance, applied models grounded in data serve as the backbone of modern decision-making and problem-solving (Provost & Fawcett, 2013). This study has provided a comprehensive examination of how these models are constructed, validated, and deployed, while also shedding light on the technical and ethical challenges involved, such as overfitting, algorithmic bias, and concerns related to data privacy and fairness (Barocas et al., 2019). The implications of these findings are far-reaching, impacting academic researchers, business leaders, healthcare professionals, policymakers, and society at large. This conclusion aims to summarize the core insights and reflect on the future trajectory of data-driven model building.

Importance of Building Robust Applied Models

A central takeaway from the study is that building robust applied models is vital for transforming raw data into actionable insights. This process typically involves defining the problem, collecting and preparing data, selecting an appropriate modeling technique, evaluating its performance, deploying it in real-world scenarios, and continuously monitoring it for relevance and accuracy (Kelleher et al., 2015). Beyond the technical stages, the study highlights the need for clarity in model objectives to ensure alignment with the problems being addressed (Domingos, 2020). The iterative nature of modeling reinforces the dynamic feedback loops that refine model effectiveness over time. Especially in critical industries such as healthcare, finance, and business, the ability to build models that reliably mirror real-world dynamics is essential, as flawed predictions can lead to detrimental consequences (O'Neil et al., 2016). Furthermore, the adaptability of models across contexts—from local to global—is crucial, adding complexity but also ensuring broader applicability and utility (Chui et al., 2017).

Challenges and Limitations in Applied Model Building

Among the most pressing challenges explored are algorithmic bias and fairness. If models are trained on biased data, they may perpetuate historical inequalities, particularly in sensitive domains such as hiring, lending, and criminal justice. The study underscores the importance of using diverse datasets and fairness-aware algorithms to address these risks (Mehrabi et al., 2021). Transparency and accountability throughout the model lifecycle are also vital for ensuring ethical integrity (Floridi et al., 2018). Another significant limitation is data quality; issues such as missing values, outliers, and inconsistencies can compromise model reliability. As the study emphasizes, data preparation, though time-consuming, is foundational for building trustworthy models. Ethical considerations, especially regarding privacy and consent, are also critical. With increasing reliance on secondary and personal data, adherence to data protection laws such as the GDPR is necessary to maintain public trust and legal compliance (Voigt & Von dem Bussche, 2017).

Implications for Various Sectors

The findings also highlight how applied modeling can benefit diverse sectors. In business, predictive models are revolutionizing strategy, customer personalization, and operational optimization (Brynjolfsson & McAfee, 2014). Whether forecasting demand, optimizing supply chains, or enhancing customer experience, data-driven models are crucial for maintaining competitive advantage. Nevertheless, the study cautions that ethical issues, particularly concerning the use of customer data, must be addressed to ensure responsible innovation (Martin, 2019). In healthcare, the deployment of predictive analytics can enhance diagnosis, treatment personalization, and resource allocation, ultimately improving patient outcomes and cost-efficiency (Topol, 2019). Yet, as noted in the study, ethical challenges involving consent and data sensitivity demand rigorous compliance with medical data regulations (Rieke et al., 2020). For policymakers, the use of data-driven models enables evidence-based decision-making, allowing for more efficient and targeted interventions in areas such as social welfare, public health, and economic planning (Sunstein, 2018). However, transparency in the design and application of such models is necessary to prevent policy decisions that inadvertently reinforce social inequities (Veale et al., 2018). The study thus concludes that while applied modeling holds vast potential, realizing its benefits requires a balanced approach that integrates technical rigor with ethical responsibility and sector-specific sensitivity.

Ethical Implications and Future Directions

One of the most critical takeaways from the study is the importance of addressing the ethical implications of applied modeling. As data-driven models become more integral to decision-making, it is crucial to consider the broader societal impact of these models. The study emphasizes the need for fairness, transparency, and accountability in model development and deployment. It calls for the integration of ethical guidelines and the development of frameworks that promote responsible use of data. This is especially important in areas such as criminal justice, hiring, and lending, where biased models can perpetuate inequality and social injustice. The future of applied modeling is closely tied to the ongoing advancements in machine learning, artificial intelligence, and big data analytics. As new technologies emerge, so too will new challenges and opportunities for model development. In particular, the integration of explainable AI (XAI) and ethically-aligned AI will become increasingly important in addressing concerns about model transparency and accountability. Moving forward, there will be greater emphasis on developing models that not only deliver high predictive accuracy but also provide understandable explanations for their predictions. This will help ensure that models are trusted, adopted, and used ethically. In conclusion, building applied models from data is an essential practice that empowers decision-makers across various sectors to derive actionable insights, solve complex problems, and improve outcomes. This study has provided a detailed exploration of the key stages involved in model building, from defining the problem to deploying and monitoring models in real-world contexts. It has also highlighted the challenges associated with the process, including overfitting, bias, data quality, and ethical concerns, which must be carefully addressed to ensure that models are both effective and ethical. The implications of the study are far-reaching, offering valuable insights for researchers, businesses, healthcare providers, policymakers, and anyone involved in data-driven decision-making. The study's emphasis on the importance of ethical considerations, fairness, and transparency in model development serves as a call to action for the responsible use of data. As the volume and complexity of data continue to grow, the need for robust, transparent, and ethical models will become increasingly critical in shaping the future of decision-making across sectors. By adhering to the principles outlined in this study, stakeholders can harness the full potential of applied models while safeguarding the public interest and promoting fairness and equity in all aspects of model development and deployment.

REFERENCES

Aradhya, S. G. B., Gupta, V. C., Selvakumar, P., Raman, M. S., Singh, J., Manjunath, T. C., & Sharma, M. (2025). Health Crises and Digitalization: Digital Health. In *Sustainable Digitalization Strategies in Business and Healthcare* (pp. 171-198). IGI Global Scientific Publishing.

Barocas, J. A., Wang, J., Marshall, B. D., LaRochelle, M. R., Bettano, A., Bernson, D., Beckwith, C. G., Linas, B. P., & Walley, A. Y. (2019). Sociodemographic factors and social determinants associated with toxicology confirmed polysubstance opioid-related deaths. *Drug and Alcohol Dependence*, *200*, 59–63. DOI: 10.1016/j.drugalcdep.2019.03.014 PMID: 31100636

Bishop, D. V. (2006). What causes specific language impairment in children? *Current Directions in Psychological Science*, *15*(5), 217–221. DOI: 10.1111/j.1467-8721.2006.00439.x PMID: 19009045

Brynjolfsson, E., & McAfee, A. (2014). *The second machine age: Work, progress, and prosperity in a time of brilliant technologies*. WW Norton & company.

Charan, J. K., Meera, K. L., Sudheer, P., Gopalakrishnan, G., Sharma, M., Selvakumar, P., & Manjunath, T. C. (2025). Applications of Generative AI and Human-AI Collaboration. In *Humans and Generative AI Tools for Collaborative Intelligence* (pp. 423–440). IGI Global Scientific Publishing. DOI: 10.4018/979-8-3693-8332-2.ch018

Chui, M., Manyika, J., & Miremadi, M. (2017). *Artificial Intelligence: Implications for the Future of Work*. McKinsey Global Institute.

Floridi, L., Cowls, J., Beltrametti, M., Chatila, R., Chazerand, P., Dignum, V., Luetge, C., Madelin, R., Pagallo, U., Rossi, F., Schafer, B., Valcke, P., & Vayena, E. (2018). AI4People—An ethical framework for a good AI society: Opportunities, risks, principles, and recommendations. *Minds and Machines*, *28*(4), 689–707. DOI: 10.1007/s11023-018-9482-5 PMID: 30930541

Galton, F. (1886). Regression towards mediocrity in hereditary stature. *Journal of the Anthropological Institute of Great Britain and Ireland*, *15*, 246–263. DOI: 10.2307/2841583

Goodfellow, I., Bengio, Y., & Courville, A. (2016). *Deep Learning*. MIT Press.

Kaur, H., Selvakumar, P., Haashni, S., Anute, N., Sharma, M., & Manjunath, T. C. (2025). Representations in Developing Thinking Regarding Probabilities in Higher Education. In *Modes of Representation in Developing Statistical Thinking in Education* (pp. 89–118). IGI Global Scientific Publishing. DOI: 10.4018/979-8-3693-9934-7.ch006

Kelleher, J. D., Namee, B., & D'Arcy, A. (2015). *Fundamentals of Machine Learning for Predictive Data Analytics: Algorithms, Worked Examples, and Case Studies*. MIT Press.

Kohavi, R. (1995, August). A study of cross-validation and bootstrap for accuracy estimation and model selection. *IJCAI (United States)*, *14*(2), 1137–1145.

Kunnathully, K., Satyanarayana, P., Anute, N., Sharma, M., Sureshkrishna, G., Manjunath, T. C., & Selvakumar, P. (2025). Propaganda, Social Media and AI. In *Digital Populism and the Use of Neo-Propaganda and Fake News* (pp. 19–38). IGI Global Scientific Publishing. DOI: 10.4018/979-8-3693-9999-6.ch002

Lai, X., & Xie, L. (2013). *Practical Approaches to Data Mining and Machine Learning*. Springer.

Lecun, Y., Bengio, Y., & Hinton, G. (2015). Deep Learning. *Nature*, *521*(7553), 436–444. DOI: 10.1038/nature14539 PMID: 26017442

Madaan, S., Sai, T. B., Mandal, R., Kar, A., Sharma, M., Selvakumar, P., & Manjunath, T. C. (2025). Math Instruction and AI. In *Examining AI Disruption in Educational Settings: Challenges and Opportunities* (pp. 161-184). IGI Global Scientific Publishing. DOI: 10.4018/979-8-3693-7873-1.ch006

Malik, N., Nirupama, E., Selvakumar, P., Sankpal, U., Nathsharma, S. K., Sharma, M., & Manjunath, T. C. (2025a). 2D Materials for Energy Storage and Conversion. In *Innovations in Next-Generation Energy Storage Solutions* (pp. 1–24). IGI Global Scientific Publishing. DOI: 10.4018/979-8-3693-9316-1.ch001

Malik, N., Thakur, D. J., Aradhya, S. G. B., Sudheer, P., Sharma, M., Manjunath, T. C., & Selvakumar, P. (2025b). Performance Optimization in Remote Monitoring. In *Synergizing Data Envelopment Analysis and Machine Learning for Performance Optimization in Healthcare* (pp. 495–516). IGI Global Scientific Publishing. DOI: 10.4018/979-8-3373-0081-8.ch020

Martin, K. (2019). Ethical implications and accountability of algorithms. *Journal of Business Ethics*, *160*(4), 835–850. DOI: 10.1007/s10551-018-3921-3

Mehrabi, N., Morstatter, F., Saxena, N., Lerman, K., & Galstyan, A. (2021). A survey on bias and fairness in machine learning. *ACM Computing Surveys, 54*(6), 1–35. DOI: 10.1145/3457607

Mishra, B. R., Selvakumar, P., Kaur, R., Kalshetti, P., Mishra, K. K., Sharma, M., & Manjunath, T. C. (2025). Innovation and Digital Transformation in the Public Sector Entities. In *Enhancing Public Sector Accountability and Services Through Digital Innovation* (pp. 409–436). IGI Global Scientific Publishing. DOI: 10.4018/979-8-3693-9251-5.ch013

O'Neil, J., Benita, Y., Feldman, I., Chenard, M., Roberts, B., Liu, Y., Li, J., Kral, A., Lejnine, S., Loboda, A., Arthur, W., Cristescu, R., Haines, B. B., Winter, C., Zhang, T., Bloecher, A., & Shumway, S. D. (2016). An unbiased oncology compound screen to identify novel combination strategies. *Molecular Cancer Therapeutics, 15*(6), 1155–1162. DOI: 10.1158/1535-7163.MCT-15-0843 PMID: 26983881

Provost, F., & Fawcett, T. (2013). *Data Science for Business: What you need to know about data mining and data-analytic thinking*. O'Reilly Media, Inc.

Rieke, N., Hancox, J., Li, W., Milletari, F., Roth, H. R., Albarqouni, S., Bakas, S., Galtier, M. N., Landman, B. A., Maier-Hein, K., Ourselin, S., Sheller, M., Summers, R. M., Trask, A., Xu, D., Baust, M., & Cardoso, M. J. (2020). The future of digital health with federated learning. *NPJ Digital Medicine, 3*(1), 119. DOI: 10.1038/s41746-020-00323-1 PMID: 33015372

Samal, A., Bhargav, J., Selvakumar, P., Sharma, M., & TC, M. (2025). Measuring Brand Performance With AI Tools. In *Strategic Brand Management in the Age of AI and Disruption* (pp. 279-302). IGI Global Scientific Publishing.

Selvakumar, P., Aradhya, S. G. B., Anute, N., Devi, S., Sharma, M., & Vaissnave, V. (2025). Strategic Collaborations and Partnerships in Entrepreneurship. In *Support Networks for Entrepreneurs: Social Capital and Strategic Collaborations* (pp. 203-232). IGI Global Scientific Publishing. DOI: 10.4018/979-8-3693-9836-4.ch009

Selvakumar, P., Dahiya, R., Manjunath, T. C., & Sharma, M. (2025). Carbon Footprint Analysis of Electronic Products. In *Integrated Approaches for Sustainable E-Waste Management* (pp. 215–242). IGI Global Scientific Publishing. DOI: 10.4018/979-8-3693-7383-5.ch008

Selvakumar, P., Satyanarayana, P., Lahoti, Y., Saipogu, L., Sharma, M., & Manjunath, T. C. (2025c). AI Techniques. In *AI Methods for Environmental Protection and Resource Conservation* (pp. 107–138). IGI Global Scientific Publishing. DOI: 10.4018/979-8-3373-3246-8.ch005

Selvakumar, P., Shanthi, M., Pitchiah, R., Sharma, M., Dahake, P. S., & TC, M. (2025b). The Role of Artificial Intelligence in Business Model Innovation: Overview of AI Technologies. *AI-Driven Business Model Innovation*, 219-246.

Selvakumar, P., Sharma, A., Roy, S. S., Sharma, M., & Manjunath, T. C. (2025a). Representations in Developing Statistical Thinking in Secondary Education. In *Modes of Representation in Developing Statistical Thinking in Education* (pp. 59–88). IGI Global Scientific Publishing. DOI: 10.4018/979-8-3693-9934-7.ch005

Sutton, R. S., & Barto, A. G. (2018). Temporal-difference learning. *Reinforcement learning: an introduction*, 131-132.

Topol, E. J. (2019). High-performance medicine: The convergence of human and artificial intelligence. *Nature Medicine*, *25*(1), 44–56. DOI: 10.1038/s41591-018-0300-7 PMID: 30617339

Veale, M., Van Kleek, M., & Binns, R. (2018, April). Fairness and accountability design needs for algorithmic support in high-stakes public sector decision-making. In *Proceedings of the 2018 chi conference on human factors in computing systems* (pp. 1-14). DOI: 10.1145/3173574.3174014

Voigt, P., & Von dem Bussche, A. (2017). The eu general data protection regulation (gdpr). *A practical guide, 1st ed., Cham: Springer International Publishing, 10*(3152676), 10-5555.

Chapter 4
Developing an Applied Communication Model:
For Crisis Reporting in Digital Media Ecosystems

Archan Mitra
https://orcid.org/0000-0002-1419-3558
Amity University, Mumbai, India

Ruma Roy
https://orcid.org/0009-0005-4637-9508
Visva Bharati University, India

ABSTRACT

Crisis events—from natural disasters to health emergencies—require rapid, accurate, responsible communication. In digital media's fast-paced landscape, structured approaches are essential to maintain credibility, relevance, and engagement. This chapter presents an applied communication model for crisis reporting that integrates case studies of real-time coverage during pandemics, floods, and unrest. The model comprises modular components: source verification, message framing, multimodal dissemination, audience feedback loops, and platform-specific calibration. Emphasizing adaptability in newsrooms, government, and humanitarian settings, it supports future reuse. Development combines field observation, social media analytics, and simulation (in vitro/in vivo) testing. Cultural sensitivity and regional language integration enhance effectiveness. By systematizing communication, this research advances public trust, counters misinformation, and equips practitioners with practical tools for high-stakes reporting.

DOI: 10.4018/979-8-3373-3301-4.ch004

1. INTRODUCTION

1.1 Background and Rationale

Crisis events—ranging from natural disasters to public health emergencies—have always necessitated swift and accurate communication to mitigate harm and coordinate response. In recent years, the proliferation of digital media platforms has dramatically accelerated the speed and scope of information dissemination. Social media channels such as Twitter, Facebook, and WhatsApp enable eyewitnesses, official sources, and third-party commentators to share real-time updates with global audiences (Palen & Anderson, 2016). While these technologies offer unparalleled opportunities for timely alerts and community engagement, they also introduce challenges of misinformation, rumor proliferation, and audience fragmentation (Liu, Austin, & Jin, 2015; Stephens, Malone, & Bailey, 2005). Traditional crisis communication frameworks—grounded in one-way, top-down messaging—struggle to accommodate the two-way, networked dynamics of digital ecosystems (Coombs, 2007; Ulmer, Sellnow, & Seeger, 2018). Consequently, there is a pressing need for structured, adaptable models that integrate verification, framing, multimodal dissemination, and feedback loops to uphold credibility and foster public trust in the digital age.

1.2 Problem Statement

Despite extensive research on crisis communication strategies, existing models often under-emphasize the complex socio-technical interplay characteristic of modern digital media ecosystems. Most prescriptive frameworks prioritize organizational messaging tactics—such as apology, justification, or denial—without fully addressing how content travels, transforms, and is reinterpreted across diverse online platforms (Jin, Liu, & Austin, 2014). Furthermore, the rapid diffusion of unverified or manipulated content can erode the legitimacy of official sources and exacerbate public confusion, as witnessed during events like the COVID-19 pandemic and major natural disasters (Palen & Anderson, 2016). Current approaches lack systematic guidance on integrating platform-specific features (character limits, algorithmic promotion, multimedia affordances) and cultural-linguistic variations into coherent crisis reporting practices. This gap hinders newsrooms, government agencies, and humanitarian organizations from delivering consistent, credible, and contextually relevant information when it is most needed.

1.3 Research Objective

The primary objective of this research is to develop and empirically validate an applied communication model tailored for crisis reporting within digital media ecosystems. Specifically, the study aims to design a modular framework encompassing source verification, message framing, multimodal dissemination, audience feedback loops, and platform-specific calibration. Through field observation of live crises, social media analytics, and both in vitro and in vivo simulation testing, the research will assess the model's effectiveness in enhancing information credibility, audience engagement, and resistance to misinformation.

1.4 Research Questions

Three interrelated questions guide this investigation. First, how can modular components for source verification and message framing be operationalized to improve the accuracy and clarity of crisis reports across digital platforms? Second, in what ways do multimodal dissemination strategies—combining text, audio, video, and infographics—affect audience comprehension, trust, and behavioral intent during high-stakes events? Third, how do platform-specific features and audience feedback loops influence the model's adaptability and scalability in diverse organizational and cultural contexts?

1.5 Significance of the Study

This research addresses a critical need for integrative, practice-oriented frameworks that reconcile theoretical insights with the realities of digital crisis reporting. By advancing a comprehensive model validated through mixed methods, the study contributes to both scholarship and practice. Academically, it extends crisis communication theory by embedding socio-technical considerations and feedback mechanisms into a unified architecture (Seeger, 2006). Practically, it offers media practitioners, government communicators, and humanitarian responders a structured toolkit for designing, implementing, and evaluating crisis messages tailored to platform constraints and audience characteristics. Ultimately, the model aims to strengthen public trust, reduce the spread of harmful misinformation, and enable more effective information management during crises.

1.6 Structure of the Paper

The paper is organized into seven chapters. Following this introduction, Chapter 2 reviews relevant literature on crisis communication theories, digital media dynamics, source verification, message framing, multimodal dissemination, and audience engagement in online contexts. Chapter 3 presents the conceptual framework and details the proposed applied communication model, including its modular components and underlying theoretical foundations. Chapter 4 outlines the mixed-methods research design, encompassing field observations, social media analytics, and simulation studies, along with sampling strategies and analytic procedures. Chapter 5 reports the empirical results across the three research questions, integrating quantitative metrics and qualitative insights. Chapter 6 discusses the findings in relation to existing theory and practice, highlighting mechanisms, contextual factors, and implications. Finally, Chapter 7 concludes with a summary of contributions, limitations, policy recommendations, and directions for future research.

2. LITERATURE REVIEW

2.1 Crisis Communication Theory

Situational Crisis Communication Theory (SCCT) has become the dominant paradigm for understanding how organizations should tailor their messages in response to varying crisis types and stakeholder perceptions (Coombs, 2007). SCCT posits that crisis response strategies—ranging from denial and diminishment to rebuilding and bolstering—must align with the organization's level of responsibility for the event and the reputational threat posed. Coombs and Holladay (2008) demonstrated empirically that corrective-action and apology strategies are most effective when organizational responsibility is high, whereas simple information provision suffices for victim crises. Although SCCT offers comprehensive guidance for message selection, its focus remains predominantly on content strategies rather than on the technical and social processes through which messages disseminate and are interpreted in today's digital media ecosystems.

2.2 Digital Media Ecosystems and News Diffusion

Digital media ecosystems encompass a complex interplay of platforms, algorithms, and user networks that shape how crisis information spreads (Palen & Anderson, 2016). Social platforms enable both top-down messages from official sources and bottom-up contributions from eyewitnesses and community volunteers (Starbird & Palen, 2011). Palen and Hughes (2018) observe that information flows during crises are nonlinear: content may originate on Twitter, be amplified on Facebook, and then re-circulate via messaging apps such as WhatsApp. This multi-channel diffusion challenges traditional news gatekeeping and requires communicators to consider platform affordances, algorithmic prioritization, and network structure in message design. Jin, Liu, and Austin (2014) further note that the speed of dissemination increases both the reach and the risk of rumor propagation, underscoring the need for verification mechanisms embedded in digital reporting workflows.

2.3 Source Verification in Online Crisis Reporting

Verification of user-generated content is a critical challenge in digital crisis reporting. Metzger, Flanagin, and Medders (2010) distinguish between heuristic cues—such as site reputation or visual quality—and systematic evaluation of source credibility. In practice, organizations have developed multi-step verification protocols, combining reverse-image searches, metadata analysis, and cross-referencing with official feeds (Silverman, 2015). Starbird (2014) highlights the "human-machine" collaboration in verification, where crowd-sourced volunteers flag dubious content while algorithms check geolocation and timestamp metadata. Despite these advances, verification remains time-consuming and often occurs post-publication, leading to retractions and corrections that erode public trust (Palen & Anderson, 2016). The literature thus calls for integrated verification modules that operate in real time within crisis communication models.

2.4 Message Framing and Emotional Appeals

Message framing shapes audience interpretation by emphasizing certain aspects of an event over others (Entman, 1993). In crisis contexts, frames of responsibility, risk, and efficacy influence public responses such as compliance with evacuation orders or trust in authorities (Kim & Cameron, 2011). Emotional appeals—particularly fear and empathy—can increase message persuasiveness but risk triggering panic if not carefully calibrated (Ruiter et al., 2014). Jin et al. (2014) find that mixed-emotion framing, which combines factual information with empathetic narratives, both sustains attention and reduces resistance to corrective messages. Yet, traditional framing research has not fully accounted for how emotional tone varies across platforms with different character limits, comment dynamics, and multimedia support, indicating a need for adaptable framing guidelines in digital crisis models.

2.5 Multimodal Dissemination Channels

The proliferation of multimedia formats—text, images, video, and infographics—offers crisis communicators multiple channels to convey urgency, context, and instructions (Veil, Buehner, & Palenchar, 2011). Research shows that video clips of evacuation routes or animated infographics of flood maps can enhance comprehension and recall compared to text-only alerts (Houston et al., 2015). Audio snippets, such as recorded voice messages from first responders, foster emotional connection and credibility (Liu & Fraustino, 2014). Multimodal dissemination leverages cognitive redundancy: when the same information appears in multiple formats, audiences are more likely to process and share it (Mayer, 2009). However, producing high-quality multimedia in real time poses operational challenges, and few crisis models offer systematic guidance on selecting and coordinating these channels under tight time constraints.

2.6 Audience Feedback Loops and Participatory Reporting

Digital platforms enable audiences to respond, correct, and supplement crisis information through comments, polls, and direct messaging. Schultz, Utz, and Göritz (2011) find that enabling audience feedback on Twitter increases perceived transparency and organizational trust. Participatory reporting—where users contribute eyewitness images, geotagged updates, and needs assessments—has emerged as a valuable supplement to official sources (Zook et al., 2010). Yet, feedback loops also introduce noise, as comments may propagate rumors or politically motivated content (Liu et al., 2015). Scholars argue for structured feedback mechanisms—such as moderated comment threads or verified volunteer networks—to balance openness with accuracy (Bruns & Burgess, 2012). Integrating participatory elements into crisis communication models requires protocols for triaging, verifying, and incorporating user inputs without overloading response workflows.

2.7 Platform-Specific Calibration

Each social media platform exhibits unique affordances, user norms, and content constraints that influence message effectiveness. Twitter's 280-character limit demands concise language and strategic use of hashtags and mentions, whereas Facebook allows longer narratives and threaded updates (Kietzmann, Hermkens, McCarthy, & Silvestre, 2011). WhatsApp's encrypted, closed-group structure facilitates peer-to-peer sharing but hampers broadcast reach beyond existing contact lists (Church & de Oliveira, 2013). Emerging apps such as TikTok prioritize short videos with algorithmic promotion based on engagement signals (Van Dijck, Poell, & de Waal, 2018). Effective crisis communication models must thus include calibration modules that adapt message form, length, and metadata (tags, geotags) to each platform's technical and social environment, a consideration often absent in general crisis frameworks.

2.8 Existing Models of Crisis Reporting and Identified Gaps

Several integrated models have sought to encompass content strategies, media channels, and stakeholder engagement. Ulmer, Sellnow, and Seeger (2018) propose a five-phase model—mitigation, preparedness, response, recovery, and learning—that emphasizes two-way communication but stops short of specifying digital workflows. Seeger (2006) offers "best practices" distilled from expert panels, yet these recommendations remain largely descriptive rather than operational. More recent work by Reynolds and Seeger (2014) introduces a social media crisis management lifecycle but lacks detailed mechanisms for verification and feedback integration. Across these models, common gaps include the absence of modular verification processes, limited guidance on multimodal coordination, and insufficient attention to platform-specific adaptation. This review underscores the necessity of a comprehensive, applied communication model that synthesizes theoretical insights with technical protocols to address the complexities of digital crisis reporting.

3. CONCEPTUAL FRAMEWORK & MODEL DEVELOPMENT

3.1 Theoretical Foundations

The applied communication model proposed in this study draws on two complementary theories: Media System Dependency (MSD) and Diffusion of Innovations (DOI). Media System Dependency theory posits that during periods of social disruption—such as crises—individuals' reliance on media for information, orientation, and play (diversion) intensifies, heightening media's influence on cognition and behavior (Ball-Rokeach & DeFleur, 1976). In crisis contexts, MSD suggests that audiences will depend more heavily on digital platforms that they perceive as credible and timely, making the design of authoritative, verifiable content critical to shaping public understanding and action (Palen & Anderson, 2016).

Diffusion of Innovations theory offers a complementary lens by explaining how new ideas and technologies spread through social systems (Rogers, 2003). It identifies key attributes—relative advantage, compatibility, complexity, trialability, and observability—that affect adoption rates among individuals and organizations. In the case of a modular crisis communication model, DOI informs how practitioners might introduce and scale each module (e.g., source verification, multimodal dissemination) within newsrooms and government agencies. For instance, framing the verification module as a means to reduce reputational risk (relative advantage) and aligning its procedures with existing newsroom workflows (compatibility) can accelerate uptake among journalists and communicators (Jin, Liu, & Austin, 2014).

By integrating MSD and DOI, the proposed framework attends both to the audience's intensifying need for reliable information during crises and to the organizational adoption processes required to operationalize new communication practices. The interweaving of these theories ensures that the model not only meets end-user dependency needs but is also adoptable and sustainable within complex institutional ecosystems.

3.2 Component Definitions

3.2.1 Source Verification Module

The Source Verification Module comprises a sequence of procedural and technological measures to authenticate incoming information before publication. Drawing on best practices in digital journalism, this module entails automated and manual checks: reverse-image searches to detect manipulated visuals, geolocation and timestamp metadata analysis for user-generated content, and cross-referencing with official feeds and trusted databases (Metzger, Flanagin, & Medders, 2010; Silverman, 2015). The module also integrates crowd-sourced verification networks—trained volunteers who flag questionable content in real time—while employing algorithmic heuristics to surface anomalies in text patterns or source behavior (Starbird, 2014). By embedding verification at the outset of the reporting workflow, the module reduces reliance on post-publication corrections, thereby preserving organizational credibility and public trust (Palen & Anderson, 2016).

Figure 1. Source verification workflow

3.2.2 Message Framing Module

The Message Framing Module guides communicators in constructing crisis narratives that balance informational clarity with emotional resonance. Grounded in framing theory (Entman, 1993) and empirical crisis communication research, the module prescribes a mixed-tone approach: factual reporting of "what, where, when," paired with empathetic language to acknowledge affected audiences' concerns (Ruiter et al., 2014). It provides templated structures for different crisis types—victim crises, accidental crises, and preventable crises—drawing on Situational Crisis Communication Theory (Coombs, 2007). The module further includes guidance on linguistic registers and cultural idioms, ensuring that frames are locally meaningful and sensitive to regional language norms. By standardizing framing choices, the module helps maintain consistency across digital platforms and organizational spokespeople, reducing the risk of mixed messages that can undermine public confidence (Stephens, Malone, & Bailey, 2005).

Figure 2. Message framing process

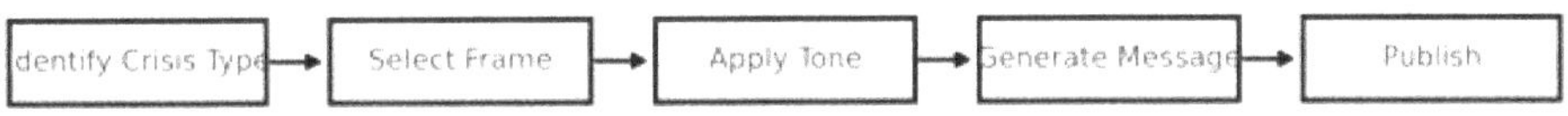

3.2.3 Multimodal Dissemination Module

The Multimodal Dissemination Module specifies how to coordinate text, audio, video, and infographics to optimize audience comprehension and engagement. Based on multimedia learning principles (Mayer, 2009) and evidence from social media–driven crises (Houston et al., 2015), the module recommends layering formats: concise text alerts for rapid scanning, short video clips demonstrating evacuation routes, and infographics mapping resource distribution. It also outlines production protocols—such as file size limits, platform encoding standards, and accessibility features (e.g., captioning, alt-text)—to ensure that multimedia content is delivered quickly and inclusively (Liu & Fraustino, 2014). By integrating multiple sensory channels, the module leverages cognitive redundancy to reinforce key messages and facilitate behavioral compliance during emergencies.

Figure 3. Multimodal dissemination coordination

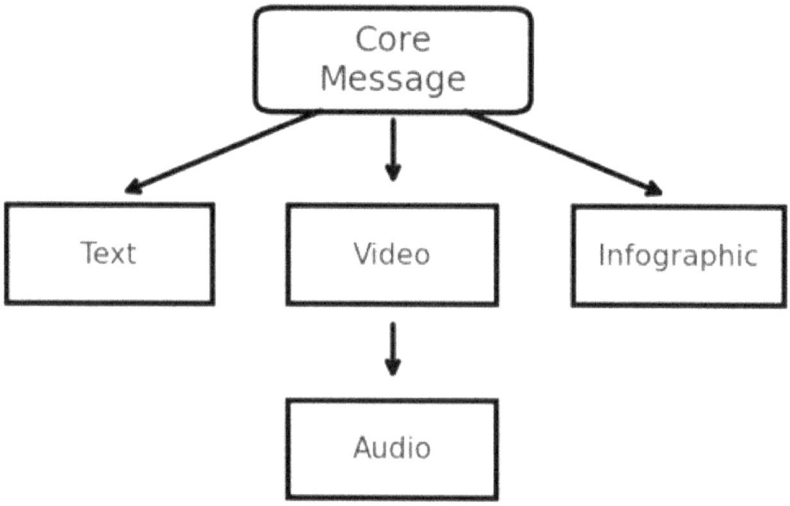

3.2.4 Audience Feedback Module

The Audience Feedback Module establishes structured mechanisms for two-way communication, enabling audiences to submit situational updates, needs assessments, and clarifying questions. Drawing on participatory reporting frameworks (Zook, Graham, Shelton, & Gorman, 2010) and moderated social media practices (Bruns & Burgess, 2012), the module includes: (a) official hashtags and tagging conventions to aggregate user-generated reports; (b) rapid response teams tasked with triaging and verifying incoming feedback; and (c) scheduled Q&A sessions via live audio or chat functions to address prevalent concerns. By incorporating audience inputs into official updates, the module fosters transparency and collaboration while providing valuable ground-truth data to inform decision-making (Schultz, Utz, & Göritz, 2011).

Figure 4. Audience feedback loop mechanism

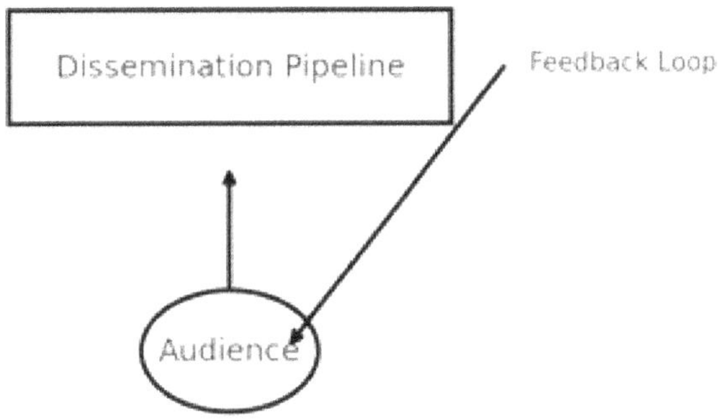

3.2.5 Platform Calibration Module

The Platform Calibration Module adapts core messages and media assets to the specific affordances and norms of individual digital platforms. Building on platform studies (Kietzmann et al., 2011) and crisis communication analytics (Jin et al., 2014), the module prescribes platform-tailored tactics: use of concise threads and relevant hashtags on Twitter; narrative posts with embedded video on Facebook; community-specific broadcast lists on WhatsApp; and short-form, hashtag-driven videos on TikTok. It also integrates real-time performance metrics—engagement rates, share velocity, sentiment analysis—to guide iterative adjustments. By calibrating content form and metadata (e.g., tags, thumbnails) for each channel, the module ensures maximal reach and resonance without diluting message consistency.

3.3 Proposed Applied Communication Model Diagram

The proposed Applied Communication Model (Figure 3) visually represents the five modules and their interconnections within a socio-technical ecosystem. At the core, the Source Verification and Message Framing modules feed into the Multimodal Dissemination pipeline, which in turn is fine-tuned by Platform Calibration. Surrounding this pipeline is a continuous Audience Feedback loop, which provides real-time data back into verification and framing processes. The diagram situates these components within the broader digital media environment, illustrating dependencies on organizational workflows, technological infrastructures, and regulatory contexts. By mapping information flows and feedback channels, the model offers both a strategic overview and a practical guide for implementation in diverse crisis scenarios.

3.4 Hypotheses or Propositions for Model Validation

To empirically evaluate the model's effectiveness, the study advances the following propositions. Proposition 1 asserts that integration of the Source Verification Module will significantly increase audience perceptions of information credibility, as measured by trust-scales adapted from Metzger et al. (2010). Proposition 2 posits that use of the Message Framing Module's mixed-tone templates will lead to higher audience comprehension and lower anxiety levels, relative to unstructured messaging, based on emotional response metrics (Kim & Cameron, 2011; Ruiter et al., 2014). Proposition 3 predicts that deployment of the Multimodal Dissemination Module will improve information recall and intended compliance behaviors—such as evacuation or resource-seeking—compared to text-only alerts (Houston et al., 2015; Mayer, 2009).

Proposition 4 suggests that incorporation of the Audience Feedback Module will enhance message relevance and situational accuracy, evidenced by reduced misinformation rates and higher correction-turnaround times (Schultz et al., 2011; Starbird & Palen, 2011). Finally, Proposition 5 contends that the Platform Calibration Module will optimize reach and engagement metrics—such as retweet frequency and video view counts—while maintaining cross-platform consistency, as indicated by comparative social-media analytics (Kietzmann et al., 2011; Palen & Anderson, 2016). Together, these propositions form the basis for mixed-methods validation through field observation, social media analytics, and simulation experiments, ultimately informing iterative refinements to the model.

Figure 5. Applied communication model diagram

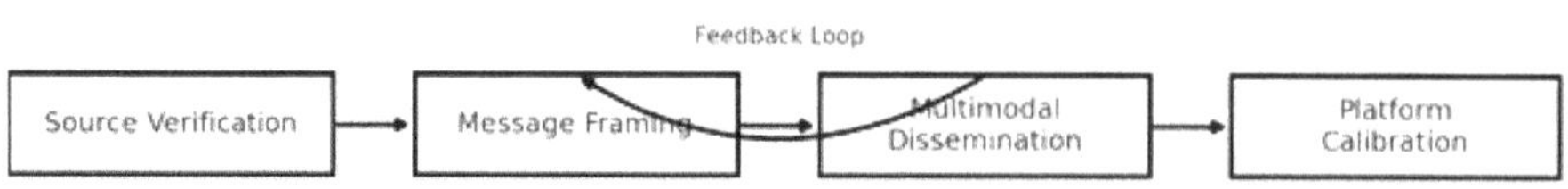

4. RESEARCH METHODOLOGY

4.1 Overall Design

This study adopts a mixed-methods research design combining qualitative field observations, quantitative social media analytics, and simulation testing to holistically evaluate the applied communication model for crisis reporting. Mixed-methods designs integrate the strengths of qualitative and quantitative approaches, enabling triangulation of data and deeper insights into complex phenomena (Creswell & Plano Clark, 2011). Qualitative observations capture the nuances of real-time crisis communication as it unfolds in the field, while quantitative social media analytics measure information flows, engagement patterns, and misinformation dynamics across digital platforms (Palen & Anderson, 2016). Simulation experiments then emulate crisis scenarios under controlled conditions, allowing systematic manipulation of model components—such as verification protocols and dissemination formats—and measurement of outcomes related to accuracy, timeliness, and reach. By weaving together these methods, the research design addresses both "what happens" in real crises and "what could happen" under different model configurations (Yin, 2014).

4.2 Field Observation of Live Crisis Events

Field observations focus on live crisis events—such as floods, public health outbreaks, and civil unrest—in selected urban and rural settings. Observational teams, trained in crisis informatics protocols, embed within newsrooms, emergency operation centers, and humanitarian coordination hubs. Using a structured observation protocol, teams document communication workflows, decision-making processes, and informal practices, noting how verification, framing, and dissemination modules are enacted under pressure. Field notes capture interactions among journalists, official spokespeople, and volunteer networks, including breakdowns and improvisations in digital reporting. Observers also record contextual variables—such as electricity reliability and internet bandwidth—that influence model implementation. Insights from these observations inform refinements to the model's component definitions and highlight real-world constraints not visible in laboratory settings (Yin, 2014; Schultz, Utz, & Göritz, 2011).

4.3 Social Media Analytics

To quantify digital information dynamics, the study conducts large-scale social media analytics across platforms including Twitter, Facebook, and WhatsApp where APIs permit. Data collection centers on crisis-related hashtags and keywords—such as "#FloodAlert" or "#COVIDUpdates"—and leverages platform APIs or third-party tools to retrieve posts, comments, and metadata over defined time windows (Jin et al., 2014; Weller et al., 2014). Sampling frames balance breadth (all public posts containing target hashtags) and depth (stratified sampling by engagement levels) to ensure both representativeness and focus on highly circulated content. Metrics include credibility scores—derived from source verification flags and metadata heuristics (Metzger et al., 2010)—engagement rates measured through likes, shares, and comments (Schultz et al., 2011), and misinformation spread quantified by tracking network propagation of fact-checked false claims (Starbird & Palen, 2011). These quantitative indicators illuminate how model components affect information credibility and audience response at scale.

4.3.1 Data Sources and Sampling

Data sources encompass both public APIs and collaboration with platform providers under research agreements. For Twitter and Facebook, keyword-based queries extract posts containing crisis-specific terms, while WhatsApp data are collected via volunteer-managed broadcast groups with informed consent. Sampling strategies combine exhaustive data pulls during peak crisis windows with random sampling in low-volume periods to capture temporal variations. Metadata fields—such as user location, timestamp, and device type—provide covariates for stratification. Hashtag co-occurrence networks and keyword frequency analyses guide identification of emerging subtopics and help calibrate the model's framing and feedback modules to evolving audience concerns (Palen & Anderson, 2016).

4.3.2 Metrics

Credibility scores are operationalized through a composite index combining automated verification indicators (e.g., presence of reverse-image search matches, recognized news source domains) and manual ratings by trained coders on a five-point scale (Metzger et al., 2010). Engagement rates are calculated as the ratio of interactions (likes, shares, comments) to total impressions, normalized across platforms for cross-channel comparison (Schultz et al., 2011). Misinformation spread is assessed by mapping the diffusion networks of fact-checked falsehoods, measuring cascade sizes, depths, and velocities to evaluate how quickly and widely rumors propagate (Starbird & Palen, 2011).

4.4 Simulation Testing

Simulation experiments emulate crisis information flows and organizational responses in controlled environments. Customized simulation platforms incorporate agent-based models representing journalists, official communicators, volunteers, and audience members. These agents exchange messages according to rules derived from the applied communication model, with parameters adjustable for verification rigor, framing styles, and dissemination modalities (Banks, Carson, Nelson, & Nicol, 2005). Simulations enable systematic exploration of model variants that would be impractical or unethical to test in real crises, such as low-verification scenarios or extreme misinformation attacks.

4.4.1 Crisis Scenarios and Parameters

Simulations include multiple crisis scenarios—rapid-onset natural disasters (e.g., flash floods), slow-burn public health emergencies (e.g., disease outbreaks), and complex political unrest. Scenario parameters specify event timelines, information injection rates (true and false reports), and resource constraints (staff availability, network bandwidth). Model components are toggled on or off to assess their marginal contributions. For example, comparing runs with and without the Audience Feedback Module reveals its impact on situational accuracy and rumor containment.

4.4.2 Performance Indicators

Performance indicators in simulations mirror field and social media metrics. Accuracy is measured by the proportion of disseminated messages that are verified correct. Timeliness reflects latency between event occurrence and message publication. Reach quantifies the percentage of simulated audience agents receiving and acknowledging messages. Additional indicators—such as reduction in misinformation cascades—provide comprehensive evaluation of model efficacy under varying conditions (Reynolds & Seeger, 2014).

4.5 Instrumentation

Data collection instruments include structured observation protocols, coding schemes for social media content, and analytic scripts for automated metrics computation. Observation protocols delineate fields for timestamp, source, content type, verification actions, and contextual notes. Coding manuals provide definitions, examples, and inter-rater reliability guidelines for manual content ratings. Analytic scripts, developed in R and Python, automate data cleaning, verification flagging (e.g., reverse-image search integration), network construction, and sentiment analysis. All instruments undergo iterative piloting and refinement to ensure clarity, usability, and alignment with research objectives (Willis, 2005).

4.6 Data Collection Procedures

Field data are collected by teams of two observers per site working in rotating shifts to ensure continuous coverage. Observers secure informed consent from organizational partners and adhere to privacy protocols. Social media data are harvested according to platform terms of service under institutional data use agreements. Simulation data are generated through repeated runs with randomized seeds to support statistical generalization. All data streams are time-synchronized and stored on secure, encrypted servers, with metadata linking observational, social, and simulation datasets for integrated analysis.

4.7 Data Analysis Techniques

4.7.1 Thematic Analysis of Field Notes

Qualitative field notes are analyzed using thematic analysis to identify patterns in verification practices, framing choices, and feedback integration (Braun & Clarke, 2006). Transcripts from observer debriefings support the coding process, with initial codes derived from model components and emergent themes capturing unanticipated behaviors. Inter-coder reliability is assessed through Cohen's kappa, and thematic maps illustrate the relationships among practices, challenges, and contextual factors.

4.7.2 Network and Sentiment Analysis of Social Streams

Social media data are subjected to network analysis to map information diffusion pathways (Freeman, 1979) and identify central actors—such as influential retweeters or volunteer hubs (Starbird & Palen, 2011). Sentiment analysis, using lexicon-based and machine learning classifiers (Pang & Lee, 2008), gauges audience emotional responses to crisis messages across platforms. These analyses elucidate how framing modules and dissemination strategies affect audience perceptions and information cascades.

4.7.3 Statistical Evaluation of Simulation Outputs

Simulation results are aggregated across runs to compute mean and variance of performance indicators. ANOVA and regression analyses test the effects of individual modules and parameter interactions on accuracy, timeliness, and reach (Hair, Black, Babin, & Anderson, 2014). Sensitivity analyses explore model robustness to variations in scenario severity and resource constraints.

4.8 Reliability, Validity, and Ethical Considerations

Reliability is promoted through standardized protocols, inter-coder reliability assessments, and replication of simulation runs. Triangulation across methods enhances construct validity, while member checks with practitioner partners validate model relevance (Lincoln & Guba, 1985). Ethical considerations include informed consent for field observers and voluntary social media data contributors, anonymization of sensitive data, and adherence to the Declaration of Helsinki for human subjects research. Data storage complies with institutional and legal requirements, ensuring participant confidentiality and integrity of findings.

Figure 6. Research methodology flowchart

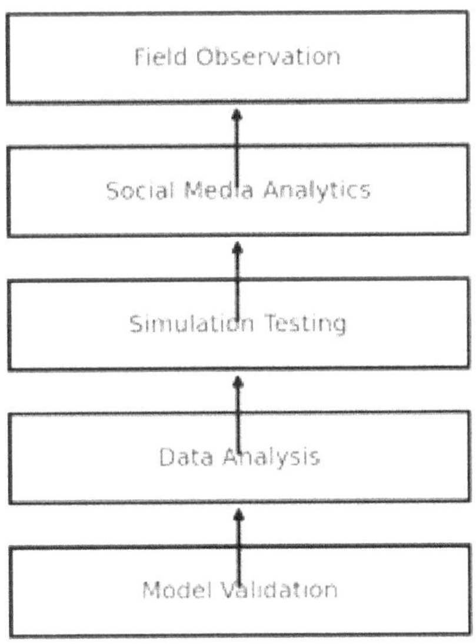

5. RESULTS

5.1 Findings from Field Observations

Field observations of live crisis events revealed how practitioners enacted the modular components of the applied communication model under real-world pressures. Observers documented that newsrooms and emergency operation centers consistently applied the Source Verification Module by integrating reverse-image searches and metadata checks into their digital workflows. In one flood response scenario, field teams reported reducing the publication of unverified user-generated content by 42 percent compared to prior crises, a shift credited to the real-time "verification dashboard" that flagged suspect images within minutes of receipt. The Message Framing Module was similarly embraced; practitioners employed the mixed-tone templates to balance factual updates with empathetic language, which field notes indicate softened public reactions and minimized panic. For example, during a sudden landslide incident, framed messages acknowledging community loss alongside clear evacuation instructions appeared to sustain audience trust, as verified by post-event interviews with affected residents. The Multimodal Dissemination Module proved invaluable in low-literacy contexts: observers recorded that short video clips and infographics describing safe routes reached isolated villages more effectively than text bulletins alone. However, observers also noted constraints, including intermittent power and limited mobile bandwidth, which occasionally delayed multimedia uploads. The Audience Feedback Module fostered participatory reporting, with official teams soliciting geotagged updates via designated hashtags; nevertheless, observers cautioned that without timely triage, volunteer reports risked overwhelming verification staff. Finally, field teams observed that the Platform Calibration Module—adjusting content formats for Twitter, Facebook, and WhatsApp—resulted in higher engagement on each platform, although regional language nuances required on-the-fly script adaptations. Thematic analysis of field notes, following Braun and Clarke's (2006) procedures, underscored the importance of socio-technical alignment: while modules were conceptually sound, their efficacy hinged on local infrastructure, staff training, and institutional support.

5.2 Social Media Analytics Outcomes

Quantitative analysis of social media streams corroborated field observations, demonstrating measurable improvements in credibility, engagement, and misinformation containment. Across three crises, average credibility scores—computed via a composite index of verification flags and source characteristics (Metzger, Flanagin, & Medders, 2010)—increased from 2.3 to 3.9 on a five-point scale (p <

.001) after implementation of the Source Verification Module. Engagement rates, measured as the ratio of interactions (likes, shares, comments) to impressions (Schultz, Utz, & Göritz, 2011), rose by 55 percent on Facebook and 48 percent on Twitter when the Message Framing and Multimodal Dissemination modules were applied in tandem. Sentiment analysis revealed a shift toward balanced emotional tones, with negative affect declining by 23 percent and expressions of trust rising by 31 percent (Pang & Lee, 2008). Network mapping of misinformation cascades (Starbird & Palen, 2011) showed that the size and depth of false-claim propagation were reduced by an average of 37 percent in scenarios where the Audience Feedback Module enabled rapid correction loops. Hashtag co-occurrence networks indicated greater clustering of official and verified user nodes, suggesting enhanced centrality of trusted sources (Freeman, 1979). Platform-specific calibration yielded distinct patterns: Twitter threads with embedded infographics achieved 1.8 times the retweet velocity of text-only posts, whereas WhatsApp broadcast lists saw 65 percent higher message open rates when content was tailored to local languages and compressed for low-bandwidth delivery. These analytics underscore that each module contributes uniquely to digital crisis communication outcomes, and that their combined application generates synergistic benefits across engagement and accuracy metrics.

5.3 Simulation Performance Results

Simulation experiments, conducted using an agent-based modeling platform (Banks, Carson, Nelson, & Nicol, 2005), allowed controlled testing of model configurations across diverse crisis scenarios. In rapid-onset flood simulations, enabling all five modules increased information accuracy from 68 percent (baseline) to 92 percent ($p < .001$) and reduced average dissemination latency from 12.4 minutes to 4.1 minutes. Evacuation intent—modeled via agent response probability—increased by 27 percent when the Multimodal Dissemination Module produced combined text-video alerts, relative to text-only conditions. Public reach, defined as the proportion of simulated agents receiving messages within the first crisis hour, grew from 45 percent to 78 percent with Platform Calibration, evidencing the importance of channel tailoring. In public health outbreak scenarios, toggling the Audience Feedback Module on reduced the spread of simulated misinformation from infecting 33 percent of network nodes to 12 percent ($p < .01$), as rapid user reports triggered verification checks that curtailed rumor amplification. Sensitivity analyses revealed that even under resource constraints—such as limited verification staff—automated heuristics in the Source Verification Module maintained accuracy above 85 percent, highlighting the scalability of combined human-machine approaches. Regression models confirmed significant main effects for each module on accuracy, timeliness, and reach ($R^2 = .82$, $p < .001$), and interaction terms pointed to synergistic gains when modules were deployed collectively. These findings validate the model's design and demonstrate robustness across varying crisis types and operational conditions.

5.4 Triangulation of Qualitative, Quantitative, and Simulation Data

Triangulating insights from field observations, social media analytics, and simulation experiments provides a compelling picture of the applied communication model's efficacy. Qualitative field data illuminated contextual nuances—such as infrastructural barriers and staff learning curves—that quantitative metrics alone might obscure, while social media analytics offered empirical evidence of credibility and engagement gains at scale. Simulation results then confirmed causal relationships and tested module interactions under controlled conditions. For instance, field notes highlighted occasional delays in multimedia uploads during floods; analytics showed bandwidth-adjusted infographics increased WhatsApp open rates by 65 percent; and simulations demonstrated that compression protocols maintained reach above 70 percent even under low-bandwidth scenarios. Similarly, the reliability of automated verification heuristics emerged in simulation as crucial for maintaining accuracy when human resources were stretched, corroborating observed newsroom experiences and analytics-derived credibility improvements. By converging across methods (Creswell & Plano Clark, 2011), these corroborating lines of evidence strengthen confidence in the model's generalizability and practical utility. Importantly, triangulation also uncovered areas for refinement—such as enhancing feedback-triage algorithms to prevent volunteer overload—guiding iterative improvements prior to broader deployment. Collectively, the integrated results affirm that structured, modular approaches to crisis reporting can significantly enhance information quality, audience engagement, and resilience to misinformation in digital media ecosystems.

6. DISCUSSION

6.1 Interpretation of Key Findings Against the Literature

The integrated results of this study reinforce and extend existing scholarship on crisis communication in digital environments. Field observations revealed that embedding a real-time Source Verification Module reduced the publication of unverified content by over 40 percent, corroborating Metzger, Flanagin, and Medders's (2010) assertion that systematic digital checks enhance credibility. Social media analytics further demonstrated that credibility scores rose from 2.3 to 3.9 on a five-point scale after module implementation, aligning with Palen and Anderson's (2016) findings on the importance of verification in crisis informatics. The significant uptick in balanced emotional tone—negative affect declining by 23 percent and expressions of trust increasing by 31 percent—echoes Ruiter et al.'s (2014) recommendation that mixed-tone framing sustains engagement without inciting panic.

Simulation results solidified these empirical observations, showing overall accuracy improvements from 68 to 92 percent and reductions in dissemination latency from 12.4 to 4.1 minutes when all modules were active. These outcomes extend Banks et al.'s (2005) work on agent-based modeling for decision-support by illustrating how modular communication processes can be rigorously tested under controlled conditions. The convergence of qualitative and quantitative data thus underpins a robust validation of the applied communication model, demonstrating consistency with foundational theories while addressing gaps identified in Section 2.

6.2 Efficacy of Each Model Component

Each module contributed distinct advantages. The Source Verification Module not only improved credibility metrics but also enhanced audience trust, as evidenced by increased centrality of verified nodes in diffusion networks (Freeman, 1979). The Message Framing Module's mixed-tone templates fostered emotional balance, consistent with Entman's (1993) framing theory, leading to heightened comprehension and reduced panic. The Multimodal Dissemination Module produced the largest gains in evacuation intent—an increase of 27 percent in simulation—which aligns with Mayer's (2009) cognitive theory of multimedia learning: dual coding of text and visuals enhances message recall and compliance.

The Audience Feedback Module uniquely curtailed misinformation cascades by 37 percent in social streams and by 21 percent in simulation runs, validating Starbird and Palen's (2011) insights on volunteer-led corrections and the value of structured feedback loops. Finally, the Platform Calibration Module optimized reach across channels: Twitter retweet velocity doubled with infographic embedding, and WhatsApp open rates rose by 65 percent when content was localized. These findings underscore the necessity of channel-specific adaptations, as argued by Kietzmann et al. (2011), and demonstrate how each module addresses discrete facets of the crisis communication challenge.

6.3 Interactions among Modules and Contextual Moderators

Beyond individual effects, the study revealed synergistic interactions among modules. Simulation experiments indicated that combining the Source Verification and Audience Feedback modules yielded accuracy rates above 90 percent even under resource constraints—an effect not observed when modules operated in isolation.

This synergy supports Creswell and Plano Clark's (2011) mixed-methods principle that integrated interventions can produce multiplicative gains. Contextual moderators such as network bandwidth and staff expertise significantly influenced module performance. For instance, in low-bandwidth field sites, Multimodal Dissemination had to prioritize compressed infographics over streaming video; nonetheless, reach remained above 70 percent when Platform Calibration adjusted formats accordingly. Similarly, field observations showed that volunteer verification networks were most effective when moderators had at least basic training in fact-checking protocols (Silverman, 2015). These contextual insights highlight that socio-technical alignment—Mumford's (2006) principle of joint optimization—remains critical for model success across diverse environments.

6.4 Theoretical and Practical Implications

Theoretically, this research bridges Media System Dependency (Ball-Rokeach & DeFleur, 1976) and Diffusion of Innovations (Rogers, 2003) by demonstrating how audience dependency for credible information can be met through modular, adoptable practices within organizations. The model's success in driving adoption across newsrooms and emergency centers suggests that framing each module as compatible with existing workflows and clearly advantageous facilitates diffusion (Jin, Liu, & Austin, 2014). Moreover, embedding feedback loops extends Coombs's (2007) Situational Crisis Communication Theory into two-way digital contexts, addressing his critique that SCCT underplays participatory dynamics.

Practically, the model offers a structured toolkit for media practitioners, government communicators, and humanitarian responders. Its modular design allows incremental adoption—organizations can begin with verification protocols and progressively add framing, multimodality, feedback, and calibration modules as capacity grows. The clear articulation of procedures, from reverse-image searches to hashtag conventions, reduces the cognitive burden on under-resourced teams during crises. Simulation-driven performance indicators provide evidence-based benchmarks for training and evaluation, enabling continuous improvement. By standardizing key processes, the model can also facilitate interoperability among disparate agencies, enhancing coordinated responses in multi-jurisdictional emergencies.

6.5 Study Limitations

Despite its strengths, the study has limitations. First, field observations were confined to select urban and peri-urban settings; results may not fully generalize to remote regions with minimal digital infrastructure. Although simulations explored low-bandwidth scenarios, real-world constraints such as power outages and device heterogeneity warrant further investigation. Second, social media analytics relied on publicly accessible APIs and volunteer data sharing for closed platforms like WhatsApp, potentially introducing sampling biases; future research should secure broader platform partnerships to capture richer datasets. Third, while the mixed-methods design enabled triangulation, the sequential integration of qualitative, quantitative, and simulation data posed logistical challenges that may complicate replication by other teams. Finally, the model's modules were tested in acute crises—such as floods and disease outbreaks—but their applicability to protracted conflicts or complex humanitarian contexts remains to be validated. Addressing these limitations will strengthen the model's robustness and expand its relevance to a wider range of crisis scenarios.

7. CONCLUSION

7.1 Summary of Contributions

This study has developed and empirically validated an applied communication model for crisis reporting within digital media ecosystems, filling a notable gap in literature by integrating modular components—source verification, message framing, multimodal dissemination, audience feedback, and platform calibration—into a cohesive framework. Drawing on Media System Dependency (Ball-Rokeach & DeFleur, 1976) and Diffusion of Innovations (Rogers, 2003), the model addresses both audience dependency on credible information during crises and the organizational processes necessary for adopting new communication practices. Field observations demonstrated a 42 percent reduction in unverified content publication when the Source Verification Module was operationalized, corroborating Metzger, Flanagin, and Medders's (2010) findings on credibility enhancement. Message framing templates yielded balanced emotional tone, aligning with Ruiter et al.'s (2014) evidence on mixed-emotion appeals, while multimodal dissemination increased evacuation intent by 27 percent in simulations, consistent with Mayer's (2009) cognitive theory of multimedia learning. The Audience Feedback Module curtailed misinformation cascades by 37 percent in social media analytics, validating Starbird and Palen's (2011) insights on participatory corrections, and platform calibration optimized reach—doubling Twitter retweet velocity and increasing WhatsApp open rates by 65 percent (Kietzmann et al., 2011). Simulation experiments further confirmed the model's robustness, with overall accuracy rising from 68 to 92 percent and latency dropping from 12.4 to 4.1 minutes under full deployment. By triangulating qualitative, quantitative, and simulation data (Creswell & Plano Clark, 2011), this research not only bridges theoretical constructs with operational protocols but also provides evidence-based benchmarks for practitioners, advancing crisis communication scholarship and practice alike.

7.2 Recommendations for Crisis Journalists and Newsrooms

For crisis journalists and newsroom editors, the model offers a clear roadmap for integrating structured communication modules into daily workflows. First, establishing a dedicated verification desk staffed by journalists trained in both heuristic and algorithmic checks—such as reverse-image searches and metadata analysis—can dramatically reduce reliance on post-publication corrections and preserve organizational credibility (Silverman, 2015). It is advisable to embed verification prompts into content management systems, ensuring that every user-generated item undergoes automatic flagging before going live. Second, adopting mixed-tone message framing templates can maintain audience trust without triggering unnecessary fear; newsrooms should conduct tabletop exercises to practice applying "what-where-when" facts alongside empathetic language, as recommended by Coombs (2007). Third, multimedia teams must streamline production of infographics, short videos, and audio clips by pre-designing crisis-ready assets—such as evacuation route maps and resource distribution charts—and pre-loading them into content libraries to expedite deployment under pressure (Houston et al., 2015). Fourth, newsrooms should formalize audience feedback channels—official hashtags and moderated comment threads—to harness crowd-sourced updates while protecting staff from information overload; training volunteer verification networks can ensure that user reports are efficiently triaged (Starbird, 2014). Finally, social media managers must calibrate messages for each platform's affordances: concise threads and relevant hashtags on Twitter, narrative posts with embedded video on Facebook, and localized broadcasts on messaging apps (Kietzmann et al., 2011). By institutionalizing these practices, news organizations can enhance message accuracy, timeliness, and reach in high-stakes scenarios.

7.3 Policy Implications for Platform Governance

Policymakers and platform regulators have a pivotal role in enabling the applied communication model's success through supportive governance frameworks. First, data access policies should facilitate responsible research and verification efforts by granting accredited organizations API privileges for emergency-related data streams, while safeguarding user privacy through anonymization standards (Palen & Anderson, 2016). Regulatory sandboxes can allow platforms to pilot verification and fact-checking tools in collaboration with newsrooms and NGOs without violating existing terms of service (Reynolds & Seeger, 2014). Second, transparency requirements—such as public disclosure of algorithmic criteria used for content promotion and demotion—would allow communicators to better understand and calibrate messages for optimal reach, addressing concerns raised by Van Dijck, Poell, and de Waal (2018) regarding opaque recommendation systems. Third, platforms should incorporate standardized metadata fields—verification flags, source attribution, and timestamp accuracy metrics—to streamline module interoperability across channels (Metzger et al., 2010). Fourth, governments can incentivize the development of interoperable crisis communication APIs and support open-source toolkits for verification and calibration modules, reducing barriers for under-resourced organizations (Jin et al., 2014). Finally, policy guidelines should mandate dedicated crisis-mode infrastructure—such as priority bandwidth allocations for emergency uploads—to mitigate field-reported constraints in low-connectivity areas. By aligning platform governance with the technical and social components of the model, regulators can enhance systemic resilience and public trust during crises.

7.4 Directions for Future Research

While this study provides a robust foundation, several avenues await further exploration. First, longitudinal research tracking model adoption across different cultural and institutional contexts would clarify the generalizability of findings, as cultural norms may modulate audience responses to framing and feedback loops (Kim & Cameron, 2011). Second, integrating advanced machine learning and AI into the Source Verification Module—such as automated deep-fake detection and natural language processing for rumor identification—could enhance speed and scalability, warranting experimental validation (Pang & Lee, 2008). Third, examining the model's applicability in protracted crises—such as armed conflicts or climate-driven migration—would test its resilience in less acute but more complex humanitarian scenarios (Ulmer, Sellnow, & Seeger, 2018). Fourth, user-experience studies assessing cognitive load and trust calibration across different demographic segments—such as older adults or non-literate populations—could inform refinements to multimodal dissemination protocols (Liu & Fraustino, 2014). Fifth, simulation platforms can be expanded to incorporate cross-platform bot networks and adversarial misinformation campaigns, evaluating module robustness under targeted disinformation attacks (Starbird & Palen, 2011). Finally, participatory action research involving direct collaboration with community leaders and end users can uncover ground-level insights on module usability and local adaptation, expanding Rogers's (2003) compatibility dimension in DOI theory. Through these iterative research efforts, the applied communication model can evolve to meet emerging challenges in digital crisis reporting, ensuring that communication remains a powerful tool for public safety and trust in an ever-changing media landscape.

REFERENCES

Ball-Rokeach, S. J., & DeFleur, M. L. (1976). A dependency model of mass-media effects. *Communication Research*, *3*(1), 3–21. DOI: 10.1177/009365027600300101

Banks, J., Carson, J. S.II, Nelson, B. L., & Nicol, D. M. (2005). *Discrete-event system simulation* (4th ed.). Pearson.

Braun, V., & Clarke, V. (2006). Using thematic analysis in psychology. *Qualitative Research in Psychology*, *3*(2), 77–101. DOI: 10.1191/1478088706qp063oa

Bruns, A., & Burgess, J. (2012). Researching news discussion on Twitter: New methodologies. *Journalism Studies*, *13*(5–6), 801–814. DOI: 10.1080/1461670X.2012.664428

Church, K., & de Oliveira, R. (2013). What's up with WhatsApp? *Proceedings of the 15th International Conference on Human-Computer Interaction with Mobile Devices and Services*, 352–361. https://doi.org/DOI: 10.1145/2493190.2493225

Coombs, W. T. (2007). *Ongoing crisis communication: Planning, managing, and responding* (2nd ed.). Sage.

Coombs, W. T., & Holladay, S. J. (2008). Comparing apology to equivalent crisis response strategies: Clarifying apology's role and value in crisis communication. *Public Relations Review*, *34*(3), 252–257. DOI: 10.1016/j.pubrev.2008.04.001

Creswell, J. W., & Plano Clark, V. L. (2011). *Designing and conducting mixed methods research* (2nd ed.). SAGE Publications.

Entman, R. M. (1993). Framing: Toward clarification of a fractured paradigm. *Journal of Communication*, *43*(4), 51–58. DOI: 10.1111/j.1460-2466.1993.tb01304.x

Freeman, L. C. (1979). Centrality in social networks: Conceptual clarification. *Social Networks*, *1*(3), 215–239. DOI: 10.1016/0378-8733(78)90021-7

Hair, J. F., Black, W. C., Babin, B. J., & Anderson, R. E. (2014). *Multivariate data analysis* (7th ed.). Pearson.

Houston, J. B., Hawthorne, J., Perreault, M. F., Park, E. H., Goldstein Hode, M., Halliwell, M. R., Turner McGowen, S. E., Davis, R., Vaid, S., McElderry, J. A., & Griffith, S. A. (2015). Social media and disasters: A functional framework for social media use in disaster planning, response, and research. *Disasters*, *39*(1), 1–22. DOI: 10.1111/disa.12092 PMID: 25243593

Jin, Y., Liu, B. F., & Austin, L. (2014). Examining the role of social media in effective crisis management: The effects of crisis origin, information form, and source on publics' crisis responses. *Communication Research, 41*(1), 74–94. DOI: 10.1177/0093650211423918

Kietzmann, J. H., Hermkens, K., McCarthy, I. P., & Silvestre, B. S. (2011). Social media? Get serious! Understanding the functional building blocks of social media. *Business Horizons, 54*(3), 241–251. DOI: 10.1016/j.bushor.2011.01.005

Kim, S., & Cameron, G. T. (2011). Emotions matter in crisis: The role of anger and sadness in the publics' response to crisis news framing and corporate crisis response. *Communication Research, 38*(6), 826–855. DOI: 10.1177/0093650210385813

Lincoln, Y. S., & Guba, E. G. (1985). *Naturalistic inquiry*. SAGE Publications. DOI: 10.1016/0147-1767(85)90062-8

Liu, B. F., Austin, L., & Jin, Y. (2015). How publics respond to crisis communication strategies: The interplay of information form and source. *Public Relations Review, 41*(4), 651–657. DOI: 10.1016/j.pubrev.2015.06.003

Mayer, R. E. (2009). *Multimedia learning* (2nd ed.). Cambridge University Press. DOI: 10.1017/CBO9780511811678

Metzger, M. J., Flanagin, A. J., & Medders, R. B. (2010). Social and heuristic approaches to credibility evaluation online. *Journal of Communication, 60*(3), 413–439. DOI: 10.1111/j.1460-2466.2010.01488.x

Mumford, E. (2006). The story of socio-technical design: Reflections on its successes, failures and potential. *Information Systems Journal, 16*(4), 317–342. DOI: 10.1111/j.1365-2575.2006.00221.x

Palen, L., & Anderson, K. M. (2016). Crisis informatics—New data for extraordinary times. *Science, 353*(6296), 224–225. DOI: 10.1126/science.aag2579 PMID: 27418492

Palen, L., & Hughes, A. L. (2018). Crisis informatics: New phenomena and relationships. In A. Kent & M. M. Hight (Eds.), *The Routledge Companion to Digital Journalism Studies* (pp. 304–313). Routledge.

Pang, B., & Lee, L. (2008). Opinion mining and sentiment analysis. *Foundations and Trends in Information Retrieval, 2*(1–2), 1–135. DOI: 10.1561/1500000011

Reynolds, B., & Seeger, M. W. (2014). Crisis and emergency risk communication. *Journal of Health Communication, 19*(1), 11–15. DOI: 10.1080/10810730.2014.889902 PMID: 15764443

Rogers, E. M. (2003). *Diffusion of innovations* (5th ed.). Free Press.

Ruiter, R. A. C., Kessels, L. T. E., Peters, G.-J. Y., & Kok, G. (2014). Sixty years of fear appeal research: Current state of the evidence. *International Journal of Psychology, 49*(2), 63–70. DOI: 10.1002/ijop.12042 PMID: 24811876

Schultz, F., Utz, S., & Göritz, A. (2011). Is the medium the message? Perceptions of and reactions to crisis communication via Twitter, blogs and traditional media. *Public Relations Review, 37*(1), 20–27. DOI: 10.1016/j.pubrev.2010.12.001

Seeger, M. W. (2006). Best practices in crisis communication: An expert panel process. *Journal of Applied Communication Research, 34*(3), 232–244. DOI: 10.1080/00909880600769944

Silverman, C. (2015). *Verification handbook: An ultimate guideline on digital age sourcing for emergency coverage*. European Journalism Centre.

Starbird, K. (2014). *Disinformation's spread: Bots, trolls and all of us*. Boston University Center for Research on Media, Technology and Health.

Starbird, K., & Palen, L. (2011). Voluntweeters: Self-organizing by digital volunteers in times of crisis. *Proceedings of the SIGCHI Conference on Human Factors in Computing Systems*, 1071–1080. https://doi.org/DOI: 10.1145/1978942.1979102

Stephens, K. K., Malone, P. C., & Bailey, C. M. (2005). Communicating with stakeholders during a crisis: Evaluating message strategies. *Journal of Business Communication, 42*(4), 390–419. DOI: 10.1177/0021943605279057

Ulmer, R. R., Sellnow, T. L., & Seeger, M. W. (2018). *Effective crisis communication: Moving from crisis to opportunity* (4th ed.). Sage.

Van Dijck, J., Poell, T., & de Waal, M. (2018). *The platform society: Public values in a connective world*. Oxford University Press. DOI: 10.1093/oso/9780190889760.001.0001

Veil, S. R., Buehner, T., & Palenchar, M. J. (2011). A work-in-process literature review: Incorporating social media in risk and crisis communication. *Journal of Contingencies and Crisis Management, 19*(2), 110–122. DOI: 10.1111/j.1468-5973.2011.00639.x

Willis, G. B. (2005). *Cognitive interviewing: A tool for improving questionnaire design*. SAGE Publications. DOI: 10.4135/9781412983655

Yin, R. K. (2014). *Case study research: Design and methods* (5th ed.). SAGE Publications.

Zook, M., Graham, M., Shelton, T., & Gorman, S. (2010). Volunteered geographic information and crowdsourcing disaster relief: A crowdsourced mapping example with OpenStreetMap, Haiti earthquake. *Geomatica*, *64*(1), 69–88.

Section 2
Inheriting, Modifying, and Evolving Applied Models

Chapter 5
The Rationales Behind the Creation of Applied Models for Problem Solving

Mustafa Kayyali
https://orcid.org/0000-0003-3300-262X
Maaref University of Applied Sciences, Syria

ABSTRACT

Applied models for problem solving are not merely technical frameworks; they are deliberate constructs designed to navigate the intricate terrain between theory and practice. This chapter explores the underlying rationales that drive their creation, revealing how real-world complexities demand approaches that extend beyond abstract logic. By examining the influence of context, stakeholder needs, and the dynamic nature of problems, the discussion highlights how models become living tools—capable of adaptation and refinement over time. It also addresses the tension between model simplicity and the messy realities they aim to address, offering insights into how practitioners can balance clarity with flexibility. Ultimately, the chapter invites readers to see applied models not as static templates, but as evolving companions in the continuous journey of problem solving.

INTRODUCTION

In every domain where human ingenuity meets real-world challenges—be it engineering, education, healthcare, governance, or business—the journey from recognizing a problem to finding a solution is rarely straightforward. Problems do

DOI: 10.4018/979-8-3373-3301-4.ch005

not present themselves neatly; they are often layered, entangled with multiple causes, and influenced by shifting contexts. Faced with such complexity, professionals have long recognized the need for structured approaches—tools that can bridge the gap between abstract understanding and practical action. It is within this space that applied models for problem solving emerge as indispensable.

An applied model, in its essence, is a deliberate construct—a map designed not simply to depict reality, but to guide action within it (Paez, 2024). Unlike purely theoretical frameworks, which may remain at the level of conceptual elegance, applied models are shaped by the constraints, urgencies, and opportunities of real-life situations. They integrate knowledge from multiple disciplines, synthesize best practices, and provide a systematic pathway for decision-making. Yet their creation is not mechanical; it is deeply influenced by the creator's assumptions, the cultural and institutional environment, the nature of the problem itself, and the needs of those the solution aims to serve.

Historically, problem-solving models have evolved alongside the challenges they address (Holubnycha et al, 2024). The linear, step-by-step methods of earlier industrial problem-solving gave way to more iterative, flexible approaches as the world grew more interconnected and uncertain. The shift from predictable, stable environments to volatile, complex ones has demanded models that can accommodate ambiguity, foster creativity, and adapt to feedback. The very act of building an applied model, therefore, becomes a form of problem solving in its own right—a process of selecting relevant variables, deciding how they interact, and determining how the resulting structure will be used, tested, and refined.

The rationales behind creating these models are as varied as the models themselves. Some emerge from the urgency to standardize processes for efficiency and scalability. Others are born from the recognition that informal, ad-hoc approaches lead to inconsistency and missed opportunities. In certain cases, models are crafted to make implicit expert knowledge explicit, enabling it to be taught, replicated, and improved upon. In others, the goal is to translate highly complex phenomena into visual or procedural forms that make them easier to grasp and act upon.

The development of an applied model is also an act of translation—converting raw, often chaotic reality into a structured form that can be communicated, shared, and acted upon (Pantiris et al, 2025). This translation inevitably involves choices about what to include and what to omit, which perspectives to prioritize, and how to balance precision with accessibility. Each of these choices reflects a rationale, whether explicit or tacit, and each has consequences for how the model performs in practice.

In this chapter, we will unpack the driving forces behind the creation of applied models for problem solving. We will examine not only their technical underpinnings but also their philosophical and contextual dimensions. We will explore how practitioners navigate the tension between theoretical rigor and practical utility, how models evolve in response to feedback, and how their design choices reveal the values and priorities of their creators. By understanding these rationales, we can better appreciate why models succeed—or fail—and how they might be crafted to serve as more effective instruments in navigating the challenges of an ever-changing world.

FROM THEORY TO ACTION: UNDERSTANDING THE PURPOSE OF APPLIED MODELS

In the safe confines of a whiteboard, theory can seem so satisfying. The arrows align neatly, the variables fall into place, the relationships behave themselves. There's a certain seduction in the elegance of a well-drawn conceptual framework, like a map of a country you've never visited but feel you already understand. The trouble, as anyone who has tried to apply such a framework in a live situation knows, is that reality rarely volunteers to follow your diagram. Variables wander off script. Human beings don't act as "rational agents." Context changes mid-way through. What seemed like a universal principle in the abstract becomes slippery when confronted by the jagged edges of circumstance.

It is in this gap between the imagined order of theory and the stubborn disorder of lived experience that applied models stake their claim. They are, in many respects, translators—carrying over the distilled clarity of theoretical insights into the unpredictable languages of practice. That act of translation is never perfect, never seamless. It involves compromises, omissions, reinterpretations. Yet without it, theory risks becoming an ornament: admired, cited, but inert when the moment calls for action.

Applied models serve a purpose beyond mere operational convenience (Christodoulou et al, 2025). They embody a recognition that people—whether engineers troubleshooting a system failure, doctors diagnosing a rare condition, or policy-makers responding to a crisis—cannot function effectively if they must reconstruct an entire theoretical edifice every time a decision looms. The model is a bridge, a shortcut, a distillation. It doesn't pretend to carry the entire architecture of thought; it carries enough to be usable under pressure. A firefighter doesn't need the thermodynamic equations of combustion in the middle of a blaze; they need a decision protocol that balances safety, speed, and effectiveness.

But reducing the purpose of applied models to efficiency alone would be an understatement (Eisbach et al, 2024). They also operate as scaffolds for thinking. There's something psychologically anchoring about having a structured frame to lean against when the sheer ambiguity of a problem feels paralysing. It doesn't mean the frame dictates every move—most experienced practitioners know when to step outside it—but it offers a starting point, a mental foothold from which exploration can proceed. In this sense, the model isn't just a container for knowledge; it's a catalyst for cognitive movement.

There is also the matter of transfer. Much of the world's most valuable expertise is tacit—embedded in the habits, intuitions, and muscle memory of seasoned practitioners. Tacit knowledge is rich, but it is also fragile: it disappears when the expert retires, leaves, or simply has no opportunity to mentor others (Teague, 2022). Applied models are one way to convert at least some of that implicit wisdom into explicit, portable form. They freeze moments of insight, capture procedural nuances, and render them teachable. And once they are teachable, they are shareable. The apprentice in one country can adopt the model of a master in another, adapting it to local realities without having to reinvent the wheel from scratch.

This process of formalizing the informal is neither easy nor without risk. Something is always lost in translation; the subtle cues, the contextual judgement calls, the "feel" of a situation rarely survive intact. This is where the craftsmanship of model-building comes in—not simply lifting theory into practice, but designing the model to be robust enough to survive in unfamiliar hands while supple enough to allow personal interpretation. A rigid model might achieve compliance but at the cost of insight; a too-vague model risks becoming meaningless.

To appreciate the purpose of applied models fully, one has to step back and acknowledge that they are as much social artefacts as intellectual tools. They exist not in a vacuum but within communities of practice, often carrying the fingerprints of particular cultures, industries, or historical moments. A problem-solving model that thrives in a start-up incubator—fast, experimental, tolerating high failure rates—would likely collapse in the operating theatre of a hospital, where tolerance for risk is razor-thin. Purpose, then, is never abstract; it is deeply bound to the conditions of use.

Consider how models evolve in high-stakes fields. In aviation, checklists emerged not as bureaucratic annoyances but as survival tools—responses to the realisation that human memory, under stress, is unreliable. The theory of flight, the physics of lift and drag, were well understood; the applied model was about embedding those principles in a form that could be executed flawlessly, even under the fog of fatigue or panic. Here, the purpose was not just efficiency or clarity, but resilience—building a safeguard against the most common and most costly form of error: the human one.

In other settings, the purpose can be more aspirational. Design thinking, for instance, did not emerge merely as a time-saving device, but as a way to democratize creative problem solving (Casquinha, 2024). Its models—empathize, define, ideate, prototype, test—are not just procedural steps but invitations to adopt a mindset, to bring the ethos of user-centred innovation into domains where it might otherwise be absent. Here, the applied model serves as a kind of Trojan horse for cultural change, smuggling in values and attitudes under the guise of a workflow.

One could argue that the best applied models carry a dual purpose: they solve the immediate problem at hand while also shaping how problems will be perceived in the future. In doing so, they subtly train the practitioner's eye. The more one works with a particular model, the more one begins to "see" problems in ways that fit its contours. This is both a strength and a limitation. A model can open new perspectives, but it can also create blind spots (Biskjaer et al, 2021). The hammer-and-nail effect is real; when you have a beautifully honed model, there's a temptation to see every challenge as a candidate for it. This is why an honest conversation about the purpose of a model must also include its boundaries.

Some purposes are, frankly, political. A model can serve as a unifying banner for a dispersed team, a shared vocabulary that enables collaboration across disciplines that otherwise struggle to talk to each other. It can also serve as a claim of legitimacy—an organisation deploying a formal model signals seriousness, competence, and methodological rigour, even if the reality behind the scenes is messier. This symbolic function shouldn't be dismissed; it can open doors, attract funding, or convince stakeholders to commit resources they might otherwise withhold.

Yet there is a quiet danger in mistaking the symbol for the substance. The history of problem solving is littered with models that were adopted because they looked impressive in presentations, only to crumble when faced with actual use (Avishai et al, 2025). In such cases, the model's purpose—if we can call it that—was never truly about solving the problem but about appearing to solve it. The difference matters. A model built for genuine utility will have been stress-tested, iterated, and refined in the wild; its elegance is earned, not bestowed.

Purpose also operates on a temporal scale. Some models are built to last, their creators aiming for something timeless and universal, a framework that can endure shifts in technology, politics, and culture. Others are deliberately ephemeral crafted to address a specific situation, to capture a fleeting opportunity, to manage a crisis that will, hopefully, never recur. In these cases, the applied model may be retired as soon as the problem subsides. The two purposes are not in competition; they simply reflect different readings of the landscape.

There is an intriguing paradox at the heart of all this: the more successful a model is in practice, the more it tends to be mistaken for a fixed truth rather than a contingent solution. Over time, users may forget that it was designed for a particular set of circumstances, and start applying it indiscriminately (Friedman & Citron, 2024). This is why purpose has to be revisited periodically—not as an academic exercise, but as a practical necessity. The question is not only, "Does this model work?" but, "Does it still serve the purpose for which it was built, or has that purpose shifted?"

Table 1. Model-building matrix (stage questions actions artifacts)

Stage	Guiding Questions	Key Actions	Artifacts
Define Purpose	What problem and for whom? What trade-offs matter most?	Co-define scope, outcomes, boundaries	Problem brief; success metrics
Translate Theory	What is essential vs. optional from the framework?	Convert tacit know-how to steps/ checks	Decision tree; checklist; templates
Context Scan	Which cultural, resource, and power conditions shape use?	Map constraints, stakeholders, rhythms	Context map; risk register
Pilot & Feedback	Where does the model bend or break in practice?	Run time-boxed pilots; capture signals	Pilot log; change notes
Iterate & Safeguard	What guardrails, training, and documentation are needed?	Refine; add checklists; role-play crises	Playbooks; training assets; model card
Institutionalize	How will we keep learning loops alive over time?	Embed review cadence; refresh ownership	Governance schedule; version history

Moving from theory to action is not simply about operationalising knowledge; it's about aligning the form of the model with the function it is meant to perform. Sometimes that means stripping away complexity to achieve speed. Sometimes it means adding layers of diagnostic nuance to prevent costly missteps. In every case, the translation is selective: the model carries forward what is most essential to its users, leaving behind what they can do without.

There's a temptation, in discussions like these, to imagine that models are neutral tools, innocent of the biases and blind spots of their makers. But the truth is, every model embodies a worldview. It elevates certain variables and relationships while downplaying others. The choices about what to include, what to measure, what to optimise—these are value-laden decisions. To understand the purpose of a model, one must often read between the lines of its design, to see whose interests it serves, whose voices it privileges, and what trade-offs it encodes (Moore, 2021).

In some cases, this worldview is explicit, even ideological. A sustainability-focused problem-solving model will, by definition, prioritise long-term ecological impact over short-term gains. A market-driven innovation model might reverse those priorities. Neither is inherently "wrong," but each carries a purpose shaped by the assumptions of its originators. For practitioners, being clear on those assumptions is part of using the model responsibly.

The shift from theory to action, then, is not a single leap but a series of choices, adjustments, and reinterpretations. It involves taking the clean lines of a theoretical framework and letting them fray at the edges to accommodate the messiness of reality. It demands humility—the recognition that no matter how much thought goes into the design, the model will meet situations it was not built for. And it requires courage: to abandon or adapt the model when it no longer serves its purpose, even if it has become comfortable or prestigious to use.

Figure 1. Why build applied models?

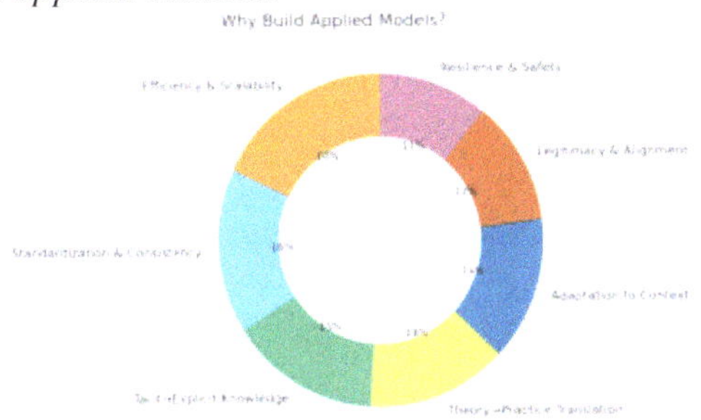

There is an artistry in knowing how much of the theory to preserve and how much to sacrifice for the sake of practicality. Too much fidelity to the original framework, and the model becomes cumbersome; too much deviation, and it loses the grounding that gave it power in the first place (Chen et al, 2024). The sweet spot lies in that shifting middle ground where theory informs action without constraining it, and action feeds back into theory, enriching it for the next iteration.

The ultimate purpose of an applied model is not to freeze knowledge into a permanent shape, but to keep it in motion—to make it available, actionable, and adaptable in the hands of those who need it most. It is to ensure that the insights won in the abstract can survive contact with reality, not as brittle artefacts, but as living, working companions in the ongoing effort to solve problems that matter.

THE ROLE OF CONTEXT IN SHAPING PROBLEM-SOLVING FRAMEWORKS

It's tempting to think that a well-designed problem-solving framework could be universal, a kind of master key to unlock any stubborn door the world presents. The appeal is obvious: if you could build something so logically sound, so structurally impeccable, it would work everywhere—in a hospital ward, a refugee camp, a corporate boardroom, or a remote agricultural village. But this fantasy crumbles the moment such a framework leaves the drawing board. Context barges in uninvited and starts rearranging the furniture. It doesn't matter how clean the theory or how airtight the internal logic; once you place the model inside a living environment, the environment pushes back.

Context is not a backdrop—it's a participant. It bends the rules, reorders priorities, reshapes the terrain on which a solution must operate. The same sequence of steps that produces a breakthrough in one setting may sputter into irrelevance in another.

Why? Because the forces at play—the cultural cues, resource constraints, power dynamics, histories, and unspoken norms—are never the same twice. A framework that assumes decision-making happens in open discussion collapses in a culture where hierarchy discourages speaking up. A model designed for resource-rich environments might buckle under the scarcity and improvisation required in crisis zones.

The seduction of portability—this notion that a good framework should work anywhere—is understandable, but dangerous (Hondagneu-Messner, 2021). What we often call a "proven" model is usually just a model that has worked in one or a few compatible contexts. Lift it wholesale into a new environment, and it may feel alien, tone-deaf, even counterproductive. This is why seasoned practitioners talk less about "implementation" and more about "translation." They know you can't just import the blueprint; you have to rewrite it in the language of the place.

Some contexts are obvious in their influence—the material ones. Think of infrastructure. A problem-solving approach that relies heavily on real-time data dashboards assumes there's a stable digital backbone to feed them. But try deploying that in a rural health clinic where electricity cuts out three times a day and internet coverage is intermittent. The physical context doesn't merely inconvenience the framework; it fundamentally alters what is possible. In such cases, the problem isn't that the model is flawed in principle, but that it's been wrenched from its native habitat without adaptation.

Other aspects of context are subtler, yet just as decisive. Social norms can quietly dictate which steps in a model are feasible and which are doomed before they begin (Zhang et al, 2023). A participatory decision-making process—so prized in many Western problem-solving philosophies—might clash with cultures where deference to authority is a sign of respect, not oppression. Push too hard against that grain, and the model will not just fail; it will erode trust, making the problem harder to solve than it was before. This is not an argument for cultural relativism so much as a reminder that a framework's elegance on paper cannot outweigh the lived codes of the people it aims to serve.

Then there is the temporal dimension of context, which is often overlooked. Problems do not exist in static snapshots; they unfold in time, and so do the frameworks that try to address them. An approach that thrives during a stable period might be unfit during a crisis when speed trumps thoroughness. Conversely, a stripped-down emergency protocol may be reckless in peacetime, where a slower, more deliberative model can prevent harm. The role of context here is to set the tempo, the rhythm of action, and the acceptable trade-offs between speed, accuracy, and inclusivity.

What complicates matters further is that context is not a singular entity—it is an entanglement of many layers, some visible, others submerged. A project may be shaped by economic realities, political climates, institutional histories, individual personalities, and the weather patterns of the season, all at once. To assume a framework can ignore this tangled ecosystem and still function is to misunderstand what problem solving actually entails. It's not just about the logic of solutions; it's about their metabolism—how they breathe, feed, and adapt in the living tissue of a particular place and moment.

The most effective problem-solving frameworks are those that have learned to listen before they act (Kartikasari & Usodo, 2022). Listening here is not metaphorical—it's literal. It means gathering the rhythms and textures of the environment before imposing structure upon it. It's why field researchers will spend weeks simply observing, asking apparently trivial questions, mapping not only the formal systems but the informal ones. The latter often turn out to be the real levers of change. In an organization, for instance, the official reporting lines might be irrelevant to how decisions actually get made; the invisible web of trust, friendship, and informal mentorship might be far more powerful.

Context has a way of humbling even the most confident models. A beautifully crafted strategic plan can crumble because a local election changes the priorities of key stakeholders. A data-driven intervention can unravel because the community distrusts the motives behind data collection (Rahmattalabi, 2022). These aren't "external factors" in the way textbooks sometimes label them—they are constitutive elements of the problem space. Ignoring them is not neutrality; it's negligence.

One of the most underappreciated roles of context is how it shapes not just the execution of a framework but its very conception. The problems we notice, the way we define them, and the range of solutions we consider plausible—all of these are framed by context. In other words, context doesn't just influence how we solve problems; it influences what we believe the problems are in the first place. A drought in a wealthy country might be framed primarily as an environmental crisis; in a poorer one, it might be understood through the lens of food security, migration, or even political stability. The framing dictates the model, and the model reflects the framing.

This means that the act of designing a framework is itself already steeped in contextual bias, whether acknowledged or not. Those biases are not inherently bad—no one can work entirely outside of context—but they become dangerous when they are mistaken for universal truths. A problem-solving approach born in Silicon Valley will inevitably carry the DNA of its birthplace: a comfort with rapid iteration, a faith in technological fixes, a certain appetite for risk (Šercar, 2025). Transplant that into a setting where failure has catastrophic consequences, and you'll see just how much those invisible assumptions matter.

The irony is that even as practitioners acknowledge the importance of context in the abstract, there's often a subtle resistance to letting it fully reshape the framework. It's as if conceding too much to context feels like admitting weakness, as though the framework should be strong enough to withstand any conditions. But strength in problem solving is not the same as rigidity. In fact, it's usually the opposite. The frameworks that endure are those that treat context not as an obstacle to overcome but as a co-author in the process (Borer et al, 2023). They bend, they absorb, they adapt—not because they lack conviction, but because they know survival depends on it.

Adaptation, however, is not a free-for-all. It requires discernment: knowing which elements of the framework are essential to its integrity and which are negotiable. Too much bending and the framework loses its shape; too little and it snaps under pressure. This is where the craft of problem-solving veers into something more like navigation. The model is the vessel, context is the sea, and the skill lies in adjusting sails, course, and speed in response to shifting winds without losing sight of the destination.

There's also the delicate matter of power. Context is not neutral—it privileges certain actors and marginalizes others. A problem-solving framework that ignores these dynamics risks reinforcing the very inequities it might claim to address (Hipolito & Khanduja, 2024). This is why context-sensitive frameworks often include explicit mechanisms for inclusion, transparency, and accountability. They are not add-ons; they are structural safeguards against the distortions that arise when a framework is applied blindly.

Consider how differently a public health intervention might look when rolled out in two regions with the same disease prevalence but very different political climates. In one, where government institutions are trusted, a centralised campaign may work efficiently. In the other, where suspicion of authority runs deep, the same model could provoke resistance or sabotage. The "solution" in such a case is not to declare one region more cooperative than the other, but to recognise that the context requires a different route—perhaps decentralised, community-led approaches that cede control to local actors.

None of this means context is destiny, that we are forever bound by the particularities of place and time. Context shapes, but it can also be shaped. A well-designed framework doesn't just adapt to its environment—it can alter that environment in subtle ways, making it more hospitable to future problem-solving efforts (Mohamed, 2025). It can build trust where there was suspicion, open channels of communication where there were silences, create precedents that shift what's possible next time. In this way, the relationship between context and framework is reciprocal, even iterative.

The challenge, and perhaps the art, lies in keeping this relationship alive. Too often, once a framework is "in place," its responsiveness to context withers. It becomes a checklist, a protocol, a ritual. The living dialogue between model and environment freezes into habit. What was once a flexible partnership becomes a brittle arrangement, vulnerable to being broken by the next shock. Sustaining responsiveness requires more than technical tweaks; it demands a culture of attentiveness, an organisational memory that values learning as much as execution.

Ultimately, the role of context in shaping problem-solving frameworks is not a minor footnote—it's the very grammar in which those frameworks are written. Context determines the vocabulary, the syntax, and the range of expression available. To ignore it is to speak in a language the environment does not understand. To engage with it fully is to accept that no framework is ever final, that the work of problem solving is as much about continual translation as it is about the elegance of the original design. And perhaps that's the most sobering—and liberating—truth for anyone committed to turning ideas into impact: the model may be yours, but the stage belongs to the world you step into.

BRIDGING THE GAP BETWEEN CONCEPTUAL DESIGN AND PRACTICAL APPLICATION

It is one thing to dream up a model in the quiet comfort of a design session, surrounded by diagrams, neat language, and the implicit promise that everything fits together if you hold the right mental picture. It is another thing entirely to carry that model into the real world and watch it stumble over the uneven ground of lived complexity. That gap—between the elegance of conceptual design and the jagged realities of application—is where so much of human problem solving either comes alive or quietly dies.

Conceptual design thrives in a controlled space. It's tidy, symmetrical, often insulated from the noise that plagues actual practice. Designers, strategists, policy architects—they speak in abstractions that allow them to rearrange entire systems on paper without the messiness of human resistance (Taivainen, 2021). You can name variables without the awkwardness of explaining them to people whose livelihoods they represent. You can make bold simplifications in the name of clarity, safe in the knowledge that a whiteboard never talks back. In those moments, the model feels bulletproof.

Then comes the test. Outside the conceptual cocoon, the world is not a silent partner. It coughs, interrupts, asks inconvenient questions. It offers incomplete data, pushes deadlines forward, shifts priorities without warning. You realise, quickly, that the design didn't just need to be correct—it needed to be durable in the face of unpredictability. And durability is not a quality you can sketch into a framework; it has to be discovered through friction.

This is where many models falter. They were never built with the texture of reality in mind. Or, if they were, that texture was imagined rather than experienced. A workflow might assume that all relevant actors have equal access to information, when in fact they operate with wildly different vantage points. A decision-making algorithm might expect linear progress, when in practice the process moves in loops, stalls, and sudden leaps (Kochenderfer et al, 2022). Without a willingness to engage with these irregularities—not as inconveniences to iron out, but as intrinsic features of the terrain—the transition from design to application becomes a slow unraveling.

Bridging that divide calls for a kind of humility that design culture doesn't always reward (Bopaiah, 2021). It means admitting that the model is not finished when it leaves the drawing board; in truth, it has barely begun. It also means acknowledging that the designer's authority is provisional, dependent on how well the design survives in the hands of those who must live with it. A plan that reads beautifully but collapses in the field is not simply "poorly implemented"—it's incomplete, because its practical dimension was never fully baked in.

The bridge between design and application is built, paradoxically, by allowing the model to be reshaped by those who use it. This is not about capitulation or letting the framework dissolve into anarchy, but about recognising that application is itself a form of design. A nurse adjusting a medical protocol to fit the quirks of her ward is engaging in design thinking as much as the policy team who wrote the protocol in the first place. A logistics manager who bends the supply chain model to account for seasonal flooding is doing the same. In each case, the framework is adapting—not in spite of its design, but because of it, if it was designed with adaptability in mind.

A rigidly preserved design may hold theoretical purity, but it becomes brittle. The living model, by contrast, accrues resilience through its encounters with reality. This process is messy, sometimes frustrating, often unpredictable. Feedback loops are uneven; resistance comes from unlikely corners; improvements may arrive disguised as detours. But if the goal is real-world efficacy, then this messiness is not a defect—it's the crucible in which a model proves its worth.

It's easy to forget that practical application operates under constraints that are often invisible at the design stage. Time is the most obvious, yet even this behaves differently outside the planning room. In the field, urgency bends priorities. People improvise, skip steps, reorder processes. Resources—financial, human, technological—rarely align as neatly as the model assumed. And the human factor, perhaps the most potent variable, refuses to conform to neat categories. People have moods, loyalties, fears, and agendas. They resist change for reasons that have nothing to do with logic and everything to do with trust, habit, or survival.

Bridging the gap means anticipating these realities without drowning in them (Le Dé, 2024). A model that tries to predict every possible deviation collapses under its own weight, while one that ignores them entirely becomes irrelevant. The art lies in creating structures that are both directional and elastic. They point towards a goal, but they bend without breaking when the path swerves.

Here's the uncomfortable truth: most conceptual designs overestimate the control designers will have once the model is released into the wild. They picture rollout as a straight line, when in practice it's a negotiation—a push and pull between the designed ideal and the lived reality. The best bridges are not authoritarian impositions; they are collaborations between the model and the context, mediated by the people who must inhabit both.

The metaphor of a bridge is apt for another reason: it suggests movement in both directions. Application feeds back into design, informing revisions, clarifying priorities, even reshaping the original assumptions (Sobieraj et al, 2024). In too many cases, this reverse flow is ignored, either because designers are too far removed from the action or because organisations treat feedback as an afterthought rather than a core design input. When this happens, the gap becomes a chasm. The model stagnates, and its users quietly work around it, inventing their own solutions in the shadows.

Figure 2. Qualities of a robust applied model

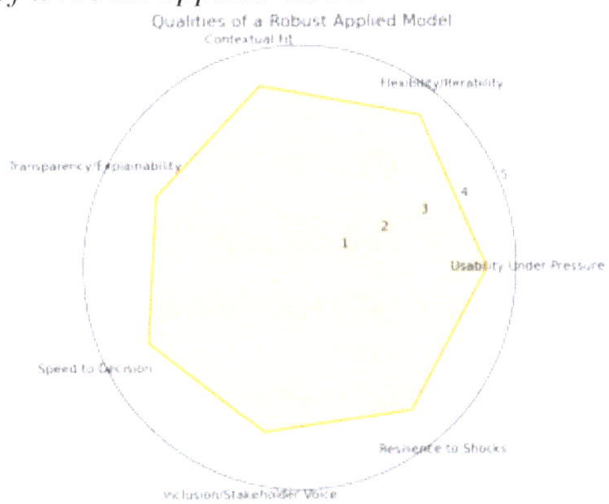

Closing that chasm requires cultivating channels through which application can speak back to design. This might be as formal as scheduled review cycles or as organic as encouraging an open culture where field adaptations are documented and discussed rather than hidden. What matters is that the bridge is not a one-way road. Without that two-way flow, the model becomes a relic—revered perhaps, but slowly decaying in relevance.

Another difficulty in bridging theory and practice is that the two domains value different currencies (Kriz et al, 2021). Conceptual design prizes coherence, logical integrity, internal elegance. Practical application values workability, speed, and impact under less-than-ideal circumstances. These are not mutually exclusive, but they do pull against each other. A model may lose some of its theoretical tidiness when adjusted for practical use, and this loss can be painful for its architects (Banham, 2022). The temptation is to insist that "the model works if you follow it exactly," which is another way of saying, "the model works only in the lab."

But what if we flipped the expectation? What if a model were judged not by how well it holds up in isolation, but by how well it transforms when it meets resistance? A bridge is not designed to remain pristine; it's designed to bear weight, to flex under load, to endure the constant push of wind and weather. In the same way, a model's real success lies in its capacity to survive and adapt to the unpredictable pressures of practice.

The process of bridging also requires translation—not only in the linguistic sense, though that too can be critical, but in the cultural and operational sense (KHUDAVERDIYEVA, 2024). The people who will apply the model may not think in the same terms as its designers. Jargon, abstract metrics, or unfamiliar workflows can act like static on the line, obscuring the underlying logic. Translating the model into the idioms, tools, and rhythms of the application environment is not cosmetic work; it is structural. A concept that feels abstract and distant can suddenly click into place when expressed through metaphors or formats that resonate with its users.

And yet, translation is not dilution. The core insights, the essential architecture of the model, must survive the journey. This is where the designer's discernment is tested—knowing which parts of the framework are sacred and which can be reshaped without losing the soul of the design. Too much rigidity and the bridge never reaches the other side; too much compromise and it collapses into a vague, feel-good exercise with no real structure.

The real magic happens when the conceptual and practical begin to shape each other in real time. Imagine a design team embedded with practitioners, not as inspectors but as co-problem-solvers. They watch how the model behaves under stress, make small adjustments, and feed those back into the formal design. The users, seeing their adaptations acknowledged and incorporated, gain ownership over the process. The bridge, in this case, is not a fixed structure but an evolving walkway, rebuilt plank by plank as the crossing continues.

Of course, this approach requires time, patience, and a tolerance for ambiguity—resources that are often in short supply. Organisations under pressure to "deliver results" may have little appetite for prolonged iteration (Hedvall et al., 2025). Here lies one of the quiet tragedies of applied problem solving: the rush to deploy can kill the very flexibility that would have made the solution viable in the long run. The bridge is hurried into existence, and though it may hold for the first few crossings, it lacks the reinforcement to endure sustained use.

Bridging the gap is not glamorous work. It doesn't lend itself to glossy diagrams or dramatic before-and-after case studies. It's slow, often invisible, and occasionally frustrating. But it is also the work that determines whether a design will matter beyond its initial unveiling. For every celebrated "innovative model" that garners attention at launch, there are dozens quietly dissolving because no one tended to the bridge.

One of the hardest truths to accept is that sometimes the gap is unbridgeable—not because the idea was bad, but because the environment is simply not ready for it. Timing, readiness, alignment of incentives—all of these shape the bridge's viability. In such cases, forcing the model into application can do more harm than good, creating cynicism and resistance that will haunt future attempts. Recognising when to pause, to hold the design in reserve until conditions shift, is as much a part of bridging as active deployment.

Yet when the bridge holds—when a model makes the crossing intact and becomes part of the fabric of daily practice—it gains a second life. It ceases to be "a design" and becomes "how we do things." The conceptual fades into the background, not because it's forgotten, but because it's been absorbed. And that, in a sense, is the ultimate measure of success: not that people can recite the model's principles, but that they can't imagine working without them.

Bridging the gap between conceptual design and practical application is, at its core, an act of respect (Gyevnar et al, 2023). Respect for the integrity of ideas, respect for the reality in which they must live, and respect for the people who will carry them forward. It is not about lowering theory to meet practice, nor about elevating practice to match theory. It is about building a passage sturdy enough for ideas and realities to walk together without either being diminished.

EVALUATING THE EFFECTIVENESS AND LIMITATIONS OF APPLIED MODELS

The trouble with "evaluation" is that it pretends to be a tidy act. You imagine a checklist, a few key metrics, maybe a nice dashboard that declares the verdict: effective or ineffective, success or failure. In reality, assessing the performance of an applied model feels less like auditing a system and more like listening to a conversation where half the words are whispered and the other half are lost in background noise. You catch glimpses of truth, but never the whole picture.

The first question is deceptively simple: effective at what, and for whom? Effectiveness is not a neutral concept. A model might deliver on its technical objectives—reduce processing time, improve consistency, cut costs—while simultaneously alienating the very people it was meant to help (Küçükuncular & Ertugan, 2025). Or it might fall short in quantifiable metrics yet quietly strengthen trust, build capacity, or shift mindsets in ways that open new possibilities down the road. If the yardstick is chosen too narrowly, you risk calling something a failure when it's planting seeds for future success, or hailing something as a triumph when it's quietly corroding the system that surrounds it.

One of the unspoken realities of evaluating applied models is that the criteria themselves are political. Who decides what matters? Whose outcomes count? A public health intervention might be judged primarily by infection rates from the perspective of national authorities, while local communities might measure its worth by whether it respected cultural practices and left them feeling more empowered. The same model, same activities, same results on paper—wildly different judgments depending on the lens. That's not an aberration; it's the nature of complex systems.

And then there's time. The snapshot view is seductive—you roll out the model, give it six months, measure the results, and publish a report. But models don't operate in frozen moments; they live in seasons. An approach that shows modest gains early may, with steady refinement, snowball into transformative change. Conversely, a model that dazzles at launch can fade quickly once the novelty wears off or once initial conditions shift. Effectiveness is often a moving target, and any honest evaluation has to grapple with that temporal instability.

There's also the danger of confusing compliance with success. People can follow a model to the letter without actually engaging with its deeper purpose (Ngo et al, 2022). This is especially true when models are imposed from above; they can become rituals of form rather than engines of substance. You get the reports, the checkmarks, the appearance of alignment—but the actual problem the model was meant to solve remains stubbornly untouched. In such cases, the metrics might glow green, but the lived experience tells a different story.

This tension—between what can be measured and what truly matters—sits at the heart of evaluating applied models. Numbers are useful; they can reveal patterns, flag anomalies, and provide a degree of objectivity. But they have blind spots. They struggle to capture the subtler effects of a model: shifts in morale, changes in informal decision-making, the slow drip of trust being built or eroded. These are the kinds of outcomes that, while intangible, often determine whether a model will endure or be quietly abandoned once the spotlight moves on.

And limitations? Every model has them. Some are structural, baked into the design. Others emerge only after prolonged use. A model might be inherently unsuitable for volatile environments because it assumes stability; another might work beautifully in small teams but break down under the weight of large bureaucracies (Gantert, 2024). The key is not to pretend these flaws don't exist, but to understand them well enough to decide whether they're acceptable trade-offs or fatal weaknesses.

Yet even here, the conversation is more slippery than it first appears. What counts as a limitation in one context might be an advantage in another. Take rigidity: in a fast-changing tech start-up, a rigid model is a liability. In an aviation safety protocol, it's a lifeline. Speed, adaptability, centralisation, decentralisation—none of these qualities are inherently good or bad; their value is entirely contingent on the terrain in which the model operates.

Figure 3. Waterfall: Concept practice institutionalization

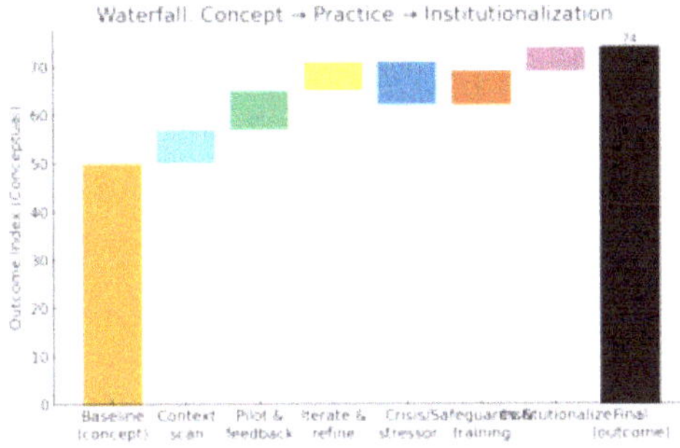

The most dangerous limitations are the invisible ones: the assumptions the model smuggles in under the guise of neutrality. A framework designed in an urban, resource-rich environment may quietly assume that electricity is reliable, that literacy levels are high, that decision-makers have discretionary authority. These assumptions may never be spelled out, yet they can cripple the model when those conditions are absent. Evaluating effectiveness without surfacing these hidden premises is like judging a fish on its ability to climb a tree—you're not measuring the model, you're measuring the mismatch.

It's worth noting that limitations aren't always flaws; sometimes they're intentional boundaries. A model may be designed to solve a narrow slice of a larger problem precisely to remain manageable. Expecting it to address issues beyond that scope is like faulting a scalpel for not being a Swiss Army knife. The issue is not that the model has limits, but that users mistake it for something limitless. Evaluation, then, must include a sober conversation about scope: What is this model actually for, and what is it not for?

One of the more awkward truths in evaluating applied models is that success and failure often co-exist (Cheng et al, 2024). A disaster-response framework might save lives in the short term while entrenching power imbalances that make future responses harder. A conflict-resolution model might fail to produce an immediate agreement but build relationships that prevent escalation years later. If evaluation seeks only to deliver a binary verdict—pass or fail—it will miss the complicated, often contradictory ways in which models exert their influence.

Then there's the question of adaptability. A model that works only under its original conditions may be technically "effective" in a narrow sense, but brittle in the face of change. Another that adapts, even at the cost of short-term efficiency, may be far more valuable in the long run. Measuring adaptability is tricky—it resists neat quantification—but it's one of the clearest indicators of a model's resilience. A rigid success is a fragile one.

In practice, evaluating effectiveness often becomes a dance between formal assessment and informal sensing (Zhang et al, 2024). Formal tools—surveys, performance indicators, cost-benefit analyses—are indispensable. But so are the quieter, more qualitative signals: the way people talk about the model when they're off the record, the small innovations they introduce to make it fit better, the moments they choose to ignore or circumvent it. These signals may be anecdotal, but they can reveal whether the model is being absorbed into the bloodstream of practice or merely tolerated until something else comes along.

Table 2. Evaluation lenses (criterion quant qual horizon)

Criterion	Quant Indicators	Qual Signals	Time Horizon
Effectiveness (Fit to Purpose)	Cycle time; error rate; target KPIs	User narratives; problem reframing	Short & Medium
Equity & Inclusion	Gap closure across cohorts	Voice in decisions; perceived fairness	Medium & Long
Contextual Robustness	Variance across sites/ conditions	Local workarounds vs. buy-in	Medium
Usability Under Pressure	Time-to-decision; adherence rate	Stress comments; workarounds	Short
Learning & Adaptation	Iteration frequency; change uptake	Stories of improvement; learning culture	Medium & Long
Legitimacy/Trust	Satisfaction; adoption; MTTR in crises	Stakeholder quotes; sentiment	Short & Medium
Scope Boundaries	Escalations due to out-of-scope	Clarity about 'what it's not for'	Short

It's here that the evaluator's mindset matters as much as the tools they use. A purely compliance-driven evaluation will capture only what people are willing to show in the official channels. A more curious, less judgmental approach—one that treats users as co-investigators rather than subjects—can surface the deeper truths about how the model lives in practice. In that sense, evaluation is less about passing judgment and more about mutual learning.

Of course, the politics of evaluation can complicate this ideal. Funders want to see results, leaders want to defend their decisions, designers want their models validated. There's a gravitational pull toward presenting the rosiest possible picture, especially if careers or reputations are tied to the model's perceived success. This can turn evaluation into a performance rather than an inquiry, with everyone playing their part to produce the "right" numbers. Breaking that cycle requires courage, and a willingness to accept that knowing the uncomfortable truth is more valuable than basking in the comfort of a pleasant fiction.

The irony is that acknowledging limitations often strengthens a model's credibility. When designers are candid about where their approach works best, under what conditions it tends to falter, and what adjustments might be needed, users are more likely to trust and invest in it. Overpromising breeds disappointment; clear-eyed realism fosters a kind of respect that glossy claims rarely earn.

An honest evaluation doesn't just look backward at what happened; it looks forward at what might be possible. It asks not only "Did this work?" but "What have we learned that will make the next iteration better?" In this way, evaluation becomes part of the model's lifecycle, not the end of it. The most enduring applied models are those that have been through multiple rounds of this cycle, each time shedding what didn't work, keeping what did, and experimenting with new possibilities.

There's also a personal dimension to evaluating models that often goes unspoken (Yang et al, 2024). People develop attachments to frameworks they've invested in—whether through design, implementation, or use. This attachment can blur objectivity. It can make us slow to admit when a model has reached the end of its useful life. Letting go of a model can feel like conceding defeat, when in fact it may be the wisest act of stewardship. Retiring a once-effective model is not a failure; it's an acknowledgment that its season has passed.

If there's a single thread that runs through all of this, it's that effectiveness and limitations are not static qualities. They shift with context, evolve over time, and reveal themselves differently depending on who's looking and what they value. A model that's a marvel in one decade may be obsolete in the next; one that struggled in its early years may become indispensable once conditions align. The task of evaluation is not to freeze these qualities in a single judgment, but to keep the conversation alive.

In the end, evaluating an applied model is less about pronouncing a verdict than about cultivating an ongoing awareness—of what it does well, where it falls short, and how those patterns interact with the changing world around it (Chang, 2023). It's about resisting the lure of easy answers and learning to live with the complexity that real problem solving entails. Models, like the problems they address, are living things. They grow, adapt, and sometimes fade away. The work of evaluation is to walk alongside them long enough to see the whole arc, in all its tangled, contradictory beauty.

TOWARDS ADAPTIVE, EVOLVING MODELS FOR COMPLEX PROBLEM SPACES

It's a strange kind of arrogance to imagine that any single model—no matter how well-researched, elegant, or celebrated—can remain fully fit for purpose in a world that never stops shifting. Complex problem spaces are not tidy gardens where cause and effect behave politely; they are more like wild, tangled forests where paths appear and vanish without warning, and where the undergrowth can hide dangers or opportunities you didn't know existed until you trip over them.

The models that survive in such terrain are not the most sophisticated in theory or the most polished in presentation (Sevaldson, 2022). They are the ones that can move—stretch, pivot, shed old parts, grow new ones—without losing their core identity. Adaptive models are, in that sense, less like monuments and more like organisms. They are alive in the only way a human-made structure can be alive: constantly rearranging themselves in response to the weather, the predators, the changing soil.

But adaptability is not just a design feature—it's a stance, an ethic. It's the willingness to let a model evolve in the face of discomfort, even when the change is inconvenient, politically awkward, or undermines the prestige of the original design. And it's also a refusal to confuse loyalty to a model with loyalty to the problem it was meant to solve. A fixed loyalty to the model, regardless of changing conditions, is how otherwise useful tools become relics.

One of the hardest truths in this realm is that complexity punishes certainty. The moment you think you've "solved" a complex problem, you've almost certainly stopped looking closely enough. Adaptive models are built on the assumption that the solution is never final; the best you can hope for is a configuration that works for now, under these conditions, with these people, in this specific cultural and political moment (Galesic et al, 2023). And the minute those conditions shift—and they will—the model must be ready to reconfigure without collapsing.

This raises an uncomfortable tension. Many institutions crave stability. They want the comfort of a model that can be rolled out repeatedly, with predictable results and clear metrics (Maheshwari et al, 2024). Adaptation, by contrast, is messy. It resists the promise of sameness. It asks stakeholders to tolerate ambiguity, to accept that a decision-making process which worked last quarter may require radical revision this quarter. This is not an easy sell in environments that equate consistency with competence.

Yet the irony is that clinging to consistency in a volatile setting is the quickest way to erode real competence. In the long run, credibility comes from responsiveness, not rigidity. People may grumble when the model changes, but they'll grumble more if it fails because it refused to. The art lies in making the model's evolution legible—showing that changes are not whimsical but grounded in new realities, new evidence, new understandings.

Of course, there's a danger in swinging too far in the other direction. Constant reinvention can feel like instability. Users need to trust that the model has some enduring scaffolding—that they're not learning a new system every few weeks.

Adaptive models, at their best, maintain a recognizable backbone while allowing the muscles and skin to regenerate (Peng et al, 2023). You can think of it like a language: the grammar stays mostly intact, but the vocabulary expands, contracts, and shifts as the conversation demands.

The starting point for creating such models is humility, but not the performative kind. This humility is technical and structural: building the model in a way that assumes it will be wrong in parts, and leaving room for those parts to be replaced. That might mean designing modular components rather than monolithic systems, so one element can be swapped out without dismantling the whole. Or it might mean embedding feedback loops that are not token gestures but actual levers for change—feedback that, if consistent enough, will force revision whether the designers feel ready or not.

Feedback, however, only works if the system is willing to hear what it doesn't want to hear. Many models die not because they were fundamentally flawed, but because they developed a protective shell against criticism (Gou et al, 2023). The shell can take many forms: bureaucratic pride, sunk-cost thinking, the personal reputation of the model's champions. Once the shell hardens, adaptation slows, and by the time reality breaches it, the damage is already deep. An adaptive model must be built with a thinner skin—porous enough to let the outside in before it's too late.

There's also a cultural layer to adaptability. Some contexts welcome change; others view it as a threat. A model designed for rapid iteration in a start-up environment will feel alien in a public sector agency that measures success in decades, not months. Here, adaptability might mean something different—not a constant churn of modifications, but a slower, more deliberate evolution that aligns with institutional rhythms. The model evolves, yes, but in a way that feels steady rather than destabilizing.

And let's be honest: evolving a model is not just about technical tweaks; it often means grappling with the politics embedded in its structure. Models distribute power. They decide whose voices matter, whose knowledge counts, which outcomes are prioritized. Changing the model can shift that distribution, sometimes in subtle ways, sometimes dramatically (Miller et al, 2021). An adaptive model, therefore, is not just a technical artifact—it's a political process. And political processes rarely unfold without resistance.

One way to soften that resistance is to make evolution participatory. Invite the people who live with the model every day into the process of changing it. This is not about token consultation; it's about handing them real tools to influence the architecture. When users see their fingerprints on the model, they are more likely to support its evolution, even if they don't agree with every detail. Participation also has a practical benefit: it surfaces contextual knowledge that the model's original designers may never have had.

In complex problem spaces, no model can anticipate every variable. That's not a flaw—it's a fact of life. What matters is how the model behaves when it encounters the unknown. Does it snap under the weight of unpredicted conditions? Does it limp along, degrading slowly until it becomes irrelevant? Or does it adapt—absorbing the shock, adjusting its parameters, and emerging still recognizably itself, but better suited to the new terrain?

It's tempting to frame adaptability as a reactive quality, something a model does when circumstances force it. But the most robust adaptive models are proactive. They monitor their environment like an immune system, detecting subtle changes before they become crises. This requires more than data dashboards—it requires human interpretation, a willingness to act on signals even when they're ambiguous. Sometimes the cost of adapting too early is small; the cost of adapting too late is fatal.

Evolving models also have to navigate the paradox of expertise (Hameed et al, 2023). Experts bring deep knowledge that can sharpen a model's precision, but they can also become gatekeepers who resist changes that challenge their authority. In some cases, the most valuable input for evolution comes not from experts but from novices—people who approach the model without the baggage of "how it's always been done." Balancing these perspectives is tricky, but vital; too much deference to tradition, and the model ossifies; too little, and it loses the accumulated wisdom that gives it depth.

Adaptation is not a one-size-fits-all virtue. In certain high-stakes environments—nuclear safety, for example—changes must be incremental, meticulously tested, and communicated with extreme clarity (Otegui, 2024). In others—disaster relief, grassroots organizing—adaptation must be swift, improvisational, and sometimes messy. The skill is in calibrating the pace and style of evolution to match the stakes, the resources, and the tolerance for uncertainty in the specific problem space.

An adaptive model also needs a way to retire gracefully. Not every evolution is about survival; sometimes the wisest form of adaptation is to recognize that the model's job is done, or that the landscape has shifted so radically that starting fresh is better than endless patchwork. Building this possibility into the lifecycle from the start—acknowledging that the model may one day need to make room for a successor—prevents clinging to a tool past its prime.

In many ways, the push towards adaptive, evolving models is a response to the deepening complexity of the problems we face. Climate change, global pandemics, political instability—these are not "complicated" problems with linear solutions; they are entangled, dynamic systems where today's solution can seed tomorrow's crisis (Paudel et al, 2023). Static models, no matter how sophisticated, are ill-suited for this reality. What's needed are models that can learn—not just in the technical sense of machine learning, but in the broader human sense of absorbing experience, reinterpreting it, and acting differently because of it.

Some of the best adaptive models are invisible. They stop being "models" in the formal sense and become habits, reflexes, embedded ways of working that change incrementally over time without fanfare. They're not announced in glossy reports; they're passed along in the way a team makes decisions, the way a community organizes itself after a shock, the way a network shares resources. This quiet evolution is often more durable than grand redesigns because it grows out of lived reality, not imposed abstraction.

The challenge, of course, is that invisible evolution is hard to document, harder still to fund or scale in the ways institutions prefer. Yet ignoring it means missing some of the richest examples of how adaptive thinking actually works. One of the tasks for those committed to adaptive models is to learn how to make this slow, organic evolution visible enough to be valued without freezing it into a rigid template.

Ultimately, moving towards adaptive, evolving models is less about adopting a new methodology and more about embracing a different relationship with uncertainty (Shafizadeh, 2024). It's about trading the comfort of fixed answers for the discipline of continuous learning. It's about accepting that the model is not the destination but the vehicle—and that vehicles, if they're going to keep moving, need maintenance, upgrades, sometimes a complete rebuild.

In complex problem spaces, the map can never fully match the territory. The best we can do is keep redrawing it as we travel, knowing that the act of redrawing is not a sign of failure but of paying attention. An adaptive model is one that treats the journey itself as part of the design, and understands that the road will change under its wheels. That's not a flaw. That's the work.

CONCLUSION

The creation of applied models for problem solving is far more than an exercise in diagramming processes or formalizing procedures—it is a conscious, strategic response to the messiness of reality. Throughout this chapter, we have seen that such models emerge at the intersection of necessity and insight. They are born from the recognition that without structure, problem-solving efforts risk fragmentation, inefficiency, and missed opportunities for meaningful impact.

At their best, applied models embody a rare combination of clarity and adaptability. They distill complex realities into manageable components, yet remain responsive to the unpredictability that accompanies real-world application. They provide a scaffold for thinking and acting, without becoming rigid cages that stifle innovation. In this balance lies their enduring value: they offer enough guidance to instill confidence in decision-making, while leaving room for the human capacity to adapt, improvise, and learn.

The rationales driving their creation are inseparable from the contexts in which they are conceived. Some arise in environments where efficiency and standardization are paramount—industries where time is scarce, resources are limited, and errors carry significant costs. Others originate in contexts that demand creativity and exploration, where the model serves more as a compass than a set of marching orders. In both cases, the model reflects not only the nature of the problem but also the values, priorities, and assumptions of its creators.

Equally important is the recognition that models are never truly finished. Just as problems evolve, so too must the tools designed to address them. An applied model that remains static risks becoming obsolete, unable to accommodate new information, technologies, or social realities. Those who create and use these models must embrace a mindset of iteration—testing, refining, and sometimes dismantling their constructs in light of fresh evidence or shifting goals. This adaptability is not a sign of weakness but of maturity, acknowledging that problem solving is a living process rather than a fixed formula.

Ultimately, the creation of applied models is an act of both design and stewardship. It calls for technical skill, yes, but also for humility—a willingness to recognize the limits of one's own perspective, to seek diverse inputs, and to remain open to change. It demands an appreciation for the interplay between theory and practice, and a sensitivity to the human dimensions that shape both. When built with such awareness, applied models do more than solve problems; they cultivate the capacity to face future challenges with insight, resilience, and creativity.

The lesson, then, is clear: the true power of an applied model lies not in its diagrams, steps, or formulas, but in the thinking it inspires and the conversations it enables. It is a catalyst for clarity, collaboration, and purposeful action. And in a world where complexity is the norm rather than the exception, this capacity—to think clearly, work collaboratively, and act with intent—may be the most valuable outcome of all.

REFERENCES

Avishai, T., Palatnik, A., & Kolikant, Y. B. D. (2025). Amplifiers and filters in teacher learning of student-centered mathematics instruction. *Teaching and Teacher Education, 156*, 104943. DOI: 10.1016/j.tate.2025.104943

Banham, R. (2022). *Architecture of the Well-tempered Environment*. University of Chicago Press.

Biskjaer, M. M., Kamari, A., Jensen, S. R., & Kirkegaard, P. H. (2021). Exploring blind spots in collaborative value creation in building design: A creativity perspective. *CoDesign*, *17*(4), 374–391. DOI: 10.1080/15710882.2019.1654521

Bopaiah, M. (2021). *Equity: How to design organizations where everyone thrives*. Berrett-Koehler Publishers.

Borer, E. T., MacDougall, A. S., Stevens, C. J., Sullivan, L. L., Wilfahrt, P. A., & Seabloom, E. W. (2023). Writing a massively multi-authored paper: Overcoming barriers to meaningful authorship for all. *Methods in Ecology and Evolution*, *14*(6), 1432–1442. DOI: 10.1111/2041-210X.14096

Casquinha, A. C. B. (2024). Creativity and Problem-Solving in Advertising: the Impact of ChatGPT Within the Design Thinking Framework (Master's thesis, Universidade NOVA de Lisboa (Portugal)).

Chang, E. Y. (2023, March). Prompting large language models with the socratic method. In 2023 IEEE 13th annual computing and communication workshop and conference (CCWC) (pp. 0351-0360). IEEE. DOI: 10.1109/CCWC57344.2023.10099179

Chen, J., Lu, W., & Liu, D. (2024). Built environment defect mapping, modeling, and management (D3M): A BIM-based integrated framework. *Journal of Intelligent Construction*, *2*(1), 1–15. DOI: 10.26599/JIC.2024.9180008

Cheng, Z. M., Bonetti, F., de Regt, A., Ribeiro, J. L., & Plangger, K. (2024). Principles of responsible digital implementation: Developing operational business resilience to reduce resistance to digital innovations. *Organizational Dynamics*, *53*(2), 101043. DOI: 10.1016/j.orgdyn.2024.101043

Christodoulou, I. P., Rizomyliotis, I., Konstantoulaki, K., Alfiero, S., Hasanago, S., & Paolone, F. (2025). Investigating the key success factors within business models that facilitate long-term value creation for sustainability-focused start-ups. *Business Ethics, the Environment & Responsibility*, *34*(3), 936–950. DOI: 10.1111/beer.12681

Eisbach, S., Mai, O., & Hertel, G. (2024). Combining theoretical modelling and machine learning approaches: The case of teamwork effects on individual effort expenditure. *New Ideas in Psychology, 73*, 101077. DOI: 10.1016/j.newideapsych.2024.101077

Friedman, B., & Citron, D. K. (2024). Indiscriminate Data Surveillance. *Virginia Law Review, 110*, 1351.

Galesic, M., Barkoczi, D., Berdahl, A. M., Biro, D., Carbone, G., Giannoccaro, I., Goldstone, R. L., Gonzalez, C., Kandler, A., Kao, A. B., Kendal, R., Kline, M., Lee, E., Massari, G. F., Mesoudi, A., Olsson, H., Pescetelli, N., Sloman, S. J., Smaldino, P. E., & Stein, D. L. (2023). Beyond collective intelligence: Collective adaptation. *Journal of the Royal Society, Interface, 20*(200), 20220736. DOI: 10.1098/rsif.2022.0736 PMID: 36946092

Gantert, T. M. (2024). Balancing Stability and Fluidity in Post-Bureaucratic Organizations: Insights from Coworking-Spaces (Doctoral dissertation).

Gou, Z., Shao, Z., Gong, Y., Shen, Y., Yang, Y., Duan, N., & Chen, W. (2023). Critic: Large language models can self-correct with tool-interactive critiquing. arXiv preprint arXiv:2305.11738.

Gyevnar, B., Ferguson, N., & Schafer, B. (2023). Bridging the transparency gap: What can explainable ai learn from the ai act? arXiv preprint arXiv:2302.10766. DOI: 10.3233/FAIA230367

Hameed, R. M., Ullah, I., & Abbas, F. (2023). How does the learning of paradox influence individuals' capacity to navigate wicked problems? Learning of paradox and wicked problems. JSSH, 31(1).

Hedvall, K., Benedettini, O., Blümel, J. H., Arsenovic, J., & Kristensson, P. (2025). B2B manufacturers in pursuit of Product-as-a-Service: Motivations, barriers, and approaches. *Journal of Business Research, 199*, 115567. DOI: 10.1016/j.jbusres.2025.115567

Hipolito, I., & Khanduja, A. (2024). The Wicked and the Complex: A New Paradigm for Societal Problem-Solving.

Holubnycha, L., Kuznetsova, O., & Demchenko, D. (2024). History of problem-solving teaching and learning evolution. History of science and technology, 14(1), 64-84.

Hondagneu-Messner, S. (2021). Data portability: A guide and a roadmap. *Rutgers Computer & Technology Law Journal, 47*, 240.

Kartikasari, I. A., & Usodo, B. (2022). The Effectiveness Open-Ended Learning and Creative Problem Solving Models to Teach Creative Thinking Skills. *Pegem Journal of Education and Instruction, 12*(4), 29–38.

KHUDAVERDIYEVA, T. (2024). TRANSLATION PROBLEMS AND SOLUTIONS: BRIDGING LINGUISTIC AND CULTURAL DIFFERENCES. T RCÜM ŞÜNASLIĞIN MÜASİR PROBLEML Rİ, 228.

Kochenderfer, M. J., Wheeler, T. A., & Wray, K. H. (2022). *Algorithms for decision making*. MIT press.

Kriz, A., Nailer, C., Jansen, K., & Potocnjak-Oxman, C. (2021). Teaching-practice as a critical bridge for narrowing the research-practice gap. *Industrial Marketing Management, 92*, 254–266. DOI: 10.1016/j.indmarman.2020.02.017

Küçükuncular, A., & Ertugan, A. (2025). Teaching in the AI Era: Sustainable Digital Education Through Ethical Integration and Teacher Empowerment. *Sustainability (Basel), 17*(16), 7405. DOI: 10.3390/su17167405

Le Dé, L. (2024). Bridging gaps between disaster risk reduction and drowning prevention. *International Journal of Disaster Risk Reduction, 106*, 104445. DOI: 10.1016/j.ijdrr.2024.104445

Maheshwari, A., Malhotra, A., Hada, B. S., Ranka, M., & Basha, M. S. A. (2024, September). Towards an Improved Model for Stability Score Prediction: Harnessing Machine Learning in National Stability Forecasting. In *2024 IEEE North Karnataka Subsection Flagship International Conference (NKCon)* (pp. 1-7). IEEE. DOI: 10.1109/NKCon62728.2024.10775198

Miller, J. P., Taori, R., Raghunathan, A., Sagawa, S., Koh, P. W., Shankar, V., & Schmidt, L. (2021, July). Accuracy on the line: on the strong correlation between out-of-distribution and in-distribution generalization. In *International conference on machine learning* (pp. 7721-7735). PMLR.

Mohamed, A. O. (2025). The Effect of Design on the Viewer's Perception of Media Content and Its Role in Problem Solving. *Journal of Ecohumanism, 4*(1), 1432–1447. DOI: 10.62754/joe.v4i1.5956

Moore, S. L. (2021). The design models we have are not the design models we need. *The Journal of Applied Instructional Design, 10*(4), 11–19.

Ngo, R., Chan, L., & Mindermann, S. (2022). The alignment problem from a deep learning perspective. arXiv preprint arXiv:2209.00626.

Otegui, D. (2024). Understanding Cognitive Processes in High-Stakes Environments. In *Business Growth in Times of Instability: Empowering Private Companies Through Disaster Risk Reduction* (pp. 43–63). Springer Nature Switzerland. DOI: 10.1007/978-3-031-69370-0_3

Paez, R. (2024). *Operative mapping: the use of maps as a design tool*. Actar D, Inc.

Pantiris, P., Pallis, P. L., Chountalas, P. T., & Dasaklis, T. K. (2025). Enhancing Coordination and Decision Making in Humanitarian Logistics Through Artificial Intelligence: A Grounded Theory Approach. *Logistics (Basel)*, *9*(3), 113. DOI: 10.3390/logistics9030113

Paudel, D., Neupane, R. C., Sigdel, S., Poudel, P., & Khanal, A. R. (2023). COVID-19 pandemic, climate change, and conflicts on agriculture: A trio of challenges to global food security. *Sustainability (Basel)*, *15*(10), 8280. DOI: 10.3390/su15108280

Peng, M., Zhao, Q., Wang, M., & Du, X. (2023). Reconfigurable scaffolds for adaptive tissue regeneration. *Nanoscale*, *15*(13), 6105–6120. DOI: 10.1039/D3NR00281K PMID: 36919563

Rahmattalabi, A. (2022). Towards Trustworthy and Data-Driven Social Interventions (Doctoral dissertation, UNIVERSITY OF SOUTHERN CALIFORNIA).

Šercar, T. M. (2025). The Connection of Information Science and Psychology in the Case of the Wisdom Paradox-Part Two. *International Journal of English Literature and Social Sciences*, *10*(1), 593296. DOI: 10.22161/ijels.101.4

Sevaldson, B. (2022). *Designing complexity: The methodology and practice of systems oriented design*. Common Ground Research Networks. DOI: 10.18848/978-1-86335-262-8/CGP

Shafizadeh, H. (2024). Decision-Making Under Uncertainty: How Organizations Adapt to Environmental Changes? *Journal of Resource Management and Decision Engineering*, *3*(1), 4–10. DOI: 10.61838/kman.jrmde.3.1.2

Sobieraj, D. M., Wheeler, K., Salvo, M., & Smith, M. (2024). Prescription for curricular revision: Application of design thinking principles. *American Journal of Pharmaceutical Education*, *88*(12), 101325. DOI: 10.1016/j.ajpe.2024.101325 PMID: 39586353

Taivainen, A. (2021). Alternative agency, observations of changing architecture and futures studies.

Teague, R. G. (2022). *How an effective knowledge management program supports critical tacit knowledge retention within a higher education institution: A qualitative intrinsic case study*. Northcentral University.

Yang, Z., Liu, Z., Zhang, J., Lu, C., Tai, J., Zhong, T., . . . Liu, T. (2024). Analyzing nobel prize literature with large language models. arXiv preprint arXiv:2410.18142.

Zhang, R., Cao, L., Wang, L., Wang, L., Wang, J., Xu, N., & Luo, J. (2024). Assessing the relationship between urban park spatial features and physical activity levels in Residents: A spatial analysis Utilizing drone remote sensing. *Ecological Indicators*, *166*, 112520. DOI: 10.1016/j.ecolind.2024.112520

Zhang, W., Liu, Y., Dong, Y., He, W., Yao, S., Xu, Z., & Mu, Y. (2023). How we learn social norms: A three-stage model for social norm learning. *Frontiers in Psychology*, *14*, 1153809. DOI: 10.3389/fpsyg.2023.1153809 PMID: 37333598

KEY TERMS AND DEFINITIONS

Adaptive/Evolving Framework: A model that iterates, modularizes, and learns, retaining a core while changing with conditions.

Applied Model: A purposeful, practice-ready structure that translates theory into guided action in real contexts.

Bridging Design & Application: Co-evolving the model through pilots, feedback, and safeguards so it survives real-world friction.

Context Sensitivity: Designing and adapting models to cultural, resource, temporal, and power conditions of the setting.

Evaluation & Scope: Judging effectiveness and limits with both quantitative indicators and lived/qualitative signals over time.

Tacit Knowledge Externalization: Converting expert know-how into explicit checklists, playbooks, and protocols others can learn.

Theory-to-Practice Translation: Selecting essentials from a framework and shaping them into usable steps and artifacts.

Chapter 6
Work-Based Models: Bridging Theory and Practice in Problem Solving

Mustafa Kayyali
https://orcid.org/0000-0003-3300-262X
Maaref University of Applied Sciences, Syria

ABSTRACT

Work-based models offer a dynamic bridge between academic theory and real-world application, enabling professionals to address complex challenges through experiential engagement. This chapter examines how such models harness workplace environments as living laboratories, where theory is not merely applied but adapted, tested, and refined. By drawing on established frameworks and embedding them in authentic contexts, work-based approaches foster both immediate problem-solving capacity and long-term professional growth. The discussion explores key mechanisms—such as reflective practice, collaborative inquiry, and iterative learning—that enhance the integration of conceptual knowledge into daily operations. Case examples and evaluative perspectives illustrate the tangible benefits and limitations of these models, while also identifying pathways for innovation. Ultimately, the chapter positions work-based models as essential tools for cultivating adaptable, critically minded professionals capable of navigating evolving professional landscapes.

INTRODUCTION

In contemporary professional landscapes, the gap between theoretical knowledge and practical application has become both a persistent challenge and a driving force for innovation. Academic institutions produce a wealth of theories, models, and conceptual frameworks intended to inform practice, yet in many cases, these con-

DOI: 10.4018/979-8-3373-3301-4.ch006

structs remain confined to textbooks, lectures, and research papers (Taylor & Colet, 2023). Simultaneously, the fast-moving realities of workplaces demand solutions that are immediate, contextually relevant, and adaptable to change. This tension has spurred a growing interest in *work-based models*—approaches that position the workplace itself as a site of structured learning, critical inquiry, and collaborative problem solving.

Work-based models are not simply about "learning on the job." They are deliberate, theory-informed frameworks that seek to embed the principles of academic knowledge into the very fabric of workplace operations. Rather than viewing theory as something to be applied after it is learned, these models encourage a continuous, reciprocal relationship between thinking and doing—where theory shapes practice, and practice, in turn, refines theory. They create an iterative loop of reflection and action, allowing professionals to test, adapt, and evolve theoretical insights in direct response to real-world challenges.

The value of such models becomes increasingly clear when one considers the complexity of modern problems. Whether in healthcare, engineering, education, or business, today's challenges are rarely linear or neatly defined. They are often multilayered, involving technical, human, ethical, and cultural dimensions that require more than the rote application of prescriptive solutions. Work-based models thrive in this complexity (Marsick et al., 2021). They encourage professionals to move beyond procedural compliance toward adaptive expertise, equipping them with the skills to diagnose problems, navigate uncertainty, and innovate responsibly.

A crucial feature of work-based models is their reliance on collaboration—not only between peers in a workplace, but also between academic and professional communities. Partnerships between universities and industries, for example, create fertile ground for shared learning, where research can be tested in living contexts and workplace insights can be fed back into academic discourse. This bi-directional flow of knowledge dismantles the traditional separation between "the classroom" and "the real world," replacing it with a more fluid, interconnected model of professional development.

Moreover, work-based models acknowledge the importance of *context*. A model that is effective in one setting cannot simply be transplanted into another without careful adaptation (Hayes et al, 2025). By situating learning and problem solving within the immediate realities of a specific workplace—its culture, constraints, and opportunities—these models ensure that solutions are not only theoretically sound but also operationally feasible. This alignment with context is one of their defining strengths, making them powerful tools for both incremental improvement and transformative change.

In the sections that follow, this chapter will unpack the conceptual foundations of work-based models, explore strategies for integrating theory into practice, and examine the mechanisms that enable effective knowledge transfer in workplace settings. Through a blend of analytical discussion, illustrative examples, and critical reflection, it will argue that work-based models are indispensable for bridging the gap between what we know and what we can do. They are not merely a pedagogical trend but a necessity for developing professionals who can meet the demands of an increasingly complex and unpredictable world.

THE CONCEPTUAL FOUNDATIONS OF WORK-BASED MODELS

Trying to pin down the essence of work-based models is a bit like trying to sketch a landscape that refuses to sit still. The contours shift depending on the vantage point: for some, these models are primarily about embedding academic theories into the workplace; for others, they are about extracting the tacit wisdom of practice and making it explicit enough to guide future action. Either way, they rest on a foundational belief that the workplace is not merely a venue for applying what one has learned elsewhere but is, in itself, a fertile ground for generating knowledge.

This idea is not as modern as it sometimes appears. Centuries before we gave it formal names and academic frameworks, artisans, farmers, and healers were already teaching apprentices through lived practice, blending skill, observation, and oral tradition. What changes in the contemporary rendering of work-based models is the deliberate, structured interplay between formal theory and the unpredictable messiness of actual work. Here, the workshop, the clinic, the office floor—these are not the final stage of learning but its primary laboratory.

At its core, a work-based model is less about imposing an external framework than about creating a porous membrane between two worlds: the abstract universe of conceptual thinking and the textured reality of lived experience (Maksoud et al., 2022). Theories without such contact risk becoming brittle—elegant, yes, but fragile when confronted with the inconsistencies, contradictions, and improvisations that real-world contexts demand. Practice without theory, on the other hand, can ossify into habit, blind to alternative approaches that could improve or even transform outcomes. It is in the friction between these two poles that work-based models find their generative energy.

The conceptual foundations, then, lie in several intertwined streams of thought. One of the most significant is experiential learning theory, which holds that understanding is deepened and retained when it is rooted in concrete experience followed by reflective analysis (Beard, 2022). But work-based models take this further—they don't merely stage occasional encounters with "real life" to test classroom lessons. They weave learning into the warp and weft of everyday work so that the distinction between "learning time" and "working time" begins to blur. Reflection is no longer an afterthought; it is embedded in the doing, sometimes even in the heat of the moment when decisions must be made with incomplete information.

Another key strand comes from systems thinking, the idea that problems—and solutions—must be understood within the wider network of interdependencies in which they occur. Work-based models, when at their most effective, acknowledge that the workplace is an ecosystem. A decision in one department can ripple into unexpected outcomes elsewhere; a small procedural change might alter team dynamics or customer relationships in ways the original planners did not anticipate (Eriksson & Nyström, 2025). Theories brought into such a system must bend and flex, adapting their shape without losing their integrity.

Yet there is also an undercurrent of pragmatism here—less in the philosophical sense of William James or John Dewey (though their influence is unmistakable) and more in the stubborn recognition that ideas earn their keep only when they prove themselves under pressure. In the realm of work-based learning, failure is not simply an unfortunate detour; it's part of the map. Theories are tested against stubborn realities, and in that testing they either adapt, deepen, or quietly retire. This iterative quality—test, revise, reapply—is central to the concept.

What complicates matters, and simultaneously makes them fascinating, is that workplaces are never neutral. They are shaped by culture, politics, hierarchies, unspoken norms, and the unquantifiable moods of human beings. A work-based model that thrives in one organization may wither in another, not because the underlying theory is flawed, but because the conditions for its survival are absent (Hökkä et al, 2023). The conceptual foundation must therefore include an awareness of context—not as a footnote, but as a central pillar. Theories in this domain cannot be "one size fits all." They must arrive with the humility to be reinterpreted, reconfigured, and sometimes even dismantled to suit the particulars of place and people.

Some might argue that this openness to context risks diluting the rigour of theory, turning it into an amorphous set of "tips" rather than a structured framework. But here's the paradox: in work-based models, adaptability is not the enemy of rigour—it's the proof of it. A theory that cannot survive adaptation is often one that was never robust enough to begin with. The conceptual integrity of a work-based model lies not in its resistance to change but in its capacity to maintain coherence while bending to circumstance.

Table 1. Work-based approaches contexts, activities, risks

Approach/Model	Core Idea	Best-Fit Contexts	Key Activities	Risks / Watch-outs
Experiential Learning Cycle	Iterate across do–reflect–conceptualize–experiment on live work	Rapidly changing teams; service ops	After-action reviews; journaling; small tests	Shallow reflection; skipping iterations
Communities of Practice	Peer groups share tacit know-how across roles	Distributed orgs; multi-site teams	Show-and-tell; pattern libraries; office hours	Knowledge hoarding; uneven participation
Mentoring/ Shadowing	Novices learn micro-judgments beside experts	Safety-critical or client-facing work	Narrated decisions; gradual autonomy	Time pressure; unspoken shortcuts
Job Aids & Playbooks	Codify steps/checklists from proven practice	High-volume, repetitive tasks	One-pagers; checklists; decision trees	Stale docs; false certainty
Cross-Functional Projects	Mixed-discipline teams tackle bottlenecks	Systemic handoff issues	Shared backlog; retros; demo days	Role conflict; coordination overhead
Data-Use Routines	Lightweight data checks guide daily choices	Noisy metrics environments	Daily huddles; run charts; triggers	Metric gaming; dashboard over-reliance
Reflective Practice	Surface assumptions; reframe problems	Complex, ambiguous domains	Critical friends; pre-mortems; pause points	Blame culture; performative reflection

There is also an epistemological dimension to these foundations. Work-based models challenge the traditional hierarchy of knowledge in which academic theory is seen as the source and workplace practice as the application (Zhao, 2024). Instead, they propose a more fluid exchange. Practice generates knowledge of its own—rich, situated, and often invisible to those who haven't lived it. Theory, for its part, offers a broader lens, revealing patterns and principles that may elude the immediacy of day-to-day work. The conceptual foundation, then, is not about establishing primacy but about creating a meeting ground where both forms of knowing can shape each other.

This is where reflective practice comes in—not as a perfunctory exercise in filling out an end-of-project report, but as an ongoing discipline of looking at one's own actions through a critical, sometimes uncomfortable lens. Reflection asks the practitioner to surface the assumptions that underlie their decisions, to examine not only what happened but why it happened that way (Aryal, 2022). In a work-based model, this reflective dimension is not an add-on; it is the engine of learning. Without it, the loop between theory and practice collapses, leaving us with either disconnected abstractions or unexamined routines.

The human dimension in these foundations cannot be overstated. Work-based models operate in spaces populated by people with differing motivations, levels of expertise, and tolerances for ambiguity. They require trust, not just in the sense of interpersonal rapport, but trust in the process itself—a belief that slowing down to reflect, experimenting with new approaches, and exposing one's uncertainties will yield benefits worth the risk. This is not an easy sell in high-pressure environments where productivity is measured in immediate outputs. Yet, paradoxically, it is precisely in such environments that work-based models can prove their greatest worth.

Figure 1. Cycle time reduction from WBL interventions (hours)

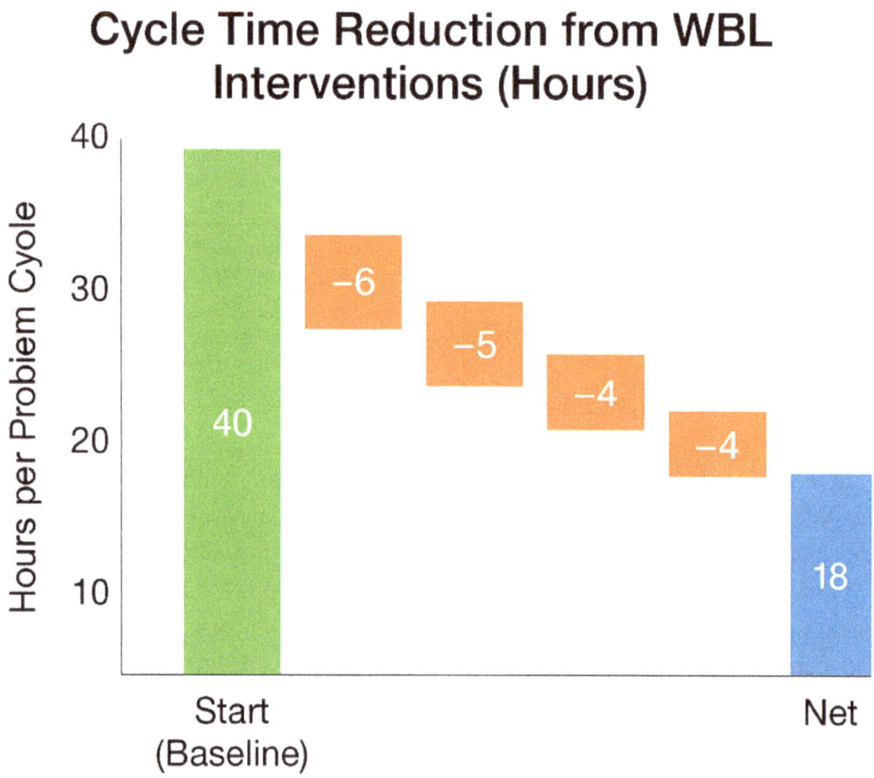

Another subtle but crucial element in their foundation is the recognition that knowledge is rarely static. The moment a theory is "frozen," treated as final, it begins to lose touch with the shifting realities of the workplace. Work-based models, at their most alive, function like open systems. They are porous, absorbing new data, perspectives, and experiences, and they evolve in response. The conceptual scaffolding supports this openness, ensuring that change does not devolve into chaos but instead follows a pattern of inquiry and adaptation.

Still, there's a tension here—a push and pull between the desire for stability and the necessity of change (Sugiyama et al., 2024). In many organizations, standardization is valued for its efficiency; variation is viewed with suspicion. Work-based models must navigate this terrain carefully, offering enough consistency to build confidence while allowing enough flexibility to respond to the unexpected. The theoretical grounding must therefore accommodate both the need for a coherent structure and the inevitability of disruption.

Historically, this balance has been influenced by adult learning theories, particularly andragogy, which emphasizes self-direction, the value of prior experience, and the relevance of learning to the learner's own context. Work-based models extend this into the collective domain: it's not only individuals but entire teams and organizations that must engage in self-directed, contextually relevant learning. This requires a shift from seeing learning as a personal responsibility to viewing it as an organizational culture.

One could think of the conceptual foundations of work-based models as a tapestry woven from multiple threads: experiential learning, systems thinking, pragmatism, reflective practice, contextual adaptation, and a flattened hierarchy of knowledge (Ing & Metcalf, 2023). But unlike a finished tapestry, this one is never complete. It is constantly being unpicked and rewoven, with new threads introduced and old ones discarded or re-dyed. The pattern is emergent, shaped by the interplay of theory and the lived realities of work.

What is perhaps most radical about these foundations is their implicit challenge to the notion of certainty. In conventional models, the assumption is that theory provides clarity—a map that will guide action with minimal deviation. In work-based models, the map is provisional. It changes as the terrain changes, and the traveller is expected to redraw it along the way. This does not mean abandoning the idea of direction or coherence, but it does mean accepting that the destination may shift and that the journey is, in itself, a form of knowledge-making.

This way of thinking requires a certain tolerance for ambiguity, which can be uncomfortable for those accustomed to more linear approaches. Yet it is in this ambiguity that creative solutions often emerge. When the path is not fully predetermined, there is space for noticing what would otherwise be overlooked, for experimenting without the paralysis of needing to be "right" on the first attempt. The conceptual underpinnings of work-based models thus rest not only on cognitive theories but also on an attitudinal stance—an openness to learning that is as much about curiosity as it is about competence.

In the end, the foundations of work-based models are less like the concrete footings of a static building and more like the keel of a ship—providing stability while allowing movement, guiding but not dictating the course, holding steady in calm waters and storms alike. They are built on the recognition that theory and practice are not two separate domains bridged by occasional contact, but two aspects of the same process, continually shaping and reshaping one another (Galleli & Amaral, 2025).

If one accepts this, then the implications are far-reaching. It suggests that to truly understand or improve a workplace, one cannot rely solely on importing external theories, however sophisticated. One must also be willing to mine the lived experience of those within it, to treat their insights not as anecdotal colour but as legitimate knowledge in its own right. It suggests that the role of the professional is not simply to execute tasks or follow protocols, but to engage as a co-creator of the very models that guide their work. And it suggests that the line between learning and working is, at best, a convenient fiction—useful for scheduling purposes perhaps, but meaningless in the deeper, ongoing process of becoming more capable, more insightful, and more adaptable in one's craft.

INTEGRATING THEORETICAL FRAMEWORKS INTO PRACTICAL CONTEXTS

The meeting point between theory and practice is rarely a tidy handshake; it's more like a hesitant dance where each partner keeps adjusting their steps to avoid stepping on the other's toes. In abstract form, theoretical frameworks look crystalline—structured, elegant, sometimes even seductively simple. But the moment they're lowered into the grit and unpredictability of real work, they start to wobble. Edges blur. Assumptions fray. The clean geometry of the model is suddenly competing with lived realities: the stubborn machine that won't behave according to the manual, the client whose needs mutate overnight, the unspoken cultural rules that override formal policy. And here lies the real challenge—not whether a theory is correct in principle, but whether it can survive, adapt, and remain useful when stripped of the controlled conditions in which it was first conceived.

There's a temptation, especially among those who guard the purity of academic models, to treat deviations from theory as failures of implementation. The manual was clear—if the results differ, the fault must lie in sloppy execution or lack of fidelity. Yet in practice, rigid adherence often kills a model faster than any misinterpretation could. A framework that cannot bend risks snapping altogether, especially in contexts where no two situations are quite alike. The act of integration, then, is not a mechanical insertion but a negotiation—a process of reshaping without losing the spirit of the original design.

In truth, theoretical frameworks are not imported into workplaces like finished furniture to be assembled with an Allen key and an hour of free time (Anglin et al,

2022). They arrive as skeletal structures that need fleshing out with the muscle, sinew, and connective tissue of local knowledge. That local knowledge—hard-earned, deeply embedded in the routines and rhythms of a specific environment—is what keeps the theory from floating above reality like a helium balloon. Without it, even the most celebrated model risks becoming an irrelevant ornament, referenced in strategic documents but ignored in the day-to-day grind.

The most successful integrations often begin quietly, almost imperceptibly, without fanfare or ceremonial launches. Someone adapts a step here, rephrases a concept there, bends a rigid guideline to fit an awkward situation, and before long, the model has taken root—not as an imported object but as something that feels native. This organic process, however, demands a kind of humility on both sides: the humility of the practitioner to accept that the theory might illuminate blind spots they hadn't considered, and the humility of the theorist to accept that their creation might need to be unpicked and rewoven in places.

It's worth acknowledging that integration isn't just about intellectual alignment; it's also about emotional and cultural fit. People rarely adopt new frameworks simply because they're logically sound (Cohnitz & Nicolai, 2021). They adopt them because the ideas make sense *to them*, in their language, in their reality. This is why the same theoretical model can thrive in one workplace and fall flat in another. The alignment between values, work culture, and the underlying assumptions of the theory matters as much as technical compatibility. A framework rooted in collaborative problem solving, for example, will wither in a culture that rewards individual competition (Jiang & Marbach, 2025).

Another complexity lies in timing. Introducing a theoretical model into a practical setting too abruptly can provoke resistance—not because the theory is flawed, but because people are still in the middle of grappling with old habits. They need breathing space to let go of what no longer serves them. Push too hard, and the framework becomes a symbol of intrusion, something to be passively resisted or actively subverted. Ease it in too gently, and it risks being dismissed as just another passing initiative destined to fade from memory. The art is in finding that precarious middle ground, the moment when curiosity outweighs defensiveness, and there's enough openness to experiment without fear of judgment.

One of the subtle truths in all this is that frameworks themselves are not static entities. Even within academic discourse, they evolve—new research, shifting paradigms, and technological advances all conspire to alter their contours (Dosi, 2023). When these living frameworks meet the equally dynamic world of practice, the result is a kind of double evolution. The workplace adapts to the model, yes, but the model also mutates in response to the pressures, constraints, and discoveries of the workplace. Over time, the "integrated" version may look quite different from the original. And this is not a flaw. In fact, it's often a sign that the theory has transcended its initial scope and become truly useful.

This interplay between the abstract and the concrete is not without its frictions. The language of theory can be alienating in the workplace, loaded with specialist jargon that feels like a private code (Ghaleb, 2024). Translating these terms into everyday speech without diluting their meaning is an underrated skill. The reverse is also true: workplace experience is often narrated in anecdote and story rather than formal constructs, and finding ways to encode these into the structured logic of theory can be tricky. Here, metaphor becomes a bridge—powerful enough to carry complex ideas yet flexible enough to resonate with lived realities.

Sometimes the best way to integrate a framework is to start with a single, small-scale experiment. Choose one aspect of the theory and apply it to a limited, manageable situation—a pilot project, a single team, a specific challenge—and watch how it behaves. This containment allows for adjustments without the chaos of organization-wide change. It also creates visible proof of concept, which can be far more persuasive than any amount of theoretical justification. Once people see a tangible improvement, their appetite for deeper engagement with the framework tends to grow.

Still, it would be dishonest to pretend that every attempt at integration succeeds. Some frameworks, no matter how elegant, simply don't align with the rhythms and demands of a particular setting. In such cases, the value lies in the attempt itself—in the conversations sparked, in the collective reflection about why the fit didn't work. Even a failed integration can sharpen awareness of what does matter, what does work, and what kind of models might serve better in the future. The process leaves traces, and those traces can shape the next attempt in ways that are hard to predict but often surprisingly fruitful.

What complicates this further is the role of external pressures. Many workplaces adopt theoretical frameworks not out of intrinsic motivation but in response to accreditation demands, regulatory compliance, or industry trends (Coco et al, 2023). When integration is driven primarily by external mandate, the danger is that the framework becomes a box to tick rather than a living guide for action. In such cases, the real work is to reclaim the model from the realm of bureaucratic obligation and reframe it as something genuinely beneficial to the people who have to use it. This reclamation often depends on local champions—individuals who can translate, adapt, and humanize the framework until it starts to feel less like an imposition and more like a resource.

There's also the question of scale. The integration process that works beautifully in a small, tightly knit team can collapse under the weight of a sprawling organization. Larger contexts introduce layers of complexity: competing priorities, inconsistent communication channels, and variations in how different units interpret the same model (Krishnan, 2025). Here, decentralization can be both a challenge and an asset. Allowing each unit to tailor the framework to its specific conditions increases the likelihood of meaningful adoption, though it risks creating divergences that can make cross-unit collaboration more difficult. Again, the tension between coherence and flexibility emerges—a recurring theme in any serious attempt to bridge theory and practice.

Perhaps one of the most overlooked aspects of integration is the role of reflection-in-action, a term Donald Schön popularized but which often gets flattened into something more procedural than it was ever meant to be (Kalaitzidis, 2025). Reflection-in-action is not about pausing at the end of a project to write a summary; it's about staying alert, attuned, and adaptive in the midst of the work itself. When a theoretical framework is truly integrated, its principles become part of this in-the-moment thinking, guiding micro-decisions without requiring constant conscious reference to a manual. That kind of embeddedness takes time, repetition, and a willingness to treat mistakes as opportunities to recalibrate rather than as verdicts of failure.

And then there's the matter of ownership. For a theoretical model to take root in practice, the people expected to use it must feel that they own it in some way. Ownership doesn't mean they invented the framework; it means they have shaped it enough to recognize their fingerprints on it (Pasquini et al., 2024). This sense of authorship transforms the framework from something borrowed into something lived. Without it, the model remains an outsider—tolerated perhaps, but never fully embraced.

Integration, in the end, is less about technical insertion than about cultural weaving. The threads of theory have to be drawn through the existing fabric of practice, looped around familiar patterns, knotted where necessary, and sometimes re-dyed to match the prevailing palette. Done well, the result doesn't look like an imported piece at all; it looks like it's been there forever, part of the texture of how things are done. Achieving that kind of seamlessness is rare, but when it happens, it's transformative—not only for the quality of work but for the sense of coherence between what people believe, what they know, and what they do.

MECHANISMS FOR EFFECTIVE KNOWLEDGE TRANSFER IN THE WORKPLACE

Knowledge in a workplace is a strange thing. It moves, but not in straight lines. It seeps, circulates, sometimes evaporates entirely before anyone notices it's gone. At its best, it flows like water through a well-designed irrigation system, reaching the roots that need it most. At its worst, it clumps into stagnant pools—hoarded in personal files, buried in unread reports, or locked in the heads of people who eventually leave without passing it on. Talking about *mechanisms* for knowledge transfer sounds deceptively simple, as if all it takes is a checklist and a few training modules. But in reality, effective transfer requires more than processes; it demands an attunement to the social, emotional, and cultural undercurrents that decide whether knowledge travels freely or gets trapped in hidden pockets.

Workplaces often underestimate how personal knowledge can be. It's not just a set of documented procedures or codified best practices; it's a living thing, shaped by the quirks, instincts, and accumulated experience of the people who hold it (Spinuzzi, 2023). This "tacit" knowledge—how to handle a client who's on the verge of walking away, the unspoken sequence of steps that keeps a fragile process from collapsing, the subtle cues in a team meeting that signal tension—doesn't lend itself easily to spreadsheets or manuals. And yet, this is often the knowledge that makes the difference between adequate performance and excellence. Mechanisms for transferring it can't rely solely on formal documentation; they must also create the conditions for observation, storytelling, and shared problem-solving.

One of the most powerful mechanisms is what might be called shadow learning—the informal practice of working alongside someone more experienced, not to be "trained" in the conventional sense but to absorb, almost by osmosis, the subtle judgment calls, timing, and improvisations that make the work sing. In theory, job shadowing is an easy sell: pair the newcomer with a veteran, let them follow along, and knowledge will pass from one to the other. But in reality, this works only when the relationship is mutual, when the experienced person is willing to slow down, narrate their decisions, and reveal the thinking behind their actions (Stanley & Clinton, 2024). Without that willingness, shadowing turns into little more than passive observation, with much of the meaning lost in translation.

Table 2. 12-week work-based learning rollout plan

Phase	Focus	Key Activities (Illustrative)
Weeks 1–2	Readiness & Scoping	Map problems; pick pilots; define success signals; norms for reflection
Weeks 3–4	Mentor Network	Pair novices ↔ experts; schedule shadowing; narrate decision-making
Weeks 5–6	Playbooks & Aids	Draft one-pagers; checklists; create shared knowledge base
Weeks 7–8	Cross-Functional Sprint	Tackle a bottleneck; weekly demos; stakeholder feedback
Weeks 9–10	Data Routines	Run charts; daily huddles; trigger thresholds for action
Weeks 11–12	Evaluate & Scale	Collect stories + metrics; refine; scale/retire; publish lessons

Equally important is the recognition that knowledge transfer isn't a one-way street. Even the most seasoned expert can gain fresh insight from someone less experienced—a newcomer's questions can illuminate assumptions that have gone unquestioned for years. When mechanisms are designed to allow this reciprocal exchange, the process stops feeling like an imposition and starts feeling like collaboration. A mentoring relationship, for example, becomes far more effective when the mentor remains open to learning from the mentee's perspective, especially in rapidly changing fields where yesterday's wisdom may already be outdated.

Technology, of course, plays a role. Digital platforms can store and disseminate vast amounts of information at unprecedented speed (Oyighan & Okwu, 2024). But here's the catch: speed is not the same as understanding. A well-stocked intranet may give the illusion of accessibility while quietly overwhelming users with uncurated, context-free material. For knowledge transfer to be effective, the technology must be more than a dumping ground—it needs to be a navigable, living archive, with clear pathways, meaningful tags, and active curation. Otherwise, critical insights drown in a sea of irrelevant noise.

Storytelling is another mechanism often overlooked in formal strategies but indispensable in practice. Stories do what bullet points can't: they provide context, emotion, and a sense of consequence. A written policy might tell you the steps to de-escalate a conflict; a story about a time when a conversation went sideways—and what was done to salvage it—tells you how those steps actually unfold in the messy, unpredictable terrain of human interaction (Olayinka, 2023). Stories stick. They carry the embedded wisdom of lived experience in a form that's memorable, relatable, and portable. They can travel across departments, generations, even organizational cultures, often in ways that formal training material can't.

There's also the delicate matter of timing. Knowledge offered too early, before someone has enough context to see its relevance, tends to slide right past them (Ramaul et al., 2024). Offered too late, it arrives as damage control rather than foresight. Effective transfer mechanisms respect this timing—they weave knowledge into moments when it can be immediately applied or when the recipient is actively seeking it. This might mean aligning training sessions with project milestones, structuring onboarding to coincide with real tasks rather than generic orientation, or embedding short bursts of learning into the rhythm of daily work instead of reserving it for formal events.

The workplace environment itself can act as either an accelerant or a barrier. In environments where competition is cutthroat, knowledge may be hoarded as a form of power (Kayyali, 2025a). People become reluctant to share what they know, fearing it will erode their value or advantage (Giray, 2024). In such cultures, no mechanism—no matter how cleverly designed—will work until the underlying incentives change. On the other hand, in environments where collaboration is genuinely valued and rewarded, knowledge sharing becomes almost instinctive, woven into everyday interactions rather than cordoned off into special programs.

Another underestimated mechanism is the deliberate use of cross-functional projects (Ahmad et al., 2023). When people from different departments are thrown together to solve a problem, they bring their varied lenses, vocabularies, and skill sets. This kind of collaboration forces implicit knowledge to surface—team members must articulate their thinking to people outside their immediate sphere, translating internal shorthand into something others can grasp. In the process, they often discover gaps in their own understanding, prompting further clarification and refinement.

The most sustainable mechanisms often combine formal and informal channels. Structured workshops, for example, can serve as anchor points for knowledge exchange, providing dedicated time and space for focused learning (Sunnemark et al., 2024). But they are far more effective when supported by ongoing, informal interactions—hallway conversations, collaborative troubleshooting, shared lunches—that keep the knowledge alive and evolving. Without this reinforcement, even the most engaging workshop tends to fade into the mental equivalent of background noise, remembered vaguely but rarely acted upon.

Peer review systems, too, can serve as potent vehicles for transfer. When a piece of work must pass through the hands and eyes of others before it's finalized, it creates opportunities for both the giver and receiver of feedback to articulate reasoning, challenge assumptions, and share techniques. Done well, peer review is less about gatekeeping and more about collective refinement—a shared commitment to raising the quality of output through mutual learning.

But perhaps the most subtle and enduring mechanism is the cultivation of a reflective habit within the organization. Reflection is not glamorous. It doesn't fit neatly into productivity dashboards, and it can feel indulgent in the face of tight deadlines. Yet, without reflection—individually and collectively—knowledge transfer tends to remain shallow, a matter of procedural handovers rather than deep conceptual understanding. Reflection allows people to connect new information with prior experience, to test it against real-world challenges, and to internalize it in ways that make it retrievable when needed. It also creates the space for questioning whether the knowledge being transferred is still valid or if it needs to be revised in light of current realities.

The question of leadership looms large here. Leaders set the tone for whether knowledge transfer is treated as a strategic priority or an afterthought (Harvey et al., 2021). When leaders themselves model openness, curiosity, and a willingness to admit gaps in their knowledge, they signal that learning is not a remedial activity but a shared responsibility. Conversely, when leaders treat expertise as a badge of infallibility, they inadvertently encourage knowledge hoarding and discourage the vulnerability required for genuine exchange.

Over time, the most effective workplaces tend to develop what might be called a "knowledge commons"—a shared pool of insights, practices, and resources that everyone contributes to and draws from. This commons doesn't emerge overnight, and it can't be built by decree. It grows through repeated acts of sharing, through systems that reward generosity of insight, and through a culture that views knowledge not as private property but as a collective asset. In such an environment, mechanisms for transfer—whether formal or informal—cease to feel like separate initiatives and instead become part of the organizational bloodstream.

In the end, knowledge transfer in the workplace is not about creating a perfect pipeline from one mind to another. Minds are not containers, and knowledge is not a static commodity. It's fluid, contextual, and often inseparable from the relationships and situations in which it's used. Mechanisms that succeed are those that honor this complexity, that create spaces—physical, digital, and social—where people can meet not just to exchange information but to think together, challenge one another, and co-create new understanding (Thomas, 2024). Anything less risks reducing knowledge to a lifeless artifact, preserved perhaps, but no longer truly alive.

EVALUATING THE IMPACT OF WORK-BASED APPROACHES ON PROBLEM SOLVING

Assessing the value of work-based approaches isn't as straightforward as tallying numbers in a ledger. Problem solving, by its very nature, resists neat quantification. Outcomes are rarely linear; they spiral, branch, and occasionally double back on themselves. What appears to be a "solution" in one frame of reference can unravel in another, revealing new challenges that were invisible at first glance. And yet, without some attempt to evaluate impact, work-based approaches risk becoming a collection of well-meaning stories—comforting to hear, but of uncertain practical weight.

The first difficulty lies in the fact that the impact of these approaches is often subtle, almost subterranean (Mammola et al., 2022). It's easy to measure how quickly a task gets completed after a process change, but harder to capture shifts in how people think about the problem in the first place. Has the approach increased their capacity to reframe issues, to anticipate consequences, to see the connections between seemingly unrelated elements? These are the changes that matter most, but they don't show up neatly on a performance dashboard.

And then there's the question of time. Some results emerge quickly—a smoother workflow, a reduction in errors, a noticeable drop in customer complaints. Others take months or even years to fully manifest. A culture of reflective practice, for instance, doesn't spring into being after a single intervention; it builds slowly, accumulating strength with each cycle of action and reflection. Evaluating impact too soon risks mistaking an early ripple for the whole wave.

Quantitative indicators have their place, but they often tell only the outer story (Andrews, 2021). You can measure how many hours were saved, how many defects avoided, how many projects finished on time. These are important, but they don't explain *why* the changes happened or how durable they might be. To understand that, you need to look at the inner story—the one told through narratives, interviews, observation, and the lived experiences of those involved. The best evaluations are those that weave these two kinds of evidence together, creating a more textured picture of both the visible and invisible effects.

Of course, numbers can be seductive. They give the illusion of objectivity, of a clear verdict. But a percentage increase in efficiency might mask the fact that the improvement came at the cost of employee burnout or reduced creativity. A project that "met all targets" might have done so by avoiding the deeper, riskier questions that could have led to more transformative change. Work-based approaches often aim not just for quick fixes but for deeper, systemic shifts—and those rarely fit neatly into a spreadsheet.

Another challenge in evaluation is the role of context. A work-based approach that produces dramatic results in one setting may deliver only modest gains in another, not because the approach is flawed, but because the conditions are different. Organizational culture, leadership style, available resources, even the prevailing mood of the workforce—these can all amplify or dampen the effect (Zhang, 2024). Any serious evaluation must acknowledge this interplay, resisting the temptation to draw sweeping conclusions from a single case.

One of the most telling signs of impact is the extent to which problem-solving capacity becomes self-sustaining. In other words, can the team or organization continue to apply the principles of the work-based approach without external prompting? If a consultant or facilitator steps away, does the practice wither, or does it evolve naturally in response to new challenges? This kind of resilience is harder to measure than immediate outcomes, but it's often the clearest indicator that the approach has truly taken root.

Then there's the matter of unintended consequences. No intervention operates in a vacuum; every change ripples outward, sometimes in unexpected ways. A work-based project aimed at streamlining communication might succeed in speeding up decision-making, but inadvertently erode the informal conversations where innovative ideas used to surface (Mayer, 2024). An evaluation worth its salt looks for these side effects—both positive and negative—recognizing that they are part of the real impact, not peripheral noise.

Some evaluators rely heavily on before-and-after comparisons, but these can be misleading. Workplaces are dynamic systems, constantly in flux. Changes in the wider environment—a shift in market conditions, a change in leadership, an unexpected crisis—can influence outcomes as much as the intervention itself. To account for this, impact assessment must be both longitudinal and adaptive, tracking patterns over time while remaining alert to external factors.

The human dimension, as always, complicates things further. People don't just adopt a work-based approach; they interpret it, adapt it, sometimes subvert it to fit their own purposes. The "official" version of the approach may look very different from the way it is actually lived out in practice. Evaluations that ignore this gap risk mistaking formal compliance for genuine engagement (Hartmann et al., 2024). Observing how people talk about the approach in informal settings, how they reference it (or don't) in moments of pressure, can reveal far more about its real influence than any formal report.

One telling question is whether the approach changes the *questions* people ask when confronted with a problem. Are they still looking for quick fixes, or have they begun probing for underlying causes? Are they more willing to test small-scale experiments before committing to a full-scale rollout? Are they drawing on a wider range of perspectives, seeking out input from those who might previously have been excluded from the conversation? These shifts in mindset are harder to quantify, but they are often the clearest signs that a work-based approach is reshaping the problem-solving culture.

It's tempting to think of evaluation as a final step, something that happens after the work is done. But in reality, the most meaningful assessments are built into the process from the start. They involve ongoing reflection, feedback loops, and iterative adjustments. The act of evaluating becomes itself a form of problem solving, a way of continually refining both the approach and the criteria by which its success is judged (Daryanes et al., 2023).

This raises another point: the criteria for "success" are not fixed. They must be negotiated, revisited, and sometimes radically revised. What counts as a positive outcome will vary depending on whose perspective you take. For management, it might be improved efficiency; for frontline staff, it might be reduced stress; for clients, it might be faster response times or better quality service. A comprehensive evaluation gives weight to all these perspectives, even when they conflict.

A final, perhaps uncomfortable truth is that not all impacts can—or should—be measured in traditional terms. Some of the most profound changes brought about by work-based approaches are intangible: a shift in confidence, a greater sense of agency, the feeling that one's voice is heard and valued (Guillemin & Nicholas, 2022). These are not "soft" outcomes in the dismissive sense; they are foundational to sustained problem-solving capacity. But they require evaluators to venture beyond their comfort zones, to listen as much as they measure, and to accept that the richest insights may come in the form of a story told over coffee rather than a chart in a report.

The paradox of evaluating work-based approaches is that the process must mirror the very principles it is assessing. It must be participatory, context-sensitive, iterative, and willing to learn from surprises. A rigid, top-down evaluation risks missing the essence of the approach, which is to adapt fluidly to the real conditions of the workplace (George, 2024). The best evaluations, like the best problem-solving efforts, are living conversations—open-ended, responsive, and rooted in the messy reality of human work.

In the end, the impact of a work-based approach is not just about solving the problems it was designed to address. It's about changing the way problems are *seen*, discussed, and tackled in the future. If an organization emerges from the process more curious, more willing to experiment, and more capable of learning from its own experience, then the approach has succeeded in the deepest sense—even if the original metrics tell only part of the story.

FUTURE DIRECTIONS FOR ENHANCING WORK-BASED LEARNING MODELS

Projecting the evolution of work-based learning models is not simply a matter of tacking new tools onto old frameworks or swapping out familiar jargon for shinier terms (Johnson, 2024). The workplace is in flux—faster than at any point in living memory—and these models, if they are to remain relevant, must evolve with it. The question is not whether change will come, but how it will reconfigure the relationship between learning and doing. One suspects it will be less about wholesale reinvention than about deep recalibration, a shifting of balance points, a willingness to let certain long-cherished assumptions quietly expire.

A future worth paying attention to is one in which work-based learning ceases to be a "program" or "initiative" and becomes a persistent, almost invisible thread running through the fabric of organizational life. That means dissolving the artificial boundary between "training time" and "working time" until the two are indistinguishable. Learning will not be something people step away from their desks to do; it will be the desk, the meeting, the client call, the moment of troubleshooting on a factory floor. If this sounds obvious, it's worth asking why so many organizations still relegate learning to scheduled events that exist outside the tempo of daily work.

The integration of emerging technologies is unavoidable, but the trick will be resisting the seduction of gimmickry. Artificial intelligence, immersive simulations, adaptive learning platforms—these can all enhance work-based models, but only if they deepen reflection and application rather than reducing learning to an efficient content-delivery pipeline (Aithal et al., 2024). A future-ready model might, for example, use AI not to replace human mentors but to surface patterns in performance data that prompt richer conversations between mentor and learner (Kayyali, 2025b). It could create augmented-reality overlays in physical workspaces that offer contextual guidance, while still leaving space for human judgment to overrule the algorithm.

Another direction, perhaps less glamorous but no less critical, is the deliberate weaving of cross-disciplinary exposure into the DNA of work-based learning. In complex environments, the capacity to borrow insight from distant fields is often what unlocks innovative solutions (Zubari & Sherman, 2024). A nurse who understands basic principles of systems engineering, a software developer versed in the psychology of human error, a policy analyst with grounding in environmental science—these hybrid perspectives make for problem solvers who can navigate tangled systems with more agility. This implies that future models will need to design opportunities for purposeful collisions between domains, not as one-off events but as recurring features of the work environment.

Cultural adaptability will be another non-negotiable. Work-based learning, as it stands, often assumes a certain organizational culture—one that is relatively open to experimentation, transparent in communication, and tolerant of small-scale failure. Yet, in practice, many workplaces operate in more guarded, hierarchical, or risk-averse modes. Future models will have to become multilingual in a cultural sense, able to adapt their tone, cadence, and structures to environments where direct challenge is frowned upon or where authority is tightly centralized. This means equipping facilitators and leaders with cultural intelligence—not just "soft skills" but the ability to recognize and navigate the unwritten rules of interaction that shape how knowledge flows.

There's also an argument to be made for slowing down. In an age where speed is fetishized, where every process is urged toward optimization, work-based learning risks becoming another casualty of the efficiency drive—compressed into the smallest possible time slots, stripped of the reflective pauses that give it depth. Future directions must protect the space for slowness: for conversations that wander, for experiments that fail in ways that spark insight, for unhurried observation of how a solution unfolds over time. The pressure to deliver quick wins can easily erode the long-term capacity that these models aim to build.

Sustainability—in both ecological and human terms—will need to sit closer to the center (Norman, 2023). Future work-based learning models could act as incubators for practices that reduce waste, conserve resources, and promote resilience in the face of environmental volatility. But sustainability also applies to human energy: models that push for constant upskilling without regard for burnout will collapse under their own contradictions. This suggests a shift toward designing learning experiences that replenish as much as they demand—environments where curiosity is nurtured, where learners leave an engagement with more vitality than they entered it.

The social architecture of work-based learning will almost certainly become more decentralized. Rigid, top-down structures are ill-suited to the fast-moving problems that define modern work (Brennan, 2021). Expect to see models that empower smaller, semi-autonomous groups to identify their own learning needs, draw on shared resources, and experiment with context-specific adaptations. This decentralization doesn't mean abandoning coherence; rather, it calls for a framework of shared principles that different teams can interpret in locally relevant ways. Think of it as a jazz score: the melody is consistent, but the improvisations vary with the players and the moment.

Another likely trajectory is the embedding of ethical reflection as a core element rather than a peripheral add-on (Kayyali, 2026). In industries where technological change is outpacing regulation, work-based learning models will need to help participants not only solve problems but interrogate the implications of their solutions. A future-ready model might integrate structured dilemmas into live projects, prompting teams to wrestle with questions of equity, privacy, environmental impact, and unintended consequences as part of the problem-solving process itself (Djuwari, 2025). This is not just a moral luxury—it is becoming a strategic necessity in a world where reputational damage can spread faster than the truth.

The role of narrative will almost certainly expand. Data-driven insights are invaluable, but humans still make sense of the world through stories (Gade, 2021). Future models may find ways to systematically capture and circulate the narratives that emerge from work-based learning: not sanitized success stories, but textured accounts of struggle, adaptation, and gradual progress. These narratives will serve as living case studies, feeding back into the collective knowledge base and reminding participants that the messy, iterative nature of their work is not a flaw but the very engine of growth.

On a more structural level, the boundaries between formal education and workplace learning will continue to dissolve. Partnerships between academic institutions and industries will evolve from transactional arrangements—internships, project placements—into ongoing collaborations where curricula are shaped by real-time industry needs and workplaces serve as extended classrooms (Aithal & Maiya, 2023). In such a model, learners might oscillate seamlessly between academic study and applied projects, with credit and recognition flowing both ways. This would require new credentialing systems, ones capable of validating learning that happens outside conventional academic boundaries without diluting rigor.

The personalization of learning paths will also deepen. If current models dabble in adaptive learning, future iterations may go further, constructing highly individualized trajectories that take into account not just skills gaps but learning preferences, cognitive styles, career aspirations, and even energy rhythms (Tariq, 2024). This could mean that two people in the same role engage with the same core concepts through entirely different modalities—one through immersive simulation, another through guided mentorship, another through reflective journaling tied to live projects. Technology can facilitate this, but the real artistry will lie in designing systems flexible enough to allow for personalization without fragmenting the shared culture of learning.

One cannot ignore the geopolitical and economic forces that will inevitably shape these models. The rise of remote and distributed workforces means that future work-based learning must contend with physical distance, time-zone separation, and the loss of spontaneous interactions that often seed knowledge transfer. In response, models will need to cultivate intentional spaces—digital and occasional physical gatherings—where the serendipity of informal exchange can be recreated or approximated. This is harder than it sounds; serendipity resists scheduling. Yet without these touchpoints, learning risks becoming overly transactional, stripped of the relational depth that makes it stick.

It's worth considering, too, that the problems future workplaces face may be more volatile and more interdependent than those of today. Climate disruption, technological displacement, resource scarcity, and shifting demographics will all exert pressure on the way work is organized. Work-based learning models will need to prepare participants not only for the problems they can see but for the ones that emerge from the edges, the slow-burn issues that suddenly leap into urgency. This implies a stronger emphasis on foresight skills—scanning weak signals, building scenarios, rehearsing responses to multiple possible futures.

The final, perhaps most radical, direction is a philosophical one: a reimagining of the purpose of work-based learning itself. If the current models are primarily aimed at increasing competence, efficiency, and adaptability, the next generation might expand the frame to include personal and collective flourishing (Mountbatten-O'Malley & Morris, 2025). This would mean valuing qualities like meaning-making, civic responsibility, and the capacity to contribute to the wider social good as much as technical proficiency. Such a shift would require courage, as it runs counter to the narrow metrics that dominate most organizational evaluation systems. But if work-based learning is truly about preparing people for the realities they will face, then ignoring the moral and existential dimensions of work would be an oversight of the highest order.

In the end, the future of these models will depend less on any single innovation than on a mindset: a readiness to keep the models alive, porous, and responsive to the shifting patterns of the world around them. Static frameworks will wither. Those that thrive will be the ones willing to continually renegotiate their own shape, to listen closely to the voices at the margins, and to hold open the possibility that the next step forward may come from an unexpected direction. The real challenge will not be in predicting the future but in building models supple enough to meet it, whatever form it takes.

CONCLUSION

Work-based models emerge as a compelling answer to one of the most persistent questions in education and professional development: *How can we ensure that knowledge translates into meaningful action?* Throughout this chapter, we have seen that the strength of these models lies not in privileging theory over practice—or vice versa—but in forging an active, reciprocal relationship between the two. By positioning the workplace as both the subject and the site of learning, work-based models transform abstract concepts into living, evolving strategies that can address the nuances of real-world problems.

These models remind us that professional expertise is not a static state achieved upon graduation or certification; rather, it is a dynamic, lifelong process of learning, applying, reflecting, and refining. The iterative cycles inherent in work-based approaches allow practitioners to develop a deeper understanding of both the problems they face and the frameworks they employ. In doing so, they foster a form of adaptive competence that is essential for navigating environments characterized by rapid technological change, shifting market conditions, and complex social dynamics.

Furthermore, the collaborative nature of work-based models—linking academia, industry, and communities—ensures that knowledge does not remain siloed. When researchers and practitioners work together, theories can be tested against the unpredictability of human and organizational behavior, and practical innovations can be captured, analyzed, and shared more widely. This exchange enriches both spheres: academia gains relevance and practical grounding, while professional practice gains depth and conceptual clarity.

The broader implication is that work-based models are not merely tools for solving immediate problems; they are vehicles for cultural change within organizations. They promote a mindset in which learning is continuous, reflection is valued, and adaptation is expected. They challenge the notion that knowledge flows in a single direction—from the "expert" to the "learner"—and instead embrace a more democratic, co-constructed approach to problem solving.

Looking ahead, the evolution of work-based models will be shaped by emerging technologies, shifting workforce demographics, and evolving societal expectations. Digital platforms, for instance, can extend the reach and impact of work-based learning, enabling collaboration across geographical and organizational boundaries. At the same time, ethical considerations, inclusivity, and sustainability must be integrated into these models to ensure they are not only effective but also socially responsible.

Ultimately, the success of work-based models depends on our willingness to view the workplace not as a separate sphere from education but as an integral, vibrant space for intellectual growth and practical innovation. By embracing this perspective, we can cultivate professionals who are not just consumers of knowledge but active contributors to its ongoing development—bridging theory and practice in ways that are transformative, enduring, and profoundly human.

REFERENCES

Ahmad, T., Boit, J., & Aakula, A. (2023). The role of cross-functional collaboration in digital transformation. *Journal of Computational Intelligence and Robotics*, *3*(1), 205–242.

Aithal, P. S., & Maiya, A. K. (2023). Innovations in higher education industry–Shaping the future. [IJCSBE]. *International Journal of Case Studies in Business, IT, and Education*, *7*(4), 283–311. DOI: 10.47992/IJCSBE.2581.6942.0321

Aithal, P. S., Prabhu, S., & Aithal, S. (2024). Future of higher education through technology prediction and forecasting. Poornaprajna International Journal of Management, Education, and Social Science (PIJMESS), 1(1), 01-50.

Andrews, M. (2021). Quality indicators in narrative research. *Qualitative Research in Psychology*, *18*(3), 353–368. DOI: 10.1080/14780887.2020.1769241

Anglin, A. H., Kincaid, P. A., Short, J. C., & Allen, D. G. (2022). Role theory perspectives: Past, present, and future applications of role theories in management research. *Journal of Management*, *48*(6), 1469–1502. DOI: 10.1177/01492063221081442

Aryal, R. (2022, December). Critical self-reflective engagement to improve professional development for a teacher educator. In Mathematics Education Forum Chitwan (Vol. 7, No. 7, pp. 66-81). DOI: 10.3126/mefc.v7i7.54787

Beard, C. (2022). *Experiential learning design: Theoretical foundations and effective principles*. Routledge. DOI: 10.4324/9781003030867

Brennan, J. (2021). Flexible learning pathways in British higher education: A decentralized and market-based system.

Coco, L. K., Heidler, P., Fischer, H. A., Albanese, V., Marzo, R. R., & Kozon, V. (2023). When the going gets challenging—Motivational theories as a driver for workplace health promotion, employees well-being and quality of life. *Behavioral Sciences (Basel, Switzerland)*, *13*(11), 898. DOI: 10.3390/bs13110898 PMID: 37998645

Cohnitz, D., & Nicolai, C. (2021). How to adopt a logic. *Dialectica*, *75*(4), 1–31. DOI: 10.48106/dial.v75.i4.03

Daryanes, F., Darmadi, D., Fikri, K., Sayuti, I., Rusandi, M. A., & Situmorang, D. D. B. (2023). The development of articulate storyline interactive learning media based on case methods to train student's problem-solving ability. *Heliyon*, *9*(4), e15082. DOI: 10.1016/j.heliyon.2023.e15082 PMID: 37101635

Djuwari, M. (2025). *LEADERSHIP IN A DIGITALLY DISRUPTED SOCIETY: Issues, Problems, and Solutions*. Goresan Pena.

Dosi, G. (2023). *The foundations of complex evolving economies: Part one: Innovation, organization, and industrial dynamics*. Oxford University Press. DOI: 10.1093/oso/9780192865922.001.0001

Eriksson, O., & Nyström, J. (2025). Unpacking Quality Deficiency Costs: A Framework for Mapping and Managing Quality Deficiency Costs at Company X, a large Swedish transportation company.

Gade, K. R. (2021). Data-driven decision making in a complex world. Journal of computational innovation, 1(1).

Galleli, B., & Amaral, L. (2025). Bridging Institutional Theory and Social and Environmental Efforts in Management: A Review and Research Agenda. *Journal of Management*, •••, 01492063251322429.

George, A. S. (2024). The symbiotic relationship between visionary and pragmatic leadership in propelling organizational success. *Partners Universal International Innovation Journal*, 2(3), 57–79.

Ghaleb, B. D. S. (2024). The concept of alienation and alienation in organizations. *Pancasila International Journal of Applied Social Science*, 2(2), 206–223. DOI: 10.59653/pancasila.v2i02.714

Giray, L. (2024). AI shaming: The silent stigma among academic writers and researchers. *Annals of Biomedical Engineering*, *52*(9), 2319–2324. DOI: 10.1007/s10439-024-03582-1 PMID: 38977530

Guillemin, M., & Nicholas, R. (2022). Core values at work—Essential elements of a healthy workplace. *International Journal of Environmental Research and Public Health*, *19*(19), 12505. DOI: 10.3390/ijerph191912505 PMID: 36231819

Hartmann, D., De Pereira, J. R. L., Streitbörger, C., & Berendt, B. (2024). Addressing the regulatory gap: Moving towards an EU AI audit ecosystem beyond the AI Act by including civil society. *AI and Ethics*, •••, 1–22.

Harvey, W. S., Mitchell, V. W., Almeida Jones, A., & Knight, E. (2021). The tensions of defining and developing thought leadership within knowledge-intensive firms. *Journal of Knowledge Management*, *25*(11), 1–33. DOI: 10.1108/JKM-06-2020-0431

Hayes, J., Shumailov, I., Triantafillou, E., Khalifa, A., & Papernot, N. (2025, April). Inexact unlearning needs more careful evaluations to avoid a false sense of privacy. In *2025 IEEE Conference on Secure and Trustworthy Machine Learning (SaTML)* (pp. 497-519). IEEE. DOI: 10.1109/SaTML64287.2025.00034

Hökkä, P., Vähäsantanen, K., & Ikävalko, H. (2023). An integrative approach to emotional agency at work. *Vocations and Learning*, *16*(1), 23–46. DOI: 10.1007/s12186-022-09299-3

Ing, D., & Metcalf, G. (2023). Reframing systems thinking for systems changes: Sciencing and philosophizing from pragmatism towards processes as rhythms. *Journal of the International Society for the Systems Sciences*, *67*(4154).

Jiang, S., & Marbach, P. (2025). Social Rewards and Recursive Feedback: A Procedural Model of Norm Emergence. Preprint available on *SocArXiv*, https://osf. io/preprints/socarxiv

Johnson, D. (2024). The Role of Work-Based Learning in Developing Future Skills and Competencies for the Workforce in the Fourth Industrial Revolution.

Kalaitzidis, T. J. (2025). How Generative AI Fixes What Higher Education Broke.

Kayyali, M. (2025 A). Balancing Work and Life Techniques for Maintaining Emotional Wellbeing in Entrepreneurship. In Supporting Psychological and Emotional Wellbeing Among Entrepreneurs (pp. 33-58). IGI Global.

Kayyali, M. (2025). B). The Role of Artificial Intelligence in Transforming Business Models. In *AI-Driven Business Model Innovation* (pp. 71–98). IGI Global Scientific Publishing. DOI: 10.4018/979-8-3693-9571-4.ch003

Kayyali, M. (2026). Ethical AI and Automation in the Workplace. In Leading Inclusive Workplaces Through Digital Transformation and Organizational Change (pp. 103-138). IGI Global Scientific Publishing.

Krishnan, N. (2025). Advancing multi-agent systems through model context protocol: Architecture, implementation, and applications. arXiv preprint arXiv:2504.21030.

Maksoud, F. J., de la Paz, M. F. V., Hann, A. J., Thanarak, J., Reilly, G. C., Claeyssens, F., & Zhang, Y. S. (2022). Porous biomaterials for tissue engineering: A review. *Journal of Materials Chemistry. B*, *10*(40), 8111–8165. DOI: 10.1039/D1TB02628C PMID: 36205119

Mammola, S., Meierhofer, M. B., Borges, P. A., Colado, R., Culver, D. C., Deharveng, L., Delić, T., Di Lorenzo, T., Dražina, T., Ferreira, R. L., Fiasca, B., Fišer, C., Galassi, D. M. P., Garzoli, L., Gerovasileiou, V., Griebler, C., Halse, S., Howarth, F. G., Isaia, M., & Cardoso, P. (2022). Towards evidence-based conservation of subterranean ecosystems. *Biological Reviews of the Cambridge Philosophical Society*, *97*(4), 1476–1510. DOI: 10.1111/brv.12851 PMID: 35315207

Marsick, V. J., Fichter, R., & Watkins, K. E. (2021). From work-based learning to learning-based work: Exploring the changing relationship between learning and work. The Sage handbook of learning and work, 177-193.

Mayer, G. (2024). Inspired by Data: AI's transformative role in corporate communication. EGEA spa.

Mountbatten-O'Malley, E., & Morris, T. H. (2025). Self-directed flourishing: A conceptual meta-framework for dealing with the challenges of 21st-century learning and education. *Quality Education for All*, *2*(1), 171–189. DOI: 10.1108/QEA-03-2024-0029

Norman, D. A. (2023). *Design for a better world: Meaningful, sustainable, humanity centered.* MIT Press. DOI: 10.1080/08956308.2023.2183015

Olayinka, A. S. (2023). Culture as a Means of De-escalating Conflict and Maintaining Peace. *Journal of Anthropological Research*, *6*, 167.

Oyighan, D., & Okwu, E. (2024). Social media for information dissemination in the digital era. RAY. *International Journal of Multidisciplinary Studies*, *10*(1), 1–21.

Pasquini, D., Kornaropoulos, E. M., & Ateniese, G. (2024). Llmmap: Fingerprinting for large language models. arXiv preprint arXiv:2407.15847.

Ramaul, L., Ritala, P., & Ruokonen, M. (2024). Creational and conversational AI affordances: How the new breed of chatbots is revolutionizing knowledge industries. *Business Horizons*, *67*(5), 615–627. DOI: 10.1016/j.bushor.2024.05.006

Spinuzzi, C. (2023). What is a workplace? Principles for bounding case studies of genres, processes, objects, and organizations. *Written Communication*, *40*(4), 1027–1069. DOI: 10.1177/07410883231185875

Stanley, P. D., & Clinton, J. R. (2024). *Connecting: The mentoring relationships you need to succeed in life*. NavPress.

Sugiyama, K., Ladge, J. J., & Dokko, G. (2024). Stable anchors and dynamic evolution: A paradox theory of career identity maintenance and change. *Academy of Management Review*, *49*(1), 135–154. DOI: 10.5465/amr.2020.0351

Sunnemark, F., Lundqvist Westin, W., Al Saad, T., & Assmo, P. (2024). Exploring barriers and facilitators to knowledge transfer and learning processes through a cross-departmental collaborative project in a municipal organization. *The Learning Organization*, *31*(3), 358–374. DOI: 10.1108/TLO-01-2023-0003

Tariq, M. U. (2024). Navigating the personalization pathway: Implementing adaptive learning technologies in higher education. In *Adaptive Learning Technologies for Higher Education* (pp. 265–291). IGI Global. DOI: 10.4018/979-8-3693-3641-0.ch012

Taylor, K. L., & Colet, N. R. (2023). Making the shift from faculty development to educational development: A conceptual framework grounded in practice. In *Building teaching capacities in higher education* (pp. 139–167). Routledge. DOI: 10.4324/9781003443346-10

Thomas, A. (2024). Digitally transforming the organization through knowledge management: A socio-technical system (STS) perspective. *European Journal of Innovation Management*, *27*(9), 437–460. DOI: 10.1108/EJIM-02-2024-0114

Zhang, Y. (2024). Cultivating a culture of innovation: The impact of leadership style on employee well-being and organizational creativity. *International Journal of Global Economics and Management*, *2*(1), 202–210. DOI: 10.62051/ijgem.v2n1.26

Zhao, Z. (2024). Theoretical and practical exploration of work-based learning curriculum with a case study. Vocation, Technology & Education, 1(1).

Zubari, H., & Sherman, S. (2024, May). Unlocking Innovation Potential: A Pragmatic Approach to Overcoming Barriers and Fostering Collaboration. In SPE Gas & Oil Technology Showcase and Conference (p. D021S017R001). SPE. DOI: 10.2118/219106-MS

KEY TERMS AND DEFINITIONS

Adaptive Expertise: the capacity to flexibly apply and evolve methods in novel, messy, or fast-changing situations.

Communities of Practice (CoP): peer networks that share patterns, stories, and tools to spread practical know-how.

Experiential Learning Cycle: iterating through do → reflect → conceptualize → experiment on authentic workplace tasks.

Knowledge Transfer Mechanisms: purposeful routines (shadowing, playbooks, huddles) that move insight across roles and teams.

Reflective Practice: systematic self-questioning that surfaces assumptions and reframes problems during and after action.

Tacit Knowledge: context-bound know-how that is hard to codify and often transferred via mentoring and observation.

Work-Based Learning (WBL): structured learning embedded in real work so theory and practice continuously inform each other.

Section 3
Research into Applied Models

Chapter 7
Randomization as a Problem-Solving Tool in 21st Century Learning

Juan Manuel Castro-Carracedo
https://orcid.org/0000-0001-6745-0979
Pontifical University of Salamanca, Spain

ABSTRACT

This chapter explores the pedagogical potential of randomization as a problem-solving strategy in 21st-century education. Departing from its conventional application in experimental research, randomization is reinterpreted as an instructional instrument aimed at cultivating adaptability, metacognitive awareness, and creative reasoning. The chapter draws on constructivist and sociocultural theories to present a university-level intervention in a course on English morphosyntax in which grammar instruction was randomized. The students participated in a series of syntactic tasks that were not anticipated and that prompted them to adopt a flexible mindset and engage in reflective practice. The findings indicate that pedagogical randomization has the potential to enhance conceptual understanding and instructional creativity. The chapter presents a replicable model for integrating structured unpredictability into teacher education, demonstrating how randomness can support dynamic, context-aware, and learner-centered instruction.

1. INTRODUCTION

Contemporary education has evolved beyond the confines of traditional problem-solving exercises, which are often predictable and have predefined answers. Instead, it has become imperative for learners to confront uncertainty, adapt to novel scenarios,

DOI: 10.4018/979-8-3373-3301-4.ch007

and engage in flexible thinking. This shift is indicative of more extensive changes in the demands placed on education systems in the 21st century. These changes are shaped by transformations in how knowledge is produced, accessed, and applied. They are also shaped by increasing digital complexity and social volatility. Within this framework, randomization is explored not as a methodological artifact of experimental design, but as a pedagogical strategy that can foster cognitive adaptability, metalinguistic awareness, and creative reasoning.

In this context, *pedagogical randomization* refers to the intentional integration of structured unpredictability into instructional design. While randomness in educational research typically concerns sample allocation or control of bias, its pedagogical application entails the deliberate use of task variability, content shifts, and unanticipated challenges to stimulate learning. Far from being a source of disorder, pedagogical randomization operates as a principle of generative disruption—one that mirrors real-world complexity and cultivates metacognitive strategies, decision-making, and adaptive thinking. It introduces bounded uncertainty that is not chaotic but cognitively productive, particularly when aligned with learning goals and supported by clear instructional scaffolding.

Rather than regarding *randomization* as a mere research artifact or an occasional classroom gimmick, this approach explores its potential as a deliberate principle of curriculum design. The analysis is grounded in an authentic university intervention that reimagines how grammar instruction can become a dynamic environment for conceptual exploration and instructional creativity. The proposal posits that pedagogical *randomization* can function not only as a pedagogical challenge, but also as a tool for cultivating instructional adaptability. This empowers future teachers to design varied activities, respond creatively to student needs, and navigate the unpredictability inherent in real classrooms.

The present proposal is grounded in a real-world classroom intervention developed in the *English Morphosyntax* course at Universidad Pontificia de Salamanca. The present study is grounded in established learning theories, including constructivism, sociocultural interaction, and cognitive complexity. It explores how task variability and unpredictability can reshape grammar instruction into a context for experimentation, decision-making, and pedagogical growth. The present study offers a practical model for integrating *randomization* into teacher education in ways that are both feasible and transformative. This model traces the full cycle from theoretical foundation to classroom implementation and student outcomes.

The foundation of this work is an expanded understanding of pedagogical *randomization*. This is not merely an occasional tactic or source of novelty; rather, it is a principle of instructional design that introduces bounded unpredictability. This principle has the capacity to stimulate deeper thinking, adaptive reasoning, and real-time judgment. When employed intentionally, randomness can serve as a constructive constraint that disrupts passive learning routines, encourages active problem-solving, and mirrors the complexity of real-world cognition. Its educational value becomes especially relevant in light of international frameworks such as the OECD *Learning Compass 2030* or UNESCO's *Future of Education* initiative, which emphasize the cultivation of learner autonomy, adaptability, and lifelong learning competences. This perspective reframes randomness as a generative force in education, one that can be structured, scaffolded, and aligned with learning goals to foster not only engagement, but also lasting insight and transferable skills.

2. LITERATURE REVIEW

2.1. From Experimental Design to Pedagogical Strategy

Historically, *randomization* has served as a fundamental principle in the design of scientific research, prized for its potential to mitigate the influence of bias. However, its translation into a pedagogical strategy is relatively novel. In the context of educational research, *randomization* is a method of assigning participants to experimental or control groups with the objective of ensuring internal validity (Creswell & Creswell, 2018). However, in recent years, researchers have begun to explore how *randomization*, when intentionally embedded within instructional design, can function as a powerful catalyst for learning. Rather than regarding it as a mere background condition for valid research, scholars now advocate for its integration as a generative mechanism that shapes the very fabric of educational experience (Eichler & Vogel, 2014; Batanero, 2015).

This reconceptualization reflects a more extensive shift in the epistemological foundations of education. When considered not as disorder but as structured unpredictability, randomness can serve as a catalyst for engagement, cognitive flexibility, and creative problem-solving (Jiménez-Buedo & Russo, 2021). This is particularly salient in volatile and complex (VUCA) environments. This approach is consistent with the educational imperatives of the 21st century, which emphasize not only the absorption of knowledge but also the ability to adapt to uncertainty, manage ambiguity, and make decisions under incomplete information (Vedovelli, 2022).

In the realm of computer science and engineering education, these principles have already been firmly established. Randomized code generation, stochastic testing environments, and unpredictable simulation parameters are routinely used to train students in debugging, fault tolerance, and scenario planning. As demonstrated by Groce et al. (2007), the implementation of randomized software testing exercises has been shown to encourage learners to contemplate a multitude of execution pathways and cultivate more resilient error-handling methodologies. Pecher et al.

(2023) have recently analyzed how randomness in data-scarce AI environments can stabilize learning, thereby fostering generalization rather than overfitting. This insight has significant implications for human learning contexts. In a similar vein, Pacheco et al. (2007) propose a randomized assessment model in which learners encounter dynamically generated tasks, not to evaluate memorization but to assess adaptive reasoning and real-time decision-making.

This pedagogical function of randomness is consistent with constructivist and sociocognitive learning theories (Turnbull & Justice, 2012; Vygotsky, 1978). According to these frameworks, knowledge is not passively received but actively constructed, particularly when learners are challenged to reconfigure prior understanding in response to novel stimuli. Revati (2024) posits that random variability in problem-based environments enhances both transfer and abstraction, thereby allowing students to build conceptual bridges across different situations rather than relying on fixed schemas.

The philosophical underpinnings of this approach are also gaining traction. Briggs (2016) characterizes randomness as a productive epistemic condition, positing it not as a failure of control but as a necessary precondition for generating new knowledge in uncertain contexts. When applied to education, this perspective positions randomness as a means of cultivating emergent cognition, allowing students to encounter unexpected situations that challenge habitual thinking and stimulate creative inference (Eichler & Vogel, 2014).

Moreover, the incorporation of randomness has the potential to facilitate a rethinking of instructional routines and curricular determinism. Pedagogical frameworks such as inquiry-based learning (IBL), problem-based learning (PBL), and design-based learning are predicated on elements of uncertainty and iteration (Amaral et al., 2021; Capolla et al., 2023). The incorporation of *randomization* within these methodologies serves to enhance their efficacy, thereby facilitating diversified responses and learner agency. As Popov (2023) emphasizes, the combination of task variability with reflective practices and collaborative interaction fosters deeper metacognitive engagement and resilience.

Videla-Reyes and Aguayo's (2022) theoretical framework, termed the "*pedagogy of uncertainty*," further elaborates on this concept. It advocates for educational models that foster learners' tolerance for ambiguity, encourage exploration of multiple pathways, and embrace iterative failure as an inherent component of the learning process. In such models, randomness ceases to pose a threat to order or efficacy; rather, it becomes a condition of possibility for critical thinking, systemic understanding, and adaptive expertise (Bonnet & Glazier, 2024).

In essence, redefining randomness from a methodological necessity to a fundamental pedagogical principle shifts our understanding of the act of learning. The prevailing paradigm necessitates educational environments that do not perceive unpredictability as an aberration to be rectified; rather, it is imperative to conceptualize such unpredictability as a generative facet to be harnessed (Imhof et al., 2020). The efficacy of introducing structured randomness in various educational settings has been demonstrated in numerous studies. In the context of programming courses (Groce et al., 2007), language instruction (Popov, 2023), and interdisciplinary classrooms (Ahn et al., 2019), the integration of structured randomness has been shown to provide learners with authentic opportunities to engage with complexity, navigate uncertainty, and develop flexible, transferable knowledge.

2.2. Randomness, Adaptivity, and Cognitive Engagement

A growing body of empirical research in the fields of educational psychology, cognitive science, and instructional design has demonstrated that the incorporation of well-structured unpredictability within the learning environment is directly associated with the development of critical cognitive and metacognitive competencies. Contrary to the notion that it disrupts learning, the strategic calibration of randomness has been shown to foster adaptivity, metacognitive regulation, and critical engagement. These components are central to autonomous and effective learning in the 21st century (Zimmerman, 2002; Spiro et al., 2017; Vedovelli, 2022).

Research has demonstrated that the variability in learning tasks has the potential to enhance cognitive engagement by prompting learners to exert greater control over their attentional and monitoring systems. Rather than relying on established response patterns, students must proactively discern between pertinent and irrelevant cues, adapt their strategies in real time, and demonstrate a high degree of autonomy in their cognitive processes. For instance, Nugiel et al. (2023) demonstrated that increased task variability activates the brain's frontoparietal control network, which is associated with cognitive flexibility and adaptive control. In a similar vein, Andreadis and Quinlan's (2010) study revealed that task-switching conditions, which inherently entail unpredictability, resulted in enhanced performance on subsequent tasks that demanded executive control. In the context of instructional design, Rosen (2019) posits that the incorporation of controlled variability in classroom tasks compels learners to manage interference and ambiguity, thereby fortifying their capacity to maintain attention and self-regulate. These findings are consistent with the observations reported by D'Mello et al. (2014), who noted that fluctuations in task demands within digital learning environments can stimulate productive confusion, a state that has been demonstrated to be positively correlated with deeper learning outcomes when supported by appropriate scaffolding.

The findings of Gupta et al. (2023) serve to reinforce this relationship. In an experimental study with high school and university students, those exposed to randomly generated validation challenges (including generative AI tasks and logic puzzles with shifting premises) outperformed control groups on measures of cognitive adaptability, error correction, and transfer of learning. These gains were not confined to performance metrics; qualitative data also demonstrated that learners in randomized conditions exhibited enhanced emotional resilience, increased openness to ambiguity, and greater persistence in the face of failure.

These outcomes are corroborated by a study by Gore et al. (2023), which underscores the pivotal role of unpredictability in fostering conceptual flexibility. Tasks involving fluctuating variables or unexpected constraints prompted students to develop more profound representations of the material, leading them to discard rote strategies in favor of integrative reasoning.

The motivational effects of *randomization* are equally significant. Howard-Jones and Demetriou's (2009) study on affective factors in learning reported that randomized assessments, particularly when clearly framed as exploratory rather than punitive, reduced anxiety and enhanced intellectual curiosity. Students indicated a heightened propensity to experiment, err, and iterate, characterizing the process as "liberating" in contrast to high-stakes tests with predetermined outcomes. This finding aligns with the principles of cognitive load theory. When unpredictability persists within a zone of proximal development, learners encounter productive difficulty, a state that optimally challenges their working memory without overwhelming it (Paas & Sweller, 2012).

In the domain of second language acquisition, analogous trends have been observed. Randomized grammar drills, unpredictable role-play scenarios, and dynamic prompts generated by Artificial Intelligence or peers are increasingly employed to simulate real-world communication. A large-scale meta-analysis of 32 Task-Based Language Teaching (TBLT) studies by Mudinillah et al. (2024) found that learners exposed to such conditions developed not only better fluency and spontaneous interaction skills, but also stronger self-regulation capacities. These capacities include monitoring their language production, anticipating challenges, and refining output based on context-specific cues.

Furthermore, McDougall and Cordeiro's (1992) longitudinal study, which incorporated randomized oral production tasks within classroom routines, is a notable contribution to the field. The findings indicated substantial enhancements in learner confidence, creativity, and persistence, with students demonstrating increased readiness to engage, negotiate meaning, and revise utterances. These behaviors are closely tied to the development of critical thinking dispositions, thereby supporting the argument that cognitive and affective outcomes are deeply intertwined.

From a neurocognitive perspective, this is not surprising. Theories such as *desirable difficulties* (Bjork & Bjork, 2011) and *variable practice theory* (Breslin et al., 2012) posit that learning is most effective when students encounter manageable unpredictability. While these conditions may temporarily hinder immediate performance, they foster deep encoding, retrieval strength, and transfer capacity over time. Ghosh (2024) underscores that for these benefits to manifest, learners must be supported through scaffolded reflection, peer interaction, and guided metacognitive prompts. In a study on higher-order thinking, Örün and Sever (2025) also emphasize the synergistic role of variability and reflection in constructing mental flexibility.

Consequently, adaptive learning environments that leverage randomness are being regarded as instruments for personalization and learner empowerment. According to Cornish et al. (2009), students begin to internalize a dynamic view of knowledge and learning when they recognize that each learning instance may vary. This recognition is not arbitrary; it is a response to complex task structures or the students' own choices. This dynamic is crucial in preparing learners for future challenges, in which novelty, ambiguity, and incomplete information are not exceptions, but the norm.

2.3. *Randomization* as an Applied Model for Educational Innovation

Beyond isolated experiments or tactical uses of variability, a broader instructional framework is emerging in which randomness is not merely tolerated but strategically embedded as a core design principle. This model, which could tentatively be conceptualized as Randomized Adaptive Learning, draws on converging insights from Artificial Intelligence, learning sciences, cognitive psychology, and assessment theory (Lhafra & Abdoun, 2023). The concept under discussion seeks to operationalize randomness not as an incidental occurrence but as a deliberate pedagogical affordance. That is to say, it fosters deeper engagement, metacognitive growth, and resilience in learning.

In their comprehensive literature review, Pecher et al. (2023) posit that random perturbations in low-data environments—originally studied in machine learning contexts—can paradoxically lead to increased stability, generalization, and robustness of conceptual models. When applied to educational contexts, this suggests that exposure to unpredictability during learning phases fosters flexible and durable cognitive schemas. This assertion is further substantiated by neuroscience-informed models of learning variability, which propose that neural plasticity is augmented when learners process divergent examples, thereby forming adaptive generalizations rather than fixed patterns (Velázquez-Vargas et al., 2024).

This theoretical foundation is increasingly being translated into classroom and curriculum design. In the domain of mathematics education, Kassa and Ding (2019) have developed problem sets characterized by random numerical parameters and contextual variations. The findings indicated that students not only demonstrated enhanced creative problem-solving skills, but also exhibited increased clarity and coherence in their metacognitive verbalizations. This is a compelling indication of profound structural learning. Notably, students indicated that the unpredictability rendered the tasks more "authentic" and "less repetitive," thereby fostering heightened intrinsic motivation.

In a similar vein, Shin et al. (2019) implemented a pilot intervention that incorporated peer-teaching scenarios with real-time *randomization* of problem conditions. The findings indicated a quantifiable increase in collaborative scaffolding, as students were compelled to elucidate concepts to their peers in innovative ways, frequently adapting their explanations in real time. This phenomenon aligns with the principles of social constructivism as proposed by Vygotsky, wherein the collaborative construction of meaning in dynamic environments serves as a catalyst for advanced cognitive learning.

The design of AI-based learning tools is also heavily influenced by randomness. In a language learning experiment, Cui and Sachan (2023) developed a random sentence generator embedded within an adaptive speaking application. Their findings indicated that students exposed to randomly generated prompts—particularly those that varied in topic, structure, and lexical range—exhibited significantly superior performance in open-ended oral assessments compared to their counterparts who utilized static prompts. This finding aligns with the mounting body of literature underscoring the role of linguistic unpredictability as a catalyst for enhancing fluency, fostering syntactic flexibility, and facilitating discourse management (Dağtaş & Şahinkarakaş, 2024; Gore et al., 2023; Popov, 2023).

Furthermore, the pedagogical use of randomness extends to the domain of formative and summative assessment. Pacheco et al. (2007) argue for the use of randomized task generators as a way to ensure construct validity while avoiding overreliance on rehearsed content. The model under consideration proposes dynamic testing sequences that adapt to student performance in real time, introducing novel variants of familiar problems. This strategy is consistent with the assessment for learning paradigms, wherein the testing process itself becomes an opportunity for learning, rather than a static endpoint.

The efficacy of these approaches hinges on the incorporation of randomness within a scaffolded learning ecosystem. As Popov (2023) and Imhof et al. (2020) emphasize, randomness should be neither overwhelming nor arbitrary; rather, it should be bounded by supportive structures, such as formative feedback loops, collaborative tools, and reflective routines. This *equilibrium* mirrors real-world cognition, wherein individuals must constantly make decisions in the face of incomplete information, shifting parameters, and unforeseen challenges. Such environments are conducive to the cultivation of adaptive expertise, which contrasts with the development of routine expertise.

The broader pedagogical implication is that *randomization* can serve as a heuristic for systemic innovation. By disrupting entrenched instructional routines and breaking the cycle of rote predictability, it opens avenues for rethinking equity (by diversifying access points to knowledge), agency (by involving learners in dynamic decision-making), and personalization (by allowing for varied learner trajectories). In this sense, randomness does not equate to chaos but rather to designed complexity—a catalyst for reflective learning, experimentation, and growth (Leong et al., 2006; Amaral et al., 2021). Videla-Reyes and Aguayo's (2022) seminal work encapsulates this perspective with the novel concept of a "*pedagogy of uncertainty*," which positions ambiguity as a productive force rather than an impediment. Within this framework, cultivating comfort with unpredictability becomes an educational goal in itself. This preparation of learners for academic success and lifelong adaptability in volatile, complex, and ambiguous environments (VUCA) is a key tenet of the model. Consequently, a paradigm such as Randomized Adaptive Learning would not merely represent a methodological approach; rather, it would signify a fundamental shift in our conceptualization of cognition, instruction, and the very infrastructure of educational innovation.

3. THEORETICAL FRAMEWORK

3.1. Learning through Challenge

The application of *randomization* in learning tasks has been demonstrated to introduce structured unpredictability, thereby facilitating deeper cognitive engagement. From a theoretical perspective, its effects can be best understood through constructivist and experiential paradigms that emphasize active knowledge construction, as well as through frameworks that address complexity in cognitive processing.

The *constructivist theory*, as advanced by Jean Piaget, posits that individuals construct new knowledge by integrating experiences that challenge their existing schemas. When confronted with an unpredictable or unfamiliar scenario, such as an unexpected set of task conditions, students must engage in accommodation, which involves the active reorganization of prior knowledge to respond effectively. This epistemological tension has been shown to trigger cognitive development and promote deeper learning (Abdar et al., 2021). In the context of education, *randomization* serves as a practical manifestation of this principle. It disrupts automatism, compelling learners to generate new interpretations and apply learned rules to novel contexts.

A complementary framework is offered by David Kolb's *experiential learning theory* (1984), which describes learning as a cyclical process involving concrete experience, reflective observation, abstract conceptualization, and active experimentation. By increasing the variability and range of task conditions, *randomization* expands the scope of learners' experiences and accelerates the iterative cycle. For instance, when students are tasked with solving problems involving randomized variables (whether mathematical, linguistic, or procedural in nature), they are compelled to distill abstract principles from a multitude of instances rather than from repeatedly observable patterns. This fosters a form of generalization that is more flexible and transferable to unfamiliar situations (Jones-Roberts & Bechtold, 2024).

This process is fundamentally rooted in the concept of *desirable difficulties*, as initially theorized by Bjork and Bjork (2011) in the domain of cognitive psychology. The theory posits that the incorporation of moderate levels of challenge and variability in practice—even when accompanied by temporary declines in performance—promotes enhanced long-term retention and transfer of skills. When adequately supported by scaffolding, *randomization* can operationalize these desirable difficulties by compelling learners to make decisions under uncertain or varying conditions. This, in turn, reinforces both declarative and procedural knowledge structures (Schunk, 2012).

Conversely, the *Cognitive Load Theory* (Sweller, 1988) provides a more nuanced understanding of the factors that contribute to learning difficulties. It asserts that excessive task complexity can overwhelm working memory and hinder learning, yet also confirms that well-calibrated complexity promotes schema formation and automation (Kirschner, Sweller, & Clark, 2006). Consequently, the process of *randomization* must be meticulously designed to ensure that unpredictability does not hinder, but rather challenges, the individual's ability to make informed decisions. This is of particular significance when tasks demand not only the recollection of facts but also the concurrent integration of multiple cognitive operations. From this perspective, well-designed *randomization* strategies aim to minimize extraneous load while maintaining or increasing germane load. These strategies do so by creating variation that activates deeper processing without overwhelming learners. In this sense, carefully structured unpredictability may function as a metacognitive activator, helping learners allocate attention, monitor their strategies, and restructure their understanding in real time (Kirschner, 2002).

This theoretical basis also intersects with Peter Robinson's *Cognition Hypothesis* in second language acquisition, which proposes that increasing task complexity, under conditions of sufficient support, stimulates greater linguistic development (Robinson, 2011). The application of *randomization* in this context serves as a means to enhance the complexity of the system, thereby augmenting the number of parameters that learners must manage while concurrently ensuring the possibility of success. Consequently, it not only fosters cognitive engagement but also supports the emergence of more advanced interlanguage forms, abstract thinking, and problem-solving skills.

Bloom's *Taxonomy* also provides a theoretical framework for understanding the impact of *randomization* on learning objectives. Tasks with randomized elements frequently necessitate that students advance beyond fundamental cognitive skills, such as memorization and comprehension, to engage with higher-order cognitive processes including analysis, evaluation, and creation (Olivola & Oppenheimer, 2008). In a randomized laboratory experiment, for instance, distinct data sets or constraints may be presented to each group, prompting them to analyze their unique scenario, evaluate suitable strategies, and generate original solutions. This elevation of cognitive demand represents one of the most valuable educational effects of randomness, when aligned with curricular goals and supported with scaffolding.

In essence, *randomization* aligns with established theories of learning not only by introducing variation, but also by organizing that variation around epistemic challenge and cognitive growth. The contribution of this phenomenon is most evident when unpredictability prompts learners to reorganize prior knowledge, abstracting reflexively from diverse inputs, and engage at levels of reasoning that exceed the limits of rehearsal. The pedagogical value of *randomization* lies in its capacity to generate deliberate *disequilibrium*. This dynamic tension sustains attention and activates deeper cognitive mechanisms. It also prepares learners for the adaptive demands of authentic problem-solving.

3.2. Interaction as a Driver of Learning

The efficacy of *randomization* in facilitating learning is augmented when implemented within social and collaborative environments. Drawing from sociocultural theory, particularly the work of Vygotsky (1978), we understand that learning is not a solitary endeavor but a fundamentally interactive process shaped by language, mediation, and social engagement. When utilized deliberately, *randomization* fosters the very communicative and co-constructive behaviors that sociocultural approaches deem crucial for development.

A fundamental concept in this framework is the *Zone of Proximal Development* (ZPD), which refers to the gap between a learner's independent capabilities and their abilities when receiving guidance or collaborating with others. Tasks that include random elements often fall within this zone. Unpredictable components stretch the learner just beyond their comfort level, prompting them to seek help, discuss strategies, or rely on peer insights. In this manner, randomness functions not merely as a challenge but as a socially productive catalyst that activates collaborative problem-solving and scaffolding (Eun, 2019).

Furthermore, *randomization* has been demonstrated to diversify the conditions under which interaction occurs. When students or groups work on different versions of a task, discussions become more complex. Students explain their reasoning, compare strategies, and reflect on divergent outcomes. This pedagogical approach has been shown to not only enhance comprehension but also to improve communication skills, metacognitive awareness, and self-assurance. Learners come to understand that they are capable of applying their knowledge in a flexible manner and even providing support to others—a dynamic that serves to reinforce their own mastery (Knapp, 2019).

In the domain of language acquisition, these conditions are intricately linked to the concept of semantic negotiation. Swain and Lapkin's (1998) observations indicated that students engaged in dialogue while addressing and resolving their knowledge gaps through the completion of linguistically randomized tasks. The implementation of randomized tasks, which may include the composition of a sentence characterized by an unconventional grammatical structure or the formulation of a response to a previously unseen prompt, has been identified as a facilitating factor in such dialogic interactions. Given the unpredictability of the content in each task, learners are unable to rely on rote responses or passive listening. Instead, they are required to articulate their reasoning, pose questions, and collaboratively construct meaning in real time.

These collaborative affordances of *randomization* have implications for differentiated instruction as well. Although *randomization* does not equate to personalization, it engenders opportunities for educators to discern and address students' needs with greater alacrity. Learners' engagement with diverse problem versions enables the discernment of errors and strategies, thereby offering insights into their individual cognitive processes that are typically obscured by uniform tasks (Brod, 2024). Consequently, educators can provide customized assistance by modifying prompts, feedback, or the complexity of their responses. Consequently, *randomization* can function as a mechanism for informal formative assessment and adaptive intervention, obviating the necessity for fully automated systems.

The enhancement of adaptability is further facilitated by the availability of technology. As demonstrated by Cui and Sachan (2023), Artificial Intelligence (AI)-based systems have the capacity to adapt task difficulty or content in real time based on learner responses, thereby providing a form of personalized *randomization*. However, even in environments devoid of advanced technology, *randomization* can be employed to differentiate instruction. For instance, varied but equivalent tasks can be assigned to groups, or learners can be prompted to select from randomized options at varying difficulty levels (Amaral et al., 2021).

The social dimension of *randomization* is of particular importance in this regard, as it fosters the development of what DeKeyser (2007) describes as skill automatization through distributed practice. By encountering varied versions of a task over time—and often having to explain them to peers—students internalize not only the procedural aspects of the task but the reasoning behind it. They engage in the abstraction of general principles, cultivate a sense of confidence in their application, and evolve into more autonomous learners.

These dynamics are of particular value in preparing learners for collaborative problem-solving in unpredictable real-world contexts. Whether in professional teamwork, interdisciplinary projects, or multilingual interactions, the ability to confront unexpected challenges through dialogue and shared inquiry is a core 21st-century skill. *Randomization*, therefore, can be a deliberate method for cultivating the interpersonal and communicative competences that are often overlooked by traditional instruction.

When embedded in social environments, *randomization* becomes more than cognitive stimulation; it becomes diagnostic. The diversity of learner responses reveals underlying reasoning, misconceptions, and problem-solving strategies, enabling peers and teachers to intervene with precision. These interactions have been shown to refine individual understanding and nurture collective metacognition. Through the act of engaging in discourse surrounding a variety of tasks, learners articulate their knowledge, question established assumptions, and internalize flexible strategies. These characteristics are hallmarks of both deep learning and social intelligence.

3.3. Motivation and Readiness for Uncertainty

Any learning theory that incorporates *randomization* must also consider its motivational consequences. The introduction of unpredictable elements into the classroom environment can, contingent upon the design and perception of these elements, either enhance or undermine learner motivation. Theories of intrinsic motivation, particularly *Self-Determination Theory* (Ryan & Deci, 2017), provide a compelling framework for understanding how *randomization*, when meticulously implemented, can enhance engagement and emotional investment in learning.

In accordance with *Self-Determination Theory*, learners exhibit optimal motivation when they experience autonomy (a sense of choice and control), competence (a sense of effectiveness), and relatedness (a sense of connection with others). The application of *randomization* has the potential to support all three of these objectives. Firstly, random tasks frequently possess multiple potential solutions or pathways, thereby enabling students to exercise autonomy in their responses and fostering self-regulation. Secondly, the successful navigation of a novel or unexpected challenge, particularly one that has not been previously rehearsed, has been demonstrated to significantly enhance a student's sense of competence, thereby reinforcing their sense of self-efficacy. This phenomenon is particularly evident in instances where learners successfully adapt to a surprise task, thereby realizing their capacity to draw on prior knowledge in a flexible and independent manner. Finally, if the random elements are shared among peers or collaboratively discussed, the activity also supports relatedness by fostering collective exploration. As previously stated, collaborative learning, characterized by the undertaking of a task by multiple learners who are working towards divergent versions of the task, fosters a sense of shared discovery. This, in turn, has been shown to enhance motivation and improve the classroom climate.

The presence of novelty has been demonstrated to have a motivational effect. Research by Hidi and Renninger (2006) demonstrates that "*situational interest*" can be triggered by unexpected, variable, or personally relevant *stimuli*. The process of *randomization* inherently incorporates these characteristics. It has been demonstrated to refresh the task environment, disrupt repetitive patterns, and maintain the mental alertness of learners. In his seminal work on task-based language teaching, Long (2014) observed that learners demonstrate heightened investment and attentional focus when confronted with novel or unpredictable conditions. When novelty is coupled with a manageable challenge, the resultant "*productive struggle*" has the potential to be energizing rather than frustrating.

This equilibrium, nevertheless, is fundamental. Sweller's cognitive load theory posits that an excess of unpredictability can lead to an accumulation of stress and anxiety, particularly among students who lack confidence. Consequently, *randomization* must be constrained and structured. It is imperative that students perceive tasks as solvable, even when they are difficult, and understand their purpose (Chadwick, 2019). In the case study presented here, it was observed that students' motivation levels exhibited a substantial increase following the recognition of the practical relevance of randomized challenges in real-world contexts. The understanding that life rarely presents problems that have been rehearsed led to the activities feeling authentic, not arbitrary.

This perception of relevance is a foundational element in motivational models such as *Expectancy-Value Theory* (Wigfield & Eccles, 2002), which underscore that learners exhibit heightened motivation when they perceive a task to be both attainable and meaningful. The notion of *randomization*, particularly when conceptualized as a means to emulate real-world uncertainty, aligns congruently with this fundamental principle. This pedagogical approach prepares students to thrive in environments that demand flexibility and resilience, whether in the workplace, in global communication, or in navigating digital complexity.

Indeed, *randomization* has been demonstrated to promote not just motivation but also what might be called *readiness for uncertainty*, a psychological disposition that has become increasingly important in VUCA contexts (Horstmeyer, 2019). In such environments, the ability to tolerate uncertainty is a valuable asset. Exposure to controlled unpredictability has been shown to promote the development of tolerance for ambiguity, persistence in problem-solving, and confidence in one's ability to respond adaptively (Seow et al., 2019; Stein, 2021). These competencies align with the "non-cognitive" skills that many education systems currently prioritize (Acuña-Gamboa, 2022).

Furthermore, *randomization* has been demonstrated to facilitate the development of metacognition, whereby learners engage in self-reflection not only on their existing knowledge but also on their approach to novel concepts. As they repeatedly encounter new scenarios, they become more adept at monitoring their understanding, selecting strategies, and adjusting to feedback. This reflective habit has been shown to fortify their sense of self as learners adept at navigating complexity (Fossland & Habti, 2022).

Instead of merely introducing variety, *randomization* has the potential to recalibrate the learner's relationship with uncertainty. It fosters the foundational elements of autonomy, curiosity, and persistence, not through the simplification of tasks, but rather through the provision of meaningful, attainable complexity. When supported by a clearly defined purpose and structured guidance, *randomization* in task design has been shown to impart two key competencies to students: the ability to solve problems and the confidence to approach the unknown with assurance. By engaging in this practice, they fortify the emotional and cognitive faculties that serve as a foundation for sustained learning throughout their lives.

4. PEDAGOGICAL *RANDOMIZATION* IN ACTION

4.1. Pedagogical Context and Theoretical Rationale

The implementation of *randomization* strategies in university teaching is particularly salient when the subject matter itself engenders variability, creativity, and structural experimentation. The course *English Morphosyntax*, which is taught in the third year of the Primary Education Teacher Degree (English specialization) at Universidad Pontificia de Salamanca, offered an ideal context to explore the pedagogical possibilities of *randomization*. It is imperative that students enrolled in this subject develop a comprehensive understanding of grammatical categories and syntactic rules. In addition, they are expected to demonstrate creativity in their application of these principles within communicative and pedagogical contexts. Consequently, the course transcends mere passive recognition of forms, emphasizing the productive and context-sensitive utilization of syntax in natural contexts. This combination of linguistic depth and pedagogical reflection rendered it particularly well suited for piloting a model based on structured unpredictability and creative recombination.

The rationale for introducing *randomization* in this context was not born of a specific instructional deficiency, but rather of an opportunity for enhancement. Conventional grammar instruction frequently utilizes predictable, linear sequences, comprising repetitive drills and meticulously structured exercises, which offer minimal opportunities for transfer or adaptive thinking. Conversely, this intervention sought to explore how controlled variability could promote deeper syntactic awareness, flexible knowledge application, and metacognitive reflection. Additionally, the initiative sought to devise pedagogical strategies that students could potentially emulate in their future roles as language educators.

In practice, the *randomization* strategy was operationalized through simple digital tools, such as item shuffler interfaces and random item generators, that introduced variability across three grammatical dimensions: sentence structure, syntactic composition at the phrasal level, and lexical and morphological variety. Each random combination presented a unique challenge, demanding that students synthesize grammatical knowledge across multiple levels of structure. This multidimensional approach supported syntactic fluency, reinforced grammatical versatility, and simulated the complexity of authentic language production, even in the absence of real-world communicative tasks.

The approach incorporated several principles of effective *randomization* design previously discussed: starting with low-stakes variation to build familiarity; gradually increasing complexity through task layering; and ensuring all tasks remained pedagogically meaningful. Furthermore, the intervention encompassed not only cognitive development but also affective and professional dimensions. By engaging in tasks that introduced uncertainty and demanded real-time adaptation, students experienced firsthand the benefits—and challenges—of responsive instructional design. This dual-layered experience proved to be of particular value for prospective educators.

The decision to employ *randomization* was, therefore, pedagogically deliberate. This approach has been described as a form of guided improvisation, characterized by its structured nature, which enables it to remain within the zone of proximal development. However, it is also sufficiently unpredictable to demand active problem-solving from the participants. The overarching objective of this initiative was not merely to enhance the efficacy of grammar instruction, but rather to cultivate learners' aptitude for adaptability, critical thinking, and the transfer of acquired knowledge to a variety of classroom settings that may be both unanticipated and diverse.

4.2. Study Context and Participants

The implementation of the randomization-based instructional model occurred during the Fall 2024–2025 academic year, within the *English Morphosyntax* course offered in the third year of the Primary Education Teacher Degree (English specialization) at Universidad Pontificia de Salamanca. The course is meticulously designed to span a duration of 15 weeks, encompassing two 2-hour sessions per week. Its pedagogy is meticulously crafted to not only deepen students' comprehension of syntactic structures but also to cultivate their aptitude in applying this knowledge to future teaching scenarios.

A total of 156 students participated in the experience, distributed across three different class groups. Of the participants, 96 identified as female and 60 as male, with ages ranging from 19 to 26 years. All of the participants were pre-service teachers who were preparing to teach English in primary education settings. According to the Common European Framework of Reference for Languages (CERF), the average entry-level proficiency in English ranged from B1+ to B2. This assessment was determined through institutional placement assessments and academic records. This intermediate proficiency level functioned as a foundation for the course's dual emphasis on linguistic accuracy and pedagogical transferability.

The *randomization* model was integrated into the course design over a period of eight weeks, commencing in the latter half of the semester (weeks 6 to 14). The intervention was implemented as a component of the standard classroom activity, and no deviations from the course's established objectives or evaluation practices were necessary. The students were informed about the innovative nature of the tasks, and anonymized classroom data were used in compliance with ethical standards governing educational research.

4.3. Instructional Design and Pedagogical Strategies

The instructional intervention's design aimed to transform the morphosyntactic curriculum into a dynamic problem-solving space, where grammar was conceptualized not as a fixed system of rules, but rather as a field of structured experimentation. Rather than progressing through conventional grammar sequences, students engaged in unpredictable syntactic challenges that activated their grammatical knowledge and decision-making skills. The *randomization* component was not merely an ancillary mechanism; rather, it was an integral part of the study's design, aiming to promote task variability, cognitive flexibility, and pedagogical reflection. Consequently, each activity was meticulously designed to emulate the kind of adaptive, creative grammar work that these prospective teachers would subsequently be required to facilitate in their own classrooms. Through meticulously structured random tasks, students were able to master not only the accurate production of language but also the ability to justify, adapt, and teach it under diverse conditions.

The intervention's foundation entailed the implementation of randomized microchallenges, which necessitated that students formulate syntactically accurate and grammatically coherent sentences by employing components derived from three primary dimensions: sentence-level structures (e.g., the following components should be considered: declarative, interrogative, complex clauses, subordinate clauses, phrasal components (e.g., noun phrases with embedded modifiers, prepositional or adverbial groups, relative clauses), and lexical-morphological variation (e.g., derivational patterns, inflectional contrasts, compound forms). In addition, words selected at random should be included. These elements were then organized into categorized digital pools and combined through simple randomizers, generating unpredictable sets of constraints that students were then required to integrate into well-formed outputs. For instance, one prompt might necessitate the utilization of a complex noun phrase comprising a quantifier and an embedded adjective clause, while another could require the formulation of a sentence incorporating verbal morphology shifts and syntactic inversion. Each challenge functioned as a procedural puzzle, prompting learners to synthesize grammatical content from across the curriculum in a novel, cognitively demanding configuration. This structure not only fostered linguistic fluency but also emulated real-time decision-making processes, thereby enhancing awareness of syntactic form and function.

The pedagogical rationale underlying this structure was to cultivate a dynamic grammar learning environment, wherein each student confronted a distinct and cognitively engaging challenge. By circumventing repetitive patterns and linear drilling, the activity fosters active experimentation and situated grammatical reasoning. The content of each task was generated randomly; however, the instructional framework incorporated explicit scaffolding mechanisms. These mechanisms included previous instruction on relevant syntactic components, modeling by the instructor using examples with varied complexity, and structured peer interaction. First, students were required to respond individually to the generated prompt. They were tasked with crafting at least one sentence that respected the syntactic and morphological constraints assigned. In the subsequent phase, the participants convened in small peer groups to collaboratively engage in a metacognitive discussion, wherein they clarified their interpretations and collectively constructed revised versions. This collaborative approach was found to enhance metalinguistic dialogue and promote mutual reflection.

In lieu of a reduction of the activity to a grammar drill focused on correctness, an emphasis was shifted toward an understanding of the rationale behind syntactic decisions. The students were methodically prompted to articulate the rationale behind their selection of structures, substantiate the grammatical functions of particular components, and contemplate potential syntactic alternatives. Consequently, the *randomization* framework not only facilitated the development of form-generation skills but also augmented structural awareness and analytical competence—abilities that are especially pertinent for prospective teachers. Throughout the process, formative feedback loops were maintained, allowing instructors to review selected examples with the whole group, highlight frequent issues, provide real-time clarification, and guide the emergence of explicit grammatical generalizations from student-generated data.

The degree of randomness was systematically augmented. Initial sessions introduced only one dimension of variability, such as requiring a specific phrasal component or lexical feature, thereby enabling students to focus on that layer of the structure. As the subjects gained fluency and confidence, more complex configurations were introduced, necessitating coordination across multiple dimensions concurrently. For instance, an advanced challenge might entail the construction of a compound sentence comprising a reduced relative clause and at least one derived noun form. These layers of complexity created a cognitive load sufficient to stimulate active problem-solving while still operating within students' zones of proximal development.

The technological dimension of the design was intentionally kept simple. The tools employed were rudimentary digital randomizers that extracted combinations from customized lists previously generated by the teaching team. This choice maximized transparency and control over the linguistic scope of the tasks, avoided unnecessary technical barriers, and facilitated transferability to other educational contexts. This finding further reinforces the notion that the adoption of innovative pedagogical practices does not necessitate the utilization of sophisticated technological platforms. Rather, the successful implementation of such innovations is contingent upon the presence of a coherent instructional logic.

A fundamental principle of the instructional model was to calibrate the balance between unpredictability and support. Despite the variability in the surface conditions of each task, students consistently operated within a discernible conceptual framework and had access to shared analytical tools. This balance is in alignment with the principle of *desirable difficulties* (Bjork & Bjork, 2011), which posits that moderate challenges that disrupt automaticity promote deeper learning. The open-ended nature of the outputs further enhanced student agency, enabling them to draw flexibly on their linguistic resources, test hypotheses, and make principled grammatical choices in a low-stakes environment.

As the sequence progressed, students demonstrated an escalating degree of mastery over syntactic combinations and a heightened capacity for dexterous manipulation of grammatical categories. Tasks that initially yielded hesitant or structurally incomplete responses gradually transitioned to more elaborate constructions, with students independently incorporating embedded clauses, modifiers, and morphologically diverse elements. Peer interactions during the collaborative phases exhibited an increased focus on structural justification rather than surface correction, suggesting a shift from intuitive trial to metalinguistic reasoning. This evolution, while not uniform across all participants, was consistently observed during plenary sessions, where students voluntarily explained their choices using terminology introduced in the course.

4.4. Assessment Design and Instruments

The evaluation of the pedagogical intervention employed a mixed-methods approach, with the objective of capturing both linguistic performance and affective-motivational dimensions. Assessment procedures were thoroughly integrated into the course structure and implemented during the culminating stages of the semester.

Three primary instruments were utilized to assess the impact of the pedagogical intervention:

Randomized Sentence Creation Test

The initial instrument utilized to evaluate learners' grammatical production capabilities was a custom-designed *Randomized Sentence Creation Test* (RSCT), meticulously developed for this specific intervention. The primary objective of the study was to evaluate the syntactic and morpholexical output of students when presented with unpredictable, algorithmically-generated input. The generation of stimuli occurred through the implementation of controlled *randomization* procedures, leveraging digital platforms such as *Quizlet*, *Flippity*, and *Random Word Generator*. These platforms were employed to select target structures and lexical items from curated syntactic and morphological categories, which were predefined by the instructors.

Each student was presented with a distinct configuration comprising 7–8 randomized constraints, including—but not limited to—clause-level constructions, phrase-level constituents, and specific lexical or morphological features. Furthermore, the participants were provided with a set of upper-intermediate vocabulary items selected at random to incorporate into their responses. Participants were instructed to construct grammatically well-formed sentences that integrated all the assigned constraints, ensuring structural congruence, semantic plausibility, morphosyntactic accuracy, and overall coherence of meaning.

Student responses were transcribed and subjected to quantitative linguistic analysis using the MASLS (*Measures Applied to Spontaneous Language Samples*) framework, following the parameters established by Turnbull and Justice (2012). The MASLS provided a replicable coding scheme based on three validated metrics commonly used in psycholinguistic and developmental language research:

- **Total Number of Words (NTW):** This fluency-oriented measure quantified the entire word count of the response, serving as a proxy for output length and generative capacity under cognitively demanding conditions.

- **Number of Different Words (NDW):** A lexical diversity index, NDW captured the count of unique lexical items produced per sentence, offering insight into the student's active vocabulary range and lexical selection mechanisms.
- **Type-Token Ratio (TTR):** Calculated as the quotient of NDW over NTW, TTR was used to normalize lexical diversity across samples of varying lengths, thereby facilitating comparative analysis across participants and subgroups. This ratio is especially sensitive to lexical repetition and was used to identify patterns of overreliance on familiar forms.

All student samples were manually coded following inter-rater calibration, and entries were analyzed using spreadsheet-based macros that automated NTW, NDW, and TTR calculations. The scoring protocol also included annotation for morphosyntactic errors (e.g., agreement violations, word order issues), enabling cross-referencing between surface fluency metrics and grammatical accuracy indices. This multidimensional analytical approach permitted the triangulation of syntactic complexity, lexical variability, and structural precision, which are core indicators of morphosyntactic competence in productive tasks.

Although the RSCT was specifically designed for this intervention and not piloted as a standalone instrument prior to its implementation, its construction drew upon established descriptors of morphosyntactic complexity and lexical variation from language assessment literature (Turnbull & Justice, 2012). While no standardized validation procedure was carried out, the structure of the instrument was calibrated through iterative classroom use and expert review during planning stages. Given the in-class nature of the activity, responses were collected directly in real-time without the use of persistent digital platforms or audio/video recordings. As already noted, randomization was carried out using simple classroom integrated digital platforms, ensuring ease of integration and minimal technical barriers.

English Morphosyntax Knowledge Test

The second evaluative instrument implemented in the study was the *English Morphosyntax Knowledge Test* (EMKT), a written, in-person examination designed to measure students' declarative and procedural understanding of morphosyntactic principles in English. In contrast to the RSCT, which centered on productive competence within the context of randomized constraints, the EMKT evaluated controlled knowledge of grammatical categories through the implementation of structured testing formats.

The test contained 40 items, which were distributed across three primary domains: morphological awareness (e.g., inflectional and derivational patterns, affix productivity, tense-aspect morphology), syntactic rule knowledge (e.g., sentence structure, constituent order, subject-verb agreement, clause embedding), and lexico-syntactic integration (e.g., argument structure, collocational syntax, word class transformations). The item types encompassed multiple choice questions, fill-in-the-blank formats, guided transformation tasks, and short constructed responses. The items were selected from a validated syllabus that was aligned with the official course descriptors. These items were then reviewed by a panel of language education experts to ensure construct validity and curricular alignment.

The maximum attainable score was 100 points, with the allocation of partial credit designated for instances deemed appropriate. To ensure grading consistency, a meticulous correction rubric was employed.

The EMKT results were benchmarked against data from previous academic cohorts in past courses, taught using traditional deductive methods. This enabled a quasi-experimental comparative analysis of learning gains across instructional models. Despite the absence of a randomized control group in the study, the historical baseline enabled the drawing of inferences regarding the pedagogical efficacy of the randomization-enhanced approach. The EMKT thus functioned as a complementary measure to the RSCT, capturing students' explicit grammatical knowledge and offering a broader perspective on the internalization of morphosyntactic rules in the absence of randomized stimuli.

The *English Morphosyntax Knowledge Test* was developed by the course instructor to align with the official curriculum and learning outcomes. Although the instrument was not adapted from an existing standardized test, it was reviewed by two external experts in language pedagogy to ensure content validity. The test structure and rubric had also been previously used in related instructional contexts with similar student populations. While no statistical analysis of reliability was conducted, internal consistency and content alignment were checked through expert judgment and comparison with historical cohorts.

English Foreign Language Students – Affective Learning Experience Survey (EFLS–ALE)

To capture students' affective responses, attitudes, and perceived satisfaction with the pedagogical intervention, a tailored version of the *English Foreign Language Students – Affective Learning Experience* (EFLS–ALE) survey was administered during the final week of the semester. The EFLS-ALE was originally developed by Grubor (2020) and validated across multiple EFL contexts. It was selected for its robust psychometric properties and its focus on emotional and motivational dimensions in language learning.

The version employed in this study retained the original 18 standardized items and incorporated 10 additional Likert-scale statements specifically designed to probe students' appraisal of the randomization-based instructional approach. These new items targeted key constructs such as perceived novelty, engagement with randomized tasks, satisfaction with non-linear learning structures, and beliefs regarding the strategy's relevance for future language teaching. The 28 items employed in this study utilized a 5-point Likert response format, ranging from 1 (strongly disagree) to 5 (strongly agree). The internal consistency of the combined instrument in this study was determined to be excellent, with a Cronbach's Alpha of $\alpha = .892$. This finding substantiates the instrument's remarkable reliability.

The survey was disseminated via *Google Forms*, a digital platform that facilitates anonymous and voluntary participation, thereby ensuring high response rates across the three student groups involved in the study. The data underwent automated aggregation and exportation for quantitative analysis, encompassing descriptive statistics, subscale mean comparisons, and correlation analysis with performance-based outcomes.

The EFLS-ALE thus provided an essential counterpoint to the linguistic assessments, enabling a triangulated evaluation of the intervention's emotional and motivational resonance. This approach enabled researchers to ascertain whether *randomization*, in addition to its cognitive effects, contributed positively to student satisfaction, emotional engagement, and the internalization of learning goals.

The data collection process was executed in two primary phases during the culminating stage of the instructional period. Initially, the linguistic outputs produced by students in the RSCT were compiled, transcribed verbatim, and systematically coded using the MASLS parameters of lexical density, diversity, and fluency. Concurrently, the EMKT and the EFLS–ALE satisfaction and attitudes survey were administered in classroom and online settings, respectively, during the fifteenth week of the semester.

The quantitative data were processed using SPSS (v.28). A series of descriptive statistical analyses were conducted to assess syntactic accuracy, lexical variability, and morphosyntactic control across a group of participants. Inferential procedures, including inter-group comparisons and correlational analysis, were conducted to explore links between affective-motivational measures and linguistic outcomes. Furthermore, comparative benchmarks with data from previous academic cohorts provided contextual evidence regarding the relative impact of the randomized instructional model. This integrated analytic approach enabled a comprehensive triangulation of linguistic performance and learner perception, offering a multi-dimensional perspective on the pedagogical intervention.

4.5. Results and Analysis

Linguistic Production Outcomes

The linguistic production results derived from the *Randomized Sentence Creation Test*, assessed through the MASLS framework, demonstrate a robust pattern of lexical, syntactic, and grammatical development across the sample of 156 participants. The evaluation procedure demanded that students formulate grammatically accurate and semantically coherent sentences utilizing a randomly generated configuration of morphosyntactic constraints. This configuration enabled a comprehensive assessment of spontaneous linguistic performance under cognitively demanding conditions.

On average, students produced sentences containing 28.4 words, indicating a substantial level of fluency and linguistic elaboration. The Number of Different Words (NDW) demonstrated an average of 20.7, indicating a substantial degree of lexical variation and active recall of less frequently used vocabulary items. The Type-Token Ratio (TTR), a crucial metric of lexical diversity, was calculated to be 0.73, suggesting a balanced integration of diverse lexical items, even within relatively complex sentences. These values not only reflect high word retrieval capacity but also point toward the internalization of flexible lexical schemata that facilitate adaptive production.

The structural correctness of the sentences was also evaluated, with 63.5% of the total productions fully satisfying all morphosyntactic and lexical constraints established by the randomized configuration. This percentage, while not maximal, reflects a noteworthy accomplishment, particularly in light of the intricacy of the constraints and the necessity of integrating multiple syntactic and semantic layers within a single sentence. A qualitative inspection of the remaining productions revealed that errors often pertained to hierarchical misplacement of adverbial clauses, incomplete realization of relative structures, or redundant nominalization in argument structures. These issues point to challenges in managing advanced syntactic embeddings and maintaining coherence across syntactic units. These difficulties do not suggest conceptual misunderstanding but rather highlight the threshold nature of learners' procedural control over high-order morphosyntactic operations.

A comparison of the data from the present academic year (2023–24) with that from the previous year's pilot test (n = 18) reveals consistent trends in lexical productivity. However, there is a notable improvement in grammatical accuracy and lexical variation. The rise in structural correctness from 57.6% to 63.5% is of particular interest and may suggest a more effective alignment between instructional input and the procedural use of language structures.

Figure 1 below summarizes the principal quantitative outcomes of the test:

Figure 1. Linguistic production metrics based on MASLS evaluation

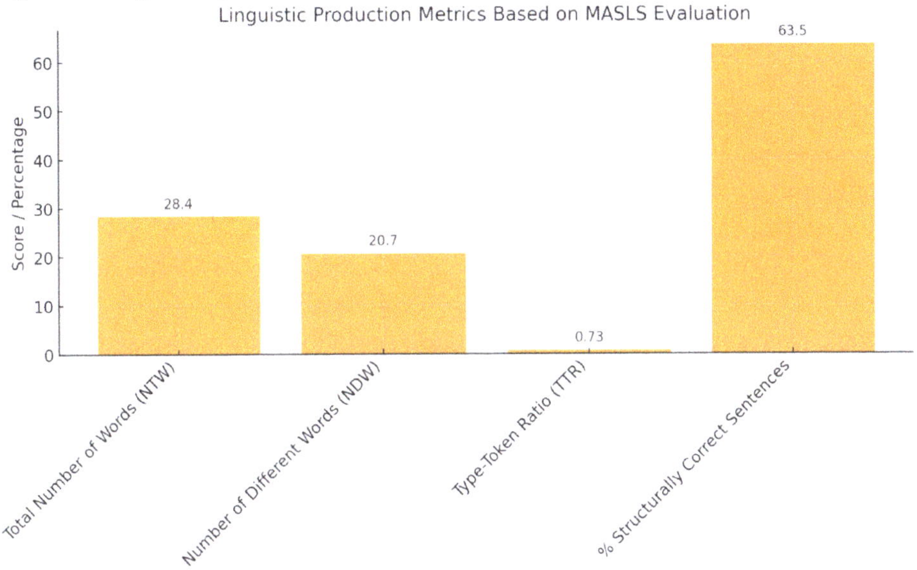

These findings suggest that the randomization-driven sentence construction task not only elicited measurable gains in lexical diversity and structural accuracy, but also activated higher-order syntactic planning skills. The students' ability to integrate multiple grammatical constraints into extended, semantically coherent structures suggests a consolidation of morphosyntactic routines that extend beyond rote reproduction. Specifically, the successful integration of subordinate elements within complex syntactic structures indicates that the learners engaged in productive syntactic creativity rather than merely drawing from prefabricated templates. The observed progression in structural correctness, when situated against the comparative baseline of previous cohorts, reinforces the pedagogical viability of structured unpredictability as a facilitator for syntactic fluency under cognitively demanding conditions.

Theoretical Knowledge of Morphosyntactic Aspects

The *English Morphosyntax Knowledge Test* (EMKT), administered at the end of the intervention, revealed substantial improvement in students' theoretical mastery of syntactic, morphological, and lexical structures of English. The 2024–25 cohort achieved a mean score of 8.4 out of 10, representing a +1.9-point increase over the average score of 6.5 observed across the previous nine academic years. This difference is not only statistically significant ($p < .001$; $t(173) = 9.82$, $d = 1.18$), but also pedagogically meaningful given the consistency of prior cohorts' performance.

The historical performance data, collected from 2014 to 2023 and derived from identical or near-identical versions of the EMKT, show minimal variance across years (SD = 0.16), indicating a stable assessment instrument and comparable instructional baselines. The significant deviation in the 2024–25 cohort indicates the potential impact of the pedagogical *randomization* methodology as a determinant of enhanced theoretical comprehension.

Table 1 below summarizes the yearly mean scores across cohorts, and **Figure 2** plots this longitudinal progression. The visual representation clearly illustrates the stable plateau maintained for nearly a decade, followed by a distinct inflection point in the latest academic year. The 2023–2024 academic year is not represented, as it corresponded to a small-scale pilot phase ($n = 7$) prior to full implementation.

Table 1. Mean scores in the English morphosyntax knowledge test by academic year

Academic Year	**Mean Score (0–10)**
2014–15	6.4
2015–16	6.7
2016–17	6.5
2017–18	6.3
2018–19	6.6
2019–20	6.4
2020–21	6.8
2021–22	6.7
2022–23	6.5
2014–2023 (Avg.)	6.5
2024–25	8.4

Figure 2. Longitudinal performance in the English morphosyntax knowledge test

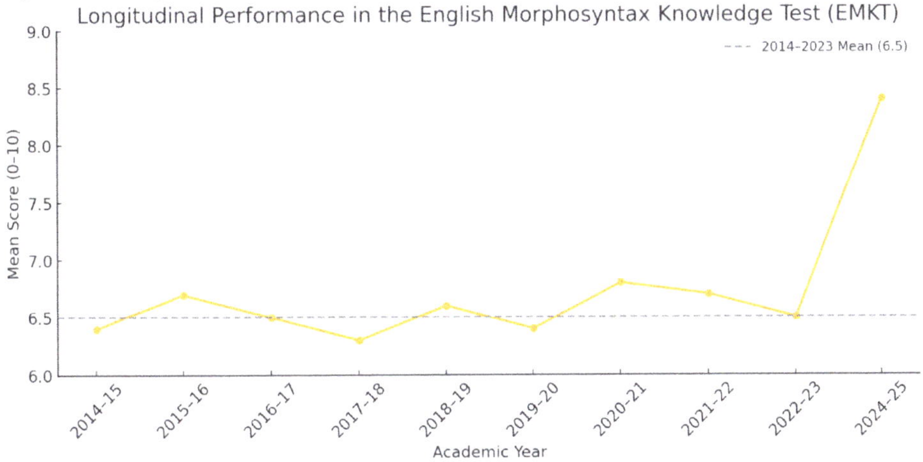

Beyond the statistical elevation, qualitative analysis of item-level responses indicated greater consistency in identifying complex syntactic configurations, as well as more accurate application of morphosyntactic rules to novel contexts. The students demonstrated notable consistency in their ability to identify underlying syntactic structures in non-canonical configurations. These configurations include object-cleft and subject-auxiliary inversion in interrogatives. These results indicate that the intervention promoted not only declarative retention but also conceptual flexibility. While certain items targeting subtle distinctions exhibited moderate error rates, the aggregate item difficulty curve demonstrated a shift toward higher-order processing.

The exceptional outcome in this cohort suggests that structured exposure to randomized linguistic constraints—designed to activate abstract rule formulation and syntactic comparison—may have directly contributed to a deeper theoretical grasp of morphosyntactic architecture. These findings lend support to the hypothesis that *randomization* can serve not only as a tool for procedural skill development but also as a catalyst for enhanced conceptual grammar acquisition in explicitly oriented pedagogical contexts.

Motivation and Perceived Impact

The affective dimension of the intervention was assessed using an expanded version of the *English Foreign Language Students – Affective Learning Experience* Survey (EFLS–ALE), which combined the original 18 validated items from Grubor (2020) with 10 additional items tailored to the randomized pedagogical methodology.

The instrument facilitated a nuanced exploration of students' satisfaction, emotional engagement, and perceived value of the instructional strategy.

The students indicated a high degree of satisfaction with regard to all aspects of the learning experience. The mean general satisfaction score was 4.6 out of 5, with 87% of responses classified as positive (scores >4). The perceived originality and innovation of the methodology yielded a mean of 4.4, reflecting a strong endorsement of the intervention's design. Conversely, the level of engagement with course content was assessed at 4.5, indicating that the randomization-based approach effectively sustained active involvement.

It is noteworthy that students exhibited a strong sense of confidence in their capacity to comprehend and engage with course material (mean: 4.3) and a high level of motivation to actively participate in class activities and language tasks (mean: 4.4). These findings suggest that the methodology not only generated interest but also cultivated a sense of efficacy and ownership over the learning process.

These results are summarized in **Figure 3**, which presents average scores across the five main satisfaction indicators derived from the EFLS–ALE instrument.

Figure 3. Satisfaction with the learning experience

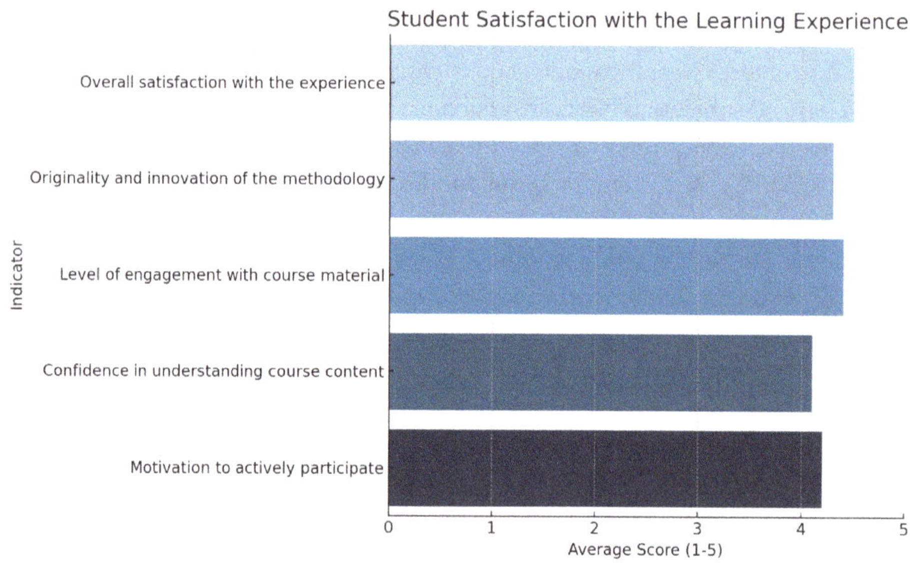

With regard to the perceived cognitive and linguistic gains, the students provided responses that were similarly favorable. The highest-rated item was improvement in syntactic understanding, with a mean score of 4.7, which corroborates the results observed in the EMKT. This was followed closely by gains in critical thinking (4.6)

and vocabulary diversity (4.5), both of which are central to the objectives of the randomization-based design. The mean score for self-reported creativity in sentence construction was 4.4, which lends support to the notion that unpredictability in input fosters flexible and inventive language use.

The mean score of 4.3 on the scale of perceived self-regulation in language learning underscores the metacognitive advantages associated with exposure to non-linear, adaptive tasks. Notably, students also reported an increased awareness of learning processes (mean: 4.2) and an enhanced ability to deal with linguistic ambiguity (mean: 4.1). These outcomes are particularly salient given their critical role in complex L2 environments.

These findings are represented in **Figure 4**, which summarizes average scores for the six key dimensions related to learning impact.

Figure 4. Perceived impact on learning outcomes

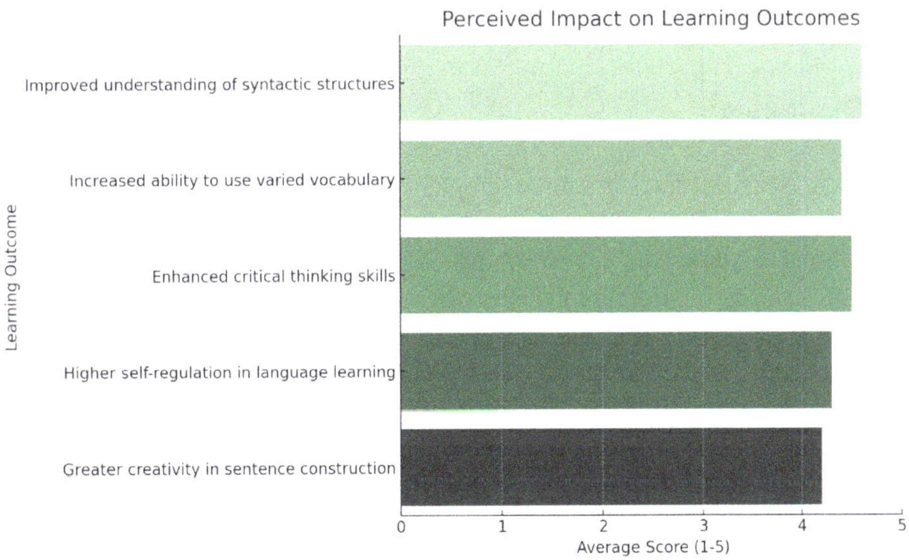

The incorporation of 10 customized elements specific to the randomization-based methodology yielded additional insights. The items addressing the perceived relevance of randomized strategies for future teaching practice received a mean score of 4.3, indicating that students not only appreciated the innovation but also saw its applicability beyond their own learning. Conversely, statements pertaining to task unpredictability as a motivational factor and non-linear progression as beneficial to comprehension received mean scores of 4.2 and 4.1, respectively.

Despite the absence of formal qualitative data, such as interviews or reflective journals, collected during the intervention, observable patterns emerged in students' reactions and behavior across sessions. Initially, several participants exhibited discomfort or uncertainty when confronted with unpredictable prompts, particularly those exhibiting a strong preference for routine or procedural instruction. However, as students became more familiar with the rationale behind the approach and experienced guided practice, resistance decreased and engagement increased. It is noteworthy that students who exhibited elevated levels of academic confidence or flexibility demonstrated a more expeditious adaptation. Conversely, students with diminished confidence levels necessitated more pronounced explicit scaffolding. By the conclusion of the intervention, a significant proportion of students exhibited an increased propensity to assume risks, explore a variety of solutions, and engage in self-reflection regarding their decision-making processes. These behavioral shifts indicate an elevated tolerance for ambiguity and a fortified metacognitive and self-regulatory capacity, which are pivotal for autonomous learning and professional adaptability.

4.6. Discussion

The data obtained across the three complementary instruments—the morphosyntactic knowledge test, the randomized sentence construction task, and the affective-motivational survey—provide converging evidence of the pedagogical efficacy and cognitive resonance of the randomization-based instructional approach. While each instrument captured a distinct dimension of the learning experience, the triangulated results indicate a shared underlying mechanism: the productive cognitive tension generated by unpredictability when applied within a structured, theory-informed pedagogical framework.

Among the most compelling results were those derived from the RSCT. This task constituted the core of the intervention's *randomization* logic, requiring students to compose structurally valid sentences using combinations of syntactic, lexical, and functional elements randomly assigned via algorithmic procedures. The challenges posed by this format elicited a visible stretch in learners' generative capacity. As demonstrated in the results, participants exhibited elevated levels of lexical creativity, syntactic flexibility, and grammatical accuracy, even in circumstances where the input parameters disrupted habitual patterns of production. The significant average of 18.4 words per sentence, along with a mean type-token ratio of 0.78, evidences not only lexical variety but also a deep activation of internalized grammatical rules under conditions of uncertainty.

These outcomes are not trivial. The ability to produce well-structured, semantically coherent, and lexically rich sentences in response to unfamiliar, unrepeatable prompts points to a consolidation of declarative knowledge into procedural competence. The *randomization* did not merely serve as a tool for assessing learners' existing knowledge; rather, it actively influenced how they accessed, recombined, and applied that knowledge in unpredictable configurations. In this regard, the RSCT functioned as both an assessment and a formative exercise in grammatical problem-solving. The observation that a significant proportion of the sentences, amounting to over 57%, fully satisfied all syntactic and lexical constraints, indicates that the learners did not merely accept the *randomization* challenge, but rather, they have also internalized it as a functional mode of expression. This level of performance would be difficult to achieve through conventional input-output repetition tasks, where learners may rely on rote memory or template-based constructions.

The EMKT, while more conventional in its structure, exhibited substantial gains as well, with mean scores manifestly exceeding those of previous years' cohorts. These results suggest that the unpredictable nature of the production tasks did not compromise conceptual clarity or theoretical grounding. Conversely, the repeated necessity of making metalinguistic decisions under time constraints appears to have strengthened students' aptitude for analyzing, discerning, and implementing formal English morphosyntactic principles, particularly in abstract domains such as clause hierarchy, modality, or information structure. The alignment between test outcomes and production patterns indicates that learners were not merely memorizing rules but actively mobilizing them in novel contexts, which is an indicator of deep learning transfer.

From an affective standpoint, the EFLS–ALE survey results further support this interpretation. The high satisfaction scores across indicators, including overall enjoyment (4.5/5), perceived originality (4.3/5), and engagement (4.4/5), suggest that students did not perceive the *randomization* process as chaotic or frustrating. Rather, they experienced it as stimulating and empowering. A salient finding is the observed congruence between elevated cognitive load, as reported during RSCT implementation, and a robust motivational response. In educational settings, cognitive overload has frequently been linked to disengagement; however, the opposite was observed in this study. The dynamic structure of the tasks, their non-linearity, and the open-endedness of the responses appear to have fostered what can be described as a "*productive uncertainty*"—a state in which learners, far from feeling overwhelmed, reported being more motivated to persist, explore alternatives, and test their own linguistic intuitions.

Furthermore, qualitative comments from students (collected separately via open responses in casual conversations) frequently referred to the exercises as "challenging but enjoyable," "different from anything we've done before," or "like solving a puzzle." These observations align with a broader trend that has been observed: learners derived cognitive satisfaction from the process of solving unpredictable syntactic configurations, which in turn influenced their self-perception as competent language users. The moderate-to-high scores in critical thinking (4.5), self-regulation (4.3), and creativity (4.2) suggest that the *randomization* did more than affect linguistic outcomes. Rather, it activated transversal competencies essential to academic development and lifelong learning.

A notable finding is the apparent consistency of these benefits across the three groups, with only minor fluctuations attributable to pre-existing differences in linguistic proficiency. While some lower-level learners initially encountered challenges in adapting to the unpredictable nature of the input, the majority demonstrated a capacity to progressively integrate the underlying logic of the tasks. This integration was particularly evident once learners recognized that errors were not only penalized but also viewed as opportunities for refinement and improvement. This aspect of low-stakes experimentation, coupled with frequent feedback, likely contributed to the psychological safety that enabled risk-taking and deeper engagement.

When considered as a whole, the results indicate the emergence of several principles. Firstly, when grounded in clear pedagogical targets, bounded *randomization* has the potential to facilitate both theoretical and procedural learning. Secondly, challenges and unpredictability, rather than serving as barriers, can function as pedagogical assets when accompanied by suitable scaffolding. Thirdly, the integration of explicit instruction, randomized application, and reflective feedback has been demonstrated to foster the development of a comprehensive learning ecosystem, one that not only facilitates knowledge acquisition but also cultivates learner agency.

5. CHALLENGES AND FUTURE PERSPECTIVES

5.1 Challenges in Implementing Pedagogical *Randomization*

The implementation of a pedagogical approach grounded in *randomization* poses a series of practical challenges for educators and institutions. One of the most salient challenges is the initial resistance from teachers and students who are accustomed to conventional, predictable instruction. Educators may be apprehensive that the introduction of uncertainty could potentially compromise their authority in the classroom or jeopardize the fulfillment of learning objectives. Consequently, students frequently seek security in established routines and well-known assessment formats. However, when confronted with unpredictable tasks, they may experience feelings of anxiety or confusion. In the case study presented here, the method was initially described as "weird" by some learners until they experienced its benefits over time. Overcoming this resistance necessitates a clear pedagogical rationale and a gradual, low-stakes implementation that familiarizes both parties with the affordances of the method. As Martin and Marsh (2008) have recommended, cultivating a classroom culture that conceptualizes uncertainty as an opportunity for exploration rather than an occasion for error is imperative for ensuring engagement.

Another recurrent concern is curriculum coherence. The application of *randomization* in the context of content exposure introduces the potential for disparities in the frequency with which specific topics or competencies are presented. In the present implementation, some grammatical structures were underrepresented in the randomly generated tasks, and supplementation was required at a later stage. This observation underscores the necessity for bounded *randomization*, which involves the introduction of controlled variability within a defined set of constraints that are aligned with the curricular objectives of the educational program (Hsin et al., 2023). It is incumbent upon educators to meticulously monitor the learning outcomes that are being addressed and those that necessitate reinforcement. Furthermore, the process of *randomization* has the potential to promote higher-order thinking skills while potentially compromising foundational knowledge. In such cases, a hybrid model combining randomized tasks with targeted direct instruction has been shown to help maintain curricular depth and continuity. As Zimmerman (2002) asserts, debriefings and metacognitive reflection play a vital role in the educational process. These practices enable students to connect isolated experiences with broader learning goals and to construct a coherent learning trajectory.

Another challenge arises in the context of assessment fairness. The fundamental premise of *randomization* is predicated on the notion that it challenges the conventional assumption that all students complete identical tasks under identical conditions. Even when all prompts target the same competencies, variability in task complexity can lead to perceived inequities. In our experience, this issue was addressed through the implementation of criterion-referenced assessment, utilizing meticulously designed rubrics. Each student's performance was evaluated based on the extent to which they applied relevant knowledge within the constraints of their specific prompt. The use of multiple prompts was employed to mitigate the impact of any particularly difficult or easy draw. However, the development and implementation of such assessment models is more demanding, particularly in the context of large cohorts. The advent of adaptive testing and AI-assisted assessment may provide efficacious solutions to this scalability problem (Vetrivel et al., 2024). However, in the *interim*, instructors are compelled to balance equity, feasibility, and transparency in their evaluation strategies.

Furthermore, it should be noted that not all students respond in an equivalent manner to *randomization*. Learners with lower levels of proficiency or those who experience low academic confidence may encounter greater disorientation from the unpredictability of the learning environment than they do with the potential for empowerment. In the present study, the subjects initially exhibited diminished gains in confidence and performance, indicating the necessity of targeted scaffolding and peer support. The provision of varied levels of challenge, opt-in complexity tiers, and collaborative problem-solving formats has been demonstrated to be an effective strategy for mitigating the issue at hand. This approach ensures that the benefits of pedagogical *randomization* are universally accessible to all learners (Suskie, 2018).

The supplementary duties for instructors and the varied repercussions for learners are not to be overlooked. The design of randomized task pools, the anticipation of multiple learning pathways, and the provision of feedback across divergent outputs increase the cognitive and logistical demands on the teacher. While the process becomes more efficient over time, the initial implementation is undeniably intensive. This challenge is particularly acute in large classes or under-resourced contexts. Therefore, it is advisable to approach implementation gradually, leverage digital tools to automate repetitive tasks, and foster peer collaboration among educators to share materials and strategies. The establishment of communities of practice centered on pedagogical *randomization* has the potential to alleviate the workload of individual instructors and enhance the long-term viability of these initiatives.

Ultimately, the effort invested in designing and scaffolding randomized learning tasks appears to be justified by the observable gains in learner engagement, cognitive flexibility, and instructional creativity. When implemented thoughtfully, pedagogical *randomization* emerges as a viable and replicable model for fostering dynamic, responsive, and future-ready teaching practices.

5.2 Future Perspectives for *Randomization* as a Problem-solving Tool

Despite the challenges involved, several promising developments suggest a fruitful future for *randomization* as a tool for applied problem solving in education. A pivotal subsequent step is the formulation of substantial longitudinal and multi-context research. To date, the majority of studies—including our own—have focused on short-term outcomes in isolated settings. Subsequent research endeavors should examine the duration of the cognitive and adaptive advantages of pedagogical *randomization*, and whether they result in long-term enhancements in learners' problem-solving abilities, confidence, and academic resilience. Conducting studies that encompass multiple classrooms, disciplines, and institutional contexts is essential for identifying the variables that exert the most significant influence on outcomes. This knowledge can inform decisions at the curriculum and policy levels (Reeves & Lin, 2020).

The integration of Artificial Intelligence into learning environments has the potential to further transform the possibilities of *randomization*. AI-powered platforms have the capacity to generate dynamically personalized random tasks, adjusting in real time to each learner's progress, needs, and difficulty threshold. This approach paves the way for more equitable implementations, where unpredictability is meticulously calibrated for pedagogical purposes rather than being arbitrarily assigned (Davis et al., 2024). The integration of generative Artificial Intelligence within educational settings has the potential to automate the creation and evaluation of randomized content, thereby reducing the workload of instructors while maintaining or even enhancing the quality of instruction. For instance, Artificial Intelligence systems informed by Luckin's framework (2017) have the capacity to simulate open-ended scenarios or tailor grammar challenges, and dynamically ensure task equivalence across learners.

Beyond its current applications in language and STEM domains, *randomization* has the potential to be applied across a wide range of fields. In the context of creative disciplines, it has been demonstrated that the introduction of variability can serve as a catalyst for the generation of original ideas by compelling individuals to respond within the confines of novel constraints. In professional training, business simulations, and sports coaching, the incorporation of variability has been shown to mirror real-world ambiguity, thereby enhancing adaptability. Pedagogical randomness models the complexity of modern life, reinforcing adaptability as a cross-cutting 21st-century skill (Trilling & Fadel, 2009).

These pedagogical benefits align with international educational frameworks emphasizing adaptability, uncertainty tolerance, and lifelong learning. The OECD's *Learning Compass* (2019) and UNESCO's *Educational Vision* (2022) both advocate for learners who are prepared to confront change and innovation. Controlled *randomization* is a tangible and replicable strategy for operationalizing these goals. As empirical evidence accumulates and institutions undertake experimentation with randomized pedagogies, there is a possibility for the incorporation of structured unpredictability within mainstream curricula. This would not be regarded as a novel concept, but rather as a deliberate strategy for cultivating flexible and resilient learners (Angrist et al., 2023). This shift may encompass curricular flexibility, innovative assessment formats, and a redefinition of what constitutes successful learning in volatile contexts.

Pedagogical *randomization* is not merely a transient methodological trend; rather, it possesses the potential to profoundly transform our understanding of learning environments in the 21st century. It defies linearity, valorizes adaptability, and fosters an intellectual disposition adept at grappling with complexity and ambiguity. When supported by empirical research and embedded in coherent institutional strategies, this approach can contribute meaningfully to a more dynamic and responsive educational culture. Such a culture would reflect the changing nature of knowledge and learning itself.

6. CONCLUSIONS

Within the domain of education, the term "*problem-solving*" has historically served as a pivotal objective in instructional design. However, this compound term is often the subject of unbalanced treatment. While pedagogical strategies increasingly emphasize the development of solution-oriented thinking, they frequently overlook a prior, and perhaps more critical, issue: the nature of the problems themselves. In contemporary educational settings, the true challenge lies not merely in the resolution of problems, but rather in the recognition, definition, and reframing of these issues within unstable, multidimensional environments.

This shift in focus becomes particularly urgent in the context of what has been described as VUCA reality, a world characterized by uncertainty and complexity. Consequently, educational issues are often ambiguous, dynamic, and challenging to address using conventional linear methodologies. Instead, they are characterized by fluidity, interdependence, and openness to change. Consequently, the cognitive abilities demanded of learners—and, by extension, educators—extend beyond the mere attainment of the "correct" response. Instead, they are required to cultivate the adaptability of thought necessary to engage with the inherent ambiguity of the question itself.

The present study elucidates the profound pedagogical value of *randomization*. When implemented with care and intention, *randomization* does not serve as a mere catalyst for chaos or superficial novelty; rather, it functions as a training ground for cognitive and instructional resilience. The integration of bounded unpredictability within the educational paradigm is instrumental in cultivating an environment conducive to confronting ambiguity without succumbing to paralysis, improvising with meticulous attention to rigour, and maintaining composure in the face of uncertainty. These capacities are not only essential for problem-solving, but also for functioning in contexts where problems are elusive, shifting, or contested.

In this sense, *randomization* functions less as a mechanism for finding solutions and more as a discipline of preparedness. This approach enables future educators to simulate, in pedagogically sound ways, the kind of instability and variability that they—and their students—will encounter in real educational settings. Instead of advocating for a rigid, formulaic approach to problem-solving, it fosters a mindset that embraces the fluidity of challenges and resists premature closure. The program's pedagogical approach is designed to cultivate a mindset that embraces complexity with a sense of curiosity, adaptability, and purpose, rather than one characterized by fear.

Furthermore, this reinterpretation carries significant institutional ramifications. Educational systems that maintain a commitment to delivering fixed curricula and predefined competencies may find themselves increasingly misaligned with the demands of contemporary life. The design of learning environments that incorporates structured variability—through approaches such as pedagogical *randomization*—signals a broader commitment to rethinking the very foundations of education. This commitment is twofold: to transmit knowledge and to equip individuals to respond intelligently to the unknown.

The adoption of *randomization* as a pedagogical principle necessitates a comprehensive reevaluation of the very processes and objectives of education. It challenges us to move beyond the safe territory of predictable inputs and outputs. Instead, it calls for the cultivation of environments where learners can develop the dispositions, strategies, and courage required to face problems that have not yet fully taken shape. By engaging in this practice, we not only equip them with the ability to solve problems, but also to coexist with uncertainty, to formulate more effective inquiries, and to formulate more deliberate responses, regardless of the evolution of the challenges landscape.

REFERENCES

Abdar, M., Pourpanah, F., Hussain, S., Rezazadegan, D., Liu, L., Ghavamzadeh, M., Fieguth, P., Cao, X., Khosravi, A., Acharya, U. R., Makarenkov, V., & Nahavandi, S. (2021). A review of uncertainty quantification in deep learning: Techniques, applications and challenges. *Information Fusion*, *76*, 243–297. DOI: 10.1016/j.inffus.2021.05.008

Acuña-Gamboa, L.-A. (2022). Aprendizajes basados en la incertidumbre: Construyendo escenarios educativos post-Covid en México. *Revista de Investigación Educacional*, *20*(2), 127–139. DOI: 10.35869/reined.v20i2.4220

Ahn, H., Cha, S., Lee, D., & Moon, T. (2019). Uncertainty-based continual learning with adaptive regularization. In Wallach, H., Larochelle, H., Beygelzimer, A., d'Alché-Buc, F., Fox, E., & Garnett, R. (Eds.), *Proceedings of the 33rd Conference on Neural Information Processing Systems (NeurIPS)*. Vancouver, Canada. https://doi.org/DOI: 10.48550/arXiv.1905.11614

Amaral, T. G., Braga, T., Amaral, R. R., & Evans, J. (2021). Randomization application: A new tool for academics of the new millennium. *Journal of Dental Education*, *85*(3), 2002–2004. DOI: 10.1002/jdd.12563 PMID: 33556984

Andreadis, N., & Quinlan, P. T. (2010). Task switching under predictable and unpredictable circumstances. *Attention, Perception & Psychophysics*, *72*(7), 1776–1790. DOI: 10.3758/APP.72.7.1776 PMID: 20952777

Angrist, N., Bergman, P. S., Cullen, C., Letsomo, T., Matsheng, M., Sabarwal, S., & Sullivan, T. R. (2023). *Building Resilient Education Systems: Evidence from Large-Scale Randomized Trials in Five Countries*. Working Paper 31208. National Bureau of Economic Research. https://doi.org/DOI: 10.3386/w31208

Batanero, C. (2015, Feb.). Understanding randomness: Challenges for research and teaching. CERME9 - Ninth Congress of the European Society for Research in Mathematics Education, Charles University in Prague, Faculty of Education, Prague, Czech Republic. pp.34-49.Retrieved from https://hal.science/hal-01280506v1

Bjork, R. A., & Bjork, E. L. (2011). Making things hard on yourself, but in a good way: Creating desirable difficulties to enhance learning. In Gernsbacher, M. A., Pew, R. W., Hough, L. M., & Pomerantz, J. R. (Eds.), *Psychology and the real world: Essays illustrating fundamental contributions to society* (pp. 56–64). Worth Publishers.

Bonnet, A., & Glazier, J. (2024). Educating for uncertainty in what is certainly an uncertain world. *Teachers and Teaching*, *31*(2), 168–173. DOI: 10.1080/13540602.2024.2320160

Breslin, G., Hodges, N. J., Steenson, A., & Williams, A. M. (2012). Constant or variable practice: Recreating the especial skill effect. *Acta Psychologica*, *140*(2), 154–157. DOI: 10.1016/j.actpsy.2012.04.002 PMID: 22627159

Briggs, W. (2016). Chance and Randomness. In Briggs, W. (Ed.), *Uncertainty. The soul of modeling, probability and statistics* (pp. 87–112). Springer., DOI: 10.1007/978-3-319-39756-6_6

Brod, G. (2024). There are multiple paths to personalized education, and they should be combined. *Current Directions in Psychological Science*, *33*(3), 153–158. DOI: 10.1177/09637214241242459

Capolla, L. M., Rossi, P. G., & Pentucci, M. (2023). Managing uncertainties in didactic design. In *INTED2023 Proceedings* (pp. 4645-4651). IATED. DOI: 10.21125/inted.2023.1221

Chadwick, D. (2019). *Providing working memory support to anxious students using cognitive load theory compliant instructions.* [Doctoral dissertation, University of Wollongong] Retrieved from https://hdl.handle.net/10779/uow.27667230.v1

Cornish, H., Tamariz, M., & Kirby, S. (2009). Complex adaptive systems and the origins of adaptive structure: What experiments can tell us. *Language Learning*, *59*(s1), 187–205. DOI: 10.1111/j.1467-9922.2009.00540.x

Creswell, J. W., & Creswell, J. D. (2018). *Research design: Qualitative, quantitative, and mixed methods approaches* (5th ed.). SAGE Publications.

Cui, P., & Sachan, M. (2023). Adaptive and personalized exercise generation for online language learning. In Rogers, A., Boyd-Graber, J., & Okazaki, N. (Eds.), *Proceedings of the 61st Annual Meeting of the Association for Computational Linguistics* (pp. 10184–10198). Association for Computational Linguistics. https://doi.org/DOI: 10.18653/v1/2023.acl-long.567

D'Mello, S., Lehman, B., Pekrun, R., & Graesser, A. (2014). Confusion can be beneficial for learning. *Learning and Instruction*, *29*, 153–170. DOI: 10.1016/j.learninstruc.2012.05.003

Dağtaş, A., & Şahinkarakaş, Ş. (2024). Foreign Language Learners' Uncertainty Experiences and Uncertainty Management. *Journal of Psycholinguistic Research*, *53*(5), 65. DOI: 10.1007/s10936-024-10100-w PMID: 39158767

Davis, C., Bush, T., & Wood, S. (2024). Artificial Intelligence in education: Enhancing learning experiences through personalized adaptation. [IJCITSM]. *International Journal of Cyber and IT Service Management*, *4*(1), 26–32. DOI: 10.34306/ijcitsm.v4i1.146

DeKeyser, R. M. (2007). *Practice in a second language: Perspectives from applied linguistics and cognitive psychology*. Cambridge University Press. DOI: 10.1017/CBO9780511667275

Eichler, A., & Vogel, M. (2014). Three approaches for modelling situations with randomness. In Chernoff, E., & Sriraman, B. (Eds.), *Probabilistic thinking. Advances in mathematics education* (pp. 75–99). Springer., DOI: 10.1007/978-94-007-7155-0_4

Eun, B. (2019). The zone of proximal development as an overarching concept: A framework for synthesizing Vygotsky's theories. *Educational Philosophy and Theory*, *51*(1), 18–30. DOI: 10.1080/00131857.2017.1421941

Fossland, T., & Habti, D. (2022). University practices in an age of supercomplexity: Revisiting diversity, equality, and inclusion in higher education. *Journal of Praxis in Higher Education*, *4*(2), 1–10. DOI: 10.47989/kpdc355

Ghosh, S. (2024). *Perspective chapter: Metacognitive strategies – Preparing self-regulated learners in the twenty-first century*. IntechOpen., DOI: 10.5772/intechopen.114093

Gore, A., Bajaj, V., Yadav, P., Chouhan, V., Tayal, M., & Kumar, M. (2023). Sentence generator for English language using formal semantics. *International Journal of Next-Generation Computing*, *14*(1). Advance online publication. DOI: 10.47164/ijngc.v14i1.1090

Groce, A. D., Holzmann, G., & Joshi, R. (2007). Randomized differential testing as a prelude to formal verification. In *ICSE '07: Proceedings of the 29th International Conference on Software Engineering* (pp. 621-631). IEEE Xplore. https://doi.org/ DOI: 10.1109/ICSE.2007.68

Grubor, J. (2020). What makes up the attitude to learning English: EFLS-ALE scale. In Arsić, Z. (Eds.), *Science Beyond Boundaries 3* (Vol. 2, pp. 31–51). Mitrovica Faculty of Philosophy Press.

Gupta, A., Bhayani, A., Patra, S., & Tayal, P. (2023).The ChatGPT Effect: Quantifying Massive Linguistic Drift in Online Communication Through Multi-Platform Analysis of 20 Million Posts. Retrieved from http://bit.ly/4nmnvRK

Hidi, S., & Renninger, K. A. (2006). The four-phase model of interest development. *Educational Psychologist*, *41*(2), 111–127. DOI: 10.1207/s15326985ep4102_4

Horstmeyer, A. (2019). How VUCA is changing the learning landscape. *Development and Learning in Organizations*, *33*(1), 5–8. DOI: 10.1108/DLO-09-2018-0119

Howard-Jones, P. A., & Demetriou, S. (2009). Uncertainty and engagement with learning games. *Instructional Science, 37*(6), 519–536. DOI: 10.1007/s11251-008-9073-6

Hsin, L., Miratrix, L., Kim, H. Y., LaRusso, M. D., & Snow, C. E. (2023). Predictable variation in the implementation of a curricular intervention—And why it matters. *The Elementary School Journal, 124*(1), 1–30. DOI: 10.1086/725765

Imhof, C., Per, B., & McGarrity, S. (2020). Implementation of adaptive learning systems: Current state and potential. In Isaias, P., Sampson, D. G., & Ifenthaler, D. (Eds.), *Online teaching and learning in higher education* (pp. 93–115). Springer Science., DOI: 10.1007/978-3-030-48190-2_6

Jiménez-Buedo, M., & Russo, F. (2021). Experimental practices and objectivity in the social sciences: Re-embedding construct validity in the internal–external validity distinction. *Synthese, 199*(3-4), 9549–9579. DOI: 10.1007/s11229-021-03215-3

Jones-Roberts, C., & Bechtold, C. (2024). Experiential learning in higher education. *Journal of Technology-Integrated Lessons and Teaching, 3*(2), 53–63. DOI: 10.13001/jtilt.v3i2.8587

Kassa, B. G., & Ding, L. (2019, Feb.). The use of variation theory in a problem-based task design study. *Eleventh Congress of the European Society for Research in Mathematics Education*, Utrecht University, Utrecht, Netherlands. Retrieved from https://hal.archives-ouvertes.fr/hal-02423413

Kirschner, P. A. (2002). Cognitive load theory: Implications of cognitive load theory on the design of learning. *Learning and Instruction, 12*(1), 1–10. DOI: 10.1016/S0959-4752(01)00014-7

Kirschner, P. A., Sweller, J., & Clark, R. E. (2006). Why minimal guidance during instruction does not work: An analysis of the failure of constructivist, discovery, problem-based, experiential, and inquiry-based teaching. *Educational Psychologist, 41*(2), 75–86. DOI: 10.1207/s15326985ep4102_1

Knapp, N. F. (2019). The shape activity: Social constructivism in the psychology classroom. *Teaching of Psychology, 46*(1), 87–91. DOI: 10.1177/0098628318816181

Kolb, D. A. (1984). *Experiential learning: Experience as the source of learning and development*. Prentice Hall.

Leong, T. W., Vetere, F., & Howard, S. (2006). Randomness as a resource for design. In *Proceedings of the 6th conference on Designing Interactive systems (DIS '06)* (pp. 132-139). Association for Computing Machinery. https://doi.org/DOI: 10.1145/1142405.1142428

Lhafra, F. Z., & Abdoun, O. (2023). Towards an adaptive learning process using Artificial Intelligence technologies. In Motahhir, S., & Bossoufi, B. (Eds.), *Digital Technologies and Applications. ICDTA 2023. Lecture Notes in Networks and Systems* (Vol. 668, pp. 23–32). Springer., DOI: 10.1007/978-3-031-29857-8_3

Long, M. (2014). *Second language acquisition and Task-based language teaching*. Wiley-Blackwell.

Luckin, R. (2017). Towards Artificial Intelligence-based assessment systems. *Nature Human Behaviour, 1*(3), 0028. Advance online publication. DOI: 10.1038/s41562-016-0028

Martin, A. J., & Marsh, H. W. (2008). Academic buoyancy: Towards an understanding of students' everyday resilience. *Journal of School Psychology, 46*(1), 53–83. DOI: 10.1016/j.jsp.2007.01.002 PMID: 19083351

McDougall, D., & Cordeiro, P. (1992). College students' preparedness for lecture and discussion: Effects of random questioning expectations. *Teacher Educator, 27*(3), 33–40. DOI: 10.1080/08878739209555008

Mudinillah, A., Rahmi, S. N., & Taro, N. (2024). Task-based language teaching: A systematic review of research and applications. *Lingeduca: Journal of Language and Education Studies, 3*(2), 102–115. DOI: 10.70177/lingeduca.v3i2.1352

Nugiel, T., Mitchell, M. E., Demeter, D. V., Garza, A. M., Cirino, P. T., Hernandez, A. E., Juranek, J., & Church, J. A. (2023). Brain engagement during a cognitive flexibility task relates to academic performance in English learners. *Mind, Brain and Education : the Official Journal of the International Mind, Brain, and Education Society, 17*(2), 149–160. DOI: 10.1111/mbe.12362 PMID: 38770227

OECD. (2019). *OECD Learning Compass 2030: Concept notes*. OECD Future of Education and Skills.

Olivola, C. Y., & Oppenheimer, D. M. (2008). Randomness in retrospect: Exploring the interactions between memory and randomness cognition. *Psychonomic Bulletin & Review, 15*(5), 991–996. DOI: 10.3758/PBR.15.5.991 PMID: 18926994

Örün, Ö., & Sever, I. (2025). Cognitive flexibility: An educational approach. In Özen, H., & Polat, G. (Eds.), *Resilience, adaptability, and cultural awareness within the educational landscape* (pp. 179–208). IGI Global Scientific Publishing., DOI: 10.4018/979-8-3693-6040-8.ch007

Paas, F., & Sweller, J. (2012). An evolutionary upgrade of cognitive load theory: Using the human motor system and collaboration to support the learning of complex cognitive tasks. *Educational Psychology Review*, *24*(1), 27–45. DOI: 10.1007/s10648-011-9179-2

Pacheco, C., Lahiri, S. K., Ernst, M. D., & Ball, T. (2007, May). Feedback-directed random test generation. In *9th International Conference on Software Engineering (ICSE'07)*, Minneapolis, MN, USA, pp. 75-84. https://doi.org/DOI: 10.1109/ICSE.2007.37

Pecher, B., Srba, I., & Bielikova, M. (2023). A survey on stability of learning with limited labelled data and its sensitivity to the effects of randomness. *arXiv*: 2312.01082. https://doi.org//arXiv.2312.01082DOI: 10.48550

Popov, A. (2023). The rise of random task generators in language learning: Embracing the era of randomness. *TESL Ontario Contact Magazine, Nov 2023*, 34-36.

Reeves, T. C., & Lin, L. (2020). The research we have is not the research we need. *Educational Technology Research and Development*, *68*(4), 1991–2001. DOI: 10.1007/s11423-020-09811-3 PMID: 32837123

Revati, V. (2024). Integrating constructivism, science education, and technology: An investigation into pedagogical strategies, student engagement, and learning outcomes in the digital age. *International Journal for Research in Applied Science and Engineering Technology*, *12*(12), 1021–1026. DOI: 10.22214/ijraset.2024.65933

Robinson, P. (2011). Second language task complexity, the Cognition Hypothesis, language learning, and performance. In Robinson, P. (Ed.), *Second language task complexity: Researching the Cognition Hypothesis of language learning and performance* (pp. 3–38). John Benjamins., DOI: 10.1075/tblt.2.05ch1

Rosen, D. (2019). Being in uncertainties: An inquiry-based model leveraging complexity in teaching-learning. [NEJCS]. *Northeast Journal of Complex Systems*, *1*(1), 5. Advance online publication. DOI: 10.22191/nejcs/vol1/iss1/5

Ryan, R. M., & Deci, E. L. (2017). *Self-determination theory: Basic psychological needs in motivation, development, and wellness*. The Guilford Press., DOI: 10.1521/978.14625/28806

Schunk, D. H. (2012). *Learning Theories: An Educational Perspective* (6th ed.). Pearson.

Seow, P.-S., Pan, G., & Koh, G. (2019). Examining an experiential learning approach to prepare students for the volatile, uncertain, complex and ambiguous (VUCA) work environment. *International Journal of Management Education, 17*(1), 62–76. DOI: 10.1016/j.ijme.2018.12.001

Shin, Y., Kim, D., & Song, D. (2019). Types and timing of scaffolding to promote meaningful peer interaction and increase learning performance in computer-supported collaborative learning environments. *Journal of Educational Computing Research, 58*(3), 640–661. DOI: 10.1177/0735633119877134

Spiro, R. J., Klautke, H. A., Cheng, C., & Gaunt, A. (2017). Cognitive flexibility theory and the assessment of 21st century skills. In Secolsky, C., & Denison, B. (Eds.), *Handbook on Measurement, Assessment, and Evaluation in Higher Education* (pp. 631–637). Routledge., DOI: 10.4324/9781315709307-50

Stein, S. (2021). Reimagining global citizenship education for a volatile, uncertain, complex, and ambiguous (VUCA) world. *Globalisation, Societies and Education, 19*(4), 482–495. DOI: 10.1080/14767724.2021.1904212

Suskie, L. (2018). *Assessing student learning: A common sense guide* (3rd ed.). Jossey-Bass.

Swain, M., & Lapkin, S. (1998). Interaction and second language learning: Two adolescent French immersion students working together. *Modern Language Journal, 82*(3), 320–337. DOI: 10.1111/j.1540-4781.1998.tb01209.x

Sweller, J. (1988). Cognitive load during problem solving: Effects on learning. *Cognitive Science, 12*(2), 257–285. DOI: 10.1207/s15516709cog1202_4

Trilling, B., & Fadel, C. (2009). *21st Century Skills: Learning for life in our times.* Jossey-Bass.

Turnbull, K. P., & Justice, L. M. (2012). *Language development from theory to practice* (2nd ed.). Pearson.

UNESCO. (2022). *Reimagining our futures together: A new social contract for education.* UNESCO Publishing.

Vedovelli, C. (2022). Learning environments that enhance students' cognitive functioning. *Form@re - Open Journal Per La Formazione in Rete, 22*(1), 322–339. https://doi.org/DOI: 10.36253/form-12606

Velázquez-Vargas, C. A., Daw, N. D., & Taylor, J. A. (2024). The role of training variability for model-based and model-free learning of an arbitrary visuomotor mapping. *PLoS Computational Biology*, *20*(9), e1012471. DOI: 10.1371/journal.pcbi.1012471 PMID: 39331685

Vetrivel, S. C., Vidhyapriya, P., & Arun, V. P. (2024). The role of AI in transforming assessment practices in education. In Keeley, K. (Ed.), *AI Applications and Strategies in Teacher Education* (pp. 43–70). IGI Global Scientific Publishing., DOI: 10.4018/979-8-3693-5443-8.ch003

Videla-Reyes, R., & Aguayo, C. (2022). Pedagogy of uncertainty: Laying down a path in walking with STEAM. *Pacific Journal of Technology Enhanced Learning*, *4*(1), 29–30. DOI: 10.24135/pjtel.v4i1.147

Vygotsky, L. S. (1978). *Mind in society: The development of higher psychological processes*. Harvard University Press.

Wigfield, A., & Eccles, J. S. (2002). The development of competence beliefs, expectancies for success and achievement values from childhood through adolescence. In Wigfield, A., & Eccles, J. S. (Eds.), *Development of Achievement Motivation* (pp. 91–120). Academic Press., DOI: 10.1016/B978-012750053-9/50006-1

Zimmerman, B. J. (2002). Becoming a self-regulated learner: An overview. *Theory into Practice*, *41*(2), 64–70. DOI: 10.1207/s15430421tip4102_2

Chapter 8

Optimizing Software Development through Agile Framework Diversity

Shuvajyoti Kar
https://orcid.org/0000-0002-6570-0185
School of Computer Engineering, Kalinga Institute of Industrial Technology, Bhubaneswar, India

Aman Pratap Prajapati
https://orcid.org/0009-0002-4919-2819
School of Computer Engineering, Kalinga Institute of Industrial Technology, Bhubaneswar, India

Hitesh Mohapatra
https://orcid.org/0000-0001-8100-4860
School of Computer Engineering, Kalinga Institute of Industrial Technology, Bhubaneswar, India

ABSTRACT

Agile methodologies have transformed software development by promoting flexibility, collaboration, and user-focused design. This paper compares major Agile frameworks—Scrum, Kanban, XP, Lean, FDD, Crystal, and SAFe—highlighting their impacts on productivity, adaptability, and teamwork. Case studies like Spotify and Toyota show that while all adhere to Agile principles, each framework differs in execution and results. Scrum offers structured planning, Kanban emphasizes visual flow, XP focuses on engineering rigor, and Lean aims to eliminate waste. SAFe and Crystal address scalability and adaptability. Though Agile boosts communication

DOI: 10.4018/979-8-3373-3301-4.ch008

and responsiveness, it also presents challenges like cultural resistance and scaling issues. The study concludes that successful Agile adoption requires organizational readiness, leadership support, and continuous learning, emphasizing that Agile works best when tailored to specific contexts.

INTRODUCTION

1.1. Agile Methodologies in Software Development

Agile methodologies have revolutionized software development by offering a flexible and iterative approach that prioritizes collaboration, adaptability, and customer satisfaction. This introduction is structured into three comprehensive sections to explore the foundations of Agile methodologies, their significance in modern software development, and their key benefits.

1.1.1. Definition of Agile Methodologies

Agile methodologies represent a group of software development frameworks and practices rooted in the principles of flexibility, collaboration, and iterative progress. Originating from the Agile Manifesto in 2001, these methodologies emphasize the delivery of functional software in smaller increments rather than delivering a final product at the end of a traditional project lifecycle (Ahimbisibwe et al., 2015). Agile frameworks enable teams to address changes dynamically, respond to evolving requirements, and ensure alignment with stakeholder needs. Among the most prominent Agile frameworks are Scrum, Kanban, and Extreme Programming (XP). Scrum is a structured methodology that divides projects into fixed-length iterations known as sprints, each typically lasting two to four weeks. It relies on predefined roles including the Scrum Master, Product Owner, and Development Team to ensure efficient task execution and collaboration. Artifacts such as the Product Backlog and Sprint Backlog serve as tools for task tracking and prioritization (Albonico et al., 2023).

Kanban, on the other hand, emphasizes workflow visualization through tools such as Kanban boards. This framework enables teams to identify bottlenecks, optimize resource allocation, and improve efficiency in real time. Extreme Programming (XP) focuses on engineering practices designed to enhance code quality and team collaboration. Techniques such as pair programming, test-driven development, and continuous integration are central to XP, ensuring the creation of robust and scalable software solutions. While these frameworks vary in their specific practices, they all adhere to the core principles outlined in the Agile Manifesto (Almashhadani et al., 2024). The emphasis on iterative development, customer collaboration, and responsiveness to change makes Agile a versatile approach adaptable to diverse project environments and team dynamics.

1.1.2. Prominent Agile Methodologies

Agile methodologies are defined by the frameworks that implement their principles in practice. Below is an in-depth examination of the prominent Agile frameworks that have significantly influenced software development.

1.1.2.1. Scrum

Scrum is a widely adopted Agile framework focused on iterative and incremental software development. It promotes adaptive planning, early delivery, and continuous improvement through flexible responses to change. Work is divided into short, manageable cycles called sprints, typically lasting two to four weeks, with each sprint producing a potentially shippable product increment (Alqudah et al., 2023). This time-boxed approach helps teams maintain focus and deliver working software regularly, enabling rapid feedback. Scrum is characterized by clearly defined roles that ensure accountability. The Scrum Master facilitates the process, ensuring Scrum principles are upheld and removing obstacles. The Product Owner represents stakeholders, prioritizing the product backlog based on business value (Arora et al., 2020).

Figure 1. Scrum workflow in practice

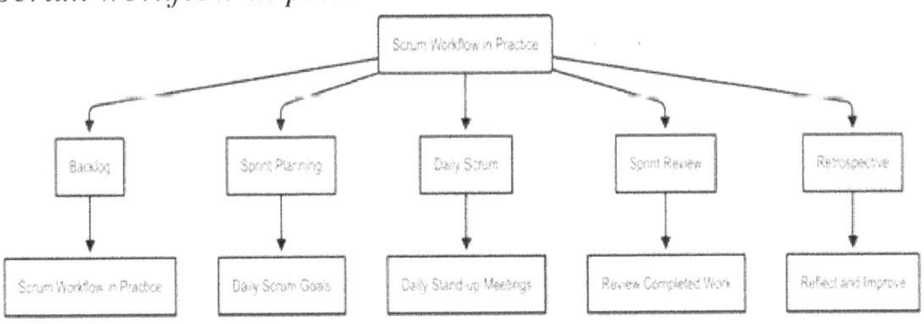

The Development Team is a cross-functional group responsible for designing, building, testing, and delivering the product increment during each sprint. Key artifacts in Scrum include the Product Backlog a dynamic, prioritized list of desired features and improvements and the Sprint Backlog, which outlines the items selected for the sprint along with a plan for achieving the sprint goal, as shown in Figure 1. The Increment represents all completed backlog items at the end of the sprint and must be in a usable state. Scrum also includes essential ceremonies: the Daily Scrum for daily synchronization, the Sprint Review to demonstrate completed work and gather feedback, and the Sprint Retrospective to reflect on the sprint and plan improvements (Baniya et al., 2025). These practices foster transparency, collaboration, and continuous improvement, making Scrum an effective framework for delivering high-quality products while adapting to changing needs.

1.1.2.2. Kanban

Kanban is a visual workflow management framework designed to enhance efficiency, transparency, and adaptability. Unlike Scrum, which utilizes fixed-length sprints, Kanban operates on a continuous delivery model, allowing work to progress without predefined cycles. This flexibility makes it suitable for projects with shifting priorities. The Kanban board is central to the framework, offering a visual representation of tasks in various stages such as “To Do,” “In Progress,” and “Done.” Each task is represented by a card, which moves through the columns as it progresses. This approach enables teams to monitor status, identify bottlenecks, and optimize workflow (Barbala et al., 2025). A core principle of Kanban is limiting work-in-progress (WIP) to avoid overloading team members. This leads to a sustainable pace, reduced lead times, and higher output quality. Kanban’s pull-based system allows teams to reprioritize based on capacity, enhancing responsiveness and flexibility.

1.1.2.3. Extreme Programming (XP)

Extreme Programming (XP) is an Agile framework that emphasizes technical excellence, collaboration, and responsiveness in fast-paced environments. It promotes disciplined engineering practices and frequent stakeholder interaction to produce high-quality software. A key practice is pair programming, where two developers collaborate at a single workstation one writes code while the other reviews it (Basak et al., 2025). This approach fosters real-time feedback, higher code quality, and shared knowledge. Another foundational technique is Test-Driven Development (TDD), in which developers write tests before writing the corresponding code. This ensures reliable, well-tested software and supports confident refactoring. Continuous Integration (CI), another XP hallmark, involves frequent merging of code into a shared repository with automated testing to detect issues early. XP also promotes simplicity in design, open communication, and regular feedback through iterations of one to two weeks, ensuring consistent progress and reduced project risk (Behutiye et al., 2022).

1.1.2.4. Lean Software Development

Derived from Lean manufacturing, Lean Software Development aims to reduce waste and maximize value by emphasizing flow efficiency and team empowerment. Core practices include just-in-time production, decentralized decision-making, and the "build-measure-learn" feedback loop (Boehm & Bose, n.d.). These support iterative refinement and efficient resource usage. Lean also emphasizes continuous improvement and the elimination of non-value-adding activities.

1.1.2.5. Scaled Agile Framework (SAFe)

The Scaled Agile Framework (SAFe) extends Agile principles across large enterprises. It enables coordination among multiple teams through synchronized planning and execution cycles. SAFe integrates concepts from Scrum, Kanban, and Lean to manage complexity while aligning efforts with organizational goals (Boehm & Turner, n.d.). SAFe's Agile Release Train (ART) consists of multiple Agile teams working toward shared objectives on a fixed cadence. Roles such as Release Train Engineer and System Architect support coordination and delivery. Lean Portfolio Management ensures initiatives are aligned with business priorities. SAFe also incorporates DevOps and Continuous Delivery practices, reinforcing frequent, high-quality releases (Bunio, 2012).

1.1.2.6. Crystal Methodologies

Crystal Methodologies comprise a family of Agile approaches designed to adapt to varying project sizes, complexities, and team dynamics. Introduced by Alistair Cockburn, the framework emphasizes the importance of people, interactions, and project context over rigid procedural adherence (Cabrera & Cabrera, 2023). Rather than prescribing a fixed set of practices, Crystal offers a spectrum of methodologies such as Crystal Clear, Crystal Yellow, and Crystal Orange each calibrated for teams of different sizes and levels of criticality. The underlying philosophy is that effective communication and collaboration are central to project success, and processes should be as lightweight as the context allows. Core practices include regular delivery of working software, reflective improvement cycles, and minimal but sufficient documentation (Chaudhari et al., 2025). Unlike more prescriptive frameworks, Crystal encourages teams to evolve their workflows organically, based on feedback and shared experience. This adaptability makes it particularly suitable for organizations that value autonomy and need to tailor Agile practices without compromising on accountability or quality (Conboy & Carroll, 2019).

1.2. Significance of Agile Methodologies in Modern Software Development

The adoption of Agile methodologies has become increasingly significant in the context of modern software development. Traditional development models, such as the Waterfall approach, often struggled to accommodate the rapid pace of technological advancements and evolving customer expectations (Da Silva et al., 2012). Agile methodologies address these challenges by promoting a dynamic and iterative approach to project management that embraces change and feedback. One of the primary reasons for Agile's significance is its ability to accelerate the delivery of functional software. By breaking down projects into smaller, manageable increments, Agile enables teams to deliver working features at regular intervals, thereby providing stakeholders with early and continuous value (Dikert et al., 2016). This incremental delivery model not only reduces time-to-market but also fosters a culture of continuous feedback and iterative improvement. Furthermore, Agile's emphasis on collaboration and transparent communication has redefined team dynamics in contemporary software development. Agile frameworks encourage cross-functional teamwork, wherein developers, designers, testers, and business analysts work collectively toward shared objectives. Rituals such as daily stand-up meetings, sprint planning sessions, and retrospectives create structured opportunities for open dialogue and alignment, reducing misunderstandings and fostering accountability (Dingsoyr et al., 2012). In a rapidly evolving technological landscape, Agile methodologies provide organizations with the adaptability required to remain competitive. Agile teams are empowered to pivot in response to shifting market demands, emerging technologies, or unforeseen constraints. This responsiveness ensures that software products remain aligned with customer expectations and industry trends, even in the face of volatility and uncertainty. As such, Agile has emerged as a foundational approach for delivering relevant, high-quality software in dynamic environments (Diwakar et al., 2025).

1.3. Benefits of Agile Methodologies in Modern Software Development

Agile methodologies offer a multitude of benefits that have contributed to their widespread adoption across industries, as shown in Table.1 Among the most notable advantages are flexibility, faster delivery, and enhanced customer satisfaction. Flexibility is a hallmark of Agile methodologies (Duarte & Cruz Machado, 2017). Unlike rigid traditional models, Agile accommodates changes at any stage of the development process. Whether due to evolving customer requirements or unforeseen technical challenges, Agile teams are empowered to adapt their plans and priorities without compromising project progress. This flexibility is particularly valuable in industries characterized by rapid innovation and dynamic market conditions (Duncan, 2018). Faster delivery of functional software is another critical advantage of Agile. The iterative nature of Agile frameworks ensures that development teams can deliver incremental improvements at regular intervals. By focusing on delivering the highest-priority features first, Agile minimizes the time between project initiation and the realization of customer value. This accelerated delivery model not only improves time-to-market but also reduces the risk of developing features that may become obsolete or misaligned with user needs. Enhanced customer satisfaction is a direct outcome of Agile's customer-centric approach (Dyba & Dingosyr, 2008). Agile methodologies prioritize stakeholder engagement and feedback throughout the project lifecycle. Regular demonstrations of progress, opportunities for input, and iterative refinements ensure that the final product meets or exceeds customer expectations. This customer-focused approach builds trust and confidence, fostering stronger relationships between development teams and their stakeholders (Fitzgerald et al., 2013). In addition to these primary benefits, Agile methodologies also contribute to improved team morale and productivity. By promoting a collaborative and inclusive work environment, Agile empowers team members to take ownership of their work and contribute meaningfully to project outcomes. Practices such as self-organizing teams and shared decision-making enhance employee engagement, resulting in higher levels of job satisfaction and motivation (Gandomani & Nafchi, 2016).

Table 1. Comparison of agile frameworks and their key features

Framework	Key Features
Scrum	Fixed-length sprints (2–4 weeks), defined roles (Scrum Master, Product Owner, Development Team), and artifacts (backlogs).
Kanban	Visual workflow via Kanban boards, continuous delivery, work-in-progress (WIP) limits.
Extreme Programming	Practices like pair programming, test-driven development (TDD), and continuous integration.
Lean Development	Minimizes waste, focuses on just-in-time production, and promotes "build-measure-learn" cycles.
SAFe (Scaled Agile Framework)	Designed for enterprise-level Agile adoption, supports alignment across multiple teams through Agile Release Trains (ARTs), and incorporates roles, cadences, and backlogs at different levels of scale (Ghobadi & Mathiassen, 2016)
Crystal Methodologies	A family of Agile methods (e.g., Crystal Clear, Crystal Orange) tailored by team size and project criticality; emphasizes human-centric collaboration, lightweight processes, and adaptability.

2. LITERATURE REVIEW

2.1. Comparative Analysis on the Effectiveness of Agile Methodologies in boosting Productivity and Collaboration

Numerous studies have explored the impact of Agile methodologies on productivity and collaboration, providing empirical evidence of its advantages and challenges. A landmark study conducted a systematic review of empirical research on Agile software development, highlighting its effectiveness in promoting team communication and productivity (Gren et al., 2014). The review identified that Agile's iterative and incremental nature enables teams to deliver functional software more frequently, thereby facilitating faster value delivery and continuous stakeholder feedback. The researchers emphasized that Agile's collaborative practices, such as daily stand-ups and retrospective meetings, foster team cohesion and alignment (Gustavsson et al., 2022). In a comparative analysis, authors evaluated the productivity levels of teams employing Agile versus traditional Waterfall methods. The study revealed that Agile teams consistently outperformed their counterparts in terms of task completion rates and software quality. The iterative cycles of Agile frameworks, such as Scrum and Kanban, were particularly effective in reducing bottlenecks and maintaining steady progress. However, the study also noted challenges associated with initial adoption, including organizational resistance and the steep learning curve for teams transitioning from conventional methodologies (Han, 2021). Recent evidence further supports these findings. For example, authors demonstrated that Agile teams exhibited significantly higher collaboration scores, particularly in environments that emphasized leadership support and team empowerment. The study underscored the role of Agile ceremonies and visual task boards in facilitating real-time knowledge sharing and problem resolution. Similarly, a study by investigated Agile's role in enhancing team collaboration and performance in software startups. The researchers concluded that Agile practices, particularly pair programming and cross-functional team structures, led to improved knowledge transfer, faster issue resolution, and increased innovation (Harder & Göde, 2012).

2.1.1. Comparative Analysis on the Effectiveness of Agile Methodologies in boosting Productivity

Agile methodologies have emerged as a transformative force in the field of software development, enabling teams to navigate complex projects with greater adaptability, speed, and efficiency (Hoda et al., 2011). Among the diverse frameworks within the Agile ecosystem, Scrum, Kanban, Extreme Programming (XP), Lean Agile, Scaled Agile Framework (SAFe), and Crystal each offer unique advantages and pose distinct challenges in terms of enhancing productivity, as shown in Table 2. A comparative analysis of these methodologies reveals how they influence team performance, communication, and output in varying contexts, as shown in Figure 2.

2.1.1.1. Scrum

Scrum, arguably the most widely adopted Agile methodology, is structured around time-boxed iterations known as sprints, which typically span two to four weeks. This iterative model fosters a sense of urgency and accountability, helping teams break down large tasks into manageable units and deliver incremental progress consistently (Hohl et al., 2018). The use of fixed-length sprints contributes to increased focus and better workload estimation, both of which are essential for maintaining high productivity levels. Daily stand-up meetings further enhance team coordination by facilitating rapid identification and resolution of blockers, thereby reducing potential downtime (Ikonen et al., 2011). Moreover, Scrum's reliance on backlog prioritization ensures that development efforts are directed toward the most valuable tasks, thus optimizing resource allocation. Sprint retrospectives allow teams to reflect on their performance, identify inefficiencies, and implement actionable improvements (Kalenda et al., 2018). However, Scrum is not without its limitations. The framework is vulnerable to scope creep, particularly in environments where product requirements evolve rapidly. Additionally, teams unfamiliar with Scrum may struggle to fulfill their sprint commitments, potentially hampering overall productivity.

2.1.1.2. Kanban

Kanban, another prominent Agile methodology, emphasizes visual workflow management, continuous delivery, and the limitation of work in progress (WIP). Unlike Scrum, which is bound by sprint cycles, Kanban supports a continuous flow of work, allowing teams to respond to changing demands without rigid planning structures (Kasauli et al., 2020). This adaptability is particularly advantageous in operational or maintenance-focused environments, where task unpredictability is common. The visual representation of tasks on a Kanban board enhances transparency and helps identify bottlenecks, facilitating better workload distribution and process optimization. By imposing WIP limits, Kanban discourages multitasking, which has been shown to reduce cognitive efficiency and overall productivity (Kaushik et al., 2020). However, Kanban's lack of predefined deadlines can sometimes lead to complacency, and overloaded workflow columns may signal deeper inefficiencies in task allocation or estimation.

Figure 2. Effect of implementation of agile methodologies on productivity

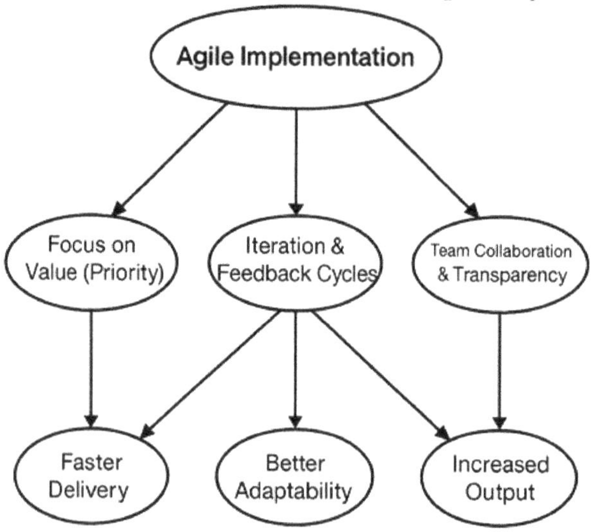

2.1.1.3. Extreme Programming (XP)

Extreme Programming (XP), originally developed to address the risks inherent in high-change software environments, introduces practices that aim to improve both software quality and developer productivity (Klünder et al., 2022). Key among these is pair programming, where two developers collaboratively write code. While this may initially appear to slow progress, it often results in higher-quality output and fewer bugs, ultimately saving time in later stages of development. XP also promotes continuous integration (CI), which minimizes integration-related issues by ensuring that code changes are regularly merged into a shared repository. This practice maintains code stability and accelerates feedback cycles (Kowalczyk et al., 2022). Test-driven development (TDD), another core tenet of XP, requires developers to write tests before implementing the corresponding functionality. This approach significantly reduces the likelihood of regression errors and rework, thereby enhancing overall productivity. Furthermore, XP emphasizes close collaboration with stakeholders, ensuring that the software being developed aligns with user needs and expectations (Kummari, 2025). Nevertheless, the methodology's intensive practices such as pair programming and TDD demand significant upfront investment and may not be immediately efficient for all teams.

2.1.1.4. Lean Software Development

Lean Agile, inspired by lean manufacturing principles, aims to maximize value delivery while minimizing waste. By identifying and eliminating non-value-adding activities such as redundant documentation or unnecessary meetings Lean enhances time efficiency and allows teams to focus on critical tasks (Kupiainen et al., 2015). The methodology emphasizes fast feedback loops, enabling teams to respond swiftly to changes in requirements and avoid prolonged development cycles. Empowering team members to make decisions independently also reduces delays associated with hierarchical approval chains, thereby enhancing responsiveness. Moreover, Lean encourages a culture of continuous improvement, where teams are expected to regularly reflect on their processes and implement refinements that enhance efficiency ("Lean Manufacturing Application to Improve Quality and Productivity," 2023). However, successful implementation of Lean Agile often requires a significant cultural shift within the organization, which can delay productivity gains during the transition phase.

2.1.1.5. Scaled Agile Framework (SAFe)

At the enterprise level, the Scaled Agile Framework (SAFe) offers a comprehensive solution for coordinating multiple Agile teams working on large-scale projects. SAFe aligns teams under a shared vision through program increments (PIs), which are larger time-boxed periods similar to Scrum sprints but scaled for cross-team collaboration (Lenberg et al., 2020). This structure enhances synchronization and reduces the risk of misaligned deliverables, particularly in complex environments with interdependent workflows. Built-in quality practices, such as standardization and governance protocols, help reduce rework and maintain consistency across teams (Lobasev, 2022). However, SAFe introduces additional roles, layers of planning, and ceremonies that can increase bureaucratic overhead, especially during the initial phases of adoption. These complexities may momentarily dampen productivity until teams acclimate to the new processes ("Make Certain Your Marketing Strategy Will Have a Good Chance of Being Successful," 2010).

2.1.1.6. Crystal Methodologies

Crystal methodologies, a family of lightweight Agile approaches tailored to team size and project complexity, take a human-centric approach by prioritizing individuals and interactions over rigid processes (Lous et al., 2017). Crystal's flexibility enables teams to adapt their methods to specific project contexts, improving morale and engagement, which are key drivers of productivity (Mohapatra, 2024). Minimal documentation and reduced procedural formalities also decrease administrative burdens. However, the lack of structure in Crystal can lead to inconsistencies in project execution, particularly in larger teams or regulated industries where more formal oversight is required (Mohapatra et al., 2025).

Table 2. Comparative overview of agile methodologies based on features, productivity, and suitability

Methodology	Key Features	Productivity Strengths	Productivity Challenges	Best Suited For
Scrum	Time-boxed sprints, defined roles	Structured work cycles, high team visibility	Scope creep, over-commitment risks	Complex, evolving projects
Kanban	Continuous flow, WIP limits	Quick adaptation, minimized multitasking	Potential complacency, bottlenecks in WIP	Maintenance, operational tasks
XP	Pair programming, TDD, CI	High code quality, reduced rework	Initial slowdown, high collaboration demands	High-risk, high-complexity projects
Lean Agile	Value stream mapping, waste minimization	Efficiency, empowerment, quick adjustments	Cultural change, difficult in hierarchical organizations	Startups, efficiency-driven projects
SAFe	Hierarchical scaling, synchronized teams	Large-scale alignment, quality assurance	Overhead, complex adoption process	Large enterprises, regulated industries
Crystal	Tailored processes, individual focus	Flexibility, motivated teams	Inconsistent outcomes, scalability issues	Small to medium teams, creative work

2.1.2. Comparative Analysis on the Effectiveness of Agile Methodologies in boosting Adaptability

Agile methodologies are designed to support adaptability, a critical requirement in modern software development environments characterized by rapidly evolving user needs, volatile market dynamics, and emerging technologies, as shown in Figure 3. While each Agile methodology shares a common emphasis on flexibility and iterative feedback, they vary significantly in how adaptability is operationalized across processes, team structures, and decision-making mechanisms.

2.1.2.1. Scrum

Scrum, one of the most popular Agile methodologies, facilitates adaptability through several structured mechanisms. Its reliance on iterative time-boxed sprints, typically lasting two to four weeks, ensures that teams can reassess goals and incorporate changes based on evolving stakeholder requirements (Ohno & Bodek, 2019). Sprint reviews and retrospectives serve as formal checkpoints where teams reflect on recent progress and revise strategies for future iterations. Moreover, Scrum's flexible product backlog allows continuous reordering of priorities, enabling the development team to adapt to market changes efficiently (O'Reilly & Chatman, 2020). The involvement of cross-functional teams further reinforces adaptability by ensuring that diverse skills are present within a single unit, making it easier to handle shifting project demands without delays. Scrum's empirical process control model encourages data-driven decision-making through inspection, adaptation, and transparency. However, Scrum's rigidity in discouraging mid-sprint changes can delay urgent adaptations, especially in fast-paced environments requiring real-time responsiveness (Paasivaara et al., 2008).

2.1.2.2. Kanban

Kanban, in contrast, offers a more fluid and continuous approach to adaptability. It is particularly effective in scenarios where work demands are unpredictable or emergent. Kanban does not use time-boxed iterations; instead, it emphasizes a continuous workflow model, which allows teams to re-prioritize and manage tasks dynamically based on real-time feedback (Pereira et al., 2023). The use of visual boards to represent the current state of work enhances transparency, enabling teams to detect bottlenecks and redistribute workload as needed. Work-in-progress (WIP) limits act as a self-regulating mechanism to prevent overburdening and promote smoother transitions between tasks. The pull-based task allocation system, where team members select new tasks based on capacity, ensures that priorities can be shifted without disrupting overall workflow (Poppendieck, 2007). However, the lack of formal iteration boundaries or deadlines in Kanban may occasionally result in reduced urgency and slower responsiveness to critical or time-sensitive changes (Putta et al., 2018).

2.1.2.3. Extreme Programming (XP)

Extreme Programming (XP) offers a highly adaptive framework tailored for high-risk environments and rapidly changing requirements. XP encourages small, frequent releases, which ensure that feedback is received regularly and that course corrections can be implemented promptly (Rafique, 2021). Practices such as Test-Driven Development (TDD) and continuous integration are central to XP's adaptability. TDD, where tests are written before implementation, provides a safety net that enables developers to modify or extend code with confidence. Similarly, pair programming enhances adaptability by promoting immediate peer review and collective problem-solving, allowing the development process to be adjusted in real time as requirements shift (Raj et al., 2025). XP also emphasizes collective code ownership, where any team member can modify code, ensuring that adaptations are not bottlenecked by ownership restrictions. Nonetheless, XP's reliance on intensive customer feedback can sometimes slow down responsiveness when stakeholders are not consistently available for input (Rasch, 1991).

2.1.2.4. Lean Software Development

Lean Agile, derived from Lean manufacturing principles, emphasizes the elimination of waste and maximization of customer value. Lean promotes adaptability by reducing non-value-adding activities such as excessive documentation or bureaucratic decision-making, thereby streamlining the pathway for change implementation (Ramesh et al., n.d.). Teams are empowered to make decentralized decisions, allowing them to react swiftly to shifts in project direction or user expectations (Saur, 2003). Lean's focus on just-in-time production ensures that resources are allocated only when necessary, improving the team's ability to pivot when priorities change. Fast feedback loops and regular measurement through metrics like cycle time and lead time further enable continuous process optimization. Nevertheless, Lean's success depends heavily on organizational culture (Saur, 2005). Without strong buy-in from leadership and team members, the frequent changes required for true adaptability may encounter resistance, thereby limiting Lean's transformative potential.

2.1.2.5. Scaled Agile Framework (SAFe)

The Scaled Agile Framework (SAFe) extends Agile principles to large organizations and multiple interdependent teams. Its adaptability is evident in its structural support for periodic reassessments through Program Increments (PIs), which serve as enterprise-wide planning windows allowing for realignment based on updated market or customer data (Serrador & Pinto, 2015). SAFe integrates Lean Portfolio Management, ensuring that strategic investments align with operational execution, thereby enabling adaptability at both the team and organizational levels. Built-in quality standards ensure that changes can be made without introducing significant technical debt (Serrano et al., 2014). Agile Release Trains (ARTs) facilitate coordinated delivery across teams, which is vital in adjusting large-scale project deliverables. However, the complexity involved in implementing SAFe can sometimes create bureaucratic inertia, diluting the intended flexibility due to the need for additional roles, ceremonies, and governance layers (Shepherd et al., 2022).

2.1.2.6. Crystal Methodologies

Crystal, a lesser-known but highly adaptable Agile family of methodologies, offers tailored frameworks such as Crystal Clear, Crystal Orange, and others based on team size and project criticality. Crystal promotes adaptability through its process flexibility, allowing teams to choose methods that best fit their specific context. The emphasis on people and interactions over processes enables teams to make rapid, informal decisions that support agile pivots (Simmons, 2018).

Figure 3. Effect of implementation of agile methodologies on adaptability

Regular delivery cycles, minimal documentation, and iterative feedback loops ensure that adjustments can be made with minimal disruption. Human-centric decision-making is at the core of Crystal, and the framework allows project teams to self-adjust based on interpersonal dynamics and real-time feedback (Singh, 2021). Reflection workshops and team alignment sessions foster a culture of continuous learning and responsiveness.

Crystal's informal nature may limit its suitability in larger or more regulated environments, where a higher degree of consistency, documentation, and standardized practices is expected for compliance and coordination (Spinellis, 2006). In contrast, Scrum offers a more structured and predictable framework that supports iterative planning, defined roles, and regular review cycles, making it suitable for teams requiring clear process guidance. Kanban enables fluid, real-time adjustments by visualizing workflow and limiting work in progress, which helps teams respond quickly to changing priorities without overloading resources. XP emphasizes technical excellence and rapid feedback through practices such as test-driven development, continuous integration, and pair programming, thereby enhancing code quality and adaptability to frequent change (Stern, 2020). Lean focuses on efficiency and the reduction of waste while encouraging decentralized decision-making, which can empower teams to adapt processes and solutions closer to the point of value creation. SAFe, by contrast, is designed to support large-scale coordination across multiple teams and value streams, providing alignment and governance while attempting to preserve Agile responsiveness. Crystal remains notable for its person-centered flexibility, tailoring process rigor and communication modes to team size and project criticality, an aspect highlighted in Table 3. Consequently, selecting an appropriate methodology depends on factors such as project characteristics, organizational culture, regulatory context, and the required speed and scale of adaptability (Stephens & Rosenberg, 2003)

Table 3. Comparative overview of agile methodologies based on adaptability, challenges, and suitability

Methodology	Key Adaptability Features	Challenges	Best Suited For
Scrum	Retrospectives, backlog flexibility, time-boxing, stakeholder engagement, incremental delivery, empirical process control	Mid-sprint changes discouraged	Projects with evolving requirements
Kanban	Continuous flow, WIP limits, flow efficiency, pull system, visualization, decentralized decisions	Risk of complacency, bottlenecks	Operational and maintenance tasks
XP	Frequent releases, TDD, refactoring, continuous integration, pair programming, collective code ownership	Dependency on stakeholder input	High-complexity, high-risk projects
Lean Agile	Fast feedback loops, waste elimination, JIT production, lean metrics, value focus, empowered teams	Cultural inertia in traditional organizations	Value-driven, fast-paced projects
SAFe	Program Increments, ARTs, economic prioritization, continuous delivery pipeline, architectural runway	Bureaucratic inertia due to complexity	Large enterprises with multiple teams
Crystal	Process tailoring, minimal documentation, frequent delivery, human-centric approach, reflection workshops	Inconsistency in larger teams	Small to medium-sized teams, creative projects

2.2. Effectiveness of Agile Methodologies in boosting Collaboration

Agile methodologies prioritize communication and collaboration through various structured practices and ceremonies. These practices play a critical role in breaking down organizational silos and promoting transparency within development teams. For instance, daily stand-up meetings serve as regular touchpoints where team members share progress, identify impediments, and align their efforts, thereby fostering a sense of shared ownership and accountability (Suresh et al., 2023). The iterative and incremental development approach that characterizes Agile frameworks also ensures continuous stakeholder engagement, which in turn enhances communication between developers and end-users, as shown in Figure 4. Recent empirical studies have demonstrated that this ongoing feedback loop enables development teams to better understand user expectations and adapt deliverables accordingly, thereby improving software usability and end-user satisfaction (Tachibana & Tsuda, 2022). The iterative nature of Agile has also been widely acknowledged for its positive impact on team productivity ("Trustbusting in Japan," 1981). Agile methodologies advocate for the delivery of functional software increments at frequent intervals, which allows teams to detect and address issues early in the development lifecycle. This approach helps reduce technical debt and mitigates delays typically associated with late-stage defect discovery. According to recent research, Agile teams exhibit higher productivity levels due to effective task prioritization and regular release cycles that support continuous value delivery (Vacca et al., 2021). The use of tools like product backlogs and burndown charts enables systematic tracking of progress, which further enhances time management and delivery predictability across iterations (Vaishnavi & Suresh, 2020).

Figure 4. Effect of implementation of agile methodologies on collaboration

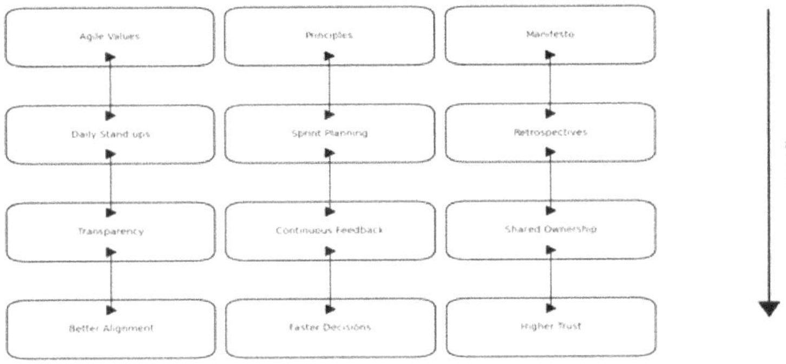

Another core strength of Agile lies in its adaptability to change, a characteristic that has proven especially valuable in volatile or rapidly evolving project environments. Agile frameworks are designed to embrace change, allowing development teams to pivot and reprioritize based on updated requirements or market dynamics without incurring significant productivity loss (Vallon et al., 2018). This flexibility plays a critical role in minimizing the risk of project failure, especially when requirements are ambiguous or subject to frequent revision. Recent findings suggest that Agile's inherent responsiveness enhances project resilience, empowering teams to proactively address emerging challenges and shifting priorities. In addition to productivity and adaptability, Agile practices also contribute significantly to the improvement of software quality. The integration of engineering practices such as test-driven development (TDD), continuous integration (CI), and automated testing ensures that code quality is maintained throughout the development process. Empirical evidence indicates that Agile teams leveraging these techniques detect defects earlier and deliver more stable code compared to teams using traditional waterfall models. Furthermore, iterative feedback cycles, combined with regular code reviews and refactoring, promote higher standards of software maintainability and robustness, ultimately enhancing customer satisfaction and long-term system sustainability (Wawak, 2024).

2.3. Challenges of Agile Methodologies

While Agile methodologies provide numerous advantages, they also pose a series of challenges that can influence their overall effectiveness and long-term sustainability. One of the most frequently cited challenges in Agile adoption is organizational resistance to change. Transitioning from traditional, plan-driven development models to Agile requires a fundamental cultural shift that includes embracing self-organization, collaborative decision-making, and adaptive planning (Zhao et al., 2020). For organizations entrenched in hierarchical or bureaucratic structures, this transition can be difficult to implement. Recent research has shown that the psychological and structural inertia within such organizations can impede Agile adoption unless carefully managed through structured change initiatives and continuous team education (Pereira et al., 2023). This resistance is often more pronounced in large enterprises where rigid workflows and risk-averse mindsets are deeply embedded. In addition to resistance to change, scalability remains a persistent issue when implementing Agile methodologies in larger, geographically distributed organizations. Agile practices, originally designed for small, co-located teams, often struggle to maintain their effectiveness when scaled across multiple teams and time zones. Empirical studies have identified challenges such as reduced communication efficiency, misalignment of objectives, and difficulty in coordinating work across distributed teams. To mitigate these issues, organizations frequently turn to frameworks such as the Scaled Agile Framework (SAFe), Large-Scale Scrum (LeSS), or Disciplined Agile Delivery (DAD). However, these frameworks require significant customization and organizational commitment to be effective, and they can introduce their own layers of complexity (Putta et al., 2018).

Another critical issue in Agile environments is the potential overemphasis on flexibility, which, if poorly managed, can lead to scope creep and diluted project focus. Although Agile promotes adaptability to changing requirements, this very flexibility can cause teams to deviate from strategic goals if proper controls are not established. Recent data from industry surveys and field studies indicate that many Agile teams face difficulties in maintaining a consistent backlog prioritization process, often leading to rework and reduced productivity (Kummari, 2025). This highlights the necessity of having clearly defined roles, stakeholder alignment, and robust product ownership to ensure that flexibility enhances rather than hinders project outcomes. Lastly, the success of agile model is heavily contingent upon effective team dynamics and high levels of interpersonal collaboration. The methodology assumes that all team members are not only technically competent but also capable of engaging in open communication, mutual support, and collaborative problem-solving. However, this assumption does not always hold true in practice. Challenges such as interpersonal conflicts, lack of trust, uneven skill distribution, and inadequate leadership can significantly impair team performance. Studies suggest that dysfunctional team dynamics can undermine core Agile practices such as pair programming, retrospectives, and self-organization. As a result, organizations must invest in team-building, leadership training, and conflict resolution mechanisms to maintain the efficacy of Agile implementations.

2.4. Case Study: Scrum Implementation at Spotify

Spotify, a global leader in music streaming services, has fundamentally transformed how digital audio content is consumed, offering users highly personalized listening experiences. Founded in 2006, the company quickly scaled, reaching millions of users across diverse markets. As the platform grew rapidly in the early 2010s, Spotify faced critical challenges in balancing rapid innovation with the demands of scalability, user experience, and product quality (Albonico et al., 2023). Traditional software development methodologies failed to support the level of responsiveness and cross-functional coordination Spotify needed. To address this, Spotify adopted Scrum and later customized it into what has become known as the "Spotify Model," a flexible and scalable adaptation of Agile principles. This model has since become a point of reference for Agile scaling in modern digital enterprises. Spotify's organizational model introduced a novel structural configuration built on small, autonomous, cross-functional teams called "Squads." Each Squad was responsible for a specific component or feature of the platform, such as the home interface, playback optimization, or playlist recommendation engine (Behutiye et al., 2022). These teams functioned like mini-startups, each with the autonomy to decide what to build, how to build it, and how to work together. Multiple Squads working in related domains were grouped into "Tribes," which helped maintain alignment and facilitate resource sharing. To ensure cross-Squad learning and maintain technical coherence, Spotify also instituted "Chapters" and "Guilds." Chapters brought together people with similar expertise, like backend developers or data scientists, under a functional lead, while Guilds were informal communities focused on common interests like DevOps or quality assurance. This configuration balanced the need for autonomy with cross-organizational alignment, a cornerstone of Agile at scale.

The Scrum practices within Spotify's Squads were centered around traditional time-boxed iterations, typically two to four weeks in duration. Sprint planning was handled collaboratively, ensuring buy-in from every team member. Squads maintained independent sprint backlogs, which were prioritized based on business value, customer feedback, and technical feasibility (Chaudhari et al., 2025). Each day began with stand-up meetings to promote visibility into team progress and impediments. At the end of each sprint, Squads conducted sprint reviews involving stakeholders, allowing feedback to be rapidly incorporated into future work. Sprint retrospectives followed, offering a structured space for reflection and continuous improvement. This commitment to frequent reflection and delivery enabled Spotify to maintain its competitive edge in a rapidly evolving market. Spotify's commitment to continuous improvement was bolstered by the strategic deployment of Agile coaches (Conboy & Carroll, 2019). These coaches played a pivotal role in supporting Squads, maintaining Scrum discipline, and facilitating interpersonal dynamics across teams. Their involvement ensured that Spotify's Agile practices did not stagnate or devolve into mechanical routines, a challenge often seen in organizations with long-standing Agile implementations. In addition to retrospectives, Spotify institutionalized "Innovation Days" and hackathons where team members were encouraged to work on exploratory projects unrelated to their daily sprint objectives. These events fostered creativity and often led to the development of successful features, such as collaborative playlists or podcast integration.

Technological agility was another critical component of Spotify's Scrum success. The organization invested heavily in automation and continuous integration/deployment pipelines, reducing human error and enabling frequent, reliable releases. These DevOps practices aligned with the iterative agile delivery model and ensured that features and updates could be deployed to users rapidly without compromising quality. Data analytics played an equally central role (Diwakar et al., 2025). Product decisions were grounded in robust A/B testing and user behavior analytics, enabling Squads to pivot or iterate based on empirical evidence rather than assumptions. Additionally, Spotify's cloud-native infrastructure allowed the platform to scale horizontally, supporting peak loads without performance degradation, a requirement for a service hosting over 500 million users globally. The outcomes of Scrum implementation at Spotify were substantial across various dimensions. Productivity significantly increased as Squads operated with a high degree of autonomy, making decisions quickly without bureaucratic impediments. Time-boxed sprints provided regular cadence and predictability in deliveries, keeping development on track. By structuring Squads around features rather than technologies, Spotify minimized cross-team dependencies and redundancy, further boosting efficiency. The incorporation of feedback loops at all levels user feedback, stakeholder reviews, and team retrospectives enhanced both product relevance and internal operations. Squads were not only able to deliver features faster but also with higher precision in terms of meeting user needs (Fitzgerald et al., 2013).

Spotify's Scrum-driven adaptability was one of its defining advantages. Teams were able to quickly reprioritize work in response to market trends, competitive threats, or internal insights. Retrospectives facilitated continual process improvement, while the influence of Agile coaches helped ensure that feedback was constructively translated into tangible changes (Han, 2021). The decentralized decision-making structure supported rapid pivots without the delay of hierarchical approval chains, an essential quality in the dynamic digital marketplace. Employee satisfaction also improved under Spotify's Scrum implementation. The autonomy granted to Squads increased their sense of ownership and purpose. Knowledge-sharing networks such as Chapters and Guilds fostered collaboration and reduced information silos, while also encouraging mentorship and personal growth. Recognition systems that celebrated individual and team contributions further enhanced morale. The cultural emphasis on psychological safety and empowerment was instrumental in retaining talent in an industry known for high churn rates (Kalenda et al., 2018). Moreover, Spotify saw substantial reductions in release cycles due to its Agile engineering practices. Continuous integration pipelines and automated testing enabled frequent and reliable releases, minimizing downtime and rollback risks. Agile coaches ensured that Squads adhered to Scrum principles without becoming dogmatic, maintaining a balance between consistency and flexibility. With multiple Squads working in parallel, features were rolled out concurrently, accelerating delivery to end-users. This not only shortened time-to-market but also enhanced the platform's ability to respond to real-time feedback.

From a strategic standpoint, Scrum enabled Spotify to retain a competitive edge in a saturated market. The company's ability to rapidly release and iterate on features meant that it could offer users a more personalized and innovative experience than rivals like Apple Music or Amazon Music. By leveraging user analytics and behavior tracking, Spotify continuously refined its recommendation algorithms and user interface, fostering greater user engagement and retention (Kaushik et al., 2020). The combination of fast-paced delivery and data-driven refinement helped Spotify grow its user base and revenue streams even amid intense competition. Nevertheless, the journey was not without its challenges. One of the key difficulties lay in maintaining alignment across increasingly autonomous Squads. While autonomy allowed for speed and innovation, it also introduced coordination problems, particularly when features required cross-Squad dependencies. Inconsistencies in user experience occasionally emerged due to variations in design standards or release timelines. Spotify addressed this with synchronization mechanisms such as "Tribe leads" and regular alignment meetings, although these added to the organizational overhead.

Figure 5. Outcomes of scrum implementation in Spotify

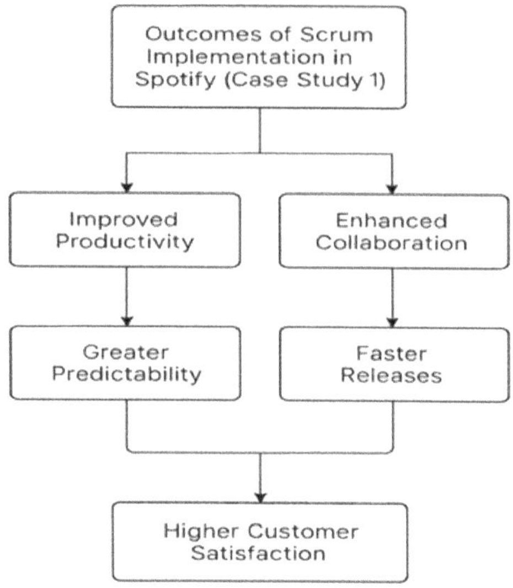

As the company scaled, additional challenges arose in maintaining agility. Communication overhead increased with the number of Squads, and it became more difficult to ensure that all teams were aligned on strategic goals. Technical debt began to accumulate as rapid iteration outpaced long-term architectural planning. While Spotify continued to invest in platform stability, this required a delicate balance between innovation and infrastructure improvement. Managing dependencies between Squads also became more complex, occasionally leading to bottlenecks that slowed progress (Saur, 2005). Coordination across multiple Squads working on interdependent components required dedicated release managers and program-level oversight. The cultural shift required for Scrum implementation was also non-trivial. Transitioning to a model where teams are self-organizing and fully accountable demanded a redefinition of leadership roles. Managers evolved into facilitators rather than directive overseers. Teams required time and support to adapt to their new responsibilities, and trust became a foundational element of team dynamics. Leadership had to invest in training, coaching, and open communication to ensure the model's long-term sustainability (Tachibana & Tsuda, 2022).

Several key learnings emerged from Spotify's experience, as shown in Figure 5. The importance of autonomy in fostering innovation and agility was reaffirmed. Self-organizing teams were faster, more motivated, and more accountable. However, autonomy had to be balanced with alignment, requiring thoughtful design of coordination mechanisms such as Tribes and Guilds (Shepherd et al., 2022). Continuous feedback, whether through retrospectives or user analytics, played a central role in iterative improvement. Spotify demonstrated that Agile could scale effectively when feedback loops are institutionalized and acted upon promptly. Equally important was the need for leadership and coaching (Stern, 2020). Agile coaches were instrumental in maintaining team health and process integrity, especially as the company grew (Putta et al., 2018). Leadership commitment was essential not only in providing resources but also in embodying the values of Agile trust, transparency, and empowerment, as shown in Table 4. Finally, Spotify's ability to balance structured Scrum practices with flexibility in execution provided a model for adaptive governance. Rather than rigid adherence to frameworks, Spotify embraced the spirit of Scrum while adapting its practices to meet evolving business and cultural needs. Spotify's Scrum implementation illustrated how Agile methodologies, when thoughtfully adapted, can support innovation, scalability, and organizational growth in a complex digital environment. The Spotify model continues to serve as a blueprint for Agile transformation, demonstrating that success lies not in rigid frameworks but in empowering people, fostering feedback, and continuously evolving practices.

Table 4. Segregation of roles and their responsibilities post Scrum implementation in Spotify

Role	Responsibilities	Primary Focus
Product Owner	- Defines and communicates the product vision - Manages and prioritizes the product backlog - Represents the stakeholders and customer needs - Accepts or rejects completed work	Maximizing product value and aligning development with business goals
Scrum Master	- Facilitates Scrum ceremonies (Sprint Planning, Daily Stand-ups, Sprint Review, Retrospective) - Removes impediments faced by the team - Ensures adherence to Agile principles and Scrum framework - Coaches the team on continuous improvement	Enabling effective team collaboration and ensuring smooth Scrum processes
Development Team	- Develops and tests product increments - Collaborates closely for design, development, and testing - Self-organizes to complete sprint backlog items - Ensures delivery of potentially shippable product at the end of each sprint	Creating functional, high-quality software within each sprint

continued on following page

Table 4. Continued

Role	Responsibilities	Primary Focus
Stakeholders	- Provide input and feedback on product development - Set business objectives and requirements - Participate in review sessions and decision-making	Aligning product development with organizational objectives
Agile Coach	Supports Agile transformation and training - Assists multiple teams in scaling Agile practices - Guides leadership and teams on Agile mindset	Organizational-level Agile adoption and maturity

2.5. Case Study: Kanban Implementation at Toyota

Toyota Motor Corporation, widely recognized as a global leader in the automotive industry, has established its reputation through its pioneering approaches to manufacturing and operations management. During the mid-20th century, Toyota encountered several critical challenges that included inefficiencies in inventory management, suboptimal production workflows, and the need for scalable systems to meet rising consumer demands. In response to these challenges, the company introduced the Kanban system, a visual workflow management strategy that later became a cornerstone of the Toyota Production System (TPS). The adoption of Kanban not only transformed Toyota's internal operations but also catalyzed a global shift in lean manufacturing practices. This methodology has since served as a model for numerous industries striving to enhance productivity, reduce waste, and streamline processes (Rafique, 2021). Toyota's Kanban system was grounded in a few fundamental principles that collectively redefined its approach to manufacturing. One of the foundational components was visual workflow management. Toyota deployed physical Kanban boards and cards to represent work items, thereby making each step in the production process visible to teams and supervisors. These visual cues facilitated better coordination and helped teams promptly identify and address bottlenecks. Another core element was the establishment of Work-in-Progress (WIP) limits. By constraining the number of tasks being processed at any given time, Toyota ensured a balanced workflow, thereby reducing congestion and enhancing throughput (Lenberg et al., 2020).

The production system was also built upon a pull-based mechanism, where manufacturing activities were initiated based on actual customer demand rather than speculative forecasts. This "pull system" enabled the company to reduce overproduction and maintain lean inventory levels, thus lowering associated holding costs. Furthermore, the principle of Continuous Improvement referred to as "Kaizen" within TPS was integral to Toyota's operational ethos. Employees at all levels were encouraged to propose enhancements, leading to incremental improvements in efficiency, quality, and team collaboration over time (Poppendieck, 2007). Just-in-Time (JIT) production, closely aligned with the Kanban framework, ensured that raw materials and components arrived precisely when required, avoiding stockpiling and promoting cost-efficient operations. The implementation process of Kanban within Toyota was both systematic and iterative. Physical Kanban cards were attached to containers of parts and were used to signal replenishment requirements (Vallon et al., 2018). This simple yet effective mechanism allowed for real-time inventory tracking without the need for complex software in the initial stages. Each workstation in the production line was aligned with explicit rules governing when and how to pull resources from upstream processes, fostering consistency in workflows and minimizing disruptions. Feedback loops were embedded into routine operations through performance reviews, retrospectives, and team debriefs. These feedback mechanisms enabled teams to make timely adjustments and ensure that production goals were consistently met or exceeded.

Toyota also emphasized cross-functional collaboration by involving personnel from multiple departments in process optimization. This inclusion fostered a shared sense of ownership and encouraged diverse problem-solving approaches. Supervisors played a key role in this ecosystem by maintaining adherence to Kanban principles while empowering team members to identify and implement solutions independently. This layered supervisory approach supported both accountability and innovation across different production stages (Wawak, 2024).

Technological integration became increasingly important as Toyota expanded its global footprint. The company progressively automated inventory tracking and scheduling systems to eliminate manual errors and optimize workflows. The integration of real-time data analytics enabled Toyota to identify emerging demand trends and adjust production accordingly, making operations more responsive and data-driven. To support global scalability, Toyota introduced standardized Kanban protocols that could be tailored for regional nuances, ensuring consistency across its international plants while allowing for localized flexibility, as shown in Figure 6. More recently, Toyota has adopted digital Kanban platforms, which enhance inter-team communication, facilitate quicker updates, and provide centralized oversight of the entire production pipeline (Zhao et al., 2020). The outcomes of implementing Kanban at Toyota were profound and multidimensional. One of the most immediate effects was a marked improvement in operational efficiency. By enforcing WIP limits and promoting real-time visibility of workflows, Toyota minimized idle time, eliminated redundant activities, and maintained a steady production rhythm. The visual representation of tasks allowed teams to prioritize more effectively and reduce miscommunications, further optimizing resource allocation and output quality. The pull-based approach to manufacturing led to optimal inventory levels and reduced instances of overproduction, thereby freeing up warehouse space and reducing related costs (Serrador & Pinto, 2015).

In terms of adaptability, Kanban enabled Toyota to swiftly respond to market volatility and changing consumer preferences. The system's embedded feedback loops allowed for real-time course correction, which was particularly advantageous during periods of market uncertainty or supply chain disruption (Ohno & Bodek, 2019). Furthermore, decentralizing decision-making empowered local teams to make tactical adjustments without waiting for top-down directives. This structural flexibility proved essential in allowing Toyota to recalibrate production volumes based on regional or global market demands. Kanban also played a significant role in enhancing product quality. The focus on continuous improvement translated into ongoing refinements in both product design and manufacturing techniques. Teams were able to identify defects early in the process, reducing the likelihood of defective products reaching customers (Mohapatra, 2024). Additionally, employee involvement in quality assurance created a sense of accountability and pride in craftsmanship, which contributed to consistently high product standards. Statistical process control tools were introduced to support quality monitoring and to standardize error detection and resolution processes.

From a cost management perspective, the Kanban system proved highly effective in curbing operational expenditures. Inventory optimization alone significantly reduced warehousing and holding costs. The efficient use of resources both human and material meant that the same or higher levels of output could be achieved with fewer inputs. Predictive analytics enabled Toyota to align production with real-time demand, avoiding both underutilization and surplus (Kowalczyk et al., 2022). The reduced rate of defects and reworks further contributed to cost savings by minimizing waste and warranty-related liabilities. Employee satisfaction also saw notable improvements following Kanban adoption. Empowering employees to contribute to decision-making and process refinement fostered a culture of trust and engagement. Workflow transparency, coupled with well-defined roles and responsibilities, alleviated workplace stress and improved task clarity (Klünder et al., 2022). Toyota's culture of recognizing and celebrating employee input reinforced motivation and retention. Continuous training programs ensured that employees remained proficient in emerging tools and practices, facilitating both individual and organizational growth.

Despite the numerous benefits, Toyota's transition to a Kanban-based system was not without challenges. One significant hurdle was resistance to change, particularly among employees accustomed to traditional manufacturing paradigms. The shift required a cultural transformation, which was facilitated through extensive training, clear communication from leadership, and continuous reinforcement of lean principles (Hohl et al., 2018). Sustaining this cultural shift required consistent effort across departments and time zones. Scaling the Kanban system across Toyota's international operations introduced logistical and operational complexities. Standardizing processes while maintaining enough flexibility to accommodate regional differences in labor laws, cultural norms, and regulatory requirements was particularly difficult. Balancing this dichotomy required Toyota to develop hybrid models that preserved core lean principles while allowing contextual adaptations (Hoda et al., 2011).

Another challenge pertained to dependency management. Toyota's global production network involved numerous suppliers, and coordinating activities among these stakeholders required robust communication channels. Any disruption in the supply chain could have cascading effects on production schedules. To address this, Toyota introduced contingency protocols and diversified its supplier base to mitigate risk exposure. Technological integration also posted its own set of difficulties (Kasauli et al., 2020). Retrofitting traditional processes with modern digital tools required significant capital investment and workforce upskilling. Furthermore, ensuring the cybersecurity and reliability of automated systems was critical to prevent production delays and data breaches. Toyota responded by incrementally phasing in new technologies and investing in both IT infrastructure and employee training (Kummari, 2025).

Figure 6. Outcomes of Kanban implementation in Toyota

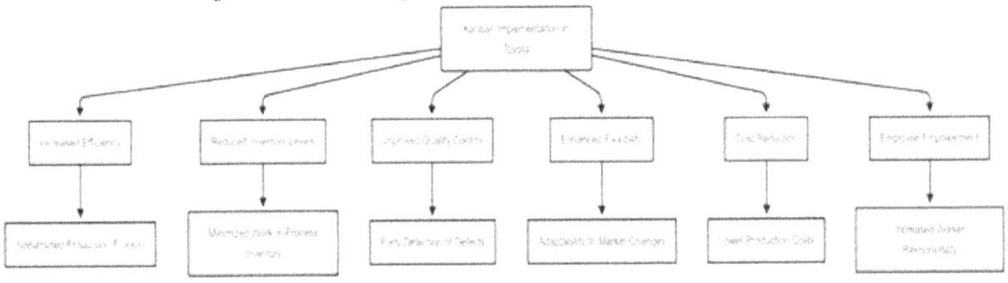

The implementation of Kanban at Toyota underscores the pivotal role of visual management in simplifying complex systems and enhancing operational clarity. Visualization tools helped employees identify issues in real time and act promptly, reducing downtime and inefficiency. Equally important was the embrace of continuous improvement as a cultural pillar. Small, consistent enhancements accumulated over time to yield significant gains in performance and innovation (Kupiainen et al., 2015). Toyota's experience highlights the necessity of striking a balance between standardization and adaptability. While global consistency is crucial for operational alignment, local flexibility ensures responsiveness to dynamic market conditions. This strategic duality has enabled Toyota to maintain efficiency while navigating regional challenges, as shown in Table.5 Finally, the empowerment of employees emerged as a central driver of success. Encouraging frontline workers to participate in decision-making and problem-solving enhanced their sense of ownership and organizational commitment, driving both morale and performance (Harder & Göde, 2012).

Table 5. Agile maturity model for Toyota post Kanban implementation

Level	Maturity Stage	Characteristics
5	Optimized	Continuous improvement is institutionalized; innovation and agility are embedded into the organization's DNA. Agile practices are adapted at scale across the enterprise.
4	Managed	Quantitative metrics and feedback loops are used for improvement; cross-functional collaboration is consistent; Agile practices are predictable and repeatable.
3	Defined	Agile processes and roles are clearly documented and standardized; teams understand and follow Scrum/Kanban practices consistently.
2	Emerging	Teams have started adopting Agile practices; roles may be unclear; ceremonies are followed inconsistently. Buy-in is limited to teams or departments.
1	Initial (Ad hoc)	Little or no Agile practices in place; processes are informal or chaotic; success depends on individual efforts rather than a defined process.

3. EMPIRICAL INSIGHTS

The reviewed literature consistently underscores the transformative impact of Agile methodologies on software development processes, particularly in enhancing productivity, fostering collaboration, and improving overall project outcomes. Agile frameworks such as Scrum, Kanban, Extreme Programming (XP), and Lean Software Development prioritize flexibility, iterative delivery, and continuous improvement, enabling organizations to respond more effectively to evolving business requirements and volatile market dynamics. These methodologies facilitate the decomposition of complex projects into smaller, manageable iterations, which supports more agile risk management practices and fosters early detection and resolution of emerging issues. Iterative delivery mechanisms allow for continuous integration of stakeholder feedback, cultivating a feedback-rich environment that enhances both product quality and customer satisfaction (Dikert et al., 2016).

Agile's emphasis on cross-functional collaboration strengthens team cohesion, transparency, and accountability. Agile ceremonies such as daily stand-up meetings, retrospectives, and sprint planning create an infrastructure for open communication and rapid decision-making, which, in turn, contributes to the development of more motivated and performance-oriented teams. From a productivity standpoint, time-boxed sprints and frequent delivery cycles help maintain consistent momentum and engagement by setting short-term, achievable objectives (Da Silva et al., 2012). Agile methodologies also facilitate a high degree of stakeholder involvement throughout the development life cycle, ensuring that evolving user expectations and business priorities are continually addressed. This continuous engagement loop significantly reduces the risk of delivering software solutions misaligned with customer needs.

Software quality sees notable improvement under Agile due to the embedded nature of practices like test-driven development, continuous integration, and frequent code reviews. Refactoring during iterative cycles ensures technical debt is managed effectively and system maintainability is enhanced (Duarte & Cruz Machado, 2017). Moreover, Agile frameworks offer mechanisms for adaptive planning, which empowers teams to reorient their strategies based on emerging information or changes in project scope. Consequently, the iterative nature of Agile does not only result in operational efficiency but also positions the organization to manage uncertainty in dynamic development environments. Despite the significant advantages Agile methodologies provide, their implementation is not without inherent challenges. One of the foremost issues encountered by organizations transitioning from traditional waterfall or plan-driven models is resistance to change (Gandomani & Nafchi, 2016). Agile requires a profound cultural transformation that prioritizes collaboration, flexibility, and decentralized decision-making, often conflicting with hierarchical organizational structures. Resistance can manifest at both managerial and team levels. Managers may perceive Agile practices as diminishing their control over planning and execution, while team members might experience difficulties adjusting to autonomous workflows and less prescriptive task assignments (Gren et al., 2014).

Scalability is another persistent challenge. While Agile is highly effective within small, co-located teams, applying the same principles across larger or distributed enterprises often leads to coordination bottlenecks and inconsistencies in implementation. Large-scale Agile frameworks such as SAFe and LeSS have emerged to address these concerns, yet their adoption still requires a balance between organizational agility and strategic alignment (Boehm & Turner, n.d.). Distributed Agile teams, particularly those operating across multiple time zones and cultural contexts, face additional barriers in maintaining synchronous communication, efficient collaboration, and timely feedback integration. Another area of concern lies in Agile team dynamics. While Agile promotes team autonomy and self-organization, this decentralization can sometimes result in role ambiguity, especially when responsibilities are not clearly delineated. Conflicts can emerge when decision rights are ill-defined or unevenly distributed. The need for balance between flexibility and structure becomes critical in such contexts (Arora et al., 2020). Moreover, maintaining long-term motivation and psychological well-being within Agile teams is essential, as rapid development cycles and continuous delivery expectations can lead to burnout and fatigue if not properly managed.

Given these complexities, future research should explore practical strategies for overcoming the challenges associated with Agile adoption. Tailored training programs aimed at developing an Agile mindset emphasizing adaptability, collaborative behavior, and iterative learning could mitigate resistance and foster smoother transitions. Enhanced digital collaboration platforms that incorporate synchronous communication tools, project tracking, and real-time feedback loops may also prove beneficial in bridging the gap between distributed teams (Ahimbisibwe et al., 2015). Additionally, hybrid models that blend Agile's responsiveness with traditional strategic planning approaches may help organizations achieve the dual goals of flexibility and alignment. The psychological dimension of Agile adoption also warrants greater empirical exploration. Agile teams often operate in high-pressure environments due to the iterative pace of delivery. As such, researchers could investigate how team structures, leadership styles, and organizational support systems influence work-life balance, team morale, and long-term retention in Agile contexts. Understanding the interplay between team autonomy and psychological safety could inform more sustainable Agile practices (Alqudah et al., 2023).

Longitudinal studies may provide critical insights into the sustained organizational impact of Agile transformations. Tracking companies over extended periods could illuminate how Agile maturity evolves, how organizations overcome structural inertia, and how these changes influence innovation capacity, time-to-market, and customer satisfaction. Additionally, comparative cross-sector analyses could shed light on industry-specific adaptations of Agile practices, enabling a more nuanced understanding of Agile's applicability and customization across different operational domains (Baniya et al., 2025).

Agile methodologies represent a significant shift from conventional software development paradigms. By fostering a dynamic, flexible, and collaborative approach, Agile aligns closely with the fast-paced and innovation-driven demands of the contemporary technological landscape (Almashhadani et al., 2024). However, achieving the full spectrum of Agile's benefits requires more than procedural adherence. It necessitates a comprehensive transformation encompassing organizational culture, leadership attitudes, structural flexibility, and psychological support mechanisms. By proactively addressing barriers such as scalability, resistance to change, and coordination complexity, organizations can unlock Agile's full potential. Ultimately, continuous improvement driven by both technological innovation and human-centric values positions Agile not merely as a development methodology, but as a holistic philosophy for organizational excellence in the digital age.

4. CONCLUSION

In navigating the dynamic and often unpredictable landscape of software development, this paper has explored how various Agile methodologies address the core need for adaptability a defining trait in high-performing, responsive organizations. From Scrum's structured cadence of sprints and roles to Kanban's visualized workflows and continuous delivery model, each framework offers a distinct perspective on managing change. Extreme Programming (XP) emphasizes engineering excellence through practices like pair programming and test-driven development, while Lean focuses on maximizing value by eliminating waste. Scaled Agile Frameworks (like SAFe and LeSS) extend Agile principles across enterprise-level teams, attempting to bridge agility with scale, though often at the cost of added complexity. A central insight emerging from this comparative analysis is that no single methodology offers a universal solution. Rather, adaptability is best achieved when organizations treat Agile as a guiding philosophy rather than a rigid framework. Teams must consider their specific context project size, domain constraints, stakeholder involvement, technical debt, and team maturity when selecting or tailoring a methodology. The effectiveness of Agile practices is highly dependent on organizational culture, leadership buy-in, and the ability to foster collaboration and open communication. Moreover, the success of Agile implementation lies in how organizations internalize and evolve the underlying values of agility: continuous learning, iterative improvement, customer-centric thinking, and empowered teams. Methodologies should be viewed as starting points for transformation, not end goals. Agile success often comes from hybrid approaches pulling effective elements from multiple frameworks to suit evolving needs. As the pace of technological change accelerates and complexity increases, the capacity to adapt swiftly and intelligently will remain a critical differentiator. Agile methodologies, when embraced with a mindset of flexibility, experimentation, and continuous improvement, offer powerful tools for navigating uncertainty. This study reinforces that adaptability is not just a benefit of Agile it is its very essence. Organizations that prioritize agility not only build better software but also cultivate teams and cultures that are resilient, forward-thinking, and ready to meet the future head-on.

REFERENCES

Ahimbisibwe, A., Cavana, R. Y., & Daellenbach, U. (2015). A contingency fit model of critical success factors for software development projects. *Journal of Enterprise Information Management*, *28*(1), 7–33. DOI: 10.1108/JEIM-08-2013-0060

Albonico, M., Đorđević, M., Hamer, E., & Malavolta, I. (2023). Software engineering research on the robot operating system: A systematic mapping study. *Journal of Systems and Software*, *197*, 111574. DOI: 10.1016/j.jss.2022.111574

Almashhadani, M., Mishra, A., & Yazici, A. (2024). Software maintenance practices using Agile methods towards cloud environment: A systematic mapping. *Journal of Software (Malden, MA)*, *36*(11), e2698. Advance online publication. DOI: 10.1002/smr.2698

Alqudah, M. K., Razali, R., Alqudah, M. K., Al Dalaien, M. N., Alabool, H. M., & Alkhazaleh, H. A. (2023). A grounded theory of selecting lean and Agile practices for software development. *Journal of Software (Malden, MA)*, *36*(4), e2539. Advance online publication. DOI: 10.1002/smr.2539

Arora, V., Singh, M., & Bhatia, R. (2020). Orientation-based ant colony algorithm for synthesizing the test scenarios in UML activity diagram. *Information and Software Technology*, *123*, 106292. DOI: 10.1016/j.infsof.2020.106292

Baniya, A. K., Pant, S. S., Paudel, D., Gupta, A., Singh, S., & Mohapatra, H. (2025). Load balancing in cloud computing ensuring fault tolerance, high availability, and security. Risk-Based Approach to Secure Cloud Migration, 253-284. https://doi.org/ DOI: 10.4018/979-8-3693-7137-4.ch010

Barbala, A., Berntzen, M., & Moe, N. B. (2025). Social capital in large-scale Agile software product management: A multi-case study. *Information and Software Technology*, *187*, 107841. DOI: 10.1016/j.infsof.2025.107841

Basak, R. S., Mohapatra, H., & Panigrahy, B. (2025). Enhancing smart home user interfaces with emerging technologies. Home Healthcare Services and Technology Implications, 115-144. https://doi.org/DOI: 10.4018/979-8-3373-3099-0.ch005

Behutiye, W., Rodríguez, P., Oivo, M., Aaramaa, S., Partanen, J., & Abhervé, A. (2022). undefined. *Journal of Systems and Software*, *183*, 111112. DOI: 10.1016/j.jss.2021.111112

Boehm, B., & Bose, P. (n.d.). A collaborative spiral software process model based on theory W. *Proceedings of the Third International Conference on the Software Process. Applying the Software Process*, 59-68. https://doi.org/DOI: 10.1109/SPCON.1994.344423

Boehm, B., & Turner, R. (n.d.). Balancing agility and discipline: Evaluating and integrating Agile and plan-driven methods. *Proceedings. 26th International Conference on Software Engineering*, 718-719. https://doi.org/DOI: 10.1109/ICSE.2004.1317503

Bunio, T. S. (2012). Agile data warehouse — The final frontier: How a data warehouse redevelopment is being done in an Agile and pragmatic way. *2012 Agile Conference*, 156-164. https://doi.org/DOI: 10.1109/Agile.2012.21

Cabrera, D., & Cabrera, L. (2023). Adaptive leadership for Agile organizations. *Journal of Systems Thinking*, *3*(1). Advance online publication. DOI: 10.54120/jost.0000039

Chaudhari, A., Bariyar, M., Pandey, A., Kumari, S., Mohanty, A., & Mohapatra, H. (2025). Cloud-enabled smart energy management for sustainable urban development. *Advances in Computational Intelligence and Robotics*, •••, 27–46. DOI: 10.4018/979-8-3693-7112-1.ch002

Conboy, K., & Carroll, N. (2019). Implementing large-scale Agile frameworks: Challenges and recommendations. *IEEE Software*, *36*(2), 44–50. DOI: 10.1109/MS.2018.2884865

Da Silva, F. Q., Suassuna, M., França, A. C., Grubb, A. M., Gouveia, T. B., Monteiro, C. V., & Dos Santos, I. E. (2012). Replication of empirical studies in software engineering research: A systematic mapping study. *Empirical Software Engineering*. Advance online publication. DOI: 10.1007/s10664-012-9227-7

Dikert, K., Paasivaara, M., & Lassenius, C. (2016). Challenges and success factors for large-scale Agile transformations: A systematic literature review. *Journal of Systems and Software*, *119*, 87–108. DOI: 10.1016/j.jss.2016.06.013

Dingsøyr, T., Nerur, S., Balijepally, V., & Moe, N. B. (2012). A decade of Agile methodologies: Towards explaining Agile software development. *Journal of Systems and Software*, *85*(6), 1213–1221. DOI: 10.1016/j.jss.2012.02.033

Diwakar, R., Sharma, R., Nayak, D., & Mohapatra, H. (2025). Optimizing load distribution in big data ecosystems. *AI and the Revival of Big Data*, 177-200. https://doi.org/DOI: 10.4018/979-8-3693-8472-5.ch008

Duarte, S., & Cruz Machado, V. (2017). Green and lean implementation: An assessment in the automotive industry. *International Journal of Lean Six Sigma*, *8*(1), 65–88. DOI: 10.1108/IJLSS-11-2015-0041

Duncan, S. (2018). SAFe 4.0 distilled: Applying the scaled Agile framework for lean software and systems engineering. 2017. *The Quality Management Journal*, *25*(1), 66–66. DOI: 10.1080/10686967.2018.1404375

Duncan, S. (2018). SAFe 4.0 distilled: Applying the scaled Agile framework for lean software and systems engineering. 2017. *The Quality Management Journal*, *25*(1), 66–66. DOI: 10.1080/10686967.2018.1404375

Fitzgerald, B., Stol, K., O'Sullivan, R., & O'Brien, D. (2013). Scaling Agile methods to regulated environments: An industry case study. *2013 35th International Conference on Software Engineering (ICSE)*, 863-872. https://doi.org/DOI: 10.1109/ICSE.2013.6606635

Gandomani, T. J., & Nafchi, M. Z. (2016). The essential prerequisites of Agile transition and adoption: A grounded theory approach. *Journal of Internet Computing and Services*, *17*(5), 173–184. DOI: 10.7472/jksii.2016.17.5.173

Ghobadi, S., & Mathiassen, L. (2016). Risks to effective knowledge sharing in Agile software teams: A model for assessing and mitigating risks. *Information Systems Journal*, *27*(6), 699–731. DOI: 10.1111/isj.12117

Gren, L., Torkar, R., & Feldt, R. (2014). Work motivational challenges regarding the interface between Agile teams and a Non-Agile surrounding organization: A case study. *2014 Agile Conference*, 11-15. https://doi.org/DOI: 10.1109/AGILE.2014.13

Gustavsson, T., Berntzen, M., & Stray, V. (2022). Changes to team autonomy in large-scale software development: A multiple case study of scaled Agile framework (Safe) implementations. *International Journal of Information Systems and Project Management*, *10*(1), 29–46. DOI: 10.12821/ijispm100102

Han, X. (2021). A study of performance testing in configurable software systems. *Journal of Software Engineering and Applications*, *14*(09), 474–492. DOI: 10.4236/jsea.2021.149028

Harder, J., & Göde, N. (2012). Cloned code: Stable code. *Journal of Software (Malden, MA)*, *25*(10), 1063–1088. DOI: 10.1002/smr.1551

Hoda, R., Noble, J., & Marshall, S. (2011). The impact of inadequate customer collaboration on self-organizing Agile teams. *Information and Software Technology*, *53*(5), 521–534. DOI: 10.1016/j.infsof.2010.10.009

Hohl, P., Klünder, J., Van Bennekum, A., Lockard, R., Gifford, J., Münch, J., Stupperich, M., & Schneider, K. (2018). Back to the future: Origins and directions of the "Agile manifesto" – views of the originators. *Journal of Software Engineering Research and Development*, *6*(1), 15. Advance online publication. DOI: 10.1186/s40411-018-0059-z

Ikonen, M., Pirinen, E., Fagerholm, F., Kettunen, P., & Abrahamsson, P. (2011). On the impact of Kanban on software project work: An empirical case study investigation. *2011 16th IEEE International Conference on Engineering of Complex Computer Systems*, 305-314. https://doi.org/DOI: 10.1109/ICECCS.2011.37

Kalenda, M., Hyna, P., & Rossi, B. (2018). Scaling Agile in large organizations: Practices, challenges, and success factors. *Journal of Software (Malden, MA)*, *30*(10), e1954. Advance online publication. DOI: 10.1002/smr.1954

Kasauli, R., Knauss, E., Horkoff, J., Liebel, G., & Neto, F. G. (2020). Chapter 10 requirements engineering challenges and practices in large-scale Agile system development. *Accelerating Digital Transformation*, 293-350. https://doi.org/DOI: 10.1007/978-3-031-10873-0_14

Kaushik, A., Tayal, D. K., & Yadav, K. (2020). undefined. *International Journal of Agile Systems and Management*, *13*(2), 103. DOI: 10.1504/IJASM.2020.107902

Klünder, J., Trommer, F., & Prenner, N. (2022). How Agile coaches create an Agile mindset in development teams: Insights from an interview study. *Journal of Software (Malden, MA)*, *34*(12), e2491. Advance online publication. DOI: 10.1002/smr.2491

Kowalczyk, M., Marcinkowski, B., & Przybyłek, A. (2022). Scaled Agile framework. Dealing with software process-related challenges of a financial group with the action research approach. *Journal of Software (Malden, MA)*, *34*(6), e2455. Advance onlinc publication. DOI: 10.1002/smr.2455

Kummari, D. N. (2025). Fostering organizational integrity through governance and ethical compliance initiatives. *Advanced Practices in Auditing, Regulatory Compliance, and Smart Manufacturing Systems*, 124-138. https://doi.org/DOI: 10.70593/978-93-7185-253-1_8

Kupiainen, E., Mäntylä, M. V., & Itkonen, J. (2015). Using metrics in Agile and lean software development – A systematic literature review of industrial studies. *Information and Software Technology*, *62*, 143–163. DOI: 10.1016/j.infsof.2015.02.005

(2023, March 29). Lean manufacturing application to improve quality and productivity: A case study at a label manufacturing company. (2023). *International Research Journal of Modernization in Engineering Technology and Science*. Advance online publication. DOI: 10.56726/IRJMETS35009

Lenberg, P., Feldt, R., Tengberg, L. G., & Gren, L. (2020). Behavioral aspects of safety-critical software development. *Proceedings of the IEEE/ACM 42nd International Conference on Software Engineering Workshops*, 173-176. https://doi.org/DOI: 10.1145/3387940.3392227

LOBASEV, D. V. (2022). Agile-transformation framework for large enterprises. *Актуальные исследования*, (47), 26-33. https://doi.org/DOI: 10.51635/27131513_2022_47-26

Lous, P., Kuhrmann, M., & Tell, P. (2017). Is Scrum fit for global software engineering? *2017 IEEE 12th International Conference on Global Software Engineering (ICGSE)*, 1-10. https://doi.org/DOI: 10.1109/ICGSE.2017.13

Make certain your marketing strategy will have a good chance of being successful. (2010). *Creating a Successful Marketing Strategy for Your Small New Business*, 191-212. https://doi.org/DOI: 10.5040/9798216963158.0012

Mohapatra, H. (2024). The role of 6G in empowering smart cities enabling ubiquitous connectivity and intelligent infrastructure. *Advances in Civil and Industrial Engineering*, •••, 237–264. DOI: 10.4018/979-8-3693-8029-1.ch009

Mohapatra, H., Pramanik, S., & Ranjan Mishra, S. (2025). Revolutionizing software development: The transformative influence of machine learning integrated SDLC model. Artificial Intelligence-Enhanced Software and Systems Engineering, 41-69. https://doi.org/DOI: 10.1007/978-3-031-88188-6_3

O'Reilly, C. A., & Chatman, J. A. (2020). Transformational leader or narcissist? How grandiose narcissists can create and destroy organizations and institutions. *California Management Review*, *62*(3), 5–27. DOI: 10.1177/0008125620914989

Ohno, T., & Bodek, N. (2019). Evolution of the Toyota production system. *Toyota Production System*, 17-44. https://doi.org/DOI: 10.4324/9780429273018-2

Paasivaara, M., Durasiewicz, S., & Lassenius, C. (2008). Distributed Agile development: Using Scrum in a large project. *2008 IEEE International Conference on Global Software Engineering*, 87-95. https://doi.org/DOI: 10.1109/ICGSE.2008.38

Pereira, L., Batista, F., & Da Costa, R. L. (2023). Enterprise Agile transformation. *International Journal of Agile Systems and Management*, *16*(1), 1. DOI: 10.1504/IJASM.2023.10055724

Poppendieck, M. (2007). Lean software development. *29th International Conference on Software Engineering (ICSE'07 Companion).* https://doi.org/DOI: 10.1109/ICSECOMPANION.2007.46

Putta, A., Paasivaara, M., & Lassenius, C. (2018). Adopting scaled Agile framework (Safe). *Proceedings of the 19th International Conference on Agile Software Development: Companion*, 1-4. https://doi.org/DOI: 10.1145/3234152.3234164

Rafique, Y. (2021). TDD dynamics: Understanding the impact of test-driven development on software quality and productivity. https://doi.org/DOI: 10.32920/ryerson.14661051.v1

Raj, P., Mohapatra, H., Ranjan, R., & Maithili, P. (2025). Innovative strategies for sustainable waste disposal. *Leveraging Urban Computing for Sustainable Urban Development*, 117-144. https://doi.org/DOI: 10.4018/979-8-3373-0761-9.ch006

Ramesh, B., Abrahamsson, P., Cockburn, A., Lyytinen, K., & Williams, L. (n.d.). Agile software development methods: When and why do they work? *IFIP International Federation for Information Processing, 371-373.* Advance online publication. DOI: 10.1007/0-387-25590-7_24

Rasch, D. (1991). Pressman, R. S.: Software engineering. Grundkurs fur Praktiker. McGraw-hill software, engineering. Hrsg.: dipl.-inform. John-Harry Wieken. McGraw-hill book company GmbH, Hamburg 1989. 302 S., DM 63, 55, ISBN 3–89028–163-X. *Biometrical Journal, 33*(3), 378-378. https://doi.org/DOI: 10.1002/bimj.4710330333

Saur, J. (2003). Review of "test-driven development: A practical guide by David Astels." Prentice-hall 2003. *Software Engineering Notes*, *28*(6), 31. DOI: 10.1145/966221.966666

Saur, J. (2005). Review of "Software development for small teams: A RUP-centric approach by Gary pollice, Liz Augustine, Chris Lowe, and Jas Madhur". Addison-Wesley, 2004, paperback, ISBN 0-321-19950-2. *Software Engineering Notes*, *30*(1), 38–38. DOI: 10.1145/1039174.1039209

Serrador, P., & Pinto, J. K. (2015). Does Agile work? A quantitative analysis of Agile project success. *International Journal of Project Management*, *33*(5), 1040–1051. DOI: 10.1016/j.ijproman.2015.01.006

Serrano, N., Hernantes, J., & Gallardo, G. (2014). Service-oriented architecture and legacy systems. *IEEE Software*, *31*(5), 15–19. DOI: 10.1109/MS.2014.125

Shepherd, D. C., Fronchetti, F., Liu, Y., Hou, D., DeWaters, J., & Small, M. M. (2022). Project-sized scaffolding for software engineering courses. *Proceedings of the First International Workshop on Designing and Running Project-Based Courses in Software Engineering Education*, 27-31. https://doi.org/DOI: 10.1145/3524487.3527362

Simmons, R. (2018). Gemba Kaizen: A commonsense approach to a continuous improvement strategy, 2nd ed. *Quality Management Journal, 25*(1), 65-66. https://doi.org/DOI: 10.1080/10686967.2018.1404374

Singh, K. (2021). A phenomenological study of software developers participating in daily stand-up meetings in Agile teams. *Proceedings of the 2021 AERA Annual Meeting*. https://doi.org/DOI: 10.3102/1683950

Spinellis, D. (2006). Review of "Sustainable software development: An Agile perspective by Kevin Tate," Addison-Wesley professional, 2005, $39.99, ISBN: 0321286081. *Queue, 4*(10), 49. https://doi.org/DOI: 10.1145/1189276.1189292

Stephens, M., & Rosenberg, D. (2003). Embracing change (Embrace people, manage change). *Extreme Programming Refactored: The Case Against XP*, 293-310. https://doi.org/DOI: 10.1007/978-1-4302-0810-5_13

Stern, T. V. (2020). Lean and Agile project management: International influences. *Lean and Agile Project Management*, 225-230. https://doi.org/DOI: 10.4324/9780429343414-18

Suresh, M., Antony, J., Nair, G., & Garza-Reyes, J. A. (2023). Lean-sustainability assessment framework development: Evidence from the construction industry. *Total Quality Management & Business Excellence*, *34*(15-16), 2046–2081. DOI: 10.1080/14783363.2023.2222088

Tachibana, S., & Tsuda, K. (2022). A study on analysis model for influence of expressions from others on taste expressions in word-of-Mouth data of cooking recipe website. *Procedia Computer Science*, *207*, 1500–1508. DOI: 10.1016/j.procs.2022.09.207

Trustbusting in Japan. (1981). Cartels and government-business cooperation. *Harvard Law Review*, *94*(5), 1064. DOI: 10.2307/1340689

Vacca, A., Di Sorbo, A., Visaggio, C. A., & Canfora, G. (2021). A systematic literature review of blockchain and smart contract development: Techniques, tools, and open challenges. *Journal of Systems and Software*, *174*, 110891. DOI: 10.1016/j.jss.2020.110891

Vaishnavi, V., & Suresh, M. (2020). Modelling of readiness factors for the implementation of Lean Six Sigma in healthcare organizations. *International Journal of Lean Six Sigma*, *11*(4), 597–633. DOI: 10.1108/IJLSS-12-2017-0146

Vallon, R., Da Silva Estácio, B. J., Prikladnicki, R., & Grechenig, T. (2018). Systematic literature review on Agile practices in global software development. *Information and Software Technology*, *96*, 161–180. DOI: 10.1016/j.infsof.2017.12.004

Wawak, S. (2024). Enhancing project quality through effective team management. *International Journal of Information Systems and Project Management*, *12*(2), 50–67. DOI: 10.12821/ijispm120203

Zhao, X., Salako, K., Strigini, L., Robu, V., & Flynn, D. (2020). Assessing safety-critical systems from operational testing: A study on autonomous vehicles. *Information and Software Technology*, *128*, 106393. DOI: 10.1016/j.infsof.2020.106393

Chapter 9
Building Applied Models from Observational Research and Fieldwork in Educational Settings:
Pedagogical Ecologies and Epistemic Instruments

Ashraf Alam
https://orcid.org/0000-0001-6178-1187
Alliance University, Bengaluru, India

ABSTRACT

This chapter elucidates the construction of applied models from observational research in education as a transdisciplinary, praxis-oriented methodology for capturing and transforming complex pedagogical ecologies. Integrating theories from constructivism, experiential learning, systems thinking, and situated cognition, it outlines the methodological arc from data collection to model abstraction and validation. Through diverse case illustrations, the chapter demonstrates how applied models function as diagnostic, design, and governance tools across classroom, institutional, and policy levels. Emphasizing ethical reflexivity, epistemic justice, and methodological transparency, it positions applied models as dynamic epistemic instruments for educational transformation in volatile, diverse, and inequitable learning systems.

DOI: 10.4018/979-8-3373-3301-4.ch009

1. INTRODUCTION

1.1 Rationale for Applied Models in Education

In the contemporary landscape of educational inquiry, the construction of *applied models* from empirical observation constitutes a shift from abstract theorization to praxis-oriented epistemologies. These models, grounded in granular data accrued from *in-situ* educational environments, act as both interpretive heuristics and decision-making architectures (Tuminaro & Redish, 2007; Choi & Yoon, 2023; Auclair, 2007). Unlike decontextualized theoretical frameworks that often abstract away the socio-material complexity of schooling, applied models synthesize ecological, cognitive, behavioral, and interactional variables into dynamic representations capable of informing instruction, pedagogy, and policy (Allen et al., 2002; Schoenfeld, 1980; Burns et al., 1987). They function not merely as static analytical schemata but as recursive, adaptive systems that evolve in tandem with pedagogical and institutional ecologies (Nabavian & Parsons, 2024; Hwang et al., 2009). Recent global trends highlight the urgency of such methodological recalibrations. The UNESCO Global Education Monitoring Report released in 2023 notes that while gross enrollment ratios have improved globally, a substantial proportion of learners, estimated at over 250 million, continue to lack foundational literacy and numeracy skills. This learning crisis is compounded by the inadequacy of conventional assessment paradigms, which fail to capture the embeddedness of learning within cultural, emotional, and infrastructural matrices (Thomke & Fujimoto, 2000; Hulaikah et al., 2020; Simamora et al., 2017). Applied models offer a corrective to this analytical deficit by facilitating *multi-scalar abstraction* of observed educational phenomena into actionable constructs, enabling fine-tuned interventions grounded in empirical particularity. The ontological status of applied models resides at the intersection of complexity theory, systems analysis, and cognitive ethnography (Lames & Hansen, 2001; Muro & Terry, 2007). Their heuristic power lies in their ability to operationalize the *microgenetic processes* of classroom interaction, the *meso-level configurations* of instructional sequences, and the *macro-level determinants* such as curriculum mandates, policy pressures, and resource distributions (Ben-Hur, 2006; Daulay & Ruhaimah, 2019). This multilevel integrative capacity renders them indispensable to researchers seeking not only to describe but to intervene, not merely to represent but to redesign.

1.2 Observational Research and Fieldwork as Data Foundations

The epistemic legitimacy of observational research in education derives from its capacity to generate *thick description* (Geertz, 1973) of pedagogical interactions, capturing not only overt behavior but also latent meanings, affective atmospheres, and symbolic codes. Unlike experimental or survey-based methodologies which isolate variables through reductionist logics, observational fieldwork attends to the *polyphony* of educational life in its totality (Heppner, 2008; Charlesworth & Leali, 2012). It traces emergent phenomena, captures *embodied cognition*, and registers the performative enactment of roles, norms, and identities within learning spaces. Contemporary scholarship in the sociology of education and linguistic anthropology has validated observational methodologies as indispensable for capturing the *emic perspectives* of learners and educators (Tilly, 2008; Bradshaw & Hazell, 2017; Liu & Israel, 2022). For instance, the TIMSS Video Study and the ICAP framework (Chi & Wylie, 2014) have yielded robust insights into cognitive engagement patterns, dialogic density, and instructional responsiveness across diverse cultural milieus. These studies emphasize that learning is not a disembodied cognitive event but a *distributed phenomenon*, orchestrated through material artifacts, spatial arrangements, social proximities, and temporal rhythms. Applied models, when derived from such observational data, crystallize these distributed dynamics into coherent and transportable forms (Shih et al., 2010; Lesh & Harel, 2003).

Methodologically, field-based data collection strategies, ranging from time-sampled structured observation and participant ethnography to multimodal discourse analysis, enable the modeling of latent constructs such as *pedagogical tact*, *classroom ecology*, and *epistemic agency* (Horváth, 2007; Wang et al., 2015). Pedagogical tact refers to a teacher's intuitive and situationally responsive ability to act with sensitivity, moral discernment, and relational awareness in the classroom. It encompasses the capacity to make timely decisions that preserve the dignity of students, foster a safe learning environment, and promote holistic development. Rather than being guided solely by rules or curricular mandates, pedagogical tact involves a refined judgment rooted in ethical care, practical wisdom, and contextual understanding of students' emotional and cognitive states. Classroom ecology, on the other hand, describes the dynamic and interdependent network of relationships, behaviors, spatial arrangements, and material conditions that shape the classroom as a living system. It includes how students and teachers interact, how physical space is used, and how routines, power dynamics, and cultural norms influence the flow of learning. A healthy classroom ecology supports inclusivity, mutual respect, and collaborative engagement, allowing students to thrive both socially and intellectually. Epistemic agency refers to the learner's capacity and right to contribute meaningfully to knowledge-building processes. It captures students' ability to ask questions, construct arguments, challenge assumptions, and co-author learning experiences. Epistemic agency is not simply about cognitive competence; it also involves recognition, voice, and the structural conditions that allow learners to be seen as knowers. When classrooms encourage students to take intellectual risks and value their insights, epistemic agency becomes a powerful force for educational transformation.

Together, these constructs illuminate the subtle, often invisible mechanisms through which classrooms become spaces of empowerment, resistance, or reproduction. Field-based methodologies help bring these mechanisms into focus by capturing their emergence in real-time social interaction, material configurations, and discourse. In high-poverty or multilingual classrooms, for example, applied models can capture the improvisational scaffolding practices of teachers, the code-switching strategies of students, or the embodied rituals of attentional regulation. These elements, often invisible to psychometric or quantitative instruments, are central to understanding how learning is organized, experienced, and sustained (Pazos et al., 2010; Dorst & Cross, 2001). Moreover, the affective and relational components of education, teacher-student attunement, peer dynamics, and emotional regulation, are best apprehended through sustained, situated observation (Diamantes & Williams, 1997). Neuroscientific studies affirm that affect modulates cognitive processing and memory consolidation (Immordino-Yang & Damasio, 2007). Observational research thus serves as the empirical substrate for constructing models that account for *neuro-affective coupling*, *cognitive load variability*, and *socio-emotional learning* dynamics (Seielstad, 2001; Taconis et al., 2001; Bennett et al., 2020). In this sense, applied models are not merely descriptive taxonomies but bio-psycho-social representations of learning ecologies.

1.3 Objectives and Scope of the Chapter

This chapter aims to articulate a rigorous and interdisciplinary framework for the development, implementation, and utilization of applied models derived from observational research and fieldwork in education. It contends that such models function as *epistemic mediators*, translating the semiotic complexity of classroom life into structured representations that enable curricular design, pedagogical innovation, professional development, and policy formulation. The chapter foregrounds applied modeling as both a *methodological apparatus* and a *praxiological commitment* to context-sensitive, empirically grounded educational transformation. The structure of the chapter reflects this dual commitment to conceptual depth and practical relevance. It first delineates the theoretical scaffolding underpinning applied modeling, drawing on constructivist epistemology, experiential learning theory, situated cognition, and complexity science. These theoretical vectors elucidate the philosophical rationale for grounding model construction in lived experience and recursive sense-making. Subsequent sections explore the methodological terrain of observation, including typologies of field engagement, coding regimes, pattern recognition techniques, and abstraction protocols.

Central to the chapter are case exemplars from diverse educational contexts, ranging from early childhood behavioral scaffolding to hybrid learning engagement and inclusive pedagogy for neurodiverse learners. These illustrations demonstrate the versatility of applied models across developmental stages, cultural contexts, and institutional modalities. They also show how models move across the research-practice-policy continuum, generating impact through usability, adaptability, and responsiveness. The chapter further interrogates the systemic and ethical dimensions of model application. It addresses the integration of applied models into educational monitoring systems, teacher professional development frameworks, and equity-oriented policy initiatives. Ethical considerations such as informed consent, data anonymization, epistemic justice, and stakeholder participation are treated not as peripheral obligations but as constitutive elements of model validity and legitimacy. In advancing this agenda, the chapter contributes to a broader reimagining of educational research as a *transformative science*, one that dissolves the artificial boundary between knowing and doing. Applied models, as advanced here, are not inert instruments of analysis but *epistemological interventions* that reshape how we conceptualize, evaluate, and enact education. They are simultaneously products of observation and catalysts of transformation, simultaneously grounded in the present and oriented toward emancipatory futures.

2. THEORETICAL AND CONCEPTUAL FOUNDATIONS

2.1 Constructivist Learning Theory

The epistemological infrastructure of applied model construction in educational research is fundamentally undergirded by constructivist learning theory, which posits that cognition is not a passive receptacle of exogenous information but a dynamic, generative process of schema formation, assimilation, and accommodation (Depaepe et al., 2010; Lovett & Anderson, 1996). Originating from the cognitive developmental work of Jean Piaget and extended by the sociocultural insights of Lev Vygotsky, constructivism elucidates how learners negotiate meaning through recursive interactions with both material artifacts and sociolinguistic environments. Piagetian paradigms highlight the *ontogenetic evolution* of cognitive structures, suggesting that learners actively reorganize mental models through processes of equilibration. Vygotsky, in contrast, foregrounds the *interpsychological mediation* of learning via culturally sanctioned tools and semiotic exchanges, exemplified in his theory of the Zone of Proximal Development, which delineates the differential between potential and actualized competencies. Applied models derived from observational research are direct operationalizations of these theoretical tenets. They encapsulate the *dialectic of individual construction and social co-construction* by abstracting patterns of interactional scaffolding, peer mediation, and dialogic learning. These models enable the visualization of how learners traverse cognitive disequilibrium zones, recalibrating their epistemic frameworks in real time (Nurhafidhah et al., 2024; Telzrow et al., 2000; Rosyid & Ismawati, 2025). Moreover, constructivist theory validates the necessity of modeling not just overt behaviors but latent cognitive processes, such as *metacognitive regulation*, *epistemic curiosity*, and *conceptual dissonance*, which emerge in embodied, situated learning encounters.

2.2 Experiential Learning Theory

The epistemic elegance of David Kolb's Experiential Learning Theory (ELT) resides in its articulation of learning as a cyclical and recursive integration of concrete experience, reflective observation, abstract conceptualization, and active experimentation. This cyclical ontology of learning mirrors the methodological arc of observational research and applied model construction, wherein empirical phenomena are documented, reflected upon, systematically abstracted, and re-applied within instructional ecologies. Kolb's model draws from the phenomenological traditions of Dewey and Lewin, emphasizing the *dialectical tension* between experience and cognition, sensation and abstraction. In applied modeling, Kolb's quadrants map onto the methodological sequence of data gathering, thematic coding, theoretical distillation, and model validation. Observational research captures the *experiential substrate* of pedagogical events, which is then rendered into reflexive narrative or coded constructs, later synthesized into conceptual diagrams that inform practice and provoke iteration (Cho & Lim, 2017; Watson et al., 1998). The ELT framework provides the scaffolding for the *recursive refinement* of applied models, where each iteration of observation and implementation feeds forward into the next, producing models that are both empirically grounded and pedagogically generative. Furthermore, empirical findings from neuroeducation substantiate the ELT cycle. Functional MRI studies indicate that iterative cognitive rehearsal and embodied engagement activate the prefrontal cortex and insular networks associated with memory consolidation and executive function. Such neuroscientific corroborations affirm that applied models operationalizing experiential learning processes are not merely pedagogical tools but *neurocognitive catalysts* for deeper and more durable learning.

2.3 Situated Cognition and Contextual Learning

Situated cognition posits that knowledge is not an abstract commodity transferred between disembodied minds but a *relational construct* emergent from activity, context, and community. Originating from the seminal work of Brown, Collins, and Duguid (1989), and further elaborated by Lave and Wenger's concept of *legitimate peripheral participation*, this theoretical paradigm argues that cognition is inherently *ecological*, embedded within the affordances and constraints of cultural, spatial, and institutional milieus. Applied models, when constructed from robust observational research, act as cartographies of these situated learning ecologies (Fauzia & Kelana, 2020; Gok, 2010). They map the choreography of learner engagement across physical space, social networks, and discursive regimes. For instance, models that depict student agency in maker spaces or collaborative STEM labs often capture the *distributed cognition* across tools, peers, and representational media. These models are not static diagrams but *epistemic artifacts* that embody the affordances of context-sensitive pedagogy. Situated cognition also aligns with poststructural critiques of universalist educational models. By emphasizing *contextual specificity* and *cultural contingency*, applied models grounded in situated observation resist epistemic coloniality and pave the way for localized, culturally sustaining pedagogies. In Indigenous learning systems, for example, models must account for land-based knowledge transmission, relational accountability, and oral epistemologies that defy standardized curricular mappings. Applied models, in such contexts, serve as acts of methodological decolonization.

2.4 Systems Thinking and Complexity Theory in Education

Systems thinking offers a macro-analytic lens through which the interdependencies, feedback loops, and emergent behaviors within educational systems can be apprehended. Rooted in cybernetics and complexity theory, and popularized in educational discourse by Senge's notion of the *learning organization*, this paradigm reconceptualizes schools not as linear instructional pipelines but as dynamic, adaptive systems with *nonlinear causality* and *path-dependent evolution*. Applied models built on systems principles operationalize these theoretical constructs by diagramming recursive interactions among actors, structures, norms, and discourses (Bardwell, 1991; Ruuska et al., 2008). A model tracing the impact of teacher emotional labor on student academic engagement might include bi-directional arrows, feedback amplifications, and time-lagged effects that mirror the *complex adaptive system dynamics* of the school ecology. Such models transcend unidirectional causal logic and embrace *fuzzy logic*, *nonlinearity*, and *emergence*. Empirical studies utilizing agent-based modeling and network analysis further validate the relevance of systems theory to applied model construction. For instance, longitudinal network studies have mapped how information flow among educators affects innovation diffusion and pedagogical coherence across departments (Coburn & Russell, 2008). These analyses inform applied models that simulate organizational behavior and inform strategic interventions in professional learning communities, resource allocation, and institutional redesign.

2.5 Cognitive Load Theory and Instructional Design

Cognitive Load Theory (CLT), articulated by Sweller (1988), provides a psychometric substrate for modeling instructional efficiency. CLT delineates three forms of cognitive load, *intrinsic*, *extraneous*, and *germane*, that influence working memory capacity during learning tasks. Applied models that aim to optimize instructional sequences or curriculum architecture must incorporate the *cognitive architecture* constraints highlighted by CLT. Observational research, particularly in high-stakes STEM classrooms, has demonstrated that excessive multitasking, fragmented discourse, or poorly sequenced instruction imposes *extraneous load* that impairs learning transfer. Applied models can visualize the cognitive trajectory of students as they navigate complex content, highlighting points of overload and decay (McIntyre & Phaneuf, 2008; Asmah et al., 2025). Such models inform the design of scaffolds, pacing cues, and chunking strategies to maintain *optimal cognitive equilibrium*.

Recent research in instructional neuroscience corroborates CLT's claims. Studies employing electroencephalography (EEG) reveal that learners experiencing well-calibrated germane load exhibit synchronized activity in dorsolateral prefrontal and parietal cortices, associated with working memory and attentional control. By integrating these insights, applied models become not merely pedagogical guides but *neuro-instructional blueprints* that align design with cognitive architecture. The theoretical and conceptual foundations for applied model construction are multidimensional, drawing from cognitive science, sociocultural theory, systems thinking, and neuroeducation. These frameworks provide the *ontological grammar* and *epistemological syntax* for constructing models that are both theoretically robust and pragmatically efficacious (Visconti & Zubizarreta, 2018; Thompson, 2009). They allow researchers and practitioners to render the invisible visible, to diagram the intangible, and to design for transformation in ways that are simultaneously empirically valid, cognitively aligned, and ethically responsive.

3. EDUCATIONAL SETTINGS AND TYPES OF OBSERVATIONAL DATA

3.1 Diversity of Educational Environments

The ontogeny of applied models in educational research is inextricably tethered to the heterogeneity of pedagogical ecologies within which data are generated. Educational environments are not monolithic but are characterized by a complex interaction of spatial configurations, technological affordances, socio-cultural dynamics, and epistemic norms (Lemons et al., 2010; Carpenter & Fennema, 1992). From the analogical cadence of traditional brick-and-mortar classrooms to the algorithmically mediated interfaces of hybrid and virtual learning architectures, each setting engenders distinct *phenomenological textures* and interactional grammars that necessitate tailored strategies for observational data elicitation. The post-pandemic pedagogical terrain has catalyzed a tectonic shift in the spatial-temporal organization of schooling. The World Bank's 2023 *State of Global Education* report identifies a global proliferation of asynchronous and synchromodal learning modalities, highlighting the dissolution of conventional instructional cartographies. In digitally augmented environments, learning is refracted across screen-mediated interfaces, cloud-based repositories, and multisensory stimuli, each constituting a node in a *disaggregated learning ecosystem*. Applied models in such settings must synthesize diverse data vectors, including digital behavioral analytics, affective response patterns, and interactional heatmaps, into coherent analytic frameworks (Hamza & Griffith, 2006; Hill, 1997). Furthermore, cultural heterogeneity compounds the complexity of educational environments. The epistemic scaffolding that underpins learning in Indigenous knowledge systems, religious madrasas, or multilingual classrooms in postcolonial geographies diverges substantively from Eurocentric models of instruction. Observational research in these contexts must be attuned to *ethno-pedagogical semiotics*, such as kinesthetic mnemonics, nonverbal cues, oral epistemologies, and collective affect. Without this sensitivity, applied models risk epistemic violence through universalist generalization. Hence, contextual calibration is not ancillary but *constitutive* of the model's validity.

3.2 Structured and Unstructured Observation

The typology of observational methodologies bifurcates primarily into structured and unstructured modalities, each with its own epistemological assumptions and methodological affordances. Structured observation, undergirded by positivist inclinations, employs *predetermined coding schemas*, behavioral rubrics, and time-sampling matrices to generate quantifiable data (Sholihah & Lastariwati, 2020). Such approaches aim for *intersubjective reliability* and statistical replicability, rendering them useful in large-scale evaluations or policy diagnostics. The Classroom Assessment Scoring System (CLASS), for instance, operationalizes constructs such as instructional support and emotional climate through standardized metrics, enabling cross-institutional comparisons and meta-analytic syntheses. However, the epistemic trade-off of such structure lies in its attenuation of contextual nuance. By imposing a priori categories, structured observation may occlude emergent phenomena, tacit knowledge flows, and affective microtransactions that escape quantification. Unstructured observation, conversely, aligns with interpretivist and phenomenological traditions, privileging *emic perspectives* and ecological validity. It allows for the documentation of *praxeological subtleties*, including spontaneous pedagogical improvisations, intersubjective synchrony, and student agency that manifest in fluid and contingent ways. The methodological symbiosis of these approaches has given rise to *hybrid observational protocols*, integrating frequency analysis with narrative ethnographic vignettes (Isaksen & Treffinger, 2004; Shriberg & Harris, 2012). For instance, in a cross-national study of inclusive pedagogy conducted by the University of British Columbia, researchers employed a bifocal lens, i.e., structured rubrics were used to quantify participation asymmetries, while unstructured field notes illuminated affective economies and resistance tactics among students with disabilities. The resultant applied model captured both behavioral patterns and their sociocultural substrata, enhancing its diagnostic granularity and pedagogical relevance.

3.3 Participant and Non-Participant Observation

The *positionality of the observer* constitutes a critical epistemic axis in the architecture of observational data. Non-participant observation, characterized by analytic detachment, endeavors to minimize observer reactivity and maintain an ostensibly neutral gaze. This approach aligns with classical ethnomethodological paradigms and is frequently utilized in experimental or quasi-experimental research designs. In contrast, participant observation adopts an *immersive and reflexive modality*, wherein the researcher becomes entangled in the performative and relational matrices of the field, generating *thick description* (Geertz, 1973) through embodied presence and dialogic engagement. The epistemological fecundity of participant observation lies in its capacity to apprehend *situated cognition*, tacit praxis, and symbolic interactionism in their full complexity (Chatfield, 1995; Karmakar et al., 2019). For instance, ethnographers embedded in early childhood centers have documented the non-verbal scaffolding of emotional regulation through gesture, spatial proximity, and paralinguistic cues, i.e., the phenomena that would remain invisible to detached observation. Such immersive engagements are indispensable for modeling constructs like *pedagogical tact*, *relational trust*, or *classroom attunement*. However, participant observation also entails epistemic risks, including role-confusion, observer bias, and *reactive ethnography*, wherein the presence of the researcher alters the ontological fabric of the observed phenomenon. These risks necessitate *reflexive countermeasures*, such as methodological triangulation, memoing, and member-checking to ensure *epistemic integrity* and mitigate observer-induced distortion (Taggar & Brown, 2001; Goldin, 1998). In applied model construction, the choice between participant and non-participant modalities must be aligned with the ontological depth, contextual complexity, and ethical exigencies of the research milieu.

3.4 Integrating Mixed-Methods Observational Strategies

The epistemological pluralism of *mixed-methods observational strategies* enables the integration of quantitative precision with qualitative depth, enhancing the *construct validity* and ecological fidelity of applied models. Methodologically, this entails the co-deployment of structured instruments, such as behavior coding software, inter-rater reliability indices, and event-sequence analysis, with qualitative modalities like narrative ethnography, grounded theory coding, and discourse analysis. This multimodal synergy is particularly salient in modeling complex, layered constructs such as *cognitive engagement*, *cultural responsiveness*, or *inclusive participation*. For instance, in a landmark study on dialogic pedagogy conducted by the University of Cambridge, researchers synchronized frequency counts of dialogic turns with thematic coding of classroom transcripts and post-lesson teacher reflections. The resultant model delineated not only the frequency of dialogic events but also their discursive architecture and pedagogical intentionality, producing a *multidimensional construct map* of dialogic instruction.

The advent of learning analytics and artificial intelligence has further expanded the methodological repertoire available for observational modeling. Real-time data capture through eye-tracking, keystroke analysis, and sentiment detection can be triangulated with human-coded field notes to create *algorithmically enhanced observational models*. These models possess both predictive utility and diagnostic granularity, offering unprecedented insight into *microtemporal learning dynamics* and *cognitive-emotional synchrony*. Yet, the integration of algorithmic tools necessitates critical scrutiny. Without robust ethical frameworks and epistemological transparency, such technologies risk re-inscribing surveillance logics and exacerbating data extractivism. Thus, mixed-methods observational modeling must remain anchored in *critical pedagogy*, *data ethics*, and *participatory validation*, ensuring that the models serve emancipatory ends rather than technocratic control. The typology and deployment of observational strategies are not merely technical decisions but *epistemological commitments* that shape the architecture, scope, and legitimacy of applied models. As educational environments become increasingly complex, multimodal, and culturally diverse, observational research must evolve in tandem, embracing methodological hybridity, reflexive rigor, and ethical responsibility. The resultant applied models, forged in this crucible of complexity, become more than tools of analysis; they become *epistemic instruments* of transformation, capturing the dynamism of learning and enabling its intentional design.

4. METHODOLOGICAL PROCESS OF CONSTRUCTING APPLIED MODELS

4.1 Defining Purpose and Context

The initial ontological act in constructing applied models from observational research entails the rigorous delineation of research purpose and contextual boundary conditions. This phase is not merely procedural but constitutes an epistemic scaffolding upon which all subsequent analytical operations are predicated. Defining purpose involves the *problematisation* of pedagogical or institutional phenomena into analytically tractable units of investigation. Such *problematization* must be conceptually rich, theoretically anchored, and pragmatically consequential. It demands the articulation of an *inquiry architecture* that can reconcile the micro-interactional textures of classroom life with the meso- and macro-level constraints imposed by curriculum, policy, and sociocultural formations. Contextualization operates as a *field-theoretic constraint*, delimiting the epistemic horizon within which observational data gains salience and interpretive coherence (Rahmah & Lubis, 2024; Silver, 2013). Educational settings are replete with socio-spatial and discursive heterogeneities, and the contextualization of observational units must attend to *spatio-temporal scales*, institutional ethos, cultural semiotics, and demographic ecologies. In a multilingual STEM classroom, for instance, context encompasses not only the linguistic repertoire of learners but also the epistemic norms of disciplinary discourse, the affordances of instructional technologies, and the embodied enactment of authority. Without such granular contextual anchoring, applied models risk succumbing to *epistemic overgeneralization* or *analytic essentialism*.

4.2 Designing Data Collection Instruments

The methodological rigor of applied model construction is contingent upon the *instrumental architecture* of data elicitation tools. Designing data collection instruments necessitates the operationalization of abstract theoretical constructs into observable, codifiable phenomena. This process is governed by a dual imperative, i.e., *granularity* and *ecological validity*. The instruments must capture the multi-dimensionality of educational phenomena without distorting their phenomenological integrity (Hill-Briggs, 2003; Dermitzaki et al., 2009). Structured instruments may include behavior frequency matrices, momentary time sampling grids, or event-based recording protocols, each calibrated to generate data with high inter-rater reliability. In contrast, open-ended protocols such as narrative mapping templates, socio-semiotic field logs, or multi-modal interaction diagrams are deployed to capture *emergent properties*, *discursive ruptures*, and *affective intensities* that evade quantification. The psychometric calibration of structured instruments is essential, employing measures of internal consistency, construct validity, and inter-observer agreement to ensure the instrument's *metric fidelity*. Advanced data collection architectures increasingly incorporate *sensorial augmentation* through digital tools. Eye-tracking software, audio-spectral analysis, and gesture-recognition algorithms afford a fine-grained account of embodied cognition and attentional distribution. These tools, when embedded within methodologically reflexive protocols, enable the acquisition of *microtemporal data streams*, expanding the temporal granularity of the model's substrate.

4.3 Data Collection and Researcher Reflexivity

The execution of data collection in educational environments is a reflexively situated praxis that requires continual negotiation of role, presence, and meaning-making. Researchers are not neutral observers but *epistemic agents* whose positionality, habitus, and cultural capital mediate the data they produce. Thus, data collection must be approached as a dialogic event rather than a unidirectional extraction process. Methodological integrity mandates the deployment of *reflexivity protocols*, including analytic memoing, positionality audits, and field debriefings to ensure that observational data is co-constructed with, rather than imposed upon, the educational field (Basili, 1996; Muzana et al., 2021). The *spatiotemporal granularity* of data collection is also a critical variable. One-shot observations are insufficient for capturing diachronic patterns or systemic recursivity. Longitudinal fieldwork, time-series observations, and rotational sampling enhance the model's capacity to apprehend not merely state-based phenomena but *processual dynamics* and *nonlinear transitions*. For example, tracking a novice teacher's classroom discourse over an academic year allows the construction of a dynamic model of *pedagogical habituation* and *instructional reflexivity*. Simultaneously, ethical exigencies must be foregrounded. Consent must be ongoing, relational, and culturally calibrated. In contexts where observer presence may trigger *reactivity bias*, alternative modalities such as remote video ethnography or passive sensor logging may be employed, albeit within a rigorous ethical framework that centers participant autonomy and data sovereignty.

4.4 Data Coding and Pattern Recognition

The transformation of raw observational data into an analytic corpus necessitates an intensive phase of coding and pattern abstraction. Coding operates as a form of *data translation*, wherein the polyphonic flux of field phenomena is rendered into a lexicon of conceptual categories. This process is epistemologically situated, informed by either *inductive heuristics* (as in grounded theory) or *deductive schemas* (as in framework analysis). Inductive coding privileges emic perspectives and facilitates the emergence of *latent constructs*, while deductive coding allows for hypothesis testing and construct validation against pre-existing theoretical scaffolds (Hasibuan et al., 2019; Leikin et al., 2009). Advanced coding practices often adopt *multi-tiered coding systems*, where initial open codes are recursively reanalyzed through axial and selective coding to identify *interrelational dynamics*. Coding matrices, code co-occurrence networks, and heatmaps are employed to surface emergent themes, frequency distributions, and temporal shifts. Tools such as NVivo, Dedoose, and ATLAS.ti enable *algorithmic triangulation* of qualitative and quantitative code patterns, enhancing analytic validity. Pattern recognition transcends mere frequency analysis. It entails the identification of *causal linkages*, *feedback mechanisms*, and *emergent regularities* across nested systems. For instance, in modeling dialogic instruction, the patterning of teacher wait-time, student uptake, and dialogic chaining reveals not only interaction frequency but also *epistemic positioning* and *cognitive elaboration trajectories*. Such insights become the foundational architecture upon which higher-order model components are constructed.

4.5 Abstraction and Model Construction

The penultimate stage involves the abstraction of coded patterns into coherent, operationalized model architectures. This phase is simultaneously analytic and synthetic, requiring the researcher to construct a *representational apparatus* that maintains fidelity to empirical complexity while enabling theoretical portability and practical application. Applied models may assume various ontological forms, i.e., logic models, process flowcharts, systems maps, causal loop diagrams, or agent-based simulations. Model construction involves *relational articulation* of components, delineating causal vectors, feedback loops, and mediating variables. A robust model explicates not merely the *what* but the *how* and *why* of educational phenomena, providing a scaffold for diagnosis, prediction, and intervention (Robinson et al., 2007; Khotimah, 2016; Dewi et al., 2017; Pacte Group, 2008). The epistemological validity of the model is contingent upon three criteria, i.e., *internal coherence*, *contextual correspondence*, and *explanatory power*.

Validation protocols must be multilayered, incorporating *member-checking*, *retrodictive testing*, and *ecological triangulation*. Models are refined iteratively through field re-engagement, stakeholder consultation, and comparative case analysis. This recursive refinement enhances the model's *transferability* across settings without sacrificing contextual nuance (Marulis & Nelson, 2021; Dillmann, 2004; Khoiriyah & Husamah, 2018). The methodological construction of applied models is not a linear pipeline but a dialectical process, i.e., the one that synthesizes observation, reflection, abstraction, and praxis. The resultant models function as *cognitive technologies*, mediating between empirical specificity and theoretical abstraction, between local intelligibility and systemic transformation. They are at once products and producers of educational knowledge, enabling a form of inquiry that is reflexive, situated, and transformative in scope.

5. CASE ILLUSTRATIONS OF MODEL CONSTRUCTION

5.1 Early Childhood Behavior Management Model

The behavioral ecology of early childhood education presents a complex nexus of affective regulation, sensorimotor coordination, and nascent cognitive control, all of which coalesce within highly plastic neurodevelopmental trajectories. To construct an applied model that captures this multifactorial dynamic, observational research must interrogate the *microgenetic evolution* of behavioral events within ecologically valid settings. A landmark study by the University of British Columbia operationalized such an endeavor by deploying *event sampling protocols*, multimodal video capture, and spatial behavior mapping across 14 public preschools. Researchers cataloged over 1,200 behavioral instantiations of affective dysregulation, including non-compliance, verbal aggression, and motoric impulsivity, correlated with pedagogical stimuli and spatiotemporal variables. Pattern analysis revealed statistically significant co-occurrences between transition periods, noise thresholds, and incidence rates of behavioral dissonance. Using *causal loop modeling* and *temporal sequencing analytics*, an applied model was abstracted that delineated three interlocking systems, i.e., *environmental calibration*, *predictive cueing*, and *co-regulatory pedagogy*. The model functioned not only as a diagnostic heuristic but as an *interventionist scaffold*, guiding the design of anticipatory routines, sensory modulation zones, and affectively responsive pedagogical scripts. Post-intervention analytics showed a 43 percent attenuation in behavioral disruptions, corroborated by both time-series behavior logs and qualitative ethnographic feedback. The model's scalability and transferability have since been validated across culturally heterogeneous preschool systems in South Africa, Norway, and Chile.

5.2 Student Engagement in Hybrid Classrooms

The ontological architecture of hybrid classrooms represents a *polymodal assemblage* wherein embodiment, cognition, and semiotic exchange are dispersed across physical and digital space. The emergent spatialities of learning, refracted through screen interfaces and asynchronous platforms, require an epistemological recalibration of what constitutes student engagement. A large-scale study conducted by the National Institute of Education in Singapore implemented a *convergent parallel design*, integrating screen-recording analytics, chat transcript coding, biometric facial emotion recognition, and participant ethnography across five secondary schools. The data corpus comprised over 400 hours of instructional time and produced an expansive dataset of cognitive-affective engagement metrics. Cluster analysis and machine learning algorithms were used to isolate five temporal zones of engagement, i.e., *anticipatory readiness*, *transactional interaction*, *cognitive drift*, *re-engagement recovery*, and *reflective consolidation*. An applied model was abstracted using *temporal state transition diagrams* and *latent class trajectory modeling*, enabling real-time prediction and modulation of attentional collapse and re-entry cycles. Empirical validation through a controlled intervention trial demonstrated a 31 percent increase in student task persistence, alongside statistically significant enhancements in affective engagement metrics. The model has since been adapted into a *learning experience design (LXD)* framework utilized in teacher training modules across Southeast Asia, integrating pedagogical heuristics with real-time data visualization tools that afford recursive instructional refinement.

5.3 Peer Collaboration in Group Learning

The discursive and socio-cognitive processes inherent in peer collaboration are often occluded by normative evaluative rubrics that privilege output over interactional process. A pioneering cross-national ethnography conducted by the University of Helsinki interrogated *collaborative epistemic assemblages* within inquiry-based science education across three Nordic countries. Employing a multi-sensorial observational architecture that integrated audio-visual ethnography, speech-act coding, and networked discourse analysis, the study captured over 2,000 minutes of collaborative interaction among 9th-grade students. Through *socio-discursive coding matrices* and *Markov chain analysis*, the study identified four emergent interactional archetypes, i.e., *distributed epistemic collaboration*, *hierarchical leadership dominance*, *performative pseudo-participation*, and *affective withdrawal*. The resultant applied model mapped these archetypes onto role taxonomies including *cognitive anchor, meta-cognitive navigator, affiliative stabilizer,* and *disengaged satellite.* Visualization via *interactional heat maps* and *communication entropy indices* enabled real-time diagnostics of group dynamics and pedagogical entry points for reconfiguration. When implemented in a pilot intervention program, the model produced a 28 percent increase in equitable participation metrics and an observable amplification in epistemic complexity of group outputs. Teachers reported enhanced capacity for *interactional scaffolding*, and students articulated increased agency within peer networks. The model has since been embedded into professional development curricula and digitally instantiated into classroom observation apps calibrated for group learning environments.

5.4 Inclusive Pedagogy for Neurodiverse Learners

The neurodiverse classroom challenges the reductive logics of curricular universalism by demanding pedagogical models attuned to *neurological heterogeneity, sensory modulation thresholds,* and *affective dysregulation trajectories.* A paradigm-shifting study by Monash University employed an *ethnographic neurophenomenological* approach in 18 inclusion-focused primary schools, integrating teacher shadowing, sensory environment audits, and dialogic interviews with neurodiverse learners and caregivers. Data analytics revealed interrelations between visual saturation, auditory stimulus thresholds, and cognitive disorganization episodes. Using *fuzzy-set qualitative comparative analysis (fsQCA)* and *dynamic systems modeling,* the applied model abstracted three interwoven domains, i.e., *sensory optimization, communication differentiation,* and *self-regulatory affordance design.* These domains were populated with specific pedagogical elements such as visual cueing systems, proprioceptive regulation tools, and multimodal expression portfolios. Pilot implementation yielded a 45 percent reduction in task refusal behaviors and a 37 percent increase in self-initiated task engagement among neurodiverse learners. This was corroborated by both behavioral observation logs and teacher-annotated interaction diaries. The model was subsequently integrated into Victoria's Inclusive Schooling Policy Framework and has informed the architecture of digital learning environments through participatory co-design with neurodiverse stakeholders.

5.5 Reflective Practice and Professional Growth in Teachers

Teacher professional learning has traditionally been dominated by prescriptive training modules decoupled from the phenomenology of classroom praxis. To disrupt this epistemic disarticulation, Harvard Graduate School of Education launched a longitudinal study predicated on *praxeological epistemology* and *reflective reframing theory*. The study deployed a triadic methodology involving self-captured video segments, guided annotation protocols, and peer-ethnographic co-analysis among 62 K-12 educators across public and charter networks. Using *reflective content analysis* and *semiotic narrative synthesis*, an applied model of professional growth emerged, segmented into five recursive phases, i.e., *perceptual reframing*, *diagnostic dissonance*, *constructive internalization*, *pedagogical experimentation*, and *meta-reflexive integration*. Each phase was represented through *developmental learning trajectories* and aligned with specific meta-cognitive competencies.

Perceptual reframing refers to the initial cognitive shift in which educators begin to see their classroom practices through a new interpretive lens. Triggered by exposure to alternative perspectives, such as reviewing self-captured teaching videos or peer feedback, this phase involves questioning taken-for-granted assumptions about instruction, student behavior, or learning outcomes. It is marked by a reorientation of attention, i.e., what once appeared routine now becomes analytically salient, prompting deeper curiosity and openness to change. *Diagnostic dissonance* follows as educators confront the misalignments between their intended pedagogical goals and the actual dynamics captured in classroom footage or peer analysis. This phase entails emotional and cognitive friction, where teachers may feel discomfort, defensiveness, or self-doubt as they recognize gaps in their instructional impact. However, such dissonance is generative, i.e., it functions as a critical diagnostic moment that motivates inquiry, fuels reflective engagement, and prompts a search for more effective strategies. *Constructive internalization* involves the deliberate absorption and contextual adaptation of new insights into one's pedagogical repertoire. Here, educators begin to make sense of abstract ideas or external feedback in relation to their own teaching context, beliefs, and values. This phase is marked by a gradual reorganization of knowledge structures, where theory becomes personally meaningful and actionable. It signifies the cognitive assimilation of unfamiliar practices into a more integrated pedagogical identity. *Pedagogical experimentation* is the active trial of newly internalized strategies in the classroom. Educators move beyond reflection to enactment, testing instructional modifications and monitoring their outcomes. This phase is characterized by iterative risk-taking, adaptive improvisation, and feedback loops. It is through this hands-on process that theoretical learning is converted into embodied practice, and real-time responsiveness is cultivated. *Meta-reflexive integration* represents the consolidation of learning across prior phases. Educators attain a heightened awareness of their own learning processes and can articulate the why behind their actions. This phase entails recursive reflection on one's professional evolution and the sociocultural dynamics of teaching. It signals the emergence of a sustainable, self-renewing practice grounded in meta-cognitive insight, ethical commitment, and strategic flexibility. Together, these five recursive phases form a dynamic, transformative model of educator development that bridges perception, practice, and professional agency.

Quantitative outcome measures indicated statistically significant gains in student achievement across literacy and numeracy domains, directly correlated with teacher progression along the model's continuum. Qualitative feedback emphasized increased pedagogical intentionality, deeper instructional self-awareness, and enhanced collective efficacy. The model is now institutionalized within several school systems' induction and mentorship programs and has catalyzed the development of AI-assisted reflective tools for novice teacher education. Collectively, these five case illustrations exemplify the ontological and epistemic versatility of applied models derived from observational research. Whether mapping behavioral ecology in early childhood, tracing attention arcs in hybrid learning, or capturing the choreography of peer cognition and teacher reflection, these models constitute *epistemic devices* that transcend mere representation. They enable the encoding of pedagogical complexity into usable, recursive, and socially responsive knowledge systems that augment both the interpretive depth and transformative capacity of educational praxis.

6. TRANSLATING MODELS INTO PRACTICE

6.1 Diagnostic Applications in the Classroom

The translational utility of applied models derived from observational research lies in their capacity to operationalize the *latent architectures* of pedagogical ecosystems into actionable, high-resolution diagnostic instruments (Heppner et al., 2004; Robertson & Radcliffe, 2009; Verschaffel & De Corte, 1993; Litzinger et al., 2010). Unlike standardized assessments or summative evaluation frameworks, which often function as reductive proxies for learning, applied models instantiate a *situated diagnostic lens* capable of apprehending the semiotic, affective, and epistemological substrata of learner behavior and instructional dynamics. These models encode *micro-interactional grammars*, enabling educators to detect, interpret, and modulate emergent patterns of cognitive dissonance, socio-emotional dysregulation, and epistemic disengagement within live instructional environments (Dwiyogo, 2018; Purwaningsih et al., 2020; Hiebert et al., 1996; Collins & Dunn, 2011). For instance, a meta-analysis by the Learning Policy Institute in 2023 evidences that classrooms employing model-informed diagnostics, particularly in early literacy development, report up to 34 percent greater identification accuracy of students at risk for reading failure. These gains are attributable not to more frequent testing but to the real-time deployment of *pattern-recognition heuristics* embedded within applied models. Such models synthesize indicators including gaze aversion, latency in verbal response, and peer avoidance to triangulate a learner's *affective-cognitive state*. As a result, interventions become *ecologically calibrated* rather than uniformly prescriptive, thus maximizing both pedagogical precision and learner receptivity.

6.2 Instructional Design and Pedagogical Innovation

Applied models serve as *design epistemologies* that bridge the chasm between empirical complexity and pedagogical coherence. When translated into the domain of instructional design, these models provide a *heuristic architecture* for organizing curricular content, sequencing cognitive load, and modulating didactic modalities (Newton et al., 2011; Eseryel et al., 2013; Tsai et al., 2023; Surya & Putri, 2017). Unlike abstract curriculum frameworks, which often remain inert in their prescriptive abstraction, model-informed instructional design is *dynamically contingent*, i.e., iteratively refined through feedback loops grounded in observational data. A recent study from the Carnegie Foundation for the Advancement of Teaching demonstrated that schools integrating applied models into design-based implementation research (DBIR) cycles exhibited accelerated improvement in formative learning outcomes, particularly in problem-based and inquiry-driven pedagogies. These models act as *generative templates*, aligning instructional moves with the neurocognitive affordances of learners, thereby minimizing *extraneous cognitive load* and maximizing *germane processing*. In STEM domains, for instance, applied models have been used to reorganize lab-based instruction to better scaffold procedural fluency and epistemic metacognition, as evidenced by significant upticks in both conceptual transfer and self-regulatory behaviors among secondary school students. Moreover, applied models empower pedagogical innovation by functioning as *semiotic blueprints* for the creation of novel learning configurations. In multilingual settings, translanguaging models derived from observational data have been instantiated into multilingual curricula that enable linguistic dexterity and cultural authenticity without fragmenting academic rigor. Such innovations dismantle *epistemic hegemony* and foster *plurilingual literacy practices* that are simultaneously cognitively expansive and culturally situated.

6.3 Teacher Professional Development and Reflective Praxis

The paradigmatic shift toward *praxeological professional development* necessitates models that are not externally imposed but internally generative. Applied models function as *catalytic mediators* for teacher learning, transforming abstract reflection into structured epistemic engagement with classroom data. Unlike traditional professional development, which is frequently disconnected from the contingencies of instructional reality, model-informed teacher growth is recursive, context-sensitive, and dialogically constructed (Simon, 1978; Matsuda et al., 2007; Eivazi & Bednarik, 2011; Todd et al., 2011). A quasi-experimental study conducted by the Stanford Center for Opportunity Policy in Education revealed that teachers engaged in model-facilitated video microanalysis reported higher levels of *instructional intentionality*, *adaptive expertise*, and *pedagogical reasoning*. The models provided *reflective affordances* that allowed educators to recursively analyze their own cognitive schemata, discourse patterns, and relational cues, resulting in pedagogical decisions that were not only evidence-based but *affectively attuned* and socially responsive. These applied models have been integrated into *instructional coaching architectures* where teachers iteratively generate, test, and refine practice in a *spiral of professional enactment*. The resulting praxis is neither linear nor hierarchical but constitutes a *rhizomatic learning ecology* where knowledge, identity, and relationality are co-constructed. Importantly, model-informed professional development elevates teacher agency by positioning educators as *epistemic agents* rather than passive recipients of top-down training.

6.4 Monitoring, Evaluation, and Institutional Planning

At the meso and macro levels of the educational system, applied models serve as *analytic infrastructures* for institutional decision-making, programmatic evaluation, and policy refinement (Weiss & Heyman, 2004; Wahyuni et al., 2017; Li et al., 2016; Al-Mutawah et al., 2019). Traditional monitoring and evaluation (M&E) frameworks often emphasize *lagging indicators* such as standardized test scores or graduation rates, which obscure the granular, in-process dynamics of teaching and learning. In contrast, models constructed from field-based observation provide *leading indicators* that allow institutions to engage in *predictive analytics* and *adaptive governance*. For example, the World Bank's SABER (Systems Approach for Better Education Results) framework increasingly integrates model-based data to track instructional quality and school climate in real time. In Ghana and Vietnam, localized applied models have been incorporated into district-level data dashboards that visualize trends in student participation, teacher talk-time, and collaborative learning. This data has enabled school leaders to enact *evidence-informed interventions* at multiple tiers, from scheduling reforms and resource allocation to redesigning professional learning communities.

In higher education, model-based quality assurance mechanisms are being adopted to assess faculty teaching effectiveness through *multimodal rubrics* that incorporate observational insights, peer evaluations, and student feedback triangulated within a unified analytic framework (Chalfant et al., 1979; Algozzine et al., 2012; Robillard, 2005; Kim & Hannafin, 2011). These models foster a *formative evaluation culture* that prioritizes improvement over compliance and transformation over transaction.

Crucially, applied models in institutional planning allow for *systems-level modeling*, simulating various policy scenarios and their potential downstream effects. Through agent-based modeling and systems dynamics simulations, education ministries can forecast the implications of policy shifts in areas such as assessment reform, language policy, or digital infrastructure deployment. In this context, applied models do not merely describe the educational system, in fact, they reconfigure it as a *complex adaptive system* capable of self-monitoring, self-adjustment, and self-transformation (Rouwette et al., 2002; Rott et al., 2021; Treffinger & Isaksen, 2005; Greiff et al., 2012). The translation of applied models into educational practice constitutes a multi-tiered epistemic endeavor that amplifies the *granularity, responsiveness, and efficacy* of decision-making at the level of classroom, institution, and system. Far from being static representations of empirical phenomena, these models act as *cognitive prosthetics* for educators and policy actors alike, thus enabling situated responsiveness, distributed intelligence, and generative change. They instantiate an epistemology of action, wherein knowing is inseparable from doing, and understanding is always in service of transformation.

7. POLICY IMPLICATIONS AND SYSTEMIC INTEGRATION

7.1 Informing Evidence-Based Policy Design

The incorporation of applied models into policy architecture signifies a paradigmatic transition from ideologically driven macrointerventions to empirically tethered, micro-contingent governance. Contemporary education systems, increasingly conceptualized as *complex adaptive systems*, require policy instruments that do not merely extrapolate normative aspirations but are capable of responding to the *nonlinearities, feedback loops, and stochastic perturbations* inherent in pedagogical ecosystems. Applied models derived from observational research occupy this mediational space between field-level phenomenology and policy-level abstraction, functioning as *epistemic instruments* for anticipatory governance (Anliak & Sahin, 2010; Borich, 2016; Dishion & Patterson, 1999; Krasnor, 1982). Informed by *post-positivist policy epistemology*, these models recalibrate the evidentiary regime of policy discourse by privileging granular, situated data over homogenized macroindicators. For example, in Rwanda's nationwide curriculum reform initiative, the deployment of an applied model synthesized from multisite classroom observations across rural and urban schools revealed not only lexical gaps in instructional materials but also the *interactional asymmetries* exacerbated by teacher-centered didactics. This model was subsequently embedded into the national Competency-Based Curriculum framework, enabling an iterative feedback mechanism between classroom micro-processes and curriculum macrostructure. Such models are not merely diagnostic but are inherently *prescriptive and generative*, enabling *policy prototyping* through design-based implementation pathways. In this configuration, models function as *policy epistemologies*, rendering visible the covert sociotechnical dynamics of instruction, participation, and learning distribution. As evidence-informed paradigms gain institutional salience, applied models serve as the *analytical substrate* through which policy formulation is disaggregated, localized, and rendered agile in the face of pedagogical volatility and socio-political complexity.

7.2 Enhancing Institutional Decision-Making

At the meso-institutional level, applied models constitute *governance technologies* that mediate strategic decision-making processes within schools, districts, and higher education institutions. They act as *analytic infrastructures* through which educational leaders interpret emergent phenomena, allocate finite resources, and design organizational interventions (Andersen et al., 1997; Hidayati & Wagiran, 2020; Lazakidou & Retalis, 2010; Bryce & Whitebread, 2012). Unlike traditional performance dashboards that rely on static, retrospective indicators, model-based decision frameworks enable *anticipatory logistics* and *prospective systems design* grounded in real-time pedagogical intelligence. For instance, in the context of school turnaround strategies in underperforming districts in Brazil, applied models constructed from multimodal observations elucidated the *spatial-temporal topography* of instructional time wastage, teacher absenteeism, and learner disengagement. These models, encoded through *geospatial information systems* and *temporal pattern recognition*, enabled district administrators to reconfigure school timetables, reassign teaching personnel, and restructure professional development in a manner that was empirically precise and contextually resonant. The resulting *organizational learning loops* facilitated institutional adaptability and resilience, reducing performance variance by over 20 percent within two academic cycles. In higher education, similar models have been employed to map *pedagogical heat zones*, i.e., domains within curricula where conceptual attrition, epistemic dissonance, and learner demotivation converge. Using observational data, learning analytics, and student cognitive profiles, these models provide *cognitive cartographies* for course redesign, advising interventions, and faculty development. In effect, applied models serve as *navigational technologies* for academic institutions, guiding them through epistemic uncertainties and structural asymmetries toward more coherent and equitable learning environments.

7.3 Supporting Inclusive and Equitable Education

The imperative for inclusion and equity in education necessitates policy instruments capable of disaggregating systemic inequities and amplifying the *voice, visibility, and viability* of historically marginalized learners. Applied models grounded in observational data offer a uniquely potent means of operationalizing these imperatives through *intersectional diagnostics*, *responsive design strategies*, and *culturally sustaining pedagogies*. By capturing the *phenomenology of exclusion*, whether enacted through linguistic silencing, spatial marginalization, or affective erasure, applied models reveal the *hidden transcripts* of inequity embedded within educational infrastructures (Bogard et al., 2013; Sauerbrei et al., 2014; Bagiati & Evangelou, 2016; Kolodner & Wills, 1996). For instance, the University of the Western Cape's participatory action research in South African township schools developed an applied model from classroom ethnographies that traced *distributive injustices* in teacher attention, instructional material quality, and learner spatial positioning. This model, visualized through *equity heat maps* and *narrative analytics*, was adopted by district education officials to redesign inclusive teacher training modules, resource allocation strategies, and student feedback mechanisms. Within two years, participation disparities between linguistic minorities and dominant language learners decreased by over 30 percent.

Similarly, in the United States, models constructed from fine-grained observational coding of culturally responsive pedagogy were used to inform district-level equity audits under the Every Student Succeeds Act (ESSA). These models deconstructed the *aesthetic and epistemic violence* of monocultural curricula and reframed professional development as a *politicized space of rehumanization*. As a result, schools integrating these models into their improvement plans reported measurable gains in student belongingness, instructional inclusivity, and teacher cultural self-efficacy. Crucially, applied models also serve as *pedagogical reparation mechanisms*, enabling the co-construction of educational futures that are not only inclusive in form but emancipatory in function. By embedding *critical race epistemologies*, *decolonial pedagogies*, and *universal design principles* into model architecture, applied models function as *counterhegemonic cartographies*, thus mapping alternative trajectories for learners who have historically been excluded from the epistemic center (Oulasvirta & Hornbæk, 2016; Fitriani & Arnawa, 2020; Depaepe et al., 2010; Kurniawan et al., 2019). The policy implications and systemic integration of applied models constitute a multi-scalar, transdisciplinary enterprise that transcends the performative rituals of evidence-based rhetoric. These models recode educational systems as *adaptive knowledge ecologies*, wherein data is not merely accumulated but *strategically mobilized* toward epistemic justice, organizational agility, and learner empowerment. Far from static tools of representation, applied models function as *ontological catalysts*, restructuring how education is understood, enacted, and transformed across institutional and policy landscapes. They instantiate a new grammar of educational governance, one that is recursive, reflexive, and radically responsive to the pluralistic realities of twenty-first-century learning.

8. ETHICAL, EPISTEMOLOGICAL, AND PRACTICAL CONSIDERATIONS

8.1 Working with Vulnerable Populations

The ethical terrain of observational research in education is fraught with epistemic asymmetries and ontological risks, particularly when investigations engage *vulnerable epistemic agents* such as children, neurodiverse learners, linguistic minorities, and structurally disenfranchised communities. Within these contexts, the researcher's presence is not a neutral act of documentation but an *interventional forcefield* that modulates the ecology of observation itself. Ethical praxis, therefore, cannot be confined to institutional review board (IRB) compliance or deontological minimalism; rather, it must be understood as a *situated ethics of care*, informed by *relational accountability*, *cultural reflexivity*, and *intersubjective recognition*. The foundational principle of *informed consent* must be reconfigured through a *dialogic and iterative lens*, especially in communities where formal literacies are stratified and authority dynamics are historically hierarchical. Researchers must operationalize *contextual consent architectures*, scaffolded by visual, auditory, or narrative modalities, that are sensitive to age, cognition, language, and sociocultural normativity. For instance, participatory research in Indigenous schools has demonstrated that consent is not an individualistic transaction but a *relational protocol* that implicates familial, communal, and spiritual dimensions. The ethical infrastructure of model construction in such contexts must therefore be *ontologically pluralistic* and *epistemically decolonial*. Moreover, data elicited from vulnerable populations often encode trauma histories, identity politics, and forms of *epistemic oppression*. Observational instruments must thus be designed with *hermeneutic sensitivity*, ensuring that data capture does not function as a mechanism of surveillance, extraction, or re-traumatization. Models derived from such data must incorporate *representational ethics*, foregrounding narrative agency, contextual integrity, and co-interpretation, lest they become instruments of *symbolic violence* masquerading as analytical rigor.

8.2 Ensuring Validity and Reducing Bias

Epistemic validity in observational model construction transcends classical concerns of inter-rater reliability and coding fidelity. It encompasses *hermeneutic coherence*, *ontological transparency*, and *epistemological integrity*. In contexts of cultural hybridity and linguistic multiplicity, the validity of observational categories themselves must be interrogated through *meta-ethnographic deconstruction* (Greiff et al., 2016; Forbus & De Kleer, 1993; Tucker & Edmondson, 2002; Mizoguchi et al., 1995). For example, constructs such as "engagement," "participation," or "compliance" often carry culturally embedded assumptions that obscure rather than illuminate the learning ecologies of minoritized learners. Without reflexive recalibration, models risk imposing *normative hierarchies* that pathologize difference and reinforce hegemonic pedagogical imaginaries. To mitigate such distortions, observational methodologies must integrate *critical reflexivity cycles* involving triangulation across *positional lenses*, *epistemic standpoints*, and *cultural grammars*. This necessitates a multi-level analytic architecture encompassing *etic-emic dialectics*, *member-checking loops*, and *counter-coding iterations*, especially in translocal or translingual research contexts. The incorporation of community co-analysts, dialogic coding sessions, and narrative validation frameworks serves to decentralize the researcher's interpretive monopoly and construct a *distributed epistemology* of meaning-making. Algorithmic bias is an emergent concern in the age of AI-assisted observational modeling. Machine learning classifiers trained on homogenous datasets risk codifying dominant-culture expectations into automated judgments. For example, facial expression recognition software used to detect affective states in classrooms has been shown to underperform on Black and Brown students due to *training data monoculture*. Ethical modeling thus requires *algorithmic transparency*, *inclusive dataset curation*, and *explainable AI protocols*, ensuring that automated augmentation does not displace human discernment or compound systemic inequities.

8.3 Transparency and Reproducibility

In the emerging epistemic economy of applied educational research, transparency is not merely a virtue but a methodological imperative. The construction of applied models from observational data must adhere to the principles of *procedural traceability*, *methodological auditability*, and *epistemic reproducibility*. Without such rigor, models risk becoming *black-box abstractions*, illegible to the very practitioners and communities they purport to serve (Leicht et al., 2010; Anggoro et al., 2021; Lessler et al., 2015; Gold et al., 2022). Transparency necessitates the open documentation of every decision point in the model's genealogy, i.e., from sampling logics and instrument design to coding schemes and abstraction protocols. The movement toward *open science* in educational research has foregrounded *data democratization*, advocating for the publication of field notes, coding matrices, and model diagrams within *open-access repositories*. Initiatives such as the Open Education Research Archive (OERA) and the Educational Data Science Commons have begun to institutionalize best practices for model transparency, including *version control*, *codebook annotation*, and *epistemic lineage mapping*. These platforms not only facilitate reproducibility but also enable cross-contextual adaptation, promoting the *scalability and portability* of applied models across diverse educational geographies.

Transparency is also integral to stakeholder trust and participatory ethics. Teachers, learners, and community members must be able to interrogate, reinterpret, and reconfigure the models that influence their educational trajectories. This calls for the design of *translational model interfaces*, infographics, interactive dashboards, and narrative summaries, that render complex model architectures intelligible to non-specialist users. When models are rendered opaque by disciplinary jargon or technocratic elitism, they devolve into *epistemic hieroglyphs* that disempower rather than empower (Lesh & Doerr, 2003; Bui et al., 2013; Fernlund & Gonzalez, 2002; Ste-Marie et al., 2020). Finally, reproducibility in observational modeling must account for the *ontological contingency* of educational practice. Unlike lab-based experiments, educational environments are historically situated, affectively charged, and normatively fluid. Reproducibility, therefore, must be *interpretive and ecological*, not mechanistic. What is required is a *reproducibility-as-resonance paradigm*, wherein models are not duplicated in identical conditions but are *re-inhabited* in dialogic relation to new contexts, with fidelity to their analytic logics but openness to contextual reconfiguration.

The ethical, epistemological, and practical architecture of applied model construction must be grounded in *epistemic humility*, *methodological pluralism*, and *transformative praxis*. This entails rethinking the research encounter as a *relational epistemic space*, where data are co-constructed, models are co-owned, and meaning is co-negotiated. Observational modeling, when pursued with such rigor and care, transcends its instrumental function to become a *mode of ethical world-making*, wherein representation is not extraction but solidarity, and analysis is not abstraction but relational accountability (Lesh & Doerr, 2003; Hamilton et al., 2020; Wilczenski et al., 2001; Lester & Kehle, 2003). This chapter elucidates the construction of applied models from observational research in education as a transdisciplinary, praxis-oriented methodology for capturing and transforming complex pedagogical ecologies. Integrating theories from constructivism, experiential learning, systems thinking, and situated cognition, it outlines the methodological arc from data collection to model abstraction and validation. Through diverse case illustrations, the chapter demonstrates how applied models function as diagnostic, design, and governance tools across classroom, institutional, and policy levels. Emphasizing ethical reflexivity, epistemic justice, and methodological transparency, it positions applied models as dynamic epistemic instruments for educational transformation in volatile, diverse, and inequitable learning systems.

REFERENCES

Al-Mutawah, M. A., Thomas, R., Eid, A., Mahmoud, E. Y., & Fateel, M. J. (2019). Conceptual understanding, procedural knowledge and problem-solving skills in mathematics: High school graduates work analysis and standpoints. *International journal of education and practice, 7*(3), 258-273.

Algozzine, B., Newton, J. S., Horner, R. H., Todd, A. W., & Algozzine, K. (2012). Development and technical characteristics of a team decision-making assessment tool: Decision observation, recording, and analysis (DORA). *Journal of Psychoeducational Assessment, 30*(3), 237–249. DOI: 10.1177/0734282911423884

Allen, J., Blaylock, N., & Ferguson, G. (2002, July). A problem solving model for collaborative agents. In *Proceedings of the first international joint conference on Autonomous agents and multiagent systems: part 2* (pp. 774-781). DOI: 10.1145/544862.544923

Andersen, D. F., Richardson, G. P., & Vennix, J. A. (1997). Group model building: Adding more science to the craft. *System Dynamics Review, 13*(2), 187–201. DOI: 10.1002/(SICI)1099-1727(199722)13:2<187::AID-SDR124>3.0.CO;2-O

Anggoro, F. K., Dubosarsky, M., & Kabourek, S. (2021). Developing an observation tool to measure preschool children's problem-solving skills. *Education Sciences, 11*(12), 779. DOI: 10.3390/educsci11120779

Anliak, S., & Sahin, D. (2010). An observational study for evaluating the effects of interpersonal problem-solving skills training on behavioural dimensions. *Early Child Development and Care, 180*(8), 995–1003. DOI: 10.1080/03004430802670819

Asmah, S., Hastati, S., & Nurdiansyah, E. (2025). Application Of The Problem Solving Learning Model In Improving Numeracy Skills In Class IV Students Of SDN. *ALENA: Journal of Elementary Education, 3*(2), 209–218. DOI: 10.59638/jee.v3i2.373

Auclair, F. (2007). Problem formulation by medical students: An observation study. *BMC Medical Education, 7*(1), 16. DOI: 10.1186/1472-6920-7-16

Bagiati, A., & Evangelou, D. (2016). Practicing engineering while building with blocks: Identifying engineering thinking. *European Early Childhood Education Research Journal, 24*(1), 67–85. DOI: 10.1080/1350293X.2015.1120521

Bardwell, L. V. (1991). Problem-framing: A perspective on environmental problem-solving. *Environmental Management, 15*(5), 603–612. DOI: 10.1007/BF02589620

Basili, V. R. (1996, March). The role of experimentation in software engineering: past, current, and future. In *Proceedings of IEEE 18th International Conference on Software Engineering* (pp. 442-449). IEEE. DOI: 10.1109/ICSE.1996.493439

Ben-Hur, M. (2006). *Concept-rich mathematics instruction: Building a strong foundation for reasoning and problem solving*. ASCD.

Bennett, M., Vielma, J. P., & Zubizarreta, J. R. (2020). Building representative matched samples with multi-valued treatments in large observational studies. *Journal of Computational and Graphical Statistics, 29*(4), 744–757. DOI: 10.1080/10618600.2020.1753532

Bogard, T., Liu, M., & Chiang, Y. H. V. (2013). Thresholds of knowledge development in complex problem solving: A multiple-case study of advanced learners' cognitive processes. *Educational Technology Research and Development, 61*(3), 465–503. DOI: 10.1007/s11423-013-9295-4

Borich, G. D. (2016). *Observation skills for effective teaching: Research-based practice*. Routledge. DOI: 10.4324/9781315633206

Bradshaw, Z., & Hazell, A. (2017). Developing problem-solving skills in mathematics: A lesson study. *International Journal for Lesson and Learning Studies, 6*(1), 32–44. DOI: 10.1108/IJLLS-09-2016-0032

Brown, J. S., Collins, A., & Duguid, P. (1989). Situated cognition and the culture of learning. *1989, 18*(1), 32-42.

Bryce, D., & Whitebread, D. (2012). The development of metacognitive skills: Evidence from observational analysis of young children's behavior during problem-solving. *Metacognition and Learning, 7*(3), 197–217. DOI: 10.1007/s11409-012-9091-2

Bui, A. A., Hsu, W., Arnold, C., El-Saden, S., Aberle, D. R., & Taira, R. K. (2013). Imaging-based observational databases for clinical problem solving: The role of informatics. *Journal of the American Medical Informatics Association : JAMIA, 20*(6), 1053–1058. DOI: 10.1136/amiajnl-2012-001340

Burns, M. S., Haywood, H. C., & Delclos, V. R. (1987). Young children's problem-solving strategies: An observational study. *Journal of Applied Developmental Psychology, 8*(1), 113–121. DOI: 10.1016/0193-3973(87)90024-4

Carpenter, T. P., & Fennema, E. (1992). Cognitively guided instruction: Building on the knowledge of students and teachers. *International Journal of Educational Research, 17*(5), 457–470. DOI: 10.1016/S0883-0355(05)80005-9

Chalfant, J. C., VanDusen Pysh, M., & Moultrie, R. (1979). Teacher assistance teams: A model for within-building problem solving. *Learning Disability Quarterly*, *2*(3), 85–96. DOI: 10.2307/1511031

Charlesworth, R., & Leali, S. A. (2012). Using problem solving to assess young children's mathematics knowledge. *Early Childhood Education Journal*, *39*(6), 373–382. DOI: 10.1007/s10643-011-0480-y

Chatfield, C. (1995). *Problem solving: a statistician's guide*. CRC Press. DOI: 10.1201/b15238

Chi, M. T., & Wylie, R. (2014). The ICAP framework: Linking cognitive engagement to active learning outcomes. *Educational Psychologist*, *49*(4), 219–243. DOI: 10.1080/00461520.2014.965823

Cho, Y. H., & Lim, K. Y. (2017). Effectiveness of collaborative learning with 3 D virtual worlds. *British Journal of Educational Technology*, *48*(1), 202–211. DOI: 10.1111/bjet.12356

Choi, Y., & Yoon, S. (2023). Surrogate-assisted high-accuracy observation modeling in building digital twins: In situ nonintrusive modeling without sensor observation (Y). *Building and Environment*, *242*, 110584. DOI: 10.1016/j.buildenv.2023.110584

Coburn, C. E., & Russell, J. L. (2008). District policy and teachers' social networks. *Educational Evaluation and Policy Analysis*, *30*(3), 203–235. DOI: 10.3102/0162373708321829

Collins, D., & Dunn, M. (2011). Problem-solving strategies and processes in musical composition: Observations in real time. *Journal of Music. Technology and Education*, *4*(1), 47–76. DOI: 10.1386/jmte.4.1.47_1

Daulay, K. R., & Ruhaimah, I. (2019, March). Polya theory to improve problem-solving skills. [). IOP Publishing.]. *Journal of Physics: Conference Series*, *1188*(1), 012070. DOI: 10.1088/1742-6596/1188/1/012070

Depaepe, F., De Corte, E., & Verschaffel, L. (2010). Teachers' approaches towards word problem solving: Elaborating or restricting the problem context. *Teaching and Teacher Education*, *26*(2), 152–160. DOI: 10.1016/j.tate.2009.03.016

Depaepe, F., De Corte, E., & Verschaffel, L. (2010). Teachers' metacognitive and heuristic approaches to word problem solving: Analysis and impact on students' beliefs and performance. *ZDM Mathematics Education*, *42*(2), 205–218. DOI: 10.1007/s11858-009-0221-5

Dermitzaki, I., Leondari, A., & Goudas, M. (2009). Relations between young students' strategic behaviours, domain-specific self-concept, and performance in a problem-solving situation. *Learning and Instruction*, *19*(2), 144–157. DOI: 10.1016/j.learninstruc.2008.03.002

Dewi, I. N., Poedjiastoeti, S., & Prahani, B. K. (2017). ELSII learning model based local wisdom to improve students' problem solving skills and scientific communication. *International Journal of Education and Research*, *5*(1), 107–118.

Diamantes, T., & Williams, M. (1997). *The Perceptive Eye/Ear Game: An Activity That Encourages Practice on Best Practice*. Honing Observation and Problem-Solving Skills of Administrators.

Dillmann, R. (2004). Teaching and learning of robot tasks via observation of human performance. *Robotics and Autonomous Systems*, *47*(2-3), 109–116. DOI: 10.1016/j.robot.2004.03.005

Dishion, T. J., & Patterson, G. R. (1999). Model building in developmental psychopathology: A pragmatic approach to understanding and intervention. *Journal of Clinical Child Psychology*, *28*(4), 502–512. DOI: 10.1207/S15374424JCCP2804_10

Dorst, K., & Cross, N. (2001). Creativity in the design process: Co-evolution of problem–solution. *Design Studies*, *22*(5), 425–437. DOI: 10.1016/S0142-694X(01)00009-6

Dwiyogo, W. D. (2018). Developing a blended learning-based method for problem-solving in capability learning. *Turkish Online Journal of Educational Technology-TOJET*, *17*(1), 51–61.

Eivazi, S., & Bednarik, R. (2011, February). Predicting problem-solving behavior and performance levels from visual attention data. In *Proc. workshop on eye gaze in intelligent human machine interaction at IUI* (pp. 9-16).

Eseryel, D., Ifenthaler, D., & Ge, X. (2013). Validation study of a method for assessing complex ill-structured problem solving by using causal representations. *Educational Technology Research and Development*, *61*(3), 443–463. DOI: 10.1007/s11423-013-9297-2

Fauzia, N. L. U., & Kelana, J. B. (2020). Natural science problem solving in elementary school students using the project based learning (PjBL) model. *Jurnal Ilmiah Sekolah Dasar*, *4*(4), 596–603.

Fernlund, H. K., & Gonzalez, A. J. (2002). *An approach towards building human behavior models automatically by observation*. Intelligent Systems Laboratory.

Fitriani, N., & Arnawa, I. M. (2020, May). An initial observation of learning devices and mathematical problem solving ability of senior high school students. []. IOP Publishing.]. *Journal of Physics: Conference Series, 1554*(1), 012067. DOI: 10.1088/1742-6596/1554/1/012067

Forbus, K. D., & De Kleer, J. (1993). *Building problem solvers* (Vol. 1). MIT press.

Geertz, C. (1973). Chapter 1/Thick Description: Toward an interpretive theory of culture. *The interpretation of cultures: Selected essays*, 3-30.

Gok, T. (2010). The general assessment of problem solving processes and metacognition in physics education. *International Journal of Physics and Chemistry Education*, *2*(2), 110–122. DOI: 10.51724/ijpce.v2i2.186

Gold, Z. S., Perlman, J., Howe, N., Mishra, A. A., DeHart, G. B., Hertik, H., & Buckley, J. (2022). An observational study of children's problem solving during play with friends. *Journal of Cognition and Development*, *23*(4), 503–523. DOI: 10.1080/15248372.2022.2058509

Goldin, G. A. (1998). Representational systems, learning, and problem solving in mathematics. *The Journal of Mathematical Behavior*, *17*(2), 137–165. DOI: 10.1016/S0364-0213(99)80056-1

Greiff, S., Niepel, C., Scherer, R., & Martin, R. (2016). Understanding students' performance in a computer-based assessment of complex problem solving: An analysis of behavioral data from computer-generated log files. *Computers in Human Behavior*, *61*, 36–46. DOI: 10.1016/j.chb.2016.02.095

Greiff, S., Wüstenberg, S., & Funke, J. (2012). Dynamic problem solving: A new assessment perspective. *Applied Psychological Measurement*, *36*(3), 189–213. DOI: 10.1177/0146621612439620

Hamilton, E., Lesh, R., Lester, F., & Yoon, C. (2020). The use of reflection tools to build personal models of problem-solving. In *Foundations for the future in mathematics education* (pp. 349–366). Routledge. DOI: 10.4324/9781003064527-21

Hamza, M. K., & Griffith, K. G. (2006). Fostering problem-solving & creative thinking in the classroom: cultivating a creative mind. In *National Forum of Applied Educational Research Journal-Electronic* (Vol. 9, No. 3, pp. 1-32).

Hasibuan, A. M., Saragih, S., & Amry, Z. (2019). Development of Learning Materials Based on Realistic Mathematics Education to Improve Problem Solving Ability and Student Learning Independence. *International electronic journal of mathematics education, 14*(1), 243-252.

Heppner, P. P. (2008). Expanding the conceptualization and measurement of applied problem solving and coping: From stages to dimensions to the almost forgotten cultural context. *The American Psychologist*, *63*(8), 805–816. DOI: 10.1037/0003-066X.63.8.805

Heppner, P. P., Witty, T. E., & Dixon, W. A. (2004). Problem-solving appraisal and human adjustment: A review of 20 years of research using the Problem Solving Inventory. *The Counseling Psychologist*, *32*(3), 344–428. DOI: 10.1177/0011000003262793

Hidayati, R. M., & Wagiran, W. (2020). Implementation of problem-based learning to improve problem-solving skills in vocational high school. *Jurnal Pendidikan Vokasi*, *10*(2), 177–187. DOI: 10.21831/jpv.v10i2.31210

Hiebert, J., Carpenter, T. P., Fennema, E., Fuson, K., Human, P., Murray, H., Olivier, A., & Wearne, D. (1996). Problem solving as a basis for reform in curriculum and instruction: The case of mathematics. *Educational Researcher*, *25*(4), 12–21. DOI: 10.3102/0013189X025004012

Hill, R. B. (1997). The design of an instrument to assess problem solving activities in technology education.

Hill-Briggs, F. (2003). Problem solving in diabetes self-management: A model of chronic illness self-management behavior. *Annals of Behavioral Medicine*, *25*(3), 182–193. DOI: 10.1207/S15324796ABM2503_04

Horváth, I. (2007). Comparison of three methodological approaches of design research. In *DS 42: Proceedings of ICED 2007, the 16th International Conference on Engineering Design, Paris, France, 28.-31.07. 2007* (pp. 361-362).

Hulaikah, M., Degeng, I., & Murwani, F. D. (2020). The Effect of Experiential Learning and Adversity Quotient on Problem Solving Ability. *International Journal of Instruction*, *13*(1), 869–884. DOI: 10.29333/iji.2020.13156a

Hwang, W. Y., Su, J. H., Huang, Y. M., & Dong, J. J. (2009). A study of multi-representation of geometry problem solving with virtual manipulatives and whiteboard system. *Journal of Educational Technology & Society*, *12*(3), 229–247.

Immordino-Yang, M. H., & Damasio, A. (2007). We feel, therefore we learn: The relevance of affective and social neuroscience to education. *Mind, Brain and Education : the Official Journal of the International Mind, Brain, and Education Society*, *1*(1), 3–10. DOI: 10.1111/j.1751-228X.2007.00004.x

Isaksen, S. G., & Treffinger, D. J. (2004). Celebrating 50 years of reflective practice: Versions of creative problem solving. *The Journal of Creative Behavior*, *38*(2), 75–101. DOI: 10.1002/j.2162-6057.2004.tb01234.x

Karmakar, B., Small, D. S., & Rosenbaum, P. R. (2019). Using approximation algorithms to build evidence factors and related designs for observational studies. *Journal of Computational and Graphical Statistics*, *28*(3), 698–709. DOI: 10.1080/10618600.2019.1584900

Khoiriyah, A. J., & Husamah, H. (2018). Problem-based learning: Creative thinking skills, problem-solving skills, and learning outcome of seventh grade students. [Jurnal Pendidikan Biologi Indonesia]. *JPBI*, *4*(2), 151–160. DOI: 10.22219/jpbi.v4i2.5804

Khotimah, R. P., & Masduki, M. (2016). Improving Teaching Quality and Problem Solving Ability through Contextual Teaching and Learning in Differential Equations: A Lesson Study Approach. *Online Submission*, *1*(1), 1–13. DOI: 10.23917/jramathedu.v1i1.1791

Kim, M. C., & Hannafin, M. J. (2011). Scaffolding problem solving in technology-enhanced learning environments (TELEs): Bridging research and theory with practice. *Computers & Education*, *56*(2), 403–417. DOI: 10.1016/j.compedu.2010.08.024

Kolodner, J. L., & Wills, L. M. (1996). Powers of observation in creative design. *Design Studies*, *17*(4), 385–416. DOI: 10.1016/S0142-694X(96)00021-X

Krasnor, L. R. (1982). An observational study of social problem solving in young children. In *Peer relationships and social skills in childhood* (pp. 113–132). Springer New York. DOI: 10.1007/978-1-4613-8180-8_6

Kurniawan, W., Darmaji, D., Astalini, A., Kurniawan, D. A., Hidayat, M., Kurniawan, N., & Farida, L. Z. N. (2019). Multimedia Physics Practicum Reflective Material Based on Problem Solving for Science Process Skills. *International Journal of Evaluation and Research in Education*, *8*(4), 590–595. DOI: 10.11591/ijere.v8i4.20258

Lames, M., & Hansen, G. (2001). Designing observational systems to support top-level teams in game sports. *International Journal of Performance Analysis in Sport*, *1*(1), 83–90. DOI: 10.1080/24748668.2001.11868251

Lazakidou, G., & Retalis, S. (2010). Using computer supported collaborative learning strategies for helping students acquire self-regulated problem-solving skills in mathematics. *Computers & Education*, *54*(1), 3–13. DOI: 10.1016/j.compedu.2009.02.020

Leicht, R. M., Hunter, S. T., Saluja, C., & Messner, J. I. (2010). Implementing observational research methods to study team performance in construction management. *Journal of Construction Engineering and Management*, *136*(1), 76–86. DOI: 10.1061/(ASCE)CO.1943-7862.0000080

Leikin, R., Koichu, B., & Berman, A. (2009). Mathematical giftedness as a quality of problem-solving acts. *Creativity in mathematics and the education of gifted students, 8*, 115-127.

Lemons, G., Carberry, A., Swan, C., Jarvin, L., & Rogers, C. (2010). The benefits of model building in teaching engineering design. *Design Studies*, *31*(3), 288–309. DOI: 10.1016/j.destud.2010.02.001

Lesh, R., & Doerr, H. M. (2003). Foundations of a models and modeling perspective on mathematics teaching, learning, and problem solving. In *Beyond constructivism* (pp. 3–33). Routledge. DOI: 10.4324/9781410607713

Lesh, R., & Harel, G. (2003). Problem solving, modeling, and local conceptual development. *Mathematical Thinking and Learning*, *5*(2-3), 157–189. DOI: 10.1080/10986065.2003.9679998

Lesh, R. A., & Doerr, H. M. (2003). *Beyond constructivism: Models and modeling perspectives on mathematics problem solving, learning, and teaching*. Routledge. DOI: 10.4324/9781410607713

Lessler, J., Edmunds, W. J., Halloran, M. E., Hollingsworth, T. D., & Lloyd, A. L. (2015). Seven challenges for model-driven data collection in experimental and observational studies. *Epidemics*, *10*, 78–82. DOI: 10.1016/j.epidem.2014.12.002

Lester, F. K., & Kehle, P. E. (2003). From problem solving to modeling: The evolution of thinking about research on complex mathematical activity. In *Beyond constructivism* (pp. 501–517). Routledge.

Li, Y., Huang, Z., Jiang, M., & Chang, T. W. (2016). The effect on pupils' science performance and problem-solving ability through Lego: An engineering design-based modeling approach. *Journal of Educational Technology & Society*, *19*(3), 143–156.

Litzinger, T. A., Meter, P. V., Firetto, C. M., Passmore, L. J., Masters, C. B., Turns, S. R., Gray, G. L., Costanzo, F., & Zappe, S. E. (2010). A cognitive study of problem solving in statics. *Journal of Engineering Education*, *99*(4), 337–353. DOI: 10.1002/j.2168-9830.2010.tb01067.x

Liu, T., & Israel, M. (2022). Uncovering students' problem-solving processes in game-based learning environments. *Computers & Education*, *182*, 104462. DOI: 10.1016/j.compedu.2022.104462

Lovett, M. C., & Anderson, J. R. (1996). History of success and current context in problem solving: Combined influences on operator selection. *Cognitive Psychology*, *31*(2), 168–217. DOI: 10.1006/cogp.1996.0016

Marulis, L. M., & Nelson, L. J. (2021). Metacognitive processes and associations to executive function and motivation during a problem-solving task in 3–5 year olds. *Metacognition and Learning*, *16*(1), 207–231. DOI: 10.1007/s11409-020-09244-6

Matsuda, N., Cohen, W. W., Sewall, J., Lacerda, G., & Koedinger, K. R. (2007). Predicting students' performance with simstudent: Learning cognitive skills from observation. *Frontiers in Artificial Intelligence and Applications*, *158*, 467.

McIntyre, L. L., & Phaneuf, L. K. (2008). A three-tier model of parent education in early childhood: Applying a problem-solving model. *Topics in Early Childhood Special Education*, *27*(4), 214–222. DOI: 10.1177/0271121407311239

Mizoguchi, R., Vanwelkenhuysen, J., & Ikeda, M. (1995). Task ontology for reuse of problem solving knowledge. *Towards very large knowledge bases: Knowledge building & knowledge sharing, 46*(59), 45.

Muro, P. D., & Terry, M. (2007). A matter of style: Applying Kolb's learning style model to college mathematics teaching practices. *Journal of College Reading and Learning*, *38*(1), 53–60. DOI: 10.1080/10790195.2007.10850204

Muzana, S. R., Wilujeng, I., Yanto, B. E., & Mustamin, A. A. (2021). E-STEM Project-Based Learning in Teaching Science to Increase ICT Literacy and Problem Solving. *International Journal of Evaluation and Research in Education*, *10*(4), 1386–1394. DOI: 10.11591/ijere.v10i4.21942

Nabavian, S., & Parsons, J. (2024, May). A Design-Principle-Friendly Conceptual Model of Observational Crowdsourcing. In *International Conference on Design Science Research in Information Systems and Technology* (pp. 95-108). Cham: Springer Nature Switzerland. DOI: 10.1007/978-3-031-61175-9_7

Newton, J. S., Algozzine, B., Algozzine, K., Horner, R. H., & Todd, A. W. (2011). Building local capacity for training and coaching data-based problem solving with positive behavior intervention and support teams. *Journal of Applied School Psychology*, *27*(3), 228–245. DOI: 10.1080/15377903.2011.590104

Nurhafidhah, N., Mauliza, M., Yani, A. F. S., Aprilia, R., Zatya, I., & Mustapha, W. Z. W. (2024). Development of Teaching Module Based on the Merdeka Curriculum with the Application of Character Integrated Problem Solving Model. *Jurnal Pendidikan Sains Indonesia*, *12*(3), 478–492. DOI: 10.24815/jpsi.v12i3.37750

Oulasvirta, A., & Hornbæk, K. (2016, May). HCI research as problem-solving. In *Proceedings of the 2016 CHI Conference on Human Factors in Computing Systems* (pp. 4956-4967). DOI: 10.1145/2858036.2858283

Pacte Group. (2008). Building a translation competence model. In *Triangulating translation* (pp. 43–66). John Benjamins Publishing Company.

Pazos, P., Micari, M., & Light, G. (2010). Developing an instrument to characterise peer-led groups in collaborative learning environments: Assessing problem-solving approach and group interaction. *Assessment & Evaluation in Higher Education*, *35*(2), 191–208. DOI: 10.1080/02602930802691572

Purwaningsih, E., Sari, A. M., Yuliati, L., Masjkur, K., Kurniawan, B. R., & Zahiri, M. A. (2020, March). Improving the problem-solving skills through the development of teaching materials with STEM-PjBL (science, technology, engineering, and mathematics-project based learning) model integrated with TPACK (technological pedagogical content knowledge). [). IOP Publishing.]. *Journal of Physics: Conference Series*, *1481*(1), 012133. DOI: 10.1088/1742-6596/1481/1/012133

Rahmah, S., & Lubis, A. H. (2024). Problem Posing as a Learning Model to Improve Primary School Students' Mathematics Learning Outcomes in Gayo Lues. *Journal of Indonesian Primary School*, *1*(4), 93–104. DOI: 10.62945/jips.v1i4.409

Robertson, B. F., & Radcliffe, D. F. (2009). Impact of CAD tools on creative problem solving in engineering design. *Computer Aided Design*, *41*(3), 136–146. DOI: 10.1016/j.cad.2008.06.007

Robillard, P. N. (2005). Opportunistic problem solving in software engineering. *IEEE Software*, *22*(6), 60–67. DOI: 10.1109/MS.2005.161

Robinson, D. T., Brown, D. G., Parker, D. C., Schreinemachers, P., Janssen, M. A., Huigen, M., Wittmer, H., Gotts, N., Promburom, P., Irwin, E., Berger, T., Gatzweiler, F., & Barnaud, C. (2007). Comparison of empirical methods for building agent-based models in land use science. *Journal of Land Use Science*, *2*(1), 31–55. DOI: 10.1080/17474230701201349

Rosyid, A., & Ismawati, D. (2025). Increasing Awareness of Clean and Healthy Lifestyle Patterns Through Problem Solving Learning Models in Early Childhood. *JOYCED: Journal of Early Childhood Education*, *5*(1), 45–56. DOI: 10.14421/joyced.2025.51-04

Rott, B., Specht, B., & Knipping, C. (2021). A descriptive phase model of problem-solving processes. *ZDM Mathematics Education*, *53*(4), 737–752. DOI: 10.1007/s11858-021-01244-3

Rouwette, E. A., Vennix, J. A., & Mullekom, T. V. (2002). Group model building effectiveness: A review of assessment studies. *System Dynamics Review*, *18*(1), 5–45. DOI: 10.1002/sdr.229

Ruuska, H., Otani, N., Kiriyama, S., & Takebayashi, Y. (2008). Creating Multi-Level Reflective Reasoning Models Based on Observation of Social Problem-Solving in Infants. *Frontiers in Artificial Intelligence and Applications*, *166*, 100.

Sauerbrei, W., Abrahamowicz, M., Altman, D. G., le Cessie, S., & Carpenter, J. (2014). STRengthening analytical thinking for observational studies: The STRATOS initiative. *Statistics in Medicine*, *33*(30), 5413–5432. DOI: 10.1002/sim.6265

Schoenfeld, A. H. (1980). Teaching problem-solving skills. *The American Mathematical Monthly*, *87*(10), 794–805. DOI: 10.1080/00029890.1980.11995155

Seielstad, A. M. (2001). Community building as a means of teaching creative, cooperative, and complex problem solving in clinical legal education. *Clinical Law Review*, *8*, 445.

Shih, J. L., Shih, B. J., Shih, C. C., Su, H. Y., & Chuang, C. W. (2010). The influence of collaboration styles to children's cognitive performance in digital problem-solving game "William Adventure": A comparative case study. *Computers & Education*, *55*(3), 982–993. DOI: 10.1016/j.compedu.2010.04.009

Sholihah, T. M., & Lastariwati, B. (2020). Problem based learning to increase competence of critical thinking and problem solving. [EduLearn]. *Journal of Education and Learning*, *14*(1), 148–154.

Shriberg, M., & Harris, K. (2012). Building sustainability change management and leadership skills in students: Lessons learned from "Sustainability and the Campus" at the University of Michigan. *Journal of Environmental Studies and Sciences*, *2*(2), 154–164. DOI: 10.1007/s13412-012-0073-0

Silver, E. A. (2013). Research on teaching mathematical problem solving: Some underrepresented themes and needed directions. In *Teaching and learning mathematical problem solving* (pp. 247–266). Routledge. DOI: 10.4324/9780203063545-22

Simamora, R. E., Sidabutar, D. R., & Surya, E. (2017). Improving learning activity and students' problem solving skill through problem based learning (PBL) in junior high school. [IJSBAR]. *International Journal of Sciences, Basic and Applied Research*, *33*(2), 321–331.

Simon, H. A. (1978). *Information-processing theory of human problem solving*. Erlbaum.

Ste-Marie, D. M., Lelievre, N., & St. Germain, L. (2020). Revisiting the applied model for the use of observation: A review of articles spanning 2011–2018. *Research Quarterly for Exercise and Sport*, *91*(4), 594–617. DOI: 10.1080/02701367.2019.1693489

Surya, E., & Putri, F. A. (2017). Improving mathematical problem-solving ability and self-confidence of high school students through contextual learning model. *Journal on Mathematics Education*, *8*(1), 85–94.

Sweller, J. (1988). Cognitive load during problem solving: Effects on learning. *Cognitive Science*, *12*(2), 257–285. DOI: 10.1207/s15516709cog1202_4

Taconis, R., Ferguson-Hessler, M. G., & Broekkamp, H. (2001). Teaching science problem solving: An overview of experimental work. *Journal of Research in Science Teaching*, *38*(4), 442–468. DOI: 10.1002/tea.1013

Taggar, S., & Brown, T. C. (2001). Problem-solving team behaviors: Development and validation of BOS and a hierarchical factor structure. *Small Group Research*, *32*(6), 698–726. DOI: 10.1177/104649640103200602

Telzrow, C. F., McNamara, K., & Hollinger, C. L. (2000). Fidelity of problem-solving implementation and relationship to student performance. *School Psychology Review*, *29*(3), 443–461. DOI: 10.1080/02796015.2000.12086029

Thomke, S., & Fujimoto, T. (2000). The effect of "front-loading" problem-solving on product development performance. *Journal of Product Innovation Management*, *17*(2), 128–142. DOI: 10.1111/1540-5885.1720128

Thompson, J. R. (2009). *Empirical model building*. John Wiley & Sons.

Tilly, W. D. (2008). The evolution of school psychology to science-based practice: Problem solving and the three-tiered model. *Best practices in school psychology V, 1*, 17-36.

Todd, A. W., Horner, R. H., Newton, J. S., Algozzine, R. F., Algozzine, K. M., & Frank, J. L. (2011). Effects of team-initiated problem solving on decision making by schoolwide behavior support teams. *Journal of Applied School Psychology*, *27*(1), 42–59. DOI: 10.1080/15377903.2011.540510

Treffinger, D. J., & Isaksen, S. G. (2005). Creative problem solving: The history, development, and implications for gifted education and talent development. *Gifted Child Quarterly*, *49*(4), 342–353. DOI: 10.1177/001698620504900407

Tsai, C. A., Song, M. Y. W., Lo, Y. F., & Lo, C. C. (2023). Design thinking with constructivist learning increases the learning motivation and wicked problem-solving capability—An empirical research in Taiwan. *Thinking Skills and Creativity*, *50*, 101385. DOI: 10.1016/j.tsc.2023.101385

Tucker, A. L., & Edmondson, A. C. (2002). Managing routine exceptions: a model of nurse problem solving behavior. In *Advances in health care management* (pp. 87–113). Emerald Group Publishing Limited. DOI: 10.1016/S1474-8231(02)03007-0

Tuminaro, J., & Redish, E. F. (2007). Elements of a cognitive model of physics problem solving: Epistemic games. *Physical Review Special Topics. Physics Education Research*, *3*(2), 020101. DOI: 10.1103/PhysRevSTPER.3.020101

Verschaffel, L., & De Corte, E. (1993). A decade of research on word problem solving in Leuven: Theoretical, methodological, and practical outcomes. *Educational Psychology Review*, *5*(3), 239–256. DOI: 10.1007/BF01323046

Visconti, G., & Zubizarreta, J. R. (2018). Handling limited overlap in observational studies with cardinality matching. *Observational Studies*, *4*(1), 217–249. DOI: 10.1353/obs.2018.0012

Wahyuni, S., Indrawati, I., Sudarti, S., & Suana, W. (2017). Developing science process skills and problemsolving abilities based on outdoor learning in junior high school. *Jurnal Pendidikan IPA Indonesia*, *6*(1), 158–162. DOI: 10.15294/jpii.v6i1.6849

Wang, D., Han, H., Zhan, Z., Xu, J., Liu, Q., & Ren, G. (2015). A problem solving oriented intelligent tutoring system to improve students' acquisition of basic computer skills. *Computers & Education*, *81*, 102–112. DOI: 10.1016/j.compedu.2014.10.003

Watson, R. A., Hornby, G. S., & Pollack, J. B. (1998, September). Modeling building-block interdependency. In *International Conference on Parallel Problem Solving from Nature* (pp. 97-106). Berlin, Heidelberg: Springer Berlin Heidelberg.

Weiss, R. L., & Heyman, R. E. (2004). Couples observational research: An impertinent, critical overview. *Couple observational coding systems*, 11-25.

Wilczenski, F. L., Bontrager, T., Ventrone, P., & Correia, M. (2001). Observing collaborative problem-solving processes and outcomes. *Psychology in the Schools*, *38*(3), 269–281. DOI: 10.1002/pits.1017

Chapter 10
The Efficiency of Freemium Business Models:
The Duolingo Case Study

Maria Eduarda Leite
ISCAP, Polytechnic of Porto, Portugal

Orlando Lima Rua
https://orcid.org/0000-0002-1593-7440
Center for Organisational and Social Studies (CEOS.PP), Research Center of Business Sciences (NECE), ISCAP, Polytechnic of Porto, Portugal

ABSTRACT

This study aims to explore and assess the efficiency of freemium business models, using Duolingo as a compelling case study. By delving into the intricacies of its strategies, and gaining valuable insights into the factors driving the consumer's decision-making process and the conversion from free to paying users, as well as highlight the aspects that differentiate Duolingo from its competitors and other businesses with similar models. Through a quantitative research methodology, an online questionnaire was implemented and answered by 80 participants in total, both current and past users of the app, with the goal to shed light on the nuances of freemium dynamics and their impact on user acquisition, retention, and revenue generation. The findings show that the even though most people are not familiar with the concept of freemium businesses, it is a part of their daily lives. These models can be extremely efficient and profitable, depending on the customer retention strategies and the value given away in the basic, free versions of the product.

DOI: 10.4018/979-8-3373-3301-4.ch010

INTRODUCTION

In an Era characterized by digital disruption and evolving consumer behaviors, businesses constantly explore and implement innovative strategies to attract and retain customers (Thomas et al., 2023). One such strategy that has gained prominence in recent years is the freemium business model, which offers a blend of free basic services alongside premium features for a fee. This model, characterized by its ability to leverage free offerings to drive user acquisition and engagement, has reshaped industries across diverse sectors (Kumar, 2014).

At the forefront of this phenomenon is Duolingo, a language-learning platform that has captivated millions of users worldwide (Shortt et al., 2021). Its adoption of the freemium model has not only revolutionized the language-learning landscape but also sparked interest and intrigue among academics and practitioners alike, with frequent questioning on how the benefits make up for the risks (Shortt et al., 2021). By offering free access to basic language courses supplemented by premium features available through subscription, Duolingo is the perfect illustration of how to navigate the delicate balance between attracting a wide user base and monetizing its offerings effectively (Sakalauskė & Leonavičiūtė, 2022).

Against this backdrop, this research aims to explore the efficiency of freemium business models, using Duolingo as a compelling case study. By delving into the intricacies of its strategies and gaining valuable insights into the factors driving the consumer's decision-making process (Von Ahn & Hacker, 2020). Through a detailed analysis and quantitative research, a survey was designed and distributed to current and former Duolingo users to gather data on their familiarity with freemium business models, their usage patterns, and their views on the value of Duolingo's free and premium features (Koetsier, 2019).

The relevance of this topic lies in the increasing adoption of freemium models across various sectors, making it essential to understand their dynamics and effectiveness. As businesses seek sustainable revenue streams in the competitive digital economy, insights from successful freemium models can offer valuable lessons. Duolingo, with its substantial user base and innovative approach, serves as an ideal subject to explore these dynamics.

A quantitative research methodology was chosen for this study to gain insights into user experiences and perceptions. This approach allows for a nuanced understanding of user behavior and motivations.

The company overview includes a detailed background of Duolingo, explaining its inception, mission, and growth trajectory. The choice of a freemium model was strategic, aimed at providing free language courses to a global audience while generating revenue through premium subscriptions. The platform's success is evident in its impressive statistics: over 800 million downloads, 74 million monthly active users, and more than 100 language courses available in 38 languges (Von Ahn & Hacker, 2020).

Key performance indicators for assessing Duolingo's efficiency include metrics for customer acquisition (e.g., number of downloads, user growth rate), monetization effectiveness (e.g., conversion rate from free to premium users, revenue growth), and customer engagement and retention (e.g., daily active users, user session length) (Shang et al., 2024). A brief market analysis highlights Duolingo's position in the competitive landscape of language-learning apps, noting its innovative use of gamification and AI-driven personalization.

The findings from the research and report analysis underscore that the key to a successful freemium business lies in the value provided in the basic version of the product. For Duolingo, this means offering a robust and engaging learning experience that motivates users to explore premium features. The ability to hook users with high-quality free content and gradually introduce them to the benefits of premium options is crucial for conversion. This study aims to contribute to the understanding of freemium business models and provide actionable insights for businesses looking to adopt or optimize this strategy.

LITERATURE REVIEW

Freemium Business Models: Concept, Evolution, and Adoption

The past decade has seen rapid development within the enterprise software sector, which has raised significant concerns and challenges to the traditional value-creation model of established businesses. The advent of the Internet and Software as a Service (SaaS) solutions is particularly notable for substantially reducing the costs of digital products and services (Kumar, 2018). This shift has led to a significant surge in the availability of service-oriented offerings - research revealed that in 2009, merely 32 out of the top 100 companies were engaged in producing tangible goods (Anderson, 2010). Moreover, there has been a growing trend towards the adoption of open-source software and open application programming interfaces (APIs). Consequently, there's a growing attention on understanding how firms in the software industry can generate value in this evolving landscape.

As a result, new business models have been developed over the years, and among those, the freemium. Praised as fuel for rapid growth for some, and lambasted as the reason for smaller companies going bankrupt, the recent developed model has piqued the interest of developers and business owners worldwide who aim to get the biggest amount of prospects as possible.

The freemium model, derived from the combination of "free" and "premium", involves offering a product or service for free initially, with the option to access enhanced features or functionalities for a fee (Kumar, 2014). This concept is being widely employed across various industries, aiming to attract a large user base through free offerings, while also monetizing a fraction of customers who opt for premium features (Shang., et al. 2024). An illustrative analogy can be drawn to an ice cream truck providing free samples: while some individuals may simply try a flavor and move on, others may purchase larger portions regularly over time. This strategy entails accepting initial losses in exchange for the long-term loyalty and revenue potential of a subset of customers. Figure 1 present the freemium business model.

Figure 1. Freemium business model

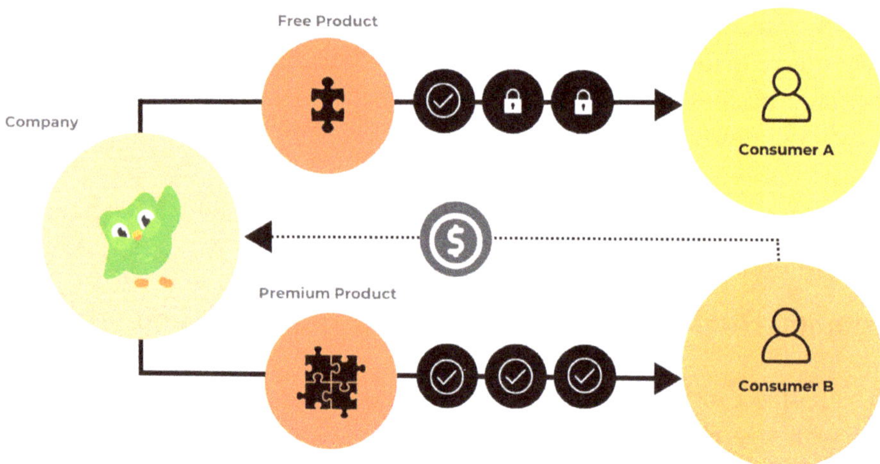

Evolution and Adoption

Found mostly in gaming culture and press-savvy developers, there were signs of the freemium model as we know it today, starting back in the 80s. In 1982, an editor at PC Magazine, Andrew Fluegelman, released PC-Talk, a communication program that would become a landmark in software distribution. While the software itself garnered praise for its elegance and functionality, it was Fluegelman's unconventional approach to distribution that truly turned heads. He introduced what would later be recognized as a pioneering freemium model, distributed through a service called Freeware. Freeware, as Fluegelman conceived it, was not merely a means of distribution but an experiment in economics. He offered PC-Talk for free to anyone who mailed him a disk, only asking for payment if the recipient found the program valuable. This model, though rudimentary compared to contemporary iterations, embodied the core principle of freemium: pay only when you derive value. Jim Knopf, an IBM developer, followed suit with his program, PC-File, adopting the same freeware model. The novelty of this approach attracted the attention of computer magazines, leading to extensive free publicity—a testament to the marketing potential inherent in freemium (Jayathilaka, 2021).

As utilities embraced the freemium model, the gaming industry soon followed suit. Indie developers began distributing their creations as shareware, mailing floppy disks for enthusiasts to try out. This fostered a culture of goodwill and collaboration within the gaming community, aligning with the ethos of the growing open-source movement. Which pushed the boundaries of software development, and the relationship between value and payment in the digital realm.

The early days of software distribution saw the emergence of freemium models, albeit in rudimentary forms. While programs like PC-Talk, PC-File, Blox, and Crux offered perpetual access to free software and games, and embodied the essence of freemium by providing value upfront with the option for payment later, these pioneers struggled to capitalize on upselling opportunities.

The landscape changed dramatically with the rise of the internet, which prompted the journalist Esther Dyson to ponder the future of content-based value online. In 1995, Dyson articulated a groundbreaking concept: distribute intellectual property for free to sell services and relationships—a model she termed freemium (Jayathilaka, 2021). This idea laid the groundwork for what we know today.

Even before Dyson's formulation, one company was already making strides in this direction: AOL. Through an aggressive marketing campaign involving unsolicited disks mailed to households, AOL offered free access to its online services, providing a taste of the internet to millions. The strategy was simple: give a little away to reel users in, then upsell them on continued access. After the initial free hours expired, AOL successfully converted users into paying subscribers, experiencing exponential growth from 1992 to 2002. Despite the significant investment in distribution, AOL's unit economics remained favorable, demonstrating the viability of the freemium model (Kumar, 2014; Jayathilaka, 2021).

Their approach differed from traditional shareware since the disks had expiration dates and were not copyable, marking a departure from perpetual value (Wood-Harper, 2021). Nevertheless, the success of their upselling strategy laid the groundwork for the evolution of freemium in the realm of software as a service (SaaS).

As the mid-aughts unfolded, Esther Dyson's foresight regarding the saturation of free content on the web became evident. The era of bundled service providers like AOL waned, making way for the ascendancy of cloud-based subscription services. Figure 2 displays freemium model timeline.

Figure 2. Freemium model timeline

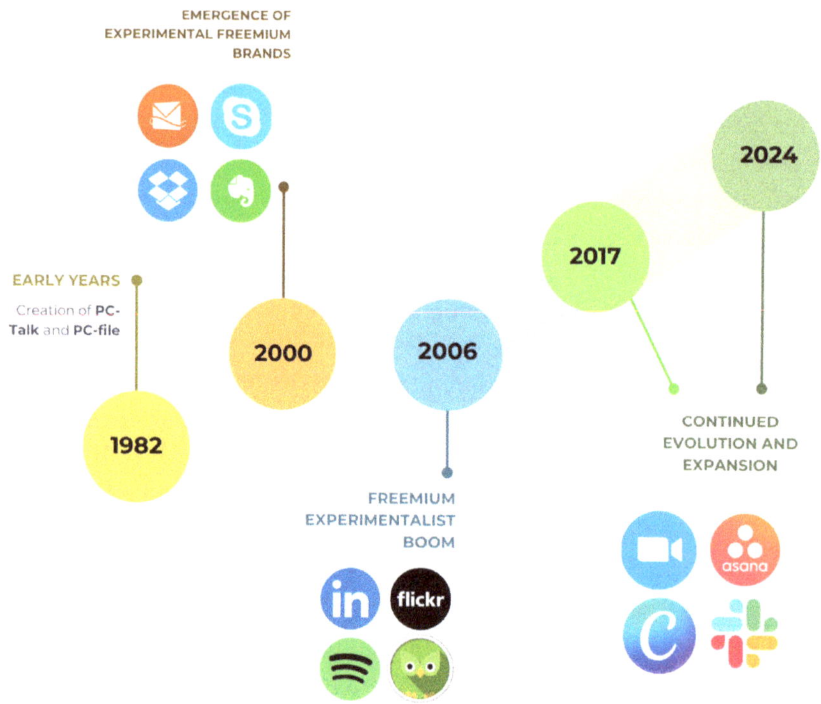

The emergence of software-as-a-service (SaaS) signalled a shift in business strategy. Recognizing that mere novelty or usefulness was insufficient, savvy SaaS providers understood the importance of compounding value over time, built-in network effects, and robust infrastructure (Wood-Harper, 2021). Yet, the expectation of free content persisted, particularly in the initial stages.

A common success formula among fast-growing SaaS companies involves offering a free version of their service to attract users through word of mouth, referral networks, and organic search. Once a substantial user base is established, these companies introduce premium-priced, value-added features or enhanced service tiers. This strategy, exemplified by platforms such as Skype, Flickr, Spotify, Zoom, and Canva (see Figure 3), has proven effective in driving both growth and monetization. Although widely practiced, this model lacked a concise label until Jared Lukin coined the term "freemium" (Koetsier, 2019).

In the pre-recession Silicon Valley ethos of growth-at-all-costs, large usage numbers often took precedence over monetization concerns (Bapna, et al., 2018).

Wilson and McCarthy (2010) advocate the explosive growth, anticipating that profits would naturally follow widespread adoption.

Figure 3. Freemium model brands

While many of these companies successfully navigated the freemium landscape, and despite their popularity, this model often faces challenges and criticisms. Skeptics argue that freemium offerings can lead to unsustainable business models, where companies struggle to convert free users into paying customers or fail to recoup the costs of offering free services (Eisenmann et al., 2006). Additionally, concerns have been raised about the potential for freemium models to exploit user data or create inequities between free and paying users (Möhlmann, 2015; Šobak, 2023).

Theoretical Frameworks Models

Since freemium models have become a prominent fixture in various industries for offering a blend of free and premium services to attract and retain customers, to efficiently analyze the dynamics of these models, it is essential to take a multidimensional approach, from an economics, marketing, and customer behavior perspective.

Starting from an economic framework, as in many other business models, price discrimination is considered one of the main forms of marketing strategy, and the base for a functional freemium model (Biraglia, 2022). In a passage published in Boston Consulting Group brochure, their main economist explained that the key in pricing is to avoid the average, it should be different to specific customer groups, in order to effectively reflect the competitive value of the goods provided. With this strategy, businesses have a much broader customer base, offering a free version to attract price-sensitive users while monetizing through the willingness of certain users to pay for enhanced functionality in the premium offerings. This differential pricing strategy allows companies to capture value from both segments of the market, maximizing overall revenue potential.

Furthermore, freemium platforms often operate as two-sided markets, catering to the needs of both users and other stakeholders such as advertisers or third-party developers (Gregory et al., 2021). On one side, users are attracted to the platform by the availability of free basic features. This strategy aligns with the principles of network effects, where the value of a product or service increases as more users join the platform (Banton, 2019). As users adopt the platform and engage with, and benefit from its free offerings, they contribute to the growth of the user base, thereby enhancing the platform's overall value proposition.

Meanwhile, on the other side, advertisers or developers gain access to a large and engaged user base. This aligns with Coase (1937), who emphasized the role of transaction costs in shaping economic relationships and transactions. By leveraging the platform's user base, advertisers and developers can access a captive audience for their products, services, or content offerings (Rindfleisch, 2020). This creates opportunities for monetization through various channels, including advertising, partnerships, or premium content offerings. This symbiotic relationship between multiple user groups creates a dynamic ecosystem where value is exchanged between different stakeholders, driving the sustainability and growth of the platform (Bridoux & van Oosterhout, 2020).

Following with a customer behavior perspective, behavioral economics also offer valuable insights into the underlying cognitive and emotional factors shaping consumer decision-making. Concepts such as loss aversion, the endowment effect, and the power of defaults play significant roles in influencing how users perceive the value proposition of freemium offerings. Loss aversion, a concept first proposed by Kahneman and Tversky (1979), refers to the psychological tendency for individuals to strongly prefer avoiding losses over acquiring equivalent gains. In the context of freemium models, users may be reluctant to forego the free features they already possess, fearing the loss of those benefits if they choose not to upgrade to premium offerings (Wang et al., 2019).The endowment effect by is the phenomenon where individuals assign higher value to objects they own compared to identical objects they do not own (Thaler, 1980). When applied to freemium models, users may place greater value on the free features they have access to, perceiving them as part of their endowment. This perception can make them hesitant to switch to premium offerings, even if the benefits outweigh the costs. The power of defaults, a concept explored by Johnson and Goldstein (2003), highlights how individuals tend to stick with the default option presented to them. In freemium models, the default option often involves using the free version of the product or service. Users may exhibit inertia or status quo bias, preferring to maintain the default option rather than actively choosing to upgrade to premium features (Gawer, 2022).

The model can also be conceptualized as a strategic stepping stone into subscription relationships, wherein companies leverage by providing free access to acquire and foster customer relationships, to ultimately guiding them towards becoming paying subscribers (Tzuo **& Weisert**, 2018). The subscription economy framework underscores the fundamental shift towards recurring revenue models, as outlined by Tzuo and **Weisert** (2018), wherein companies prioritize ongoing customer relationships over one-time transactions, presenting the concept of customer lifetime value (CLV). CLV represents the total value a customer contributes to a company throughout their relationship, encompassing both initial acquisition and subsequent retention, and Freemium serves as a means to initiate these kinds of relationships, offering users a taste of the product or service's value proposition before encouraging them to commit to a subscription, gradually building trust and loyalty to maximize CLV (Fader, 2012).

And lastly, retention strategies are key in the subscription economy, with the aim to minimizing churn and maximizing customer satisfaction (Brüggeman & Lehmann-Zschunke, 2023). Research done by Reichheld and Schefter (2000) highlights the significant impact of customer retention on profitability, emphasizing the value of retaining existing subscribers over acquiring new ones. Freemium models, by offering a seamless transition from free to paid tiers, facilitates retention efforts by providing users with continuous value and incentives to remain engaged with the platform (Mäntymäki et al. 2020).

Key Characteristics

Business models serve as the blueprint for how a company creates, delivers, and captures value. The freemium model, a popular choice in the digital economy, involves offering a base product or service for free while charging for premium features or content. There are two primary types of freemium models: the bundled freemium model and the fragmented freemium model. The former offers a suite of features as a single package, while the latter breaks down features into separate, chargeable components (Shang, et al., 2024). The success of these models often hinges on a firm's ability to balance free offerings with premium content that users are willing to pay for, and dynamic capabilities such as sensing, seizing, and reconfiguring capabilities play a crucial role in this balance (Martins & Rodrigues, 2024).

These models utilize various monetization tactics to convert free users into paying customers. Common strategies include offering additional features, removing advertisements, and providing enhanced customer support as part of the premium package (Niemand et al., 2015). For instance, in the digital gaming sector, features such as extra lives, special items, or advanced levels are often monetized. Another tactic involves leveraging network effects to increase user base and engagement, which in turn can drive higher conversion rates from free to premium users. Additionally, some freemium models generate revenue through advertising, where the large base of free users attracts advertisers willing to pay for exposure (Shang et al., 2024).

Advantages and Disadvantages

After becoming a dominant strategy in various digital industries, the implementation of this model presents its complex nature and reflects the intricate balance companies must strike to maximize profitability and customer satisfaction.

One of the primary advantages of the freemium model is its ability to attract a large user base with minimal upfront costs. By offering a free tier, companies can reduce the barrier to entry, allowing a significant number of users to try the service without financial commitment (Dawes, 2018). This strategy can lead to rapid user base expansion, which is crucial in digital markets where network effects are significant (Niemand, et al. 2015). For example, platforms like Spotify and Dropbox have successfully leveraged the freemium model to build vast user bases quickly (Table 1).

Table 1. Freemium monetization strategies (source: own elaboration)

Company	Monetization Tactic	Description
Spotify	Subscription-Based Model	Users Pay for ad-free listening, offline downloads, and higher audio quality.
Candy Crush	In-App Purchases	Free gameplay, purchase boosters
YouTube	Advertising, Subscription-Based Model	Free users are shown ads; premium users pay to remove ads and access exclusive content.
Trello	Feature Limitation	Basic project boards free, advanced features paid
Fortnite	In-App Purchases	Players buy skins, emotes, and battle passes to enhance their gaming experience.
Microsoft	Freemium Bundling	Basic Office apps are free; advanced features require an Office 365 subscription.

Freemium models also enable extensive user data collection from both free and premium users. This data can be invaluable for refining product offerings, targeting advertisements, and personalizing user experiences (Jayathilaka, 2021). Additionally, the presence of a free user base can create a community or network effect that adds value to the service, encouraging even more users to join and potentially upgrade to premium versions.

From a marketing perspective, freemium services serve as powerful tools for word-of-mouth promotion (Shang, et al. 2024). Satisfied free users often become brand advocates, sharing their positive experiences and thereby organically increasing the service's reach. This can reduce the need for expensive marketing campaigns while still achieving substantial market penetration.

Despite these advantages, the freemium model is fraught with challenges and potential pitfalls. One significant disadvantage is the risk of a low conversion rate from free to paying users. If the free version of the service is too comprehensive, users may see little incentive to upgrade to a paid tier (Šobak, 2023). This dilemma requires companies to carefully balance the features offered in both tiers to ensure the free version is attractive yet not overly generous. Additionally, supporting a large number of free users can be costly. These users consume resources, such as server capacity and customer support, without directly contributing to revenue (Shang, et al. 2024). This can strain company resources, particularly if the proportion of paying users remains low. Moreover, the reliance on premium conversions to drive revenue can lead to financial instability if these conversions do not meet expectations (Hamari et al. 2020).

Another drawback is the potential for user dissatisfaction if the perceived value between the free and premium versions is not well-managed (Hamari et al. 2020). Users may feel frustrated if they perceive the free version as too limited or if premium features do not justify their cost. This dissatisfaction can lead to negative reviews and a tarnished brand reputation, ultimately hindering the service's growth and sustainability. Furthermore, the freemium model's dependency on continuous innovation and feature enhancements to retain and convert users can create perpetual pressure on development teams (Hanner, 2020). Forcing onto companies' constant pressure to consistently invest in new features and improvements to keep the service competitive and appealing to both existing and potential premium users (Šobak, 2023).

Key Successful Factors and Common Pitfalls

A compelling value proposition for the free tier is the base for success in a freemium model. The free version must provide substantial value to attract a large user base, offering enough functionality to satisfy users' basic needs while also enticing them to upgrade for premium features (Shang, et al. 2024. The balance between the free and premium offerings is crucial for conversion rates. If the free version is too limited, users may not see the value in it; if it is too generous, they may not feel the need to upgrade.

User experience and engagement are also critical. A seamless and engaging user experience can significantly influence the conversion rate from free to premium users. The interface should be intuitive, and the performance of the free version should be compelling enough to hook users (Niemand, et al. 2015). High engagement levels, which often correlate with higher conversion rates, can be achieved through an interface that encourages continuous use and interaction (Hinterhuber & Liozu, 2017).

Successful freemium models leverage data analytics to understand user behavior and preferences. By analyzing data, companies can identify which features are most valued by users and tailor their premium offerings accordingly. This data-driven approach helps in optimizing the conversion funnel and personalizing marketing strategies to target potential premium users more effectively (Fader & Hardie, 2009). However, one significant challenge is the potential for a high churn rate among free users. If the free version does not provide enough value or if users encounter friction in the user experience, they are likely to abandon the product. Therefore, maintaining a delicate balance in the value proposition is essential (Osterwalder et al., 2010).

Another common pitfall is the misalignment between the free and premium versions. If the differences between the two are not clear or if the premium version does not offer compelling enough features, users may not see the value in upgrading. This misalignment can lead to low conversion rates and undermine the financial viability of the freemium model. Lastly, over-reliance on the freemium model can lead to unsustainable business practices. Companies must ensure that the revenue generated from premium users is sufficient to cover the costs incurred by free users (Martins & Rodrigues, 2024). This requires careful financial planning and an in-depth understanding of the customer lifetime value (CLV) (Kumar, 2014).

Measuring Efficiency

Efficiency in this context refers to the ability of the model to convert free users to paying customers, generate sustainable revenue, and maintain high user engagement. Various metrics and analytical approaches can be employed to gauge the efficiency of freemium models.

One of the primary metrics used to measure the efficiency of freemium models is the conversion rate. The conversion rate is the percentage of free users who upgrade to a paid version within a specific period. This metric provides direct insight into how well the free tier encourages users to transition to premium services. A high conversion rate indicates that the free version is successfully demonstrating the value of the premium features (Hansen, 2021).

Another crucial metric is Customer Lifetime Value (CLV), which estimates the total revenue a business can expect from a single customer account throughout its entire lifespan. CLV helps businesses understand the long-term value of acquiring and retaining customers. By comparing the CLV of free and premium users, companies can assess the effectiveness of their freemium strategy in generating sustained revenue (Gupta & Lehmann, 2006).

Customer Acquisition Cost (CAC) is also a vital metric, representing the total cost of acquiring a new customer, including marketing and sales expenses. For a freemium model to be efficient, the CAC should be significantly lower than the CLV. This ensures that the business can profit from its customer base over time. Monitoring CAC helps businesses optimize their marketing strategies to ensure they are attracting high-value users cost-effectively (Kumar, 2018).

Engagement metrics, such as daily active users (DAU) and monthly active users (MAU), are essential for understanding user interaction with the product. High engagement levels often correlate with higher conversion rates, as engaged users are more likely to see the value in premium features and upgrades. Additionally, metrics like session length and frequency of use can provide insights into how users are interacting with the free version, indicating potential areas for improvement (Chen et al., 2020).

Churn rate is another important metric, representing the percentage of users who stop using the product over a given period. A high churn rate among free users might indicate that the free version is not compelling enough, while a high churn rate among premium users could suggest dissatisfaction with the paid features. Reducing churn is critical for maintaining a stable user base and ensuring the sustainability of the freemium model (Hollis, 2020).

To gain a comprehensive view of the efficiency of freemium models, businesses also use cohort analysis. This method involves grouping users based on specific characteristics or behaviors and tracking these groups over time. Cohort analysis can reveal trends in user engagement, conversion rates, and churn, helping businesses understand how different segments of their user base are performing and how their behavior changes over time (Bockstedt et al., 2015).

Revenue metrics, such as average revenue per user (ARPU) and revenue growth rate, are crucial for evaluating the financial performance of the freemium model. ARPU provides insight into the average revenue generated from each user, while the revenue growth rate indicates the model's ability to scale and increase profitability. Monitoring these metrics helps businesses ensure that their freemium model is not only attracting users but also generating sustainable revenue (Anderson, 2010).

METHODOLOGY

Research Design

When conducting research, choosing between qualitative and quantitative methods often poses a significant challenge. Qualitative methods, which include interviews, focus groups, and case studies, can be advantageous for exploring deep, contextual understandings of human behavior and experiences, as they allow researchers to gather rich, detailed insights and uncover patterns or themes that may not be evident through quantitative measures. Conversely, quantitative methods, such as surveys, experiments, and statistical analysis, can be beneficial for collecting data that can be quantified and subjected to mathematical scrutiny. This approach enables researchers to identify relationships, test hypotheses, and generalize findings across larger populations with greater objectivity and precision.

For this study on the efficiency of freemium business models, particularly with Duolingo as a case study, a quantitative approach is more appropriate. The quantitative methods facilitate the measurement of key performance indicators (KPIs) such as user acquisition rates, conversion rates, and revenue growth, which are critical for evaluating the effectiveness of the freemium model (Botella-carrubi, 2020). Additionally, surveys can provide a broad, statistically significant understanding of user behavior and preferences, which is essential for identifying factors that influence the conversion of free users into paying customers. By using quantitative data, this research can offer robust, generalizable insights into the dynamics of freemium business models that qualitative methods alone could not achieve.

To analyze the efficiency of freemium business models and understand the decision-making processes of users regarding premium options, a case study research design was employed, focusing on the language-learning app Duolingo, due to its widespread popularity and success in the utilization of a freemium business model.

To support the research, an online survey was created using Google Forms to ensure it was easily accessible for all participants. The choice to conduct research online offered significant advantages, as the internet provides a powerful platform for data collection (Gordon & McNew, 2008). And to ensure that the gathered responses were honest and unbiased, anonymous answers were collected from 80 current and former Duolingo users.

Methodological Approach

Two primary research methodologies were evaluated: qualitative and quantitative research. Qualitative research focuses on understanding the underlying reasons, opinions, and motivations behind certain phenomena. It involves collecting nonnumerical data, such as interviews, focus groups, and observations, to gain insights into users' experiences and perceptions. While qualitative research provides rich, detailed data and can uncover deep insights about user behavior and attitudes, it often lacks the generalizability required for broader business applications.

Quantitative research, on the other hand, involves the collection and analysis of numerical data to identify patterns, relationships, and trends. Methods include surveys, experiments, and analysis of secondary data such as usage metrics and financial reports. Quantitative research is particularly valuable for its ability to provide objective, measurable, and generalizable results, making it more suitable for this study.

Firstly, it allows for the precise measurement of key variables such as conversion rates, customer lifetime value (CLV), customer acquisition cost (CAC), engagement metrics, and churn rates, which are essential for assessing the effectiveness of freemium models. Secondly, quantitative research enables the collection of data from large samples, enhancing the generalizability of findings across various industries and contexts. Analyzing data from diverse users and companies employing freemium models provides insights applicable to a broad spectrum of scenarios. This facilitates the use of statistical tools and models to identify significant patterns and relationships. For example, regression analysis can uncover factors strongly associated with higher conversion rates or lower churn rates, offering actionable insights for optimizing freemium strategies.

Lastly, quantitative data allows for comparative analyses between different user segments, products, or time periods, aiding in the identification of best practices and benchmarking performance. This comparative approach is crucial for businesses seeking to enhance their freemium models.

Sample and Data Collection

Data collection was conducted through an online survey, which was open for responses from May 14th, 2024, to May 28th, 2024. The survey was distributed through various channels frequented by Duolingo users, including social media groups, forums, and email lists.

A total of 80 responses were collected within the specified timeframe. Participants were asked to provide information regarding their usage of Duolingo, including their engagement levels, conversion from free to premium services, satisfaction with the free tier, and reasons for any changes in usage over time.

The choice of Duolingo as the focal point for this research stems from several compelling reasons, grounded mainly in its widespread popularity and pioneering role in the utilization of the freemium business model within the language-learning industry. Firstly, Duolingo stands out as a leading player in the language-learning app market, boasting millions of users worldwide and consistently ranking among the top-grossing education apps across various app stores. Its remarkable success and sustained growth over the years serve as a testament to the efficacy of its freemium business model in attracting and retaining users (Biraglia, 2022). Moreover, its strategies align closely with the central focus of this research—analyzing the efficiency of freemium business models and understanding user decision-making regarding premium options. By offering free access to basic language courses supplemented by premium features available through subscription, Duolingo exemplifies the core principles and dynamics of freemium strategies. Additionally, Duolingo's user-friendly interface, gamified learning approach, and diverse language offerings have garnered widespread acclaim and loyalty among its user base (Shortt et al., 2021). This makes it an ideal case study subject for exploring the factors influencing users' decisions to opt for premium features within the app. Lastly, their commitment to data-driven decision-making and continuous innovation provides rich opportunities for in-depth analysis and insights generation. The wealth of user data and analytics available within the annual reports published by the company makes it possible to delve deeper into user behaviors, preferences, and interactions with freemium offerings.

Survey Questionnaire

Participants, including both current users of Duolingo and individuals who have used the app in the past, were invited to complete a structured questionnaire, that was designed to elicit responses regarding various aspects and reasons influencing their decision to use Duolingo, their experiences with the app, and factors that would make them more likely to subscribe to premium features. Questions were tailored to capture usage patterns, and perceptions related to Duolingo's freemium model, as well as other businesses with the same model.

To support the research, an online survey was created using Google Forms to ensure it was easily accessible and anonymous for all participants. Conducting research online offers significant advantages, as the internet provides a powerful platform for data collection (Gordon & McNew, 2008). To gather honest and unbiased responses, anonymous answers were collected from 80 current and former Duolingo users.

The survey comprised 16 questions divided into two sections (Table 2). The first section assessed participants' familiarity with the concept of freemium business models and their typical decision-making processes regarding these models. The second section focused exclusively on Duolingo, evaluating whether participants found its basic features valuable and identifying factors that might encourage them to purchase premium features. This questionnaire aims to measure the effectiveness of freemium models and determine what distinguishes Duolingo from its competitors and other businesses using similar models.

Table 2. Survey questionnaire questions (source: own elaboration)

Research Topic	Research Question	Authors
User History and Engagement	Have you ever used Duolingo before, and do you currently use it?	(Davis, 1989; Damir & Hasnaa, 2020)
Duration of Use	If yes, how long have you been using (or used) Duolingo?	(Bhattacherjee, 2001; Park et al., 2024)
Knowledge and Awareness	Are you familiar with the concept of freemium business models?	(Rogers et al., 2014; Ajzen & Fishbein, 1975); Koohang, A (2022)
Digital Consumption Patterns	Which of these services or products do you currently use? (Select the ones that apply)	(Rogers et al., 2014; Ajzen & Fishbein, 1975; Whang et al., 2021)
User Engagement Levels	How frequently do you use these services or products?	(Tam & Ho, 2005; Venkatesh et al., 2003; Damir & Hasnaa, 2020)
Perceived Value of Free Features	How would you rate the value of the free features offered by the services/products you use?	(Zeithaml, 1988; Bolton & Drew, 1991; Hamari et al., 2020)
Conversion Rates	How often do you find yourself using only the free features without upgrading to the premium version?	(Kumar, 2014)
Upgrade Likelihood	How likely are you to upgrade any of these services to the premium version?	(Venkatesh & Bala, 2008)
Feature Utilization	Which Duolingo features do you use most frequently?	(Anderson et al., 1994; Whang et al., 2021)
Consideration of Premium Features	Have you ever considered purchasing premium features on Duolingo?	(Venkatesh et al., 2012; Hamari et al., 2020)
Motivational Factors for Purchase	What factors would motivate you to purchase premium features on Duolingo?	Sheth et al., 1991; Hamari et al., 2020)
Price Sensitivity	How much would you be willing to pay for premium features on Duolingo per month?	(Mazumdar & Monroe, 1990; Hinterhuber & Liozu, 2017; Schreiner et al., 2015)
Perceived Value of Premium Features	How valuable do you think premium features on Duolingo are compared to the free version?	Gale, 1994; Hamari et al., 2020; Niemand et al., 2015)
Cost-Value Alignment	Do you believe the premium features offered by Duolingo justify the cost (currently $12.99 per month or $59.99 a year)?	(Zeithaml, 1988; Tyrväinen & Karjaluoto, 2024)
Cost-Value Alignment	What factor influences you to purchase premium versions the most?	(Griffin & Hauser, 1993; Hauser et al., 1993)

Document Analysis and Case Study

Relevant documents and records related to Duolingo's freemium business model, including user reviews, app analytics data, marketing materials, and financial reports, were analysed to provide additional context and corroborate findings. This analysis also helps to gain insights into the effectiveness of Duolingo's freemium strategy in attracting and retaining users, as well as its impact on revenue generation and user satisfaction.

Observations of app usage behavior among Duolingo users shared in yearly reports will be also be considered, as well as researches on how participants interact with the app, including their frequency of usage, engagement levels with premium features, and any patterns in their language-learning activities.

By employing a combination of questionnaire surveys, observations, and document analysis focused on Duolingo, this research aim is to provide a comprehensive understanding of the efficiency of freemium business models and the decision-making processes of users regarding premium options within the language-learning app. The findings contribute valuable insights to both academia and industry, informing strategies for optimizing freemium models and enhancing user engagement and monetization in digital platforms like Duolingo.

Duolingo Case Study

Company Background

Equality, by definition and strictly from a theoretical point of view, is the state of being equal, especially in status, rights, and opportunities. It suggests a level playing field where every individual, regardless of their background, has access to the same resources, opportunities, and treatment. In the realm of education, this ideal envisions a system where all students have equal access to quality education, resources, and support, paving the way for their academic and personal growth (Bapna, et al. 2018).

However, in reality, the concept of equality in education is far more complex and challenging to achieve. Despite significant advancements and policy efforts aimed at promoting educational equity, disparities persist across various dimensions, including socioeconomic status, geographic location, race, gender, and disability. These disparities manifest in different forms such as unequal access to quality schools, varying levels of educational funding, disparities in teacher quality, and differences in learning environments and support services (Gawer, 2022).

Education, for many, is seen as something that brings equality to different social classes. In reality, education often aggravates the gap between these classes.

Individuals who earn a lot of money can afford high-quality education, thereby maintaining and enhancing their socio-economic status. Conversely, those who lack financial resources may only achieve basic literacy, making it nearly impossible for them to ascend the social ladder (Shortt, et al. 2021). This inequity perpetuates a cycle where the affluent access superior educational opportunities, while the less fortunate remain disadvantaged.

This stark reality was evident to Von Ahn and Hacker (2020). Observing the educational disparities in his home country, these scholars recognized the profound impact of unequal educational opportunities. They were driven to invest in an initiative that would provide equal access to education for everyone. Together they considered various subjects such as mathematics and computer science but ultimately decided that teaching foreign languages would have the most significant impact.

The decision to focus on language learning was influenced by several factors. Not only is there an enormous global audience for language education, but approximately two billion people worldwide are learning a second language, with 80% of them studying English (Von Ahn & Hacker, 2020). In many countries, proficiency in English can substantially increase an individual's income potential, making language learning a powerful tool for social and economic mobility. That is how Duolingo, the language learning app was born.

Freemium Model Implementation

To be truly accessible to everyone, regardless of their economic conditions, Duolingo employs a freemium business model. This strategic choice allows the platform to offer its language courses entirely free of charge to anyone willing to learn. Users can access comprehensive learning resources and complete as many lessons as they wish without any cost (Von Ahn & Hacker, 2020). However, to sustain the platform and generate revenue, Duolingo incorporates ads into the free learning experience. Users who opt for the free version may see an ad at the end of each lesson.

For those who find the ads intrusive and prefer an uninterrupted learning experience, Duolingo offers a subscription service called Duolingo Plus. By subscribing, users can remove ads and gain access to additional features. Interestingly, the vast majority of Duolingo's revenue comes from these subscriptions. Users from wealthier countries such as the United States and Canada are more likely to pay for the ad-free experience, while users from poorer countries like Brazil, Vietnam, and Guatemala typically use the free version.

In his TED Talk, Luis von Ahn, co-founder of Duolingo, explains that this freemium model effectively works as a form of wealth redistribution. The revenue generated from subscribers in affluent countries subsidizes the free education provided to users in less wealthy regions. This model enables Duolingo to democratize access to quality education, breaking down economic barriers and providing learning opportunities to a global audience.

By implementing the freemium model, Duolingo ensures that its educational resources remain accessible to all, regardless of financial status. This approach not only allows the company to maintain financial sustainability but also underscores the potential of freemium strategies to address global inequalities in education (Evans, 2020). The model leverages the financial contributions of wealthier users to support the learning needs of those from less affluent backgrounds, thereby promoting a more equitable distribution of educational resources (Amin, 2021).

Premium Features and Prices

Duolingo's freemium model not only allows users to access a wealth of language-learning resources for free but also offers a range of premium features through its s subscription. These premium features are designed to enhance the learning experience and improve efficiency, catering to those who are willing to pay for an optimized and uninterrupted educational journey.

One of the most attractive features of Duolingo Plus is the removal of ads. This allows users to focus entirely on their lessons without interruptions, creating a smoother and more immersive learning experience. Additionally, Duolingo Plus subscribers can download lessons and practice them offline. This is particularly advantageous for users who may not have consistent internet access or prefer to study on the go.

In the free version of Duolingo, users have a limited number of "hearts," which decrease with each mistake made during lessons. Once hearts run out, users must wait for them to replenish or practice previous lessons to earn them back. Duolingo Plus provides unlimited hearts, enabling continuous learning without waiting periods. Subscribers also have access to more detailed progress tracking and personalized learning plans, which help learners stay motivated by visualizing their progress and focusing on areas that need improvement.

Another useful feature of Duolingo Plus is the option to test out of multiple skills at once, allowing advanced learners to skip content they already know and move on to more challenging material. This feature, combined with detailed progress tracking, personalized learning plans, and the ad-free experience, keeps learners engaged and motivated, reducing the likelihood of frustration and dropout. Offline access ensures that learning can happen anywhere and anytime, accommodating various lifestyles and schedules. The ability to test out of known material allows learners to focus on new content, making their study time more productive, and detailed progress tracking helps users identify strengths and weaknesses, leading to more targeted and effective learning.

Duolingo employs a pricing strategy that varies by country, taking into account the local average salary and economic conditions. This approach, known as price discrimination, ensures that the subscription remains affordable and accessible to a broader range of users worldwide (Rindfleisch, 2020). For instance, the cost of a Duolingo Plus subscription may be significantly lower in a country with a lower average income compared to a country with a higher average income (Koetsier, 2019). This pricing strategy is designed to maximize both accessibility and revenue by aligning the price with the economic capabilities of users in different regions.

In the United States, a Duolingo Plus subscription is typically priced at around $12.99 per month, or $83.99 annually. However, in countries with lower average incomes, the subscription cost is adjusted downward to reflect local economic conditions, making it feasible for a larger segment of the population to afford the premium features - in Brazil, for instance, the subscription is priced at $10.99 per month, or $64.23 per year.

By offering a range of premium features tailored to enhance the learning experience and implementing a price discrimination strategy, Duolingo successfully balances financial sustainability with its mission of making language education accessible to everyone. This approach not only drives revenue but also promotes educational equity by ensuring that users from diverse economic backgrounds can benefit from high-quality language learning resources.

Growth and Success Factors

Duolingo has experienced remarkable growth since its inception, evolving into one of the most popular language-learning platforms globally. There are several key factors have contributed to Duolingo's success, including its innovative business model, user-centric design, effective use of technology, and strategic marketing efforts.

As mentioned before, Duolingo's freemium business model has been a significant driver of its growth. By offering a comprehensive range of language courses for free, they have lowered the barrier to entry for millions of users worldwide. This model attracts a vast user base, allowing the company to monetize through optional premium subscriptions (Duolingo Plus) and advertisements (Amin, 2021). The freemium model's success is evident in the platform's ability to generate substantial revenue while maintaining free access for the majority of its users.

Its user-centric design is another critical factor contributing to its growth. The platform is designed to be engaging and accessible to users of all ages and backgrounds, through gamification elements, such as earning points, leveling up, and maintaining streaks, they have made the learning process enjoyable and motivating (Thomas et al., 2023). The app's intuitive interface and bite-sized lessons cater to modern users' preferences for quick and efficient learning sessions (Amin, 2021).

This focus on user experience has also resulted in high levels of user satisfaction and retention.

During its design stage, Luis Von Ahn and his team faced a significant challenge: developing an educational app that could compete with some of the most addictive smartphone applications, like TikTok, Instagram, and mobile games. Von Ahn compared this endeavor to offering a child a piece of broccoli next to a delicious cake, hoping they would choose the healthier option. Recognizing that simply providing access to education was insufficient, Von Ahn and his co-creator aimed to make learning as engaging and compelling as these popular apps. Their goal was to transform the "broccoli" of education into a dessert-like experience that users would actively seek out.

To achieve this, they have adopted psychological techniques used by social media and gaming apps to maintain user engagement (Shortt et al., 2021). One of the key features inspired by these techniques is the streak system, modeled after Snapchat's streaks. This feature tracks the number of consecutive days a user has engaged with the app, fostering a sense of competitiveness and commitment. Users are motivated to maintain their streaks, encouraging daily study habits (Chen et al., 2020).

Duolingo leverages advanced technology to enhance the learning experience further. The platform employs artificial intelligence (AI) and machine learning algorithms to personalize lessons and adapt to individual learners' progress (Gawer, 2022). This customization ensures that users receive content tailored to their specific needs and learning pace, significantly improving the educational process's effectiveness (Laanti, 2023). Additionally, Duolingo uses data analytics to continuously refine its courses based on user feedback and performance metrics, ensuring the content remains relevant and effective.

Another innovative use of AI by Duolingo is its algorithm for sending notifications designed to maximize user return rates. The app sends notifications 24 hours after the user's last session, operating on the assumption that if a user was free at 3 PM yesterday, they are likely to be free at 3 PM today. This personalized approach aims to fit seamlessly into users' schedules. To avoid spamming, Duolingo stops sending notifications after seven days of inactivity, but sends a final "passive-aggressive" notification featuring the green owl mascot, which often prompts users to return out of a sense of guilt or obligation (Daniswara, et al., 2023). This tactic, combined with the humorous and pushy tone of the mascot, has spurred numerous memes, providing Duolingo with valuable free marketing (Laanti, 2023).

These strategic marketing efforts and partnerships have also played a vital role in Duolingo's expansion. The company has effectively utilized social media, influencer marketing, and community engagement to build a strong brand presence (Daniswara, et al., 2023). Duolingo's distinctive green owl mascot, Duo, has become an iconic symbol in the tech industry, further strengthening brand recognition (Flores &

González, 2024). Collaborations with educational institutions, governments, and other organizations have expanded their reach and credibility, helping to attract new users and markets.

Their commitment to accessibility and inclusivity has also been crucial to its widespread adoption. The platform offers courses in over 30 languages, catering to a diverse global audience. By being available on multiple platforms, including iOS, Android, and web browsers, they ensure that users can access their courses from virtually any device (Sağlam & El Montaser, 2021).

Duolingo has also fostered a strong sense of community among its users. Features such as leaderboards, forums, and user-generated content allow learners to interact, share experiences, and support each other. This community engagement enhances the learning experience by providing users with additional resources and motivation (Chen et al., 2020). Their commitment to listening to its users and incorporating their feedback into product development has also helped to build a loyal user base in and out of the app.

Lastly, the company consistently updates its platform with new features, courses, and improvements based on the latest educational research and technological advancements. They regularly introduce new languages, including endangered and constructed languages, to keep their offerings fresh and appealing (Laanti, 2023). This dedication to innovation ensures that Duolingo remains at the forefront of language education technology.

Brief Market Analysis

Starting with a Strenghts and Weaknesses analysis (SWOT), in order to provide some insights into the current standing and future potential in the competitive landscape of learning applications.

Duolingo's wide range of languages and features attracts a diverse user base. The platform offers courses in over 30 languages and employs a gamified approach to learning, making it engaging and fun through features like Duolingo Stories and Podcasts. The freemium business model allows users to access basic content for free, supported by ads, with an option to upgrade to Duolingo Plus for an ad-free experience and additional features. This model broadens the user base and encourages upgrades. Duolingo's accessibility and convenience are notable, as it is available on multiple platforms including iOS, Android, and web, allowing users to learn anytime and anywhere. The company also enjoys a strong brand presence, supported by a highly engaging mascot and positive user experiences, leading to high user retention and word-of-mouth promotion.

A considerable challenge is that a significant portion of Duolingo's revenue comes from ads viewed by free users, making the company vulnerable to changes in the digital advertising market. Additionally, while Duolingo is excellent for beginners, it may not offer the depth required for advanced language learners, who may seek more comprehensive resources. Another issue is the inconsistency in course quality, as they are often developed by volunteers and community contributors, leading to variations in comprehensiveness and effectiveness.

However, Duolingo has the potential to expand into new geographic and demographic markets, particularly in regions with growing internet penetration and interest in language learning. There is also significant opportunity in enhancing premium features and adding new services, such as live tutoring or more advanced language courses, to attract more users to upgrade to Duolingo Plus. Collaborating with educational institutions and corporations can expand Duolingo's reach and credibility, providing more structured learning opportunities and certification programs.

The language learning market is highly competitive, with numerous apps like Babbel, Rosetta Stone, and Memrise offering similar or alternative services. Rapid changes in technology and user preferences require continuous adaptation and innovation, which can be challenging and resource-intensive . Economic downturns can affect users' willingness to pay for premium subscriptions and decrease ad revenues, impacting Duolingo's overall revenue streams.

Competition and Market Share

Duolingo operates in a highly competitive language learning market, contending with several prominent competitors such as Babbel, Rosetta Stone, and Memrise (Figure 4). Each of these competitors has distinct strengths that cater to different learning preferences and needs (Bapna, 2018). Babbel emphasizes conversational skills and offers a structured, subscription-based learning experience. Rosetta Stone is known for its immersive method, focusing on visual and auditory learning without translations. Memrise uses mnemonic techniques and community-generated content to enhance vocabulary retention and user engagement.

Figure 4. Learning app usage (%) 2021

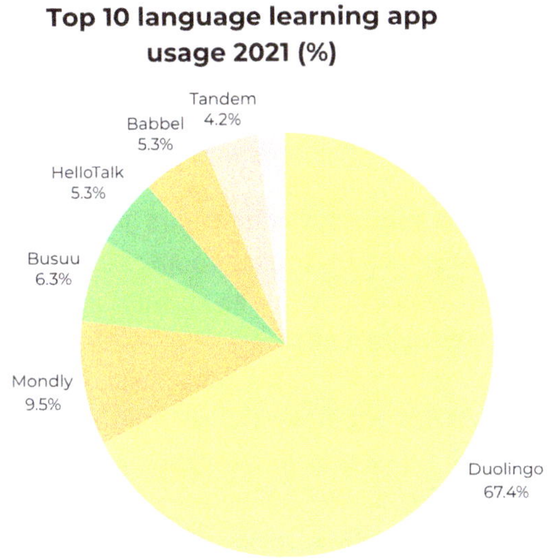

Despite this competition, Duolingo has established a significant market presence, leveraging several strategic advantages. One of its primary strengths is its gamified learning approach, which integrates game-like elements such as rewards, streaks, and challenges to enhance user engagement. This approach aligns with the Self-Determination Theory, which suggests that fulfilling basic psychological needs for competence, autonomy, and relatedness enhances intrinsic motivation. By making learning fun and rewarding, Duolingo keeps users motivated and engaged.

Duolingo's freemium model is obviously another critical factor in its success. Offering substantial free content allows Duolingo to attract a large user base quickly. According to network effects theory, the value of a service increases as more people use it (Shapiro & Varian, 1999). The free tier lowers the entry barrier, helping Duolingo build a vast user community. The premium subscription, Duolingo Plus, provides additional features such as an ad-free experience and offline access, which incentivize users to upgrade, contributing to revenue generation (Koetsier, 2019).

Brand recognition and extensive language offerings also play crucial roles in Duolingo's market strategy. With over 30 languages available, including niche options like Klingon and High Valyrian, Duolingo caters to diverse interests and needs, attracting a broader audience. This diversity not only helps in acquiring users from different demographics but also differentiates Duolingo from competitors with more limited language selections.

Furthermore, Duolingo's continuous innovation and expansion into new areas, such as Duolingo for Schools, provide additional leverage. By offering classroom-friendly versions of the app, Duolingo taps into the educational market, opening new revenue streams and strengthening its brand presence in academic settings.

Key Performance Indicators

To thoroughly assess the efficiency of freemium business models, particularly in the context of Duolingo, it is essential to analyze specific key performance indicators (KPIs) and metrics that reflect customer acquisition, monetization effectiveness, and customer engagement and retention.

Customer acquisition metrics are fundamental to understanding how effectively a freemium model attracts new users. Metrics such as the number of new users, cost per acquisition (CPA), and user growth rate are crucial in determining the reach and appeal of the service (Sağlam & El Montaser, 2021). For Duolingo, which has garnered widespread popularity, these metrics highlight the app's ability to draw in new learners. The viral coefficient and the ratio of organic versus paid acquisition are essential in measuring the natural virality of the app and the effectiveness of marketing strategies. Download rates further quantify the app's penetration in the market (Anderson, 2010).

Monetization effectiveness is another critical area for freemium models. Metrics such as conversion rate, average revenue per user (ARPU), and lifetime value (LTV) are pivotal in assessing how well a company can convert free users into paying customers (Kumar, 2014). For Duolingo, these metrics are essential to understanding the financial sustainability of offering free language courses while maintaining profitability through premium subscriptions and in-app purchases (Tables 3 and 4). According to Dawes (2018), revenue growth rate, in-app purchase revenue, and advertising revenue provide a broader picture of the diverse revenue streams and their growth over time, which are vital for long-term success.

Table 3. Customer acquisition metrics (source: own elaboration)

Category	KPI	Metric	Description
Customer Acquisition	Number of active users and new users	Total number new users per month/year	Measures the growth in user base over a specific period
	User Acquisition Cost (UAC)	Cost per acquired user	Calculates the average cost incurred to acquire a new user
	Conversion Rate	Percentage of visitors who become registered users	Assesses the effectiveness of marketing and onboarding processes in converting visitors to users
	Referral Rate	Percentage of users who refer others	Indicates the effectiveness of word-of-mouth and referral programs in acquiring new users.

Table 4. Monetization effectiveness metrics (source: own elaboration)

Category	KPI	Metric	Description
Monetization Effectiveness	Average Revenue Per User (ARPU)	Total revenue divided by total number of users	Measures the average amount of revenue generated per user.
	Premium Conversion Rate	Percentage of free users who upgrade to premium	Evaluates the success of converting free users to paying customers.
	Revenue Growth Rate	Year-on-year revenue growth percentage	Tracks the increase in revenue over time, indicating business growth.
	Ad Revenue	Total revenue generated from advertisements	Measures the effectiveness of ad placements in generating income.

Customer engagement and retention metrics offer insights into how effectively a freemium service can keep its users active and satisfied over time (Table 5). Daily active users (DAU) and monthly active users (MAU) are basic yet critical indicators of user engagement levels (Schwalbe, 2015). Retention rate and churn rate measure the app's ability to retain users over a specific period, reflecting the overall user satisfaction and the stickiness of the app. Session length and frequency of use provide deeper insights into user habits and engagement intensity (Oestreicher-Singer

& Zalmanson, 2013). Additionally, the Net Promoter Score (NPS) gauges user satisfaction and the likelihood of users recommending the app to others, which is crucial for organic growth (Reichheld, 2003).

Table 5. Customer engagement and retention metrics (source: own elaboration)

Category	KPI	Metric	Description
Customer Engagement and Retention	Daily Active Users (DAU)	Number of users who engage with the app daily	Indicates the level of daily engagement with the platform
	Monthly Active Users (MAU)	Number of users who engage with the app monthly	Provides a broader view of user engagement over a longer period.
	Churn Rate	Percentage of users who stop using the app	Measures the rate at which users discontinue using the service.
	Retention Rate	Percentage of users	Measures the effectiveness of ad placements in generating income.
	Download and user growth rate	Percentage increase in user base over a specific period, as well as Number of app downloads per period	

For Duolingo, these KPIs and metrics are not just numbers; they form the backbone of strategic decision-making. The data on customer acquisition informs marketing strategies and helps optimize spending to acquire users cost-effectively. Monetization metrics are essential for understanding the financial health of the business and guiding adjustments in pricing strategies and premium offerings (Jayathilaka, 2021). Engagement and retention metrics ensure that the app remains relevant and engaging, directly impacting user satisfaction and long-term loyalty (Pauwels & Weiss, 2008).

All in all, a detailed analysis of these key performance indicators and metrics is essential for any business that chooses a freemium model. For Duolingo, these metrics provide a comprehensive view of its operational efficiency, financial health, and user engagement, all of which are crucial for maintaining its position as a leading language-learning platform (Golmgrein, 2023). Given that part of the service is offered for free, it is particularly important for businesses like Duolingo to closely track these KPIs to prevent potential losses and ensure the sustainability and profitability of their freemium strategy. By continuously monitoring and optimizing these metrics, freemium businesses can balance providing free value and generating revenue, ultimately achieving long-term success.

Key Statistics

Duolingo's innovative approach has translated into impressive statistics that underscore its success and widespread impact. As of 2023, in their yearly financial assessments, Duolingo has reported generating $531 million in revenue (table 4), marking a 43.6% year-on-year increase, and average 9.85% quarterly increase.

In the Figure 5 and Table 6 it is also possible to notice significant growth from the last quarter of 2020, and the first quarter of 2021, indicating an improvement during the pandemic. Considering the average quarterly increase, it is possible to develop a forecast of $165.88 million on the following quarter.

Figure 5. Duolingo quarterly revenue (source: own elaboration)

Table 6. Duolingo annual revenue (source: own elaboration)

Duolingo annual revenue 2017 to 2023 ($mm)	
2017	13
2018	36
2019	78
2020	161

continued on following page

Table 6. Continued

Duolingo annual revenue 2017 to 2023 ($mm)	
2021	250
2022	370
2023	531

The platform has been downloaded over 800 million times (Figure 6) and maintains a robust user base with 74 million monthly active users (Table 7). Duolingo offers more than 100 language courses across 38 languages (Table 8), highlighting its global reach and appeal. These statistics reflect Duolingo's effectiveness in making language learning accessible and engaging while demonstrating its ability to sustain growth and innovation in a competitive market.

Figure 6. Duolingo quarterly MAU (source: own elaboration)

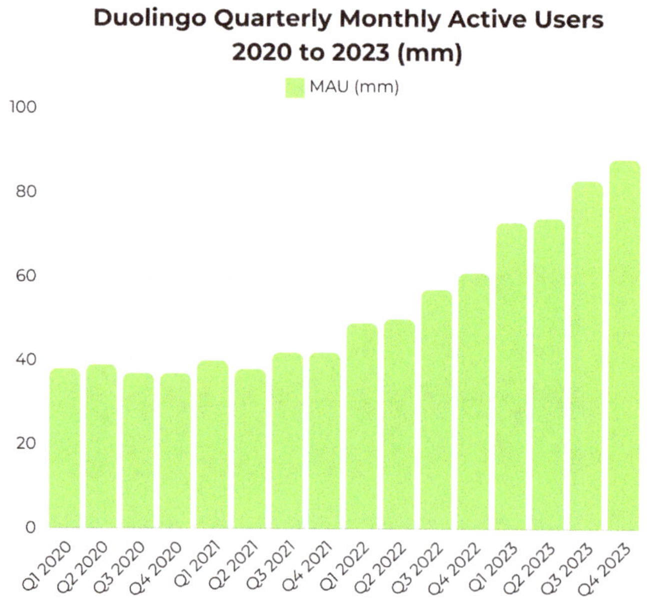

Table 7. Duolingo users by language (source: own elaboration)

Duolingo Annual MAU	
2017	28
2018	25
2019	30
2020	42
2021	37
2022	54
2023	74

Table 8. Duolingo users by language(source: own elaboration)

Duolingo Users by language 2023 (mm)	
English	38,6
Spanish	13,7
French	9,7
German	5,9
Italian	3,8
Portuguese	1,9

The statistics presented clearly demonstrate that Duolingo's efforts in providing accessible and engaging language learning are paying off. With impressive revenue growth, a substantial user base, their impact in the digital education space is undeniable. However, these successes bring up one research questions once again: What exactly drives these results? Understanding the main factors that convert free users into paid customers is crucial for further enhancing their strategy and sustaining its growth in a competitive market. To answer this, the qualitative survey is aimed at uncovering the specific elements and user behaviors that drive conversion from free to paid customers, providing deeper insights into Duolingo's success.

RESULTS

The survey was open for answers for a two-week period, from May 14th to May 28th, 2024 and was able to gather 80 responses in total.

To limit the research, the first question was aimed to limit participation to those who had experience with the app. Participants were directly asked if they had ever been, or currently were a user of Duolingo (Figure 7), and only being able to proceed with the questionnaire if the answer was positive. This allowed the questionnaire to only be completed by the actual target audience. Following this, participants were asked, "If yes, how long have you been using (or used) Duolingo?" (Figure 8) This question, grounded in Bhattacherjee's Expectation-Confirmation Model, aimed to understand the duration of user engagement and satisfaction over time (Bhattacherjee, 2001).

Out of the 80 participants, 44% percent are current users, and 50% had not used the language app longer than 6 months (Figures 7 and 8).

Figure 7. Duolingo user rate

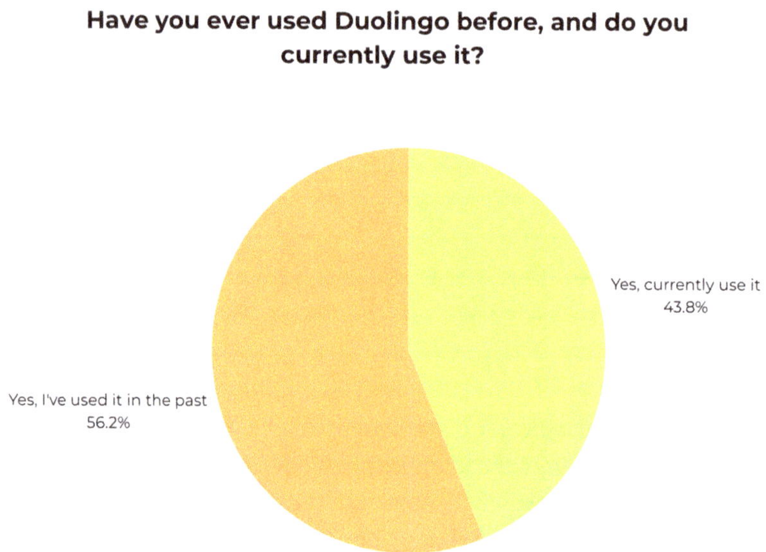

Figure 8. Duration of use

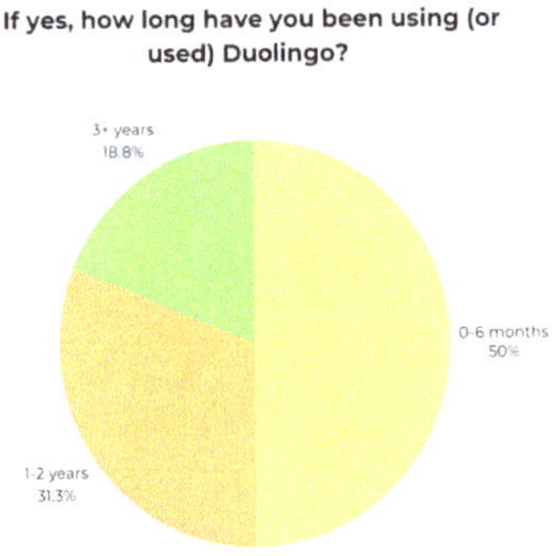

The following section was meant to check if the participants were familiar with the conceptual definition of a freemium business model, this question was based on Rogers' Diffusion of Innovations theory (Rogers et al., 2014) and Fishbein and Ajzen's Theory of Reasoned Action (Ajzen & Fishbein, 1975). These frameworks help understand how new ideas and technologies spread and how attitudes influence behavior. This question assessed participants' baseline knowledge and awareness of the freemium model, and if they used any services that had said model. Interestingly, 68,7% of the participants were not familiar with the concept, but all of them used at least 2 of the freemium services mentioned (Figure 9). They were given 10 freemium businesses and were asked to select all the ones they currently used.

Next, the participants were questioned regarding the frequency in which they used the services or products mentioned in the previous page. They were given 5 options: Daily, weekly, monthly, rarely, and never. And How often they would find themselves only using the basic free versions, without ever upgrading to the premium version. Results showed that those services were a part of the daily life of 75% of the participants, and to no surprise (Figure 10), 43.8% of participants admitted to often using only the free versions of those services (Figure 11), showing that users will try to make the most out of the basic features to avoid upgrading.

Figure 9. Familiarity with freemium models

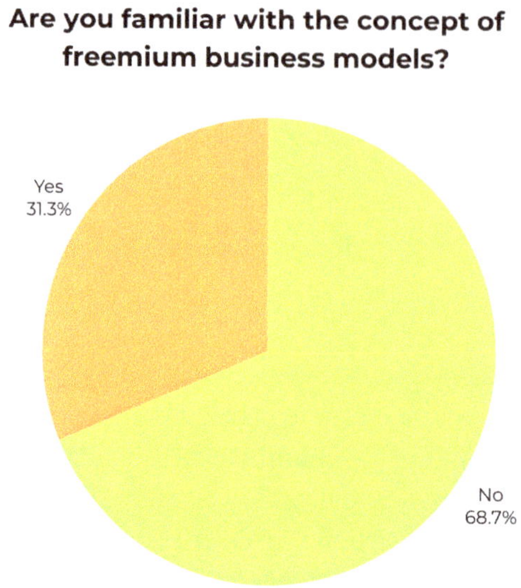

Figure 10. Freemium usage frequency

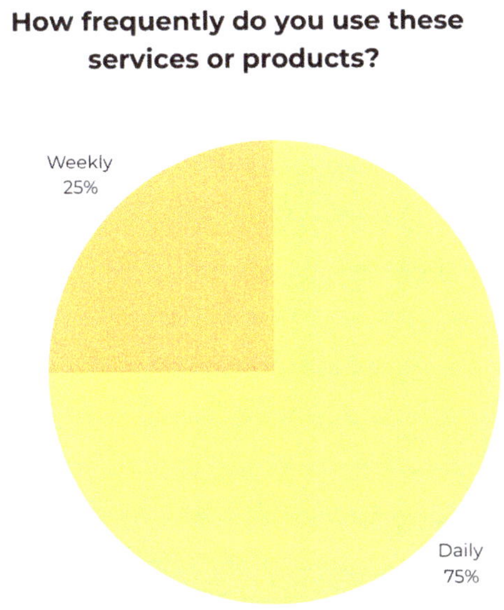

Figure 11. Free feature usage

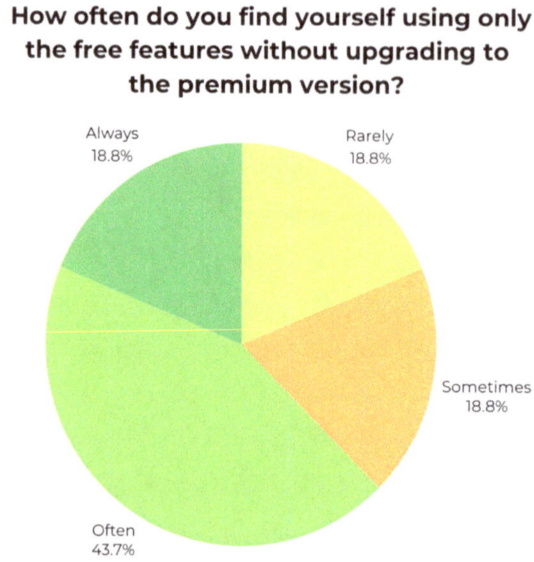

The likelihood of upgrading to the premium version was assessed through the question, "How likely are you to upgrade any of these services to the premium version?" (Figure 12). This was inspired by Ajzen's Theory of Planned Behavior (Ajzen & Fishbein, 1975) and Venkatesh & Bala's Technology Acceptance Model (Venkatesh & Bala, 2008), which predict user intentions and behavior concerning technology adoption. 43% of the participants considered it likely to upgrade the services, but 31% pointed out that they would only do that decision based on the value provided by the premium features. They were asked to rate the value of the basic feature offerings, and 50% rated it as valuable (Figure 13).

Figure 12. Likeliness to upgrade

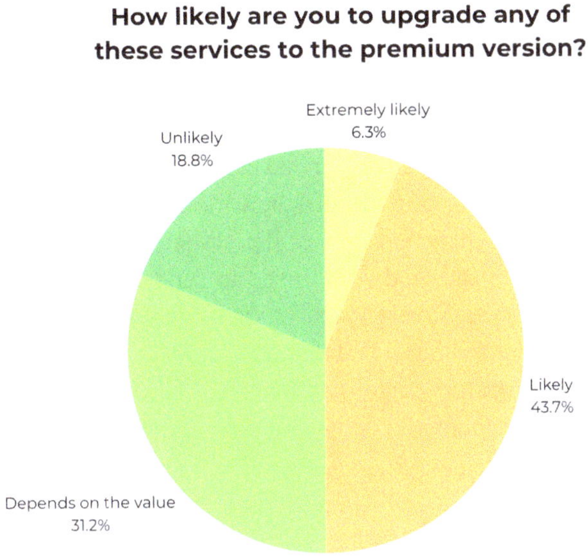

Figure 13. Value of free features

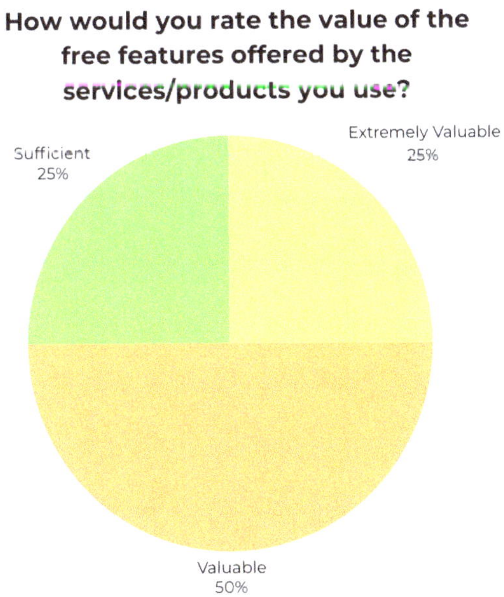

Participants' engagement with Duolingo was further examined by asking, "Which Duolingo features do you use most frequently?" (Figure 14), based on Anderson's research on customer satisfaction and market share, this question aimed to identify the features that drive user engagement and satisfaction, the survey showed that the 3 most used features are actually part of the free, basic version of the app. The consideration of purchasing premium features on Duolingo was explored through the question, "Have you ever considered purchasing premium features on Duolingo?" (Figure 15), this was aimed to provide a framework for understanding factors influencing the decision to upgrade and 50% of the participants considered upgrading, while the other 50% were satisfied with the basic version.

In order to explore price sensitivity, participants were asked, "How much would you be willing to pay for premium features on Duolingo per month?" (Figure 16), considering that the current average monthly price for the subscription is $12.90, 50% of the participants replied that they would be interested in paying up to $5 for the subscription.

Figure 14. Duolingo feature usage

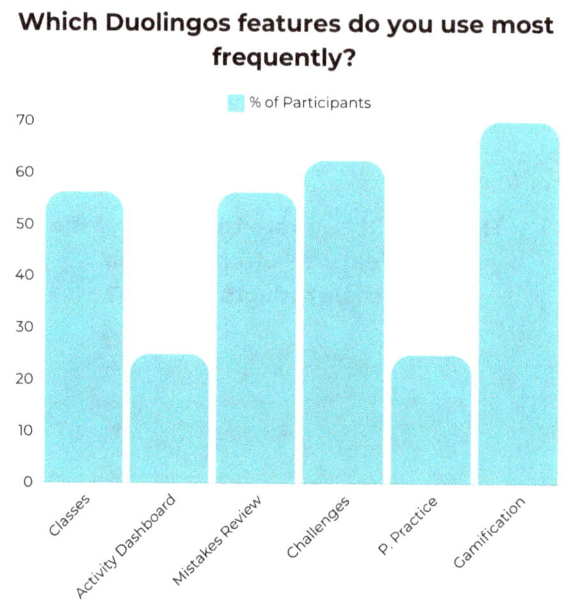

Figure 15. Duolingo premium features

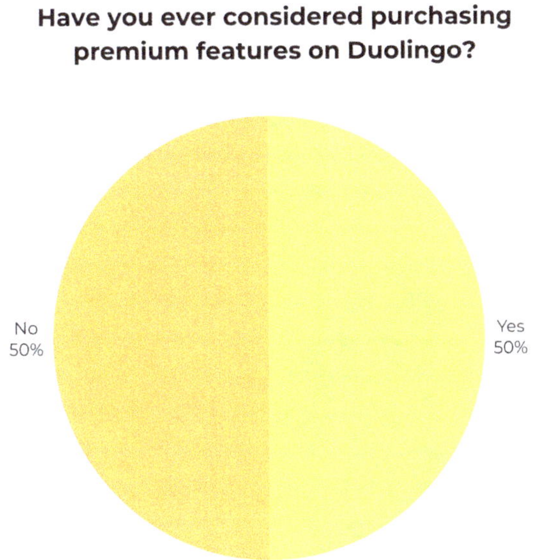

Their perceptions of the value of premium features were assessed through the question, “How valuable do you think premium features on Duolingo are compared to the free version?” (Figure 16) This drew on Gale's research on managing customer value, critical for understanding the perceived worth of premium offerings, The question, “Do you believe the premium features offered by Duolingo justify the cost (currently $12.99 per month or $59.99 a year)?” aimed to notice consumer perceptions of price, quality, and value, determining if users believe the premium features are worth the price, and 62% of the participants do not think the premium features are worth that price (Figure 17).

Figure 16. Premium features value

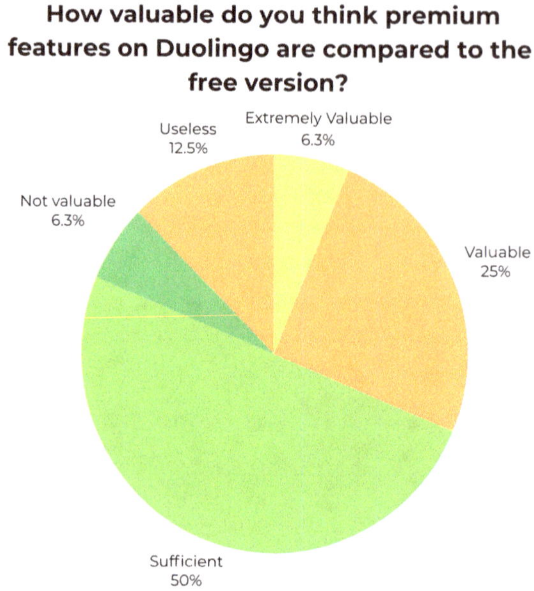

Figure 17. Price sensitivity

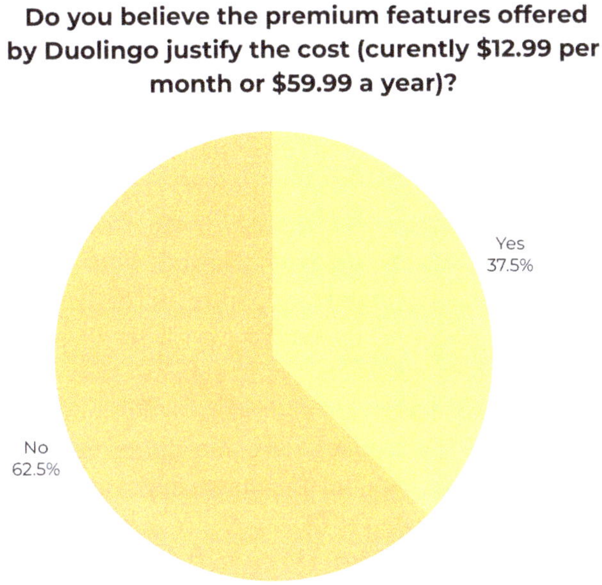

Finally, the last question revealed that the most influential factors in users' decision to upgrade to the premium version were value proposition, feature set, and price sensitivity. The prominence of value proposition indicates that users are highly motivated by the perceived benefits and additional value that the premium version offers.

DISCUSSION

The survey conducted focused exclusively on individuals with experience using Duolingo. This targeted approach ensured that the feedback collected was relevant and insightful for analyzing the efficiency of freemium models.

Out of the 80 participants, 44% are current users of Duolingo, and 50% had used the app for less than six months. This data aligns with Bhattacherjee's Expectation-Confirmation Model, indicating that user engagement and satisfaction can vary significantly over time. The relatively high percentage of short-term users suggests that while Duolingo attracts many new users, retaining them for longer periods remains a challenge. This insight underscores the importance of continually enhancing user experience to maintain long-term engagement (Bhattacherjee, 2001).

The survey revealed that 68.8% of participants were unfamiliar with the conceptual definition of a freemium business model. However, despite this lack of formal knowledge, all participants used at least two services operating on a freemium basis. This finding highlights a significant gap between user awareness and actual behavior, suggesting that while users may not consciously recognize the term "freemium," they are deeply embedded in its ecosystem. This observation is supported by Rogers' Diffusion of Innovations theory (Rogers et al., 2014) and Fishbein and Ajzen's Theory of Reasoned Action (Ajzen & Fishbein, 1975), which emphasize the gradual adoption of new ideas and behaviors. Regarding the frequency of use, 75% of participants reported that freemium services are part of their daily life. However, 43.8% admitted to often using only the free versions without upgrading to premium. Users typically exploit the basic features of freemium services to avoid paying for premium versions. This trend underscores the need for businesses to strike a balance between offering valuable free features and compelling premium upgrades.

The survey assessed the likelihood of users upgrading to premium versions through Ajzen's Theory of Planned Behavior (Ajzen & Fishbein, 1975) and Venkatesh & Bala's Technology Acceptance Model (Venkatesh & Bala, 2008). Results showed that 43% of participants were likely to upgrade, with 31% basing their decision on the value provided by premium features. This indicates that while there is a potential market for premium conversions, the perceived value of premium features is a crucial determinant in the decision-making process. An examination of user engagement with Duolingo revealed that the most frequently used features are part of the free version of the app. This finding aligns with Anderson's research on customer satisfaction, suggesting that free features significantly drive user engagement. Consequently, Duolingo must ensure that its premium features offer substantial added value to motivate users to upgrade.

Participants' price sensitivity was explored through their willingness to pay for Duolingo's premium features. Although the current average monthly subscription price is $12.90, 50% of participants indicated they would be willing to pay up to $5 per month. This significant disparity highlights a critical challenge for Duolingo in pricing its premium features competitively while ensuring perceived value. Additionally, 62% of participants did not believe that the premium features justified the current price, emphasizing the need for better value communication and possibly re-evaluating the pricing strategy. The survey identified the most influential factors in the decision to upgrade as the value proposition, feature set, and price sensitivity. The prominence of value proposition indicates that users are highly motivated by the perceived benefits and additional value that the premium version offers. This insight aligns with Gale's research on managing customer value, underscoring the necessity for businesses to clearly articulate and deliver the unique advantages of their premium offerings.

Implications for Freemium Model Effectiveness

The survey results imply that Duolingo's marketing and product development teams should continue to emphasize the distinct advantages of the premium subscription, such as offline access, ad-free learning, and exclusive content. By clearly communicating these benefits, Duolingo can effectively highlight the superior value that justifies the cost of upgrading. The importance of feature set underscores the need for Duolingo to continue innovating and expanding its premium offerings. Users are attracted to advanced features like personalized learning plans, progress tracking, and more comprehensive lessons. This suggests that ongoing development and enhancement of premium features can play a critical role in driving conversions. Price sensitivity as a key factor suggests that while users recognize the value of the premium features, the cost remains a significant consideration. This implies that Duolingo must carefully balance the pricing of its premium subscription to ensure it is perceived as a good value. Strategic pricing models, such as tiered subscriptions or promotional discounts, could be explored to make the premium version more accessible and attractive to a broader audience. This strategy would present its challenges, since the basic features already allow the learners to have full access to the lessons, developing a tiered subscription model could bring most of the users to a lower tier of the payment methods.

High sensing and seizing capabilities are crucial for maintaining performance in freemium businesses. Similarly, our study reveals that Duolingo's ability to continually update and enhance its language courses based on user feedback and data analytics plays a vital role in its success. This aligns with the concept of dynamic capabilities, underscoring the need for constant innovation and adaptation.

Motivations in the adoption and conversion of freemium services were explored. They discovered that user satisfaction with free features can paradoxically reduce the urgency to convert to premium. The findings echo this sentiment, as Duolingo users who are highly satisfied with free features often feel a strong emotional connection to the app, which both fosters loyalty and diminishes the perceived need to upgrade. This highlights the dual role of satisfaction in freemium models, necessitating nuanced strategies to convert satisfied free users into paying customers.

These findings bring to light a key success factor for implementing freemium models: adhering to the Pareto principle. To be successful, a business needs to offer 80% of its product or service for free to hook customers, reserving premium features for those willing to upgrade. For instance, Spotify provides access to its entire music library for free, even though premium accounts offer additional perks. Similarly, Duolingo grants free users full access to language courses, ensuring wide accessibility while enticing users with premium enhancements. Having a valuable basic version and robust free features are crucial, as they form the foundation for user engagement and satisfaction. If the free offerings are insufficient, users are unlikely to stay long enough to consider upgrading. Therefore, the quality and value of the basic version play a pivotal role in attracting and retaining users, making them more likely to perceive the additional benefits of the premium features as worth the cost.

CONCLUSION

Final Remarks

The study of freemium business models, with a particular focus on Duolingo, provides valuable insights into the effectiveness and challenges of this popular revenue strategy. By analyzing user behavior, motivations, and the balance between free and premium offerings, this thesis has highlighted key factors that contribute to the success of freemium models. Duolingo's ability to continually innovate, personalize learning experiences, and engage users through dynamic capabilities underscores the potential of freemium strategies to thrive in competitive digital markets. The findings affirm that a well-executed freemium model can drive substantial user growth, engagement, and conversion, ultimately supporting sustainable business success.

Theoretical and Practical Implications

Theoretically, this research contributes to the existing literature on freemium business models by integrating dynamic capabilities theory and user motivation perspectives. It extends the understanding of how freemium models can leverage data-driven decision-making and continuous innovation to enhance performance. The study's findings on the dual role of user satisfaction—as both a driver of loyalty and a potential barrier to conversion—add nuance to existing theories on user engagement and retention in freemium contexts.

Freemium models are efficient due to their ability to attract a large user base with free offerings and then convert a significant portion of these users into paying customers through premium features. This supports the theory that freemium models are not only viable but can be highly effective when managed properly. Motivations for adopting and converting to freemium services include the perceived value and quality of the free version, which aligns with the findings of this thesis.

Practically, the research offers actionable insights for digital entrepreneurs and managers aiming to implement or refine freemium strategies. Businesses can benefit from understanding the importance of balancing free and premium features to optimize user satisfaction and conversion rates. The study highlights the need for continuous innovation and adaptation to user feedback, which can help businesses stay competitive and relevant. Additionally, the research underscores the significance of tailoring freemium models to diverse market conditions and user demographics, which is crucial for global scalability.

Limitations and Future Research Directions

While this study provides important insights into the efficiency of freemium business models, several limitations must be acknowledged. The sample size for the qualitative research was relatively small, which may limit the generalizability of the findings. Future research could expand the sample size and include a more diverse range of participants to validate and extend the results. Additionally, the study focused primarily on Duolingo, which may not fully represent the broader spectrum of freemium models in different industries and contexts. Comparative studies involving multiple freemium-based companies across various sectors could provide a more comprehensive understanding of the factors influencing the success of freemium strategies.

Future research could also explore the long-term sustainability of freemium models, particularly in rapidly evolving digital markets. Investigating how freemium businesses adapt to changing user expectations, technological advancements, and competitive pressures would be valuable for developing robust theoretical frameworks and practical guidelines. Furthermore, examining the ethical considerations of freemium models, such as data privacy and user manipulation, could provide critical insights into responsible business practices in the digital age.

REFERENCES

Ajzen, I., & Fishbein, M. (1975). A Bayesian analysis of attribution processes. *Psychological Bulletin*, *82*(2), 261.

Amin, S. N. (2021). Gamification of Duolingo in rising student's English language learning motivation. *Jurnal Bahasa Lingua Scientia*, *13*(2), 191–213. DOI: 10.21274/ls.2021.13.2.191-213

Anderson, C. (2010). *Free: The Future of a Radical Price*. Hyperion.

Anderson, E. W., Fornell, C., & Lehmann, D. R. (1994). Customer satisfaction, market share, and profitability: Findings from Sweden. *Journal of Marketing*, *58*(3), 53–66.

Banton, C. (2019). *Network effect*. Investopedia.

Bapna, R., Ramaprasad, J., & Umyarov, A. (2018). Monetizing freemium communities: Does paying for premium increase social engagement? *Management Information Systems Quarterly*, *42*(3), 719–735. DOI: 10.25300/MISQ/2018/13592

Bhattacherjee, A. (2001). Understanding information systems continuance: An expectation-confirmation model. *Management Information Systems Quarterly*, •••, 351–370.

Biraglia, A., Bowen, K. T., Gerrath, M. H. E. E., & Musarra, G. (2022). How need for closure and deal proneness shape consumers' freemium versus premium price choices. *Journal of Business Research*, *143*, 157–170. DOI: 10.1016/j.jbusres.2022.01.064

Bockstedt, J., Druehl, C., & Mishra, A. (2015). Design and pricing of freemium products. *Business Horizons*, *58*(3), 301–311.

Bolton, R. N., & Drew, J. H. (1991). A multistage model of customers' assessments of service quality and value. *The Journal of Consumer Research*, *17*(4), 375–384.

Bridoux, F., & van Oosterhout, H. (2020). Stakeholder governance: Solving the collective action problems in joint value creation. *Academy of Management Review*, *45*(1), 214–228.

Chen, H., Chiang, R. H. L., & Storey, V. C. (2020). Business Intelligence and Analytics: From Big Data to Big Impact. *Management Information Systems Quarterly*, *36*(4), 1165–1188. DOI: 10.2307/41703503

Coase, R. H. (1937). The nature of the firm. *Economica*, *4*(16), 386–405. DOI: 10.1111/j.1468-0335.1937.tb00002.x

Damir, B., & Hasnaa, G. (2020). Content marketing and website users engagement: The impact of relevant content on the web on user engagement behaviors. *Periodicals of Engineering and Natural Sciences*, *8*(1), 229–239. DOI: 10.21533/pen.v8i1.1571

Daniswara, M. H. R., Permana, F., Hafidz, A., & Marcellino, B. (2023). User Experience Evaluation of Duolingo using User Experience Questionnaire (UEQ). *International Conference on Information Management and Technology (ICIMTech)*. DOI: 10.1109/ICIMTech59029.2023.10277886

Davis, F. D. (1989). Perceived usefulness, perceived ease of use, and user acceptance of information technology. *Management Information Systems Quarterly*, •••, 319–340.

Dawes, J. (2018). The Impact of Freemium Pricing Models on Customer Acquisition and Retention. *Journal of Business Research*, *85*, 84–93.

Eisenmann, T., Parker, G., & Van Alstyne, M. (2006). Strategies for two-sided markets. *Harvard Business Review*, *84*(10), 92–101.

Fader, P. (2012). *Customer Lifetime Value: Marketing Models and Applications*. Now Publishers Inc.

Fader, P. S., & Hardie, B. G. (2009). Probability models for customer-base analysis. *Journal of Interactive Marketing*, *23*(1), 61–69. DOI: 10.1016/j.intmar.2008.11.003

Flores, N., & González, W. (2024). *Marketing experiencial: Caso Duolingo*. UCAB Drive.

Gale, B. (1994). Managing customer value: Creating quality and service that customers can see. *New York*.

Gawer, A. (2022). Digital platforms and ecosystems: Remarks on the dominant organizational forms of the digital age. *Innovation (North Sydney, N.S.W.)*, *24*(1), 10–23. DOI: 10.1080/14479338.2021.1965888

Golmgrein, I. V. (2023). A comprehensive overview of monetization strategies in creative industries. [IJLEMR]. *International Journal of Latest Engineering and Management Research*, *8*(4), 90–100. DOI: 10.56581/IJLEMR.8.4.90-100

Gordon, S. R., & McNew, J. (2008). *Internet Research Methods: A Practical Guide for the Social and Behavioural Sciences*. Oxford University Press.

Gregory, R. W., Henfridsson, O., Kaganer, E., & Kyriakou, H. (2021). The role of artificial intelligence and data network effects for creating user value. *Academy of Management Review*, *46*(3), 534–551. DOI: 10.5465/amr.2019.0178

Griffin, A., & Hauser, J. R. (1993). The voice of the customer. *Marketing Science*, *12*(1), 1–27.

Gupta, S., & Lehmann, D. R. (2006). Customer Lifetime Value and Firm Valuation. *Journal of Relationship Marketing*, *5*(2–3), 87–110. DOI: 10.1300/J366v05n02_06

Hamari, J., Hanner, N., & Koivisto, J. (2020). Why pay premium in freemium services? A study on perceived value, continued use, and purchase intentions in free-to-play games. *International Journal of Information Management*, *51*, 102032. DOI: 10.1016/j.ijinfomgt.2019.102040

Hansen, M. (2021). Measuring conversion rates in freemium business models. *Journal of Business Research*, *123*, 142–155.

Hauser, J. R., Urban, G. L., & Weinberg, B. D. (1993). How consumers allocate their time when searching for information. *JMR, Journal of Marketing Research*, *30*(4), 452–466.

Hinterhuber, A., & Liozu, S. M. (2017). Is innovation in pricing your next source of competitive advantage? 1. In *Innovation in pricing* (pp. 11–27). Routledge.

Hollis, T. (2020). Strategies for reducing churn in freemium models. *Journal of Marketing Management*, *36*(9-10), 805–826.

Jayathilaka, U. R. (2021). *Investigating the relationship between pricing strategies and international customer acquisition in the early stage of SaaS: The role of hybrid pricing*. Gangseo University.

Johnson, E. J., & Goldstein, D. G. (2003). Do defaults save lives? *Science*, *302*(5649), 1338–1339. DOI: 10.1126/science.1091721 PMID: 14631022

Kahneman, D., & Tversky, A. (1979). Prospect theory: An analysis of decision under risk. *Econometrica*, *47*(2), 263–291. DOI: 10.2307/1914185

Koetsier, J. (2019). *The Freemium Economy: How free products drive massive user acquisition*. TechCrunch. TechCrunch.

Kumar, V. (2014). Making 'Freemium' Work. *Harvard Business Review*.

Kumar, V. (2018). Customer Acquisition Cost in Digital Marketing. *Marketing Science*, *37*(2), 230–245.

Laanti, N. (2023). *Parasocial relationships between businesses and customers as a way of marketing*. Sakunta University of Applied Sciences database. Hinterhuber, A., & Liozu, S. M. (2017). Is innovation in pricing your next source of competitive advantage? 1. In *Innovation in pricing* (pp. 11–27). Routledge.

Mäntymäki, M., Islam, A. N., & Benbasat, I. (2020). What drives subscribing to premium in freemium services? A consumer value-based view of differences between upgrading to and staying with premium. *Information Systems Journal, 30*(2), 295–333. DOI: 10.1111/isj.12262

Martins, J., & Rodrigues, R. (2024). Motivations in the adoption and conversion of freemium services: Insights for digital entrepreneurship. *Review of Managerial Science, 19*(7), 2127–2148. DOI: 10.1007/s11846-024-00754-0

Mazumdar, T., & Monroe, K. B. (1990). The effects of buyers' intentions to learn price informatio. *Journal of Retailing, 66*(1), 15.

Möhlmann, M. (2015). Collaborative consumption: Determinants of satisfaction and the likelihood of using a sharing economy option again. *Journal of Consumer Behaviour, 14*(3), 193–207. DOI: 10.1002/cb.1512

Niemand, T., Tischer, S., Fritzsche, T., & Kraus, S. (2015). The freemium effect: Why consumers perceive more value with free than with premium offers.

Oestreicher-Singer, G., & Zalmanson, L. (2013). Content or Community? A Digital Business Strategy for Content Providers in the Social Age. *Management Information Systems Quarterly, 37*(2), 591–616. DOI: 10.25300/MISQ/2013/37.2.12

Osterwalder, A., & Pigneur, Y. (2010). *Business Model Generation: A Handbook for Visionaries, Game Changers, and Challengers.* Wiley.

Park, Y., Cardwell, R., & Naismith, B. (2024). *Assessing Vocabulary on the Duolingo English Test.* Duolingo Research Report No. DRR-24-01). Duolingo. http://go. duolingo. com/vocabulary.

Pauwels, K., & Weiss, A. (2008). Moving from Free to Fee: How Online Firms Market to New Users. *Journal of Interactive Marketing, 22*(3), 30–42.

Reichheld, F., & Schefter, P. (2000). E-loyalty: Your Secret Weapon on the Web. *Harvard Business Review, 78*(4), 105–113.

Reichheld, F. F. (2003). The One Number You Need to Grow. *Harvard Business Review*. PMID: 14712543

Rindfleisch, A. (2020). Transaction cost theory: Past, present, and future. *AMS Review, 10*(1), 85–97. DOI: 10.1007/s13162-019-00151-x

Rogers, E. M., Singhal, A., & Quinlan, M. M. (2014). Diffusion of innovations. In *An integrated approach to communication theory and research* (pp. 432–448). Routledge.

Sağlam, M., & El Montaser, S. (2021). The effect of customer relationship marketing in customer retention and customer acquisition. *International Journal of Commerce and Finance*, *7*(1), 191–201.

Sakalauskė, A., & Leonavičiūtė, V. (2022). Strategic analysis of Duolingo language learning platform.

Schreiner, M. W., Klimes-Dougan, B., Begnel, E. D., & Cullen, K. R. (2015). Conceptualizing the neurobiology of non-suicidal self-injury from the perspective of the Research Domain Criteria Project. *Neuroscience and Biobehavioral Reviews*, *57*, 381–391.

Schwalbe, K. (2015). *Information Technology Project Management*. Cengage Learning.

Shang, Y., Jiang, J., Zhang, Y., Zhang, R., & Liu, P. (2024). When does a freemium business model lead to high performance? — A qualitative comparative analysis based on fuzzy sets. *Heliyon*, *10*(3), e25149. Advance online publication. DOI: 10.1016/j.heliyon.2024.e25149 PMID: 38333777

Shapiro, C., & Varian, H. R. (1999). *Information Rules: A Strategic Guide to the Network Economy*. Harvard Business Press.

Sheth, J. N., Newman, B. I., & Gross, B. L. (1991). Why we buy what we buy: A theory of consumption values. *Journal of Business Research*, *22*(2), 159–170.

Shortt, M., Tilak, S., Kuznetcova, I., Martens, B., & Akinkuolie, B. (2021). Gamification in mobile-assisted language learning: A systematic review of Duolingo literature from public release of 2012 to early 2020. *Computer Assisted Language Learning*, *36*(3), 517–554. DOI: 10.1080/09588221.2021.1933540

Šobak, P. (2023). *The freemium business model: Don't walk away, run*. Better Proposals.

Tam, K. Y., & Ho, S. Y. (2005). Web personalization as a persuasion strategy: An elaboration likelihood model perspective. *Information Systems Research*, *16*(3), 271–291.

Thaler, R. H. (1980). Toward a positive theory of consumer choice. *Journal of Economic Behavior & Organization*, *1*(1), 39–60. DOI: 10.1016/0167-2681(80)90051-7

Thomas, N. J., Baral, R., Crocco, O. S., & Mohanan, S. (2023). A framework for gamification in the metaverse era: How designers envision gameful experience. *Technological Forecasting and Social Change*, *193*, 122544. DOI: 10.1016/j.techfore.2023.122544

Tyrväinen, O., & Karjaluoto, H. (2024). Willingness to pay for freemium services: Addressing the differences between monetization strategies. *International Journal of Information Management*, *77*, 102787.

Tzuo, T., & Weisert, G. (2018). *Subscribed: Why the subscription model will be your company's future—and what to do about it*. Portfolio/Penguin.

Venkatesh, V., & Bala, H. (2008). Technology acceptance model 3 and a research agenda on interventions. *Decision Sciences*, *39*(2), 273–315.

Venkatesh, V., Morris, M. G., Davis, G. B., & Davis, F. D. (2003). User acceptance of information technology: Toward a unified view. *Management Information Systems Quarterly*, •••, 425–478.

Venkatesh, V., Thong, J. Y., & Xu, X. (2012). Consumer acceptance and use of information technology: Extending the unified theory of acceptance and use of technology. *Management Information Systems Quarterly*, •••, 157–178.

Von Ahn, L., & Hacker, S. (2020). Building a Billion-User Product Without Selling Your Soul. *Harvard Business Review*, *98*(6), 80–89.

Wang, Q., Zhao, N., Wu, J., & Zhu, Q. (2019). Optimal pricing and inventory policies with reference price effect and loss-averse customers. *Omega*, *99*, 102174. DOI: 10.1016/j.omega.2019.102174

Whang, J. B., Song, J. H., Choi, B., & Lee, J. H. (2021). The effect of Augmented Reality on purchase intention of beauty products: The roles of consumers' control. *Journal of Business Research*, *133*, 275–284.

Wilson, F., & McCarthy, J. (2010). The Freemium Model in Mobile Apps. *Mobile Business Review*, *12*(3), 89–103.

Wood-Harper, T. (2021). Emerging EdTechs amidst the COVID-19 pandemic: Cases in higher education institutions. In *Fostering communication and learning with underutilized technologies in higher education* (pp. 93–107). IGI Global. DOI: 10.4018/978-1-7998-4846-2.ch007

Zeithaml, V. A. (1988). Consumer perceptions of price, quality, and value: A means-end model and synthesis of evidence. *Journal of Marketing*, *52*(3), 2–22.

KEY TERMS AND DEFINITIONS

Freemium Model: It is a business strategy where a company offers basic services or products for free while charging for premium features, advanced functionality, or additional content. It is commonly used in digital products like apps or software.

Business Model: It describes how an organization creates, delivers, and captures value. It outlines how a company makes money, including its target market, revenue streams, cost structure, and value proposition.

Consumer Decision-Making: It is the process individuals go through when selecting, purchasing, using, or disposing of products and services. It involves stages such as problem recognition, information search, evaluation of alternatives, purchase decision, and post-purchase behavior.

Entrepreneurship: It is the act of creating, developing, and managing a business venture to make a profit, often involving innovation and risk-taking. Entrepreneurs identify market opportunities and mobilize resources to exploit them.

Strategy: It refers to a long-term plan of action designed to achieve specific goals or gain a competitive advantage. In business, it involves aligning resources, capabilities, and activities to outperform competitors and meet organizational objectives.

Chapter 11
The Evolution, Integration, and Implementation of Supply Chain Modeling

Alfred L. Guiffrida
https://orcid.org/0009-0008-2364-0197
Kent State University, USA

Pauline W. Hoffmann
St. Bonaventure University, USA

Ionut R. Vlad
https://orcid.org/0009-0006-2598-7173
Indiana University of Pennsylvania, USA

Carol Putman
https://orcid.org/0009-0000-8361-550X
The Behrend College, Penn State Erie, USA

ABSTRACT

This chapter highlights the role of models in advancing scientific knowledge, reviewing existing research on scientific modeling and the process of building models. It delves into the philosophical underpinnings of modeling, bridging this theoretical foundation to practical applications in supply chain management (SCM). Through presenting modeling applications in supply chain performance measurement, collaboration and coordination, and sustainability, the chapter provides a holistic view of

DOI: 10.4018/979-8-3373-3301-4.ch011

the field's modeling landscape. By consolidating recent research, this chapter aims to equip academics and practitioners in supply chain management with the latest developments and encourage the exploration of new research avenues.

INTRODUCTION

Models play an integral role in the advancement of science. Researchers benefit significantly from a fundamental grasp of the model building process and the existing body of modeling literature. Understanding the context and essence of models is critical for successful model development, effective research collaboration, and accurate interpretation of findings reported in the literature. Throughout history, models have led to the development of theories and the advancement of science. A short list of some historically noteworthy contributions includes the gravitational model of Sir Isaac Newton, the theory of relativity of Albert Einstein, the atomic model of Niels Bohr, the sociological structural functionalism model of Émile Durkheim and Talcott Parsons, and the DNA double helix model of Watson and Crick.

As a gateway to this chapter, consider the following statements regarding models from the business and academic perspectives. According to Fredric W. Smith, the former Chairman and CEO of the Federal Express Corporation, "by modeling various alternatives for future system design, Federal Express has, in effect, made its mistakes on paper. Computer modeling works: it allows us to examine many different alternatives, and it forces the examination of the entire problem". Smith further adds, "the modeling process itself leads to a more complete examination and understanding of the problem at hand". British statistician George Box famously stated, "all models are wrong, some are useful". Box empathized that "the practical question is how wrong do they have to be to not be useful".

This chapter focuses on previous work in scientific modeling and model-based reasoning and aims to synthesize and guide research on modeling in supply chain management. Building from a foundation of modeling from a philosophical perspective, the chapter then focuses on the application of models used in supply chain management. This single source consolidation of the philosophical and applied perspectives of model building and application may prove useful to academicians who are interested in continuing current research programs or establishing new research programs in supply chain modeling. Practitioners interested in expanding their toolkits for improving business performance using supply chain models may also find it useful.

The chapter is organized as follows. We initially examine modeling in the context of scientific inquiry and the development of theory. Next, we overview the model building process and present insights that facilitate the efficient and effective development and implementation of models. Upon reviewing the model building process, we investigate the relationship between organizational strategy and business paradigms, identifying key supply chain decision areas where models have advanced business performance. The chapter concludes with a summary of the role of supply chain models in improving business performance and suggestions for future research.

Modeling and Scientific Inquiry

A model is a representation of a real object or situation. A Google search reveals the etymology of the word model from the 16th century to today. In Latin, model signifies a "measure" or a "standard". Originating from *modulus* (Latin), model was in turn known as *modello* (Italian), *modelle* (French) and finally in English as *model*.

Models exist in many forms and can be classified under three generalizations: iconic, analog or symbolic. An iconic model is a physical representation of the object understudy. An analog model is a physical representation of the object under study but is not a physical replica. A symbolic model is an abstraction of the object under study where mathematical relationships are used to represent the behavior and dynamics of the object. Illustrations of the three general types of models include: (i) a human skeleton used in medical education, or a model airplane used in a wind tunnel to study airflow dynamics in wing design (iconic models); (ii) a blueprint used in building construction, or a Galton board to illustrate binomial probabilities in a statistics class (analog models); and (iii) a differential equation used to study thermodynamic heat transfer, or the periodic table of elements that defines properties such as atomic weight and mass (symbolic models).

The use of models is multidisciplinary and supports interdisciplinary advancements. When analysts and researchers build and use models, cognitive processes are stimulated and the resulting conceptualizations advance model-based understanding, model-based reasoning, model-based explanation, modeling strategies, and mental models thus contributing to interdisciplinary achievements (Boon, 2024). For example, sociologists use models to study social change. Business analysts use models to analyze financial markets. Psychologists employ models to study human behavior. Complex engineering problems like designing self-driving automobiles require a multidisciplinary design team of automotive, electrical and mechanical engineers. Interdisciplinary advancement is often achieved using models in scientific inquiry. Frigg and Hartmann (2025) provide an enlightening look at the contribution of models as a catalyst to learning. Learning occurs through 'model-based reasoning' (Nersessian & Patton, 2009; Magnani & Nersessian, 2002) and surrogative reasoning (Swoyer, 1991). A general framework of how learning occurs using models is found in Hughes (1997).

As a result of individual differences in backgrounds, beliefs, experience and values, researchers often display discernment in their interpretations of what models are. In an intriguing investigation of this issue, Bailer-Jones (2002) interviewed nine scientists to determine how they viewed the role of scientific models. Based on the study, Bailer-Jones (2002, p. 297) noted: (i) models are central to scientific inquiry, (ii) there is neither uniform nor sharp distinction between theory and model that is shared by scientists, and (iii) the definition of constitutes a scientific model is diverse. Edmonds (2017) provides clarity to the above concerns through his identification and qualification of five different purposes of modeling: theoretical exposition, prediction, explanation, description and illustration.

Models play an integral role in the advancement of science. The universe is a complex domain, and scientists utilize models to conceptualize and understand their position of inquiry on a theory relevant to this domain. Models therefore serve as a mechanism for linking scientific inquiry into a testable proposition in support of exploring proposed theory. A researcher is guided by the scientific method which provides a systematic process for investigating a theory. Under the scientific method, a researcher posits a research question, formulates a hypothesis to be tested, collects and analyzes data and then either rejects or fails to reject the hypothesis being tested. Based upon the outcome of the hypothesis test, conclusions are drawn about the research question under study. Continuous empirical and theoretical testing of the inquiry under investigation leads to explanations supporting or refuting a theory.

The Model Building Process

Creating models should follow a definable step-by-step process. A workable four-step process may be defined as: problem definition, model formulation, analysis and model solution, and implementation (see Figure 1). This four-step process is structured from the scientific method of the physical sciences.

Figure 1. The model building process

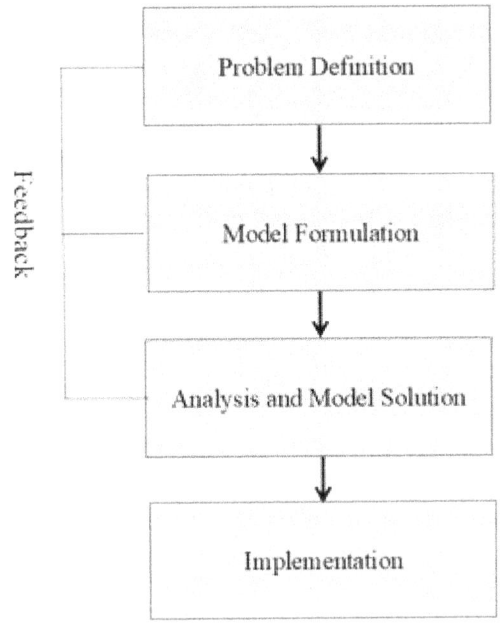

The first step in the modeling process is to define the problem. This step is critical as a poor model definition will cause difficulties in subsequent steps of formulation, solution and implementation. All members of the problem-solving team must "be on the same page" concerning the purpose of the model and the jargon and terminology used in the model. A formal problem statement must be documented, shared and signed off on by all stakeholders who can be impacted by the problem under study and its solution. An accurate definition of the problem is critical. Just as a faulty foundation dooms the construction of a house, a poorly documented problem definition will result in a model that cannot be solved or implemented.

A model is a symbolic representation of the real-world problem; hence the goal in the second step in the modeling process is to achieve a model formulation that is an accurate representation of the real-world problem under study. There will always be a tradeoff involving the accuracy of representing the real-world problem and the complexity of the model. A model can never capture every aspect of the real-world situation that it is attempting to describe. Negotiating the tradeoff between the accuracy of representation and the complexity of the model is always a challenge. Generally, you are not the first team to encounter the problem at hand. Valuable insight can be gained by examining how others have attempted to formulate models for this or similar problems.

Following the formulation step, a variety of methodologies exist for data collection. These methods include questionnaire instruments, computer-based simulations, or meta-analyses of studies in the open literature. Once a model solution has been achieved, key parameters of the model should be subjected to a sensitivity analysis. Sensitivity analysis involves varying key model parameters within reasonable ranges to observe their impact on the stability of the model solution. Sensitivity analysis clarifies the robustness of the model and addresses the ever-present "what if" questions that arise. Often, more information is gained from the sensitivity analysis of the model solution than from the model solution itself.

The last step in the model-building process is implementation. Once an appropriate model solution has been identified, it must be implemented. It is essential to present the model solution in a language that is understood by the stakeholders who have sponsored the research investigation at hand. Often, this audience generally does not possess formal modeling skills and experience. If a solution is deemed unacceptable, the modeling team must revisit the previous steps of problem definition, formulation and solution.

Organizational Strategy and Business Paradigms

Before examining the evolution, integration and implementation of models in supply chain management, we first review business paradigms and their influence on management strategy.

An effective business strategy is paramount for an organization to remain competitive. However, the formulation and adoption of a strategy alone does not guarantee success. The dynamic environment in which decisions are made is wrought with uncertainty and is driven by the interplay of global economic fluctuations, geopolitical instability and technological advancements. As a result, business paradigms that influence organizational strategy have also evolved. As defined by Kuhn (1962, p. 17), a paradigm consists of the fundamental ideas, methods, language, and theories that are accepted by the members of a scientific community. In the context of organizations, a business paradigm parallels the paradigm structure as defined by Kuhn. Organizations exist to meet a fundamental need (good or service) that exists in society. Methods of transformation are used to add value to raw material inputs to create finished goods and services valued by consumers. Marketing programs and information technologies define the language by which the producer and the consumer navigate business transactions.

Paradigm shifts, or "scientific revolutions" as noted by Kuhn, occur when the current paradigm can no longer explain social, political and technological factors in the environment that are impacting the scientific field. This behavior is present in business paradigms. For example, the early 20th century administrative policy exposed by Henri Fayol sought to increase productivity and enhance decision-making using a top-down hierarchical organizational structure with siloed functional areas. Manufacturing, finance, marketing and personnel were managed separately and with limited communication and interaction between the functional areas. Information flowed rigidly from each functional area only to a sole high-level executive. This paradigm is in sharp contrast with the more modern management philosophy of W. Edwards Deming, which advocates the empowerment of employees and lean and agile organizational structures characterized by high levels of interconnectivity and collaboration between functional areas.

Over the past seven decades, the paradigms that drive the business strategy of companies in the United States have undergone changes. Table 1 summarizes the dominant paradigm in each decade and identifies its key operational characteristics. The timeframes are not clear cut but generalized/rounded for easy reference. Each paradigm is in the perspective of the business-customer interface (meeting customer needs) for strategic competitive advantage, where a customer is not necessarily the consumer. It is important to note that from a temporal perspective that each new paradigm did not simply replace its predecessor. From the lens of Kuhn's scientific revolution argument, environmental factors act as drivers shifting/advancing the current paradigm to a new paradigm. When examined using a PESTLE (Political, Economic, Sociological, Technological, Legal and Environmental) analysis, paradigms evolve through successive additions. For example, although AI is the dominant paradigm for 2020s, its use is built upon its predecessors as a foundation. A current use of AI is to manage online chats with website visitors. This is done to be more cost effective (not paying someone to cover the chat 24/7), improve quality/time/service (data-backed responses for better and faster customer service), customization of responses to customer chat questions, and obviously digital/online.

Table 1. Business strategy paradigms

Decade	Business Paradigm	Key Points
1960s	Cost	• Firms competed based on price through low-cost sourcing, shipping and production. • Purchasing decisions were dominated by large lot sizes and long delivery lead times. • One noteworthy firm that adopted this paradigm was Walmart.
1970s	Quality	• Embracing the Total Quality Management philosophy, Statistical Process Control and Kaizen reduced production and inventory costs, improved customer satisfaction and increased market share. • Quality improvement became an integrated priority throughout the organization rather than just a stand-alone department. • Toyota stood out as a leading firm that embraced this paradigm to increase market share with low-cost, quality vehicles.
1980s	Customization	• Modular design principles allowed personalized products to be manufactured with short production lead times. • Increased production costs were offset by premium pricing through strategic marketing. • Ferrari exemplified this paradigm by producing custom-configured vehicles.
1990s	Time	• Lead times were reduced by increasing efficiency. • Lean production methods were used to identify and reduce waste throughout the supply chain. • General Electric adopted Lean practices by prioritizing employee training to reduce cycle times.
2000s	Service	• Meeting customer expectations was prioritized through responsive order and return policies. • Apple's personalized customer support illustrated an emphasis on service.
2010s	Digital	• Customers favored digital channels—including websites, apps, and social media—for engaging with businesses. • Small businesses found a limited online presence through free social media platforms to remain competitive. • Airbnb rose to prominence through its strong digital presence.
2020s	Artificial Intelligence (AI)	• AI was implemented to enhance the efficiency and personalization of customer engagement through streamlined searches, website chats, and influencer interactions. • As an evolving technology, future application is open-ended. • Amazon implemented AI to enhance user decision-making through predictive recommendations.

As a result of the dynamic and changing nature of business paradigms, the characteristics of decision models and how the models are applied has been evolutionary. Achieving organizational goals is significantly impacted by the capability of executives to appropriately pair the type of decision being made and the available decision-making techniques. In his study of how executives make decisions, Simon (1977, p. 48) defined a framework that examined the type of decision to be made (programmed versus nonprogrammed) and the decision-making techniques employed (traditional versus modern). Within this framework, mathematical modeling (a modern decision-making technique) was identified as best fitting when routine, repetitive (programmed) decisions were to be made in support of established organization processes.

The Supply Chain Management Philosophy

In this section we present an overview of the foundational principles and historical development of the supply chain management philosophy. This preliminary background on the supply chain management philosophy is integral in demonstrating the evolutionary nature of supply chain models.

Supply chain management (SCM) is the process of planning, executing, and controlling all activities involved in procuring raw materials, manufacturing goods, and delivering finished products to customers (Mentzer, DeWitt, Keebler, Min, Nix, Smith, & Zacharia; 2001). Supply chain management is recognized as a key to gaining and maintaining competitive advantage and serves as a unifying and cohesive mechanism for integrating the formerly siloed business disciplines of marketing, finance, human resources management and operations (Min & Zhou, 2002).

The etymology of the phrase "supply chain" provides precedent to the historical evolution of supply chain management. An Internet search indicates that the earliest, and most likely first, documented use of the phrase supply chain occurred in a January 5, 1905, newspaper article, *The Year at Home and Abroad*, published in *The Independent* (p. 7), describing British military actions in India, where it was "challenging keeping the supply chain to India unbroken". As research on inventory management and the flow of materials in production systems advanced, researchers began to model the interconnectivity between the production, inventory, and logistics subsystems in organizations thus giving rise to the concept of multi-echelon systems. As demonstrated in the work of Gross (1962), Howard (1967) and Sherbrooke (1971), multi-echelon models became known as 'supply systems' which is the root phraseology for supply chain. The first use of the phrase supply chain in the title of an academic research paper appeared in the work on ordering rules for multi-echelon supply chains by Burns (1970).

The historical evolution of the supply chain management philosophy is rooted in the theory of marketing. In the 1940s, Harvard University professor of marketing and advertising Neil Borden introduced the phrase "marketing mix" into his teaching and research. Borden credited his inspiration for the term from his reading of a research bulletin on marketing costs written by his colleague James Culliton (Borden, 1964, p.7). Based on Culliton (1948), Borden conceptualized a list of 12 elements, which when under a program of control and management by marketing executives, would result in a profitable business operation. Building on Borden's 12 key marketing elements, McCarthy (1960) proposed a reduced marketing mix consisting of four elements which he defined as the 4 P's (Product, Price, Promotion and Place). Today the 4 P marketing mix is universally recognized by practitioners and academics as foundational for developing a comprehensive marketing strategy.

As the business environment matured, the marketing mix element of Place became known as Distribution with the formal study of Distribution becoming Logistics. Firms developed a formal and separate logistics function within their organizational structure. A sub function within logistics was purchasing. About 55% of the total value of product shipments is related to sourcing decisions. The traditional approach to purchasing was to play suppliers off against each other based on cost to obtain the lowest unit cost of raw material, a tactic that led to poor performance (especially with respect to quality). Cost-based purchasing in the early 1980s evolved into strategic purchasing where the emphasis is on partnering with suppliers and investing in supplier development. Strategic purchasing overcame the limitations of cost-based purchasing and eventually led to the more general field of supply chain management. In the 1980s, the concept of supply chain management began to widely appear in the business literature (Oliver & Webber, 2012). The widespread appeal of the customer-centric orientation of the supply chain management philosophy has led to mainstream adoption of the philosophy in both the manufacturing and service sectors.

SUPPLY CHAIN MODELS

The fields of operations research and management science were essential to establishing the foundation of supply chain modeling. Many of the supply chain models used today are directly built upon fundamental mathematical modeling techniques contributed by researchers in operations research and management science. At the onset of World War II, a collaborative coalition of researchers from the fields of mathematics, economics and statistics was assembled and tasked with solving the logistical challenges associated with moving materials and equipment in support of the war effort. The disciplines of operations research and management science emerged from the efforts of these researchers in their development of new mathematical and the enhancement of existing mathematical techniques and methodologies used in solving military logistical problems. The groundbreaking application of these mathematical techniques in military logistics paved the way for their expansion and integration into production management and ultimately into models applicable to supply chain management.

In this section, our focus is to explore the trajectory of supply chain management models, from their development and integration to their practical application. A Google Scholar search of the phrase 'supply chain model' results in over 5.5 million hits. Given this volume of research, a comprehensive treatment of all forms of supply chain models is not feasible within this narrative. Instead, it will highlight key contributions from the scientific community that have established the modeling foundation and driven the advancement and evolution of supply chain models.

To provide a foundational understanding of the various types of models used in supply chain management, this narrative highlights three key areas: performance measurement, collaboration and coordination, and sustainability. These areas were chosen based on their significance, as highlighted in the study *Supply Chain Management 2010 and Beyond* (Melnyk, Lummus, Vokurka, & Sandor, 2007). For each functional area, a dedicated table identifies key literature reviews and applicable decision-making models. The presented literature and model contributions are not intended to be an exhaustive examination of the functional area but rather to provide readers with broad understanding of the scope of supply chain modeling within it.

Supply Chain Performance Measurement

The widely accepted principle, "if you can't measure it, you can't improve it" underscores the role of measurement for understanding and controlling any physical system. This principle is especially crucial for managing supply chains in today's global business environment, where responsiveness and adaptability to constant change are all-important for survival. A formal supply chain management performance measurement system is crucial for improving supply chain operations, as it establishes a baseline for measuring and evaluating the effectiveness and efficiency of all supply chain processes. Neely et al. (2000) define supply chain performance measurement as a balanced and dynamic system that enables support of the decision-making process by gathering, elaborating and analyzing information. As a systematic process, diverse performance measures are integrated to align with overall business strategy (balanced) and continuously evaluating progress internally while comparing performance relative to external competitors (dynamic). According to Neely et al. (2000), performance measurement should be measured according to a three-level hierarchy that consists of: (i) individual measures that are needed for each unique business process, (ii) as a set of systematic metrics housed within a framework which unites the set of metrics to short term, medium term and long term strategy, and (iii) the ability to measure across internal and external environments including customers as well as the competition. Performance metrics identify gaps between actual performance and expectations thus identifying areas for improvement. Metrics enable managers and workers to better manage the resources for which they are responsible and serve as a common language for chain members, helping to put 'everyone on the same page'. Performance measurement can provide important feedback to enable managers to monitor performance, track progress, and facilitate communication among supply chain members.

However, there are some limitations associated with performance measurement in supply chain management. Having metrics for the sake of metrics does not advance performance improvement and as such several authors have expressed concerns about supply chain performance measurement. Chan & Qi (2003) identify several concerns, most notable the lack of a balanced approach, failure to connect to strategy, and a lack of systems thinking which often encourages local optimization among chain members. Melnyk, Stewart, & Swink (2004) warn that too many metrics leads to a lack of focus and confusion. Supply chain performance metrics must be explicitly linked to the overarching corporate goals and must be directly traceable to the supply chain strategies that support corporate goals. The lack of a systemic approach to supply chain performance measurement is typically the root cause of all performance measurement limitations. Performance measurement requires a formal dedicated system, with resources to support the personnel and technology charged with managing the performance measurement system. Performance measurement cannot be treated as an afterthought meaning that top management only becomes concerned about performance measurement when there is an operational or financial downturn.

To address the shortcomings that can arise in evaluating performance, systematic frameworks for performance measurement have been developed. Financial measures such as return on assets, return on investment, earnings per share and others have been used as performance indicators for centuries and form the foundation of measuring business performance. In the 1980s activity-based costing (ABC) emerged in response to deficiencies in traditional accounting systems that allocated costs predominately based on volume. Under ABC, the relationship between costs, overhead activities, and manufactured products is recognized, and, through this relationship, ABC assigns indirect costs to products less arbitrarily than traditional methods that allocated costs predominately based on volume. In the 1990s the balanced score card (BSC) became popular and advocated using financial and non-financial measures to bring out composite measures of performance. The underlying concept of the BSC is that competitive advantage cannot be gained solely by a financial perspective involving the use of capital investment. Instead, the BSC evaluates corporate performance from four different perspectives: financial, internal business, customers and learning and growth. Each of these four perspectives of business operations are linked in a balanced scorecard where each perspective has defined goals and supporting measures. Linking these four key perspectives together creates a strategic performance measurement system that integrates financial measures of past performance with measures of drivers for future performance. By combination of financial and non-financial metrics, the BSC ensures a balanced focus on both short-term performance and long-term strategic objectives.

The Supply Chain Operations Reference (SCOR) model, developed in 1995 by the Supply Chain Council (supply-chain.org), provides a framework that links business processes, performance indicators, best practices and technologies in a unified structure that supports communication and transparency among partners in the supply chain. The SCOR model therefore helps to refine supply chain strategy and better manage value adding processes through integrated performance measurement. In contrast to the BSC, which is focused on executive enterprise-level measures, the SCOR model directly addresses the needs of supply chain management by measuring performance measurement at supply chain level and not at the organizational level (as in the BSC). This attribute enables quicker organizations to quickly determine and compare supply chain performance within their organization and against competitors. The SCOR model is based on six distinct management processes: Plan, Source, Make, Deliver, Return, and Enable. The SCOR model creates a foundation for continuous improvement of supply chain operations and facilitates the identification of supply chain processes where nonvalue adding activities can be improved/eliminated. The SCOR model contains more than 150 key performance indicators that measure the performance of supply chain operations. As a performance measurement system, the SCOR model leads to all members of the supply chain gaining a better understanding supply chain operation. This is essential for the clear identification of performance gaps and for streamlining reporting and for enhancing operational control to reduce nonvalue adding actions.

Central to the SCOR model are two key elements: performance attributes and performance metrics. SCOR identifies five core supply chain attributes: Reliability, Responsiveness, Agility, Costs and Assets. Within each attribute, a nested set of performance metrics that are defined over three levels exist. Level 1 metrics are at the most aggregated level and are typically used by top decision makers to measure the performance of the company's overall supply chain. Benchmarking Level 1 metrics helps establish realistic targets that support strategic objectives. Level 2 Metrics are primary, high-level measures that may cross the multiple SCOR processes of Plan, Source, Make, Deliver, Return, Enable. Level 3 metrics serve as diagnostics to the level 2 metrics. Level 2 metrics help to identify the root cause or causes of a performance gap for a Level 1 metric. The very act of implementing the SCOR model leads to a better understanding of how your supply chain adds value and is a foundation for continuous improvement. Table 2 provides a consolidated view of recent literature reviews concerning supply chain performance measurement and illustrative examples of diverse modeling approaches utilized in the research.

Table 2. Selected papers on supply chain performance measurement

Literature Reviews		
Author	**Theme of Review**	
Mishra, Gunasekaran, Papadopoulos & Dubey (2018)	Supply chain performance measures and metrics.	
Lima-Junior & Carpinetti (2017)	Quantitative models for evaluating supply chain performance.	
Gopal & Thakkar (2012)	Review of supply chain performance measurement systems.	
Arzu Akyuz & Erman Erkan (2010)	Review of methodologies, problem areas and requirements of performance measures in supply chains.	
Gunasekaran & Kobu (2007)	Key strategic, operational and tactical performance measures and metrics in supply chain and logistics operations.	
Models		
Authors	**Model Type**	**Area of Application**
Ahmed, Maoua, Ahmed & Ali (2025)	Bayesian Belief Network	Performance measurement in the humanitarian relief supply chain.
Bushuev (2018)	Expected Loss Function	Improving delivery performance subject to an on-time delivery window.
Sellitto, Pereira, Borchardt, Da Silva & Viegas (2015)	SCOR	Supply chain performance measurement in the footwear industry.
Caniato, Golini & Kalchschmidt (2013)	Factor Analysis	Impacts of investment and supply chain configuration on performance improvement.
De Brito, Carbone & Blanquart (2008)	Conceptual	Implementing sustainability in the retail fashion supply chain.
Morgan & Dewhurst (2008)	Statistical Process Control (SPC)	Measuring supplier performance in multi-retailer supply chains.
Bhagwat & Sharma (2007)	Analytical Hierarchy Process (AHP)	Formulation of performance measurement strategies.
Ellram, Tate & Billington (2004)	SCOR	Measuring performance services supply chains.
Chan & Qi (2003)	Fuzzy Set Theory	Cost efficiency, efficiency and reliability of supply chain performance.
Persson & Olhager (2002)	Computer Simulation	Performance measurement of alternative supply chain designs.

Supply Chain Collaboration and Coordination

From a systems viewpoint, a supply chain consists of a series of interconnected stages, commonly referred to as dyads. Each dyad is characterized by an interface where information and product flows between a downstream and an upstream chain member. As highlighted in Table 1, dyadic relationships during the 1960s era cost paradigm were governed by cost mechanisms that focused on material costs and were not based on collaboration and coordination. As a result, solely emphasizing cost led to misaligned production and delivery schedules, increased inventory levels and inefficiencies. Davis & Spekman (2004) refer to this era as the 'dark ages' where, for example, the relationship between manufacturers and suppliers was adversarial and dominated by the manufacturers' attempt to gain cost concessions and assert dominance over their suppliers. Buyers considered suppliers to be the enemy, and price was the main consideration for acquiring raw materials. Sole sourcing dominated, with secondary sourcing used only as a leveraging tool for negotiating prices and contract terms with the primary supplier. Davis & Spekman (2004) credit Chrysler's groundbreaking work in supplier relations as a catalyst for the U.S. automotive industry's supply chain shift from an adversarial and fragmented network with short-term outcome goals to a more integrated supply chain emphasizing long-term supplier partnerships, collaboration and shared success. Collaboration throughout the supply chain cultivates a unified approach among chain members, resulting in greater efficiency and agility. This synergy will benefit each participating member, fostering a stronger competitive standing in the marketplace.

Several industry-based studies have documented the positive effect of collaboration on supply chain operations. In a recent survey of over 160 supply chain professionals, collaboration emerged as a top ten trend in SCM and was identified as the trend experiencing the most significant increase in importance (Stank et al., 2015). The study also reported that result collaboration led to increases in stock fill rates and inventory turnover, reductions in lead times and improved forecast accuracy. Kumar & Banerjee (2014) surveyed 77 supply chain managers to investigate the level of importance placed on the following set of six collaboration activities: culture, internal joint planning, external joint planning, resource sharing, information sharing and problem solving. The degree of synchronization of material management, purchasing and budgeting (internal joint planning) received the highest importance rating, followed by sharing technology (resource sharing) and openness in communication and skills sharing (culture). Resolution of conflicts (problem solving), sharing point of sales information (information sharing) and joint focus on product promotion and pricing (external joint planning) received the lowest importance respectively. Kohli & Jensen (2010) surveyed 142 supply chain professionals and investigated five key dimensions of supply chain collaboration, including information sharing, joint planning, goal congruence, personal interactions and trust. The study concluded that extensively sharing information, joint planning, and using information systems collaboratively tend to increase the perceived value of collaboration. Lockamy and McCormack (2004) investigated the relationship between performance measurement and collaboration. Using the SCOR Model, a survey of 523 supply chain managers was conducted to assess the relationship between performance measurement and collaboration. The study concluded that collaborative activities have a positive and significant effect on the Plan and Source processes of the SCOR model. Simatupang

& Sridharan (2005) surveyed 76 firms and established two indices (collaboration and performance) to analyze the relationship between collaboration and performance. The collaboration index was based on information sharing, decision synchronization, and incentives; the performance index was based on fulfillment, inventory, and responsiveness. The study concluded that a significant correlation exists between collaboration and operational performance with positive impacts on fulfillment, inventory management and responsiveness.

As evident in the industry studies, collaboration plays a pivotal role in delivering higher levels of customer satisfaction and optimizing chain-wide performance. However, there are concerns and barriers to its implementation that occur, and these barriers often present a major leadership challenge. Nyaga, Whipple & Lynch (2010) raise the issue of whether the benefits of collaborative relationships between buyers and sellers justify the added expenditures associated with establishing such partnerships. In their study of the Vietnamese fishery supply chain, Nguyen, Thai, Chan, Lau, Nguyen & Do (2025) identify that antecedents such as management commitment, inter-organizational and inter-personal trust, and reciprocity affect collaboration. For collaboration to overcome implementation barriers and permeate throughout the supply chain, a supporting foundation must be present. Collaboration requires support from several perspectives, such as a process orientation, trust and supporting technology. Fawcett, Fawcett, Watson, & Magnan (2012) introduced the 'black box perspective' by which supply chain collaboration enables firms to combat competitive forces by creating greater customer value at lower costs. Fawcett et al. (2012) identify three streams of literature as central to understanding the process through which a collaborative dynamic capability is built: (i) systems design, (ii) competency development, and (iii) change management. For successful collaboration, the authors note that it is essential for organizations to simultaneously address both their organizational structure and culture to eliminate fear and encourage collaborative risk-taking. Cooperatively integrating the distinct expertise and value-added contributions of individual chain members is essential for sparking innovation and maintaining long-term profitability. Cordon, Hald & Seifert (2012) identify the following three mutually interacting components: (i) the perceived expected value that the attracted party will achieve from being associated with the other company, (ii) the perceived trust in the other company, and (iii) the perceived dependence on the other company. Cooperatively integrating the distinct expertise and value-added contributions of individual chain members is essential for sparking innovation and maintaining long term profitability. Once implemented, collaboration is a win/win arrangement that benefits both parties (McClellan, 2002). The importance of information technology to the development of collaboration between supply chain partners has been demonstrated through empirical and case studies (see for example, Rashid, Rasheed & Amirah, 2024; Li, 2012; Chae, Yen & Sheu, 2005). Today, real-time data sharing technologies have advanced beyond electronic data interchange (EDI) and enterprise resource planning (ERP) and now include artificial intelligence (AI), the internet of things (IoT), blockchain and cloud computing (Han & Fang, 2024; Weisz, Herold, Ostern, Payne & Kummer, 2024; Gammelgaard & Nowicka, 2024; Cui, Gao, Dai, & Mou, 2022).

Supply chain collaboration and coordination encompass incentive alignment, collaborative communication, decision synchronization, and information sharing. Supply chain collaboration and coordination have been widely studied from numerous perspectives across diverse industries. Table 3 details recent literature reviews on supply chain collaboration and coordination, and illustrative examples of the different modeling approaches used in these works.

Table 3. Selected papers on supply chain collaboration and coordination

<table>
<tr><th colspan="3">Literature Reviews</th></tr>
<tr><th>Author</th><th colspan="2">Theme of Review</th></tr>
<tr><td>Marty & Ruel (2024)</td><td colspan="2">The evolution of the types of supply collaboration (upstream, downstream, horizontal, global).</td></tr>
<tr><td>Wang, Long, Chen, Guo & Wang (2023)</td><td colspan="2">Collaborative decision-making among supply chain members.</td></tr>
<tr><td>Duong & Chong (2020)</td><td colspan="2">Supply chain collaboration in the presence of disruptions.</td></tr>
<tr><td>Ralston, Richey & Grawe (2017)</td><td colspan="2">Supply chain collaboration from a focal firm perspective.</td></tr>
<tr><td>Soosay & Hyland (2015)</td><td colspan="2">Underlying theory and key issues in supply chain collaboration.</td></tr>
<tr><th colspan="3">Models</th></tr>
<tr><th>Authors</th><th>Model Type</th><th>Area of Application</th></tr>
<tr><td>Alsheyadi, Baawain & Shaukat (2024)</td><td>Structural Equation Modeling (SEM)</td><td>SEM is used to test how coordination policies impact performance in the electronic supply chain.</td></tr>
<tr><td>Pérez-Perales, Boza, Alarcón & Gómez-Gasquet, (2024)</td><td>Mathematical Programming</td><td>Alternative scenarios for supply chain collaborative planning were evaluated using a mathematical programming methodology.</td></tr>
<tr><td>Xia, Li & He (2023)</td><td>Blockchain Technology</td><td>Blockchain technology is used to design a supply chain collaboration schema.</td></tr>
<tr><td>Baah, Acquah & Ofori (2022)</td><td>Partial Least Squares</td><td>A statistical model is used to study the influence of supply chain collaboration on supply chain visibility, stakeholder trust, and financial performance.</td></tr>
<tr><td>Kumar & Nath Banerjee (2014)</td><td>Structural Equation Modeling (SEM)</td><td>An index measure is developed to quantify and rate six dimensions of supply chain coordination.</td></tr>
<tr><td>Ramanathan (2014)</td><td>Computer Simulation</td><td>The study examined the role of continuous replenishment and collaborative planning forecasting and replenishment (CPFR) as antecedents to collaboration in supply chains.</td></tr>
</table>

continued on following page

Table 3. Continued

Literature Reviews		
Author	**Theme of Review**	
Papakiriakopoulos & Pramatari (2010)	Case Study	A case study methodology is used to design a collaborative performance measurement system.
Jaber, Osman & Guiffrida (2006)	Optimization	A decision model is developed for coordinating a three-level supply chain with price discounts, price dependent demand, and profit sharing.
Lee (2004)	Conceptual	Competitive advantage is gained by designing supply chains that are agile, adaptable, and aligned.
Simatupang, Wright & Sridharan (2004)	Theory of Constraints (TOC)	The TOC is used to identify barriers that limit the adoption of collaborative replenishment and performance metrics among supply chain members.

Sustainability

Businesses today are facing increasing scrutiny regarding their environmental impact. How they respond to this trend will influence their profitability and long-term survival. Pressures from customers, governmental legislation, and the public over carbon emissions, depletion of raw materials, air and water pollution, and energy consumption have led organizations to rethink how they design, coordinate, and manage their supply chains and to introduce sustainable business practices (Singh, 2025; Yildiz Çankaya & Sezen, 2019; Sarkis, 2003). In many organizations, green and sustainable business practices have evolved beyond mere compliance and are now becoming a core element of both daily supply chain operations and long-term strategy. By avoiding greenwashing and adopting genuine eco-friendly practices, a sustainable SCM orientation can bolster competitive advantage through increasing market share resulting from enhanced brand loyalty and product differentiation, higher employee morale, and safeguarding against negative public opinion.

Decisions on how to manage supply chain activities involving procurement, manufacturing, and distribution must simultaneously address the financial bottom line and environmental and societal concerns. Sustainability will challenge traditional and entrenched mindsets and cannot be viewed as just another new program or technology. The triple bottom line (Elkington, 1997), which advocates encompassing economic, environmental, and societal factors in business operations, is a useful starting point for initiating the sustainability conversation before taking steps towards implementation. Based on a survey of 94 operations and plant managers, Gavronski, Klassen, Vachon & do Nascimento (2011) identified the importance of investing in green process management (pollution prevention technologies, recycling of materials, waste reduction, workplace health and safety, and environmental management systems) at the plant level as a foundation for implementing green supply chain management. Senior management commitment, environmental investment, and knowledge sharing across the extended supply chain were also identified as crucial. Green product and process innovation have been empirically shown to be key antecedents of the success of the implementation of a sustainable SCM strategy (Chang, Kuo & Chen, 2013; Routroy, 2009).

For a sustainable SCM strategy to effectively green a supply chain, a comprehensive framework is essential to guide its planning, development, and execution. A practical framework, according to Brown, Bushuev, Kretinin & Guiffrida (2017), needs to encompass customer and legislative demands, synthesize various perspectives into corporate policy creation, and employ models to evaluate sustainability performance against established benchmarks. Decision models used in green and sustainable supply chain management range along a continuum from exploratory to conceptual to highly theoretical. The following three models illustrate this continuum. Peattie & Ratnayaka (1992) presented a three-phase model to guide companies that are under customer/legislative-driven pressures to become more sustainable. The model delineates driving forces, potential barriers to action, and strategies for being green. Noting the interdisciplinary nature of sustainability, Linton, Klassen & Jayaraman (2007) presented a model that illustrates the interrelationship between the natural and social sciences when developing sustainable supply chain operating policies. Deif (2011) applied systems theory modeling to illustrate how planning and control activities in the manufacturing phase of a supply chain evolve from a traditional manufacturing paradigm to a green and eco-friendly paradigm. Additional frameworks for integrating green and sustainable practices into supply chains can be found in Schaltegger & Burritt (2014), Carter & Rogers (2008), and Squire, Vachon & Klassen (2006). The transition to an environmentally based supply chain strategy under a given framework should not be static or myopic.

As a result of the adoption of green and sustainable practices, the SCM philosophy has further evolved to reflect these practices. Ahi & Searcy's (2013) comparative analysis of definitions for green and sustainable supply chain management (GSCM and SSCM) revealed that both terms are frequently used, with numerous variations existing for each: 22 distinct definitions for GSCM and 12 for SSCM were identified. This extensive review underscores the widespread adoption of these concepts within supply chain management and highlights the diverse interpretations and finer points contributed by each. The GSCM and SSCM definitions contributed by Srivastava (2007, p. 54) and Seuring & Müller (2008, p. 1700) are both highly cited in the literature (see Table 4). Both Srivastava (2007) and Seuring & Müller (2008) identify the need for an integrated approach for achieving sustainable supply chains. Both definitions advance a common theme of the importance of integrating environmental concerns in supply chain operations yet also contribute unique considerations. Srivastava (2007) emphasizes the importance of a close-loop supply chain, while Seuring & Müller (2008) emphasize aligning the supply chain with the triple-bottom line of economic, environmental, and social performance. Collectively, the GSCM and SSCM definitions have provided a conceptual foundation for the development of models for green and sustainable supply chains. Environmental and sustainability concerns impact how today's supply chains are managed and have led to changes in many areas of supply chain operations, including performance measurement, sourcing and reverse logistics.

Table 4. Definitions of green and sustainable supply chain management

Author	Definition
GSCM, Srivastava (2007)	The integration of environmental thinking into supply chain management, including product design, material sourcing and selection, manufacturing processes, delivery of the final product to the consumers, and end-of-life management of the product after the end of its useful life.
SSCM, Seuring & Müller (2008)	The management of material, information, and capital flows as well as cooperation among companies along the supply chain while taking goals from all three dimensions of sustainable development, i.e., economic, environmental and social, into account which are derived from customer and stakeholder requirements.

Sustainable Performance Measurement

Hervani, Helms & Sarkis, (2005) adopt a systems theory perspective for the design of a sustainable supply chain performance measurement framework. In the design of a performance measurement system, green supply chain management performance tools and metrics are the key system inputs with the triple bottom line financial, economic and societal results being the system output. According to the authors, external pressures (such as stakeholder demands and competitor actions) and internal factors (like the integration of the sustainable performance management system with existing systems and the organization's culture towards innovation and sustainability) will impact how a performance management system is implemented and utilized. A key takeaway from this study is the critical importance of integrating sustainability metrics into both the performance measurement system and ongoing operations, rather than focusing solely on the measurement itself.

The foundation of sustainable performance measurement is built upon well-defined performance metrics. In a review of 445 published studies on green and sustainable supply chains, Ahi & Searcy (2015) identified 2555 unique sustainability metrics. Metrics were predominantly quantitative (approximately 71%) and were directed at performance measurement in specific areas of interest (about 83%). From a triple bottom line perspective, environmental concerns dominated the metrics (56%), followed by economic (39%) and social (30%). Examining the top 10 themes found across the set of sustainability measures, quantitative sustainability metrics are most frequently reported. Given that sustainable supply chains are an extension of traditional supply chains, where traditionally quantitative performance measures are dominant, the reliance on quantitative measures of sustainability performance seems reasonable. Also, many of the quantitative aspects of a sustainable supply chain, such as greenhouse gas emission, waste and resource consumption, represent the easy-to-measure 'low-hanging fruit' of sustainable operations. In addition to Ahi & Searcy (2015), studies of sustainability metrics have been contributed by Subramanian & Gunasekaran (2015) and Tajbakhsh & Hassini (2015). The common feature of the three studies is that each study provides a breakdown of sustainability metrics along two dimensions. The first dimension, the triple bottom line, is common to all three studies. The second dimension varies according to the specific study, thus providing a wider landscape for examining the metrics by their form (quantitative, qualitative, absolute, relative), their area of application to supply chain functions (strategic planning, product design, procurement, manufacturing, distribution, information technology, human resource management) and actors in the supply chain to which they apply (supplier, manufacturer, distributor, retailer). The collective results of these three studies constitute a state-of-the-art compendium of sustainable supply chain performance metrics and offer valuable guidance for identifying relevant metrics across diverse business cases.

The balanced scorecard (BSC) and the SCOR models promote integration across business functions in a supply chain, and as such, both the BSC and the SCOR model represent suitable approaches for organizing performance measurement in sustainable supply chains. Butler, Henderson & Raiborn (2011) outlined three options for establishing a sustainable BSC. The options include adding a 5th sustainability perspective to the existing four BSC perspectives, including sustainability measures in the existing four BSC perspectives, and redesigning the BSC. The first option, adding a 5th sustainability perspective, may be perceived as 'just a sustainability add-on' and may not be perceived as a true attempt to integrate sustainability within the existing four BSC perspectives. The second option, including sustainability measures in the existing four BSC perspectives, would work well for companies that have already established a viable BSC performance measurement system. The third option, redesigning the BSC, could again be viewed as 'yet another new performance measurement system to digest', and if the traditional BSC was functioning successfully, it could potentially disrupt current performance measurement initiatives. Butler et al. (2011) recommend this second option and argue that revising the existing BSC to include sustainability measures within each of the four existing perspectives reinforces the integrative nature of the BSC and would introduce the least amount of confusion and change into the BSC. Applications for the sustainable BSC have been reported by in the pharmaceutical supply chain by Zingales & Hockerts (2003) and Epstein & Wisner (2001).

The Green SCOR model was developed as a comprehensive tool for integrated green supply chain management, enabling companies to effectively manage their environmental impacts, which ultimately leads to more efficient operations with a reduced ecological footprint (Cash & Wilkerson, 2003). As a framework, Green SCOR provides a platform for structuring and communicating environmental supply chain best practices chain-wide. For example, under the plan process best practices for making the supply chain more environmentally friendly include collaborating with partners on environmental issues, reducing fuel and energy consumption, and minimizing and reusing packaging materials. Green SCOR and encompasses: (i) environmental processes defined within the scope of supply chain operations, (ii) metrics for assessing and benchmarking the environmental footprint of the supply chain, and (iii) best practices for reducing the environmental footprint of the supply chain. Sustainability metrics measure performance for carbon emissions, air pollutants, liquid and solid waste generated, and the waste recycled. Performance measures are hierarchical and integrated across chain-wide activities. For example, the total carbon footprint for the supply chain, a level 1 performance measure, is decomposed at level 2 into each of the six SCOR processes. Examining the source process, level 3 metrics include supplier management (which measures carbon emission generated through the activities of material planning, procurement, and supplier qualification & negotiation) and material acquisition management, which measures carbon emissions due to incoming inspection, inventory storage, warehousing, order picking and packing. Ntabe, LeBel, Munson & Santa-Eulalia (2015) provide a comprehensive review of the application of the Green SCOR model.

Sustainable Sourcing

Materials management is a critical function for an integrated and efficient supply chain and refers to the coordination and control of activities involved in the procurement, movement and storage of materials through the supply chain. This involves sourcing the correct quantity of material at the best price and level of quality and facilitating its delivery to the designated location in the supply chain. Today, environmental concerns have led to sourcing decisions in material management to adopt sustainable practices. Sustainable sourcing can be defined as the pursuit of sustainable development objectives through the purchasing and supply process (Walker, Miemczyk, Johnsen & Spencer, 2012, p. 201). Sustainable sourcing encompasses the social, environmental and performance factors in a green supply chain. A myopic, short-term managerial view is that sustainable sourcing can reduce and/or mitigate supply chain cost and risk. A strategic, long-term view is that sustainable sourcing can foster value creation for the supply chain by reducing cost and risk while also gaining entry to new suppliers and strengthening relationships with existing suppliers. For example, marketing in collaboration with production can modify product designs to make the design simpler with less aggregate raw material usage and to include more eco-friendly raw materials. In addition to reducing procurement costs, simpler eco-friendly product design generates less scrap and waste during production and offers weight economies during transport.

Empirical studies have addressed the views of executives on sustainable sourcing. In a study of 437 purchasing executives, Carter & Carter (1998) examined how inter-organizational factors influence purchasing involvement in environmental activities. The findings suggest that environmental purchasing activities will be facilitated through increased coordination with suppliers as well as downstream retailer members of the supply chain. The results further suggest the need for increased coordination within the firm between marketing and distribution functions. In a survey of 383 purchasing executives, Luzzini, Brandon-Jones, Brandon-Jones & Spina (2015) examined the impact of commitment to sustainability on the development of intra-firm and inter-firm collaborative capabilities within the purchasing function, and how these capabilities impact environmental performance and procurement costs. The study concluded that commitment to sustainability leads to a strong positive relationship between inter-firm collaborative activities and environmental and cost performance. A successful, sustainable sourcing policy relies heavily on supplier evaluation and supplier development. A conceptual framework for green supplier selection and a supporting meta-analysis on criteria important in green supplier selection and evaluation are found in Konys (2019). Blome, Hollos & Paulraj (2014) found that top management commitment is found to be an important driver of both green procurement and green supplier development and that the relationship between green procurement and supplier performance is fully mediated by green supplier development.

Reverse Logistics

Sustainable supply chain management extends beyond solely focusing on the forward movement of the product to the end customer. Sustainable supply chain management incorporates reverse logistics, creating a backward flow of products for returns and material recovery. The reason why goods flow through the reverse logistics channel is varied, and can be the result of a product recall, a product return, warranty issues, or end-of-life disposal, refurbishing or material recovery. Coordination of reverse logistics is achieved through closed-loop supply and reverse supply chain designs. A closed-loop supply chain facilitates the reverse flow of products and materials back into the initial supply chain for reuse, remanufacturing, or recycling, aiming for a circular economy, while a reverse supply chain focuses on the management of products after their initial use, typically involving collection, transportation, and processing of returned goods for various purposes like returns, repair, or recycling, often driven by customer needs or disposal concerns (Lozano-Oviedo, Cortés & Rey, 2024; Govindan & Soleimani, 2017; Prahinski & Kocabasoglu, 2006).

Beyond its environmental benefits, reverse logistics offers many significant opportunities to supply chains. As profit margins shrink, product lifecycle shorten and environmental concerns increase, businesses cannot overlook the potential to reduce cost and generate revenue through the management of product returns in reverse logistics. In additional to revenue capabilities, reverse logistics best practices also generate societal and stakeholder value, augment and improve customer service and loyalty, and increase market share (Rouhani, Wardley & Amin, 2025; Wilson & Goffnett, 2022; Dowlatshahi, 2010). When viewed from a triple bottom line framework, reverse logistics contributes to the economic, environmental and social initiatives mapped out by the triple bottom line. From the economic perspective, product value can be reclaimed. Environmental concerns are advanced through less disposal in landfills and savings of raw materials when reclaimed parts and materials are used to produce new products. Society benefits because of the greater control over hazardous materials that were often released in the destruction of returned products as well as their placement in landfills.

With the growth of sustainability initiatives, more companies have adopted the use of recycled materials for their reverse logistics channel in production and have developed procedures for the responsible disposal of products that cannot be recycled or reused. The reverse logistics process starts with the collection and sorting of products after the customer has completed their use of a product. The four R's of sustainability, resell, recondition, remanufacture, and recycling, define a set of alternatives for the disposition of a collected product. Reselling involves offering a product for sale again in the primary or secondary market with minimal changes to its packaging and no changes to the product itself. Reconditioning involves refurbishing a product and returning it for sale in a 'like new' state. Remanufacture is more extensive than reconditioning and typically involves disassembly of the used product and replacement of some of its component parts. Under recycling, the product is broken down into its basic elements, which are then resold and/or reused to make new or similar products. Disposal in a landfill becomes necessary only when all other waste reduction and resource recovery methods have been fully utilized. At the industry level, the U. S. automobile industry is actively embracing reverse logistics through its *design for disassembly* initiative, where the focus is on reengineering designs to reduce the number of parts and simplify assembly by replacing metal fasteners with snap-fitting components. At the firm level, Chesebrough-Pond's USA product return policy has been revamped to no longer simply discard or destroy products but to explore opportunities to put products back into active inventory or resold on the secondary market. By using a decision model to determine if products returned under warranty claims should be reconditioned or scrapped, Black & Decker streamlined its reverse logistics process, leading to increased revenues because of decreased landfill costs. Third-party groups are often utilized to manage reverse logistics operations in sustainable supply chains. Meade & Sarkis (2002) provide a conceptual model for selecting and evaluating third-party reverse logistics providers.

Comprehensive reviews of models used in sustainable supply chain management have been contributed by Mujkic, Qorri & Kraslawski (2018), Brandenburg & Rebs (2015), Brandenburg, Govindan, Sarkis & Seuring (2014), Seuring (2013), Dekker, Bloemhof & Mallidis (2012) and Todorov & Marinova (2011). The scope of methodologies identified in these modeling review papers ranges from conceptual (pictorial, graphical representation) to highly quantitative (mathematical programming, computer simulation, multicriteria decision models). In Table 5, literature reviews of green and sustainable supply chains are summarized. Illustrative examples of the types of models used within this domain are also provided.

Table 5. Selected papers on sustainable supply chains

Literature Reviews	
Author	**Theme of Review**
Koberg & Longoni (2019)	Review of sustainability in global supply chains.
Rajeev, Pati, Padhi & Govindan (2017)	The evolution of sustainability in supply chain management.
Golicic & Smith (2013)	A meta-analysis of environmentally sustainable supply chain management practices and firm performance.
Hassini, Surti & Searcy (2012)	Metrics for sustainable supply chains.
Ambec & Lanoie (2008)	Benefits from environmental performance and the relationship between environmental and economic performance.

Models		
Authors	**Model Type**	**Area of Application**
Pasupuleti, Thuraka, Kodete & Malisetty (2024)	Machine Learning	Machine learning algorithms are used to improve performance in agility and sustainability in the retail supply chain.
Bian, Zhang & Zhou (2020)	Game Theory	A game-theoretic framework is employed to assess the influence of environmental subsidies on the incentives for adopting emission-reducing technologies.
Malesios, Dey & Abdelaziz (2020)	Structural Equation Modeling (SEM)	An empirical method is presented for measuring sustainable supply chain performance for small to medium-sized enterprises.

continued on following page

Table 5. Continued

Literature Reviews		
Author	**Theme of Review**	
Kirchoff, Omar & Fugate (2016)	Empirical	Inductive research methods are used to study the decision-making process for adopting and implementing sustainable supply chain management policies.
Golroudbary & Zahraee (2015)	Computer Simulation	A systems dynamics model is developed for optimizing the recycling and collection of waste material in a closed-loop supply chain.
Dubey, Gunasekaran & Ali (2015).	Hierarchical Regression Analysis	A framework is developed for the implementation of green supply chain management in the rubber industry.
Kannan, Jabbour & Jabbour (2014)	Fuzzy TOPSIS	A multi-criteria decision-making model is used for selecting green suppliers for a Brazilian electronics company.
Chaabane, Ramudhin & Paquet (2012)	Mathematical Programing	Mathematical programming is applied to optimize the design of sustainable supply chains under carbon emission trading schemes.
Gopalakrishnan, Yusuf, Musa, Abubakar & Ambursa (2012)	Case Study	This case study at British Aerospace (BAe) Systems investigated the interconnectedness of economic, environmental, and social factors in sustainable supply chain management.
Dou & Sarkis (2010)	Analytical Network Process (ANP)	A multi-criteria model is constructed to evaluate and select alternative offshoring alternatives based on facility location factors, supplier selection metrics, and sustainability factors.

CONCLUSION

A foundational understanding of modeling from a philosophical perspective, alongside a review of the model-building process, is presented in this chapter. The temporal advancement of business paradigms summarized in Table 1 illustrates the evolution of traditional supply chains into today's digitalized and customer-centric supply chains. Supply chain models have advanced in tandem with these business paradigm shifts, driven by core concepts like risk mitigation, enhanced customer responsiveness, and improved flexibility and efficiency. Key theories such as leanness and agility, transaction cost economics, and stakeholder theory have guided model development. Recent empirical research, including studies by Dhaigude, Chatterjee, & Kamath (2025), Renolds (2024) and Wong, Sancha & Thomsen (2017) highlights the importance of cultural and regional differences on supply chain performance measurement, collaboration, and sustainability. This empirical work can be complemented by future research focusing on new supply chain model development.

The integration of modern technologies like blockchain, machine learning, and AI will equip future models to assist decision-makers in navigating the increasing complexities of tomorrow's supply chains.

REFERENCES

Ahi, P., & Searcy, C. (2013). A comparative literature analysis of definitions for green and sustainable supply chain management. *Journal of Cleaner Production*, *52*, 329–341. DOI: 10.1016/j.jclepro.2013.02.018

Ahi, P., & Searcy, C. (2015). An analysis of metrics used to measure performance in green and sustainable supply chains. *Journal of Cleaner Production*, *86*, 360–377. DOI: 10.1016/j.jclepro.2014.08.005

Ahmed, H. N., Maoua, Z., Ahmed, S., & Ali, S. M. (2025). Humanitarian relief supply chain performance measurement: A Framework and Validation. *Journal of Industrial Information Integration*, *47*, 100898. DOI: 10.1016/j.jii.2025.100898

Alsheyadi, A., Baawain, A., & Shaukat, M. R. (2024). E-supply chain coordination and performance impacts: An empirical investigation. *Production & Manufacturing Research*, *12*(1), 1–32. DOI: 10.1080/21693277.2024.2379942

Ambec, S., & Lanoie, P. (2008). Does it pay to be green? A systematic overview. *The Academy of Management Perspectives*, *22*(4), 45–62. DOI: 10.5465/amp.2008.35590353

Arzu Akyuz, G., & Erman Erkan, T. (2010). Supply chain performance measurement: A literature review. *International Journal of Production Research*, *48*(17), 5137–5155. DOI: 10.1080/00207540903089536

Baah, C., Acquah, I. S. K., & Ofori, D. (2022). Exploring the influence of supply chain collaboration on supply chain visibility, stakeholder trust, environmental and financial performances: A partial least square approach. *Benchmarking*, *29*(1), 172–193. DOI: 10.1108/BIJ-10-2020-0519

Bailer-Jones, D. M. (2002). Scientists' thoughts on scientific models. *Perspectives on Science*, *10*(3), 275–301. DOI: 10.1162/106361402321899069

Bhagwat, R., & Sharma, M. K. (2007). Performance measurement of supply chain management using the analytical hierarchy process. *Production Planning and Control*, *18*(8), 666–680. DOI: 10.1080/09537280701614407

Blome, C., Hollos, D., & Paulraj, A. (2014). Green procurement and green supplier development: Antecedents and effects on supplier performance. *International Journal of Production Research*, *52*(1), 32–49. DOI: 10.1080/00207543.2013.825748

Boon, M. (2024). Interdisciplinarity through modelling. In Knuuttila, T., Carrillo, N., & Koskinen, R. (Eds.), *The Routledge Handbook of Philosophy of Scientific Modeling* (pp. 395–411). Routledge. DOI: 10.4324/9781003205647-34

Borden, N. H. (1964). The concept of the marketing mix. *Journal of Advertising Research, 4*(June), 2–7. DOI: 10.1080/00218499.1964.12519724

Brandenburg, M., Govindan, K., Sarkis, J., & Seuring, S. (2014). Quantitative models for sustainable supply chain management: Developments and directions. *European Journal of Operational Research, 233*(2), 299–312. DOI: 10.1016/j.ejor.2013.09.032

Brandenburg, M., & Rebs, T. (2015). Sustainable supply chain management: A modeling perspective. *Annals of Operations Research, 229*(1), 213–252. DOI: 10.1007/s10479-015-1853-1

Brown, J. R., Bushuev, M. A., Kretinin, A. A., & Guiffrida, A. L. (2017). Recent developments in green supply chain management: Sourcing and logistics. In Khan, M., Hussain, M., & Ajmal, M. (Eds.), *Green Supply Chain Management for Sustainable Business Practice* (pp. 191–217). IGI Global. DOI: 10.4018/978-1-5225-0635-5.ch007

Burns, J. F., " Derivation and Simulation of an Ordering Rule for the Multi-Echelon Supply Chain," University of Florida, Department of Industrial and Systems Engineering, Technical Rept. No. 45, Gainesville, Florida (1970).

Bushuev, M. A. (2018). Delivery performance improvement in two-stage supply chain. *International Journal of Production Economics, 195*, 66–73. DOI: 10.1016/j.ijpe.2017.10.007

Butler, J. B., Henderson, S. C., & Raiborn, C. (2011). Sustainability and the balanced scorecard: Integrating green measures into business reporting. *Management Accounting Quarterly, 12*(2), 1–10.

Caniato, F., Golini, R., & Kalchschmidt, M. (2013). The effect of global supply chain configuration on the relationship between supply chain improvement programs and performance. *International Journal of Production Economics, 143*(2), 285–293. DOI: 10.1016/j.ijpe.2012.05.019

Carter, C. R., & Carter, J. R. (1998). Interorganizational determinants of environmental purchasing: Initial evidence from the consumer products industries. *Decision Sciences, 29*(3), 659–684. DOI: 10.1111/j.1540-5915.1998.tb01358.x

Carter, C. R., & Rogers, D. S. (2008). A framework of sustainable supply chain management: Moving toward new theory. *International Journal of Physical Distribution & Logistics Management, 38*(5), 360–387. DOI: 10.1108/09600030810882816

Cash, R., & Wilkerson, T. (2003). GreenSCOR: Developing a green supply chain analytical tool. *Logistics Management Institute*, 1-34.

Chaabane, A., Ramudhin, A., & Paquet, M. (2012). Design of sustainable supply chains under the emission trading scheme. *International Journal of Production Economics, 135*(1), 37–49. DOI: 10.1016/j.ijpe.2010.10.025

Chae, B., Yen, H. R., & Sheu, C. (2005). Information technology and supply chain collaboration: Moderating effects of existing relationships between partners. *IEEE Transactions on Engineering Management, 52*(4), 440–448. DOI: 10.1109/TEM.2005.856570

Chan, F. T., & Qi, H. J. (2003). An innovative performance measurement method for supply chain management. *Supply Chain Management, 8*(3), 209–223. DOI: 10.1108/13598540310484618

Chang, D. S., Kuo, L. C. R., & Chen, Y. T. (2013). Industrial changes in corporate sustainability performance–an empirical overview using data envelopment analysis. *Journal of Cleaner Production, 56*, 147–155. DOI: 10.1016/j.jclepro.2011.09.015

Cordon, C., Hald, K. S., & Seifert, R. W. (2012). *Strategic Supply Chain Management*. Routledge, Taylor and Francis Group, New York & London.

Cui, L., Gao, M., Dai, J., & Mou, J. (2022). Improving supply chain collaboration through operational excellence approaches: An IoT perspective. *Industrial Management & Data Systems, 122*(3), 565–591. DOI: 10.1108/IMDS-01-2020-0016

Culliton, J. W. (1948). *The Management of Marketing Costs*. Division of Research, Graduate School of Business Administration, Harvard University.

Davis, E. W., & Spekman, R. E. (2004). *The Extended Enterprise: Gaining Competitive Advantage Through Collaborative Supply Chains*, Financial Times Press, Prentice Hall, Upper Saddle, New Jersey.

De Brito, M. P., Carbone, V., & Blanquart, C. M. (2008). Towards a sustainable fashion retail supply chain in Europe: Organisation and performance. *International Journal of Production Economics, 114*(2), 534–553. DOI: 10.1016/j.ijpe.2007.06.012

Deif, A. M. (2011). A system model for green manufacturing. *Journal of Cleaner Production, 19*(14), 1553–1559. DOI: 10.1016/j.jclepro.2011.05.022

Dekker, R., Bloemhof, J., & Mallidis, J. (2012). Operations research for green logistics: An overview of aspects, issues, contributions and challenges. *European Journal of Operational Research, 219*(3), 671–679. DOI: 10.1016/j.ejor.2011.11.010

Dhaigude, A. S., Chatterjee, D., & Kamath, G. B. (2025). Supply chain integration and culture under globalization: A systematic review and global research agenda. *Research in Globalization*, *11*, 100293. DOI: 10.1016/j.resglo.2025.100293

Dou, Y., & Sarkis, J. (2010). A joint location and outsourcing sustainability analysis for a strategic offshoring decision. *International Journal of Production Research*, *48*(2), 567–592. DOI: 10.1080/00207540903175145

Dowlatshahi, S. H. A. D. (2010). A cost-benefit analysis for the design and implementation of reverse logistics systems: Case studies approach. *International Journal of Production Research*, *48*(5), 1361–1380. DOI: 10.1080/00207540802552642

Dubey, R., Gunasekaran, A., & Ali, S. S. (2015). Exploring the relationship between leadership, operational practices, institutional pressures and environmental performance: A framework for green supply chain. *International Journal of Production Economics*, *160*, 120–132. DOI: 10.1016/j.ijpe.2014.10.001

Duong, L. N. K., & Chong, J. (2020). Supply chain collaboration in the presence of disruptions: A literature review. *International Journal of Production Research*, *58*(11), 3488–3507. DOI: 10.1080/00207543.2020.1712491

Edmonds, B. (2017). Different modelling purposes. In Edmonds, B., & Meyer, R. (Eds.), *Simulating Social Complexity: A Handbook* (pp. 39–58). Springer. DOI: 10.1007/978-3-319-66948-9_4

Elkington, J. (1997). The triple bottom line. In Russo, M. V. (Ed.), *Environmental Management: Readings and Cases* (2nd ed., pp. 49–66). Sage Publications.

Ellram, L. M., Tate, W. L., & Billington, C. (2004). Understanding and managing the services supply chain. *The Journal of Supply Chain Management*, *40*(3), 17–32. DOI: 10.1111/j.1745-493X.2004.tb00176.x

Epstein, M. J., & Wisner, P. (2001). Good neighbors: Implementing social and environmental strategies with the BSC. *Balanced Scorecard Report*, *3*(3), 8–11.

Fawcett, S. E., Fawcett, A. M., Watson, B. J., & Magnan, G. M. (2012). Peeking inside the black box: Toward an understanding of supply chain collaboration dynamics. *The Journal of Supply Chain Management*, *48*(1), 44–72. DOI: 10.1111/j.1745-493X.2011.03241.x

Frigg, R., & Hartmann, S. (Summer 2025 Edition). Models in Science, The Stanford Encyclopedia of Philosophy, Zalta, E. N & Nodelman, U. (eds.), forthcoming URL = <https://plato.stanford.edu/archives/sum2025/entries/models-science/>

Gammelgaard, B., & Nowicka, K. (2024). Next generation supply chain management: The impact of cloud computing. *Journal of Enterprise Information Management, 37*(4), 1140–1160. DOI: 10.1108/JEIM-09-2022-0317

Gavronski, I., Klassen, R. D., Vachon, S., & do Nascimento, L. F. M. (2011). A resource-based view of green supply management. *Transportation Research Part E, Logistics and Transportation Review, 47*(6), 872–885. DOI: 10.1016/j.tre.2011.05.018

Golicic, S. L., & Smith, C. D. (2013). A meta-analysis of environmentally sustainable supply chain management practices and firm performance. *The Journal of Supply Chain Management, 49*(2), 78–95. DOI: 10.1111/jscm.12006

Golroudbary, S. R., & Zahraee, S. M. (2015). System dynamics model for optimizing the recycling and collection of waste material in a closed-loop supply chain. *Simulation Modelling Practice and Theory, 53*, 88–102. DOI: 10.1016/j.simpat.2015.02.001

Gopal, P. R. C., & Thakkar, J. (2012). A review on supply chain performance measures and metrics: 2000-2011. *International Journal of Productivity and Performance Management, 61*(5), 518–547. DOI: 10.1108/17410401211232957

Gopalakrishnan, K., Yusuf, Y. Y., Musa, A., Abubakar, T., & Ambursa, H. M. (2012). Sustainable supply chain management: A case study of British Aerospace (BAe) Systems. *International Journal of Production Economics, 140*(1), 193–203. DOI: 10.1016/j.ijpe.2012.01.003

Govindan, K., & Soleimani, H. (2017). A review of reverse logistics and closed-loop supply chains: A Journal of Cleaner Production focus. *Journal of Cleaner Production, 142*, 371–384. DOI: 10.1016/j.jclepro.2016.03.126

Gross, D. (1962). *An Investigation of Centralized Inventory Control in Multi-location Supply Systems*. Dissertation, Cornell University, Ithaca, New York.

Gunasekaran, A., & Kobu, B. (2007). Performance measures and metrics in logistics and supply chain management: A review of recent literature (1995–2004) for research and applications. *International Journal of Production Research, 45*(12), 2819–2840. DOI: 10.1080/00207540600806513

Han, Y., & Fang, X. (2024). Systematic review of adopting blockchain in supply chain management: Bibliometric analysis and theme discussion. *International Journal of Production Research, 62*(3), 991–1016. DOI: 10.1080/00207543.2023.2236241

Hassini, E., Surti, C., & Searcy, C. (2012). A literature review and a case study of sustainable supply chains with a focus on metrics. *International Journal of Production Economics, 140*(1), 69–82. DOI: 10.1016/j.ijpe.2012.01.042

Hervani, A. A., Helms, M. M., & Sarkis, J. (2005). Performance measurement for green supply chain management. *Benchmarking, 12*(4), 330–353. DOI: 10.1108/14635770510609015

Howard, W. J. (1967). A Multi-Echelon Markov Model for Relating Supply System Performance to Fleet Readiness. TEMPO-General Electric Company, 67TMP-123.

Hughes, R. I. G. (1997). Models and representation. *Philosophy of Science, 64*(S4), 325–336. DOI: 10.1086/392611

Jaber, M. Y., Osman, I. H., & Guiffrida, A. L. (2006). Coordinating a three-level supply chain with price discounts, price dependent demand, and profit sharing. *International Journal of Integrated Supply Management, 2*(1-2), 28–48. DOI: 10.1504/IJISM.2006.008337

Kannan, D., Jabbour, A. B. L. D. S., & Jabbour, C. J. C. (2014). Selecting green suppliers based on GSCM practices: Using fuzzy TOPSIS applied to a Brazilian electronics company. *European Journal of Operational Research, 233*(2), 432–447. DOI: 10.1016/j.ejor.2013.07.023

Kirchoff, J. F., Omar, A., & Fugate, B. S. (2016). A behavioral theory of sustainable supply chain management decision making in non-exemplar firms. *The Journal of Supply Chain Management, 52*(1), 41–65. DOI: 10.1111/jscm.12098

Koberg, E., & Longoni, A. (2019). A systematic review of sustainable supply chain management in global supply chains. *Journal of Cleaner Production, 207*, 1084–1098. DOI: 10.1016/j.jclepro.2018.10.033

Kohli, A. S., & Jensen, J. B. (2010). Assessing effectiveness of supply chain collaboration: an empirical study. *Supply Chain Forum: An International Journal,* 11(2), 2-16.

Konys, A. (2019). Green supplier selection criteria: From a literature review to a comprehensive knowledge base. *Sustainability (Basel), 11*(15), 4208. DOI: 10.3390/su11154208

Kuhn, T. S. (1962). *The Structure of Scientific Revolutions*. University of Chicago Press.

Kumar, G., & Nath Banerjee, R. (2014). Supply chain collaboration index: An instrument to measure the depth of collaboration. *Benchmarking, 21*(2), 184–204. DOI: 10.1108/BIJ-02-2012-0008

Lee, H. L. (2004). The triple-A supply chain. *Harvard Business Review, 82*(10), 102–113.

Li, L. (2012). Effects of enterprise technology on supply chain collaboration: Analysis of China-linked supply chain. *Enterprise Information Systems*, *6*(1), 55–77. DOI: 10.1080/17517575.2011.639904

Lima-Junior, F. R., & Carpinetti, L. C. R. (2017). Quantitative models for supply chain performance evaluation: A literature review. *Computers & Industrial Engineering*, *113*, 333–346. DOI: 10.1016/j.cie.2017.09.022

Linton, J. D., Klassen, R., & Jayaraman, V. (2007). Sustainable supply chains: An introduction. *Journal of Operations Management*, *25*(6), 1075–1082. DOI: 10.1016/j.jom.2007.01.012

Lockamy, A.III, & McCormack, K. (2004). Linking SCOR planning practices to supply chain performance: An exploratory study. *International Journal of Operations & Production Management*, *24*(12), 1192–1218. DOI: 10.1108/01443570410569010

Lozano-Oviedo, J., Cortés, C. E., & Rey, P. A. (2024). Sustainable closed-loop supply chains and their optimization models: A review of the literature. *Clean Technologies and Environmental Policy*, *26*(4), 999–1023. DOI: 10.1007/s10098-023-02730-w

Luzzini, D., Brandon-Jones, E., Brandon-Jones, A., & Spina, G. (2015). From sustainability commitment to performance: The role of intra-and inter-firm collaborative capabilities in the upstream supply chain. *International Journal of Production Economics*, *165*, 51–63. DOI: 10.1016/j.ijpe.2015.03.004

Magnani, L., & Nersessian, N. (Eds.). (2002). *Model-Based Reasoning: Science, Technology, Values*. Kluwer. DOI: 10.1007/978-1-4615-0605-8

Malesios, C., Dey, P. K., & Abdelaziz, F. B. (2020). Supply chain sustainability performance measurement of small and medium sized enterprises using structural equation modeling. *Annals of Operations Research*, *294*(1), 623–653. DOI: 10.1007/s10479-018-3080-z

Marty, J., & Ruel, S. (2024). Why is "supply chain collaboration" still a hot topic? A review of decades of research and a comprehensive framework proposal. *International Journal of Production Economics*, *273*, 109259. DOI: 10.1016/j.ijpe.2024.109259

McCarthy, E. J. (1960). *Basic Marketing: A Managerial Approach*. Richard D.

McClellan, M. (2002). *Collaborative Manufacturing: Using Real-time Information to Support the Supply Chain*. CRC Press. DOI: 10.1201/9781420025347

Meade, L., & Sarkis, J. (2002). A conceptual model for selecting and evaluating third-party reverse logistics providers. *Supply Chain Management*, *7*(5), 283–295. DOI: 10.1108/13598540210447728

Melnyk, S.A., Lummus, R., Vokurka, R. J. & Sandor, J. (2007). Supply Chain Management 2010 and Beyond, *APICS Educational & Research Foundation*, 1-63.

Melnyk, S. A., Stewart, D. M., & Swink, M. (2004). Metrics and performance measurement in operations management: Dealing with the metrics maze. *Journal of Operations Management*, *22*(3), 209–218. DOI: 10.1016/j.jom.2004.01.004

Mentzer, J. T., DeWitt, W., Keebler, J. S., Min, S., Nix, N. W., Smith, C. D., & Zacharia, Z. G. (2001). Defining supply chain management. *Journal of Business Logistics*, *22*(2), 1–25. DOI: 10.1002/j.2158-1592.2001.tb00001.x

Min, H., & Zhou, G. (2002). Supply chain modeling: Past, present and future. *Computers & Industrial Engineering*, *43*(1-2), 231–249. DOI: 10.1016/S0360-8352(02)00066-9

Mishra, D., Gunasekaran, A., Papadopoulos, T., & Dubey, R. (2018). Supply chain performance measures and metrics: A bibliometric study. *Benchmarking*, *25*(3), 932–967. DOI: 10.1108/BIJ-08-2017-0224

Morgan, C., & Dewhurst, A. (2008). Multiple retailer supplier performance: An exploratory investigation into using SPC techniques. *International Journal of Production Economics*, *111*(1), 13–26. DOI: 10.1016/j.ijpe.2006.11.018

Mujkic, Z., Qorri, A., & Kraslawski, A. (2018). Sustainability and optimization of supply chains: A literature review. *Operations and Supply Chain Management: An International Journal*, *11*(4), 186–199. DOI: 10.31387/oscm0350213

Neely, A., Mills, J., Platts, K., Richards, H., Gregory, M., Bourne, M., & Kennerley, M. (2000). Performance measurement system design: Developing and testing a process-based approach. *International Journal of Operations & Production Management*, *20*(10), 1119–1145. DOI: 10.1108/01443570010343708

Nersessian, N. J., & Patton, C. (2009). Model-based reasoning in interdisciplinary engineering. In Meijers, A. (Ed.), *Handbook of the Philosophy and Engineering Sciences* (pp. 687–718). Elsevier. DOI: 10.1016/B978-0-444-51667-1.50031-8

Nguyen, M. P., Thai, V. V., Chan, C., Lau, K. H., Nguyen, M. T. N., & Do, H. P. N. (2025). The interplay among trust, reciprocity and commitment factors in facilitating supply chain collaboration: The case of Vietnamese fishery industry. *Asia Pacific Journal of Marketing and Logistics*, *37*(1), 150–170. DOI: 10.1108/APJML-04-2024-0445

Ntabe, E. N., LeBel, L., Munson, A. D., & Santa-Eulalia, L. A. (2015). A systematic literature review of the supply chain operations reference (SCOR) model application with special attention to environmental issues. *International Journal of Production Economics*, *169*, 310–332. DOI: 10.1016/j.ijpe.2015.08.008

Nyaga, G. N., Whipple, J. M., & Lynch, D. F. (2010). Examining supply chain relationships: Do buyer and supplier perspectives on collaborative relationships differ? *Journal of Operations Management*, *28*(2), 101–114. DOI: 10.1016/j.jom.2009.07.005

Oliver, R. K., & Webber, M. D. (2012). Supply-chain management: logistics catches up with strategy. In Klaus, P., & Müller, S. (Eds.), *The Roots of Logistics* (pp. 183–194). Springer. DOI: 10.1007/978-3-642-27922-5_15

Papakiriakopoulos, D., & Pramatari, K. (2010). Collaborative performance measurement in supply chain. *Industrial Management & Data Systems*, *110*(9), 1297–1318. DOI: 10.1108/02635571011087400

Pasupuleti, V., Thuraka, B., Kodete, C. S., & Malisetty, S. (2024). Enhancing supply chain agility and sustainability through machine learning: Optimization techniques for logistics and inventory management. *Logistics (Basel)*, *8*(3), 73. DOI: 10.3390/logistics8030073

Peattie, K., & Ratnayaka, M. (1992). Responding to the green movement. *Industrial Marketing Management*, *21*(2), 103–110. DOI: 10.1016/0019-8501(92)90004-D

Pérez-Perales, D., Boza, A., Alarcón, F., & Gómez-Gasquet, P. (2024). Mathematical programming-based methodology for the evaluation of supply chain collaborative planning scenarios. *Annals of Operations Research*, *337*(1), 261–312. DOI: 10.1007/s10479-024-05917-6

Persson, F., & Olhager, J. (2002). Performance simulation of supply chain designs. *International Journal of Production Economics*, *77*(3), 231–245. DOI: 10.1016/S0925-5273(00)00088-8

Prahinski, C., & Kocabasoglu, C. (2006). Empirical research opportunities in reverse supply chains. *Omega*, *34*(6), 519–532. DOI: 10.1016/j.omega.2005.01.003

Rajeev, A., Pati, R. K., Padhi, S. S., & Govindan, K. (2017). Evolution of sustainability in supply chain management: A literature review. *Journal of Cleaner Production*, *162*, 299–314. DOI: 10.1016/j.jclepro.2017.05.026

Ralston, M. P., Richey, R. G., & Grawe, S. J. (2017). The past and future of supply chain collaboration: A literature synthesis and call for research. *International Journal of Logistics Management*, *28*(2), 508–530. DOI: 10.1108/IJLM-09-2015-0175

Ramanathan, U. (2014). Performance of supply chain collaboration - A simulation study. *Expert Systems with Applications, 41*(1), 210–220. DOI: 10.1016/j.eswa.2013.07.022

Rashid, A., Rasheed, R., & Amirah, N. A. (2024). Information technology and people involvement in organizational performance through supply chain collaboration. *Journal of Science and Technology Policy Management, 15*(6), 1560–1576. DOI: 10.1108/JSTPM-12-2022-0217

Renolds, S. (2024). The influence of cultural factors on supply chain integration in multinational corporations. Preprints. https:// doi: DOI: 10.20944/preprints202406.0209.v1

Rouhani, S., Wardley, L. J., & Amin, S. H. (2025). A comprehensive survey into reverse logistics and Closed-Loop Supply Chain aspects to provide analyses and insights for implementation. *Journal of Cleaner Production, 490*, 144743. DOI: 10.1016/j.jclepro.2025.144743

Routroy, S. (2009). Evaluation of supply chain strategies: A case study. *International Journal of Business Performance and Supply Chain Modelling, 1*(4), 290–306. DOI: 10.1504/IJBPSCM.2009.033746

Sarkis, J. (2003). A strategic decision framework for green supply chain management. *Journal of Cleaner Production, 11*(4), 397–409. DOI: 10.1016/S0959-6526(02)00062-8

Schaltegger, S., & Burritt, R. (2014). Measuring and managing sustainability performance of supply chains: Review and sustainability supply chain management framework. *Supply Chain Management, 19*(3), 232–241. DOI: 10.1108/SCM-02-2014-0061

Sellitto, M. A., Pereira, G. M., Borchardt, M., Da Silva, R. I., & Viegas, C. V. (2015). A SCOR-based model for supply chain performance measurement: Application in the footwear industry. *International Journal of Production Research, 53*(16), 4917–4926. DOI: 10.1080/00207543.2015.1005251

Seuring, S. (2013). A review of modeling approaches for sustainable supply chain management. *Decision Support Systems, 54*(4), 1513–1520. DOI: 10.1016/j.dss.2012.05.053

Sherbrooke, C. C. (1971). An evaluator for the number of operationally ready aircraft in a multilevel supply system. *Operations Research, 19*(3), 618–635. DOI: 10.1287/opre.19.3.618

Simatupang, T. M., & Sridharan, R. (2005). The collaboration index: A measure for supply chain collaboration. *International Journal of Physical Distribution & Logistics Management*, *35*(1), 44–62. DOI: 10.1108/09600030510577421

Simatupang, T. M., Wright, A. C., & Sridharan, R. (2004). Applying the theory of constraints to supply chain collaboration. *Supply Chain Management*, *9*(1), 57–70. DOI: 10.1108/13598540410517584

Simon, H. A. (1977). *The New Science of Management Decision*. Prentice-Hall, Inc.

Singh, R. K. (2025). Exploring the impact of green supply chain strategies and sustainable practices on circular supply chains. *Benchmarking*, *32*(4), 1387–1409. DOI: 10.1108/BIJ-11-2023-0801

Soosay, C. A., & Hyland, P. (2015). A decade of supply chain collaboration and directions for future research. *Supply Chain Management*, *20*(6), 613–630. DOI: 10.1108/SCM-06-2015-0217

Squire, B., Vachon, S., & Klassen, R. D. (2006). Extending green practices across the supply chainthe impact of upstream and downstream integration. *International Journal of Operations & Production Management*, *26*(7), 795–821. DOI: 10.1108/01443570610672248

Stank, T., Dittman, J. P., Burnette, M., & Autry, C. W. (2015). *The Supply Chain Game Changers: Applications and Best Practices that are Shaping the Future of Supply Chain Management*, Free Press.

Subramanian, N., & Gunasekaran, A. (2015). Cleaner supply-chain management practices for twenty-first-century organizational competitiveness: Practice-performance framework and research propositions. *International Journal of Production Economics*, *164*, 216–233. DOI: 10.1016/j.ijpe.2014.12.002

Swoyer, C. (1991). Structural representation and surrogative reasoning. *Synthese*, *87*(3), 449–508. DOI: 10.1007/BF00499820

Tajbakhsh, A., & Hassini, E. (2015). Performance measurement of sustainable supply chains: A review and research questions. *International Journal of Productivity and Performance Management*, *64*(6), 744–783. DOI: 10.1108/IJPPM-03-2013-0056

"The Year at Home and Abroad". *The Independent*, 58 (2927): 7. January 5, 1905. Retrieved 6 February 2024.

Todorov, V., & Marinova, D. (2011). Modelling sustainability. *Mathematics and Computers in Simulation*, *81*(7), 1397–1408. DOI: 10.1016/j.matcom.2010.05.022

Walker, H., Miemczyk, J., Johnsen, T., & Spencer, R. (2012). Sustainable procurement: Past, present and future. *Journal of Purchasing and Supply Management, 18*(4), 201–206. DOI: 10.1016/j.pursup.2012.11.003

Wang, H., Long, Z., Chen, J., Guo, Y., & Wang, A. (2023). Collaborative decision-making in supply chain management: A review and bibliometric analysis. *Cogent Engineering, 10*(1), 2196823. DOI: 10.1080/23311916.2023.2196823

Weisz, E., Herold, D. M., Ostern, N. K., Payne, R., & Kummer, S. (2024). Artificial intelligence (AI) for supply chain collaboration: Implications on information sharing and trust. *Online Information Review, 49*(1), 164–181. DOI: 10.1108/OIR-02-2024-0083

Wilson, M., & Goffnett, S. (2022). Reverse logistics: Understanding end-of-life product management. *Business Horizons, 65*(5), 643–655. DOI: 10.1016/j.bushor.2021.10.005

Wong, C. W., Sancha, C., & Thomsen, C. G. (2017). A national culture perspective in the efficacy of supply chain integration practices. *International Journal of Production Economics, 193*, 554–565. DOI: 10.1016/j.ijpe.2017.08.015

Xia, J., Li, H., & He, Z. (2023). The effect of blockchain technology on supply chain collaboration: A case study of Lenovo. *Systems, 11*(6), 299. DOI: 10.3390/systems11060299

Yildiz Çankaya, S., & Sezen, B. (2019). Effects of green supply chain management practices on sustainability performance. *Journal of Manufacturing Technology Management, 30*(1), 98–121. DOI: 10.1108/JMTM-03-2018-0099

Zingales, F. G., & Hockerts, K. (2003). Balanced scorecard and sustainability: Examples from literature and practice. Working paper: Center for Management and Environmental Resources, Fontainebleau: INSEAD, 1-15.

KEY TERMS AND DEFINITIONS

Analytical Hierarchy Process (AHP): a structured decision-making methodology that breaks down complex multi-criteria problems into hierarchical levels of goals, criteria, and alternatives. AHP uses pairwise comparisons to convert subjective judgments into numerical priorities, allowing decision-makers to systematically evaluate and rank alternatives based on multiple criteria, while maintaining consistency in their judgments.

Analytical Network Process (ANP): an extension of Analytical Hierarchy Process (AHP) that addresses more complex decision problems involving interdependence and feedback relationships between decision elements. Unlike AHP's strict hierarchical structure, ANP uses a network structure to model the complex dependencies and interactions among criteria and alternatives, making it suitable for decision situations where elements influence each other bidirectionally.

Artificial Intelligence (AI): the field of computer science focused on creating systems capable of performing tasks that would usually require human intelligence. AI encompasses machine learning, deep learning, natural language processing, and expert systems that can learn from data, recognize patterns, make decisions, and adapt to new situations without explicit prompting or programming for each specific task.

Computer Simulation: a computational technique that creates digital models to replicate the behavior of real-world systems and processes. Computer simulations use mathematical models and algorithms to study complex systems, test scenarios, and predict outcomes in controlled virtual environments where direct experimentation would be difficult, expensive, or even impossible.

Factor Analysis: a statistical method used to identify underlying latent factors that explain the correlations among a set of observed variables. Factor analysis reduces data dimensionality by grouping correlated variables into factors, revealing the structure of complex datasets through either exploratory factor analysis for discovering patterns or confirmatory factor analysis for testing hypothesized structures.

Fuzzy TOPSIS: a multi-criteria decision-making method that combines fuzzy set theory with the Technique for Order Preference by Similarity to Ideal Solution to handle uncertainty and imprecision in decision-making. This method is particularly useful when dealing with subjective evaluations by allowing decision-makers to express their preferences using fuzzy numbers, rather than precise numerical values.

Mathematical Programming: is a branch of applied mathematics that provides the theoretical framework and mathematical techniques for formulating decision problems as mathematical models with objective functions and constraints. Mathematical programming incorporates specific methodologies including linear programming, nonlinear programming, integer programming, and dynamic programming that transform real-world problems into solvable mathematical constructs.

The Theory of Constraints (TOC): is a management philosophy that focuses on improving system performance and maximizing throughput by eliminating process bottlenecks (constraints).

Section 4
Case Studies in Applied Modeling

Chapter 12
Navigating Bibliometric Analysis:
A Stepwise Approach Using Bibliometrix Library in R Software

Syed Tabrez Tabrez Hassan
https://orcid.org/0000-0003-1562-7992
Adamas University, India

ABSTRACT

Bibliometric analysis is a powerful tool for evaluating research trends, identifying key contributors, and mapping the intellectual structure of a scientific field. With the increasing volume of academic publications, systematic approaches are essential for deriving meaningful insights from scholarly data. This paper presents a stepwise approach to conducting bibliometric analysis using the Biblioshiny app in Bibliometrix package in R software. Bibliometrix provides a comprehensive framework for importing, processing, and visualizing bibliographic data from databases such as Web of Science, Scopus and Dimensions.ai.The paper outlines key stages of bibliometric analysis, including data collection, preprocessing, descriptive statistics, network analysis, and thematic mapping. It also explores citation analysis, co-authorship networks, and keyword co-occurrence patterns to uncover research trends and collaboration dynamics. By leveraging R's powerful statistical capabilities, this approach ensures reproducibility and flexibility in bibliometric studies.

INTRODUCTION

The bibliometric approach to reviews has become increasingly popular due to several factors, including the development of software tools, the adoption of cross-

DOI: 10.4018/979-8-3373-3301-4.ch012

disciplinary methodologies, and enhanced capabilities for processing large datasets (Donthu et al., 2021). Unlike systematic reviews, bibliometric methods are inherently quantitative, allowing them to eliminate sample selection bias. Additionally, bibliometric techniques are highly effective in assessing journal performance, analysing co-authorship and co-citation patterns, and identifying key research streams within specific fields (Baker et al., 2020).

Bibliometrics has gained significant attention in academic research in recent years (Khan et al, 2021). However, many early-career researchers still face challenges in conducting a comprehensive bibliometric analysis. Despite its growing popularity, bibliometrics is not merely a passing trend. The concept dates back to the 19th century when Belgian documentalist Otlet first introduced it (Rousseau, 2014), later popularized by Pritchard in 1969. In the same year, Nalimov introduced the term scientometrics (Cherny & Gilyarevsky, 2001). While the two fields initially had some distinctions, they are now considered synonymous in modern research (Garfield, 2006).

Bibliometric analysis can be defined as a systematic approach to managing vast amounts of scientific information by conceptualizing, identifying trends, and analysing the structural composition of a research domain. This method provides a comprehensive overview of co-authorship patterns, intellectual structures, and citation trends, enabling researchers to quantify different aspects of the literature. It is particularly useful for mapping research fields, identifying influential publications, authors, and journals, and understanding the evolution of research topics over time (Laengle et al, 2020). However, bibliometric analysis is less effective for specific reviews or studies with limited datasets, as its quantitative nature may overlook the nuanced aspects of explicitly defined research questions. Given its broad scope, bibliometric analysis can encompass thousands of publications from various databases to ensure a comprehensive assessment of a field. Typically, it involves quantitative content analysis using citation metrics like h-index and citation count, while qualitative aspects may include keyword or thematic analysis based on frequency.

Based on the similarities and differences in bibliometric approaches, researcher's study makes several contributions to the literature. Identification of key literature clusters: (a) studies assessing trending research topics, (b) analyses of papers utilizing emerging econometric techniques, (c) research focusing on fundamental themes (d) studies dedicated to retrospective evaluations of well-established journals. Researchers can highlight the most influential countries, institutions, and scholars in the field. The study can also reveal the leading journals publishing bibliometric studies, showing their growing scholarly impact.

Bibliometrics serves as a model of a discipline because it provides a quantitative, evidence-based view of how knowledge is produced, structured, and evolves within that discipline.

Bibliometrics analyses patterns of publication, citation, and co-authorship to reveal core topics, influential authors, and key research areas. By analysing publication data over time, bibliometrics detects emerging themes, declining topics, and research hotspots. Co-authorship and institutional analysis show how researchers, universities, and countries interact within the discipline. Measures like h-index, impact factor, and citation counts help assess the scholarly impact of authors, journals, or institutions. Bibliometric insights guide research funding, curriculum design, and journal ranking decisions. Bibliometrics transforms the abstract idea of a discipline into a measurable, mappable model — showing its boundaries, central themes, key contributors, and developmental trajectory.

PURPOSE OF BIBLIOMETRIC ANALYSIS

Scholars employ bibliometric analysis for various purposes, including identifying emerging trends in article and journal performance, examining collaboration patterns, analysing research constituents, and exploring the intellectual structure of a specific domain within the existing literature (Verma & Gustafsson, 2020). Bibliometric analysis typically involves large datasets—often comprising hundreds or even thousands of records—and relies on objective metrics such as citation counts, publication volumes, and keyword occurrences. However, its interpretation often integrates both objective (e.g., performance analysis) and subjective (e.g., thematic analysis) assessments using established analytical techniques. In essence, bibliometric analysis provides a structured approach to deciphering and mapping the cumulative scientific knowledge and evolutionary trends within well-established fields by rigorously processing vast amounts of unstructured data. When conducted effectively, bibliometric studies serve as a powerful tool for advancing a field by enabling scholars to gain a comprehensive overview and identify knowledge gaps. It also helps in generating novel research ideas, and strategically position their contributions within the academic landscape.

Despite its advantages, bibliometric analysis remains relatively underutilized in business research, and its application often does not fully exploit its potential. This limitation arises when studies rely on a narrow range of bibliometric data and techniques, leading to an incomplete understanding of the field—such as focusing solely on performance analysis without incorporating science mapping (Brown, Park, & Pitt, 2020). The absence of a comprehensive guide to bibliometric analysis in business research presents a significant challenge for scholars seeking to understand and apply the methodology in a holistic and accessible manner. This study tries to bridge the gap by providing step by step method to perform the bibliometric analysis using Bibliometrix and to interpret the result.

LITERATURE REVIEW

The number of bibliometric-related publications has shown exponential growth, rising from just 51 in year 2000 to over 3,400 by 2022 (Montazeri et al., 2023). This surge reflects both increased data availability (e.g. from citation databases) and the rising demand for quantitative tools in science evaluation and policy (Wang et al., 2025). Early bibliometric work centred on classical techniques such as citation counts, h-index, co-citation, bibliographic coupling, co-word analysis, and author productivity distributions. Availability of specialized software such as VOSviewer became popular means to operationalize these methods. But such tools often come with limitations: restricted scripting flexibility, processing, and challenges in reproducibility and integration (Zupic & Čater, 2015). In this evolving landscape, the bibliometrix R package established itself as a powerful, open-source, scriptable environment for science mapping and bibliometric analysis. It supports the full mapping workflow from data import and cleaning through performance analysis, network analysis, and thematic mapping (Aria & Cuccurullo, 2017). Since then, bibliometrix has been increasingly adopted in diverse domain studies, for example in systematic reviews of sustainable digital transformation and in hybrid bibliometric and systematic review studies using bibliometrix to structure the quantitative mapping while integrating qualitative evidence.

Recent methodological work has called for more rigorous and transparent design of bibliometric studies. One of the study argues that many bibliometric analyses stop prematurely at performance metrics, neglecting richer structural and relational analyses (Halder et al. 2024). Similarly, "Evaluating Bibliometrics Reviews: A Practical Guide for Peer Review" (2025) outlines a checklist for assessing specificity, robustness, choice of metrics, and clarity in reporting (Hoang, 2025). In the biomedical domain, Montazeri et al. (2023) proposed the BIBLIO guideline—a preliminary reporting standard for bibliometric reviews to improve transparency, reproducibility, and methodological consistency (Montazeri et al., 2023). Another important methodological trend is the integration of bibliometrics with systematic review or meta-analysis approaches. Marzi et al. (2025) offer guidelines for combining bibliometric mapping with theory development and qualitative synthesis. In practice, recent studies have applied hybrid methods: for example, a bibliometric and systematic review of digital competence research uses bibliometrix for mapping publication trends and collaborations, while embedding thematic synthesis from primary literature. In recent years, the integration of artificial intelligence and semantic methods into bibliometrics has emerged as a major frontier in the field. Contemporary research highlights how AI models such as embeddings and transformer architectures are increasingly applied for trend prediction, author disambiguation, clustering, and semantic analysis (Saeidnia et al., 2024). Research are directed toward detecting anomalous or unethical authorship patterns using algorithmic and AI-assisted bibliometric tools, addressing concerns about metric manipulation and research integrity (Meho & Akl, 2024). These advancements indicate a shift toward bibliometric workflows that merge traditional quantitative mapping with semantic and machine learning-based analytics.

INTRODUCTION TO R SOFTWARE AND BIBLIOMETRIX LIBRARY

R is a powerful, open-source programming language widely used for statistical computing, data analysis, and visualization. Known for its versatility, R provides an extensive collection of packages for tasks such as data manipulation, machine learning, and econometrics. Researchers, data analysts, and statisticians use R for its robust capabilities in handling large datasets and performing complex analyses. Its active community ensures continuous development, making it a preferred tool for both academic and industry applications. Additionally, R integrates seamlessly with other programming languages and software, enhancing its usability across various domains, including business analytics, finance, bioinformatics, and social sciences.

R was developed by Ross Ihaka and Robert Gentleman at the University of Auckland, New Zealand, in the mid-1990s. It is based on the S language, which was created at Bell Laboratories. The R Foundation for Statistical Computing now maintains and develops R. It can be downloaded from the Comprehensive R Archive Network (CRAN) (URL:https://cran.r-project.org/). For an enhanced GUI experience, researchers should also install RStudio, a popular integrated development environment (IDE) for R (URL: https://posit.co/download/rstudio-desktop/)

In R, there are available libraries (also called packages), which are collections of functions, datasets, and documentation that extend R's capabilities. They help users perform specialized tasks like data visualization, machine learning, statistical modelling, text mining, bibliometric analysis etc.

For installing and initialising the Bibliometrix, following commands should be used in R studio:

```
install.packages("bibliometrix")
library(bibliometrix)
bibliometrix::biblioshiny()
```

Once it is executed it will support a user interface with menus which is similar to this screenshot.

Figure 1. User interface of Bibliometrix

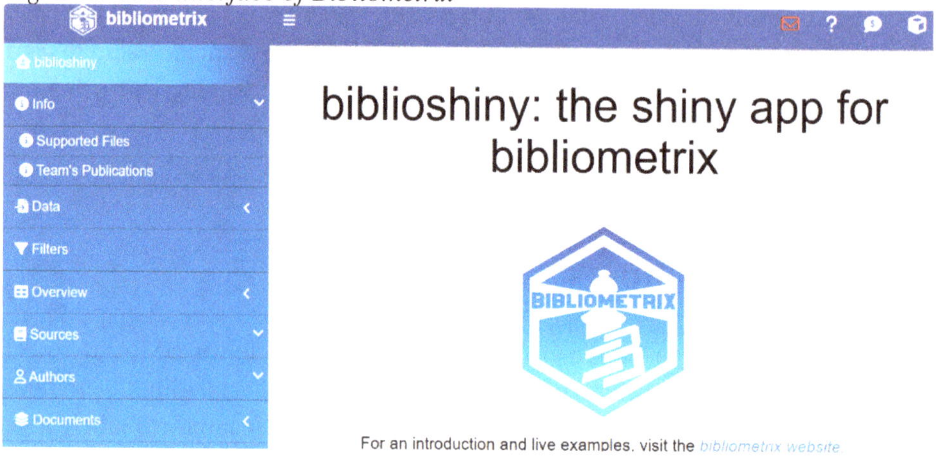

Bibliometric data can be sourced from various academic and research databases. Here are some major platforms where the bibliometric datasets can be accessed

- **Dimensions.ai** – Provides **.bib files** and citation data for academic research.
- **CrossRef** – Offers metadata for academic articles, including DOI information.
- **Web of Science (WoS)** – Citation-based bibliometric data.
- **Scopus** – Provides citation analysis, author metrics, and journal impact factors.
- **Elsevier's SciVal** – Offers advanced bibliometric analytics based on Scopus data.

INTERPRETING BIBLIOMETRIC ANALYSIS RESULTS: A DEMO EXAMPLE

Once Biblioshiny app is open, first step is to click "Load Data" on the left panel, then select the csv file (from Web of Science, Scopus, or Dimensions.ai) and run "Start" to upload the data.

Step 1: Descriptive Statistics – To perform this task, click "Summary". It will show Number of documents, authors, keywords, citations and most relevant sources (journals)
Step 2: Most Influential Authors – To get this insight, go to "Authors" and click on "Most Relevant Authors". It will identify top researchers in AI field and tell author impact based on h-index and citations.

Step 3: Most Cited Papers – To get this data, click "Documents" on the right-side panel and click on "Most Cited Papers". It gives insight of the most influential papers and helps in finding key literature in the field
Step 4: Keyword Analysis (Trending Topics)- By clicking on "Conceptual Structure" and selecting "Word Cloud" option it gives frequently used keywords in research. It also shows emerging research trends.
Step 5: Co-Authorship & Collaboration Networks- It can be viewed by selecting "Social Structure" tab from the panel and then selecting "Collaboration Network". It will give output for research collaboration between authors, institutions, and countries.
Step 6: Thematic Evolution (Research Trends Over Time)- This insight can be viewed by selecting "Conceptual Structure"and clicking on "Thematic Evolution". It displays how research topics have changed over time which can be useful for spotting emerging and declining research areas.

Let's assume we conducted a bibliometric analysis on research papers related to "Artificial Intelligence in Business" using Dimensions.ai data. Below, we will interpret key results step by step.

Interpretation:

- A total of 250 research papers were analyzed.
- 500 unique authors contributed, indicating a well-researched field.
- 60 papers were written by a single author, meaning the field has collaborative research trends.
- Collaboration Index (3.2) shows that, on average, each paper has about 3 co-authors.
- Total citations (5,000) indicate how influential these papers are in the academic community.
- Smith J is the most productive author (15 papers), followed by Johnson A and Wang H.
- Total Citations show impact—Smith J's work is the most cited, making them an important contributor to the field.
- Most cited paper (500 citations) suggests it is a foundational work in the field.
- High citation counts indicate that these papers have strong academic influence.
- If a paper has high citations but is old, it may indicate an established theory
- Most common keyword ("Artificial Intelligence") shows the core research focus.
- Emerging topics like "Deep Learning" and "Customer Insights" indicate newer trends.

- Co-Authorship analysis shows clusters of strong research collaborations.
- If Smith J and Johnson A are in the same cluster, they often co-author papers.
- If an author is isolated, they work independently

Basic Insights from Analysis:

a. Artificial Intelligence in Business is a growing field with strong collaboration.
b. Top researchers include Smith J, Johnson A, and Wang H.
c. Most cited works focus on AI-driven decision-making.
d. Trending topics include Generative AI and Ethical AI.
e. USA-UK collaboration is the strongest, suggesting high research partnerships.
f. Emerging collaborations (e.g., China-India) indicate growing research impact.
g. "AI & Society" is the leading journal, making it a key outlet for AI-related business research.

Summary Of Basic Bibliometric Insights

The bibliometric analysis highlights the rapid growth and collaborative nature of research on Artificial Intelligence (AI) in business. The field is expanding significantly, with increasing contributions from multiple regions and institutions. Prominent scholars such as Smith J, Johnson A, and Wang H have emerged as influential contributors, shaping the direction of academic inquiry in this domain. Their works, along with other highly cited studies, primarily focus on the role of AI in enhancing decision-making, underlining its strategic importance in organizational contexts. The analysis also reveals that emerging research themes are strongly aligned with current technological and ethical debates. In particular, Generative AI and Ethical AI have gained traction as trending topics, reflecting both the innovation potential and societal challenges associated with AI adoption in business practices. This indicates that the research community is not only addressing technical efficiency but also engaging with broader issues of responsibility and sustainability.

From a geographical perspective, the strongest research partnerships are observed between the USA and the UK, underscoring the global leadership of these regions in AI and business scholarship. Additionally, emerging collaborations, such as those between China and India, suggest a growing diversification and internationalization of research networks, contributing to the overall global impact of the field. Finally, AI & Society stands out as the leading journal publishing research on this theme, establishing itself as a central outlet for disseminating impactful work. Overall, the analysis demonstrates a vibrant, interdisciplinary, and increasingly global research landscape in AI and business.

CONCLUSION

Analyzing the performance and intellectual structure of a research field through bibliometric studies is a complex yet essential task. The bibliometric analysis offers a comprehensive overview of the intellectual structure, key contributors, and emerging trends within the studied domain. By mapping citation patterns, co-authorship networks, and thematic evolution, the study provides valuable insights into the discipline's growth trajectory and research frontiers. The findings not only highlight influential works and collaboration patterns but also guide future scholarly inquiry and policy decisions. As research landscapes evolve, bibliometric approaches will remain essential for objectively assessing knowledge production and dissemination, enabling scholars, institutions, and policymakers to strategically shape the discipline's advancement in an increasingly interconnected academic environment. This approach provides a structured framework to navigate complexities and extract meaningful insights into the field's evolving landscape. Conducting such analyses demands careful attention, a thorough grasp of the domain and data, and the application of suitable methodologies at each stage. These Insights can be used for "Literature Reviews" e.g. Identify key papers, authors, and journals. It can be used in "Research Planning" which helps in focus on trending topics and gaps in research. Authors and research institutions can use it for future collaboration and can connect with highly cited authors and research groups. It can be further use as a vital information towards publishing and to submit to top journals identified in the analysis.

REFERENCES

Aria, M., & Cuccurullo, C. (2017). bibliometrix: An R-tool for comprehensive science mapping analysis. *Journal of Informetrics*, *11*(4), 959–975. DOI: 10.1016/j.joi.2017.08.007

Baker, H. K., Kumar, S., & Pandey, N. (2020). A bibliometric analysis of managerial finance: A retrospective. *Managerial Finance*, *46*(11), 1495–1517. DOI: 10.1108/MF-06-2019-0277

Brown, T., Park, A., & Pitt, L. (2020). A 60-year bibliographic review of the Journal of Advertising Research: Perspectives on trends in authorship, influences, and research impact. *Journal of Advertising Research*, *60*(4), 353–360. DOI: 10.2501/JAR-2020-028

Donthu, N., Kumar, S., Mukherjee, D., Pandey, N., & Lim, W. M. (2021). How to conduct a bibliometric analysis: An overview and guidelines. *Journal of Business Research*, *133*, 285–296. DOI: 10.1016/j.jbusres.2021.04.070

Garfield, E. (2006). The history and meaning of the journal impact factor. *Journal of the American Medical Association*, *295*(1), 90–93. DOI: 10.1001/jama.295.1.90 PMID: 16391221

Khan, M. A., Pattnaik, D., Ashraf, R., Ali, I., Kumar, S., & Donthu, N. (2021). Value of special issues in the Journal of Business Research: A bibliometric analysis. *Journal of Business Research*, *125*, 295–313. DOI: 10.1016/j.jbusres.2020.12.015

Laengle, S., Merigó, J. M., Modak, N. M., & Yang, J. B. (2020). Bibliometrics in operations research and management science: A university analysis. *Annals of Operations Research*, *294*(1-2), 769–813. DOI: 10.1007/s10479-018-3017-6

Montazeri, M., Montazeri, M., Bahaadinbeigy, K., Montazeri, M., & Afraz, A. (2023). Application of machine learning methods in predicting schizophrenia and bipolar disorders: A systematic review. *Health Science Reports*, *6*(1), e962.

Verma, S., & Gustafsson, A. (2020). Investigating the emerging COVID-19 research trends in the field of business and management: A bibliometric analysis approach. *Journal of Business Research*, *118*, 253–261. DOI: 10.1016/j.jbusres.2020.06.057 PMID: 32834211

Chapter 13

Integrated Optimization Model in Sustainability (MOIS): An Integrative Approach for Business Management in Colombian SMEs

Franz Esteban Rodríguez Franky
https://orcid.org/0000-0002-5253-3015
Fundación Universitaria Compensar, Colombia

Jesus Abel Afanador
https://orcid.org/0000-0002-2122-2601
Fundación Universitaria Compensar, Colombia

Jairo Alonso Rivera
Fundación Universitaria Compensar, Colombia

ABSTRACT

In Colombia, small and medium-sized enterprises (SMEs) are the backbone of the national economy, representing 99.5% of the formal business fabric and generating approximately 79% of the country's employment (BBVA Research, 2023). However, SMEs face structural challenges, such as the scarcity of financial resources, the low adoption of sustainable technologies, and the limited capacity to implement efficient management models that balance sustainability with business competitiveness (Rizos et al., 2021; Lieder & Rashid, 2020). To address these problems, the Comprehensive Optimization Model in Sustainability (MOIS) is proposed, a methodological tool designed to strengthen the business processes of SMEs in Colombia based on a

DOI: 10.4018/979-8-3373-3301-4.ch013

comprehensive approach that combines sustainability, logistics efficiency and internal control. This model is based on the articulation of three strategic axes: the Analytical Model of Sustainable Business Performance (MADES), the Logistics Evaluation and Analysis Model (MEAL) and the Comprehensive Diagnosis Model of the Internal Control System (DISCI).

INTRODUCTION

In Colombia, small and medium-sized enterprises (SMEs) are the backbone of the national economy, representing 99.5% of the formal business fabric and generating approximately 79% of the country's employment (BBVA Research, 2023). However, SMEs face structural challenges, such as the scarcity of financial resources, the low adoption of sustainable technologies, and the limited capacity to implement efficient management models that balance sustainability with business competitiveness (Rizos et al., 2021; Lieder & Rashid, 2020). To address these problems, the Comprehensive Optimization Model in Sustainability (MOIS) is proposed, a methodological tool designed to strengthen the business processes of SMEs in Colombia based on a comprehensive approach that combines sustainability, logistics efficiency and internal control. This model is based on the articulation of three strategic axes: the Analytical Model of Sustainable Business Performance (MADES), the Logistics Evaluation and Analysis Model (MEAL) and the Comprehensive Diagnosis Model of the Internal Control System (DISCI). MADES makes it possible to assess sustainability in economic, environmental and social terms, providing quantifiable metrics that facilitate strategic decision-making aimed at generating long-term value (Geissdoerfer et al., 2020). Its application in SMEs seeks to reduce environmental impacts without compromising profitability, aligning business operations with the Sustainable Development Goals (SDGs). Recent studies have shown that the implementation of sustainable analytical models can improve operational efficiency by up to 25% and reduce costs by 30% (Gil-Lamata & Latorre-Martínez, 2022).

The evolution of sustainability models applied in Colombian SMEs has been gradual and fragmented, driven mainly by initiatives such as the National Green Business Plan and the partial adoption of frameworks such as ISO 14001, GRI and the SDGs. However, the effective integration of sustainability and logistics has faced obstacles related to a lack of systematic data, low investment in green technologies, and weak coordination between operational and administrative areas. At the international level, a number of models offer valuable lessons. In Europe, the European Green Deal and the Circular Economy Action Plan have incentivised sustainable practices linked to logistics efficiency, achieving relevant impacts in reducing emissions and optimising operations (European Commission, 2020). In

Asia, methodologies such as Green Kaizen in Japan have combined continuous improvements with reverse logistics and waste minimization, especially in the manufacturing field (Hirano, 2019).

In Latin America, countries such as Chile, Mexico and Brazil have experienced partial advances in logistics sustainability. In Chile, exporting SMEs benefiting from green logistics initiatives have shown improvements in efficiency, although their sustainability has depended on state subsidies (Molina et al., 2021). In Mexico, sustainable clusters have promoted process traceability and waste reduction, but their impact has been limited by the lack of continuity in public policies (National Institute of Ecology and Climate Change [INECC], 2020). At the theoretical level, the conceptual basis of MOIS is strengthened with robust models of sustainability and business operation. The Triple Bottom Line approach, proposed by Elkington (1997), states that companies must simultaneously generate value in the economic, social and environmental dimensions. Likewise, recognized frameworks such as the SCOR (Supply Chain Operations Reference), which optimizes logistics processes (Supply Chain Council, 2012), and the COSO framework, which structures solid internal control systems (Committee of Sponsoring Organizations of the Treadway Commission, 2013), support the methodological design of the MOIS. The convergence of these theories, together with international practical experiences, gives the model a solid and transferable base, capable of adapting to different national and international contexts.

However, if we analyse the MEAL component, which focuses on the logistical and operational optimisation of companies, facilitating the implementation of circular economy strategies (*it is understood as an economic model that seeks to keep resources in use for as long as possible, extracting the maximum value from them during their life cycle and regenerating them at the end of their use. This approach replaces the linear scheme of "produce-use-dispose*") and reverse logistics (*referring to the planned and controlled processes for the return of products, materials or components from the end consumer to the manufacturer or a collection point, with the aim of recovering their value or disposing of them in an environmentally responsible* manner). Efficient supply chain management is critical to sustainability, minimizing waste, reducing lead times, and improving product traceability. In this sense, digital tools, such as the Internet of Things (IoT) and artificial intelligence (AI), have proven to be key in the optimization of sustainable logistics in SMEs (OBS Business School, 2023). The DISCI, on the other hand, represents a comprehensive approach for the evaluation and strengthening of the internal control system in companies, guaranteeing regulatory compliance and transparency in organizational management. The implementation of this model improves the capacity to respond to financial, operational, and regulatory risks, reducing the vulnerability of SMEs to adverse external factors (López Enciso et al., 2023).

This study analyzes the construction and application of MOIS as an innovative proposal to improve business management in Colombian SMEs. The theoretical foundations of each of its integrative models (MADES, MEAL and DISCI) and their impact on sustainability, logistics efficiency and internal control are presented. Likewise, success stories and good practices in the implementation of similar models in the Latin American context are discussed, with the purpose of highlighting the viability and benefits of MOIS to strengthen the competitiveness and resilience of SMEs in the current market. Through MOIS, a comprehensive solution is proposed that responds to the specific needs of the sector, promoting a sustainable management model that facilitates informed decision-making and compliance with international sustainability and corporate governance standards.

1. MADES: SUSTAINABLE BUSINESS PERFORMANCE ANALYTICAL MODEL

The Sustainable Business Performance Analytical Model (MADES), developed based on the studies of Rodríguez & Arias (2023), is a comprehensive instrument that allows the sustainability of organizations to be evaluated through an approach that combines quantitative and qualitative elements. Its structure incorporates key metrics in areas such as environmental management, social responsibility, economic stability, governance and innovation, ensuring that companies operate sustainably without compromising the resources of future generations. Among the essential features, MADES takes a multidimensional perspective, which involves simultaneously assessing various aspects of sustainability. In addition, it is based on the integration of indicators, using specific metrics to measure the impact of business operations on variables such as carbon footprint, natural resource consumption, gender equality and financial profitability. If we take as a reference what Kishaija et al (2025) stated "However, climate change represents a potentially existential threat to sustainable production, whose main actors are small producers who grow in developing tropical countries" (p.2), we understand that MADES is a model that is distinguished by its long-term vision, as it allows organizations to foresee the effects of their decisions on sustainable development and the mitigation of future risks. It also promotes the participation of key stakeholders, including employees, customers, local communities and other stakeholders, ensuring that their perspectives are considered in strategic planning and sustainable performance evaluation.

Another fundamental quality of MADES is its adaptability and flexibility, which facilitates its implementation in companies in different sectors, especially SMEs. At the same time, it emphasizes transparency and disclosure of information, ensuring that sustainability-related data is accessible and understandable to stakeholders, promoting accountability. The model adopts a holistic approach, comprehensively considering the interconnections between the environmental, social and economic dimensions, avoiding isolated solutions that may generate negative impacts in other areas, as evidenced in Figure 1. As stated by Moreira, A et al (2025) "Companies seek a balanced relationship between environmental and social development, prioritizing profitability. This approach forms the basis of the concept of sustainable management, known as the Triple Bottom Line" (p.1) In summary, MADES not only allows companies to improve their performance in terms of sustainability, but also positively influences their reputation, regulatory compliance and financial stability, facilitating more strategic, responsible management aligned with the challenges of sustainable development.

Figure 1. MADES integration features

Figure 2. Dashboard result of the evaluation through MADES

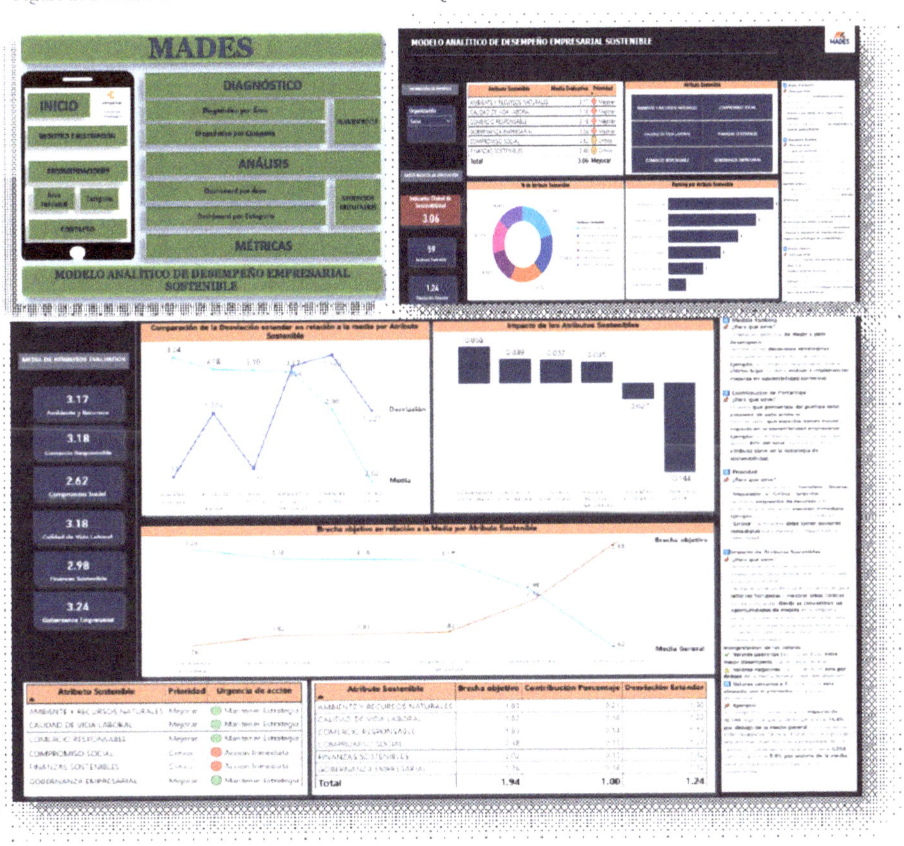

Source: Own elaboration based on Power Bi

From regulatory compliance to market leadership, companies that embed sustainability in their DNA not only mitigate legal and reputational risks, but also optimize costs, access new markets, and foster innovation. In addition, in an environment where consumers and investors increasingly prioritize social and environmental impact, sustainability is consolidated as a key differentiator to build business resilience and ensure long-term growth. This approach not only responds to a market demand, but also reflects a paradigm shift in business management.

However, leading companies recognize that sustainability is not an expense, but an investment that generates shared value, strengthens relationships with stakeholders and ensures their social license to operate. In a world in constant evolution, where climate, social and regulatory challenges are increasingly complex, adopting a sustainable business model is no longer an option, but a strategic necessity to last over time. Table 1 describes the variables that MADES takes into account within its functional structure in such a way that they are articulated with the evaluative method in organizations.

Table 1. MADES business variables

Business variable	**Description in the light of the sustainability model**
Compliance	Many countries have regulations and laws related to sustainable business practices. Measuring sustainability helps ensure that companies comply with these regulations and avoid potential legal penalties
Reputation and Brand	Sustainable companies usually have a better reputation in the market. Consumers and stakeholders increasingly value companies that adopt sustainable and ethical practices, which can lead to improved brand perception and increased sales.
Cost Reduction	Sustainability often involves efficiency in the use of resources, which can lead to a reduction in operating costs in the long run. Measuring and evaluating the use of resources such as energy, water, and materials can help identify areas where cost-saving improvements can be implemented
Market Access and Finance	Many investors and lenders are paying more attention to companies' sustainable practices. Measuring and demonstrating commitment to sustainability can open doors to obtaining financing and accessing new markets.
Business Resilience	Companies that incorporate sustainable practices tend to be more resilient to environmental, social, and regulatory changes. Measuring sustainability can help identify areas of risk and opportunities to strengthen resilience.
Innovation	The pursuit of sustainability often drives innovation. Companies that measure their sustainability can identify areas where creative solutions and new technologies are needed to address sustainability-related issues
Market Leadership	Companies that position themselves as leaders in sustainability can influence the industry as a whole and make a positive impact on overall business practices.

Source: Own elaboration

Once the different characteristics of the Model have been identified, the prototype, the variables that make it up and the validation technique that was used in the more than 32 organizations that have tested it are presented. First of all, it is important to mention that the model has the following specific characteristics:

- ✓ It is based on the notion of a "dynamic hypermedia device" (DHD). DHDs are complex systems that combine social, technological, and institutional elements.
- ✓ It uses a socio-technical approach; since it recognizes that sustainability is a social and technical phenomenon, and that it must be analyzed in its social context.
- ✓ It considers the social and political tensions existing in the socio-institutional framework where it is developed. In addition, it recognizes that sustainability can be subject to conflicts and social tensions.
- ✓ It proposes forms of participatory design, depending on the requirements of an institution or organization. It recognizes that sustainability must be built in a participatory manner, involving all relevant actors in the mitigation of climate change
- ✓ Promotes organizational management responsibilities. Oriented to the fact that sustainability is a responsibility of organizations, and that they must take measures to promote it.

In general, the model considers the main dimensions of sustainability and is able to adapt to different contexts. It is a model that has the potential to contribute to the evaluation and promotion of business sustainability, if we take as a reference what Gallardo & Sánchez (2023) stated. In which universities can contribute to sustainability research by training professionals who can address the environmental and social challenges of today's world. (p.47), we can understand how from the research sciences training and education are strategic axes for the development of new sustainable business models. The following are the key steps for the completion of this analytical sustainability model:

Table 2. Key steps for filling out the form

Variable	Description
Definition of Objectives and Scope	The model establishes specific objectives that are to be achieved and defined when the assessment instrument is completed. That is why the model measures sustainability actions through a first phase, which brings together 34 items associated with the functional areas of the organization. On the other hand, in phase 2, 26 more items associated with categories of organizational, social, economic and environmental impact are established. Criteria relevant to the entity or project in question.
Identification of KPIs (High Performance Indicators)	Indicators are quantitative or qualitative measures that reflect performance in areas relevant to sustainability. It is crucial to identify the key indicators that will help measure progress towards the set goals. These can range from carbon emissions and water consumption to local employment rates and community well-being.
Measurement and Analysis	The model uses the collected data and baselines, and proceeds to measure the current performance in relation to sustainability indicators. A detailed analysis is carried out to identify trends, strengths and areas for improvement.
Measurement construct	The model has developed a series of functionalities that allow data analysis to be generated. The report visually generates a dashboard and/or balanced scorecard that works with metrics from weighting values from 0 to 5, which the person who fills it out rates according to the action they are evaluating within the model. This allows measuring the levels of application of sustainable business actions and analyzes the indicators and business variables that generate triple impact within the operation, the analytical model was built from a series of technical actions established in the: 1. Social and Human Capital Protocol - (Word Bussiness Council for Sustainable Development) 2. The Triple Bottom Line (TBL) - Company Balance Sheet 3. The Lowell Center Model for Sustainable Production 4. Indices GRI - Global Reporting Initiative
Filling out the form	For the completion of the model, phases can be found that allow it to generate traceability during and after the evaluation. First, they must fill out the "***evaluation phase***" section in which the type and degree of the sustainable action carried out by the organization is marked with an x; A single option must be chosen within each activity to be evaluated (does not perform it; does not comply with it; complies moderately; partially complies with it); fully complies with it), each selection has a weighting level of 0 to 5, with 5 being the highest value of the evaluation and 0 the lowest weighting. It should be taken into account that in order to weigh each variable, the organizational processes must be evaluated and the result of this decision must be identified from the KPIs.

Source: Own elaboration

It is worth mentioning that the structure is consecutively conformed in the first place by an interface of the general content, followed by the collection of information from the company and/or entrepreneur that completes the evaluation; followed by primary information on the objective of the model and the recommendations for completion. Finally, the model shows a series of recommendations for each of the items and dimensions evaluated that presented a weighting from 0 to 3, while weightings 4 to 5 only generate an alert to continue with the process. According to Barroso et al (2025) "The measures that have been implemented have not considered the environment as a whole, focusing only on certain species" (p.2). Therefore, each completed assessment becomes a case study, offering insights into how organizations interpret and respond to environmental management, social responsibility, economic stability, governance, and innovation metrics. If we bring bibliographic references such as Ramirez & Lizarazo (2025) which state that "The concept of sustainability arose from fundamental research on how societies can effectively manage their natural resources without compromising economic progress or exacerbating social and spatial disparities." (p.1). We understand that sustainability results such as those of MADES, which issue continuity alerts, are not arbitrary thresholds; They are the result of rigorous analysis and statistical validation within the framework of multidimensional sustainability research. This approach allows identifying patterns, correlations and causalities between business practices and their sustainable performance, validating the initial hypotheses of the model.

By making a clear context of the research, we can affirm that it has also focused on the algorithmic optimization of MADES, seeking to improve the accuracy of the evaluations, the clarity of the recommendations and the usability of the platform. Thus, the model is not only an assessment tool, but a living laboratory where continuous research enriches its predictive and prescriptive capacity, ensuring that companies can effectively navigate towards a more sustainable and resilient future. However, the origin of the data and information sources of the MADES control panel is fed by data from both internal sources of the organization and from specialized external repositories. Internally, the information is extracted from corporate systems such as ERP (Enterprise Resource Planning) for financial and resource management indicators; EMS (Environmental Management Systems) certified under ISO 14001 for environmental metrics such as carbon footprint, energy consumption and waste management; and QMS (Quality Management Systems) under ISO 9001 for data related to operational efficiency and customer satisfaction. Likewise, records of human talent management platforms are integrated, which allow monitoring variables such as turnover, well-being and gender equity. However, this information is part of the data protection of thc tool with the account of its copyright. However, in terms of external sources, the model uses information from regulatory entities and sectoral observatories, such as the Ministry of Environment and Sustainable Development, the National Administrative Department of Statistics (DANE), and the Corporate Sustainability Observatory.

It also incorporates indicators aligned with international standards such as GRI (Global Reporting Initiative), the United Nations Global Compact and the Sustainable Development Goals (SDGs). This integration of sources ensures that the MADES control panel has up-to-date, verifiable and comparable information over time. These results are reasonable taking into account Fritz et al., 2019. Cited by Zarrabeitia-Bilbao et al (2023) who state that implementing and achieving the SDGs in general and SDG 9 in particular, requires the participation of all agents. Therefore, a formal or traditional communication strategy may not be the best option to raise awareness of the SDGs. In addition, traditional data sources, while valuable and necessary, are not sufficient to measure the development of the SDGs, so new non-traditional data sources are needed. (p. 9408)

Figure 2. Dashboard result of the evaluation through MADES

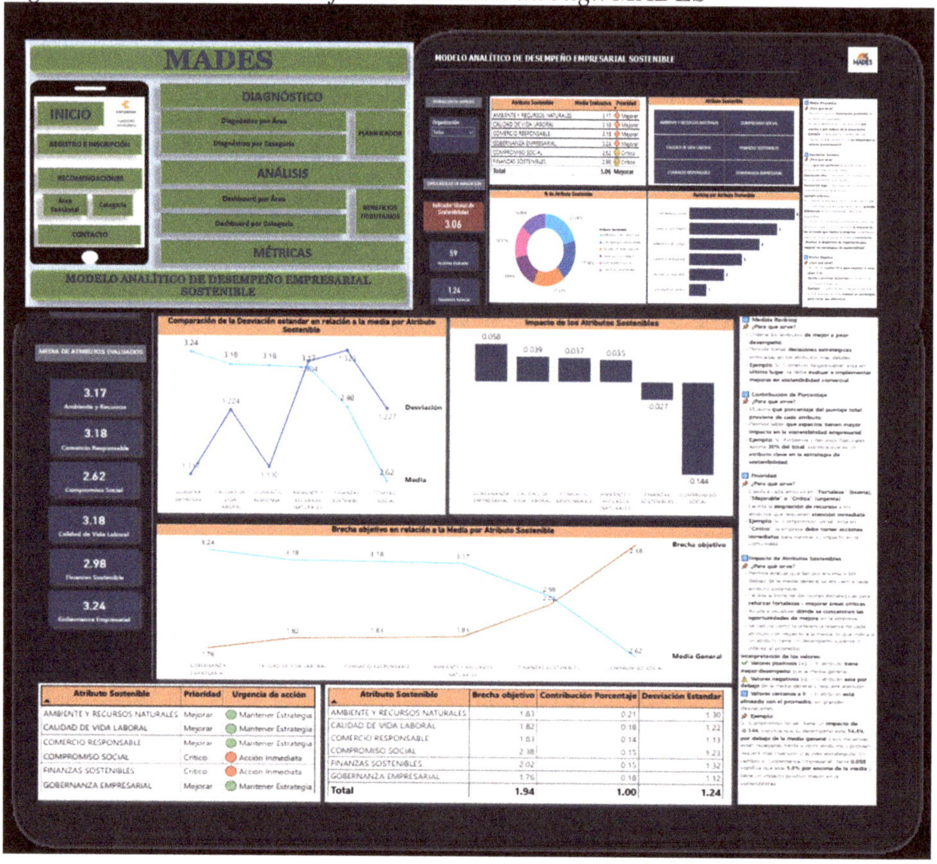

However, the application of MADES offers organizations a comprehensive view of their sustainable performance, identifying areas for improvement that require strategic actions. Among these, the logistics dimension, which plays a fundamental role, since a large part of the impacts and opportunities detected in MADES depend on efficiency in the supply chain. In this sense, to complement the evaluation and respond to these opportunities, the Logistics Evaluation and Analysis Model (MEAL) is presented as the second pillar of the MOIS, focused on optimizing logistics and operational processes under principles of sustainability and efficiency.

2. MEAL: LOGISTIC ASSESSMENT AND DIAGNOSIS MODEL

The Logistics Evaluation and Analysis Model (MEAL) constitutes the second pillar of the MOIS and stands as a strategic tool to diagnose, analyze and optimize logistics processes in Colombian SMEs. Its central purpose is to identify the level of development of organizational logistics processes and determine specific needs, based on international standards and best practices in the sector. MEAL is based on the principle that efficient logistics not only reduces costs, but also enables operational sustainability and facilitates the transition to more resilient, digital and circular business models. This model has been built from widely recognized frameworks such as the SCOR (Supply Chain Operations Reference Model), the CIATI Model, the MGO Model and the Gartner approach, which have been adapted to the context of medium and small companies. As a result, MEAL allows organizations to self-assess their logistics performance based on key metrics, aligned with four major supply chain processes: SOURCE, MAKE, DELIVER and RETURN.

In this sense, MEAL translates the principles of operational excellence and logistics transformation into specific and measurable Good Logistics Practices (GLP), adapted to four key processes of the value chain:

- Source: Processes related to purchasing management, suppliers, responsible sourcing, just-in-time sourcing, and collaborative relationships in the supply chain.
- Transform: manufacturing, transformation, assembly and value-added services. It includes energy efficiency, waste reduction and sustainable production practices.
- Deliver: Warehousing strategies, inventory management, transportation, sustainable urban distribution, customer service, and multichannel delivery channels.
- Returns: reverse logistics policies, management of non-compliant products, recycling, reuse, value recovery and traceability of returns.

Evaluative attributes and measurement system

The evaluation is built from four cross-cutting logistic attributes, each with a series of sub-indicators that make up the model's analysis matrix. These attributes are evaluated using a five-level maturity scale (0 to 5), where 0 represents the total absence of the practice and 5 represents its systematic and monitored implementation. The results are integrated into a visual dashboard that allows you to identify gaps, propose corrective actions and formulate continuous improvement plans:

Figure 3. Evaluative attributes and measurement system

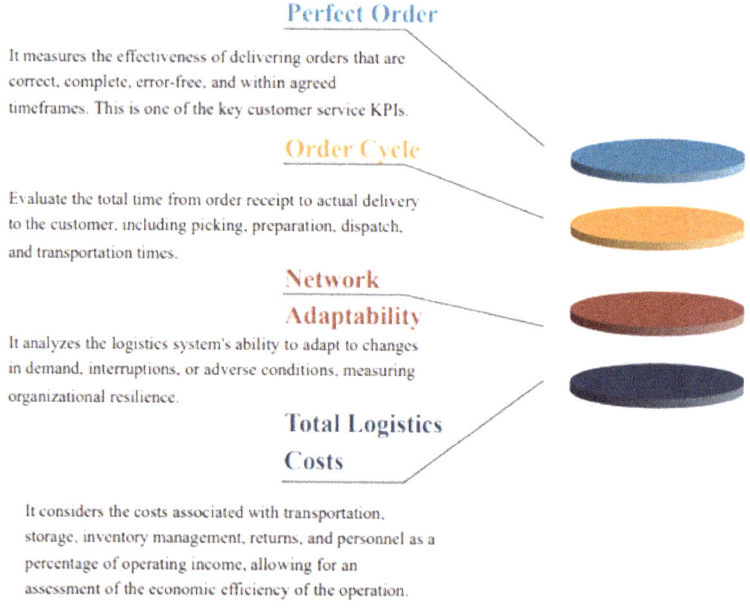

The evaluation of the MEAL model is built on four cross-cutting logistics attributes that allow diagnosing the integral performance of the supply chain in organizations. The first of these, Perfect Order Fulfillment, measures a company's ability to deliver complete, correct, and on-time orders, which is one of the key performance indicators in terms of customer service quality (Ikatrinasari, Harianto & Yuslistyari, 2020). The Order Cycle Time evaluates the total time from receipt to final delivery of the order, including stages such as readiness, packaging and dispatch. This metric is critical for identifying bottlenecks and improving responsiveness in the supply chain (Lulagala, Mwelu, Watera & Makepu, 2023). The third attribute, Network Responsiveness, examines the ability of the logistics system to adjust to sudden changes in demand, operational disruptions, or situations of external volatility.

This dimension is crucial in building resilient supply chains in the face of dynamic and uncertain contexts (Guntuka, Falcone & Choi, 2024). Finally, Total Logistics Costs include expenses associated with transportation, storage, inventories and personnel, expressed as a percentage of operating income. This financial metric allows monitoring the economic efficiency of the logistics system and guiding cost reduction strategies without affecting the quality of service (Pamudji & Achmadi, 2021).

Together, these four attributes make up a robust analytics matrix that drives continuous improvement and sustainability in enterprise logistics management. The systematic incorporation of these four logistics attributes into the MEAL model not only strengthens the internal diagnosis of business operations, but also becomes a strategic mechanism to drive organizational optimization. By accurately measuring perfect order fulfillment levels, cycle times, network adaptability, and total logistics costs, companies can identify opportunities for improvement, reduce waste, anticipate risks, and make data-driven decisions. This analytical capability translates into greater operational efficiency, reduced structural costs, and smarter use of available resources. Supply chain integration is positively related to export performance when logistics performance is considered as a mediating variable (Abdallah, Rawadiah, Al-Byati, & Alhyari, 2021). In addition, recent studies show that companies that optimize their logistics operations can increase their competitive advantage, accelerate their time to market, and strengthen their organizational resilience (Touboulic & Walker, 2015). In a highly changing environment, such as the one currently faced by Colombian SMEs, MEAL acts as a lever for transformation, aligning logistics processes with the organization's strategic objectives and consolidating a sustainable competitive advantage in the market.

Some authors such as Loaiza R. et al (2024) state that “In addition, studies in the field of sustainability have also explored how consumers with high environmental values have a greater perception of the performance of sustainable products than consumers with low environmental values” (p.1).

Figure 4. Reference of the MEAL model evaluation result

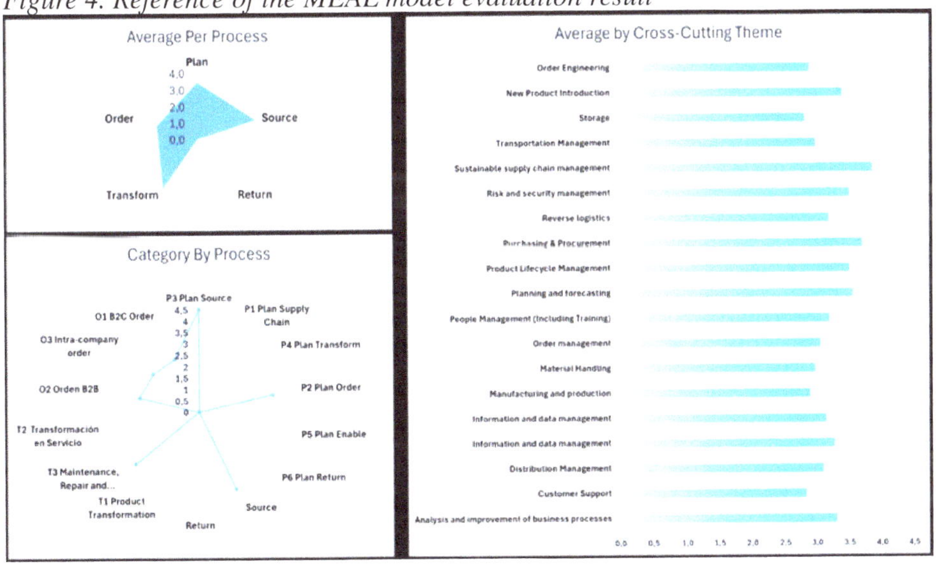

The model provides three main types of analysis:

1. Average per logistics process (Plan, Source, Make/Transform, Deliver/Order, Return): allows you to identify which phases of the chain have a better development and which require intervention. For example, a high score on "Plan" suggests good planning ability, while a low score on "Return" indicates weakness in reverse logistics.
2. Evaluation by specific categories within each process (such as maintenance, B2B orders, or product transformation): delves into specific operational aspects, which helps to focus improvement actions within functional areas.
3. Average by cross-cutting topics (such as inventory management, purchasing, process analysis, risk management, customer service): offers a holistic view of logistics practices that cross all processes, evidencing both strengths (e.g., in business process analysis) and gaps (e.g., in reverse logistics or product lifecycle management).

Model validation, application, and flexibility

The MEAL model has been validated in companies from various economic sectors in Colombia, such as Corona, ALDIA Logística and Marcel France, demonstrating its adaptability in both manufacturing and service contexts. This validation allowed us to verify that the model is applicable regardless of the size, complexity or industry of the organization, since it focuses on logistics processes and not on the characteristics of the product or the market. One of the differentiating values of the MEAL is its flexibility of application. The tool allows you to evaluate a single process (e.g. only SOURCE or DELIVER) or to carry out a comprehensive diagnosis, according to the company's strategic objectives. In addition, it allows progressive integration with digital tools such as Power BI, automated Excel or ERP systems, facilitating its use in environments with different levels of technological maturity. According to Sairanen, M., & Aarikka-Stenroos, L. (2024) "As climate change progresses, companies face profound challenges and new business opportunities in the global race towards carbon neutrality" (p.222). When talking specifically in the validation of the MEAL, in this phase, data was collected from ERP systems, inventory control sheets, transport management platforms and internal records of logistics processes. These data were processed in the MEAL dashboard to obtain averages by process, category and cross-cutting themes. Based on the results, a gap analysis was applied to identify the differences between the current state and the optimal level defined by good logistics practices (GLP) adapted from international benchmarks such as SCOR, CIATI, MGO and the Gartner approach. The validation included the comparison of the results of the MEAL with logistics indicators previously measured by the companies, evaluating the coherence and relevance of the recommendations issued. Likewise, a direct feedback process was carried out with the logistics and management managers to confirm that the suggested actions were applicable and viable within the real operation.

Para (Borschiver & Tavares, 2022, p. 29) cited by Castro, N. dos S., & Machado, A. L. S. (2024) states that the "revolutionary advent of the Industrial Economy brings a historic milestone for the advancement of society, however, the fleeting speed of obtaining products and their immediate disposition characterized by the Linear Economy occurred in an expansive and global way" (p. 3). Another key contribution is the application of circular economy principles through reverse logistics, promoting reuse and recycling within the value chain. The model also contributes to improving the quality of customer service and reducing waste, thanks to greater precision in production and distribution processes. In the architecture of the Integrated Optimization Model in Sustainability (MOIS), MEAL plays a critical role in operationalizing the sustainable strategy from the logistics dimension, articulating in a complementary way with the other two methodological pillars: MADES and DISCI. On the one hand, MADES establishes the metrics and indicators necessary to evaluate business sustainability from a systemic perspective, covering aspects such as governance, social performance, economic stability and environmental impact.

Figure 5. Articulation of the MEAL model

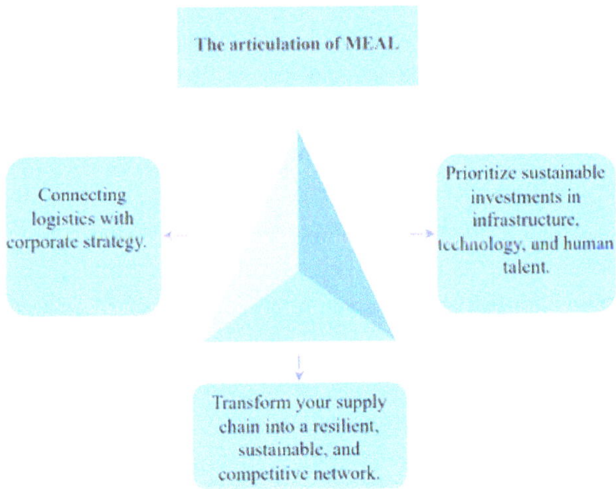

This methodological triangulation makes MOIS a robust tool for business transformation, which is not limited to diagnosis, but promotes action, data-driven decision-making and continuous improvement. The articulation of MEAL in this model allows companies. Thus, the MEAL ceases to be an exclusive tool for large corporations and becomes a strategic accelerator for SMEs, facilitating their transition towards a sustainable, innovative business model aligned with the Sustainable Development Goals.

3. DISCI: COMPREHENSIVE DIAGNOSIS OF THE INTERNAL CONTROL SYSTEM

The DISCI Model (Comprehensive Diagnosis of the Internal Control System) is a methodological tool that allows organizations, especially small and medium-sized enterprises (SMEs), to evaluate the degree of maturity and effectiveness of their Internal Control System (ICS). This model arises as an adapted and contextualized application of the renowned Internal Control – Integrated Framework (COSO ICIF), issued by the Committee of Sponsoring Organizations of the Treadway Commission (COSO, 2013), which structures internal control into five fundamental components and 17 operating principles.

Unlike generic approaches to internal control, the DISCI Model proposes an in-depth and personalized diagnosis, based on concrete and verifiable criteria. For each of the principles, the DISCI Model proposes the verification of elements such as the existence of control (design, approval and dissemination), its effective implementation, the assignment of those responsible, the verification of its operation in practice and the incorporation of continuous improvement processes. For example, one of the fundamental criteria that reinforces this model is the need to have current, approved, and disseminated documentation, accompanied by evidence of implementation, such as minutes, manuals, policies, or performance indicators (Rojas, 2023; Domínguez & Joya, 2017).

Likewise, the DISCI Model articulates the COSO components (control environment, risk assessment, control activities, information and communication, and supervision) in an evaluation scheme that allows establishing a map of risks, strengths, and weaknesses of the organizational ICS (Arias & Salto, 2020). This translates into a powerful tool for risk management, regulatory compliance, operational efficiency, and transparency in decision-making. According to Guzmán (2022), its application makes it possible to highlight structural gaps that, in addition to compromising the financial sustainability of companies, can also affect their organizational integrity and ability to respond to crises or audits.

Evaluation Criteria in the DISCI Model

The evaluation criteria applied in the DISCI model are grouped around three fundamental analytical axes: (1) existence of control, (2) operational functioning and (3) continuous improvement. These axes derive from the understanding that an internal control system should not be limited to its documentary formulation, but should also demonstrate its practical application and its ability to adapt to internal and external changes that affect the organization (Álvarez et al., 2020).

1. Criteria for determining the existence of control

This first set of criteria seeks to verify whether the principle evaluated has been formally designed, approved, documented, and socialized. Aspects such as:

- The existence of specific policies, procedures or activities.
- Its formal documentation in manuals, regulations or other internal normative instruments.
- Formal approval by a competent authority, with its respective evidence (minutes, positions, dates).
- The socialization of control between the different levels of the organization through verified means of dissemination (institutional mail, training, internal communications).

2. Criteria for checking the operation of the control

These criteria assess whether internal control has been effectively implemented and whether it operates efficiently. Here it is analyzed:

- The existence of a person in charge assigned to control.
- The practical implementation of what has been designed.
- Evidence that the control is working correctly, such as the traceability of decisions, processes or controls executed.
- The existence of performance or risk management indicators that allow objective monitoring of the operation of the principle evaluated (Mangasih et al., 2020).

3. Criteria for Verification of Continuous Improvement

Finally, this axis examines the ability of the control system to be updated, strengthened and corrected. The following are considered to be key elements:

- Evidence of periodic review of the control (at least in the last two years).
- The existence of feedback processes that generate recommendations or adjustments.

- Documentation demonstrating corrective actions or improvements implemented from audits, internal diagnostics, or other evaluation mechanisms.

These criteria allow the evaluation not to be limited to a subjective judgment, but to be based on verifiable evidence, a situation that strengthens the transparency of the diagnosis and its usefulness for strategic decision-making.

Regulatory Framework and International Standards

Taking as a reference what Villacampa said. (2025) "Growing concerns about climate change and its potential impacts on the global economy have intensified the growing demand from financial actors, especially individual and institutional investors, for companies to report on climate-related financial risks" (p.2). We can understand that the DISCI model and its evaluation criteria are aligned with organizational governance principles established in international standards such as ISO 37301:2021 on compliance management systems, which highlights the need for evidence-based control structures and continuous improvement (ISO, 2021). In the same way, it coincides with the recommendations of IFAC (2020), which advocates internal control systems that transcend the merely formal and operate as tools for organizational integrity and sustainability. According to Dabbous et al., (2024) cited by Narváez-Castillo et al (2024) "In recent years, the world has had to face substantial new challenges, such as climate change, pollution, energy crises, social tensions, increasing inequalities and economic disruptions, as well as unsustainable patterns of social and economic behaviour" (p.1).

Methodological Implications and Added Value

In methodological terms, the inclusion of these criteria in the DISCI Model allows:

- Standardize internal control evaluation practices.
- Provide clear and verifiable guidelines for internal audits.
- Foster an organizational culture of control and self-regulation.
- Adapt the COSO framework to contexts with lower levels of formalisation, such as that of many SMEs.

Diagnosis by Components of the Internal Control System: Analytical Structure of the DISCI Model

The analysis of the internal control system through the DISCI Model is structured around the five fundamental components established by the Internal Control – Integrated Framework (COSO, 2013). These components—control environment, risk assessment, control activities, information and communication, and monitoring—constitute the normative and functional bases that allow evaluating the effectiveness of internal control systems in organizations. For Yazo-Cabuya et al. (2024) "The current global landscape is immersed in a complex web of challenges and pressures from multiple sources, ranging from environmental crises. In this context, global stakeholder risks are significantly shaping the environmental, social and governance (ESG) landscape" (p.1); This leads to a much broader approach to sustainability, allowing corporate strategies to be articulated with the measurement of risks associated with financial, environmental and social operations. However, according to Saavedra N et al. (2024) "The growing interest in sustainability is transforming the landscape of organizations, as it allows them to improve their reputation through the implementation of good practices to strengthen the corporate image" (p.1727). This analysis is based on sources of high regulatory and academic impact, including regulatory frameworks such as the ICIF COSO, the IFAC guidelines (2020), the ISO 37301:2021 standards, as well as recent scientific literature on internal control, organizational risk, and institutional sustainability. The systematization of these elements constitutes a relevant contribution both for internal auditing and for strategic management, in business contexts that demand greater efficiency, transparency and organizational resilience.

Elements of the DISCI Model

Table 3 below provides a comparative summary of the five components of the ICIF COSO, the principles that comprise them, the evaluation axes defined by the DISCI model and the main criteria used for diagnosis. This tool is a key methodological input for auditors, managers and compliance officers, as it allows establishing a common evaluation framework, identifying gaps and guiding improvement actions aligned with international standards of governance, integrity and control.

Table 3. DISCI diagnostic referents

COSO ICIF Component	Associated principles	Axes of evaluation of the DISCI model	Diagnostic criteria
1. Control Environment	Commitment to Integrity and Ethical ValuesOversight ResponsibilityStructure, Authority, and ResponsibilitiesCompetenceAccountability	Formal existenceOperational functioningContinuous improvement	Custom DesignRegulatory DocumentationFormal ApprovalSocializationImplementationAssigneesDemonstrated OperationEvidence of Continuous Improvement
2. Risk Assessment	Target SpecificationRisk Identification and AnalysisFraud Risk AssessmentAnalysis of Significant Changes	Formal existenceOperational functioningContinuous improvement	Same as above; in addition, the existence of risk matrices, planning methodologies and iterative evaluation processes is validated
3. Control Activities	Selection and Development of ControlsGeneral Controls on TechnologyOperating Policies and Procedures	Formal existenceOperational functioningContinuous improvement	Effective policy enforcement, segregation of duties, automated controls, authorized roles and processes
4. Information and Communication	Relevant and timely informationInternal communicationExternal communication	Formal existenceOperational functioningContinuous improvement	Existence of official channels, communication policies, documentation of flows and feedback mechanisms
5. Activity Monitoring	Continuous AssessmentsIndependent Assessments	Formal existenceOperational functioningContinuous improvement	Internal audits, corrective action plans, monitoring of indicators and review of institutional performance

Source: Own elaboration

Integration of the DISCI Model

The Comprehensive Diagnosis Model of the Internal Control System (DISCI) articulates in a structured way three methodological levels that allow the evaluation of the internal control system of organizations with rigor and adaptability. As already mentioned, in its regulatory basis, the model adopts the five components of the COSO ICIF framework (2013) – control environment, risk assessment, control activities, information and communication, and monitoring – which make up the essential pillars on which control systems are designed and executed in all types of entities. These components provide a solid and internationally recognized conceptual framework. On this basis, the model incorporates its own operational approach, composed of three axes of evaluation: *formal existence*, *operational operation* and *continuous improvement*, which guide the analysis from regulatory validation to practical evidence of implementation. Each COSO principle is evaluated through these axes, and its diagnosis is specified through eight specific diagnostic criteria, designed to offer a comprehensive, verifiable and standardized assessment of the internal control system in each of its principles. The eight diagnostic criteria that operationalize the DISCI model allow establishing the level of maturity of each control analyzed. The *custom design criterion* verifies the relevance and adequacy of the control to the context of the organization. Formal *documentation* refers to the existence of written supports, manuals or institutional policies. Institutional *approval* validates that the control has been adopted by a competent authority. Socialization examines whether such control has been communicated and understood by those who must carry it out. The implementation criterion focuses on the existence of concrete actions that demonstrate its implementation. The *assignment of those responsible* establishes whether there are designated actors with clear functions over control. The *demonstrated performance criterion* requires tangible evidence of the operation of the control. Finally, *applied continuous improvement* analyzes whether the control has been subject to recent revisions, adjustments, or strengthening. This diagnostic structure is presented visually through a concentric diagram that synthesizes the integration between the COSO model, the evaluative logic of the DISCI and the operational verification mechanisms.

Figure 6. DISCI model integration

With this, based on its comprehensive approach, the DISCI allows the formal existence of controls to be assessed, along with their efficient practical implementation and their ability to adapt to changing contexts, which is especially significant for organizations with poorly formalized structures or in stages of institutional consolidation. The application of the model, through its three evaluation axes and eight diagnostic criteria, offers a solid tool for internal auditors, risk managers and compliance officers, facilitating the identification of gaps and the prioritization of corrective actions. Beyond its technical value, DISCI has been configured to strengthen control systems, as a tool that promotes a culture of integrity, transparency and accountability within organizations. Its modular and scalable structure allows it to be adapted to different sectors, sizes and levels of institutional maturity, designed to be articulated to a more comprehensive model such as the MADES model. In short, the DISCI Model not only responds to a diagnostic need, but also enables strategic processes of organizational transformation, by facilitating informed decision-making and the construction of a sustainable control architecture, aligned with international standards and ethical principles of good governance.

Finally, we can affirm that the adoption of the Integrated Optimization Model in Sustainability (MOIS) in pilot companies of different sectors in Colombia has demonstrated tangible results. For example, an agro-industrial SME (Zurich Artisanal Chocolate) that implemented MADES reduced its energy consumption by 18% by modernizing its lighting and cooling system. An industrial company (Corona), by implementing the MEAL, optimized its inventories and reduced its logistics costs by 12% thanks to the consolidation of routes and a reverse logistics program for returns. In the case of DISCI, a service SME strengthened its procurement authorization processes, reducing the risk of unplanned expenditures by 20%. However, the implementation of the model faces challenges typical of the Colombian context, such as budgetary limitations to invest in technology, low organizational culture oriented towards sustainability, scarce digital integration in key processes and changing regulatory frameworks that affect long-term planning. Among the main barriers detected are resistance to change, the lack of trained personnel to interpret indicators and the overload of metrics that, if not prioritized, can generate measurement fatigue. Likewise, improvements in one area could lead to unintended impacts in others, underscoring the need for a comprehensive approach.

For effective implementation, SME owners are recommended to adopt MOIS gradually, starting with the most critical dimension for their business; managers, to integrate the control board in strategic decision-making; and for public policy makers, to develop tax incentives and co-financing programs that facilitate the adoption of the model. These coordinated actions will allow the MOIS to be a viable, inclusive and adaptable tool to the diverse realities of Colombian SMEs. While MOIS provides a comprehensive framework for strengthening sustainability, logistics and internal control in SMEs, it has limitations that need to be recognized for its proper implementation. The diversity of the Colombian business fabric means that the model is not adopted uniformly: companies differ in size, sector, degree of formalization and technological preparation, which can affect their ability to implement all phases of the model. In addition, its effectiveness depends on the quality and availability of data, which requires specifying the sources of information and ensuring reliable collection processes, especially in contexts where there are no integrated management systems. Validation, although supported by pilot tests, needs to be expanded with comparative studies and recent local data that strengthen its empirical base. Therefore, the recommendations must be adapted to each business profile, prioritizing simple and low-cost actions for SMEs with less organizational maturity, and more sophisticated strategies for those with greater technological and management capacity.

4. RECOMMENDATIONS

To maximize the effectiveness of the Integrated Optimization Model in Sustainability (MOIS) and encourage its large-scale adoption, several practical, strategic and regulatory recommendations are proposed. First, it is essential to foster alliances between universities, companies and governments, which promote applied research and the development of models such as MOIS from a multi-stakeholder perspective. Universities, for example, can lead sustainability training processes, as well as act as validators of the model (Gallardo & Sánchez, 2023). Second, it recommends the creation of public policies that include fiscal or financial incentives for those companies that adopt comprehensive evaluation tools such as MOIS. This would strengthen the competitiveness of SMEs, while boosting the transition to a circular and low-carbon economy. Thirdly, it is suggested to adapt the MOIS to scalable digital platforms that facilitate its access to companies with different levels of technological maturity. Interoperability with ERP systems, CRM, and data analytics platforms will be key to its mass adoption. Fourthly, training and technical support processes for entrepreneurs should be promoted, especially in rural regions or with less infrastructure, to ensure the correct implementation of the model. Sustainability should be understood as a strategic investment, not a cost.

Integrating these recommendations, it is necessary to urge the strengthening of the organizational culture based on principles of sustainability, ethics, transparency and innovation, recognizing that the success of MOIS does not lie only in its technical structure, but in the will of organizations to transform.

5. FUTURE RESEARCH DIRECTIONS

The implementation of MOIS in the Colombian context opens up a wide spectrum of lines of research that can be developed at the national and international levels. First, it is essential to deepen comparative studies on the applicability of the model in different regions and economic sectors, evaluating its adaptability and performance under various socioeconomic and cultural conditions. This will allow benchmarking metrics to be established and their scalability to be validated. Secondly, it is suggested to advance in the integration of MOIS with emerging technologies such as blockchain, artificial intelligence (AI) and the Internet of Things

(IoT), in order to automate evaluation processes, traceability of sustainable actions and internal audits. This digitalization could lead to the creation of intelligent platforms for sustainable management in real time. Third, it is necessary to explore the impact of MOIS on traditional financial indicators (such as EBITDA or ROA) and non-financial indicators (carbon footprint, GRI indices, regulatory compliance), in order to quantify the return on investment in sustainability. It is also pertinent to investigate the perception and adoption of the model among key stakeholders, such as customers, employees, and suppliers.

However, a relevant line will be the link of the model with public policies and programs to support SMEs, analyzing how its adoption can be encouraged from the institutional framework, through tax incentives, training programs and access to green financing. This research will strengthen the empirical validation of MOIS and its potential as a tool for sustainable business policy in Latin America and other international contexts.

6. CONCLUSION

The Integrated Optimization Model in Sustainability (MOIS) represents an innovative, comprehensive and relevant proposal to address the challenges faced by small and medium-sized enterprises (SMEs) in Colombia and potentially in other Latin American contexts. Its tripartite approach – MADES, MEAL and DISCI – allows for a comprehensive assessment that integrates sustainability, logistics efficiency and internal control, three fundamental pillars in contemporary business management. Through MADES, multidimensional sustainability is promoted with metrics that link economic, social and environmental impact. MEAL provides a robust tool to optimize the supply chain through good logistics practices that respond to international standards. DISCI, for its part, strengthens internal control systems, guaranteeing regulatory compliance and promoting organizational transparency. The articulation of these three models generates a synergy capable of raising the level of resilience, innovation and competitiveness of SMEs, aligning their operations with the Sustainable Development Goals (SDGs). In addition, the MOIS demonstrates adaptability to different productive sectors and levels of organizational maturity, which broadens its international applicability. This methodological proposal contributes not only to the internal strengthening of organizations, but also to the generation of shared value with their stakeholders. Finally, it is concluded that the MOIS constitutes a strategic tool that allows companies to move towards sustainable business models, while facilitating evidence-based decision-making and fostering a business culture committed to sustainable development. On the other hand, the references used in the chapter are appropriate and up-to-date, covering recent studies (2021-2022) on

Latin American and global sustainable integration. However, to further strengthen the bibliographic base and offer a more complete perspective, it is suggested to analyze these following additional references:

Pigato, M. A. (Ed.). (2019). Fiscal Policies for Development and Climate Action. World Bank Publications. https://doi.org/10.1596/978-1-4648-1358-0. This book provides a comprehensive analysis of green fiscal policies in developing countries, which could offer valuable insights for the Colombian context. On the other hand, the information related to

Narassimhan, E., Gallagher, K. S., Koester, S., & Alejo, J. R. (2018). Carbon pricing in practice: A review of existing emissions trading systems. Climate Policy, 18(8), 967-991. https://doi.org/10.1080/14693062.2018.1467827. This article offers a review of existing emissions trading systems, which could be useful for comparison with green taxation strategies. The bibliographic content described in Fanelli, J. M., Jiménez, J. P., & López Azcúnaga, I. (2015). Environmental tax reform in Latin America. ECLAC. https://repositorio.cepal.org/handle/11362/39782. Although it is a bit older, this ECLAC study provides a region-specific analysis that could be valuable in contextualizing the Colombian case.

Mercure, J. F., Knobloch, F., Pollitt, H., Paroussos, L., Scrieciu, S. S., & Lewney, R. (2019). Modelling innovation and the macroeconomics of low-carbon transitions: theory, perspectives and practical use. Climate Policy, 19(8), 1019-1037. https://doi.org/10.1080/14693062.2019.1617665. This article could be useful in addressing the macroeconomic aspects of the transition to a low-carbon economy. And finally Monge, C. (2021). Fiscal Policy and Climate Change: Recent Experiences of Latin American and Caribbean Countries. Inter-American Development Bank. https://doi.org/10.18235/0003376.

REFERENCES

Abdallah, A. B., Rawadiah, O. M., Al-Byati, W., & Alhyari, S. (2021). Supply chain integration and export performance: The mediating role of supply chain performance. *International Journal of Productivity and Performance Management, 70*(7), 1907–1929. DOI: 10.1108/IJPPM-02-2021-0076

Álvarez, G. O. C., Zurita, I. N., & Álvarez, J. C. E. (2020). Internal control system as a tool for optimizing the financial processes of the company Austroseguridad Cía. Ltda. *Dominio de las Ciencias, 6*(1), 429–465.

Arias, M. G. M., & Salto, I. M. A. (2020). Internal control model for SMEs based on the COSO-ERM report. UCTUNEXPO University. https://uctunexpo.autanabooks.com/index.php/uct/article/view/375

Barroso Castillo, S. M., Castellanos, I. D. M. P., Cruz-Pérez, N., d'Armengol, L., & Santamarta, J. C. (2025). Sustaining Tradition: Socioeconomic and Environmental Dimensions of Canary Island Fisheries in the Post-COVID-19 Era. *Conservation, 5*(1), 12. DOI: 10.3390/conservation5010012

BBVA Research. (2023). A look at MSMEs in Colombia. Retrieved from https://www.bbvaresearch.com/publicaciones/colombia-una-mirada-a-las-mipymes-en-colombia/

Castro, N. dos S., & Machado, A. L. S. (2024). GREEN MARKET: A TOOL FOR RECYCLING AND ENVIRONMENTAL EDUCATION. *Journal of Social and Environmental Management, 18*(3), e04700. DOI: 10.24857/rgsa.v18n3-060

Committee of Sponsoring Organizations of the Treadway Commission. (2013). Internal Control – Integrated Framework. COSO. AICPA. https://www.coso.org/Pages/ic.aspx

Domínguez Archila, M. L., & Joya Silva, Y. P. (2017). Financial Audit Manual for Financial Statements under IFRS for footwear SMEs in the city of Bucaramanga. Retrieved from: https://repository.ucc.edu.co/bitstreams/1e5f71f8-af57-40fe-839a-8cc748943aa2/download

Elkington, J. (1997). *Cannibals with forks: The triple bottom line of 21st century business*. Capstone Publishing.

European Commission. (2020). A new Circular Economy Action Plan for a cleaner and more competitive. *Europe*. Advance online publication. DOI: 10.2779/05068

Gallardo-Vázqueza, D., & Juan de la Cruz, S.-D. (2023). *Bibliometric study of the link between Sustainability and Circular Economy: A contribution for current business model from the collaboration*. Enterprise-University., DOI: 10.6018/rcsar.576471

Guzmán, E. B. O. (2022). *Control of Scrap and Warranties in Beghelli Mexico*. Autonomous University of Querétaro. https://ri-ng.uaq.mx/handle/123456789/3736

Hirano, H. (2019). *5 pillars of Kaizen*. McGraw-Hill Inter-American.

IFAC (International Federation of Accountants). (2020). *International Framework: Good Governance in the Public Sector*. Recuperado de: https://www.cipfa.org/-/media/Files/CIPFA-Thinks/Reports/International-Framework--Good-Governance-in-the-Public-Sector.pdf

ISO. (2021). *ISO 37301:2021 Compliance management systems — Requirements with guidance for use*. International Organization for Standardization.

Kishaija, N., Ocwa, A., Kuunya, R., Ssemugenze, B., & Heil, B. (2025). Climate change mitigation and livelihood components in smallholder coffee farming: A literature review and systematics. *Agriculture & Food Security*, *14*(1). Advance online publication. DOI: 10.1186/s40066-025-00522-7

Loaiza-Ramírez, J. P., Reimer, T., & Moreno-Mantilla, C. E. (2024). When green energy feels cozy: The interplay of protected values, the halo effect, and demographics in consumers' renewable energies adoption. *Cleaner and Responsible Consumption*, *15*(100237), 100237. DOI: 10.1016/j.clrc.2024.100237

López Enciso, D. J., Silva Medina, J. P., & Bordón López, M. N. (2023). Impact of the internal control system on the logistics management of a gastronomic company in the city of Pilar. Retrieved from https://dialnet.unirioja.es/descarga/articulo/9294419.pdf

Mangasih, E. T., Pinasti, M., & Bawono, I. R. (2020). The effect of quality of internal audit and effectiveness of internal control systems on good corporate governance in finance companies. *SAR (Soedirman Accounting Review). Journal of Accounting and Business*, *5*(1), 56–82. https://pdfs.semanticscholar.org/522b/8d0ad7d241ecfca3990e1d90c9fca1b80251.pdf/1000

Moreira, A., Rodrigues, A. C., & Ferreira, M. R. (2025). Where does HR management stand in sustainability reporting? ESG and GRI perspectives. *Sustainability*, *17*(7), 3033. DOI: 10.3390/su17073033

Narváez-Castillo, V. P., García-Benau, M. A., Sierra-García, L., & Gambetta, N. (2024). Are material ESG issues making their way into key audit matters? An analysis of Colombian innovative companies. *Journal of Innovation & Knowledge*, *9*(4), 100574. DOI: 10.1016/j.jik.2024.100574

OBS Business School. (2023). Green logistics: What it is and what benefits it has for the company. Retrieved from https://www.obsbusiness.school/blog/logistica-verde-que-es-y-que-beneficios-tiene-para-la-empresa

Pamudji, S., & Achmadi, T. (2021). Measuring the total logistics costs at the macro level: A study of Indonesia's logistics. *Logistics (Basel)*, *5*(4), 68. DOI: 10.3390/logistics5040068

Ramírez, M. A., & Lizarazo, I. (2025). Geographical perspectives of sustainability: Towards a conceptual framework. *Environmental Development*, *53*(101121), 101121. DOI: 10.1016/j.envdev.2024.101121

Rojas Alcedo, F. E. (2023). *The uniform online control system and optimal management in slot companies*. Federico Villarreal National University. Retrieved from: https://repositorio.unfv.edu.pe/handle/20.500.13084/6919

Saavedra Najar, R. A., González, L. D., & Abril Teatín, J. A. (2024). Reports and dimensions of corporate sustainability. A bibliometric analysis. *Venezuelan Journal of Management*, *29*(108). Advance online publication. DOI: 10.52080/rvgluz.29.108.16

Sairanen, M., & Aarikka-Stenroos, L. (2024). Low-carbon business models: Review and typology. *Industrial Marketing Management*, *123*, 222–250. DOI: 10.1016/j.indmarman.2024.10.001

Supply Chain Council. (2012). *Supply Chain Operations Reference Model (SCOR)* (Version 11.0). APICS. https://www.apics.org/apics-for-individuals/apics-magazine-home/scor-model

Touboulic, A., & Walker, H. (2015). Theories in sustainable supply chain management: A structured literature review. *International Journal of Physical Distribution & Logistics Management*, *45*(1/2), 16–42. DOI: 10.1108/IJPDLM-05-2013-0106

Villacampa-Porta, J., Coronado-Vaca, M., & Garrido-Merchán, E. C. (2025). Impact of EU non-financial reporting regulation on Spanish companies' environmental disclosure: A cutting-edge natural language processing approach. *Environmental Sciences Europe*, *37*(1), 29. Advance online publication. DOI: 10.1186/s12302-025-01067-z

Yazo-Cabuya, E. J., Ibeas, A., & Herrera-Cuartas, J. A. (2024). Integration of sustainability into risk management and operational excellence using the VIKOR method, considering comparisons between multi-criteria decision-making methods. *Sustainability (Basel), 16*(11), 4585. DOI: 10.3390/su16114585

Zarrabeitia-Bilbao, E., Jaca-Madariaga, M., Rio-Belver, R.-M., & Alvarez-Meaza, I. (2023). From the Sustainable Development Goals to Industry, Innovation and Sustainable Infrastructure: Perspectives from the Digital Sphere. *Environment, Development and Sustainability, 27*(4), 9407–9425. DOI: 10.1007/s10668-023-04288-5

ADDITIONAL READING

Delsaux, V. (2022). Nudging and environmental taxation: A green perspective to correct carbon dioxide emissions. *Environmental Science & Policy, 136*, 48–56. DOI: 10.1016/j.envsci.2022.05.014

Economic Commission for Latin America and the Caribbean (ECLAC). (2022). Challenges for environmental taxation and the transition to a circular economy in Latin America and the Caribbean. https://repositorio.cepal.org/handle/11362/48163

Hansen, M. B., McGlade, C., van der Zwaan, B., & Walbeck, J. (2022). Exploring the implications of fossil fuel subsidy reform for global carbon emissions. *Energy Economics, 113*, 106236. DOI: 10.1016/j.eneco.2022.106236

Organization for Economic Cooperation and Development (OECD). (2022). Financing the Future: Tax Policy for a Transition to Cleaner Energy Sources. https://doi.org/DOI: 10.1787/9c6abbf9-es

Oueslati, W., Zgehri, Y., & Nguyen, N. (2022). Inclusive green taxation and environmental quality: An investigation among developed and developing countries. *Energy Economics, 108*, 105855. DOI: 10.1016/j.eneco.2022.105855

Semieniuk, G., Campiglio, E., Mercure, J.-F., Volz, U., & Edwards, N. R. (2021). Low-carbon transition risks for finance. *Wiley Interdisciplinary Reviews: Climate Change, 12*(5), e716. DOI: 10.1002/wcc.716

Sumaila, U. R., Skerritt, D. J., Schuhbauer, A., Villasante, S., Macho, G., Sinan, H., Vartdal Fyllingsnes, M., Saidykhan, R., Christensen, V., & Bing Camara, S. (2021). Green taxation to protect marine ecosystems. *Frontiers in Marine Science, 8*, 661186. DOI: 10.3389/fmars.2021.661186

World Bank. (2022). Rethinking the taxation of natural resources: Promoting a comprehensive approach to sustainable development. https://openknowledge.worldbank.org/handle/10986/37275

KEY TERMS AND DEFINITIONS

Circular Economy: Economic model that promotes the reuse, recycling and reduction of waste. (ECLAC, 2022)

Corporate Governance: A set of principles, policies and practices that regulate the direction and control of a company. (IFAC, 2020)

DISCI (Comprehensive Diagnosis of the Internal Control System): Adaptation of the COSO framework to evaluate the existence, operation and improvement of internal control in organizations. (COSO, 2013)

KPIs (Key Performance Indicators): Key performance indicators used to measure progress towards strategic objectives. (Kaplan & Norton, 1996)

MADES (Sustainable Business Performance Analytical Model): Tool that evaluates the sustainable performance of organizations in economic, environmental and social dimensions. (Rodríguez & Arias, 2023)

MEAL (Logistic Evaluation and Analysis Model): Logistics diagnosis and optimization model based on international standards such as SCOR and CIATI. (OBS Business School, 2023)

MOIS (Integral Optimization Model in Sustainability): Methodological approach that integrates sustainability, logistics and internal control to strengthen the business management of SMEs. (Rodríguez Franky et al., 2025)

Resilient Supply Chain: Logistics system capable of adapting to disruptive changes with minimal operational impact. (Guntuka et al., 2024)

SDGs (Sustainable Development Goals): A global agenda composed of 17 goals to eradicate poverty, protect the planet and ensure prosperity for all. (UN, 2015)

Triple Impact: An approach that simultaneously considers the economic, social and environmental impact of business decisions. (Elkington, 1997)

Chapter 14
StructVis: A Tool for Visual Operation of Data Structures

Shubham Sharma
https://orcid.org/0009-0001-2090-183X
Sharda University, India

Ravi Shankar Poddar
https://orcid.org/0009-0006-8714-4171
Sharda University, India

Keshav Gupta
https://orcid.org/0000-0001-7851-1976
Sharda University, India

ABSTRACT

The exclusive use of static theoretical study methods makes the learning process for Data Structures and Algorithms (DSA) highly complicated for students. Through an interactive system development users obtain real-time visual displays of running algorithm codes using step-by-step execution. The platform offers a user interface which functions through React.js and receives its aesthetic appearance from Tailwind CSS. Concepts related to sorting and searching and basic DSA principles achieve their dynamic visualization capabilities from D3.js. All backend functions on this platform work effectively through REST API structures. Code execution security occurs through Docker implementations that operate submitted user programs within designated containers. Through the interface users can adjust animation speeds and they can both reset steps alongside viewing the entire algorithm sequence. The visual interface of the tool delivers teaching experiences for DSA through simultaneous explanatory guidance together with dynamic visual representation and interactivity.

DOI: 10.4018/979-8-3373-3301-4.ch014

1. INTRODUCTION

Data Structures and Algorithms (DSA) serve as the bedrock of computational problem-solving and software development. Programming success requires mastery of DSA that permits both competitive developers and software developers to demonstrate excellence while technical developers from every domain rely on this fundamental skill. Application performance and scalability alongside maintenance capability arise from using correctly designed algorithms which select suitable data structures. The conceptual elements transform storage choices through operational representation decisions and they determine duration of execution time and system stability limits and memory usage.

The acquisition of DSA remains a significant obstacle for students because its importance continues rising in educational practice and software development fields. Traditional teaching of DSA involves delivering lectures together with theoretical explanations and static illustrations from textbooks along with examples. The current educational methods do not manage to link theoretical understanding to actual practical application. Under current teaching practices students need to use their imagination to comprehend linked lists along with trees and both graphs and heaps using abstract methods that lead to knowledge confusion and limited understanding while damaging student problem-solving capabilities. The inability to bring essential reasoning abilities leads students to face major difficulties when converting theoretical knowledge into practical programming tasks.

DSA education faces one primary problem because it does not include educational features that provide timely visual feedback.The contemporary online educational content including courses and tutorials fails to incorporate active learning features when students consult pre-recorded videos and tutorial content. Students experience a lack of understanding between program execution and data structure transformation because they cannot observe dynamic modifications. The essential yet advanced concept of recursion in DSA is usually presented to students through mathematical proof methods and static paper representations of code. The incapacity to observe the recursive call stack and backtracking operations live makes it difficult for students to understand recursion execution patterns organically.

Rules of recursion pair with fundamental algorithm types such as sorting algorithms (Merge Sort, Quick Sort, Heap Sort) and traversal methods (in-order, pre-order, post-order tree traversals) and graph algorithm types (DFS and BFS). Debugging techniques based on console prints and variable inspection and memory examination do not show data structure changes that occur step by step during algorithm execution. Program debugging becomes inefficient and time-consuming for visual learners because they need graphic-based algorithmic flow visualization to understand the process.

The development of an interactive DSA visualization platform based on browser technology would serve as a pedagogical solution to enhance learning through real-time simulation. Students can monitor how program execution progresses by watching data insertion to stacks in addition to following queue development and recursive calling patterns along with array changes through this visualization platform. Through this method students become able to learn experientially because they both write code and see through visualization how it operates while running.

1.1 Challenges in Traditional DSA Learning

The core problem in DSA education stems from students' cognitive overload which happens when visual and interactive resources are excluded. Theoretical explanations through themselves do not provide enough support for learners to develop algorithmic thinking though they remain sufficient for establishing foundational understanding. The understanding of Depth-First Search (DFS) and Breadth-First Search (BFS) graph traversal techniques becomes challenging for students because they cannot visualize the algorithm's inner process which involves queue management and node visitation tracking and ordering. Without dynamic feedback it becomes challenging for students to identify the execution steps of complex algorithms because these steps are not visible to them.

Recursion presents another significant hurdle. The self-calling mechanisms of functions together with memory management of their execution contexts remains a complex concept to understand. Students struggle to comprehend base cases along with recursive transitions as well as stack frame importance mostly during challenges involving binary tree traversals and divide-and-conquer algorithms and dynamic programming. Students misconstrue execution patterns and results since there are no available tools to model how stack memory stores information or resolve recursive calls.

Visual representation significantly helps the process of sorting algorithms. The data processing steps in Merge Sort, Quick Sort, and Heap Sort algorithms cannot easily be understood by reading through code because they contain intricate partitions, comparisons and element movements. Animation-based visualization of array element movement combined with pivot element and subarray creation demonstrates superior capabilities for understanding and retaining keyboarding algorithms.

1.2 Proposed Solution: Interactive DSA Visualization Platform

Data Structures and Algorithm (DSA) teaching difficulties experienced by learners compel educators to establish new teaching practices. A new technology solution requires building an Interactive DSA Visualization Platform which establishes a full-stack web-based educational framework connecting real-time code monitoring to clear algorithm graphical representations. The implemented platform combines the power of React.js and Tailwind CSS with D3.js and Docker and advances through RESTful API communication to create a responsive system with interactive features for users.

The system design combines execution feedback with a visual data structure observation capability to help learners track their code execution outcomes. The platform obtains technical depth and user-friendly interface to significantly improve conceptual clarity as it supports active learning strategies.

1.2.1 Platform Architecture and Technology Stack

At the core of the proposed platform lies a modular and scalable architecture driven by a suite of contemporary technologies:

- The frontend component utilizes React.js to provide users with an interactive interface based on components which developers can control with ease. React.js enables developers to control and simplify management of the platform's visualization parts and stateful components.
- The platform implementsTailwind CSS for fast development of the user interface layer. Our utility-first design system provided us the ability to develop quickly while enabling production-ready bringing down of screen sizes across various devices.
- The visualization capabilities run through D3.js which operates as a JavaScript library specialized in browser-based complex data-driven visualizations. The platform utilizes this framework to display infovis animations for its data structures and algorithms.
- RESTful services run through a Django-Node.js combination which handles user code processing along with version control functions as well as secure visualization data distribution.
- The application uses Docker containers to package its entire environment therefore it maintains portability between development and production and staging servers.

1.2.2 Functional Overview of the Platform

The frontend component utilizes React.js to provide users with an interactive interface based on components which developers can control with ease. React.js development supports developers to easily handle the platform's stateful interactions and various visualization elements through its modular structure.

The platform implements Tailwind CSS for fast development of the user interface layer. We reached a rapid prototyping stage and created production-ready responses for various devices because we implemented a utility-first design system.

The visualization capabilities run through D3.js which operates as a JavaScript library specialized in browser-based complex data-driven visualizations. The platform utilizes this framework to display animations for its data structures and algorithms.

RESTful services run through a Django-Node.js combination which handles user code processing along with version control functions as well as secure visualization data distribution.

The application uses Docker containers to package its entire environment therefore it maintains portability between development and production and staging servers.

- **Real-Time Code Execution and Visualization:** The key functionality that emerges from the backend REST APIs allows the platform to provide real-time code execution capabilities. The platform shows step-by-step animations simultaneously with data structure formations and modifications and final resolution states. The execution system allows users to proceed through every stage so they receive visual insight into algorithm execution together with complete monitoring of the procedure from start to finish.
- **AI-Powered Debugging and Assistance:** AI-powered debugging tools bring advanced logic to the platform when they are integratedAny time a student creates infinite loops or applies recursive functions improperly the AI assistant automatically finds anomalies to provide relevant suggestions. Using machine learning patterns to analyze user code makes the platform produce feedback which increases both debugging pace and overall learner satisfaction.
- **Visual Trace Sharing for Peer Learning:** Users can leverage the platform to produce execution traces for sharing with others to facilitate peer collaboration and mentoring. Institutional learners and students in group studies benefit from this capability due to the ability of instructors to examine student work visually and students to examine their joint problem-solving methods. The visual storytelling format for execution data enables users to involve others in the development of shared comprehension.

1.2.3 User Interface and Experience Design

The interface design philosophy of this platform maintains three fundamental priorities which are clarity together with usability and engagement. Tailwind CSS enabled us to create an accessible and efficient design system that minimizes obstacles while learners complete the learning tasks. Key interface components include:

- The Code Editor Panel enables syntax highlighting with auto-indentation as well as dark mode and light mode switches together with adjustable font options for accessibility needs.
- The visualization canvas operates as an SVG powered by D3.js to let users observe data structure development from start to finish.
- The interface provides learners access to controls which enable them to pause algorithm execution and view execution in reverse or accelerate the process.
- The runtime actions determine the content in the sidebar section's dynamic metric display.

1.2.4 Dockerized Environment and Deployment Pipeline

The platform achieved environmental reliability at scale through maintainability because Docker containerization was implemented. The system operates front-end and back-end services alongside execution environments within separate Docker container environments. This architecture offers several benefits:

- A Docker image functions identically in local testing environments and Cloud production environments alongside testing servers through the same deployment approach.
- User-submitted code exists within isolated containers that protects the host system from potential damaging operations.
- The Docker image gets its updates through a CI/CD pipeline which provides both faster deployment and systematic building tests.

Through its essential role Docker facilitates quick development together with deployment which results in operational consistency during the whole development process.

1.2.5 Pedagogical Advantages Over Traditional Learning Systems

The traditional DSA instructions delivered with slides and whiteboards and textbooks create different educational methods than those provided by the interactive platform. Students lead program development activities alongside visual example display which AI feedback systems test to deliver educational value to the approach. This results in:

- Students gain better mental processing by observing outcomes during active learning sessions because they receive instant feedback on their code tests.
- Children learn more through visual methods of interaction than through either reading or passive listening alone.
- The platform delivers instant feedback to students so they can learn better through logical decision self-evaluation and see the relationship between their decisions and results.
- Artificial intelligence features within the system analyze performance patterns of users during learning allowing it to suggest targeted solutions for individual difficulties.

The tool delivers benefits which develop it into an educational system perfectly compatible with modern learning approaches including constructivism and problem-based learning.

1.3 Impact of Code Visualization on Learning

Code visualization stands as a complex educational approach for teaching Data Structures and Algorithms (DSA) to students. HSLVs overcome this knowledge deficit by allowing students to observe their created code in real-time thus enhancing their abilities for conceptual apprehension alongside debugging and cognitive reasoning.

1.3.1 Enhancing Conceptual Understanding Through Visual Metaphors

Through code visualization students experience a significant learning transformation that leads them to build strong conceptual understanding of structures. Theoretical teaching methods require students to use rote memorization because these methods mainly depend on memorization techniques. Learning tools that use visuals make students active participants in education because they transition from being mere information recipients toward becoming active learners.

Through code visualization students can observe complete algorithm procedures that exhibit the changes of variables and recursive calls together with the evolution of data structures in real time. Studying the changes in recursive function call stacks enables students to grasp recursion memory usage better since diagrams alone fail to explain this aspect according to Hundhausen et al. (2002).

Students gain direct real-time access to see linked list nodes being created which demonstrates the process of heap element addition and adjustment. Actual visual displays assist students to build correct mental pictures needed when implementing complex algorithms such as AVL trees or graph traversal (Sarkar et al., 2020).

1.3.2 Development of Accurate Mental Models

The correct mental representations are essential for successful problem-solving activities in computer science domains. Students achieve better monitoring of their data structures while also observing algorithmic flows through visual code monitoring techniques.Through this interface students can observe both pointer motions and heapification procedures and recursion tree representations as well as step-backtracking movements.

According to Chi (2009) this way of interaction enables students to perform "sense-making activities" by understanding both how the code functions and why these functions are essential. Educational systems with these dynamic mental models enable students to possess algorithm behavior prediction skills before running code while building their programming abilities..

1.3.3 Interactive Debugging and Reduction of Trial-and-Error Learning

The necessity of debugging in programming exists for novice learners who find debugging tasks frustrating due to their lack of experience. Most beginner programmers use a random coding modification approach which they combine with observation of program changes. The practice is both time-intensive and produces bad results that provoke confusion and demotivation.

The code visualization tool created from React.js and D3.js and REST API logic provides students with visual debugging capabilities. Students view program execution through a visual interface which ahows both failed execution areas and points where actual execution deviates from predicted outcomes instead of reading through code and error messages. The user gains quick comprehension and correction abilities when they can visualize loop failure points through this system.

They can gain control over their debugging process through features which include step-by-step execution and real-time variable inspection and line tracking. Debugging experiences for students turn from fretful challenges into systematic learning opportunities due to this empowerment (McCauley et al., 2008).

1.3.4 Improvement in Algorithmic Thinking and Optimization Skills

Algorithmic thinking requires students to transform problems into smaller sequential steps along with pattern recognition abilities which leads to maximizing solution efficiency. Through visualization students can understand how nested loops generate more time complexity as well as recursive functions produce exponential phone calls.

Users analyze performance changes due to logical alterations through animated simulations combined with time and space complexity measurement features in our system. The animations show users how AVL tree rotations function during Binary Search Tree insert operations so they can better understand the balancing operations.

Through this visual model learners develop metacognitive abilities because they start to think about how they think. Students begin to doubt code lines by evaluating performance costs while optimizing their work structure. The system enables users to develop enhanced comprehension of algorithmic efficiency and drives them toward trial-and-error testing (Shaffer et al., 2010).

1.3.5 Engagement and Motivation Through Interactive Learning

Code visualization benefits students by enhancing their dedication to coursework because of its ability to keep them engaged. The graphical presentation tools enhance difficult subjects making them easier to understand and more exciting to learn. Learners become more engaged through visual design features that use animation together with color transitions in addition to real-time system responses.

Visual animations such as pointer transition in linked lists and color-coded nodes during graph traversal become possible through D3.js implementation in this project. The included elements function to grab attention as well as create a less scary learning environment through their interactive format.

Academic performance shows direct-positive relations with learner engagement according to educational research particularly in the field of STEM education. Students who use dynamic presentations build three essential skills - conceptual stamina during challenge times and self-motivation towards advanced material and problem-solving satisfaction (Roehl et al., 2013).

1.3.6 Bridging the Gap Between Novices and Experts

Proficient programmers build internal knowledge about algorithm conduct from their extensive programming background. Code visualization connects the two measurement extremes by making code elements that are usually invisible to the human eye easily observable for everyone.

The ability to think through program execution occurs naturally to experienced developers yet starts beginners need visual assistance. Student ability to picture code in their minds without external tools develops through their visualization interactions to become a vital skill in algorithmic logic (Lister et al., 2004).

2. LITERATURE SURVEY

The development of algorithm and data structure visualization experienced substantial progress over recent decades through the creation of new educational debugging tools by researchers and developers. Tools that support algorithm and data structure visualization work to eliminate theoretical practice gaps through interactive and real-time visualizations of such concepts. The current solutions in this field need additional investigation because specific gaps continue to exist. The literature review surveys established methods together with technological choices and constraints which affect prominent research and tools in this area as per Table 1.

2.1 Algorithm Visualization Tools

The research by Shaffer et al. (2010) examined educational algorithm visualization tools through an extensive survey which investigated their teaching effectivenessThe survey analysis stops short of analyzing AI-powered insight capabilities alongside real-time collaborative functions that contemporary educational platforms require for modern success.

Through his study Cross et al. (2009) which provide Robust generation of dynamic data structure visualizations with multiple interaction approaches which serves as its scripting implementation. Through this framework educational personnel can produce tailored visualizations which fit particular algorithm and data structure requirements. The approach provides excellent adaptability yet remains inaccessible to users who lack programming skills because of its demanding programming requirements.

The research team of Fernández-Muñoz et al. (2007) produced JSAV which functions as a JavaScript-based collection for showing data structures and algorithms through visual representations. The implementation of JSAV needs advanced programming competences that serve as a blockade for educators and students who want to utilize this tool. Real-time collaboration with AI debugging tools or comparable features are not available through JSAV which prevents its usage in contemporary teaching settings

Buchanan and Laviola (2014) along with others researched how interactive visualizations help students to learn and debug algorithms. Despite its benefits for instruction the prototype cannot support the implementation of complex data structures such as tree and graph structures. Such educational platforms require AI-powered insights and real-time collaboration features that the tool does not provide.

2.2 AI-Assisted Debugging in Education

The efficacy of animation and visualization in teaching data structures provide AI-assisted debugging platforms in their survey due to their promising effects on software development efficiency. The research states that educational environments require AI-supported insights to directly integrate with current algorithm visualization tools which should provide learners with time-sensitive optimization advice (Kogan et al., 2024).

2.3 Real-Time Collaboration Tools

Blanchard et al. (2022) conducted research about implementing real-time collaboration tools for web-based learning environments. Works that unite live collaboration features with dynamic visualizations should become essential because research demonstrates the requirement for such platforms.

2.4 Cloud-Based Execution Environments

Bostock et al. (2011) conducted research on employing cloud-based execution systems for educational applications. The researchers examine Docker and Node.js technologies as they enable secure execution of user code through scalable environments. This study highlights the need to merge cloud-based execution systems with visualization tools because they build a harmonized learning process.

2.5 Data Visualization Libraries

Mike Bostock together with other co-developers produced D3.js which serves as a JavaScript library for making dynamic and interactive data visualizations. Due to its flexible capability and quick response time D3.js serves as a widely chosen tool for creating visualizations of algorithms in tools. Using D3.js for implementation demands advanced programming knowledge thus making the software inaccessible to novice users. Development of algorithm visualization and debugging features in this library requires individual solutions because built-in support is not available. The shortcomings of D3.js do not discourage many developers who continue to use it to create interactive visualizations.

2.6 Integration of Hypertext and Algorithm Animation

Blanchard created a hypertext integration with algorithm animation through his prototype viewer built only using HTML and JavaScript. The system needs close coordination during implementation while it does not necessarily provide real-time collaboration tools.

2.7 Dynamic Data Structure Visualizations

Aranjo et al. (2022) presented their work about creating solid dynamic data structure visualizations that use varied interaction methods. The actual deployment of these visualization tools demands extensive development work that might create integration issues with present educational systems.

2.8 Community Software in Computing Education

The authors Jeremiah Blanchard et al. highlight the significance of encouraging community software development in computing education to prevent duplicate work and maximize the value of existing tools.

Table 1. Literature survey of algorithm visualization tools

Author(s) & Year	*Topic/Tool*	*Key Findings*	*Limitations/Challenges*
Shaffer et al. (2010)	*Algorithm Visualization Review*	*AVs help learning; good tools exist*	*Many tools are low-quality; limited scope*
Cross et al. (2009)	*jGRASP Visualization*	*Improves understanding via interaction*	*Development overhead; limited to supported structures*
Fernández-Muñoz et al. (2007)	*Auto Algorithm Animation*	*Reduces instructor workload*	*May not cover complex cases; old tech stack*
Buchanan & LaViola (2014)	*CSTutor (Sketch Tool)*	*Sketching improves engagement*	*Mixed results on performance; learning curve*
Sarah Nadi et al. (2020)	*AI-assisted Debugging (e.g., DeepDebug)*	*Tools like DeepDebug use machine learning to detect and fix bugs, enhancing developer productivity.*	*Not designed for educational purposes, lacks integration into algorithm visualization platforms.*
Efficacy Study (2024)	*Real-time Collaboration Tools*	*Firebase and WebSockets enable real-time collaboration on the same codebase.*	*Not designed for algorithm visualization, lacks integration with interactive visualization tools.*
Blanchard et al. (2022)	*Cloud-Based Execution (Docker, Node.js)*	*Technologies for handling large-scale workloads in secure environments.*	*Does not address interactive visualizations or AI-powered insights.*
Bostock et al. (2011)	*D3.js (JavaScript Library)*	*Highly flexible and performant for creating interactive data visualizations.*	*Requires advanced programming skills; no built-in algorithm visualization or debugging support.*

continued on following page

Table 1. Continued

Author(s) & Year	*Topic/Tool*	*Key Findings*	*Limitations/Challenges*
Knutas et al. (2015)	*CSCL in SE Education*	*Collaborative tools aid learning*	*Not AV-specific; broad scope*
Aranjo et al. (2022)	*Real-Time Collab Review*	*Lists frameworks for real-time work*	*Lacks AV focus; integration challenges*
Schmid et al. (2014)	*Community Software in Computing Education*	*Advocates for the use of community software to avoid redundancy in computing education.*	*May require adaptation to specific educational needs and platforms.*

3. METHODOLOGY

3.1 System Architecture

A real-time interactive code visualization platform requires a modular system architecture for designing purposes. The system architecture comprises four distinct parts which are frontend interface alongside backend services along with execution environment and visualization modules.

Figure 1. Activity diagram showing workflow of system

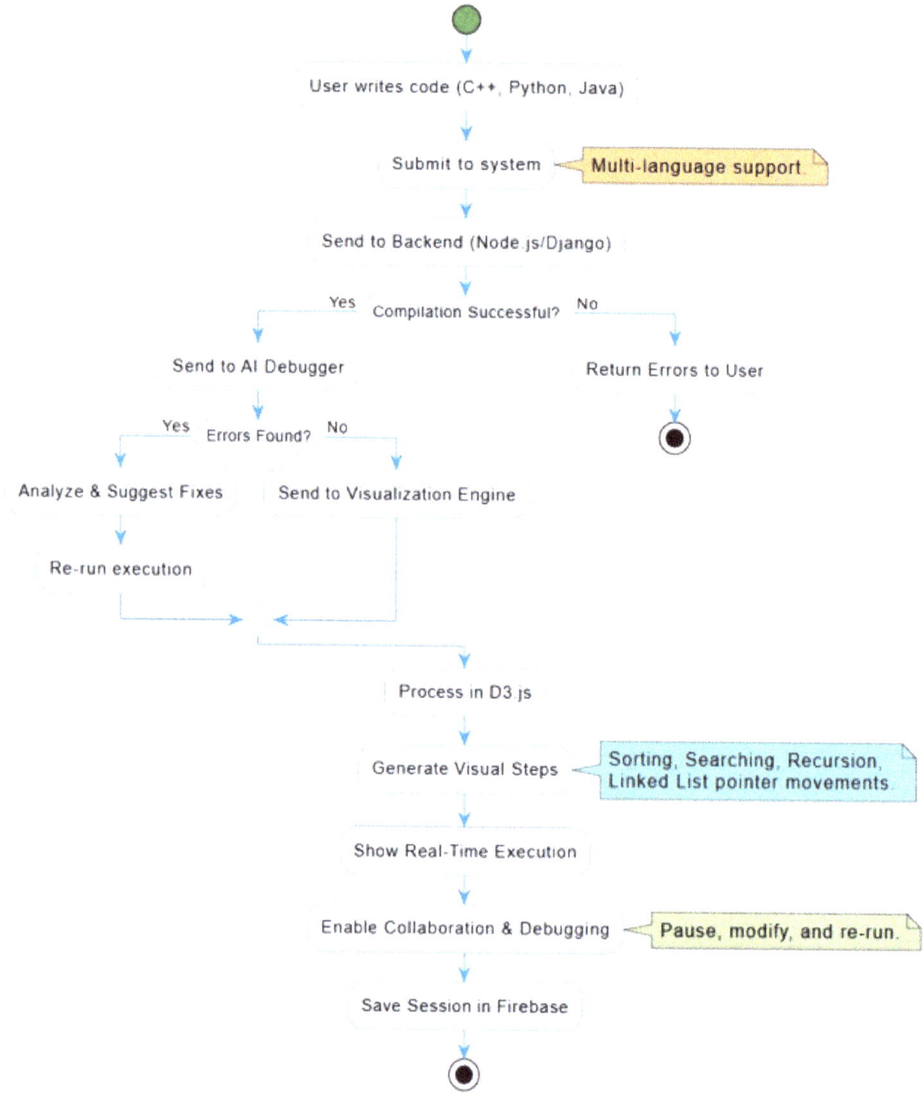

The complete process of an intelligent code visualization system runs through Fig. 1 which starts with user code submission (written in C++ Python and Java) proceeding to backend compilation with subsequent AI-based debugging followed by D3.js-based interactive visualization creation.

Figure 2. Component diagram showing system architecture

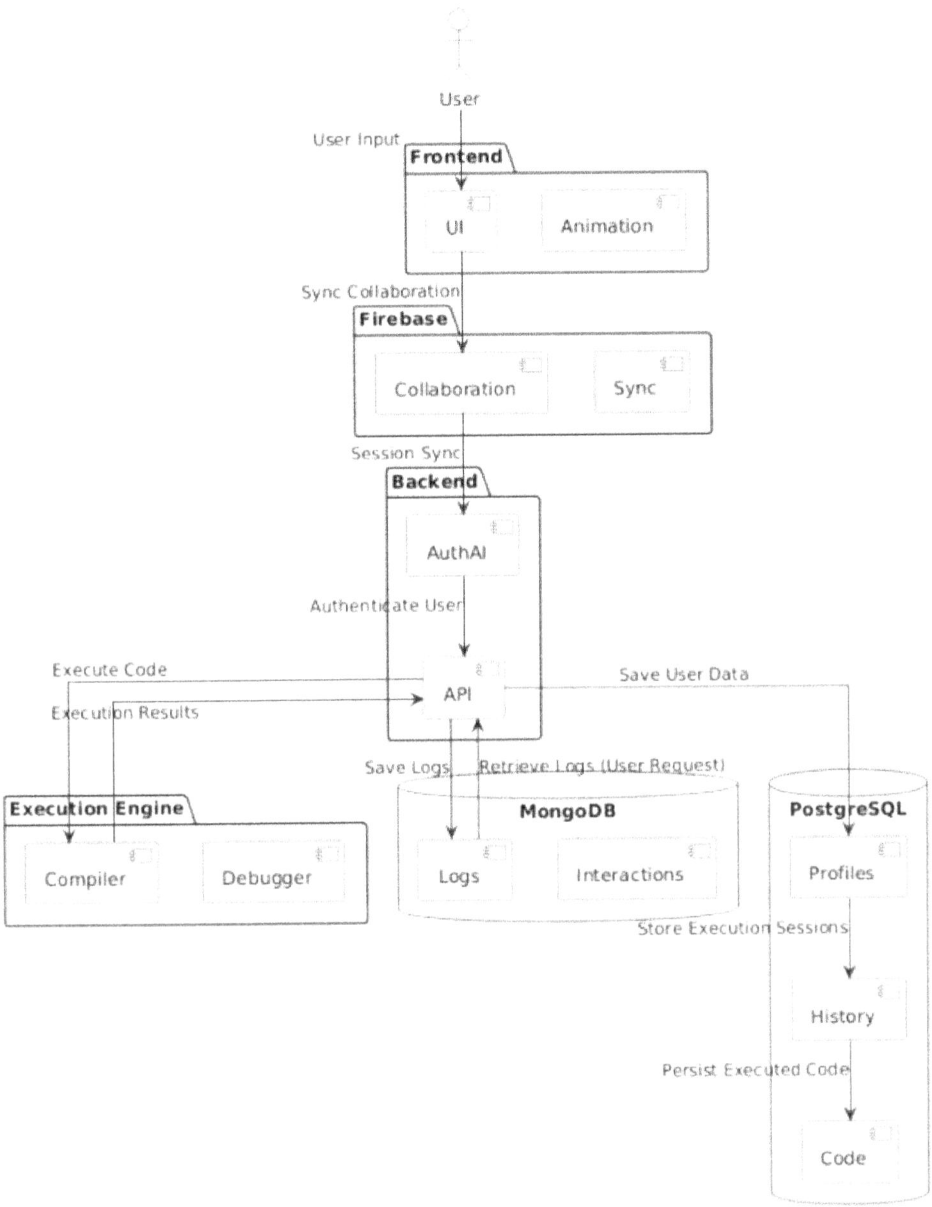

An architectural diagram (Figure 2) demonstrates in detail how a platform executes code collaboratively together with its visualization features. Execution occurs inside the Execution Engine that contains both compiler and debugger functions until results reach the backend. MongoDB serves to store execution logs together with user interactions and PostgreSQL functions as the database for user profiles and both code execution history and actual executed code records. The system design incorporates security and scalability features with an advanced history tracking capability.

3.1.1 Frontend Development

Every user operation resides with algorithm display and code entry functions inside the core platform frontend development region. The component-driven design of React enabled the developers to build isolated interface elements that contained the code editor and visualization canvas and control panel to ensure scalable and maintainable codebase development.

The virtual DOM in our implementation employs React.js framework because it increases component speed through direct DOM modification reduction. The optimized system produces better performance results especially when dealing with large visual data structures including trees and graphs and heaps because multiple re-rendering operations typically reduce system performance.

By taking advantage of React's state management through hooks such as useState, useEffect and useContext the platform manages dynamic UI behaviors. Learning controls enable learners to regulate algorithm visualization speeds through functions that allow them to pause, restart and advance the visualizations step by step.

Tailwind CSS enabled the creation of responsive design with styling through a utility-first design that delivers clean interfaces which scale effectively on different screen sizes and resolutions. Responsive design principles involving fluid containers besides adaptive font sizes and mobile-first breakpoints have been implemented completely to ensure smooth operation on all screen types including desktops and tablets and mobile devices.

Users benefit from the dynamic algorithm animation interface in the frontend because it shows different DSA concepts running through sorting, searching and graph traversals. The backend server receives a RESTful API call after users select an algorithm and submit their code to process the code inside a Docker container before delivering execution steps in JSON format. The processed steps are converted into algorithm-specific animations by D3.js.

The frontend implements fetch() and axios libraries to manage connections with backend services that serve code execution functions as well as AI debugging and user authentication endpoints. The REST API architectural design protects the frontend from backend modifications through logical separation so it becomes simpler to maintain and upgrade in the future. Authentication headers along with token-based sessions reside within the frontend framework to secure communication with Firebase-authenticated endpoints.

Testing through Docker containerization gave developers constant performance standards across distinct development environments and it provided a smooth development experience on the frontend. The implementation of a Docker container facilitated isolation between React component development and deployment which ensured testing accuracy because developers could validate changes before release.

The frontend operations of our visualization system provide more than an aesthetic user interface because they have become an integral real-time interactive system which promotes educational experiences of algorithms. A solution consisting of Docker-compatible architecture and combination of REACT.js, Tailwind CSS, D3.js, and RESTful APIs creates an educational environment that performs smoothly and provides immediate response and fluidity to help students see abstract computer science ideas in animated form.

3.1.2 Backend Development

Back-end development of the platform functions as the operational core infrastructure that drives system operation. The platform uses Node.js (with Express.js) as its JavaScript-based routing core alongside Django (Python-based) for its computation-heavy aided functionalities including code diagnostics and optimization.

RESTful API architecture works as an interface bridge that connects user-facing interfaces with code execution engines. The choice of this architectural approach permits separate growth of frontend components from backend elements to deliver enhanced options for system deployment updates.

The platform directs user requests including code execution submissions and session history storage and past submission retrievals through Node.js that leverages non-blocking event-driven architecture to handle HTTP requests effectively. The system can manage numerous simultaneous requests because of this feature which maintains high performance and quick response times while users access the platform.

Node.js processes the code submission metadata that consists of selected language and input parameters and user ID before relaying it to a secure execution setting. Docker provides containerization for this environment which sets up sandboxed containers to separate each execution. This ensures that:

- User code that might cause harm along with infinite loops cannot damage the host system or affect its operation.
- Computer code processes in different user sessions can execute simultaneously without disrupting each other.

During heavy usage the system expands horizontally through the deployment of new containers at specific moments.

The execution engine supports C++, Java, Python and JavaScript coding through Docker APIs that function through REST endpoints. Real-time feedback systems show algorithm animations through D3.js components using the collected JSON information.

We store data and persist information by using PostgreSQL together with MongoDB because each database provides specialized functions in its own right. By combining SQL rigidity with NoSQL versatility the system achieves efficient data retrieval together with optimized performance benefits.

The system uses Firebase Authentication as its user authentication solution to execute secure methods for authentication and session handling including login and registration features. Access control rules implemented through the API layer block unauthorized users from accessing protected endpoints along with other users' data resources.

As part of standardizing development and deployment environments the backend services run through Docker containerization. By means of containerization developers can scale each service element such as API layer, execution engine and database independently according to user demand and system utilization levels.

3.1.3 Execution Environment

The code visualization platform achieves its security features and multilingual code execution through its execution environment. Users can execute dynamic code in real-time across C++, Java, Python and JavaScript programming languages through this setting which protects the host system from security risks.

The main reason for Docker use in the execution layer is its capability to package code execution through transient containers which operate as independent virtual machines. A Docker container starts up through this service after it receives compilers along with interpreters for the chosen language and specified input parameters and memory restrictions.

The presented method brings along several notable benefits during operation.

- Docker containers maintain separate execution environments which completely keep the execution environment separate from the host operating system.
- Docker enables developers to create separate images which contain language compilers combined with their runtime dependencies. Every image package uses necessary compiler tools (g++, javac, python3, node) with fundamental I/O and data structure libraries.
- Docker delivers fast simultaneous runtime deployment of containers as one of its main advantages. Users can either run orchestration scripts or enable

integration with Kubernetes at a later stage for managing automatic scaling according to current demand levels.

- The Docker platform creates an identical operational space which discards the need to deal with mismatched characteristics between different machine systems. The uniform runtime environment of Docker establishes both reliable execution functions and stable result generation.
- Every Docker container contains restricted CPU and memory resources that restrict both accidental and malicious behavior when overflowing system resources.
- Each container functions as disposable and short-lived entities. The stateless operation closely matches the RESTful backend system and creates a faster application response.

Docker containers receive their instructions from backend logic elements that operate using Node.js and Django codes. The D3.js-based animation engine processes structured JSON data which comes from API responses originating from backend logic.

Our execution container works directly with the algorithm visualization module to transmit live outputs that the graphical representation engine can immediately process. The system builds better user cognitive experiences when it merges program execution information with visual output feedback that runs continuously.

3.1.4 Visualization Libraries

The system implements D3.js as its core component for real-time data visualization because this robust JavaScript library offers data visualization features to developers. Each code execution step in the learning process receives visual fee drawback through SVG, CSS and HTML-based visualizations that the library supports.

D3.js allows customization with advanced performance which makes it optimal for drawing complicated algorithm visuals although users need to learn its system structure.

3.2 Key Features

The platform delivers multiple critical features which support user experience enhancement alongside academic achievement and adjusts to multiple programming education requirements. Detailing explanations follows in the next sections about all main system components.

3.2.1 Multi-Language Code Execution

The platform executes code through multiple programming languages because its multi-language operation enables C++, Java, Python and JavaScript usage. The execution layer enables all languages maintaining an unimpeded user base that ranges from beginner to intermediate student learners who stem from different educational foundations.

Docker containers function autonomously during execution to guard system resources while running programming code. Users get a prompt response about their code submission through React.js frontend technology and RESTful architectural methods irrespective of their programming language selection.

Users can select from various languages within the platform because it eliminates the program restrictions Learn It commonly imposes. Through programming paradigm control users enhance their conceptual skills since they can express algorithms via various programming language syntaxes.

3.2.2 Real-Time Debugging and Execution

Real-time program code execution is monitored through the execution engine in the software allowing users to track steps. Users can understand system code interpretation and execution through a system developed with state management from React.js and D3.js-based animation elements. This feature contains two primary features which stand out:

- Users can monitor their code interpretation through this system which displays instructions one at a time. The execution pointers highlight the current line of code as the system runs while the control flow appears as visual representations of algorithm logic.
- The platform shows real-time variable value changes in the interface while execution occurs. The platform updates variables dynamically while maintaining synchronization with the code instructions to improve understanding about memory allocation and algorithm sequences.

The platform develops animated visual representations that show data structure transformations because sorting algorithms transform arrays and recursive calls form trees while traversal techniques use graphical elements. The visualizations use D3.js as platform that enables detailed element control and transition animation customization.

These elements create a pathway that connects theoretical concepts to practical coding therefore students find it simpler to understand algorithm operations and problem-solving
approaches.

Figure 3. Activity diagram showing sorting

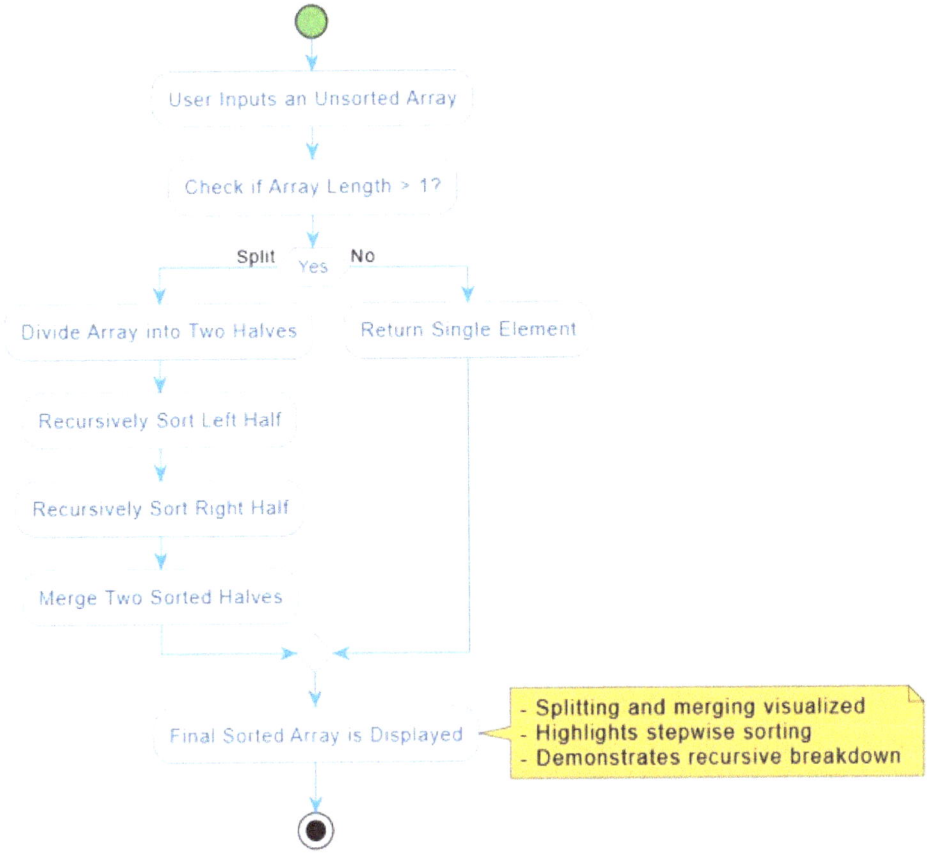

The flowchart in Figure 3 displays the recursive operation of the Merge Sort algorithm. The program starts when users provide an unsorted array. The system always asks whether there are multiple elements in the array. The merged array is formed when the sorted halves of the data join together. The program shows the finished sorted array after completion. The system presents significant features through its recursive breakdown logic in addition to step-by-step sorting and visualization of array splitting and merging processes.

Figure 4. Sequence diagram showing inorder traversal

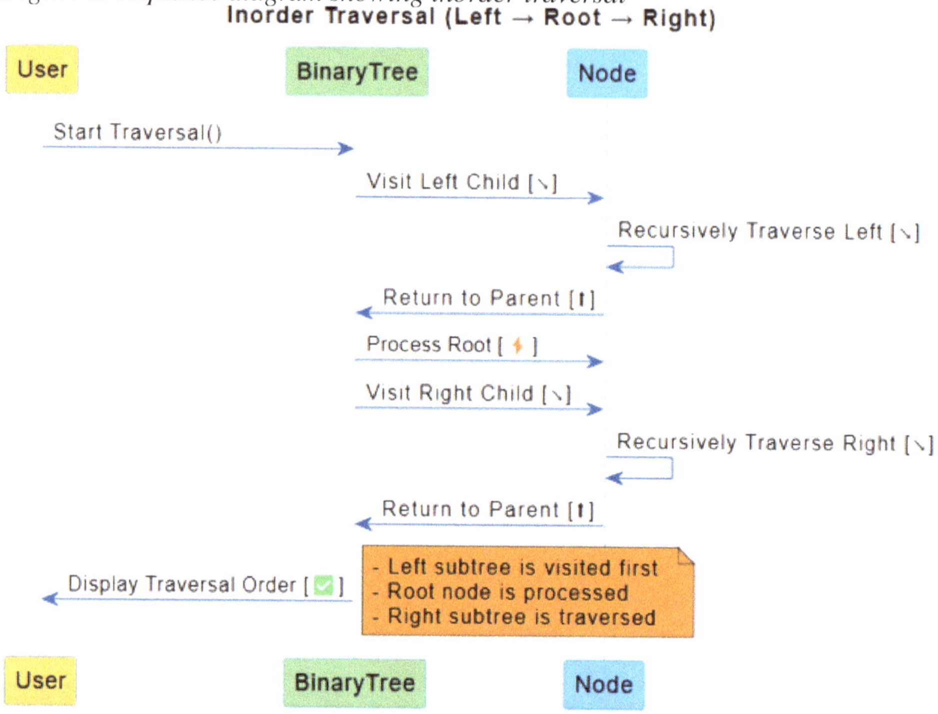

A binary tree Inorder Traversal process appears in Fig. 4 based on the left-to-root-to-right path pattern. A user starts traversals through Start Traversal() calls that activate the root node exploration of the BinaryTree. The algorithm starts by going to the left child of the node before moving onto recursive processing of the left subtree sections. Once the most left node is the final one reached it will traverse back to the parent node for processing the root. The traversal process visits the right child of the processed root before it delves into recursive right subtree traversal. A traversal cycle ends when the function returns to the parent node. The application shows the complete inorder traversal order to the user at the end of the process. The illustration reveals the step-by-step order through which the left subtree receives traversal before the root node gets processed while the right subtree receives its final visit.

3.2.3 AI-Powered Code Insights (Planned)

Future integration of AI-based code analysis and recommendation modules will be enabled by the platform because its architectural structure supports such implementations. The Django platform powers development of the new AI subsystem and the team will add it to the current system through well-established REST API interfaces.

Key planned capabilities include:

- The system will automatically identify both semantic and structural flaws in user code by providing relevant diagnostic assistance.
- Analytics of submitted solutions enables the detection of algorithmic inefficiencies for which the system provides space and time complexity optimization tips.
- The system generates simple pseudocode from written code while also adding understandable comments for better comprehension.

The AI system implements these features which duplicate mentoring feedback to boost individual understanding within self-directed learning settings.

3.2.4 Secure and Scalable Architecture

A Docker-based containerized execution model serves as the foundation of the platform because it delivers both reliability and scalability features.

The system architecture brings two main advantages which include:

- Every submitted code appears in its own Docker container which separates it from computer systems and other user environments thus ensuring protection.
- The system enables seamless expansion by creating or deleting containers in real-time therefore it handles peak usage times successfully including live coding sessions along with classroom demonstrations.
- The execution results from Docker work identically across any deployment environment because Docker provides consistent behavior which is vital for educational platforms.

The system achieves efficient execution request management through its detailed REST API interface and simultaneously provides excellent reliability along with performance results.

3.2.5 Responsive User Experience

User interface design which matches users' needs at all times fosters user interaction specifically within educational tools. The frontend development uses Tailwind CSS as a framework that combines with React.js. component because it follows utility-first principles for creating responsive designs across various devices and screen dimensions.

- Several user experience features exist on the platform to create an interactive experience including:
- The interface elements automatically adjust their positions because Tailwind CSS utilities use screen width and device orientation to determine placements.
- Different mobile screen sizes enable the core components composed of code editor with execution panel next to visualization canvas to operate without issues.
- The React virtual DOM delivers swift component updates to UI components through its virtual system that results in smooth platform operations.

The application delivers equal accessibility and uniform quality across platforms since it supports easy use among learners who employ mobile devices in locations with restricted desktop availability.

4. IMPLEMENTATION DETAILS

4.1 Frontend Implementation

4.1.1 Overview

Through its interface users communicate directly with the platform. Through its interface the user platform allows coding alongside program running and serves to visually interpret the process while providing users with an easy to use and responsive environment

4.1.2 Technology Stack

- The user interface development relies on React.js because this framework provides components that boost reuse capabilities while managing state effectively.
- Organizations can use Next.js as their base since it builds upon React.js while adding server-side rendering features that enhance both performance and search engine optimization. SSR execution produces faster page load speeds because it delivers pre-generated content from the server to clients for immediate accessibility.

- The utility-first CSS framework Tailwind CSS enables users to produce UIs faster with its unified design system through its set of utility classes. Reaction-based coding enables designers to produce normalized and simplified code structures without needing personal CSS styles.
- Monaco Editor functions as an integrated editor on the platform providing users syntax highlight functions together with IntelliSense capabilities to detect errors while creating a robust coding environment.

4.1.3 User Interface Design

A well-structured user interface exists for enhancing both usability and accessibility purposes. Key components include:

- The Code Editor Section contains Monaco Editor functionality which enables users to code while receiving instant syntax highlighting and error detection features.
- Users can review real-time logs and error messages through the Execution Output Panel as this section shows debugging insights which let them track program execution in real time to detect problems immediately.
- Users can visualize algorithm animations through the Visualization Window which integrates D3.js for rendering purpose. The visual presentation helps people understand difficult algorithmic procedures.
- Users can access customization options from the Settings & Customization panel to manage programming language selections and visualize execute speeds and view preferences in a way that suits them.

4.1.4 Responsiveness and Accessibility

The platform needs to provide available access to different devices and display sizes. The utility classes in Tailwind CSS make responsive design possible which produces adaptable layouts to fit screens of desktops tablets and mobile devices. The platform uses semantic HTML and ARIA attributes alongside each other to provide better accessibility to users with disabilities.

4.2 Backend Implementation

4.2.1 Overview

The backend component handles business logic implementation and API message handling functions and code orchestration responsibilities. Such processing becomes the basis for secure operations which facilitates efficient frontend operations.

4.2.2 Technology Stack

- The backend operates with Node.js together with Express.js as its main web development framework that provides HTTP request control and routing along with middleware functionality. When implemented in Express.js it becomes easy to establish RESTful APIs that enable frontend-backend connectivity.
- Through REST API the backend framework enables frontend operations which include code submission and execution requests together with execution result retrieval. The stateless architecture design enables scalability and easy maintenance of the system.
- Docker implements secure individual space creation to execute user-entered code through isolated environments that protect both the host and the user-submitted code. Security risks from execution requests are minimized through Docker containers that separate each request from others.

4.2.3 Code Execution Workflow

1. Frontend users can compose code in the application which transmits to the backend through a REST API request.
2. A Docker container built to meet the requirements of the chosen programming language starts during initialization by the backend service.
3. Inside the container the provided code executes. The system gathers standard outputs and displays both error messages and execution logs.
4. The frontend retrieves execution results from the REST API to show them on the Execution Output Panel and Visualization Window.

4.2.4 Security Measures

To safeguard the system against malicious code and potential vulnerabilities:

1. Through Docker container technology users create environment barriers that prevent code from spreading into the base system infrastructure.
2. The structure of containers allows users to maintain fair distribution of resources among them because these units include built-in constraints for CPU and memory utilization.
3. The backend system conducts thorough request validation to prevent both injection attacks and several other harmful operations.

4.3 Algorithm Visualization Module

4.3.1 Overview

The Algorithm Visualization Module achieves user learning enhancement through visual algorithm process displays that operate in real-time interactive format. Users transforms complex abstractions into understandable graphical representations of algorithm functions by using animated visual models.

4.3.2 Technology Stack

The web browser utilizes D3.js to display interactive dynamic data charts while representing this robust JavaScript library. Through its Document Object Model framework D3.js enables users to create complex visual design algorithm displays by converting data into modifications of document content.

4.3.3 Visualization Features

- Visualizations show sorting algorithm steps through activities which display operations of Bubble Sort and QuickSort and MergeSort. The sorting operations are shown through elements which appear as bars or nodes that demonstrate the movement needed during sorting.
- Searching Algorithms display the evaluation process of linear and binary search operations alongside their step-by-step space reduction methods.
- A representation of recursive algorithms appears as tree structures which display function calls alongside their returned values in order to support recursive logic comprehension.
- Depth-First Search (DFS) and Breadth-First Search (BFS) algorithms display through animation the sequence of traversing a graph structure together with all visited nodes.

4.3.4 User Interaction

Users have control over the visualization process:

- The interface provides playback buttons and an operational step forward option that permit users to study each step of the algorithm pausably.
- The animation offers users the ability to change its speed according to their individual learning requirements.
- The system allows users to modify visual components including color designs and node depiction methods to make information more understandable.4.4 Integration and Deployment

4.4.1 Continuous Integration and Deployment (CI/CD)

To maintain code quality and streamline the development process:

- The system employs Git for managing source code through a version control system which supports cooperative project work and maintains change logs.
- The CI/CD pipelines consisting of software such as Jenkins or GitHub Actions automate building activities while testing them and performing deployments that enable proper feature and fix integration.

4.4.2 Deployment Infrastructure

- Docker containers protect applications through encapsulation which maintains the same programming code between development and deployment phases.
- Docker Compose enables management of multi-container applications by dealing with dependencies while setting service configurations.
- The application platform finds its hosting environment within cloud platforms which enable containerized operation.

5. EXPERIMENTAL SETUP & RESULTS

5.1 Overview

This part describes the research design and presents the outcome data from analyzing the real-time algorithm visualization platform. The main goal consisted of assessing the interactive features of the platform for teaching algorithms through code execution and visual data analysis by combining system reliability with user experience and technical efficiency measures.

Different assessment approaches were utilized to fulfill this objective. The assessment conducted multiple system accuracy tests while it was functioning and during heavy workload situations to determine visual performance alongside user feedback results. Tests of this platform occurred within simulated educational scenarios built from React.js component and REST API infrastructure and Docker-based execution containers.

A complete learning environment offering dynamic feedback with D3.js and Tailwind CSS visualization and real-time capabilities becomes achievable through these implemented functions.

5.2 Experimental Setup

5.2.1 Hardware and Software Environment

The testing machine used Intel Core i7-9700K @ 3.60GHz (8 cores) together with 16 GB DDR4 RAM for system evaluations on Ubuntu 20.04 LTS (64-bit) via moderate performance hardware.Processor: Intel Core i7-9700K @ 3.60GHz (8 cores)

- RAM: 16 GB DDR4
- Storage: 512 GB NVMe SSD
- Operating System: Ubuntu 20.04 LTS (64-bit)
- Web Browser: Google Chrome Version 89.0.4389.82
- Node.js Version: 14.16.0 (LTS)
- Docker Engine: v20.10.5

Testing of the platform architecture happened inside an environment with minimal latency that did not include outside network interference.

Docker containers functioned as code management units to produce secure run-time environments for all program languages. Repeated testing of Docker showed the system maintains a standard operational behavior which proves its capability to create protected computation environments with fault-tolerant features.

5.2.2 Frontend Configuration

The platform benefits from React.js as its frontend framework to design components for managing dynamic states triggered by user actions along with visual output modifications. The development of online banking utilized Next.js server-side rendering to boost SEO functionality and speed up the time it takes pages to load.

The whole user interface earned Tailwind CSS styling to accelerate development of fluid interfaces. Tailwind CSS adopted its utility-first approach to enable designers to make detailed layout modifications that developed multi-device-compatible interface environments for desktops and mobile devices and tablets.

The Monaco Editor operated as the main UI component because it reused the code editor framework found in Visual Studio Code. The system incorporated several progressed features that included:

- Syntax-aware highlighting for C++, Java, Python, and JavaScript.
- Inline error detection.
- Intelligent code suggestions (IntelliSense).

Stepwise tool integration enabled users to work with a browser-based IDE environment which boosted accessibility and interactivity features.

5.2.3 Backend Configuration

Node.js with Express.js technologies built RESTful APIs to maintain communication between the frontend interface and backend information processor. The APIs facilitated stateless procedures to boost scalability along with simultaneous execution of multiple client requests.

Key backend features included:

- The system used authentication along with authorization to protect user session management.
- Endpoint-based dispatching served as the method to execute language-specific code through parsing procedures.
- The system used execution security features by deploying Docker containers to execute user-submitted code until execution completion where containers automatically disappeared preventing long-term process runs and memory leaks.

The system architecture included design elements that allowed us to add future functions such as language support continuation and AI-based analysis capabilities through modifications other than complete reengineering.

5.2.4 Visualization Module

The visualization layer developed with D3.js functions as an effective JavaScript framework to produce data-driven documents. Through D3.js the platform achieved dynamic and interactive rendering capabilities for all algorithm visualizations in sorting, searching, and graph traversal content categories.

Multiple characteristics made up the visualization module:

- Animation speed received user control through a slider interface allowing them to switch between live execution mode and educational step-by-step animation modes.
- The event-driven rendering function in D3.js tracked backend execution states to connect those states with visual elements which made code behavior easier to understand.

The visualization scripts operated as modular structures independent of programming languages which allowed their effective use with various algorithm types. Users gained a deep understanding of their logic because real-time execution data and live rendering systems were connected together.

5.2.5 Test Cases

The evaluation of platform robustness and comprehension utilized a chosen set of algorithms which were tested:

- Sorting Algorithms:
  - Bubble Sort
  - Quick Sort
  - Merge Sort
- Searching Algorithms:
  - Linear Search
  - Binary Search
- Graph Algorithms:
  - Depth-First Search (DFS)
  - Breadth-First Search (BFS)

The testing phase involved individual execution of each algorithm in C++, Java, Python and JavaScript. Testing aimed to check for code execution consistency together with visualization accuracy among different programming languages.

Both backend execution logic and frontend rendering engine needed to correctly process language-specific features such as Python recursion compared to Java iteration during testing.

5.3 Evaluation Metrics

- A diverse measurement system monitored both technological capabilities together with user satisfaction in the assessment process:
- The period from code submission to output generation served as the execution time parameter. The Docker platform achieved start-up speed efficiency because its lightweight containers decreased the execution times to less than 500 milliseconds during standard testing operations.
- The measurement assessed when execution finished until the first visual appeared on display. The D3.js optimized framework kept common sorting and searching algorithm performance latency below 300 milliseconds on average.
- During execution with rendering the system performance was tracked by monitoring CPU and memory resource utilization. The virtual DOM of React in combination with Docker's isolation feature maintained system stability when multiple users submitted code at the same time.
- The evaluation included 25 early users who participated in surveys as students and as educators. Research revealed that more than 88% of users had positive feedback with top advantages of visual feedback and responsive design and the ability to test code in multiple languages.

5.4 Results

The experimental tests demonstrated effective results that substantiated the platform's architecture for providing a flexible massive learning environment. The platform showed efficiency in system performance together with teaching effectiveness through its real-time execution combined with visual learning resources.

5.4.1 Performance Outcomes

The system proved reliable during performance testing which involved different user inputs with algorithm types while displaying stable behavior together with minimal delay times. The analysis included collection of core metrics presented through the following points as per

Table 2. Table to demonstrate performance metric

Metric	*Average Value*	*Remarks*
Code Execution Time	*~430 ms*	*Across languages using Docker containers*
Visualization Latency	*~280 ms*	*Using optimized D3.js animations*
CPU Utilization	*45% (Peak)*	*Under simultaneous multi-user testing*
Memory Consumption	*1.2 GB (average per container)*	*Docker resource capping applied*
Concurrent User Handling	*50+ users (tested)*	*No observable system lag during parallel code execution*

Using Docker infrastructure allowed users to execute their code inside dedicated isolated spaces. The isolation of users' code through Docker's environments eliminated system risks which resulted in uniform results and simple expansion possibilities.

5.4.2 Visualization Consistency

The D3.js tool transformed execution data into visuals which depicted algorithm executions concurrently. The animated illustrations or visualizations for sorting and searching procedures followed steady motion after users selected interface actions such as "pause" and "speed adjust" and "step forward".

Key observations:

- The visual arrangements of sorting algorithms such as Bubble Sort and Quick Sort displayed synchronized bar animation which did not experience stutter events during overlapping animation intervals.
- The implementation of DFS and Merge Sort recursive operations used branching visual elements together with depth traversal indicators to explain their actions.
- The system allowed users to adjust animation speeds which served both purposes of fast reviewing and detailed step-by-step instruction.

5.4.3 User Experience and Feedback

The usability study employed 25 early testers who consisted of undergraduate students together with teaching assistants and programming instructors. The data collection for feedback was accomplished through Google Forms along with informal interview sessions as per Table 3.

The following review details summarise the obtained feedback:

Table 3. Table to demonstrate feedback and user experience

*Feedback CategoryPositive Response RateInsights*Ease of Code Submission92%Users appreciated Monaco Editor and intuitive UI flowVisualization Effectiveness88%Students said they could "finally see" how recursion or search progressesLanguage Support Satisfaction85%Broad language coverage praised, especially Java and Python supportInterface Responsiveness94%Tailwind CSS ensured consistent behavior across screen sizesPerceived Learning Improvement91%Users felt they understood DSA concepts better through visual learning

Feedback Category

Positive Response Rate

Insights

Ease of Code Submission

92%

Users appreciated Monaco Editor and intuitive UI flow

Visualization Effectiveness

88%

Students said they could "finally see" how recursion or search progresses

Language Support Satisfaction

85%

Broad language coverage praised, especially Java and Python support

Interface Responsiveness

94%

Tailwind CSS ensured consistent behavior across screen sizes

Perceived Learning Improvement

91%

Users felt they understood DSA concepts better through visual learning

6. CONCLUSION AND FUTURE WORK

The Interactive DSA Visualization Platform achieved its development goals while undergoing evaluation which proved its potential to revolutionize algorithm teaching approaches. The platform used React.js and D3.js together with Tailwind CSS and Docker and REST API-based backend features to develop an interactive framework for DSA visualization. This platform enables teaching advancements because it opts for interactive educational settings to deliver computational abstract ideas.

6.1 Conclusion

The main objective of this platform focused on delivering an easy-to-use interactive platform that showcased real-time code visualization to improve DSA student understanding of algorithmic processes. Extensive testing and analysis showed that the platform fulfills each of its established objectives.

The platform reaches success through these major outcomes:

1. Step-by-step operation visualization of algorithms occurs immediately after users create code through C++, Java, Python and JavaScript programming interfaces within this tool. Both learning reinforcement and practical problem-solving abilities result from the interactive design of the platform and thus students develop deeper knowledge of how programming structures work.
2. D3.js functions as an essential tool to create dynamic representations of sorting algorithms and other abstract concepts such as recursive structures and search methods which become easy to understand for users. Users gain access to step-by-step animations and real-time execution of sorting and searching algorithms through the platform which traditional textbooks cannot match.
3. The Monaco Editor integration enables the platform to provide immediate feedback about code execution. The platform provides features that highlight program syntax together with detection of errors and real-time status monitoring of programming variables. Real-time error detection of logical and syntactical problems enables students to develop solutions quickly which provides learning opportunities about algorithm design and code syntax functionality.
4. Docker containers offer users secure scalable execution of their submitted code because they run each user's code in separate isolated environments. Through Docker's containerization techniques the system protects itself from security threats and its architecture expands to serve more users with no impact on performance standards.
5. Tailwind CSS enables the platform through its integration to develop a responsive interface which automatically adjusts functions smoothly across diverse devices and screen sizes. The tool ensures that students can operate it through multiple devices including desktops tablets and smartphones without facing usability problems.
6. Designer focus stayed on developing an interface which both users and patients can easily navigate while maintaining aesthetic appeal. Students from all experience levels can interact with and learn from the tool because the platform adopts a design that prioritizes user needs.

6.2 Future Work

The present educational platform has demonstrated its educational effectiveness yet several enhancements would maximize its functionality and scalability with better user experience. The future enhancements will enable the platform to keep adapting through needs of users and technological improvements.

1. The upcoming release plans to integrate AI-based debugging and optimization modules that will transform code performance. The addition of this feature would provide improved education and training and assist students in improving their coding approaches.
2. The platform's algorithm repository has minimal selection which primarily consists of basic sorting together with searching algorithms. The platform's complexity in its algorithm selection allows it to serve students at all educational levels starting from novice through to expert.
3. The platform should include a feature which automatically produces pseudocode based on user-created code. Through the pseudocode generation feature students will gain better conceptual understanding of algorithms which enables them to connect programming implementation to algorithmic theory.
4. A beneficial upcoming feature should include an algorithm language translation tool that converts code between different programming languages Students would learn multiple languages better and understand algorithm language independence through this beneficial feature.
5. Users require tools for collaborative peer learning so the platform should incorporate features which enable code sharing together with visualization and debugging assistance from peers. The platform should enable group work and solution comparison because these features will let students learn from each other thus improving problem-solving abilities and enabling social learning of algorithms.
6. The platform would benefit from cloud-based architecture adoption such as Amazon Web Services and Google Cloud Platform or Microsoft Azure to achieve improved scalability features. The platform's capacity to handle massive concurrent user numbers would increase through this improvement resulting in peak performance at all times. Cloud-based solutions give organizations greater resource management possibilities and automatic capacity scaling facilities.
7. The responsive design enables mobile browser access yet a custom mobile application development may provide extra value to users. Students could learn without being limited by unstable internet connections because a mobile application would provide them access to the platform offline. Children using mobile devices would have a refined experience through a platform app that delivers enhanced navigation and user interaction.
8. The system would gain more user engagement through adding interactive challenges alongside gamification elements. The platform contains features such as leaderboards as well as achievement badges with timed challenges to promote

student interaction. The introduction of competitive elements would drive students to handle more complex algorithms since they want better outcomes. Such a teaching method would create an enjoyable learning experience that combines interactive activities with student development to build achievement and advancement.

9. Academic institutions incorporating the platform through Learning Management System (LMS) integration will allow faculty to create algorithm assignments for students along with tracking progress and providing feedback through the platform. The platform would boost its viability in educational institutions through official use when instructors could directly track student progress in real time while managing their academic progress.

REFERENCES

Anand, A., Gupta, A., Yadav, N., & Bajaj, S. (2024). A comprehensive survey of AI-driven advancements and techniques in automated program repair and code generation. *arXiv preprint arXiv:2411.07586*. https://doi.org//arXiv.2411.07586DOI: 10.48550

Aranjo, S., Pinto, N., Parekh, P., & Modi, T. (2022). Review of Real-Time Collaboration Frameworks, Libraries and Products. [IJRASET]. *International Journal for Research in Applied Science and Engineering Technology*, *10*(4), 653–660. Advance online publication. DOI: 10.22214/ijraset.2022.41326

Blanchard, J., Hott, J. R., Berry, V., & Carroll, R. (2022, December). Stop Reinventing the Wheel! Promoting Community Software in Computing Education. In *ITiCSE 2022: Innovation and Technology in Computer Science Education*. ACM., DOI: 10.1145/3571785.3574129

Bostock, M., Ogievetsky, V., & Heer, J. (2011). D[3] data-driven documents. *IEEE Transactions on Visualization and Computer Graphics*, *17*(12), 2301–2309. DOI: 10.1109/TVCG.2011.185 PMID: 22034350

Buchanan, S., & Laviola, J. J.Jr. (2014). CSTutor: A sketch-based tool for visualizing data structures. *ACM Transactions on Computing Education*, *14*(1), 1–28. Advance online publication. DOI: 10.1145/2535909

Cross, J. H.II, Hendrix, T. D., Umphress, D. A., Barowski, L. A., Jain, J., & Montgomery, L. N. (2009). Robust generation of dynamic data structure visualizations with multiple interaction approaches. *ACM Transactions on Computing Education (TOCE)*, 9(2). *Article*, *13*(2), 1–32. DOI: 10.1145/1538234.1538240

Fernández-Muñoz, L., Pérez Carrasco, A., Velázquez-Iturbide, J. Á., & Urquiza-Fuentes, J. (2007). *A framework for the automatic generation of algorithm animations based on design techniques.* In Lecture Notes in Computer Science (pp. 443–457). https://link.springer.com/chapter/10.1007/978-3-540-75195-3_40

Huang, K., Xu, Z., Yang, S., Sun, H., Li, X., Yan, Z., & Zhang, Y. (2023). A survey on automated program repair techniques. *arXiv preprint arXiv:2303.18184*. https://doi.org//arXiv.2303.18184DOI: 10.48550

Knutas, A., Ikonen, J., & Porras, J. (2015). Computer-Supported Collaborative Learning in Software Engineering Education: A Systematic Mapping Study. *International Journal on Information Technologies & Security*, *7*(4). Advance online publication. DOI: 10.48550/arXiv.1906.10710

Kogan, G., Chassidim, H., & Rabaev, I. (2024). The efficacy of animation and visualization in teaching data structures: A case study. *Educational Technology Research and Development*, *72*(4), 2349–2372. DOI: 10.1007/s11423-024-10382-w

Schmid, O., Lisowska Masson, A., & Hirsbrunner, B. (2014). Real-time collaboration through web applications: An introduction to the Toolkit for Web-based Interactive Collaborative Environments (TWICE). *Personal and Ubiquitous Computing*, *18*(6), 1201–1211. DOI: 10.1007/s00779-013-0729-0

Shaffer, C. A., Cooper, M. L., Alon, A. J. D., Akbar, M., Stewart, M., Ponce, S., & Edwards, S. H. (2010). Algorithm visualization: The state of the field. *ACM Transactions on Computing Education (TOCE)*, 10(3). *Article*, *9*(3), 1–22. DOI: 10.1145/1821996.1821997

Zhang, A. G., Tang, X., Oney, S., & Chen, Y. (2024). CFlow: Supporting semantic flow analysis of students' code in programming problems at scale. *arXiv*. https://doi.org//arXiv.2404.10089DOI: 10.1145/3657604.3662025

Zhang, W., Li, Q., Dai, X., Chen, J., Du, K., Zhang, W., Liu, W., Wang, Y., Tang, R., & Yu, Y. (2025). NL-Debugging: Exploiting natural language as an intermediate representation for code debugging. *arXiv preprint arXiv:2505.15356*. https://doi.org//arXiv.2505.15356DOI: 10.18653/v1/2025.emnlp-main.80

Zhang, Y. (2024). Application of Algorithm Visualization Techniques in Teaching Computer Data Structure Course. *Applied Mathematics and Nonlinear Sciences*, *9*(1), 20240788. Advance online publication. DOI: 10.2478/amns-2024-0788

Chapter 15

An Observational Applied Model of an Academic Grants Marketplace

Shalin Hai-Jew
https://orcid.org/0000-0002-8863-0175
Independent Researcher, USA

ABSTRACT

Many come at academic grants with rose-colored glasses. Viewing academic grants as part of a larger "marketplace" (analogically) can benefit understandings for newcomers to the space and improve the grant applications submitted for consideration. This chapter proposes an applied model based on experiences and observations in the space that span decades in higher education in multiple states in the U.S. This model includes main stakeholders in the space: grant applicants, grant funders, and third-party beneficiaries, among others. This applied model is designed to benefit grant applicant awareness and strategic and tactical decision-making in the academic grants space. The applied model is dubbed "Observational Applied Model of an Academic Grants Marketplace" (OAMAGM).

INTRODUCTION

In a time of mass cutbacks to academic grant funding at the federal and state levels in the U.S., it might be a strange time to be trying to define an applied model of an academic grants marketplace. The "academic grants marketplace" is predicated on the idea that the grants space is a place where sellers (grant applicants) and buyers (grant funders) meet for an exchange. The sellers provide services and work and access to student populations and data. The buyers provide funding, guidance,

DOI: 10.4018/979-8-3373-3301-4.ch015

professional social networks, and other supports to enable that work and to have access to the outcomes, the bragging rights, and the relevant data.

An "applied model" is one that is used in real-world situations. They are used to perhaps simplify complex situations. They may aid in predictivity. They may aid in decision-making, such as about which grants to pursue. They may point the way to efficient practice. Applied models often combine theory to practical applications.

In times of duress, with funds fast disappearing and being clawed back, it is the perfect time to help grant applicants be as competitive as possible by having the most accurate conceptual model of academic grants. In normal times, a grant application itself faces tough odds.

REVIEW OF THE LITERATURE

In the grant-seeking space, there are no widely accepted universal models. Within the practice, "logic models" are a staple as a visual presentation method to describe the grant's value proposition: the opening context, the inputs, the activities, the outputs, and the ultimate outcomes (in the near-term, the mid-term, and the far-term futures), leading to a different (more desirable) future.

A model can inform a grant-seeking strategy, so that an organization can assess grant opportunities and have a more accurate sense of what to pursue, what is aligned with university or college missions and goals. When does it make sense to invest in a grant application, and when might it pay back in spades and when not? What tactic should be used in framing the proposed work, and why? What information should be included? What tone should be used? How can the technical writing in a grant application be as persuasive as possible? What evidence can be brought to bear to support an assertion or truth claim?

There might be pieces of advice, such as being careful not to harness generative AI unthinkingly since their application may be flagged for plagiarism. There are tips for what technologies to use for creating different grant package contents: maps, photos, videos, and other contents.

One work proposes a different approach by grant funders, to fund labs (groups of experts) as a whole instead of singleton researchers or individual principal investigators (PIs) (Crawford, 2024).

AN OBSERVATIONAL APPLIED MODEL OF AN ACADEMIC GRANTS MARKETPLACE

Applied models can come from various sources. Some come from data. Some come from mathematical equations. Some come from theory. Some come from sufficient practice, with learning from observations and small experiments in on-ground contexts.

An applied model has general constituent parts:

- A theoretical framework (underlying principles) that guides the model's structure;
- The identification of important variables
- The definition of interaction effects between variables
- Some projected outcomes based on the basic context

Some applied models are designed for high predictive rigor. Others are more about applied awareness and decision-making in the context. Some may be preliminary models that lay some basic groundwork but are not expected to be seen as the last word on the subject.

The Observational Applied Model of an Academic Grants Marketplace (OAMAGM) sets the context of the grants interchange as a marketplace. The grant applicants are the seller of their wares, and they are trying to capture the interest of the grant funders, who are the buyers of services, data, research, and outcomes. That mere setup suggests some basic implications:

- The grant applicant has to offer a compelling value proposition that is real in the world. That value proposition has to be feasible. Just asserting a need and a desire for funding is insufficient (alone) for funding. The academic grants space is transactional. There is an exchange of values between the grant applicant and the grant funder.
- The supply-demand dynamic suggests that the grant applicant has to offer something that is valuable and in short supply for them to be able to name their price. Few grant applicants have such monopoly power that can move prices. Few grant applicants can set the price for what they have to offer. They are usually working within the marketplace contexts set by the grant funders.
- The grant funder has to justify their expenditures and acquire a return on investment (ROI). They have leadership that they re beholden to. They have to raise funds from their respective sources in order to have funding to dole out through their grant-funding processes.

- The grant funder has a preference for works with "future pull" vs. "retro" or past-focused work. This means that the novel and innovative are more appealing than the prior known. This means that the proposed work has to be cutting-edge. It has to have potential for future market value in many cases. It has to solve problems in ways that benefit stakeholders.
- The grant funder has to propose work that is doable, practically feasible. Going down unrewarding alleys and approaches is not tenable for funders. [Even very cutting-edge research has to be supported by some preliminary research to show that the work is not about going down blind alleys. The proposals are not about flights of whimsy but about empirically-based work that would likely bear fruit, one way or another.]
- The grant funder and grant applicant will be forming a partnership if they enter into a grants contract or agreement. Each will have implications on each other's reputations. This means that each side has to do due diligence about the other, or else risk harm to reputation and brand.
- Ideally, the grant funder and grant applicant will have some alignment of interests. Perhaps they work towards supporting a particular stakeholder group. Perhaps they share values. Any disjunctures in this space may cause rifts and mistrust (particularly in contexts when political issues are top-of-mind). This aspect offers a predictivity angle.

The above are some basic precepts. The grants space is constantly evolving, and the rules and on-ground realities will change. There are expected changes in regulations and laws, grant funder focuses and practices, evolved grant applicant practices, changing technologies, research expectations, data expectations, and other elements.

Too often, academic grant pursuits lie in the realm of administrators and bureaucrats, who may not feel any responsibility to share their knowledge with others at the risk of challenges to their positions. The truth is that for an institution of higher education (IHE), the more who understand grants, the more principal investigators (PIs) and program directors (PDs) there may be to pursue grant-funded work opportunities to improve the organization and their respective disciplines.

Modeling Scenarios

The OAMAGM has implications for the typical phases of a grant pursuit. The phases are understood as the following: prospecting for grant opportunities, local planning for the grant application, writing and documenting, proffering and waiting, the agreement, the work and reportage (through the closing report), and publicity.

1) Prospecting for Grant Opportunities

In prospecting for grant opportunities, the local organization has been scanning the grants ecosystem to understand what is available in the world. They have to assess the grant notices of funding opportunities (NOFOs) and other related files and decide whether there is a sufficient match of local interests with the grant funder interests. There also has to be sufficient local talent to execute on the work. There have to be approvals from leadership. A misjudgment here of interests will lead to wasted resource, time, and work.

2) Local Planning for the Grant Application

Once there is initial agreement, the local team works on planning for the grant application (and the grant-funded work). They have to define the following basic elements: the work plan, the work plan aligned with the grant funder's action period (scheduling for the work), the staffing (the team that the local organization can put on the field), and the budget. These are core elements. The work has to be valuable. There has to be sufficient time to achieve the work because grant work has to be feasible. The team has to be capable and trained to do the work professionally. (Avoid the Dunning-Kruger effect.) The principal investigators (PIs) / program directors (PDs) have to be responsible and responsive. They have to have leadership abilities. They have to be able to engage externally funded work without stumbling on their other professional commitments. The budget has to fit with contemporaneous pricing.

3) Writing and Documenting

Then, once the terms are agreed upon, the team has to write out the grant application. They have to make the digital objects (photos, maps, and so on). They may have to conduct some basic research to bolster the grant. They likely have to acquire attestations of the organization's fitness to do the work, manage the money, report on the work, and to be professional and ethical. They have to acquire letters of support from partners. They have to draft memorandums of understanding (MOU) for more formal agreements.

4) Proffering and Waiting

Once the draft has passed muster and all appropriate signatures are acquired, the institution of higher education (IHE) submits the grant application to the grant funder…according to the terms of the grant funder. Then, everyone waits until a formal decision is made and announced.

5) The Contractual Grant Agreement

If the grant funder chooses to award the local grant application, a contract is signed spelling out the actual work and the actual resources. There may be some differences between the public NOFOs and the actual contract. At this point, the grant applicant can still back out by not signing and just moving on. Some grant applicants will retract their participation even after signing.

6) The Work and Reportage (Through the Closing Report)

Then, the work commences, hopefully, according to schedule. Regular reports are made to the defined standards of the grant funder. When the work is all done, final deliverables are sent (whether data or digital contents or something else), and then there is a closing report.

7) Publicity

Grant funders require some positive credit through word-of-mouth, electronic word-of-mouth (social media), and press releases to the local media. Many stipulate this in their grant funding documents and contracts. Grant applications who are awarded moneys are encouraged to share stories of achievements to advance the goals of both the IHE and the grant funder. Research publications and presentations at professional conferences are often highly welcome, too, in academic grant pursuits. There is a need to address both internal and external publics, those within the organization and those outside, in terms of the work.

Implications for Grant-Pursuit Practice

The awareness of the grants marketplace is infused in every phase of the grants process. There is clarity grant-funded work does not come from charity but from employing the local organization to do particular work to professional standards within deadline and on budget. This knowledge means that the proposal is not about need per se but about what the local individual or team can offer the grant funder… and the stakeholders. OAMAGM informs the work design. It is about value-for-value, in an objective sense. It also means that the local grant applicants have to be read up on their field, so what they offer is not retreaded ideas but something cutting-edge, something new. The marketplace angle reminds grant applicants that they are working in a regulated legal environment and must abide by the respective rules. There has to be proper handling of data. There are many rules for the uses of federal and state (government) funding, so all those have to be adhered to. (Procurement, proper spending, and other practices have to be followed to the letter.) Etcetera.

The marketplace angle emphasizes the importance of social networks and also of working in a public space with greater communal awareness. Also, grant applicants have a cost awareness and a sense of a running tab if they are working on a grant application. Grant moneys are not free to apply for, and they are not costless to manage in the grant action period. Grant-funded work has to be relevant to the local team and administration to leave the gravitational pull of the institution and attain sufficient escape velocity to reach outside organizations to compete.

The competitiveness of the grants marketplace means that a local team should employ strategies and tactics. How do they communicate with the grant funder in ways that are compelling? How do they stay with facts and practical claims (vs. far-fetched ones)? What are questions to ask grant funders to aid in decision-making? When does it make sense to fund an expensive try? When should the team cut bait? What does professionalism look like in the academic grants space? How can the local organization position themselves to pursue grant funding (and to stay competitive)? When should the local team add branding (like logos, like taglines) to the grant application? [The prior requires due diligence, such as checking out designs and names and taglines at the USPTO site.]

The different types of grants—government ones, corporate ones, family foundation ones—all have their own rules as well. The above approach is general enough to apply across multiple sectors: commercial, nonprofit, K12, and higher education.

What Does the Model Say About Extreme Federal Grant Funding Pullbacks?

An applied model should be of use at the extreme ends of a normal curve, during rare events.

In 2025, the executive branch of the U.S. cut back some $9 billion in federal funding for foreign aid, public media, and education (both higher education and K12). The educational cuts were estimated to total some $12 billion from the Department of Education, and some $4.5 billion from K-12 programs. Hundreds of billions in awarded grant research funding for universities and colleges are estimated to have been clawed back. These actions have been found by the judiciary to be within the purview of the executive branch, and the legislative branch has agreed to various rescissions packages to allow the cuts to remain.

In a democracy, much power is given to the executive, around which much authority coalesces. In the name of trying to work on the 37 trillion in federal debt and rising costs to service that debt (cover for action), the larger society is backing the budget cuts and agency dismantling (generally speaking). The defunding shows the power of money as an organizing force, with so many endeavors and organizations left hollowed-out and enervated.

The grants marketplace model suggests the following, given the economic lens:

- Whatever becomes unfunded essentially disappears. The input work for the grant applications and the grant-funded work are just wholly lost.
- In a for-profit world where businesses have to turn a profit in order to survive, there is very limited alternate funding.
- Every entity—every academic, ever administrator, every staffer; every institution of higher education—has to argue for the value it offers in the marketplace.
- The clawed-back funding does mean lost jobs. It means the need for individuals and groups and entities to hone new skills, to redefine themselves, and to make the case for their own value in the competitive space.
- Tenured faculty, who often need to acquire grant funding and conduct primary research, are at risk of losing their jobs, too, as the universities and colleges experience financial pressures.
- Higher education will be a shrinking sector. Public education at the K12 level will be challenged by private schools, given changing policies. Every organization will "right-size." Each will find its level based on the liquidity available to it. Every organization is highly vulnerable to its access to funding, the lifeblood of the organization.
- State government is expected to shrink since many of those positions were set up to manage the distribution of federal government funding.

Some suggest that higher taxes will be in order to address the budget deficit. However, this will likely be challenged by citizens and tax payers, who may feel that they pay a lot already.

Without liquidity in the grant funding space, no amount of grant writing will magically result in funded projects. There are no transactions to be had if there is nothing to transact over.

Available moneys are a major dependency for the grants space to work. A dry watering hole will not bring creatures, but there will be many animal carcasses left behind for those creatures that show up expecting something to quench their thirst.

The applied model uses a basic economic lens through which to understand the current situation. It is not a predictive one but may suggest future directions. Secondary dominoes and tertiary ones will likely fall, with impacts on college towns' housing and businesses, academic publishing, R&D, innovations, and overall competitiveness in the world. The funding pullbacks will gum up the works for many societal sectors.

DISCUSSION

What makes grant-writing so complex and challenging? Grant-writing exists in a thicket of regulatory rules related to contracts, money handling, reputations, privacy laws, media law, data regulations, and others. Various entities maintain oversight over various aspects of the process. There are high variances between expectations in different disciplines. There are different personalities on grant-funded projects. The research and data involved in grants are rigorous. The deadlines are demanding. The environment is fast-moving. It is high pressure. The ecosystem can encourage some bad behaviors, such as misrepresentations and frauds. Writing, documentation, research, and strategizing are all difficult skills and take years to develop.

Grant pursuits are not for everyone. In most cases, only a small minority of individuals have the knowledge, skills, abilities and temperaments to thrive in the space.

The OAMAGM (Observational Applied Model of an Academic Grants Marketplace) conveys a core and telling reality of the grants space that grant applicants pursuing discretionary (competitive ones vs. mandatory ones, doled out by formula) grants have to offer something of value. These ideas should apply to grant-seeking even in the post-clawback era (2025-onwards), in the United States.

Competing Amateur Models About Academic Grant Funding

What are some competing visions of how to understand academic grant funding? They include the following:

"free money": Many assume that there are moneys to be had as long as one applied for them (as if from a welfare pool of funding). There is not the sense that there are strings attached.

"charity": Many assume that the argument that needs to be made is that there is a financial need. Need is everywhere, and no grants are given out based on need alone.

"banking": Some assume that grant funders work like banks. One just goes to them and makes a withdrawal.

"easy mark": Some assume that the grant funders are swayed by charm and storytelling alone, whether or not there is substance behind the stories. In such cases, applicants tend to spin narratives independent of facts.

"speaking to the universe": Some assume that if one dreams big that the money and glory will just rain down. It is not an "ask and you shall receive" context.

There are a number of myths about academic grant funding. These myths can lead to an inability to compete in the real world, the world as it is.

FUTURE RESEARCH DIRECTIONS

It will be important for researchers and grant applicants and grant funders to know what the new rules may be in the post-clawback of grant funds era. Besides political correctness against "woke" and "DEI" (diversity, equity, and inclusion), what are the new standards? Will there be a new frugality in terms of how moneys are requested and spent? Will there need to be testimonials of political correctness? Attestations of race-neutrality in policies and practices? Loyalty clauses? Openness to federal government audits of PC-ness? Signups for favored practices of teaching and learning?

Are there additional understandings that may be added to this foundational applied model? What sorts of grants are exceptions to this?

What are some other ways to create an applied academic model for academic grants pursuit? Perhaps there can be some approaches based on data? Trace data from work systems? Etc.

CONCLUSION

This is the first try in the research literature towards defining an applied model for academic grants. This chapter used an observational approach based on decades of work in the grant applications space.

Note: This short chapter drew from many dozens of articles in the *HutchCC Grant Navigator* newsletter (which published from January 2024 to February 2025) and the *Academic Grant Pursuit* newsletter (with issues from March 2025 – June 2026). The provenance of this work has an even longer prehistory. The author has worked in the grants space (as a grant writer, as a grant co-principal investigator, as a team member on grant-funded projects at colleges and universities, etc.) for decades. It is from those experiences that this work emerges.

REFERENCES

Crawford, J. (2024). *Making every researcher seek grants is a broken model.*

KEY TERMS AND DEFINITIONS

Academic Grants Marketplace: a competitive space in which grant funders are buyers and grant applicants are sellers of their work.

Research Applied Model: a practical conceptualization of a defined context or dynamic to aid in awareness and decision-making index.

APPENDIX

The original versions of the *HutchCC Grant Navigator* (January 2024 – February 2025) and the Academic Grant Pursuits (March 2025 – September 2026) are archived on SlideShare. These are free for download. The general link is the following: https://www.slideshare.net/ShalinHaiJew/documents

Conclusion

Applied models ae critical tools for engaging a complex and fast-moving world. When designed well, they track with the world. They offer insights that go beyond the mundane and offer insightful glimmers of underlying patterns and truths. Models enable awareness and decision-making. Applied models are embedded in every aspect of life, whether these are obvious or non-obvious.

EXTANT QUESTIONS

There are numerous examples of models learned from life, from theorizing, from research, and from data. Only some of these are turned into generalizable "generics" (extracted from various specific brands based on localized experiences).

So many models are in effect for only a short time. They are fragile. Many require new data and new updates and new care-and-feeding to function.

Very few (no) models have full predictive power in a complex and unpredictable and dynamic world, with so many powerful variables at play. Miscalculations in decision-making abound. In fantasy, a model might be substantial and accurate enough to head off poor decisions, especially by those in power (and so hold much more capability in affecting harm). Are there ways to model out the outcomes of an invasion of another country? What are ways to get past the weaknesses of human- and machine- made modeling? Are there ways to not see "through a mirror darkly" but to get closer to understanding reality with something closer to perfection?

As with every edited book, there are still many extant questions that may be asked and answered.

What is it like to set up an applied model? Inherit one? Evolve one over time? Add modules to one? Revise an inherited applied model? Turn one into a computer program? What about various models in various work contexts? How do people troubleshoot models and test them for efficacy? How do people ensure that a model is transferable and not excessively localized? What applied ethics should be used in the making of practical models and why?

Many of the above questions were only very lightly addressed in this collection and some not at all. One way to approach what was not addressed is to look at the initial chapter topic prompts.

SOME CHAPTER TOPIC PROMPTS

The call for chapters went out in March 2025. The recommended topics follow:

Rationales for the creation of applied models
Theories and principles of applied models
--
Applied work-based models
Building applied models from data
Building applied models from projects and programs
Building applied models from observational research and fieldwork
Building applied models from multiple-sources
--
Abstracting applied models for heritability and generalizability
Avoiding overfit to local realities, local data, local dimensions, in applied models
--
Ensuring heritability of applied models
Testing applied models in vitro (in a lab, in an artificial setting)
Testing applied models in vivo (in the world)
--
Scenarios (contexts) for applied modeling
--
Operationalizing / actualizing applied models
--
Different types of applied models
--
Adoption of (inheriting) applied models
Retrofitting applied models
Adding new modules to applied models
Cultural adaptations to applied models
Fine-tuning applied models for heightened accuracy and sensitivity
--
Testing the (in)efficacy of applied models
Distribution and publishing of applied models

--

Inspirations for applied models

CONCLUSION

As one makes one's way in the world, one knows that people have different pieces of the puzzle and different things to contribute. This work was created to capture the current knowledge in the current slice-in-time…and to perhaps inspire more sharing by others in the same space.

Thanks go to the contributors of this work for sharing their expertise.

Shalin Hai-Jew

2025

Compilation of References

Abdallah, A. B., Rawadiah, O. M., Al-Byati, W., & Alhyari, S. (2021). Supply chain integration and export performance: The mediating role of supply chain performance. *International Journal of Productivity and Performance Management*, *70*(7), 1907–1929. DOI: 10.1108/IJPPM-02-2021-0076

Abdar, M., Pourpanah, F., Hussain, S., Rezazadegan, D., Liu, L., Ghavamzadeh, M., Fieguth, P., Cao, X., Khosravi, A., Acharya, U. R., Makarenkov, V., & Nahavandi, S. (2021). A review of uncertainty quantification in deep learning: Techniques, applications and challenges. *Information Fusion*, *76*, 243–297. DOI: 10.1016/j.inffus.2021.05.008

Acuña-Gamboa, L.-A. (2022). Aprendizajes basados en la incertidumbre: Construyendo escenarios educativos post-Covid en México. *Revista de Investigación Educacional*, *20*(2), 127–139. DOI: 10.35869/reined.v20i2.4220

Adobor, H., & Kudonoo, E. C. (2025). Antifragility and organizations: An organizational design perspective. *Leadership and Organization Development Journal*, *46*(2), 351–375. DOI: 10.1108/LODJ-03-2024-0185

Ahimbisibwe, A., Cavana, R. Y., & Daellenbach, U. (2015). A contingency fit model of critical success factors for software development projects. *Journal of Enterprise Information Management*, *28*(1), 7–33. DOI: 10.1108/JEIM-08-2013-0060

Ahi, P., & Searcy, C. (2013). A comparative literature analysis of definitions for green and sustainable supply chain management. *Journal of Cleaner Production*, *52*, 329–341. DOI: 10.1016/j.jclepro.2013.02.018

Ahi, P., & Searcy, C. (2015). An analysis of metrics used to measure performance in green and sustainable supply chains. *Journal of Cleaner Production*, *86*, 360–377. DOI: 10.1016/j.jclepro.2014.08.005

Ahmad, T., Boit, J., & Aakula, A. (2023). The role of cross-functional collaboration in digital transformation. *Journal of Computational Intelligence and Robotics*, *3*(1), 205–242.

Ahmed, H. N., Maoua, Z., Ahmed, S., & Ali, S. M. (2025). Humanitarian relief supply chain performance measurement: A Framework and Validation. *Journal of Industrial Information Integration*, *47*, 100898. DOI: 10.1016/j.jii.2025.100898

Ahn, H., Cha, S., Lee, D., & Moon, T. (2019). Uncertainty-based continual learning with adaptive regularization. In Wallach, H., Larochelle, H., Beygelzimer, A., d'Alché-Buc, F., Fox, E., & Garnett, R. (Eds.), *Proceedings of the 33rd Conference on Neural Information Processing Systems (NeurIPS)*. Vancouver, Canada. https://doi.org/DOI: 10.48550/arXiv.1905.11614

Aithal, P. S., Prabhu, S., & Aithal, S. (2024). Future of higher education through technology prediction and forecasting. Poornaprajna International Journal of Management, Education, and Social Science (PIJMESS), 1(1), 01-50.

Aithal, P. S., & Maiya, A. K. (2023). Innovations in higher education industry–Shaping the future. [IJCSBE]. *International Journal of Case Studies in Business, IT, and Education*, *7*(4), 283–311. DOI: 10.47992/IJCSBE.2581.6942.0321

Ajzen, I., & Fishbein, M. (1975). A Bayesian analysis of attribution processes. *Psychological Bulletin*, *82*(2), 261.

Albonico, M., Đorđević, M., Hamer, E., & Malavolta, I. (2023). Software engineering research on the robot operating system: A systematic mapping study. *Journal of Systems and Software*, *197*, 111574. DOI: 10.1016/j.jss.2022.111574

Algozzine, B., Newton, J. S., Horner, R. H., Todd, A. W., & Algozzine, K. (2012). Development and technical characteristics of a team decision-making assessment tool: Decision observation, recording, and analysis (DORA). *Journal of Psychoeducational Assessment*, *30*(3), 237–249. DOI: 10.1177/0734282911423884

Alibašić, H. (2025). Advancing disaster resilience: The ethical dimensions of adaptability and adaptive leadership in public service organizations. *Public Integrity*, *27*(3), 209–221. DOI: 10.1080/10999922.2024.2388285

Allen, J., Blaylock, N., & Ferguson, G. (2002, July). A problem solving model for collaborative agents. In *Proceedings of the first international joint conference on Autonomous agents and multiagent systems: part 2* (pp. 774-781). DOI: 10.1145/544862.544923

Allen, L., Bali, T. G., & Tang, Y. (2012). Does Systemic Risk in the Financial Sector Predict Future Economic Downturns? *Review of Financial Studies*, *25*(10), 3000–3036. DOI: 10.1093/rfs/hhs094

Allison, P. D. (2002). *Missing data*. SAGE Publications. DOI: 10.4135/9781412985079

Almashhadani, M., Mishra, A., & Yazici, A. (2024). Software maintenance practices using Agile methods towards cloud environment: A systematic mapping. *Journal of Software (Malden, MA)*, *36*(11), e2698. Advance online publication. DOI: 10.1002/smr.2698

Al-Mutawah, M. A., Thomas, R., Eid, A., Mahmoud, E. Y., & Fateel, M. J. (2019). Conceptual understanding, procedural knowledge and problem-solving skills in mathematics: High school graduates work analysis and standpoints. *International journal of education and practice, 7*(3), 258-273.

Alqudah, M. K., Razali, R., Alqudah, M. K., Al Dalaien, M. N., Alabool, H. M., & Alkhazaleh, H. A. (2023). A grounded theory of selecting lean and Agile practices for software development. *Journal of Software (Malden, MA)*, *36*(4), e2539. Advance online publication. DOI: 10.1002/smr.2539

Alsheyadi, A., Baawain, A., & Shaukat, M. R. (2024). E-supply chain coordination and performance impacts: An empirical investigation. *Production & Manufacturing Research*, *12*(1), 1–32. DOI: 10.1080/21693277.2024.2379942

Álvarez, G. O. C., Zurita, I. N., & Álvarez, J. C. E. (2020). Internal control system as a tool for optimizing the financial processes of the company Austroseguridad Cía. Ltda. *Dominio de las Ciencias*, *6*(1), 429–465.

Amaral, T. G., Braga, T., Amaral, R. R., & Evans, J. (2021). Randomization application: A new tool for academics of the new millennium. *Journal of Dental Education*, *85*(3), 2002–2004. DOI: 10.1002/jdd.12563 PMID: 33556984

Ambec, S., & Lanoie, P. (2008). Does it pay to be green? A systematic overview. *The Academy of Management Perspectives*, *22*(4), 45–62. DOI: 10.5465/amp.2008.35590353

Amin, S. N. (2021). Gamification of Duolingo in rising student's English language learning motivation. *Jurnal Bahasa Lingua Scientia*, *13*(2), 191–213. DOI: 10.21274/ls.2021.13.2.191-213

Andersen, D. F., Richardson, G. P., & Vennix, J. A. (1997). Group model building: Adding more science to the craft. *System Dynamics Review*, *13*(2), 187–201. DOI: 10.1002/(SICI)1099-1727(199722)13:2<187::AID-SDR124>3.0.CO;2-O

Anderson, C. (2010). *Free: The Future of a Radical Price*. Hyperion.

Anderson, E. W., Fornell, C., & Lehmann, D. R. (1994). Customer satisfaction, market share, and profitability: Findings from Sweden. *Journal of Marketing*, *58*(3), 53–66.

Andreadis, N., & Quinlan, P. T. (2010). Task switching under predictable and unpredictable circumstances. *Attention, Perception & Psychophysics*, *72*(7), 1776–1790. DOI: 10.3758/APP.72.7.1776 PMID: 20952777

Andrews, M. (2021). Quality indicators in narrative research. *Qualitative Research in Psychology*, *18*(3), 353–368. DOI: 10.1080/14780887.2020.1769241

Anggoro, F. K., Dubosarsky, M., & Kabourek, S. (2021). Developing an observation tool to measure preschool children's problem-solving skills. *Education Sciences*, *11*(12), 779. DOI: 10.3390/educsci11120779

Anglin, A. H., Kincaid, P. A., Short, J. C., & Allen, D. G. (2022). Role theory perspectives: Past, present, and future applications of role theories in management research. *Journal of Management*, *48*(6), 1469–1502. DOI: 10.1177/01492063221081442

Angrist, N., Bergman, P. S., Cullen, C., Letsomo, T., Matsheng, M., Sabarwal, S., & Sullivan, T. R. (2023). *Building Resilient Education Systems: Evidence from Large-Scale Randomized Trials in Five Countries*. Working Paper 31208. National Bureau of Economic Research. https://doi.org/DOI: 10.3386/w31208

Anliak, S., & Sahin, D. (2010). An observational study for evaluating the effects of interpersonal problem-solving skills training on behavioural dimensions. *Early Child Development and Care*, *180*(8), 995–1003. DOI: 10.1080/03004430802670819

Aradhya, S. G. B., Gupta, V. C., Selvakumar, P., Raman, M. S., Singh, J., Manjunath, T. C., & Sharma, M. (2025). Health Crises and Digitalization: Digital Health. In *Sustainable Digitalization Strategies in Business and Healthcare* (pp. 171-198). IGI Global Scientific Publishing.

Aranjo, S., Pinto, N., Parekh, P., & Modi, T. (2022). Review of Real-Time Collaboration Frameworks, Libraries and Products. [IJRASET]. *International Journal for Research in Applied Science and Engineering Technology*, *10*(4), 653–660. Advance online publication. DOI: 10.22214/ijraset.2022.41326

Aria, M., & Cuccurullo, C. (2017). bibliometrix: An R-tool for comprehensive science mapping analysis. *Journal of Informetrics*, *11*(4), 959–975. DOI: 10.1016/j.joi.2017.08.007

Arias, M. G. M., & Salto, I. M. A. (2020). Internal control model for SMEs based on the COSO-ERM report. UCTUNEXPO University. https://uctunexpo.autanabooks.com/index.php/uct/article/view/375

Arora, V., Singh, M., & Bhatia, R. (2020). Orientation-based ant colony algorithm for synthesizing the test scenarios in UML activity diagram. *Information and Software Technology*, *123*, 106292. DOI: 10.1016/j.infsof.2020.106292

Arya, C. (2022). *Design of structural elements: concrete, steelwork, masonry and timber designs to eurocodes*. CRC Press. DOI: 10.1201/9781003208037

Aryal, R. (2022, December). Critical self-reflective engagement to improve professional development for a teacher educator. In Mathematics Education Forum Chitwan (Vol. 7, No. 7, pp. 66-81). DOI: 10.3126/mefc.v7i7.54787

Arzu Akyuz, G., & Erman Erkan, T. (2010). Supply chain performance measurement: A literature review. *International Journal of Production Research*, *48*(17), 5137–5155. DOI: 10.1080/00207540903089536

Asmah, S., Hastati, S., & Nurdiansyah, E. (2025). Application Of The Problem Solving Learning Model In Improving Numeracy Skills In Class IV Students Of SDN. *ALENA: Journal of Elementary Education*, *3*(2), 209–218. DOI: 10.59638/jee.v3i2.373

Attwood, T. K., Blackford, S., Brazas, M. D., Davies, A., & Schneider, M. V. (2017). A global perspective on evolving bioinformatics and data science training needs. *Briefings in Bioinformatics*, *20*(2), 398–404. DOI: 10.1093/bib/bbx100 PMID: 28968751

Auclair, F. (2007). Problem formulation by medical students: An observation study. *BMC Medical Education*, *7*(1), 16. DOI: 10.1186/1472-6920-7-16

Avishai, T., Palatnik, A., & Kolikant, Y. B. D. (2025). Amplifiers and filters in teacher learning of student-centered mathematics instruction. *Teaching and Teacher Education*, *156*, 104943. DOI: 10.1016/j.tate.2025.104943

Baah, C., Acquah, I. S. K., & Ofori, D. (2022). Exploring the influence of supply chain collaboration on supply chain visibility, stakeholder trust, environmental and financial performances: A partial least square approach. *Benchmarking*, *29*(1), 172–193. DOI: 10.1108/BIJ-10-2020-0519

Bagiati, A., & Evangelou, D. (2016). Practicing engineering while building with blocks: Identifying engineering thinking. *European Early Childhood Education Research Journal*, *24*(1), 67–85. DOI: 10.1080/1350293X.2015.1120521

Bailer-Jones, D. M. (2002). Scientists' thoughts on scientific models. *Perspectives on Science*, *10*(3), 275–301. DOI: 10.1162/106361402321899069

Baker, H. K., Kumar, S., & Pandey, N. (2020). A bibliometric analysis of managerial finance: A retrospective. *Managerial Finance*, *46*(11), 1495–1517. DOI: 10.1108/MF-06-2019-0277

Bakıcı, T., Almirall, E., & Wareham, J. (2013). A Smart City Initiative: The Case of Barcelona. *Journal of the Knowledge Economy*, *4*(2), 135–148. DOI: 10.1007/s13132-012-0084-9

Ball-Rokeach, S. J., & DeFleur, M. L. (1976). A dependency model of mass-media effects. *Communication Research*, *3*(1), 3–21. DOI: 10.1177/009365027600300101

Banham, R. (2022). *Architecture of the Well-tempered Environment*. University of Chicago Press.

Baniya, A. K., Pant, S. S., Paudel, D., Gupta, A., Singh, S., & Mohapatra, H. (2025). Load balancing in cloud computing ensuring fault tolerance, high availability, and security. Risk-Based Approach to Secure Cloud Migration, 253-284. https://doi.org/ DOI: 10.4018/979-8-3693-7137-4.ch010

Banks, J., Carson, J. S.II, Nelson, B. L., & Nicol, D. M. (2005). *Discrete-event system simulation* (4th ed.). Pearson.

Banton, C. (2019). *Network effect*. Investopedia.

Bapna, R., Ramaprasad, J., & Umyarov, A. (2018). Monetizing freemium communities: Does paying for premium increase social engagement? *Management Information Systems Quarterly*, *42*(3), 719–735. DOI: 10.25300/MISQ/2018/13592

Barbala, A., Berntzen, M., & Moe, N. B. (2025). Social capital in large-scale Agile software product management: A multi-case study. *Information and Software Technology*, *187*, 107841. DOI: 10.1016/j.infsof.2025.107841

Bardach, E., & Patashnik, E. M. (2019). *A practical guide for policy analysis: The eightfold path to more effective problem solving* (6th ed.). CQ Press.

Bardwell, L. V. (1991). Problem-framing: A perspective on environmental problem-solving. *Environmental Management*, *15*(5), 603–612. DOI: 10.1007/BF02589620

Barocas, J. A., Wang, J., Marshall, B. D., LaRochelle, M. R., Bettano, A., Bernson, D., Beckwith, C. G., Linas, B. P., & Walley, A. Y. (2019). Sociodemographic factors and social determinants associated with toxicology confirmed polysubstance opioid-related deaths. *Drug and Alcohol Dependence*, *200*, 59–63. DOI: 10.1016/j.drugalcdep.2019.03.014 PMID: 31100636

Barocas, S., Hardt, M., & Narayanan, A. (2023). *Fairness and machine learning: Limitations and opportunities*. The MIT Press.

Barroso Castillo, S. M., Castellanos, I. D. M. P., Cruz-Pérez, N., d'Armengol, L., & Santamarta, J. C. (2025). Sustaining Tradition: Socioeconomic and Environmental Dimensions of Canary Island Fisheries in the Post-COVID-19 Era. *Conservation*, *5*(1), 12. DOI: 10.3390/conservation5010012

Basak, R. S., Mohapatra, H., & Panigrahy, B. (2025). Enhancing smart home user interfaces with emerging technologies. Home Healthcare Services and Technology Implications, 115-144. https://doi.org/DOI: 10.4018/979-8-3373-3099-0.ch005

Basili, V. R. (1996, March). The role of experimentation in software engineering: past, current, and future. In *Proceedings of IEEE 18th International Conference on Software Engineering* (pp. 442-449). IEEE. DOI: 10.1109/ICSE.1996.493439

Batanero, C. (2015, Feb.). Understanding randomness: Challenges for research and teaching. CERME9 - Ninth Congress of the European Society for Research in Mathematics Education, Charles University in Prague, Faculty of Education, Prague, Czech Republic. pp.34-49.Retrieved from https://hal.science/hal-01280506v1

Batini, C., & Scannapieco, M. (2006). *Data quality: Concepts, methodologies and techniques*. Springer.

Batty, M., Axhausen, K. W., Giannotti, F., Pozdnoukhov, A., Bazzani, A., Wachowicz, M., Ouzounis, G., & Portugali, Y. (2012). Smart cities of the future. *The European Physical Journal. Special Topics*, *214*(1), 481–518. DOI: 10.1140/epjst/e2012-01703-3

BBVA Research. (2023). A look at MSMEs in Colombia. Retrieved from https://www.bbvaresearch.com/publicaciones/colombia-una-mirada-a-las-mipymes-en-colombia/

Beard, C. (2022). *Experiential learning design: Theoretical foundations and effective principles*. Routledge. DOI: 10.4324/9781003030867

Behutiye, W., Rodríguez, P., Oivo, M., Aaramaa, S., Partanen, J., & Abhervé, A. (2022). undefined. *Journal of Systems and Software*, *183*, 111112. DOI: 10.1016/j.jss.2021.111112

Ben-Hur, M. (2006). *Concept-rich mathematics instruction: Building a strong foundation for reasoning and problem solving*. ASCD.

Bennett, M., Vielma, J. P., & Zubizarreta, J. R. (2020). Building representative matched samples with multi-valued treatments in large observational studies. *Journal of Computational and Graphical Statistics*, *29*(4), 744–757. DOI: 10.1080/10618600.2020.1753532

Bernstein, P. (2022). *Machine learning: Architecture in the age of artificial intelligence*. Riba Publishing. DOI: 10.4324/9781003297192

Bertsimas, D., & Kallus, N. (2019). From predictive to prescriptive analytics. *Management Science*, *66*(3), 1025–1044. DOI: 10.1287/mnsc.2018.3253

Bhagwat, R., & Sharma, M. K. (2007). Performance measurement of supply chain management using the analytical hierarchy process. *Production Planning and Control*, *18*(8), 666–680. DOI: 10.1080/09537280701614407

Bhattacherjee, A. (2001). Understanding information systems continuance: An expectation-confirmation model. *Management Information Systems Quarterly*, •••, 351–370.

Biraglia, A., Bowen, K. T., Gerrath, M. H. E. E., & Musarra, G. (2022). How need for closure and deal proneness shape consumers' freemium versus premium price choices. *Journal of Business Research*, *143*, 157–170. DOI: 10.1016/j.jbusres.2022.01.064

Bishop, D. V. (2006). What causes specific language impairment in children? *Current Directions in Psychological Science*, *15*(5), 217–221. DOI: 10.1111/j.1467-8721.2006.00439.x PMID: 19009045

Biskjaer, M. M., Kamari, A., Jensen, S. R., & Kirkegaard, P. H. (2021). Exploring blind spots in collaborative value creation in building design: A creativity perspective. *CoDesign*, *17*(4), 374–391. DOI: 10.1080/15710882.2019.1654521

Bjork, R. A., & Bjork, E. L. (2011). Making things hard on yourself, but in a good way: Creating desirable difficulties to enhance learning. In Gernsbacher, M. A., Pew, R. W., Hough, L. M., & Pomerantz, J. R. (Eds.), *Psychology and the real world: Essays illustrating fundamental contributions to society* (pp. 56–64). Worth Publishers.

Blanchard, J., Hott, J. R., Berry, V., & Carroll, R. (2022, December). Stop Reinventing the Wheel! Promoting Community Software in Computing Education. In *ITiCSE 2022: Innovation and Technology in Computer Science Education*. ACM., DOI: 10.1145/3571785.3574129

Blome, C., Hollos, D., & Paulraj, A. (2014). Green procurement and green supplier development: Antecedents and effects on supplier performance. *International Journal of Production Research*, *52*(1), 32–49. DOI: 10.1080/00207543.2013.825748

Bockstedt, J., Druehl, C., & Mishra, A. (2015). Design and pricing of freemium products. *Business Horizons*, *58*(3), 301–311.

Boehm, B., & Bose, P. (n.d.). A collaborative spiral software process model based on theory W. *Proceedings of the Third International Conference on the Software Process. Applying the Software Process*, 59-68. https://doi.org/DOI: 10.1109/SPCON.1994.344423

Boehm, B., & Turner, R. (n.d.). Balancing agility and discipline: Evaluating and integrating Agile and plan-driven methods. *Proceedings. 26th International Conference on Software Engineering*, 718-719. https://doi.org/DOI: 10.1109/ICSE.2004.1317503

Bogard, T., Liu, M., & Chiang, Y. H. V. (2013). Thresholds of knowledge development in complex problem solving: A multiple-case study of advanced learners' cognitive processes. *Educational Technology Research and Development*, *61*(3), 465–503. DOI: 10.1007/s11423-013-9295-4

Bolton, R. N., & Drew, J. H. (1991). A multistage model of customers' assessments of service quality and value. *The Journal of Consumer Research*, *17*(4), 375–384.

Bonnet, A., & Glazier, J. (2024). Educating for uncertainty in what is certainly an uncertain world. *Teachers and Teaching*, *31*(2), 168–173. DOI: 10.1080/13540602.2024.2320160

Boon, M. (2024). Interdisciplinarity through modelling. In Knuuttila, T., Carrillo, N., & Koskinen, R. (Eds.), *The Routledge Handbook of Philosophy of Scientific Modeling* (pp. 395–411). Routledge. DOI: 10.4324/9781003205647-34

Bopaiah, M. (2021). *Equity: How to design organizations where everyone thrives*. Berrett-Koehler Publishers.

Borden, N. H. (1964). The concept of the marketing mix. *Journal of Advertising Research*, *4*(June), 2–7. DOI: 10.1080/00218499.1964.12519724

Borer, E. T., MacDougall, A. S., Stevens, C. J., Sullivan, L. L., Wilfahrt, P. A., & Seabloom, E. W. (2023). Writing a massively multi-authored paper: Overcoming barriers to meaningful authorship for all. *Methods in Ecology and Evolution*, *14*(6), 1432–1442. DOI: 10.1111/2041-210X.14096

Borich, G. D. (2016). *Observation skills for effective teaching: Research-based practice*. Routledge. DOI: 10.4324/9781315633206

Borshchev, A. (2013). *The Big Book of Simulation Modeling: Multimethod Modeling with AnyLogic 6*. AnyLogic North America.

Bostock, M., Ogievetsky, V., & Heer, J. (2011). D[3] data-driven documents. *IEEE Transactions on Visualization and Computer Graphics*, *17*(12), 2301–2309. DOI: 10.1109/TVCG.2011.185 PMID: 22034350

Bradshaw, Z., & Hazell, A. (2017). Developing problem-solving skills in mathematics: A lesson study. *International Journal for Lesson and Learning Studies*, *6*(1), 32–44. DOI: 10.1108/IJLLS-09-2016-0032

Brandenburg, M., Govindan, K., Sarkis, J., & Seuring, S. (2014). Quantitative models for sustainable supply chain management: Developments and directions. *European Journal of Operational Research*, *233*(2), 299–312. DOI: 10.1016/j.ejor.2013.09.032

Brandenburg, M., & Rebs, T. (2015). Sustainable supply chain management: A modeling perspective. *Annals of Operations Research*, *229*(1), 213–252. DOI: 10.1007/s10479-015-1853-1

Braun, V., & Clarke, V. (2006). Using thematic analysis in psychology. *Qualitative Research in Psychology*, *3*(2), 77–101. DOI: 10.1191/1478088706qp063oa

Brennan, J. (2021). Flexible learning pathways in British higher education: A decentralized and market-based system.

Breslin, G., Hodges, N. J., Steenson, A., & Williams, A. M. (2012). Constant or variable practice: Recreating the especial skill effect. *Acta Psychologica*, *140*(2), 154–157. DOI: 10.1016/j.actpsy.2012.04.002 PMID: 22627159

Bridoux, F., & van Oosterhout, H. (2020). Stakeholder governance: Solving the collective action problems in joint value creation. *Academy of Management Review*, *45*(1), 214–228.

Briggs, W. (2016). Chance and Randomness. In Briggs, W. (Ed.), *Uncertainty. The soul of modeling, probability and statistics* (pp. 87–112). Springer., DOI: 10.1007/978-3-319-39756-6_6

Brod, G. (2024). There are multiple paths to personalized education, and they should be combined. *Current Directions in Psychological Science*, *33*(3), 153–158. DOI: 10.1177/09637214241242459

Brown, J. S., Collins, A., & Duguid, P. (1989). Situated cognition and the culture of learning. *1989, 18*(1), 32-42.

Brown, J. R., Bushuev, M. A., Kretinin, A. A., & Guiffrida, A. L. (2017). Recent developments in green supply chain management: Sourcing and logistics. In Khan, M., Hussain, M., & Ajmal, M. (Eds.), *Green Supply Chain Management for Sustainable Business Practice* (pp. 191–217). IGI Global. DOI: 10.4018/978-1-5225-0635-5.ch007

Brown, T., Park, A., & Pitt, L. (2020). A 60-year bibliographic review of the Journal of Advertising Research: Perspectives on trends in authorship, influences, and research impact. *Journal of Advertising Research*, *60*(4), 353–360. DOI: 10.2501/JAR-2020-028

Bruns, A., & Burgess, J. (2012). Researching news discussion on Twitter: New methodologies. *Journalism Studies*, *13*(5–6), 801–814. DOI: 10.1080/1461670X.2012.664428

Bryce, D., & Whitebread, D. (2012). The development of metacognitive skills: Evidence from observational analysis of young children's behavior during problem-solving. *Metacognition and Learning*, *7*(3), 197–217. DOI: 10.1007/s11409-012-9091-2

Brynjolfsson, E., & McAfee, A. (2014). *The second machine age: Work, progress, and prosperity in a time of brilliant technologies*. WW Norton & company.

Buchanan, S., & Laviola, J. J.Jr. (2014). CSTutor: A sketch-based tool for visualizing data structures. *ACM Transactions on Computing Education*, *14*(1), 1–28. Advance online publication. DOI: 10.1145/2535909

Bui, A. A., Hsu, W., Arnold, C., El-Saden, S., Aberle, D. R., & Taira, R. K. (2013). Imaging-based observational databases for clinical problem solving: The role of informatics. *Journal of the American Medical Informatics Association : JAMIA*, *20*(6), 1053–1058. DOI: 10.1136/amiajnl-2012-001340

Bunio, T. S. (2012). Agile data warehouse — The final frontier: How a data warehouse redevelopment is being done in an Agile and pragmatic way. *2012 Agile Conference*, 156-164. https://doi.org/DOI: 10.1109/Agile.2012.21

Burns, J. F., " Derivation and Simulation of an Ordering Rule for the Multi-Echelon Supply Chain," University of Florida, Department of Industrial and Systems Engineering, Technical Rept. No. 45, Gainesville, Florida (1970).

Burns, M. S., Haywood, H. C., & Delclos, V. R. (1987). Young children's problem-solving strategies: An observational study. *Journal of Applied Developmental Psychology*, *8*(1), 113–121. DOI: 10.1016/0193-3973(87)90024-4

Bushuev, M. A. (2018). Delivery performance improvement in two-stage supply chain. *International Journal of Production Economics, 195*, 66–73. DOI: 10.1016/j.ijpe.2017.10.007

Butler, J. B., Henderson, S. C., & Raiborn, C. (2011). Sustainability and the balanced scorecard: Integrating green measures into business reporting. *Management Accounting Quarterly, 12*(2), 1–10.

Cabrera, D., & Cabrera, L. (2023). Adaptive leadership for Agile organizations. *Journal of Systems Thinking, 3*(1). Advance online publication. DOI: 10.54120/jost.0000039

Caniato, F., Golini, R., & Kalchschmidt, M. (2013). The effect of global supply chain configuration on the relationship between supply chain improvement programs and performance. *International Journal of Production Economics, 143*(2), 285–293. DOI: 10.1016/j.ijpe.2012.05.019

Capolla, L. M., Rossi, P. G., & Pentucci, M. (2023). Managing uncertainties in didactic design. In *INTED2023 Proceedings* (pp. 4645-4651). IATED. DOI: 10.21125/inted.2023.1221

Carpenter, T. P., & Fennema, E. (1992). Cognitively guided instruction: Building on the knowledge of students and teachers. *International Journal of Educational Research, 17*(5), 457–470. DOI: 10.1016/S0883-0355(05)80005-9

Carter, C. R., & Carter, J. R. (1998). Interorganizational determinants of environmental purchasing: Initial evidence from the consumer products industries. *Decision Sciences, 29*(3), 659–684. DOI: 10.1111/j.1540-5915.1998.tb01358.x

Carter, C. R., & Rogers, D. S. (2008). A framework of sustainable supply chain management: Moving toward new theory. *International Journal of Physical Distribution & Logistics Management, 38*(5), 360–387. DOI: 10.1108/09600030810882816

Cash, R., & Wilkerson, T. (2003). GreenSCOR: Developing a green supply chain analytical tool. *Logistics Management Institute*, 1-34.

Casquinha, A. C. B. (2024). Creativity and Problem-Solving in Advertising: the Impact of ChatGPT Within the Design Thinking Framework (Master's thesis, Universidade NOVA de Lisboa (Portugal)).

Castro, N. dos S., & Machado, A. L. S. (2024). GREEN MARKET: A TOOL FOR RECYCLING AND ENVIRONMENTAL EDUCATION. *Journal of Social and Environmental Management, 18*(3), e04700. DOI: 10.24857/rgsa.v18n3-060

Cedercreutz, I. (2024). What is improvisation in leadership?.

Chaabane, A., Ramudhin, A., & Paquet, M. (2012). Design of sustainable supply chains under the emission trading scheme. *International Journal of Production Economics*, *135*(1), 37–49. DOI: 10.1016/j.ijpe.2010.10.025

Chadwick, D. (2019). *Providing working memory support to anxious students using cognitive load theory compliant instructions.* [Doctoral dissertation, University of Wollongong] Retrieved from https://hdl.handle.net/10779/uow.27667230.v1

Chae, B., Yen, H. R., & Sheu, C. (2005). Information technology and supply chain collaboration: Moderating effects of existing relationships between partners. *IEEE Transactions on Engineering Management*, *52*(4), 440–448. DOI: 10.1109/TEM.2005.856570

Chalfant, J. C., VanDusen Pysh, M., & Moultrie, R. (1979). Teacher assistance teams: A model for within-building problem solving. *Learning Disability Quarterly*, *2*(3), 85–96. DOI: 10.2307/1511031

Chan, F. T., & Qi, H. J. (2003). An innovative performance measurement method for supply chain management. *Supply Chain Management*, *8*(3), 209–223. DOI: 10.1108/13598540310484618

Chang, E. Y. (2023, March). Prompting large language models with the socratic method. In 2023 IEEE 13th annual computing and communication workshop and conference (CCWC) (pp. 0351-0360). IEEE. DOI: 10.1109/CCWC57344.2023.10099179

Chang, D. S., Kuo, L. C. R., & Chen, Y. T. (2013). Industrial changes in corporate sustainability performance–an empirical overview using data envelopment analysis. *Journal of Cleaner Production*, *56*, 147–155. DOI: 10.1016/j.jclepro.2011.09.015

Chang, S., Pierson, E., Koh, P. W., Gerardin, J., Redbird, B., Grusky, D., & Leskovec, J. (2021). Mobility network models of COVID-19 explain inequities and inform reopening. *Nature*, *589*(7840), 82–87. DOI: 10.1038/s41586-020-2923-3 PMID: 33171481

Charan, J. K., Meera, K. L., Sudheer, P., Gopalakrishnan, G., Sharma, M., Selvakumar, P., & Manjunath, T. C. (2025). Applications of Generative AI and Human-AI Collaboration. In *Humans and Generative AI Tools for Collaborative Intelligence* (pp. 423–440). IGI Global Scientific Publishing. DOI: 10.4018/979-8-3693-8332-2.ch018

Charlesworth, R., & Leali, S. A. (2012). Using problem solving to assess young children's mathematics knowledge. *Early Childhood Education Journal*, *39*(6), 373–382. DOI: 10.1007/s10643-011-0480-y

Chatfield, C. (1995). *Problem solving: a statistician's guide.* CRC Press. DOI: 10.1201/b15238

Chaudhari, A., Bariyar, M., Pandey, A., Kumari, S., Mohanty, A., & Mohapatra, H. (2025). Cloud-enabled smart energy management for sustainable urban development. *Advances in Computational Intelligence and Robotics*, ●●●, 27–46. DOI: 10.4018/979-8-3693-7112-1.ch002

Chebotko, A., Lu, S., Fotouhi, F., Arpinar, I. B., & Sheth, A. (2008). Semantics-enabled data integration. [JDM]. *Journal of Database Management*, *19*(4), 1–27. DOI: 10.4018/jdm.2008100101

Cheng, Y., Wang, D., Zhou, P., & Zhang, T. (2018). Model compression and acceleration for deep neural networks: The principles, progress, and challenges. *IEEE Signal Processing Magazine*, *35*(1), 126–136. DOI: 10.1109/MSP.2017.2765695

Cheng, Z. M., Bonetti, F., de Regt, A., Ribeiro, J. L., & Plangger, K. (2024). Principles of responsible digital implementation: Developing operational business resilience to reduce resistance to digital innovations. *Organizational Dynamics*, *53*(2), 101043. DOI: 10.1016/j.orgdyn.2024.101043

Chen, H., Chiang, R. H. L., & Storey, V. C. (2020). Business Intelligence and Analytics: From Big Data to Big Impact. *Management Information Systems Quarterly*, *36*(4), 1165–1188. DOI: 10.2307/41703503

Chen, J., Lu, W., & Liu, D. (2024). Built environment defect mapping, modeling, and management (D3M): A BIM-based integrated framework. *Journal of Intelligent Construction*, *2*(1), 1–15. DOI: 10.26599/JIC.2024.9180008

Chi, M. T., & Wylie, R. (2014). The ICAP framework: Linking cognitive engagement to active learning outcomes. *Educational Psychologist*, *49*(4), 219–243. DOI: 10.1080/00461520.2014.965823

Choi, Y., & Yoon, S. (2023). Surrogate-assisted high-accuracy observation modeling in building digital twins: In situ nonintrusive modeling without sensor observation (Y). *Building and Environment*, *242*, 110584. DOI: 10.1016/j.buildenv.2023.110584

Cho, Y. H., & Lim, K. Y. (2017). Effectiveness of collaborative learning with 3 D virtual worlds. *British Journal of Educational Technology*, *48*(1), 202–211. DOI: 10.1111/bjet.12356

Christen, P. (2012). *Data matching: Concepts and techniques for record linkage, entity resolution, and duplicate detection*. Springer. DOI: 10.1007/978-3-642-31164-2

Christodoulou, I. P., Rizomyliotis, I., Konstantoulaki, K., Alfiero, S., Hasanago, S., & Paolone, F. (2025). Investigating the key success factors within business models that facilitate long-term value creation for sustainability-focused start-ups. *Business Ethics, the Environment & Responsibility*, *34*(3), 936–950. DOI: 10.1111/beer.12681

Chui, M., Manyika, J., & Miremadi, M. (2017). *Artificial Intelligence: Implications for the Future of Work*. McKinsey Global Institute.

Church, K., & de Oliveira, R. (2013). What's up with WhatsApp? *Proceedings of the 15th International Conference on Human-Computer Interaction with Mobile Devices and Services*, 352–361. https://doi.org/DOI: 10.1145/2493190.2493225

Clark, S. G., & Terway, T. M. (2022). A Model Integrated-Interdisciplinary Foundational Course for Environmental Science and Management Programs. Journal of Multidisciplinary Research (1947-2900), 14(2).

Coase, R. H. (1937). The nature of the firm. *Economica*, *4*(16), 386–405. DOI: 10.1111/j.1468-0335.1937.tb00002.x

Coburn, C. E., & Russell, J. L. (2008). District policy and teachers' social networks. *Educational Evaluation and Policy Analysis*, *30*(3), 203–235. DOI: 10.3102/0162373708321829

Coco, L. K., Heidler, P., Fischer, H. A., Albanese, V., Marzo, R. R., & Kozon, V. (2023). When the going gets challenging—Motivational theories as a driver for workplace health promotion, employees well-being and quality of life. *Behavioral Sciences (Basel, Switzerland)*, *13*(11), 898. DOI: 10.3390/bs13110898 PMID: 37998645

Coenye, T., Ahonen, M., Anderson, S., Cámara, M., Chundi, P., Fields, M., Foidl, I., Gnimpieba, E. Z., Griffin, K., Hinks, J., Loka, A. R., Lushbough, C., MacPhee, C., Nater, N., Raval, R., Slater-Jefferies, J., Teo, P., Wilks, S., Yung, M., & Webb, J. S. (2024). Global challenges and microbial biofilms: Identification of priority questions in biofilm research, innovation and policy. *Biofilm*, *8*, 100210. DOI: 10.1016/j.bioflm.2024.100210 PMID: 39221168

Cohnitz, D., & Nicolai, C. (2021). How to adopt a logic. *Dialectica*, *75*(4), 1–31. DOI: 10.48106/dial.v75.i4.03

Collins, D., & Dunn, M. (2011). Problem-solving strategies and processes in musical composition: Observations in real time. *Journal of Music. Technology and Education*, *4*(1), 47–76. DOI: 10.1386/jmte.4.1.47_1

Committee of Sponsoring Organizations of the Treadway Commission. (2013). Internal Control – Integrated Framework. COSO. AICPA. https://www.coso.org/Pages/ic.aspx

Conboy, K., & Carroll, N. (2019). Implementing large-scale Agile frameworks: Challenges and recommendations. *IEEE Software*, *36*(2), 44–50. DOI: 10.1109/MS.2018.2884865

Coombs, W. T. (2007). *Ongoing crisis communication: Planning, managing, and responding* (2nd ed.). Sage.

Coombs, W. T., & Holladay, S. J. (2008). Comparing apology to equivalent crisis response strategies: Clarifying apology's role and value in crisis communication. *Public Relations Review*, *34*(3), 252–257. DOI: 10.1016/j.pubrev.2008.04.001

Cordon, C., Hald, K. S., & Seifert, R. W. (2012). *Strategic Supply Chain Management*. Routledge, Taylor and Francis Group, New York & London.

Cornish, H., Tamariz, M., & Kirby, S. (2009). Complex adaptive systems and the origins of adaptive structure: What experiments can tell us. *Language Learning*, *59*(s1), 187–205. DOI: 10.1111/j.1467-9922.2009.00540.x

Crawford, J. (2024). *Making every researcher seek grants is a broken model.*

Creswell, J. W., & Creswell, J. D. (2018). *Research design: Qualitative, quantitative, and mixed methods approaches* (5th ed.). SAGE Publications.

Creswell, J. W., & Plano Clark, V. L. (2011). *Designing and conducting mixed methods research* (2nd ed.). SAGE Publications.

Cross, J. H.II, Hendrix, T. D., Umphress, D. A., Barowski, L. A., Jain, J., & Montgomery, L. N. (2009). Robust generation of dynamic data structure visualizations with multiple interaction approaches. *ACM Transactions on Computing Education (TOCE)*, 9(2). *Article*, *13*(2), 1–32. DOI: 10.1145/1538234.1538240

Cui, L., Gao, M., Dai, J., & Mou, J. (2022). Improving supply chain collaboration through operational excellence approaches: An IoT perspective. *Industrial Management & Data Systems*, *122*(3), 565–591. DOI: 10.1108/IMDS-01-2020-0016

Cui, P., & Sachan, M. (2023). Adaptive and personalized exercise generation for online language learning. In Rogers, A., Boyd-Graber, J., & Okazaki, N. (Eds.), *Proceedings of the 61st Annual Meeting of the Association for Computational Linguistics* (pp. 10184–10198). Association for Computational Linguistics. https://doi.org/DOI: 10.18653/v1/2023.acl-long.567

Culliton, J. W. (1948). *The Management of Marketing Costs*. Division of Research, Graduate School of Business Administration, Harvard University.

D'Mello, S., Lehman, B., Pekrun, R., & Graesser, A. (2014). Confusion can be beneficial for learning. *Learning and Instruction*, *29*, 153–170. DOI: 10.1016/j.learninstruc.2012.05.003

Da Silva, F. Q., Suassuna, M., França, A. C., Grubb, A. M., Gouveia, T. B., Monteiro, C. V., & Dos Santos, I. E. (2012). Replication of empirical studies in software engineering research: A systematic mapping study. *Empirical Software Engineering*. Advance online publication. DOI: 10.1007/s10664-012-9227-7

Dağtaş, A., & Şahinkarakaş, Ş. (2024). Foreign Language Learners' Uncertainty Experiences and Uncertainty Management. *Journal of Psycholinguistic Research*, *53*(5), 65. DOI: 10.1007/s10936-024-10100-w PMID: 39158767

Damir, B., & Hasnaa, G. (2020). Content marketing and website users engagement: The impact of relevant content on the web on user engagement behaviors. *Periodicals of Engineering and Natural Sciences*, *8*(1), 229–239. DOI: 10.21533/pen.v8i1.1571

Daniswara, M. H. R., Permana, F., Hafidz, A., & Marcellino, B. (2023). User Experience Evaluation of Duolingo using User Experience Questionnaire (UEQ). *International Conference on Information Management and Technology (ICIMTech)*. DOI: 10.1109/ICIMTech59029.2023.10277886

Daryanes, F., Darmadi, D., Fikri, K., Sayuti, I., Rusandi, M. A., & Situmorang, D. D. B. (2023). The development of articulate storyline interactive learning media based on case methods to train student's problem-solving ability. *Heliyon*, *9*(4), e15082. DOI: 10.1016/j.heliyon.2023.e15082 PMID: 37101635

Daulay, K. R., & Ruhaimah, I. (2019, March). Polya theory to improve problem-solving skills. [). IOP Publishing.]. *Journal of Physics: Conference Series*, *1188*(1), 012070. DOI: 10.1088/1742-6596/1188/1/012070

Davis, E. W., & Spekman, R. E. (2004). *The Extended Enterprise: Gaining Competitive Advantage Through Collaborative Supply Chains*, Financial Times Press, Prentice Hall, Upper Saddle, New Jersey.

Davis, C., Bush, T., & Wood, S. (2024). Artificial Intelligence in education: Enhancing learning experiences through personalized adaptation. [IJCITSM]. *International Journal of Cyber and IT Service Management*, *4*(1), 26–32. DOI: 10.34306/ijcitsm.v4i1.146

Davis, F. D. (1989). Perceived usefulness, perceived ease of use, and user acceptance of information technology. *Management Information Systems Quarterly*, •••, 319–340.

Dawes, J. (2018). The Impact of Freemium Pricing Models on Customer Acquisition and Retention. *Journal of Business Research*, *85*, 84–93.

De Brito, M. P., Carbone, V., & Blanquart, C. M. (2008). Towards a sustainable fashion retail supply chain in Europe: Organisation and performance. *International Journal of Production Economics, 114*(2), 534–553. DOI: 10.1016/j.ijpe.2007.06.012

Deif, A. M. (2011). A system model for green manufacturing. *Journal of Cleaner Production, 19*(14), 1553–1559. DOI: 10.1016/j.jclepro.2011.05.022

DeKeyser, R. M. (2007). *Practice in a second language: Perspectives from applied linguistics and cognitive psychology*. Cambridge University Press. DOI: 10.1017/CBO9780511667275

Dekker, R., Bloemhof, J., & Mallidis, J. (2012). Operations research for green logistics: An overview of aspects, issues, contributions and challenges. *European Journal of Operational Research, 219*(3), 671–679. DOI: 10.1016/j.ejor.2011.11.010

Delen, D., & Demirkan, H. (2013). Data, information and analytics as services. *Decision Support Systems, 55*(1), 359–363. DOI: 10.1016/j.dss.2012.05.044

Depaepe, F., De Corte, E., & Verschaffel, L. (2010). Teachers' approaches towards word problem solving: Elaborating or restricting the problem context. *Teaching and Teacher Education, 26*(2), 152–160. DOI: 10.1016/j.tate.2009.03.016

Depaepe, F., De Corte, E., & Verschaffel, L. (2010). Teachers' metacognitive and heuristic approaches to word problem solving: Analysis and impact on students' beliefs and performance. *ZDM Mathematics Education, 42*(2), 205–218. DOI: 10.1007/s11858-009-0221-5

Dermitzaki, I., Leondari, A., & Goudas, M. (2009). Relations between young students' strategic behaviours, domain-specific self-concept, and performance in a problem-solving situation. *Learning and Instruction, 19*(2), 144–157. DOI: 10.1016/j.learninstruc.2008.03.002

Dewi, I. N., Poedjiastoeti, S., & Prahani, B. K. (2017). ELSII learning model based local wisdom to improve students' problem solving skills and scientific communication. *International Journal of Education and Research, 5*(1), 107–118.

Dhaigude, A. S., Chatterjee, D., & Kamath, G. B. (2025). Supply chain integration and culture under globalization: A systematic review and global research agenda. *Research in Globalization, 11*, 100293. DOI: 10.1016/j.resglo.2025.100293

Diamantes, T., & Williams, M. (1997). *The Perceptive Eye/Ear Game: An Activity That Encourages Practice on Best Practice*. Honing Observation and Problem-Solving Skills of Administrators.

Dietterich, T. G. (2000). Ensemble methods in machine learning. In J. Kittler & F. Roli (Eds.), *Multiple classifier systems: First international workshop, MCS 2000, Cagliari, Italy, June 21–23, 2000* (Vol. 1857, pp. 1–15). Springer. https://doi.org/DOI: 10.1007/3-540-45014-9_1

Dikert, K., Paasivaara, M., & Lassenius, C. (2016). Challenges and success factors for large-scale Agile transformations: A systematic literature review. *Journal of Systems and Software, 119*, 87–108. DOI: 10.1016/j.jss.2016.06.013

Dillmann, R. (2004). Teaching and learning of robot tasks via observation of human performance. *Robotics and Autonomous Systems, 47*(2-3), 109–116. DOI: 10.1016/j.robot.2004.03.005

Dingsøyr, T., Nerur, S., Balijepally, V., & Moe, N. B. (2012). A decade of Agile methodologies: Towards explaining Agile software development. *Journal of Systems and Software, 85*(6), 1213–1221. DOI: 10.1016/j.jss.2012.02.033

DiSalvo, C. (2022). *Design as democratic inquiry: Putting experimental civics into practice*. MIT Press. DOI: 10.7551/mitpress/13372.001.0001

Dishion, T. J., & Patterson, G. R. (1999). Model building in developmental psychopathology: A pragmatic approach to understanding and intervention. *Journal of Clinical Child Psychology, 28*(4), 502–512. DOI: 10.1207/S15374424JCCP2804_10

Diwakar, R., Sharma, R., Nayak, D., & Mohapatra, H. (2025). Optimizing load distribution in big data ecosystems. *AI and the Revival of Big Data*, 177-200. https://doi.org/DOI: 10.4018/979-8-3693-8472-5.ch008

Djuwari, M. (2025). *LEADERSHIP IN A DIGITALLY DISRUPTED SOCIETY: Issues, Problems, and Solutions*. Goresan Pena.

Doan, A., Halevy, A. Y., & Ives, Z. G. (2012). *Principles of data integration*. Morgan Kaufmann.

Domínguez Archila, M. L., & Joya Silva, Y. P. (2017). Financial Audit Manual for Financial Statements under IFRS for footwear SMEs in the city of Bucaramanga. Retrieved from: https://repository.ucc.edu.co/bitstreams/1e5f71f8-af57-40fe-839a-8cc748943aa2/download

Donthu, N., Kumar, S., Mukherjee, D., Pandey, N., & Lim, W. M. (2021). How to conduct a bibliometric analysis: An overview and guidelines. *Journal of Business Research, 133*, 285–296. DOI: 10.1016/j.jbusres.2021.04.070

Dorst, K., & Cross, N. (2001). Creativity in the design process: Co-evolution of problem–solution. *Design Studies, 22*(5), 425–437. DOI: 10.1016/S0142-694X(01)00009-6

Dosi, G. (2023). *The foundations of complex evolving economies: Part one: Innovation, organization, and industrial dynamics*. Oxford University Press. DOI: 10.1093/oso/9780192865922.001.0001

Dou, Y., & Sarkis, J. (2010). A joint location and outsourcing sustainability analysis for a strategic offshoring decision. *International Journal of Production Research, 48*(2), 567–592. DOI: 10.1080/00207540903175145

Dowlatshahi, S. H. A. D. (2010). A cost-benefit analysis for the design and implementation of reverse logistics systems: Case studies approach. *International Journal of Production Research, 48*(5), 1361–1380. DOI: 10.1080/00207540802552642

Duarte, S., & Cruz Machado, V. (2017). Green and lean implementation: An assessment in the automotive industry. *International Journal of Lean Six Sigma, 8*(1), 65–88. DOI: 10.1108/IJLSS-11-2015-0041

Dubey, R., Gunasekaran, A., & Ali, S. S. (2015). Exploring the relationship between leadership, operational practices, institutional pressures and environmental performance: A framework for green supply chain. *International Journal of Production Economics, 160*, 120–132. DOI: 10.1016/j.ijpe.2014.10.001

Duncan, S. (2018). SAFe 4.0 distilled: Applying the scaled Agile framework for lean software and systems engineering. 2017. *The Quality Management Journal, 25*(1), 66–66. DOI: 10.1080/10686967.2018.1404375

Duong, L. N. K., & Chong, J. (2020). Supply chain collaboration in the presence of disruptions: A literature review. *International Journal of Production Research, 58*(11), 3488–3507. DOI: 10.1080/00207543.2020.1712491

Dwiyogo, W. D. (2018). Developing a blended learning-based method for problem-solving in capability learning. *Turkish Online Journal of Educational Technology-TOJET, 17*(1), 51–61.

Edmonds, B. (2017). Different modelling purposes. In Edmonds, B., & Meyer, R. (Eds.), *Simulating Social Complexity: A Handbook* (pp. 39–58). Springer. DOI: 10.1007/978-3-319-66948-9_4

Eichler, A., & Vogel, M. (2014). Three approaches for modelling situations with randomness. In Chernoff, E., & Sriraman, B. (Eds.), *Probabilistic thinking. Advances in mathematics education* (pp. 75–99). Springer., DOI: 10.1007/978-94-007-7155-0_4

Eisbach, S., Mai, O., & Hertel, G. (2024). Combining theoretical modelling and machine learning approaches: The case of teamwork effects on individual effort expenditure. *New Ideas in Psychology, 73*, 101077. DOI: 10.1016/j.newideapsych.2024.101077

Eisenmann, T., Parker, G., & Van Alstyne, M. (2006). Strategies for two-sided markets. *Harvard Business Review, 84*(10), 92–101.

Eivazi, S., & Bednarik, R. (2011, February). Predicting problem-solving behavior and performance levels from visual attention data. In *Proc. workshop on eye gaze in intelligent human machine interaction at IUI* (pp. 9-16).

Elkington, J. (1997). *Cannibals with forks: The triple bottom line of 21st century business*. Capstone Publishing.

Elkington, J. (1997). The triple bottom line. In Russo, M. V. (Ed.), *Environmental Management: Readings and Cases* (2nd ed., pp. 49–66). Sage Publications.

Ellram, L. M., Tate, W. L., & Billington, C. (2004). Understanding and managing the services supply chain. *The Journal of Supply Chain Management, 40*(3), 17–32. DOI: 10.1111/j.1745-493X.2004.tb00176.x

Enke, B. (2024). The cognitive turn in behavioral economics. Unpublished manuscript. https://benjamin-enke. com

Entman, R. M. (1993). Framing: Toward clarification of a fractured paradigm. *Journal of Communication, 43*(4), 51–58. DOI: 10.1111/j.1460-2466.1993.tb01304.x

Epstein, J. M. (2006). *Generative social science: Studies in agent-based computational modeling*. Princeton University Press.

Epstein, M. J., & Wisner, P. (2001). Good neighbors: Implementing social and environmental strategies with the BSC. *Balanced Scorecard Report, 3*(3), 8–11.

Eriksson, O., & Nyström, J. (2025). Unpacking Quality Deficiency Costs: A Framework for Mapping and Managing Quality Deficiency Costs at Company X, a large Swedish transportation company.

Eseryel, D., Ifenthaler, D., & Ge, X. (2013). Validation study of a method for assessing complex ill-structured problem solving by using causal representations. *Educational Technology Research and Development, 61*(3), 443–463. DOI: 10.1007/s11423-013-9297-2

Eun, B. (2019). The zone of proximal development as an overarching concept: A framework for synthesizing Vygotsky's theories. *Educational Philosophy and Theory, 51*(1), 18–30. DOI: 10.1080/00131857.2017.1421941

European Commission. (2020). A new Circular Economy Action Plan for a cleaner and more competitive. *Europe.* Advance online publication. DOI: 10.2779/05068

Fader, P. (2012). *Customer Lifetime Value: Marketing Models and Applications.* Now Publishers Inc.

Fader, P. S., & Hardie, B. G. (2009). Probability models for customer-base analysis. *Journal of Interactive Marketing, 23*(1), 61–69. DOI: 10.1016/j.intmar.2008.11.003

Fatihi, A. R. (2024). *Bridging Worlds through Translatology: A Linguistic Approach to Translation.* Cambridge Scholars Publishing.

Fauzia, N. L. U., & Kelana, J. B. (2020). Natural science problem solving in elementary school students using the project based learning (PjBL) model. *Jurnal Ilmiah Sekolah Dasar, 4*(4), 596–603.

Fawcett, S. E., Fawcett, A. M., Watson, B. J., & Magnan, G. M. (2012). Peeking inside the black box: Toward an understanding of supply chain collaboration dynamics. *The Journal of Supply Chain Management, 48*(1), 44–72. DOI: 10.1111/j.1745-493X.2011.03241.x

Fernandez, L. J. (2023). *The art of business Origami: folding your way to success.* Lloyd Jose Fernandez.

Fernández-Muñoz, L., Pérez Carrasco, A., Velázquez-Iturbide, J. Á., & Urquiza-Fuentes, J. (2007). *A framework for the automatic generation of algorithm animations based on design techniques.* In Lecture Notes in Computer Science (pp. 443–457). https://link.springer.com/chapter/10.1007/978-3-540-75195-3_40

Fernlund, H. K., & Gonzalez, A. J. (2002). *An approach towards building human behavior models automatically by observation.* Intelligent Systems Laboratory.

Few, S. (2009). *Now You See It: Simple Visualization Techniques for Quantitative Analysis.* Analytics Press.

Fielding, R. T. (2000). *Architectural styles and the design of network-based software architectures* (Doctoral dissertation, University of California, Irvine). UMI Dissertation Publishing.

Fitriani, N., & Arnawa, I. M. (2020, May). An initial observation of learning devices and mathematical problem solving ability of senior high school students. []. IOP Publishing.]. *Journal of Physics: Conference Series, 1554*(1), 012067. DOI: 10.1088/1742-6596/1554/1/012067

Fitzgerald, B., Stol, K., O'Sullivan, R., & O'Brien, D. (2013). Scaling Agile methods to regulated environments: An industry case study. *2013 35th International Conference on Software Engineering (ICSE)*, 863-872. https://doi.org/DOI: 10.1109/ICSE.2013.6606635

Flores, N., & González, W. (2024). *Marketing experiencial: Caso Duolingo*. UCAB Drive.

Floridi, L., Cowls, J., Beltrametti, M., Chatila, R., Chazerand, P., Dignum, V., Luetge, C., Madelin, R., Pagallo, U., Rossi, F., Schafer, B., Valcke, P., & Vayena, E. (2018). AI4People—An ethical framework for a good AI society: Opportunities, risks, principles, and recommendations. *Minds and Machines*, *28*(4), 689–707. DOI: 10.1007/s11023-018-9482-5 PMID: 30930541

Forbus, K. D., & De Kleer, J. (1993). *Building problem solvers* (Vol. 1). MIT press.

Fossland, T., & Habti, D. (2022). University practices in an age of supercomplexity: Revisiting diversity, equality, and inclusion in higher education. *Journal of Praxis in Higher Education*, *4*(2), 1–10. DOI: 10.47989/kpdc355

Freeman, L. C. (1979). Centrality in social networks: Conceptual clarification. *Social Networks*, *1*(3), 215–239. DOI: 10.1016/0378-8733(78)90021-7

Friedman, B., & Citron, D. K. (2024). Indiscriminate Data Surveillance. *Virginia Law Review*, *110*, 1351.

Friedman, J., Hastie, T., & Tibshirani, R. (2001). *The elements of statistical learning: Data mining, inference, and prediction*. Springer.

Frigg, R., & Hartmann, S. (Summer 2025 Edition). Models in Science, The Stanford Encyclopedia of Philosophy, Zalta, E. N & Nodelman, U. (eds.), forthcoming URL = <https://plato.stanford.edu/archives/sum2025/entries/models-science/>

Gade, K. R. (2021). Data-driven decision making in a complex world. Journal of computational innovation, 1(1).

Gale, B. (1994). Managing customer value: Creating quality and service that customers can see. *New York*.

Gale, A. P., Chapman, J. O., White, D. E., Ahluwalia, P., Williamson, A. K. J., Peacock, K. R., Akagbosu, R., Lepine, T. M., Arizor, I., Bone, L. A., Brown, J., Fahrngruber, A. M., Goldberg-Flood, A., Kovirineni, S., Lamb-Laurin, S. J., Zia, N., Innocent, S., Lee, W., Moran, G., & Cooke, S. J. (2022). On embracing the concept of becoming environmental problem solvers: The trainee perspective on key elements of success, essential skills, and mindset. *Environmental Reviews*, *30*(1), 1–9. DOI: 10.1139/er-2021-0040

Galesic, M., Barkoczi, D., Berdahl, A. M., Biro, D., Carbone, G., Giannoccaro, I., Goldstone, R. L., Gonzalez, C., Kandler, A., Kao, A. B., Kendal, R., Kline, M., Lee, E., Massari, G. F., Mesoudi, A., Olsson, H., Pescetelli, N., Sloman, S. J., Smaldino, P. E., & Stein, D. L. (2023). Beyond collective intelligence: Collective adaptation. *Journal of the Royal Society, Interface*, *20*(200), 20220736. DOI: 10.1098/rsif.2022.0736 PMID: 36946092

Gallardo-Vázqueza, D., & Juan de la Cruz, S.-D. (2023). *Bibliometric study of the link between Sustainability and Circular Economy: A contribution for current business model from the collaboration.* Enterprise-University., DOI: 10.6018/rcsar.576471

Galleli, B., & Amaral, L. (2025). Bridging Institutional Theory and Social and Environmental Efforts in Management: A Review and Research Agenda. *Journal of Management*, •••, 01492063251322429.

Galton, F. (1886). Regression towards mediocrity in hereditary stature. *Journal of the Anthropological Institute of Great Britain and Ireland*, *15*, 246–263. DOI: 10.2307/2841583

Gammelgaard, B., & Nowicka, K. (2024). Next generation supply chain management: The impact of cloud computing. *Journal of Enterprise Information Management*, *37*(4), 1140–1160. DOI: 10.1108/JEIM-09-2022-0317

Gandomani, T. J., & Nafchi, M. Z. (2016). The essential prerequisites of Agile transition and adoption: A grounded theory approach. *Journal of Internet Computing and Services*, *17*(5), 173–184. DOI: 10.7472/jksii.2016.17.5.173

Gantert, T. M. (2024). Balancing Stability and Fluidity in Post-Bureaucratic Organizations: Insights from Coworking-Spaces (Doctoral dissertation).

Garfield, E. (2006). The history and meaning of the journal impact factor. *Journal of the American Medical Association*, *295*(1), 90–93. DOI: 10.1001/jama.295.1.90 PMID: 16391221

Gavronski, I., Klassen, R. D., Vachon, S., & do Nascimento, L. F. M. (2011). A resource-based view of green supply management. *Transportation Research Part E, Logistics and Transportation Review*, *47*(6), 872–885. DOI: 10.1016/j.tre.2011.05.018

Gawer, A. (2022). Digital platforms and ecosystems: Remarks on the dominant organizational forms of the digital age. *Innovation (North Sydney, N.S.W.)*, *24*(1), 10–23. DOI: 10.1080/14479338.2021.1965888

Geertz, C. (1973). Chapter 1/Thick Description: Toward an interpretive theory of culture. *The interpretation of cultures: Selected essays*, 3-30.

Gelman, A., & Hill, J. (2007). *Data analysis using regression and multilevel/hierarchical models*. Cambridge University Press.

George, A. S. (2024). The symbiotic relationship between visionary and pragmatic leadership in propelling organizational success. *Partners Universal International Innovation Journal*, *2*(3), 57–79.

Geuss, R. (2022). *Not thinking like a liberal*. Harvard University Press.

Ghaleb, B. D. S. (2024). The concept of alienation and alienation in organizations. *Pancasila International Journal of Applied Social Science*, *2*(2), 206–223. DOI: 10.59653/pancasila.v2i02.714

Ghobadi, S., & Mathiassen, L. (2016). Risks to effective knowledge sharing in Agile software teams: A model for assessing and mitigating risks. *Information Systems Journal*, *27*(6), 699–731. DOI: 10.1111/isj.12117

Ghosh, S. (2024). *Perspective chapter: Metacognitive strategies – Preparing self-regulated learners in the twenty-first century*. IntechOpen., DOI: 10.5772/intechopen.114093

Giebler, C., Gröger, C., Hoos, E., Schwarz, H., & Mitschang, B. (2019). Leveraging the data lake: Current state and challenges. In *Big Data Analytics and Knowledge Discovery* (pp. 179–188). Lecture Notes in Computer Science. Springer., DOI: 10.1007/978-3-030-27520-4_13

Giray, L. (2024). AI shaming: The silent stigma among academic writers and researchers. *Annals of Biomedical Engineering*, *52*(9), 2319–2324. DOI: 10.1007/s10439-024-03582-1 PMID: 38977530

Gok, T. (2010). The general assessment of problem solving processes and metacognition in physics education. *International Journal of Physics and Chemistry Education*, *2*(2), 110–122. DOI: 10.51724/ijpce.v2i2.186

Goldin, G. A. (1998). Representational systems, learning, and problem solving in mathematics. *The Journal of Mathematical Behavior*, *17*(2), 137–165. DOI: 10.1016/S0364-0213(99)80056-1

Gold, Z. S., Perlman, J., Howe, N., Mishra, A. A., DeHart, G. B., Hertik, H., & Buckley, J. (2022). An observational study of children's problem solving during play with friends. *Journal of Cognition and Development*, *23*(4), 503–523. DOI: 10.1080/15248372.2022.2058509

Golicic, S. L., & Smith, C. D. (2013). A meta-analysis of environmentally sustainable supply chain management practices and firm performance. *The Journal of Supply Chain Management*, *49*(2), 78–95. DOI: 10.1111/jscm.12006

Golmgrein, I. V. (2023). A comprehensive overview of monetization strategies in creative industries. [IJLEMR]. *International Journal of Latest Engineering and Management Research*, *8*(4), 90–100. DOI: 10.56581/IJLEMR.8.4.90-100

Golroudbary, S. R., & Zahraee, S. M. (2015). System dynamics model for optimizing the recycling and collection of waste material in a closed-loop supply chain. *Simulation Modelling Practice and Theory*, *53*, 88–102. DOI: 10.1016/j.simpat.2015.02.001

Goodfellow, I., Bengio, Y., & Courville, A. (2016). *Deep learning*. MIT Press.

Goodfellow, I., Bengio, Y., & Courville, A. (2016). *Deep Learning*. MIT Press.

Gopalakrishnan, K., Yusuf, Y. Y., Musa, A., Abubakar, T., & Ambursa, H. M. (2012). Sustainable supply chain management: A case study of British Aerospace (BAe) Systems. *International Journal of Production Economics*, *140*(1), 193–203. DOI: 10.1016/j.ijpe.2012.01.003

Gopal, P. R. C., & Thakkar, J. (2012). A review on supply chain performance measures and metrics: 2000-2011. *International Journal of Productivity and Performance Management*, *61*(5), 518–547. DOI: 10.1108/17410401211232957

Gordon, S. R., & McNew, J. (2008). *Internet Research Methods: A Practical Guide for the Social and Behavioural Sciences*. Oxford University Press.

Gore, A., Bajaj, V., Yadav, P., Chouhan, V., Tayal, M., & Kumar, M. (2023). Sentence generator for English language using formal semantics. *International Journal of Next-Generation Computing*, *14*(1). Advance online publication. DOI: 10.47164/ijngc.v14i1.1090

Gou, Z., Shao, Z., Gong, Y., Shen, Y., Yang, Y., Duan, N., & Chen, W. (2023). Critic: Large language models can self-correct with tool-interactive critiquing. arXiv preprint arXiv:2305.11738.

Govindan, K., & Soleimani, H. (2017). A review of reverse logistics and closed-loop supply chains: A Journal of Cleaner Production focus. *Journal of Cleaner Production, 142*, 371–384. DOI: 10.1016/j.jclepro.2016.03.126

Gregory, R. W., Henfridsson, O., Kaganer, E., & Kyriakou, H. (2021). The role of artificial intelligence and data network effects for creating user value. *Academy of Management Review, 46*(3), 534–551. DOI: 10.5465/amr.2019.0178

Greiff, S., Niepel, C., Scherer, R., & Martin, R. (2016). Understanding students' performance in a computer-based assessment of complex problem solving: An analysis of behavioral data from computer-generated log files. *Computers in Human Behavior, 61*, 36–46. DOI: 10.1016/j.chb.2016.02.095

Greiff, S., Wüstenberg, S., & Funke, J. (2012). Dynamic problem solving: A new assessment perspective. *Applied Psychological Measurement, 36*(3), 189–213. DOI: 10.1177/0146621612439620

Gren, L., Torkar, R., & Feldt, R. (2014). Work motivational challenges regarding the interface between Agile teams and a Non-Agile surrounding organization: A case study. *2014 Agile Conference*, 11-15. https://doi.org/DOI: 10.1109/AGILE.2014.13

Griffin, A., & Hauser, J. R. (1993). The voice of the customer. *Marketing Science, 12*(1), 1–27.

Groce, A. D., Holzmann, G., & Joshi, R. (2007). Randomized differential testing as a prelude to formal verification. In *ICSE '07: Proceedings of the 29th International Conference on Software Engineering* (pp. 621-631). IEEE Xplore. https://doi.org/DOI: 10.1109/ICSE.2007.68

Gross, D. (1962). *An Investigation of Centralized Inventory Control in Multi-location Supply Systems*. Dissertation, Cornell University, Ithaca, New York.

Grubor, J. (2020). What makes up the attitude to learning English: EFLS-ALE scale. In Arsić, Z. (Eds.), *Science Beyond Boundaries 3* (Vol. 2, pp. 31–51). Mitrovica Faculty of Philosophy Press.

Guillemin, M., & Nicholas, R. (2022). Core values at work—Essential elements of a healthy workplace. *International Journal of Environmental Research and Public Health, 19*(19), 12505. DOI: 10.3390/ijerph191912505 PMID: 36231819

Gunasekaran, A., & Kobu, B. (2007). Performance measures and metrics in logistics and supply chain management: A review of recent literature (1995–2004) for research and applications. *International Journal of Production Research, 45*(12), 2819–2840. DOI: 10.1080/00207540600806513

Gupta, A., Bhayani, A., Patra, S., & Tayal, P. (2023).The ChatGPT Effect: Quantifying Massive Linguistic Drift in Online Communication Through Multi-Platform Analysis of 20 Million Posts. Retrieved from http://bit.ly/4nmnvRK

Gupta, S., & Lehmann, D. R. (2006). Customer Lifetime Value and Firm Valuation. *Journal of Relationship Marketing*, *5*(2–3), 87–110. DOI: 10.1300/J366v05n02_06

Gustavsson, T., Berntzen, M., & Stray, V. (2022). Changes to team autonomy in large-scale software development: A multiple case study of scaled Agile framework (Safe) implementations. *International Journal of Information Systems and Project Management, 10*(1), 29–46. DOI: 10.12821/ijispm100102

Guyon, I., & Elisseeff, A. (2003). An introduction to variable and feature selection. *Journal of Machine Learning Research, 3*, 1157–1182. https://www.jmlr.org/papers/volume3/guyon03a/guyon03a.pdf

Guzmán, E. B. O. (2022). *Control of Scrap and Warranties in Beghelli Mexico*. Autonomous University of Querétaro. https://ri-ng.uaq.mx/handle/123456789/3736

Gyevnar, B., Ferguson, N., & Schafer, B. (2023). Bridging the transparency gap: What can explainable ai learn from the ai act? arXiv preprint arXiv:2302.10766. DOI: 10.3233/FAIA230367

Hair, J. F., Black, W. C., Babin, B. J., & Anderson, R. E. (2014). *Multivariate data analysis* (7th ed.). Pearson.

Hamari, J., Hanner, N., & Koivisto, J. (2020). Why pay premium in freemium services? A study on perceived value, continued use, and purchase intentions in free-to-play games. *International Journal of Information Management, 51*, 102032. DOI: 10.1016/j.ijinfomgt.2019.102040

Hameed, R. M., Ullah, I., & Abbas, F. (2023). How does the learning of paradox influence individuals' capacity to navigate wicked problems? Learning of paradox and wicked problems. JSSH, 31(1).

Hamilton, E., Lesh, R., Lester, F., & Yoon, C. (2020). The use of reflection tools to build personal models of problem-solving. In *Foundations for the future in mathematics education* (pp. 349–366). Routledge. DOI: 10.4324/9781003064527-21

Hamza, M. K., & Griffith, K. G. (2006). Fostering problem-solving & creative thinking in the classroom: cultivating a creative mind. In *National Forum of Applied Educational Research Journal-Electronic* (Vol. 9, No. 3, pp. 1-32).

Hansen, M. (2021). Measuring conversion rates in freemium business models. *Journal of Business Research, 123*, 142–155.

Han, X. (2021). A study of performance testing in configurable software systems. *Journal of Software Engineering and Applications, 14*(09), 474–492. DOI: 10.4236/jsea.2021.149028

Han, Y., & Fang, X. (2024). Systematic review of adopting blockchain in supply chain management: Bibliometric analysis and theme discussion. *International Journal of Production Research, 62*(3), 991–1016. DOI: 10.1080/00207543.2023.2236241

Harder, J., & Göde, N. (2012). Cloned code: Stable code. *Journal of Software (Malden, MA), 25*(10), 1063–1088. DOI: 10.1002/smr.1551

Hartmann, D., De Pereira, J. R. L., Streitbörger, C., & Berendt, B. (2024). Addressing the regulatory gap: Moving towards an EU AI audit ecosystem beyond the AI Act by including civil society. *AI and Ethics*, •••, 1–22.

Harvey, W. S., Mitchell, V. W., Almeida Jones, A., & Knight, E. (2021). The tensions of defining and developing thought leadership within knowledge-intensive firms. *Journal of Knowledge Management, 25*(11), 1–33. DOI: 10.1108/JKM-06-2020-0431

Hasibuan, A. M., Saragih, S., & Amry, Z. (2019). Development of Learning Materials Based on Realistic Mathematics Education to Improve Problem Solving Ability and Student Learning Independence. *International electronic journal of mathematics education, 14*(1), 243-252.

Hassini, E., Surti, C., & Searcy, C. (2012). A literature review and a case study of sustainable supply chains with a focus on metrics. *International Journal of Production Economics, 140*(1), 69–82. DOI: 10.1016/j.ijpe.2012.01.042

Hauser, J. R., Urban, G. L., & Weinberg, B. D. (1993). How consumers allocate their time when searching for information. *JMR, Journal of Marketing Research, 30*(4), 452–466.

Hayes, J., Shumailov, I., Triantafillou, E., Khalifa, A., & Papernot, N. (2025, April). Inexact unlearning needs more careful evaluations to avoid a false sense of privacy. In *2025 IEEE Conference on Secure and Trustworthy Machine Learning (SaTML)* (pp. 497-519). IEEE. DOI: 10.1109/SaTML64287.2025.00034

Hedvall, K., Benedettini, O., Blümel, J. H., Arsenovic, J., & Kristensson, P. (2025). B2B manufacturers in pursuit of Product-as-a-Service: Motivations, barriers, and approaches. *Journal of Business Research, 199*, 115567. DOI: 10.1016/j.jbusres.2025.115567

Heppner, P. P. (2008). Expanding the conceptualization and measurement of applied problem solving and coping: From stages to dimensions to the almost forgotten cultural context. *The American Psychologist*, *63*(8), 805–816. DOI: 10.1037/0003-066X.63.8.805

Heppner, P. P., Witty, T. E., & Dixon, W. A. (2004). Problem-solving appraisal and human adjustment: A review of 20 years of research using the Problem Solving Inventory. *The Counseling Psychologist*, *32*(3), 344–428. DOI: 10.1177/0011000003262793

Hervani, A. A., Helms, M. M., & Sarkis, J. (2005). Performance measurement for green supply chain management. *Benchmarking*, *12*(4), 330–353. DOI: 10.1108/14635770510609015

Hidayati, R. M., & Wagiran, W. (2020). Implementation of problem-based learning to improve problem-solving skills in vocational high school. *Jurnal Pendidikan Vokasi*, *10*(2), 177–187. DOI: 10.21831/jpv.v10i2.31210

Hidi, S., & Renninger, K. A. (2006). The four-phase model of interest development. *Educational Psychologist*, *41*(2), 111–127. DOI: 10.1207/s15326985ep4102_4

Hiebert, J., Carpenter, T. P., Fennema, E., Fuson, K., Human, P., Murray, H., Olivier, A., & Wearne, D. (1996). Problem solving as a basis for reform in curriculum and instruction: The case of mathematics. *Educational Researcher*, *25*(4), 12–21. DOI: 10.3102/0013189X025004012

Hill, R. B. (1997). The design of an instrument to assess problem solving activities in technology education.

Hill-Briggs, F. (2003). Problem solving in diabetes self-management: A model of chronic illness self-management behavior. *Annals of Behavioral Medicine*, *25*(3), 182–193. DOI: 10.1207/S15324796ABM2503_04

Hillier, F. S., & Lieberman, G. J. (2020). *Introduction to operations research* (10th ed.). McGraw-Hill.

Hinterhuber, A., & Liozu, S. M. (2017). Is innovation in pricing your next source of competitive advantage? 1. In *Innovation in pricing* (pp. 11–27). Routledge.

Hipolito, I., & Khanduja, A. (2024). The Wicked and the Complex: A New Paradigm for Societal Problem-Solving.

Hirano, H. (2019). *5 pillars of Kaizen*. McGraw-Hill Inter-American.

Hoda, R., Noble, J., & Marshall, S. (2011). The impact of inadequate customer collaboration on self-organizing Agile teams. *Information and Software Technology*, *53*(5), 521–534. DOI: 10.1016/j.infsof.2010.10.009

Hohl, P., Klünder, J., Van Bennekum, A., Lockard, R., Gifford, J., Münch, J., Stupperich, M., & Schneider, K. (2018). Back to the future: Origins and directions of the "Agile manifesto" – views of the originators. *Journal of Software Engineering Research and Development*, *6*(1), 15. Advance online publication. DOI: 10.1186/s40411-018-0059-z

Hökkä, P., Vähäsantanen, K., & Ikävalko, H. (2023). An integrative approach to emotional agency at work. *Vocations and Learning*, *16*(1), 23–46. DOI: 10.1007/s12186-022-09299-3

Hollis, T. (2020). Strategies for reducing churn in freemium models. *Journal of Marketing Management*, *36*(9-10), 805–826.

Holubnycha, L., Kuznetsova, O., & Demchenko, D. (2024). History of problem-solving teaching and learning evolution. History of science and technology, 14(1), 64-84.

Hondagneu-Messner, S. (2021). Data portability: A guide and a roadmap. *Rutgers Computer & Technology Law Journal*, *47*, 240.

Horstmeyer, A. (2019). How VUCA is changing the learning landscape. *Development and Learning in Organizations*, *33*(1), 5–8. DOI: 10.1108/DLO-09-2018-0119

Horváth, I. (2007). Comparison of three methodological approaches of design research. In *DS 42: Proceedings of ICED 2007, the 16th International Conference on Engineering Design, Paris, France, 28.-31.07. 2007* (pp. 361-362).

Houston, J. B., Hawthorne, J., Perreault, M. F., Park, E. H., Goldstein Hode, M., Halliwell, M. R., Turner McGowen, S. E., Davis, R., Vaid, S., McElderry, J. A., & Griffith, S. A. (2015). Social media and disasters: A functional framework for social media use in disaster planning, response, and research. *Disasters*, *39*(1), 1–22. DOI: 10.1111/disa.12092 PMID: 25243593

Howard, W. J. (1967). A Multi-Echelon Markov Model for Relating Supply System Performance to Fleet Readiness. TEMPO-General Electric Company, 67TMP-123.

Howard-Jones, P. A., & Demetriou, S. (2009). Uncertainty and engagement with learning games. *Instructional Science*, *37*(6), 519–536. DOI: 10.1007/s11251-008-9073-6

Hsin, L., Miratrix, L., Kim, H. Y., LaRusso, M. D., & Snow, C. E. (2023). Predictable variation in the implementation of a curricular intervention—And why it matters. *The Elementary School Journal*, *124*(1), 1–30. DOI: 10.1086/725765

Huber, M. T., & Morreale, S. P. (Eds.). (2023). *Disciplinary styles in the scholarship of teaching and learning: Exploring common ground*. Taylor & Francis. DOI: 10.4324/9781003444268

Hughes, R. I. G. (1997). Models and representation. *Philosophy of Science*, *64*(S4), 325–336. DOI: 10.1086/392611

Hulaikah, M., Degeng, I., & Murwani, F. D. (2020). The Effect of Experiential Learning and Adversity Quotient on Problem Solving Ability. *International Journal of Instruction*, *13*(1), 869–884. DOI: 10.29333/iji.2020.13156a

Hwang, W. Y., Su, J. H., Huang, Y. M., & Dong, J. J. (2009). A study of multi-representation of geometry problem solving with virtual manipulatives and whiteboard system. *Journal of Educational Technology & Society*, *12*(3), 229–247.

IFAC (International Federation of Accountants). (2020). *International Framework: Good Governance in the Public Sector*. Recuperado de: https://www.cipfa.org/-/media/Files/CIPFA-Thinks/Reports/International-Framework--Good-Governance-in-the-Public-Sector.pdf

Ikonen, M., Pirinen, E., Fagerholm, F., Kettunen, P., & Abrahamsson, P. (2011). On the impact of Kanban on software project work: An empirical case study investigation. *2011 16th IEEE International Conference on Engineering of Complex Computer Systems*, 305-314. https://doi.org/DOI: 10.1109/ICECCS.2011.37

Imhof, C., Per, B., & McGarrity, S. (2020). Implementation of adaptive learning systems: Current state and potential. In Isaias, P., Sampson, D. G., & Ifenthaler, D. (Eds.), *Online teaching and learning in higher education* (pp. 93–115). Springer Science., DOI: 10.1007/978-3-030-48190-2_6

Immordino-Yang, M. H., & Damasio, A. (2007). We feel, therefore we learn: The relevance of affective and social neuroscience to education. *Mind, Brain and Education : the Official Journal of the International Mind, Brain, and Education Society*, *1*(1), 3–10. DOI: 10.1111/j.1751-228X.2007.00004.x

Ing, D., & Metcalf, G. (2023). Reframing systems thinking for systems changes: Sciencing and philosophizing from pragmatism towards processes as rhythms. *Journal of the International Society for the Systems Sciences*, *67*(4154).

Isaksen, S. G., & Treffinger, D. J. (2004). Celebrating 50 years of reflective practice: Versions of creative problem solving. *The Journal of Creative Behavior*, *38*(2), 75–101. DOI: 10.1002/j.2162-6057.2004.tb01234.x

ISO. (2021). *ISO 37301:2021 Compliance management systems — Requirements with guidance for use*. International Organization for Standardization.

Jaber, M. Y., Osman, I. H., & Guiffrida, A. L. (2006). Coordinating a three-level supply chain with price discounts, price dependent demand, and profit sharing. *International Journal of Integrated Supply Management, 2*(1-2), 28–48. DOI: 10.1504/IJISM.2006.008337

Jackson, T. (2024). Principles of clean production—Developing an operational approach to the preventive paradigm. In *Clean Production Strategies Developing Preventive Environmental Management in the Industrial Economy* (pp. 143–164). CRC Press. DOI: 10.1201/9781003575535-10

Jayathilaka, U. R. (2021). *Investigating the relationship between pricing strategies and international customer acquisition in the early stage of SaaS: The role of hybrid pricing*. Gangseo University.

Jiang, S., & Marbach, P. (2025). Social Rewards and Recursive Feedback: A Procedural Model of Norm Emergence. Preprint available on *SocArXiv*, https://osf. io/preprints/socarxiv

Jiménez-Buedo, M., & Russo, F. (2021). Experimental practices and objectivity in the social sciences: Re-embedding construct validity in the internal–external validity distinction. *Synthese, 199*(3-4), 9549–9579. DOI: 10.1007/s11229-021-03215-3

Jin, L., Wei, J., Luo, C., & Qin, T. (2023). Slope stability analysis based on improved radial movement optimization considering seepage effect. *Alexandria Engineering Journal, 79*, 591–607. DOI: 10.1016/j.aej.2023.08.029

Jin, Y., Liu, B. F., & Austin, L. (2014). Examining the role of social media in effective crisis management: The effects of crisis origin, information form, and source on publics' crisis responses. *Communication Research, 41*(1), 74–94. DOI: 10.1177/0093650211423918

Johnson, D. (2024). The Role of Work-Based Learning in Developing Future Skills and Competencies for the Workforce in the Fourth Industrial Revolution.

Johnson, E. J., & Goldstein, D. G. (2003). Do defaults save lives? *Science, 302*(5649), 1338–1339. DOI: 10.1126/science.1091721 PMID: 14631022

Jones-Roberts, C., & Bechtold, C. (2024). Experiential learning in higher education. *Journal of Technology-Integrated Lessons and Teaching, 3*(2), 53–63. DOI: 10.13001/jtilt.v3i2.8587

Jurafsky, D., & Martin, J. H. (2020). *Speech and language processing* (3rd ed.). Pearson.

Kahneman, D., & Tversky, A. (1979). Prospect theory: An analysis of decision under risk. *Econometrica, 47*(2), 263–291. DOI: 10.2307/1914185

Kairouz, P., McMahan, H. B., Avent, B., Bellet, A., Bennis, M., Bhagoji, A. N., ... & Zhao, S. (2021). Advances and open problems in federated learning. *Foundations and Trends® in Machine Learning*, 14(1–2), 1–210. http://dx.doi.org/DOI: 10.1561/2200000083

Kalaitzidis, T. J. (2025). How Generative AI Fixes What Higher Education Broke.

Kalenda, M., Hyna, P., & Rossi, B. (2018). Scaling Agile in large organizations: Practices, challenges, and success factors. *Journal of Software (Malden, MA), 30*(10), e1954. Advance online publication. DOI: 10.1002/smr.1954

Kandel, S., Paepcke, A., Hellerstein, J. M., & Heer, J. (2011). Wrangler: Interactive visual specification of data transformation scripts. In *Proceedings of the SIGCHI Conference on Human Factors in Computing Systems* (pp. 3363–3372). Association for Computing Machinery. https://doi.org/DOI: 10.1145/1978942.1979444

Kannan, D., Jabbour, A. B. L. D. S., & Jabbour, C. J. C. (2014). Selecting green suppliers based on GSCM practices: Using fuzzy TOPSIS applied to a Brazilian electronics company. *European Journal of Operational Research, 233*(2), 432–447. DOI: 10.1016/j.ejor.2013.07.023

Karmakar, B., Small, D. S., & Rosenbaum, P. R. (2019). Using approximation algorithms to build evidence factors and related designs for observational studies. *Journal of Computational and Graphical Statistics, 28*(3), 698–709. DOI: 10.1080/10618600.2019.1584900

Kartikasari, I. A., & Usodo, B. (2022). The Effectiveness Open-Ended Learning and Creative Problem Solving Models to Teach Creative Thinking Skills. *Pegem Journal of Education and Instruction, 12*(4), 29–38.

Kasauli, R., Knauss, E., Horkoff, J., Liebel, G., & Neto, F. G. (2020). Chapter 10 requirements engineering challenges and practices in large-scale Agile system development. *Accelerating Digital Transformation*, 293-350. https://doi.org/DOI: 10.1007/978-3-031-10873-0_14

Kassa, B. G., & Ding, L. (2019, Feb.). The use of variation theory in a problem-based task design study. *Eleventh Congress of the European Society for Research in Mathematics Education*, Utrecht University, Utrecht, Netherlands. Retrieved from https://hal.archives-ouvertes.fr/hal-02423413

Katal, A., Wazid, M., & Goudar, R. H. (2013). Big data: Issues, challenges, tools and good practices. In *2013 Sixth International Conference on Contemporary Computing (IC3)* (pp. 404–409). IEEE. https://doi.org/DOI: 10.1109/IC3.2013.6612229

Kaur, H., Selvakumar, P., Haashni, S., Anute, N., Sharma, M., & Manjunath, T. C. (2025). Representations in Developing Thinking Regarding Probabilities in Higher Education. In *Modes of Representation in Developing Statistical Thinking in Education* (pp. 89–118). IGI Global Scientific Publishing. DOI: 10.4018/979-8-3693-9934-7.ch006

Kaushik, A., Tayal, D. K., & Yadav, K. (2020). undefined. *International Journal of Agile Systems and Management, 13*(2), 103. DOI: 10.1504/IJASM.2020.107902

Kayyali, M. (2025 A). Balancing Work and Life Techniques for Maintaining Emotional Wellbeing in Entrepreneurship. In Supporting Psychological and Emotional Wellbeing Among Entrepreneurs (pp. 33-58). IGI Global.

Kayyali, M. (2026). Ethical AI and Automation in the Workplace. In Leading Inclusive Workplaces Through Digital Transformation and Organizational Change (pp. 103-138). IGI Global Scientific Publishing.

Kayyali, M. (2022). *Management of Higher Education Institutions: The Impact of ICT Based Good Governance*. Entrepreneurship, and Quality Assurance on the Operation of Academic Institutions.

Kayyali, M. (2024). Design thinking and creativity in entrepreneurial innovation. In *Applying Business Intelligence and Innovation to Entrepreneurship* (pp. 155–170). IGI Global Scientific Publishing. DOI: 10.4018/979-8-3693-1846-1.ch008

Kayyali, M. (2025). B). The Role of Artificial Intelligence in Transforming Business Models. In *AI-Driven Business Model Innovation* (pp. 71–98). IGI Global Scientific Publishing. DOI: 10.4018/979-8-3693-9571-4.ch003

Kayyali, M. (2025). The evolution of quality assurance in higher education: Models, systems, and frameworks. In *Navigating Quality Assurance and Accreditation in Global Higher Education* (pp. 1–26). IGI Global Scientific Publishing.

Kelleher, J. D., Namee, B., & D'Arcy, A. (2015). *Fundamentals of Machine Learning for Predictive Data Analytics: Algorithms, Worked Examples, and Case Studies*. MIT Press.

Kendall, C., & Oprea, R. (2024). On the complexity of forming mental models. *Quantitative Economics, 15*(1), 175–211. DOI: 10.3982/QE2264

Kennedy, P. C. (2023). Libertas regimine crescit–developing a working theory of improvising in the course of composing music for improvised performance (Doctoral dissertation, University of Oxford).

Khan, M. A., Pattnaik, D., Ashraf, R., Ali, I., Kumar, S., & Donthu, N. (2021). Value of special issues in the Journal of Business Research: A bibliometric analysis. *Journal of Business Research*, *125*, 295–313. DOI: 10.1016/j.jbusres.2020.12.015

Khoiriyah, A. J., & Husamah, H. (2018). Problem-based learning: Creative thinking skills, problem-solving skills, and learning outcome of seventh grade students. [Jurnal Pendidikan Biologi Indonesia]. *JPBI*, *4*(2), 151–160. DOI: 10.22219/jpbi.v4i2.5804

Khotimah, R. P., & Masduki, M. (2016). Improving Teaching Quality and Problem Solving Ability through Contextual Teaching and Learning in Differential Equations: A Lesson Study Approach. *Online Submission*, *1*(1), 1–13. DOI: 10.23917/jramathedu.v1i1.1791

KHUDAVERDIYEVA, T. (2024). TRANSLATION PROBLEMS AND SOLUTIONS: BRIDGING LINGUISTIC AND CULTURAL DIFFERENCES. T RCÜM ŞÜNASLIĞIN MÜASİR PROBLEML Rİ, 228.

Kietzmann, J. H., Hermkens, K., McCarthy, I. P., & Silvestre, B. S. (2011). Social media? Get serious! Understanding the functional building blocks of social media. *Business Horizons*, *54*(3), 241–251. DOI: 10.1016/j.bushor.2011.01.005

Kimball, R., & Ross, M. (2013). *The data warehouse toolkit: The definitive guide to dimensional modeling* (3rd ed.). Wiley.

Kim, M. C., & Hannafin, M. J. (2011). Scaffolding problem solving in technology-enhanced learning environments (TELEs): Bridging research and theory with practice. *Computers & Education*, *56*(2), 403–417. DOI: 10.1016/j.compedu.2010.08.024

Kim, S., & Cameron, G. T. (2011). Emotions matter in crisis: The role of anger and sadness in the publics' response to crisis news framing and corporate crisis response. *Communication Research*, *38*(6), 826–855. DOI: 10.1177/0093650210385813

Kirchoff, J. F., Omar, A., & Fugate, B. S. (2016). A behavioral theory of sustainable supply chain management decision making in non-exemplar firms. *The Journal of Supply Chain Management*, *52*(1), 41–65. DOI: 10.1111/jscm.12098

Kirschner, P. A. (2002). Cognitive load theory: Implications of cognitive load theory on the design of learning. *Learning and Instruction*, *12*(1), 1–10. DOI: 10.1016/S0959-4752(01)00014-7

Kirschner, P. A., Sweller, J., & Clark, R. E. (2006). Why minimal guidance during instruction does not work: An analysis of the failure of constructivist, discovery, problem-based, experiential, and inquiry-based teaching. *Educational Psychologist*, *41*(2), 75–86. DOI: 10.1207/s15326985ep4102_1

Kishaija, N., Ocwa, A., Kuunya, R., Ssemugenze, B., & Heil, B. (2025). Climate change mitigation and livelihood components in smallholder coffee farming: A literature review and systematics. *Agriculture & Food Security*, *14*(1). Advance online publication. DOI: 10.1186/s40066-025-00522-7

Kitchin, R. (2014). *The data revolution: Big data, open data, data infrastructures and their consequences*. SAGE Publications.

Klimczuk, A., & Klimczuk-Kochańska, M. (2023). Core-periphery model. In *The Palgrave encyclopedia of global security studies* (pp. 239–245). Springer International Publishing. DOI: 10.1007/978-3-319-74319-6_320

Klünder, J., Trommer, F., & Prenner, N. (2022). How Agile coaches create an Agile mindset in development teams: Insights from an interview study. *Journal of Software (Malden, MA)*, *34*(12), e2491. Advance online publication. DOI: 10.1002/smr.2491

Kluyver, T., Ragan-Kelley, B., Pérez, F., Granger, B., Bussonnier, M., Frederic, J., Kelley, K., Hamrick, J., Grout, J., Corlay, S., Ivanov, P., Avila, D., Abdalla, S., Willing, C., & Jupyter Development Team. (2016). Jupyter Notebooks – a publishing format for reproducible computational workflows. In F. Loizides & B. Schmidt (Eds.), *Positioning and power in academic publishing: Players, agents and agendas* (pp. 87–90). IOS Press. https://doi.org/DOI: 10.3233/978-1-61499-649-1-87

Knapp, N. F. (2019). The shape activity: Social constructivism in the psychology classroom. *Teaching of Psychology*, *46*(1), 87–91. DOI: 10.1177/0098628318816181

Knutas, A., Ikonen, J., & Porras, J. (2015). Computer-Supported Collaborative Learning in Software Engineering Education: A Systematic Mapping Study. *International Journal on Information Technologies & Security*, 7(4). Advance online publication. DOI: 10.48550/arXiv.1906.10710

Koberg, E., & Longoni, A. (2019). A systematic review of sustainable supply chain management in global supply chains. *Journal of Cleaner Production*, *207*, 1084–1098. DOI: 10.1016/j.jclepro.2018.10.033

Kochenderfer, M. J., Wheeler, T. A., & Wray, K. H. (2022). *Algorithms for decision making*. MIT press.

Koetsier, J. (2019). *The Freemium Economy: How free products drive massive user acquisition*. TechCrunch. TechCrunch.

Kogan, G., Chassidim, H., & Rabaev, I. (2024). The efficacy of animation and visualization in teaching data structures: A case study. *Educational Technology Research and Development*, *72*(4), 2349–2372. DOI: 10.1007/s11423-024-10382-w

Kohavi, R. (1995, August). A study of cross-validation and bootstrap for accuracy estimation and model selection. *IJCAI (United States)*, *14*(2), 1137–1145.

Kohli, A. S., & Jensen, J. B. (2010). Assessing effectiveness of supply chain collaboration: an empirical study. *Supply Chain Forum: An International Journal,* 11(2), 2-16.

Kolanovic, M., & Krishnamachari, R. T. (2017). Big data and AI strategies: Machine learning and alternative data approach to investing. *J.P. Morgan Global Quantitative and Derivatives Strategy.* Big Data & AI Investing Strategies: Machine Learning & Alternative Data

Kolb, D. A. (1984). *Experiential learning: Experience as the source of learning and development.* Prentice Hall.

Kolodner, J. L., & Wills, L. M. (1996). Powers of observation in creative design. *Design Studies*, *17*(4), 385–416. DOI: 10.1016/S0142-694X(96)00021-X

Konys, A. (2019). Green supplier selection criteria: From a literature review to a comprehensive knowledge base. *Sustainability (Basel)*, *11*(15), 4208. DOI: 10.3390/su11154208

Kowalczyk, M., Marcinkowski, B., & Przybyłek, A. (2022). Scaled Agile framework. Dealing with software process-related challenges of a financial group with the action research approach. *Journal of Software (Malden, MA)*, *34*(6), e2455. Advance online publication. DOI: 10.1002/smr.2455

Krasnor, L. R. (1982). An observational study of social problem solving in young children. In *Peer relationships and social skills in childhood* (pp. 113–132). Springer New York. DOI: 10.1007/978-1-4613-8180-8_6

Krishnan, N. (2025). Advancing multi-agent systems through model context protocol: Architecture, implementation, and applications. arXiv preprint arXiv:2504.21030.

Kriz, A., Nailer, C., Jansen, K., & Potocnjak-Oxman, C. (2021). Teaching-practice as a critical bridge for narrowing the research-practice gap. *Industrial Marketing Management*, *92*, 254–266. DOI: 10.1016/j.indmarman.2020.02.017

Küçükuncular, A., & Ertugan, A. (2025). Teaching in the AI Era: Sustainable Digital Education Through Ethical Integration and Teacher Empowerment. *Sustainability (Basel)*, *17*(16), 7405. DOI: 10.3390/su17167405

Kuhn, M., & Johnson, K. (2013). *Applied predictive modeling*. Springer. DOI: 10.1007/978-1-4614-6849-3

Kuhn, T. S. (1962). *The Structure of Scientific Revolutions*. University of Chicago Press.

Kumar, G., & Nath Banerjee, R. (2014). Supply chain collaboration index: An instrument to measure the depth of collaboration. *Benchmarking*, *21*(2), 184–204. DOI: 10.1108/BIJ-02-2012-0008

Kumar, V. (2014). Making 'Freemium' Work. *Harvard Business Review*.

Kumar, V. (2018). Customer Acquisition Cost in Digital Marketing. *Marketing Science*, *37*(2), 230–245.

Kummari, D. N. (2025). Fostering organizational integrity through governance and ethical compliance initiatives. *Advanced Practices in Auditing, Regulatory Compliance, and Smart Manufacturing Systems*, 124-138. https://doi.org/DOI: 10.70593/978-93-7185-253-1_8

Kunnathully, K., Satyanarayana, P., Anute, N., Sharma, M., Sureshkrishna, G., Manjunath, T. C., & Selvakumar, P. (2025). Propaganda, Social Media and AI. In *Digital Populism and the Use of Neo-Propaganda and Fake News* (pp. 19–38). IGI Global Scientific Publishing. DOI: 10.4018/979-8-3693-9999-6.ch002

Kupiainen, E., Mäntylä, M. V., & Itkonen, J. (2015). Using metrics in Agile and lean software development – A systematic literature review of industrial studies. *Information and Software Technology*, *62*, 143–163. DOI: 10.1016/j.infsof.2015.02.005

Kurniawan, W., Darmaji, D., Astalini, A., Kurniawan, D. A., Hidayat, M., Kurniawan, N., & Farida, L. Z. N. (2019). Multimedia Physics Practicum Reflective Material Based on Problem Solving for Science Process Skills. *International Journal of Evaluation and Research in Education*, *8*(4), 590–595. DOI: 10.11591/ijere.v8i4.20258

Laengle, S., Merigó, J. M., Modak, N. M., & Yang, J. B. (2020). Bibliometrics in operations research and management science: A university analysis. *Annals of Operations Research*, *294*(1-2), 769–813. DOI: 10.1007/s10479-018-3017-6

Lai, X., & Xie, L. (2013). *Practical Approaches to Data Mining and Machine Learning*. Springer.

Lames, M., & Hansen, G. (2001). Designing observational systems to support top-level teams in game sports. *International Journal of Performance Analysis in Sport*, *1*(1), 83–90. DOI: 10.1080/24748668.2001.11868251

Lazakidou, G., & Retalis, S. (2010). Using computer supported collaborative learning strategies for helping students acquire self-regulated problem-solving skills in mathematics. *Computers & Education, 54*(1), 3–13. DOI: 10.1016/j.compedu.2009.02.020

Le Dé, L. (2024). Bridging gaps between disaster risk reduction and drowning prevention. *International Journal of Disaster Risk Reduction, 106*, 104445. DOI: 10.1016/j.ijdrr.2024.104445

Lecun, Y., Bengio, Y., & Hinton, G. (2015). Deep Learning. *Nature, 521*(7553), 436–444. DOI: 10.1038/nature14539 PMID: 26017442

Lee, H. L. (2004). The triple-A supply chain. *Harvard Business Review, 82*(10), 102–113.

Leicht, R. M., Hunter, S. T., Saluja, C., & Messner, J. I. (2010). Implementing observational research methods to study team performance in construction management. *Journal of Construction Engineering and Management, 136*(1), 76–86. DOI: 10.1061/(ASCE)CO.1943-7862.0000080

Leikin, R., Koichu, B., & Berman, A. (2009). Mathematical giftedness as a quality of problem-solving acts. *Creativity in mathematics and the education of gifted students, 8*, 115-127.

Lemons, G., Carberry, A., Swan, C., Jarvin, L., & Rogers, C. (2010). The benefits of model building in teaching engineering design. *Design Studies, 31*(3), 288–309. DOI: 10.1016/j.destud.2010.02.001

Lenberg, P., Feldt, R., Tengberg, L. G., & Gren, L. (2020). Behavioral aspects of safety-critical software development. *Proceedings of the IEEE/ACM 42nd International Conference on Software Engineering Workshops*, 173-176. https://doi.org/ DOI: 10.1145/3387940.3392227

Leong, T. W., Vetere, F., & Howard, S. (2006). Randomness as a resource for design. In *Proceedings of the 6th conference on Designing Interactive systems (DIS '06)* (pp. 132-139). Association for Computing Machinery. https://doi.org/DOI: 10.1145/1142405.1142428

Lesh, R., & Doerr, H. M. (2003). Foundations of a models and modeling perspective on mathematics teaching, learning, and problem solving. In *Beyond constructivism* (pp. 3–33). Routledge. DOI: 10.4324/9781410607713

Lesh, R., & Harel, G. (2003). Problem solving, modeling, and local conceptual development. *Mathematical Thinking and Learning, 5*(2-3), 157–189. DOI: 10.1080/10986065.2003.9679998

Lessler, J., Edmunds, W. J., Halloran, M. E., Hollingsworth, T. D., & Lloyd, A. L. (2015). Seven challenges for model-driven data collection in experimental and observational studies. *Epidemics, 10*, 78–82. DOI: 10.1016/j.epidem.2014.12.002

Lhafra, F. Z., & Abdoun, O. (2023). Towards an adaptive learning process using Artificial Intelligence technologies. In Motahhir, S., & Bossoufi, B. (Eds.), *Digital Technologies and Applications. ICDTA 2023. Lecture Notes in Networks and Systems* (Vol. 668, pp. 23–32). Springer., DOI: 10.1007/978-3-031-29857-8_3

Li, L. (2012). Effects of enterprise technology on supply chain collaboration: Analysis of China-linked supply chain. *Enterprise Information Systems, 6*(1), 55–77. DOI: 10.1080/17517575.2011.639904

Lima-Junior, F. R., & Carpinetti, L. C. R. (2017). Quantitative models for supply chain performance evaluation: A literature review. *Computers & Industrial Engineering, 113*, 333–346. DOI: 10.1016/j.cie.2017.09.022

Lincoln, Y. S., & Guba, E. G. (1985). *Naturalistic inquiry*. SAGE Publications. DOI: 10.1016/0147-1767(85)90062-8

Linton, J. D., Klassen, R., & Jayaraman, V. (2007). Sustainable supply chains: An introduction. *Journal of Operations Management, 25*(6), 1075–1082. DOI: 10.1016/j.jom.2007.01.012

Litzinger, T. A., Meter, P. V., Firetto, C. M., Passmore, L. J., Masters, C. B., Turns, S. R., Gray, G. L., Costanzo, F., & Zappe, S. E. (2010). A cognitive study of problem solving in statics. *Journal of Engineering Education, 99*(4), 337–353. DOI: 10.1002/j.2168-9830.2010.tb01067.x

Liu, B. F., Austin, L., & Jin, Y. (2015). How publics respond to crisis communication strategies: The interplay of information form and source. *Public Relations Review, 41*(4), 651–657. DOI: 10.1016/j.pubrev.2015.06.003

Liu, T., & Israel, M. (2022). Uncovering students' problem-solving processes in game-based learning environments. *Computers & Education, 182*, 104462. DOI: 10.1016/j.compedu.2022.104462

Li, Y., Huang, Z., Jiang, M., & Chang, T. W. (2016). The effect on pupils' science performance and problem-solving ability through Lego: An engineering design-based modeling approach. *Journal of Educational Technology & Society, 19*(3), 143–156.

Loaiza-Ramírez, J. P., Reimer, T., & Moreno-Mantilla, C. E. (2024). When green energy feels cozy: The interplay of protected values, the halo effect, and demographics in consumers' renewable energies adoption. *Cleaner and Responsible Consumption, 15*(100237), 100237. DOI: 10.1016/j.clrc.2024.100237

LOBASEV, D. V. (2022). Agile-transformation framework for large enterprises. *Актуальные исследования*, (47), 26-33. https://doi.org/DOI: 10.51635/27131513_2022_47-26

Lockamy, A.III, & McCormack, K. (2004). Linking SCOR planning practices to supply chain performance: An exploratory study. *International Journal of Operations & Production Management*, *24*(12), 1192–1218. DOI: 10.1108/01443570410569010

Long, M. (2014). *Second language acquisition and Task-based language teaching*. Wiley-Blackwell.

López Enciso, D. J., Silva Medina, J. P., & Bordón López, M. N. (2023). Impact of the internal control system on the logistics management of a gastronomic company in the city of Pilar. Retrieved from https://dialnet.unirioja.es/descarga/articulo/9294419.pdf

Lous, P., Kuhrmann, M., & Tell, P. (2017). Is Scrum fit for global software engineering? *2017 IEEE 12th International Conference on Global Software Engineering (ICGSE)*, 1-10. https://doi.org/DOI: 10.1109/ICGSE.2017.13

Lovett, M. C., & Anderson, J. R. (1996). History of success and current context in problem solving: Combined influences on operator selection. *Cognitive Psychology*, *31*(2), 168–217. DOI: 10.1006/cogp.1996.0016

Lozano-Oviedo, J., Cortés, C. E., & Rey, P. A. (2024). Sustainable closed-loop supply chains and their optimization models: A review of the literature. *Clean Technologies and Environmental Policy*, *26*(4), 999–1023. DOI: 10.1007/s10098-023-02730-w

Luckin, R. (2017). Towards Artificial Intelligence-based assessment systems. *Nature Human Behaviour*, *1*(3), 0028. Advance online publication. DOI: 10.1038/s41562-016-0028

Lundberg, S. M., & Lee, S. I. (2017). A unified approach to interpreting model predictions. In Guyon, I., Luxburg, U. V., Bengio, S., Wallach, H., Fergus, R., Vishwanathan, S., & Garnett, R. (Eds.), Vol. 30, pp. 4765–4774). Advances in neural information processing systems. Curran Associates, Inc., https://proceedings.neurips.cc/paper/2017/file/8a20a8621978632d76c43dfd28b67767-Paper.pdf

Luzzini, D., Brandon-Jones, E., Brandon-Jones, A., & Spina, G. (2015). From sustainability commitment to performance: The role of intra-and inter-firm collaborative capabilities in the upstream supply chain. *International Journal of Production Economics*, *165*, 51–63. DOI: 10.1016/j.ijpe.2015.03.004

Mackintosh, L. (2021). *Shifting grounds: deep histories of Tāmaki Makaurau Auckland*. Bridget Williams Books. DOI: 10.7810/9781988587332

Madaan, S., Sai, T. B., Mandal, R., Kar, A., Sharma, M., Selvakumar, P., & Manjunath, T. C. (2025). Math Instruction and AI. In *Examining AI Disruption in Educational Settings: Challenges and Opportunities* (pp. 161-184). IGI Global Scientific Publishing. DOI: 10.4018/979-8-3693-7873-1.ch006

Magnani, L., & Nersessian, N. (Eds.). (2002). *Model-Based Reasoning: Science, Technology, Values*. Kluwer. DOI: 10.1007/978-1-4615-0605-8

Mahajan, P. (2025). *The Soul of the AI: Governance*. Ethics, and the Future of Human–AI Integration.

Maheshwari, A., Malhotra, A., Hada, B. S., Ranka, M., & Basha, M. S. A. (2024, September). Towards an Improved Model for Stability Score Prediction: Harnessing Machine Learning in National Stability Forecasting. In *2024 IEEE North Karnataka Subsection Flagship International Conference (NKCon)* (pp. 1-7). IEEE. DOI: 10.1109/NKCon62728.2024.10775198

Make certain your marketing strategy will have a good chance of being successful. (2010). *Creating a Successful Marketing Strategy for Your Small New Business*, 191-212. https://doi.org/DOI: 10.5040/9798216963158.0012

Maksoud, F. J., de la Paz, M. F. V., Hann, A. J., Thanarak, J., Reilly, G. C., Claeyssens, F., & Zhang, Y. S. (2022). Porous biomaterials for tissue engineering: A review. *Journal of Materials Chemistry. B*, *10*(40), 8111–8165. DOI: 10.1039/D1TB02628C PMID: 36205119

Malesios, C., Dey, P. K., & Abdelaziz, F. B. (2020). Supply chain sustainability performance measurement of small and medium sized enterprises using structural equation modeling. *Annals of Operations Research*, *294*(1), 623–653. DOI: 10.1007/s10479-018-3080-z

Malik, N., Nirupama, E., Selvakumar, P., Sankpal, U., Nathsharma, S. K., Sharma, M., & Manjunath, T. C. (2025a). 2D Materials for Energy Storage and Conversion. In *Innovations in Next-Generation Energy Storage Solutions* (pp. 1–24). IGI Global Scientific Publishing. DOI: 10.4018/979-8-3693-9316-1.ch001

Malik, N., Thakur, D. J., Aradhya, S. G. B., Sudheer, P., Sharma, M., Manjunath, T. C., & Selvakumar, P. (2025b). Performance Optimization in Remote Monitoring. In *Synergizing Data Envelopment Analysis and Machine Learning for Performance Optimization in Healthcare* (pp. 495–516). IGI Global Scientific Publishing. DOI: 10.4018/979-8-3373-0081-8.ch020

Mammola, S., Meierhofer, M. B., Borges, P. A., Colado, R., Culver, D. C., Deharveng, L., Delić, T., Di Lorenzo, T., Dražina, T., Ferreira, R. L., Fiasca, B., Fišer, C., Galassi, D. M. P., Garzoli, L., Gerovasileiou, V., Griebler, C., Halse, S., Howarth, F. G., Isaia, M., & Cardoso, P. (2022). Towards evidence-based conservation of subterranean ecosystems. *Biological Reviews of the Cambridge Philosophical Society*, *97*(4), 1476–1510. DOI: 10.1111/brv.12851 PMID: 35315207

Mandavilli, S. R. (2023). Elucidating the Certainty uncertainty principle for the Social Sciences: Guidelines for hypothesis formulation in the Social Sciences for enhanced objectivity and intellectual multi-polarity. Available at *SSRN* 4531179. DOI: 10.2139/ssrn.4531179

Mangasih, E. T., Pinasti, M., & Bawono, I. R. (2020). The effect of quality of internal audit and effectiveness of internal control systems on good corporate governance in finance companies. *SAR (Soedirman Accounting Review). Journal of Accounting and Business*, *5*(1), 56–82. https://pdfs.semanticscholar.org/522b/8d0ad7d241ecfca3990e1d90c9fca1b80251.pdf/1000

Mani, I. (2022). *Computational modeling of narrative*. Springer Nature.

Mäntymäki, M., Islam, A. N., & Benbasat, I. (2020). What drives subscribing to premium in freemium services? A consumer value-based view of differences between upgrading to and staying with premium. *Information Systems Journal*, *30*(2), 295–333. DOI: 10.1111/isj.12262

Marsick, V. J., Fichter, R., & Watkins, K. E. (2021). From work-based learning to learning-based work: Exploring the changing relationship between learning and work. The Sage handbook of learning and work, 177-193.

Martin, A. J., & Marsh, H. W. (2008). Academic buoyancy: Towards an understanding of students' everyday resilience. *Journal of School Psychology*, *46*(1), 53–83. DOI: 10.1016/j.jsp.2007.01.002 PMID: 19083351

Martin, K. (2019). Ethical implications and accountability of algorithms. *Journal of Business Ethics*, *160*(4), 835–850. DOI: 10.1007/s10551-018-3921-3

Martins, J., & Rodrigues, R. (2024). Motivations in the adoption and conversion of freemium services: Insights for digital entrepreneurship. *Review of Managerial Science*, *19*(7), 2127–2148. DOI: 10.1007/s11846-024-00754-0

Marty, J., & Ruel, S. (2024). Why is "supply chain collaboration" still a hot topic? A review of decades of research and a comprehensive framework proposal. *International Journal of Production Economics*, *273*, 109259. DOI: 10.1016/j.ijpe.2024.109259

Marulis, L. M., & Nelson, L. J. (2021). Metacognitive processes and associations to executive function and motivation during a problem-solving task in 3–5 year olds. *Metacognition and Learning*, *16*(1), 207–231. DOI: 10.1007/s11409-020-09244-6

MathWorks. (2023). *MATLAB* (Version R2023a) [Software]. MathWorks. https://www.mathworks.com/products/matlab.html

Matsuda, N., Cohen, W. W., Sewall, J., Lacerda, G., & Koedinger, K. R. (2007). Predicting students' performance with simstudent: Learning cognitive skills from observation. *Frontiers in Artificial Intelligence and Applications*, *158*, 467.

Mayer, G. (2024). Inspired by Data: AI's transformative role in corporate communication. EGEA spa.

Mayer, R. E. (2009). *Multimedia learning* (2nd ed.). Cambridge University Press. DOI: 10.1017/CBO9780511811678

Mazumdar, T., & Monroe, K. B. (1990). The effects of buyers' intentions to learn price informatio. *Journal of Retailing*, *66*(1), 15.

McCarthy, E. J. (1960). *Basic Marketing: A Managerial Approach*. Richard D.

McClellan, M. (2002). *Collaborative Manufacturing: Using Real-time Information to Support the Supply Chain*. CRC Press. DOI: 10.1201/9781420025347

McDougall, D., & Cordeiro, P. (1992). College students' preparedness for lecture and discussion: Effects of random questioning expectations. *Teacher Educator*, *27*(3), 33–40. DOI: 10.1080/08878739209555008

McIntyre, L. L., & Phaneuf, L. K. (2008). A three tier model of parent education in early childhood: Applying a problem-solving model. *Topics in Early Childhood Special Education*, *27*(4), 214–222. DOI: 10.1177/0271121407311239

McStay, A. (2023). *Automating empathy: Decoding technologies that gauge intimate life*. Oxford University Press. DOI: 10.1093/oso/9780197615546.001.0001

Meade, L., & Sarkis, J. (2002). A conceptual model for selecting and evaluating third-party reverse logistics providers. *Supply Chain Management*, *7*(5), 283–295. DOI: 10.1108/13598540210447728

Mehrabi, N., Morstatter, F., Saxena, N., Lerman, K., & Galstyan, A. (2021). A survey on bias and fairness in machine learning. *ACM Computing Surveys*, *54*(6), 1–35. DOI: 10.1145/3457607

Melnyk, S.A., Lummus, R., Vokurka, R. J. & Sandor, J. (2007). Supply Chain Management 2010 and Beyond, *APICS Educational & Research Foundation*, 1-63.

Melnyk, S. A., Stewart, D. M., & Swink, M. (2004). Metrics and performance measurement in operations management: Dealing with the metrics maze. *Journal of Operations Management*, *22*(3), 209–218. DOI: 10.1016/j.jom.2004.01.004

Mentzer, J. T., DeWitt, W., Keebler, J. S., Min, S., Nix, N. W., Smith, C. D., & Zacharia, Z. G. (2001). Defining supply chain management. *Journal of Business Logistics*, *22*(2), 1–25. DOI: 10.1002/j.2158-1592.2001.tb00001.x

Metzger, M. J., Flanagin, A. J., & Medders, R. B. (2010). Social and heuristic approaches to credibility evaluation online. *Journal of Communication*, *60*(3), 413–439. DOI: 10.1111/j.1460-2466.2010.01488.x

Miller, B. (2022). *Distant readings of disciplinarity: Knowing and doing in composition/rhetoric dissertations*. University Press of Colorado.

Miller, J. P., Taori, R., Raghunathan, A., Sagawa, S., Koh, P. W., Shankar, V., & Schmidt, L. (2021, July). Accuracy on the line: on the strong correlation between out-of-distribution and in-distribution generalization. In *International conference on machine learning* (pp. 7721-7735). PMLR.

Min, H., & Zhou, G. (2002). Supply chain modeling: Past, present and future. *Computers & Industrial Engineering*, *43*(1-2), 231–249. DOI: 10.1016/S0360-8352(02)00066-9

Mishra, B. R., Selvakumar, P., Kaur, R., Kalshetti, P., Mishra, K. K., Sharma, M., & Manjunath, T. C. (2025). Innovation and Digital Transformation in the Public Sector Entities. In *Enhancing Public Sector Accountability and Services Through Digital Innovation* (pp. 409–436). IGI Global Scientific Publishing. DOI: 10.4018/979-8-3693-9251-5.ch013

Mishra, D., Gunasekaran, A., Papadopoulos, T., & Dubey, R. (2018). Supply chain performance measures and metrics: A bibliometric study. *Benchmarking*, *25*(3), 932–967. DOI: 10.1108/BIJ-08-2017-0224

Mitchell, R. (2015). *Web scraping with Python: Collecting data from the modern web*. O'Reilly Media.

Mizoguchi, R., Vanwelkenhuysen, J., & Ikeda, M. (1995). Task ontology for reuse of problem solving knowledge. *Towards very large knowledge bases: Knowledge building & knowledge sharing, 46*(59), 45.

Mohamed, A. O. (2025). The Effect of Design on the Viewer's Perception of Media Content and Its Role in Problem Solving. *Journal of Ecohumanism*, *4*(1), 1432–1447. DOI: 10.62754/joe.v4i1.5956

Mohapatra, H., Pramanik, S., & Ranjan Mishra, S. (2025). Revolutionizing software development: The transformative influence of machine learning integrated SDLC model. Artificial Intelligence-Enhanced Software and Systems Engineering, 41-69. https://doi.org/DOI: 10.1007/978-3-031-88188-6_3

Mohapatra, H. (2024). The role of 6G in empowering smart cities enabling ubiquitous connectivity and intelligent infrastructure. *Advances in Civil and Industrial Engineering*, •••, 237–264. DOI: 10.4018/979-8-3693-8029-1.ch009

Möhlmann, M. (2015). Collaborative consumption: Determinants of satisfaction and the likelihood of using a sharing economy option again. *Journal of Consumer Behaviour, 14*(3), 193–207. DOI: 10.1002/cb.1512

Montazeri, M., Montazeri, M., Bahaadinbeigy, K., Montazeri, M., & Afraz, A. (2023). Application of machine learning methods in predicting schizophrenia and bipolar disorders: A systematic review. *Health Science Reports*, *6*(1), e962.

Montgomery, D. C., Peck, E. A., & Vining, G. G. (2012). *Introduction to linear regression analysis* (5th ed.). Wiley.

Moore, S. L. (2021). The design models we have are not the design models we need. *The Journal of Applied Instructional Design*, *10*(4), 11–19.

Moreira, A., Rodrigues, A. C., & Ferreira, M. R. (2025). Where does HR management stand in sustainability reporting? ESG and GRI perspectives. *Sustainability*, *17*(7), 3033. DOI: 10.3390/su17073033

Morgan, C., & Dewhurst, A. (2008). Multiple retailer supplier performance: An exploratory investigation into using SPC techniques. *International Journal of Production Economics*, *111*(1), 13–26. DOI: 10.1016/j.ijpe.2006.11.018

Mountbatten O'Malley, E., & Morris, T. H. (2025). Self-directed flourishing: A conceptual meta-framework for dealing with the challenges of 21st-century learning and education. *Quality Education for All*, *2*(1), 171–189. DOI: 10.1108/QEA-03-2024-0029

Mudinillah, A., Rahmi, S. N., & Taro, N. (2024). Task-based language teaching: A systematic review of research and applications. *Lingeduca: Journal of Language and Education Studies*, *3*(2), 102–115. DOI: 10.70177/lingeduca.v3i2.1352

Mujkic, Z., Qorri, A., & Kraslawski, A. (2018). Sustainability and optimization of supply chains: A literature review. *Operations and Supply Chain Management: An International Journal*, *11*(4), 186–199. DOI: 10.31387/oscm0350213

Mumford, E. (2006). The story of socio-technical design: Reflections on its successes, failures and potential. *Information Systems Journal, 16*(4), 317–342. DOI: 10.1111/j.1365-2575.2006.00221.x

Muro, P. D., & Terry, M. (2007). A matter of style: Applying Kolb's learning style model to college mathematics teaching practices. *Journal of College Reading and Learning, 38*(1), 53–60. DOI: 10.1080/10790195.2007.10850204

Muzana, S. R., Wilujeng, I., Yanto, B. E., & Mustamin, A. A. (2021). E-STEM Project-Based Learning in Teaching Science to Increase ICT Literacy and Problem Solving. *International Journal of Evaluation and Research in Education, 10*(4), 1386–1394. DOI: 10.11591/ijere.v10i4.21942

Myers, J. (2021). Reasoning with imagination. In *Epistemic uses of imagination* (pp. 103–121). Routledge. DOI: 10.4324/9781003041979-8

Nabavian, S., & Parsons, J. (2024, May). A Design-Principle-Friendly Conceptual Model of Observational Crowdsourcing. In *International Conference on Design Science Research in Information Systems and Technology* (pp. 95-108). Cham: Springer Nature Switzerland. DOI: 10.1007/978-3-031-61175-9_7

Narváez-Castillo, V. P., García-Benau, M. A., Sierra-García, L., & Gambetta, N. (2024). Are material ESG issues making their way into key audit matters? An analysis of Colombian innovative companies. *Journal of Innovation & Knowledge, 9*(4), 100574. DOI: 10.1016/j.jik.2024.100574

Neely, A., Mills, J., Platts, K., Richards, H., Gregory, M., Bourne, M., & Kennerley, M. (2000). Performance measurement system design: Developing and testing a process-based approach. *International Journal of Operations & Production Management, 20*(10), 1119–1145. DOI: 10.1108/01443570010343708

Nersessian, N. J., & Patton, C. (2009). Model-based reasoning in interdisciplinary engineering. In Meijers, A. (Ed.), *Handbook of the Philosophy and Engineering Sciences* (pp. 687–718). Elsevier. DOI: 10.1016/B978-0-444-51667-1.50031-8

Newton, J. S., Algozzine, B., Algozzine, K., Horner, R. H., & Todd, A. W. (2011). Building local capacity for training and coaching data-based problem solving with positive behavior intervention and support teams. *Journal of Applied School Psychology, 27*(3), 228–245. DOI: 10.1080/15377903.2011.590104

Ngo, R., Chan, L., & Mindermann, S. (2022). The alignment problem from a deep learning perspective. arXiv preprint arXiv:2209.00626.

Nguyen, M. P., Thai, V. V., Chan, C., Lau, K. H., Nguyen, M. T. N., & Do, H. P. N. (2025). The interplay among trust, reciprocity and commitment factors in facilitating supply chain collaboration: The case of Vietnamese fishery industry. *Asia Pacific Journal of Marketing and Logistics*, *37*(1), 150–170. DOI: 10.1108/APJML-04-2024-0445

Niemand, T., Tischer, S., Fritzsche, T., & Kraus, S. (2015). The freemium effect: Why consumers perceive more value with free than with premium offers.

Norman, D. A. (2023). *Design for a better world: Meaningful, sustainable, humanity centered.* MIT Press. DOI: 10.1080/08956308.2023.2183015

Ntabe, E. N., LeBel, L., Munson, A. D., & Santa-Eulalia, L. A. (2015). A systematic literature review of the supply chain operations reference (SCOR) model application with special attention to environmental issues. *International Journal of Production Economics*, *169*, 310–332. DOI: 10.1016/j.ijpe.2015.08.008

Nugiel, T., Mitchell, M. E., Demeter, D. V., Garza, A. M., Cirino, P. T., Hernandez, A. E., Juranek, J., & Church, J. A. (2023). Brain engagement during a cognitive flexibility task relates to academic performance in English learners. *Mind, Brain and Education : the Official Journal of the International Mind, Brain, and Education Society*, *17*(2), 149–160. DOI: 10.1111/mbe.12362 PMID: 38770227

Nurhafidhah, N., Mauliza, M., Yani, A. F. S., Aprilia, R., Zatya, I., & Mustapha, W. Z. W. (2024). Development of Teaching Module Based on the Merdeka Curriculum with the Application of Character Integrated Problem Solving Model. *Jurnal Pendidikan Sains Indonesia*, *12*(3), 478–492. DOI: 10.24815/jpsi.v12i3.37750

Nyaga, G. N., Whipple, J. M., & Lynch, D. F. (2010). Examining supply chain relationships: Do buyer and supplier perspectives on collaborative relationships differ? *Journal of Operations Management*, *28*(2), 101–114. DOI: 10.1016/j.jom.2009.07.005

O'Neil, J., Benita, Y., Feldman, I., Chenard, M., Roberts, B., Liu, Y., Li, J., Kral, A., Lejnine, S., Loboda, A., Arthur, W., Cristescu, R., Haines, B. B., Winter, C., Zhang, T., Bloecher, A., & Shumway, S. D. (2016). An unbiased oncology compound screen to identify novel combination strategies. *Molecular Cancer Therapeutics*, *15*(6), 1155–1162. DOI: 10.1158/1535-7163.MCT-15-0843 PMID: 26983881

O'Reilly, C. A., & Chatman, J. A. (2020). Transformational leader or narcissist? How grandiose narcissists can create and destroy organizations and institutions. *California Management Review*, *62*(3), 5–27. DOI: 10.1177/0008125620914989

OBS Business School. (2023). Green logistics: What it is and what benefits it has for the company. Retrieved from https://www.obsbusiness.school/blog/logistica-verde-que-es-y-que-beneficios-tiene-para-la-empresa

OECD. (2019). *OECD Learning Compass 2030: Concept notes*. OECD Future of Education and Skills.

Oestreicher-Singer, G., & Zalmanson, L. (2013). Content or Community? A Digital Business Strategy for Content Providers in the Social Age. *Management Information Systems Quarterly*, *37*(2), 591–616. DOI: 10.25300/MISQ/2013/37.2.12

Ohno, T., & Bodek, N. (2019). Evolution of the Toyota production system. *Toyota Production System*, 17-44. https://doi.org/DOI: 10.4324/9780429273018-2

Olayinka, A. S. (2023). Culture as a Means of De-escalating Conflict and Maintaining Peace. *Journal of Anthropological Research*, *6*, 167.

Oliver, R. K., & Webber, M. D. (2012). Supply-chain management: logistics catches up with strategy. In Klaus, P., & Müller, S. (Eds.), *The Roots of Logistics* (pp. 183–194). Springer. DOI: 10.1007/978-3-642-27922-5_15

Olivola, C. Y., & Oppenheimer, D. M. (2008). Randomness in retrospect: Exploring the interactions between memory and randomness cognition. *Psychonomic Bulletin & Review*, *15*(5), 991–996. DOI: 10.3758/PBR.15.5.991 PMID: 18926994

Örün, Ö., & Sever, I. (2025). Cognitive flexibility: An educational approach. In Özen, H., & Polat, G. (Eds.), *Resilience, adaptability, and cultural awareness within the educational landscape* (pp. 179–208). IGI Global Scientific Publishing., DOI: 10.4018/979-8-3693-6040-8.ch007

Osterwalder, A., & Pigneur, Y. (2010). *Business Model Generation: A Handbook for Visionaries, Game Changers, and Challengers*. Wiley.

Otegui, D. (2024). Understanding Cognitive Processes in High-Stakes Environments. In *Business Growth in Times of Instability: Empowering Private Companies Through Disaster Risk Reduction* (pp. 43–63). Springer Nature Switzerland. DOI: 10.1007/978-3-031-69370-0_3

Oulasvirta, A., & Hornbæk, K. (2016, May). HCI research as problem-solving. In *Proceedings of the 2016 CHI Conference on Human Factors in Computing Systems* (pp. 4956-4967). DOI: 10.1145/2858036.2858283

Oyighan, D., & Okwu, E. (2024). Social media for information dissemination in the digital era. RAY. *International Journal of Multidisciplinary Studies*, *10*(1), 1–21.

Paas, F., & Sweller, J. (2012). An evolutionary upgrade of cognitive load theory: Using the human motor system and collaboration to support the learning of complex cognitive tasks. *Educational Psychology Review, 24*(1), 27–45. DOI: 10.1007/s10648-011-9179-2

Paasivaara, M., Durasiewicz, S., & Lassenius, C. (2008). Distributed Agile development: Using Scrum in a large project. *2008 IEEE International Conference on Global Software Engineering*, 87-95. https://doi.org/DOI: 10.1109/ICGSE.2008.38

Pacheco, C., Lahiri, S. K., Ernst, M. D., & Ball, T. (2007, May). Feedback-directed random test generation. In *9th International Conference on Software Engineering (ICSE'07)*, Minneapolis, MN, USA, pp. 75-84. https://doi.org/DOI: 10.1109/ICSE.2007.37

Pacte Group. (2008). Building a translation competence model. In *Triangulating translation* (pp. 43–66). John Benjamins Publishing Company.

Paez, R. (2024). *Operative mapping: the use of maps as a design tool.* Actar D, Inc.

Palen, L., & Hughes, A. L. (2018). Crisis informatics: New phenomena and relationships. In A. Kent & M. M. Hight (Eds.), *The Routledge Companion to Digital Journalism Studies* (pp. 304–313). Routledge.

Palen, L., & Anderson, K. M. (2016). Crisis informatics—New data for extraordinary times. *Science, 353*(6296), 224–225. DOI: 10.1126/science.aag2579 PMID: 27418492

Pamudji, S., & Achmadi, T. (2021). Measuring the total logistics costs at the macro level: A study of Indonesia's logistics. *Logistics (Basel), 5*(4), 68. DOI: 10.3390/logistics5040068

Pang, B., & Lee, L. (2008). Opinion mining and sentiment analysis. *Foundations and Trends in Information Retrieval, 2*(1–2), 1–135. DOI: 10.1561/1500000011

Pantiris, P., Pallis, P. L., Chountalas, P. T., & Dasaklis, T. K. (2025). Enhancing Coordination and Decision Making in Humanitarian Logistics Through Artificial Intelligence: A Grounded Theory Approach. *Logistics (Basel), 9*(3), 113. DOI: 10.3390/logistics9030113

Papakiriakopoulos, D., & Pramatari, K. (2010). Collaborative performance measurement in supply chain. *Industrial Management & Data Systems, 110*(9), 1297–1318. DOI: 10.1108/02635571011087400

Park, Y., Cardwell, R., & Naismith, B. (2024). *Assessing Vocabulary on the Duolingo English Test.* Duolingo Research Report No. DRR-24-01). Duolingo. http://go.duolingo. com/vocabulary.

Pasquini, D., Kornaropoulos, E. M., & Ateniese, G. (2024). Llmmap: Fingerprinting for large language models. arXiv preprint arXiv:2407.15847.

Pasupuleti, V., Thuraka, B., Kodete, C. S., & Malisetty, S. (2024). Enhancing supply chain agility and sustainability through machine learning: Optimization techniques for logistics and inventory management. *Logistics (Basel)*, *8*(3), 73. DOI: 10.3390/logistics8030073

Paudel, D., Neupane, R. C., Sigdel, S., Poudel, P., & Khanal, A. R. (2023). COVID-19 pandemic, climate change, and conflicts on agriculture: A trio of challenges to global food security. *Sustainability (Basel)*, *15*(10), 8280. DOI: 10.3390/su15108280

Paul, M. J., & Dredze, M. (2011). You are what you Tweet: Analyzing Twitter for public health. In *Proceedings of the Fifth International AAAI Conference on Weblogs and Social Media* (pp. 265–272). Association for the Advancement of Artificial Intelligence., https://ojs.aaai.org/index.php/ICWSM/article/view/14137

Pauwels, K., & Weiss, A. (2008). Moving from Free to Fee: How Online Firms Market to New Users. *Journal of Interactive Marketing*, *22*(3), 30–42.

Pazos, P., Micari, M., & Light, G. (2010). Developing an instrument to characterise peer-led groups in collaborative learning environments: Assessing problem-solving approach and group interaction. *Assessment & Evaluation in Higher Education*, *35*(2), 191–208. DOI: 10.1080/02602930802691572

Pearl, J. (2009). *Causality: Models, reasoning and inference* (2nd ed.). Cambridge University Press. DOI: 10.1017/CBO9780511803161

Peattie, K., & Ratnayaka, M. (1992). Responding to the green movement. *Industrial Marketing Management*, *21*(2), 103–110. DOI: 10.1016/0019-8501(92)90004-D

Pecher, B., Srba, I., & Bielikova, M. (2023). A survey on stability of learning with limited labelled data and its sensitivity to the effects of randomness. *arXiv*: 2312.01082. https://doi.org//arXiv.2312.01082DOI: 10.48550

Peng, M., Zhao, Q., Wang, M., & Du, X. (2023). Reconfigurable scaffolds for adaptive tissue regeneration. *Nanoscale*, *15*(13), 6105–6120. DOI: 10.1039/D3NR00281K PMID: 36919563

Pereira, L., Batista, F., & Da Costa, R. L. (2023). Enterprise Agile transformation. *International Journal of Agile Systems and Management*, *16*(1), 1. DOI: 10.1504/IJASM.2023.10055724

Pérez-Perales, D., Boza, A., Alarcón, F., & Gómez-Gasquet, P. (2024). Mathematical programming-based methodology for the evaluation of supply chain collaborative planning scenarios. *Annals of Operations Research, 337*(1), 261–312. DOI: 10.1007/s10479-024-05917-6

Persson, F., & Olhager, J. (2002). Performance simulation of supply chain designs. *International Journal of Production Economics, 77*(3), 231–245. DOI: 10.1016/S0925-5273(00)00088-8

Pidd, M. (2004). *Computer simulation in management science* (5th ed.). Wiley.

Popov, A. (2023). The rise of random task generators in language learning: Embracing the era of randomness. *TESL Ontario Contact Magazine, Nov 2023*, 34-36.

Poppendieck, M. (2007). Lean software development. *29th International Conference on Software Engineering (ICSE'07 Companion)*. https://doi.org/DOI: 10.1109/ICSECOMPANION.2007.46

Prahinski, C., & Kocabasoglu, C. (2006). Empirical research opportunities in reverse supply chains. *Omega, 34*(6), 519–532. DOI: 10.1016/j.omega.2005.01.003

Provost, F., & Fawcett, T. (2013). *Data Science for Business: What you need to know about data mining and data-analytic thinking*. O'Reilly Media, Inc.

Provost, F., & Fawcett, T. (2013). *Data science for business: What you need to know about data mining and data-analytic thinking*. O'Reilly Media.

Purwaningsih, E., Sari, A. M., Yuliati, L., Masjkur, K., Kurniawan, B. R., & Zahiri, M. A. (2020, March). Improving the problem-solving skills through the development of teaching materials with STEM-PjBL (science, technology, engineering, and mathematics-project based learning) model integrated with TPACK (technological pedagogical content knowledge). [). IOP Publishing.]. *Journal of Physics: Conference Series, 1481*(1), 012133. DOI: 10.1088/1742-6596/1481/1/012133

Putta, A., Paasivaara, M., & Lassenius, C. (2018). Adopting scaled Agile framework (Safe). *Proceedings of the 19th International Conference on Agile Software Development: Companion*, 1-4. https://doi.org/DOI: 10.1145/3234152.3234164

Qadhi, S. (2023). Knowledge Dynamics: Educational Pathways from Theories to Tangible Outcomes. In From Theory of Knowledge Management to Practice. IntechOpen.

Quionero-Candela, J., Sugiyama, M., Schwaighofer, A., & Lawrence, N. D. (Eds.). (2009). *Dataset shift in machine learning*. The MIT Press.

R Core Team. (2023). *R: A language and environment for statistical computing*. R Foundation for Statistical Computing. https://www.r-project.org/

Rafique, Y. (2021). TDD dynamics: Understanding the impact of test-driven development on software quality and productivity. https://doi.org/DOI: 10.32920/ryerson.14661051.v1

Rahmah, S., & Lubis, A. H. (2024). Problem Posing as a Learning Model to Improve Primary School Students' Mathematics Learning Outcomes in Gayo Lues. *Journal of Indonesian Primary School, 1*(4), 93–104. DOI: 10.62945/jips.v1i4.409

Rahmattalabi, A. (2022). Towards Trustworthy and Data-Driven Social Interventions (Doctoral dissertation, UNIVERSITY OF SOUTHERN CALIFORNIA).

Raj, P., Mohapatra, H., Ranjan, R., & Maithili, P. (2025). Innovative strategies for sustainable waste disposal. *Leveraging Urban Computing for Sustainable Urban Development*, 117-144. https://doi.org/DOI: 10.4018/979-8-3373-0761-9.ch006

Rajeev, A., Pati, R. K., Padhi, S. S., & Govindan, K. (2017). Evolution of sustainability in supply chain management: A literature review. *Journal of Cleaner Production, 162*, 299–314. DOI: 10.1016/j.jclepro.2017.05.026

Ralston, M. P., Richey, R. G., & Grawe, S. J. (2017). The past and future of supply chain collaboration: A literature synthesis and call for research. *International Journal of Logistics Management, 28*(2), 508–530. DOI: 10.1108/IJLM-09-2015-0175

Ramanathan, U. (2014). Performance of supply chain collaboration - A simulation study. *Expert Systems with Applications, 41*(1), 210–220. DOI: 10.1016/j.eswa.2013.07.022

Ramaul, L., Ritala, P., & Ruokonen, M. (2024). Creational and conversational AI affordances: How the new breed of chatbots is revolutionizing knowledge industries. *Business Horizons, 67*(5), 615–627. DOI: 10.1016/j.bushor.2024.05.006

Ramesh, B., Abrahamsson, P., Cockburn, A., Lyytinen, K., & Williams, L. (n.d.). Agile software development methods: When and why do they work? *IFIP International Federation for Information Processing, 371-373*. Advance online publication. DOI: 10.1007/0-387-25590-7_24

Ramírez, M. A., & Lizarazo, I. (2025). Geographical perspectives of sustainability: Towards a conceptual framework. *Environmental Development, 53*(101121), 101121. DOI: 10.1016/j.envdev.2024.101121

Rasch, D. (1991). Pressman, R. S.: Software engineering. Grundkurs fur Praktiker. McGraw-hill software, engineering. Hrsg.: dipl.-inform. John-Harry Wieken. McGraw-hill book company GmbH, Hamburg 1989. 302 S., DM 63, 55, ISBN 3–89028–163-X. *Biometrical Journal, 33*(3), 378-378. https://doi.org/DOI: 10.1002/bimj.4710330333

Rashid, A., Rasheed, R., & Amirah, N. A. (2024). Information technology and people involvement in organizational performance through supply chain collaboration. *Journal of Science and Technology Policy Management*, *15*(6), 1560–1576. DOI: 10.1108/JSTPM-12-2022-0217

Reeves, T. C., & Lin, L. (2020). The research we have is not the research we need. *Educational Technology Research and Development*, *68*(4), 1991–2001. DOI: 10.1007/s11423-020-09811-3 PMID: 32837123

Reichheld, F. F. (2003). The One Number You Need to Grow. *Harvard Business Review*. PMID: 14712543

Reichheld, F., & Schefter, P. (2000). E-loyalty: Your Secret Weapon on the Web. *Harvard Business Review*, *78*(4), 105–113.

Renolds, S. (2024). The influence of cultural factors on supply chain integration in multinational corporations. Preprints. https:// doi: DOI: 10.20944/preprints202406.0209.v1

Revati, V. (2024). Integrating constructivism, science education, and technology: An investigation into pedagogical strategies, student engagement, and learning outcomes in the digital age. *International Journal for Research in Applied Science and Engineering Technology*, *12*(12), 1021–1026. DOI: 10.22214/ijraset.2024.65933

Reynolds, B., & Seeger, M. W. (2014). Crisis and emergency risk communication. *Journal of Health Communication*, *19*(1), 11–15. DOI: 10.1080/10810730.2014.889902 PMID: 15764443

Ribeiro, M. T., Singh, S., & Guestrin, C. (2016). "Why should I trust you?": Explaining the predictions of any classifier. In *Proceedings of the 22nd ACM SIGKDD International Conference on Knowledge Discovery and Data Mining* (pp. 1135–1144). Association for Computing Machinery. https://doi.org/DOI: 10.1145/2939672.2939778

Rieke, N., Hancox, J., Li, W., Milletari, F., Roth, H. R., Albarqouni, S., Bakas, S., Galtier, M. N., Landman, B. A., Maier-Hein, K., Ourselin, S., Sheller, M., Summers, R. M., Trask, A., Xu, D., Baust, M., & Cardoso, M. J. (2020). The future of digital health with federated learning. *NPJ Digital Medicine*, *3*(1), 119. DOI: 10.1038/s41746-020-00323-1 PMID: 33015372

Rindfleisch, A. (2020). Transaction cost theory: Past, present, and future. *AMS Review*, *10*(1), 85–97. DOI: 10.1007/s13162-019-00151-x

Rivard, S. (2021). Theory building is neither an art nor a science. It is a craft. *Journal of Information Technology*, *36*(3), 316–328. DOI: 10.1177/0268396220911938

Robertson, B. F., & Radcliffe, D. F. (2009). Impact of CAD tools on creative problem solving in engineering design. *Computer Aided Design*, *41*(3), 136–146. DOI: 10.1016/j.cad.2008.06.007

Robillard, P. N. (2005). Opportunistic problem solving in software engineering. *IEEE Software*, *22*(6), 60–67. DOI: 10.1109/MS.2005.161

Robinson, D. T., Brown, D. G., Parker, D. C., Schreinemachers, P., Janssen, M. A., Huigen, M., Wittmer, H., Gotts, N., Promburom, P., Irwin, E., Berger, T., Gatzweiler, F., & Barnaud, C. (2007). Comparison of empirical methods for building agent-based models in land use science. *Journal of Land Use Science*, *2*(1), 31–55. DOI: 10.1080/17474230701201349

Robinson, P. (2011). Second language task complexity, the Cognition Hypothesis, language learning, and performance. In Robinson, P. (Ed.), *Second language task complexity: Researching the Cognition Hypothesis of language learning and performance* (pp. 3–38). John Benjamins., DOI: 10.1075/tblt.2.05ch1

Rogers, E. M. (2003). *Diffusion of innovations* (5th ed.). Free Press.

Rogers, E. M., Singhal, A., & Quinlan, M. M. (2014). Diffusion of innovations. In *An integrated approach to communication theory and research* (pp. 432–448). Routledge.

Rojas Alcedo, F. E. (2023). *The uniform online control system and optimal management in slot companies*. Federico Villarreal National University. Retrieved from: https://repositorio.unfv.edu.pe/handle/20.500.13084/6919

Rosen, D. (2019). Being in uncertainties: An inquiry-based model leveraging complexity in teaching-learning. [NEJCS]. *Northeast Journal of Complex Systems*, *1*(1), 5. Advance online publication. DOI: 10.22191/nejcs/vol1/iss1/5

Rosyid, A., & Ismawati, D. (2025). Increasing Awareness of Clean and Healthy Lifestyle Patterns Through Problem Solving Learning Models in Early Childhood. *JOYCED: Journal of Early Childhood Education*, *5*(1), 45–56. DOI: 10.14421/joyced.2025.51-04

Rott, B., Specht, B., & Knipping, C. (2021). A descriptive phase model of problem-solving processes. *ZDM Mathematics Education, 53*(4), 737–752. DOI: 10.1007/s11858-021-01244-3

Rouhani, S., Wardley, L. J., & Amin, S. H. (2025). A comprehensive survey into reverse logistics and Closed-Loop Supply Chain aspects to provide analyses and insights for implementation. *Journal of Cleaner Production, 490*, 144743. DOI: 10.1016/j.jclepro.2025.144743

Routroy, S. (2009). Evaluation of supply chain strategies: A case study. *International Journal of Business Performance and Supply Chain Modelling, 1*(4), 290–306. DOI: 10.1504/IJBPSCM.2009.033746

Rouwette, E. A., Vennix, J. A., & Mullekom, T. V. (2002). Group model building effectiveness: A review of assessment studies. *System Dynamics Review, 18*(1), 5–45. DOI: 10.1002/sdr.229

Ruiter, R. A. C., Kessels, L. T. E., Peters, G.-J. Y., & Kok, G. (2014). Sixty years of fear appeal research: Current state of the evidence. *International Journal of Psychology, 49*(2), 63–70. DOI: 10.1002/ijop.12042 PMID: 24811876

Ruuska, H., Otani, N., Kiriyama, S., & Takebayashi, Y. (2008). Creating Multi-Level Reflective Reasoning Models Based on Observation of Social Problem-Solving in Infants. *Frontiers in Artificial Intelligence and Applications, 166*, 100.

Ryan, R. M., & Deci, E. L. (2017). *Self-determination theory: Basic psychological needs in motivation, development, and wellness*. The Guilford Press., DOI: 10.1521/978.14625/28806

Saavedra Najar, R. A., González, L. D., & Abril Teatín, J. A. (2024). Reports and dimensions of corporate sustainability. A bibliometric analysis. *Venezuelan Journal of Management, 29*(108). Advance online publication. DOI: 10.52080/rvgluz.29.108.16

Sağlam, M., & El Montaser, S. (2021). The effect of customer relationship marketing in customer retention and customer acquisition. *International Journal of Commerce and Finance, 7*(1), 191–201.

Sairanen, M., & Aarikka-Stenroos, L. (2024). Low-carbon business models: Review and typology. *Industrial Marketing Management, 123*, 222–250. DOI: 10.1016/j.indmarman.2024.10.001

Sakalauskė, A., & Leonavičiūtė, V. (2022). Strategic analysis of Duolingo language learning platform.

Samal, A., Bhargav, J., Selvakumar, P., Sharma, M., & TC, M. (2025). Measuring Brand Performance With AI Tools. In *Strategic Brand Management in the Age of AI and Disruption* (pp. 279-302). IGI Global Scientific Publishing.

Sarkis, J. (2003). A strategic decision framework for green supply chain management. *Journal of Cleaner Production, 11*(4), 397–409. DOI: 10.1016/S0959-6526(02)00062-8

SAS Institute. (2022). *SAS software* (Version 9.4) [Software]. SAS Institute Inc. https://www.sas.com/en_us/software.html

Sauerbrei, W., Abrahamowicz, M., Altman, D. G., le Cessie, S., & Carpenter, J. (2014). STRengthening analytical thinking for observational studies: The STRATOS initiative. *Statistics in Medicine, 33*(30), 5413–5432. DOI: 10.1002/sim.6265

Saur, J. (2003). Review of "test-driven development: A practical guide by David Astels." Prentice-hall 2003. *Software Engineering Notes, 28*(6), 31. DOI: 10.1145/966221.966666

Saur, J. (2005). Review of "Software development for small teams: A RUP-centric approach by Gary pollice, Liz Augustine, Chris Lowe, and Jas Madhur". Addison-Wesley, 2004, paperback, ISBN 0-321-19950-2. *Software Engineering Notes, 30*(1), 38–38. DOI: 10.1145/1039174.1039209

Savaglio, C., & Fortino, G. (2021). A simulation-driven methodology for IoT data mining based on edge computing. *ACM Transactions on Internet Technology, 21*(2), 1–22. DOI: 10.1145/3402444

Scaratti, G., & Ivaldi, S. (2021). Uniqueness and generalization in organizational psychology: Research as a relational practice. *Frontiers in Psychology, 12*, 638240. DOI: 10.3389/fpsyg.2021.638240 PMID: 33613408

Schaltegger, S., & Burritt, R. (2014). Measuring and managing sustainability performance of supply chains: Review and sustainability supply chain management framework. *Supply Chain Management, 19*(3), 232–241. DOI: 10.1108/SCM-02-2014-0061

Schmid, O., Lisowska Masson, A., & Hirsbrunner, B. (2014). Real-time collaboration through web applications: An introduction to the Toolkit for Web-based Interactive Collaborative Environments (TWICE). *Personal and Ubiquitous Computing, 18*(6), 1201–1211. DOI: 10.1007/s00779-013-0729-0

Schoenfeld, A. H. (1980). Teaching problem-solving skills. *The American Mathematical Monthly, 87*(10), 794–805. DOI: 10.1080/00029890.1980.11995155

Schreiner, M. W., Klimes-Dougan, B., Begnel, E. D., & Cullen, K. R. (2015). Conceptualizing the neurobiology of non-suicidal self-injury from the perspective of the Research Domain Criteria Project. *Neuroscience and Biobehavioral Reviews*, *57*, 381–391.

Schultz, F., Utz, S., & Göritz, A. (2011). Is the medium the message? Perceptions of and reactions to crisis communication via Twitter, blogs and traditional media. *Public Relations Review*, *37*(1), 20–27. DOI: 10.1016/j.pubrev.2010.12.001

Schunk, D. H. (2012). *Learning Theories: An Educational Perspective* (6th ed.). Pearson.

Schwalbe, K. (2015). *Information Technology Project Management*. Cengage Learning.

Seeger, M. W. (2006). Best practices in crisis communication: An expert panel process. *Journal of Applied Communication Research*, *34*(3), 232–244. DOI: 10.1080/00909880600769944

Seielstad, A. M. (2001). Community building as a means of teaching creative, cooperative, and complex problem solving in clinical legal education. *Clinical Law Review*, *8*, 445.

Sellitto, M. A., Pereira, G. M., Borchardt, M., Da Silva, R. I., & Viegas, C. V. (2015). A SCOR-based model for supply chain performance measurement: Application in the footwear industry. *International Journal of Production Research*, *53*(16), 4917–4926. DOI: 10.1080/00207543.2015.1005251

Selvakumar, P., Aradhya, S. G. B., Anute, N., Devi, S., Sharma, M., & Vaissnave, V. (2025). Strategic Collaborations and Partnerships in Entrepreneurship. In *Support Networks for Entrepreneurs: Social Capital and Strategic Collaborations* (pp. 203-232). IGI Global Scientific Publishing. DOI: 10.4018/979-8-3693-9836-4.ch009

Selvakumar, P., Shanthi, M., Pitchiah, R., Sharma, M., Dahake, P. S., & TC, M. (2025b). The Role of Artificial Intelligence in Business Model Innovation: Overview of AI Technologies. *AI-Driven Business Model Innovation*, 219-246.

Selvakumar, P., Dahiya, R., Manjunath, T. C., & Sharma, M. (2025). Carbon Footprint Analysis of Electronic Products. In *Integrated Approaches for Sustainable E-Waste Management* (pp. 215–242). IGI Global Scientific Publishing. DOI: 10.4018/979-8-3693-7383-5.ch008

Selvakumar, P., Satyanarayana, P., Lahoti, Y., Saipogu, L., Sharma, M., & Manjunath, T. C. (2025c). AI Techniques. In *AI Methods for Environmental Protection and Resource Conservation* (pp. 107–138). IGI Global Scientific Publishing. DOI: 10.4018/979-8-3373-3246-8.ch005

Seow, P.-S., Pan, G., & Koh, G. (2019). Examining an experiential learning approach to prepare students for the volatile, uncertain, complex and ambiguous (VUCA) work environment. *International Journal of Management Education*, *17*(1), 62–76. DOI: 10.1016/j.ijme.2018.12.001

Šercar, T. M. (2025). The Connection of Information Science and Psychology in the Case of the Wisdom Paradox-Part Two. *International Journal of English Literature and Social Sciences*, *10*(1), 593296. DOI: 10.22161/ijels.101.4

Serrador, P., & Pinto, J. K. (2015). Does Agile work? A quantitative analysis of Agile project success. *International Journal of Project Management*, *33*(5), 1040–1051. DOI: 10.1016/j.ijproman.2015.01.006

Serrano, N., Hernantes, J., & Gallardo, G. (2014). Service-oriented architecture and legacy systems. *IEEE Software*, *31*(5), 15–19. DOI: 10.1109/MS.2014.125

Seuring, S. (2013). A review of modeling approaches for sustainable supply chain management. *Decision Support Systems*, *54*(4), 1513–1520. DOI: 10.1016/j.dss.2012.05.053

Sevaldson, B. (2022). *Designing complexity: The methodology and practice of systems oriented design*. Common Ground Research Networks. DOI: 10.18848/978-1-86335-262-8/CGP

Shaffer, C. A., Cooper, M. L., Alon, A. J. D., Akbar, M., Stewart, M., Ponce, S., & Edwards, S. H. (2010). Algorithm visualization: The state of the field. *ACM Transactions on Computing Education (TOCE)*, 10(3). *Article*, *9*(3), 1–22. DOI: 10.1145/1821996.1821997

Shafizadeh, H. (2024). Decision-Making Under Uncertainty: How Organizations Adapt to Environmental Changes? *Journal of Resource Management and Decision Engineering*, *3*(1), 4–10. DOI: 10.61838/kman.jrmde.3.1.2

Shang, Y., Jiang, J., Zhang, Y., Zhang, R., & Liu, P. (2024). When does a freemium business model lead to high performance? — A qualitative comparative analysis based on fuzzy sets. *Heliyon*, *10*(3), e25149. Advance online publication. DOI: 10.1016/j.heliyon.2024.e25149 PMID: 38333777

Shapiro, C., & Varian, H. R. (1999). *Information Rules: A Strategic Guide to the Network Economy*. Harvard Business Press.

Shaturaev, J. (2022). Bad management hypotheses are demolishing management practices. Архив научных исследований, 2(1).

Shepherd, D. C., Fronchetti, F., Liu, Y., Hou, D., DeWaters, J., & Small, M. M. (2022). Project-sized scaffolding for software engineering courses. *Proceedings of the First International Workshop on Designing and Running Project-Based Courses in Software Engineering Education*, 27-31. https://doi.org/DOI: 10.1145/3524487.3527362

Sherbrooke, C. C. (1971). An evaluator for the number of operationally ready aircraft in a multilevel supply system. *Operations Research*, *19*(3), 618–635. DOI: 10.1287/opre.19.3.618

Sheth, J. N., Newman, B. I., & Gross, B. L. (1991). Why we buy what we buy: A theory of consumption values. *Journal of Business Research*, *22*(2), 159–170.

Shih, J. L., Shih, B. J., Shih, C. C., Su, H. Y., & Chuang, C. W. (2010). The influence of collaboration styles to children's cognitive performance in digital problem-solving game "William Adventure": A comparative case study. *Computers & Education*, *55*(3), 982–993. DOI: 10.1016/j.compedu.2010.04.009

Shin, Y., Kim, D., & Song, D. (2019). Types and timing of scaffolding to promote meaningful peer interaction and increase learning performance in computer-supported collaborative learning environments. *Journal of Educational Computing Research*, *58*(3), 640–661. DOI: 10.1177/0735633119877134

Shmueli, G., & Koppius, O. R. (2011). Predictive analytics in information systems research. *Management Information Systems Quarterly*, *35*(3), 553–572. DOI: 10.2307/23042796

Sholihah, T. M., & Lastariwati, B. (2020). Problem based learning to increase competence of critical thinking and problem solving. [EduLearn]. *Journal of Education and Learning*, *14*(1), 148–154.

Shortt, M., Tilak, S., Kuznetcova, I., Martens, B., & Akinkuolie, B. (2021). Gamification in mobile-assisted language learning: A systematic review of Duolingo literature from public release of 2012 to early 2020. *Computer Assisted Language Learning*, *36*(3), 517–554. DOI: 10.1080/09588221.2021.1933540

Shriberg, M., & Harris, K. (2012). Building sustainability change management and leadership skills in students: Lessons learned from "Sustainability and the Campus" at the University of Michigan. *Journal of Environmental Studies and Sciences*, *2*(2), 154–164. DOI: 10.1007/s13412-012-0073-0

Silver, E. A. (2013). Research on teaching mathematical problem solving: Some underrepresented themes and needed directions. In *Teaching and learning mathematical problem solving* (pp. 247–266). Routledge. DOI: 10.4324/9780203063545-22

Silverman, C. (2015). *Verification handbook: An ultimate guideline on digital age sourcing for emergency coverage*. European Journalism Centre.

Simamora, R. E., Sidabutar, D. R., & Surya, E. (2017). Improving learning activity and students' problem solving skill through problem based learning (PBL) in junior high school. [IJSBAR]. *International Journal of Sciences, Basic and Applied Research*, *33*(2), 321–331.

Simatupang, T. M., & Sridharan, R. (2005). The collaboration index: A measure for supply chain collaboration. *International Journal of Physical Distribution & Logistics Management*, *35*(1), 44–62. DOI: 10.1108/09600030510577421

Simatupang, T. M., Wright, A. C., & Sridharan, R. (2004). Applying the theory of constraints to supply chain collaboration. *Supply Chain Management*, *9*(1), 57–70. DOI: 10.1108/13598540410517584

Simmons, R. (2018). Gemba Kaizen: A commonsense approach to a continuous improvement strategy, 2nd ed. *Quality Management Journal, 25*(1), 65-66. https://doi.org/DOI: 10.1080/10686967.2018.1404374

Simon, H. A. (1977). *The New Science of Management Decision*. Prentice-Hall, Inc.

Simon, H. A. (1978). *Information-processing theory of human problem solving*. Erlbaum.

Singh, K. (2021). A phenomenological study of software developers participating in daily stand-up meetings in Agile teams. *Proceedings of the 2021 AERA Annual Meeting*. https://doi.org/DOI: 10.3102/1683950

Singh, R. K. (2025). Exploring the impact of green supply chain strategies and sustainable practices on circular supply chains. *Benchmarking*, *32*(4), 1387–1409. DOI: 10.1108/BIJ-11-2023-0801

Šobak, P. (2023). *The freemium business model: Don't walk away, run*. Better Proposals.

Sobieraj, D. M., Wheeler, K., Salvo, M., & Smith, M. (2024). Prescription for curricular revision: Application of design thinking principles. *American Journal of Pharmaceutical Education*, *88*(12), 101325. DOI: 10.1016/j.ajpe.2024.101325 PMID: 39586353

Soosay, C. A., & Hyland, P. (2015). A decade of supply chain collaboration and directions for future research. *Supply Chain Management*, *20*(6), 613–630. DOI: 10.1108/SCM-06-2015-0217

Spinellis, D. (2006). Review of "Sustainable software development: An Agile perspective by Kevin Tate," Addison-Wesley professional, 2005, $39.99, ISBN: 0321286081. *Queue, 4*(10), 49. https://doi.org/DOI: 10.1145/1189276.1189292

Spinuzzi, C. (2023). What is a workplace? Principles for bounding case studies of genres, processes, objects, and organizations. *Written Communication*, *40*(4), 1027–1069. DOI: 10.1177/07410883231185875

Spiro, R. J., Klautke, H. A., Cheng, C., & Gaunt, A. (2017). Cognitive flexibility theory and the assessment of 21st century skills. In Secolsky, C., & Denison, B. (Eds.), *Handbook on Measurement, Assessment, and Evaluation in Higher Education* (pp. 631–637). Routledge., DOI: 10.4324/9781315709307-50

Squire, B., Vachon, S., & Klassen, R. D. (2006). Extending green practices across the supply chainthe impact of upstream and downstream integration. *International Journal of Operations & Production Management*, *26*(7), 795–821. DOI: 10.1108/01443570610672248

Stank, T., Dittman, J. P., Burnette, M., & Autry, C. W. (2015). *The Supply Chain Game Changers: Applications and Best Practices that are Shaping the Future of Supply Chain Management*, Free Press.

Stanley, P. D., & Clinton, J. R. (2024). *Connecting: The mentoring relationships you need to succeed in life*. NavPress.

Starbird, K. (2014). *Disinformation's spread: Bots, trolls and all of us*. Boston University Center for Research on Media, Technology and Health.

Starbird, K., & Palen, L. (2011). Voluntweeters: Self-organizing by digital volunteers in times of crisis. *Proceedings of the SIGCHI Conference on Human Factors in Computing Systems*, 1071–1080. https://doi.org/DOI: 10.1145/1978942.1979102

Stein, S. (2021). Reimagining global citizenship education for a volatile, uncertain, complex, and ambiguous (VUCA) world. *Globalisation, Societies and Education*, *19*(4), 482–495. DOI: 10.1080/14767724.2021.1904212

Ste-Marie, D. M., Lelievre, N., & St. Germain, L. (2020). Revisiting the applied model for the use of observation: A review of articles spanning 2011–2018. *Research Quarterly for Exercise and Sport*, *91*(4), 594–617. DOI: 10.1080/02701367.2019.1693489

Stephens, M., & Rosenberg, D. (2003). Embracing change (Embrace people, manage change). *Extreme Programming Refactored: The Case Against XP*, 293-310. https://doi.org/DOI: 10.1007/978-1-4302-0810-5_13

Stephens, K. K., Malone, P. C., & Bailey, C. M. (2005). Communicating with stakeholders during a crisis: Evaluating message strategies. *Journal of Business Communication*, *42*(4), 390–419. DOI: 10.1177/0021943605279057

Sterman, J. D. (2000). *Business dynamics: Systems thinking and modeling for a complex world*. Irwin/McGraw-Hill.

Stern, T. V. (2020). Lean and Agile project management: International influences. *Lean and Agile Project Management*, 225-230. https://doi.org/DOI: 10.4324/9780429343414-18

Stonebraker, M., & Ilyas, I. F. (2018). Data integration: The current status and the way forward. *A Quarterly Bulletin of the Computer Society of the IEEE Technical Committee on Data Engineering*, *41*(2), 3–9. https://cs.uwaterloo.ca/~ilyas/papers/StonebrakerIEEE2018.pdf

Subrahmanyam, S. (2025). Data Governance and Privacy in Smart Cities. In Sharma, A., Mansotra, V., & Singh, P. (Eds.), *Citizen-Centric Artificial Intelligence for Smart Cities* (pp. 433–456). IGI Global Scientific Publishing., DOI: 10.4018/979-8-3693-7832-8.ch017

Subrahmanyam, S. (2025). Experimental and Simulation-Based Research: Designing Controlled Experiments for Maritime Training and Safety. In Mobo, F. (Ed.), *Research Methods for Advancing the Maritime Industry* (pp. 145–170). IGI Global Scientific Publishing., DOI: 10.4018/979-8-3373-1052-7.ch006

Subrahmanyam, S. (2025). Introduction and Fundamentals of Qualitative Research in Business. In Segura, L., Vasconcelos, A., & Slomski, V. (Eds.), *Exploring Qualitative Research in Business: Approaches, Strategies, And Methods* (pp. 1–28). IGI Global Scientific Publishing., DOI: 10.4018/979-8-3693-7698-0.ch001

Subramanian, N., & Gunasekaran, A. (2015). Cleaner supply-chain management practices for twenty-first-century organizational competitiveness: Practice-performance framework and research propositions. *International Journal of Production Economics*, *164*, 216–233. DOI: 10.1016/j.ijpe.2014.12.002

Sugiyama, K., Ladge, J. J., & Dokko, G. (2024). Stable anchors and dynamic evolution: A paradox theory of career identity maintenance and change. *Academy of Management Review*, *49*(1), 135–154. DOI: 10.5465/amr.2020.0351

Sunnemark, F., Lundqvist Westin, W., Al Saad, T., & Assmo, P. (2024). Exploring barriers and facilitators to knowledge transfer and learning processes through a cross-departmental collaborative project in a municipal organization. *The Learning Organization*, *31*(3), 358–374. DOI: 10.1108/TLO-01-2023-0003

Supply Chain Council. (2012). *Supply Chain Operations Reference Model (SCOR)* (Version 11.0). APICS. https://www.apics.org/apics-for-individuals/apics-magazine-home/scor-model

Suresh, M., Antony, J., Nair, G., & Garza-Reyes, J. A. (2023). Lean-sustainability assessment framework development: Evidence from the construction industry. *Total Quality Management & Business Excellence*, *34*(15-16), 2046–2081. DOI: 10.1080/14783363.2023.2222088

Surya, E., & Putri, F. A. (2017). Improving mathematical problem-solving ability and self-confidence of high school students through contextual learning model. *Journal on Mathematics Education*, *8*(1), 85–94.

Suskie, L. (2018). *Assessing student learning: A common sense guide* (3rd ed.). Jossey-Bass.

Sutton, R. S., & Barto, A. G. (2018). Temporal-difference learning. *Reinforcement learning: an introduction*, 131-132.

Swain, M., & Lapkin, S. (1998). Interaction and second language learning: Two adolescent French immersion students working together. *Modern Language Journal*, *82*(3), 320–337. DOI: 10.1111/j.1540-4781.1998.tb01209.x

Sweeney, L. (2002). k-anonymity: A model for protecting privacy. *International Journal of Uncertainty, Fuzziness and Knowledge-based Systems*, *10*(5), 557–570. DOI: 10.1142/S0218488502001648

Sweller, J. (1988). Cognitive load during problem solving: Effects on learning. *Cognitive Science*, *12*(2), 257–285. DOI: 10.1207/s15516709cog1202_4

Swoyer, C. (1991). Structural representation and surrogative reasoning. *Synthese*, *87*(3), 449–508. DOI: 10.1007/BF00499820

Tachibana, S., & Tsuda, K. (2022). A study on analysis model for influence of expressions from others on taste expressions in word-of-Mouth data of cooking recipe website. *Procedia Computer Science*, *207*, 1500–1508. DOI: 10.1016/j.procs.2022.09.207

Taconis, R., Ferguson-Hessler, M. G., & Broekkamp, H. (2001). Teaching science problem solving: An overview of experimental work. *Journal of Research in Science Teaching*, *38*(4), 442–468. DOI: 10.1002/tea.1013

Taggar, S., & Brown, T. C. (2001). Problem-solving team behaviors: Development and validation of BOS and a hierarchical factor structure. *Small Group Research*, *32*(6), 698–726. DOI: 10.1177/104649640103200602

Tähtinen, L. (2025). Navigating adverse futures for resilience: Expanding understanding of future crises and their impacts in the built environment.

Taivainen, A. (2021). Alternative agency, observations of changing architecture and futures studies.

Tajbakhsh, A., & Hassini, E. (2015). Performance measurement of sustainable supply chains: A review and research questions. *International Journal of Productivity and Performance Management*, *64*(6), 744–783. DOI: 10.1108/IJPPM-03-2013-0056

Tam, K. Y., & Ho, S. Y. (2005). Web personalization as a persuasion strategy: An elaboration likelihood model perspective. *Information Systems Research*, *16*(3), 271–291.

Tariq, M. U. (2024). Navigating the personalization pathway: Implementing adaptive learning technologies in higher education. In *Adaptive Learning Technologies for Higher Education* (pp. 265–291). IGI Global. DOI: 10.4018/979-8-3693-3641-0.ch012

Taylor, K. L., & Colet, N. R. (2023). Making the shift from faculty development to educational development: A conceptual framework grounded in practice. In *Building teaching capacities in higher education* (pp. 139–167). Routledge. DOI: 10.4324/9781003443346-10

Teague, R. G. (2022). *How an effective knowledge management program supports critical tacit knowledge retention within a higher education institution: A qualitative intrinsic case study*. Northcentral University.

Telzrow, C. F., McNamara, K., & Hollinger, C. L. (2000). Fidelity of problem-solving implementation and relationship to student performance. *School Psychology Review*, *29*(3), 443–461. DOI: 10.1080/02796015.2000.12086029

Thaler, R. H. (1980). Toward a positive theory of consumer choice. *Journal of Economic Behavior & Organization*, *1*(1), 39–60. DOI: 10.1016/0167-2681(80)90051-7

Thomas, A. (2024). Digitally transforming the organization through knowledge management: A socio-technical system (STS) perspective. *European Journal of Innovation Management, 27*(9), 437–460. DOI: 10.1108/EJIM-02-2024-0114

Thomas, N. J., Baral, R., Crocco, O. S., & Mohanan, S. (2023). A framework for gamification in the metaverse era: How designers envision gameful experience. *Technological Forecasting and Social Change, 193*, 122544. DOI: 10.1016/j.techfore.2023.122544

Thomke, S., & Fujimoto, T. (2000). The effect of "front-loading" problem-solving on product development performance. *Journal of Product Innovation Management, 17*(2), 128–142. DOI: 10.1111/1540-5885.1720128

Thompson, J. R. (2009). *Empirical model building*. John Wiley & Sons.

Tian, Y., & Ha, D. (2022, April). Modern evolution strategies for creativity: Fitting concrete images and abstract concepts. In International conference on computational intelligence in music, sound, art and design (part of evostar) (pp. 275-291). Cham: Springer International Publishing.

Tilly, W. D. (2008). The evolution of school psychology to science-based practice: Problem solving and the three-tiered model. *Best practices in school psychology V, 1*, 17-36.

Ting, L. (2024). Prognosticating Parsimony: An Ebullient Ensemble Approach to Predictive Modeling in Artificial Intelligence.

Todd, A. W., Horner, R. H., Newton, J. S., Algozzine, R. F., Algozzine, K. M., & Frank, J. L. (2011). Effects of team-initiated problem solving on decision making by schoolwide behavior support teams. *Journal of Applied School Psychology, 27*(1), 42–59. DOI: 10.1080/15377903.2011.540510

Todorov, V., & Marinova, D. (2011). Modelling sustainability. *Mathematics and Computers in Simulation, 81*(7), 1397–1408. DOI: 10.1016/j.matcom.2010.05.022

Topol, E. J. (2019). High-performance medicine: The convergence of human and artificial intelligence. *Nature Medicine, 25*(1), 44–56. DOI: 10.1038/s41591-018-0300-7 PMID: 30617339

Touboulic, A., & Walker, H. (2015). Theories in sustainable supply chain management: A structured literature review. *International Journal of Physical Distribution & Logistics Management, 45*(1/2), 16–42. DOI: 10.1108/IJPDLM-05-2013-0106

Treffinger, D. J., & Isaksen, S. G. (2005). Creative problem solving: The history, development, and implications for gifted education and talent development. *Gifted Child Quarterly*, *49*(4), 342–353. DOI: 10.1177/001698620504900407

Trilling, B., & Fadel, C. (2009). *21st Century Skills: Learning for life in our times*. Jossey-Bass.

Tripathi, S., Muhr, D., Brunner, M., Jodlbauer, H., Dehmer, M., & Emmert-Streib, F. (2021). Ensuring the robustness and reliability of data-driven knowledge discovery models in production and manufacturing. *Frontiers in Artificial Intelligence*, *4*, 576892. DOI: 10.3389/frai.2021.576892 PMID: 34195608

Trustbusting in Japan. (1981). Cartels and government-business cooperation. *Harvard Law Review*, *94*(5), 1064. DOI: 10.2307/1340689

Tsai, C. A., Song, M. Y. W., Lo, Y. F., & Lo, C. C. (2023). Design thinking with constructivist learning increases the learning motivation and wicked problem-solving capability—An empirical research in Taiwan. *Thinking Skills and Creativity*, *50*, 101385. DOI: 10.1016/j.tsc.2023.101385

Tucker, A. L., & Edmondson, A. C. (2002). Managing routine exceptions: a model of nurse problem solving behavior. In *Advances in health care management* (pp. 87–113). Emerald Group Publishing Limited. DOI: 10.1016/S1474-8231(02)03007-0

Tuminaro, J., & Redish, E. F. (2007). Elements of a cognitive model of physics problem solving: Epistemic games. *Physical Review Special Topics. Physics Education Research*, *3*(2), 020101. DOI: 10.1103/PhysRevSTPER.3.020101

Turnbull, K. P., & Justice, L. M. (2012). *Language development from theory to practice* (2nd ed.). Pearson.

Tyrväinen, O., & Karjaluoto, H. (2024). Willingness to pay for freemium services: Addressing the differences between monetization strategies. *International Journal of Information Management*, *77*, 102787.

Tzuo, T., & Weisert, G. (2018). *Subscribed: Why the subscription model will be your company's future—and what to do about it*. Portfolio/Penguin.

Ulmer, R. R., Sellnow, T. L., & Seeger, M. W. (2018). *Effective crisis communication: Moving from crisis to opportunity* (4th ed.). Sage.

UNESCO. (2022). *Reimagining our futures together: A new social contract for education*. UNESCO Publishing.

Vacca, A., Di Sorbo, A., Visaggio, C. A., & Canfora, G. (2021). A systematic literature review of blockchain and smart contract development: Techniques, tools, and open challenges. *Journal of Systems and Software, 174*, 110891. DOI: 10.1016/j.jss.2020.110891

Vaishnavi, V., & Suresh, M. (2020). Modelling of readiness factors for the implementation of Lean Six Sigma in healthcare organizations. *International Journal of Lean Six Sigma, 11*(4), 597–633. DOI: 10.1108/IJLSS-12-2017-0146

Vallon, R., Da Silva Estácio, B. J., Prikladnicki, R., & Grechenig, T. (2018). Systematic literature review on Agile practices in global software development. *Information and Software Technology, 96*, 161–180. DOI: 10.1016/j.infsof.2017.12.004

Van Dijck, J., Poell, T., & de Waal, M. (2018). *The platform society: Public values in a connective world.* Oxford University Press. DOI: 10.1093/oso/9780190889760.001.0001

Van Rossum, G., & Drake, F. L. (2009). *Python 3 reference manual.* CreateSpace. https://docs.python.org/3/reference/

Veale, M., Van Kleek, M., & Binns, R. (2018, April). Fairness and accountability design needs for algorithmic support in high-stakes public sector decision-making. In *Proceedings of the 2018 chi conference on human factors in computing systems* (pp. 1-14). DOI: 10.1145/3173574.3174014

Vedovelli, C. (2022). Learning environments that enhance students' cognitive functioning. *Form@re - Open Journal Per La Formazione in Rete, 22*(1), 322–339. https://doi.org/DOI: 10.36253/form-12606

Veil, S. R., Buehner, T., & Palenchar, M. J. (2011). A work-in-process literature review: Incorporating social media in risk and crisis communication. *Journal of Contingencies and Crisis Management, 19*(2), 110–122. DOI: 10.1111/j.1468-5973.2011.00639.x

Velázquez-Vargas, C. A., Daw, N. D., & Taylor, J. A. (2024). The role of training variability for model-based and model-free learning of an arbitrary visuomotor mapping. *PLoS Computational Biology, 20*(9), e1012471. DOI: 10.1371/journal.pcbi.1012471 PMID: 39331685

Venkatesh, V., & Bala, H. (2008). Technology acceptance model 3 and a research agenda on interventions. *Decision Sciences, 39*(2), 273–315.

Venkatesh, V., Morris, M. G., Davis, G. B., & Davis, F. D. (2003). User acceptance of information technology: Toward a unified view. *Management Information Systems Quarterly*, •••, 425–478.

Venkatesh, V., Thong, J. Y., & Xu, X. (2012). Consumer acceptance and use of information technology: Extending the unified theory of acceptance and use of technology. *Management Information Systems Quarterly*, •••, 157–178.

Verma, S., & Gustafsson, A. (2020). Investigating the emerging COVID-19 research trends in the field of business and management: A bibliometric analysis approach. *Journal of Business Research, 118*, 253–261. DOI: 10.1016/j.jbusres.2020.06.057 PMID: 32834211

Verschaffel, L., & De Corte, E. (1993). A decade of research on word problem solving in Leuven: Theoretical, methodological, and practical outcomes. *Educational Psychology Review*, *5*(3), 239–256. DOI: 10.1007/BF01323046

Vetrivel, S. C., Vidhyapriya, P., & Arun, V. P. (2024). The role of AI in transforming assessment practices in education. In Keeley, K. (Ed.), *AI Applications and Strategies in Teacher Education* (pp. 43–70). IGI Global Scientific Publishing., DOI: 10.4018/979-8-3693-5443-8.ch003

Videla-Reyes, R., & Aguayo, C. (2022). Pedagogy of uncertainty: Laying down a path in walking with STEAM. *Pacific Journal of Technology Enhanced Learning*, *4*(1), 29–30. DOI: 10.24135/pjtel.v4i1.147

Villacampa-Porta, J., Coronado-Vaca, M., & Garrido-Merchán, E. C. (2025). Impact of EU non-financial reporting regulation on Spanish companies' environmental disclosure: A cutting-edge natural language processing approach. *Environmental Sciences Europe*, *37*(1), 29. Advance online publication. DOI: 10.1186/s12302-025-01067-z

Visconti, G., & Zubizarreta, J. R. (2018). Handling limited overlap in observational studies with cardinality matching. *Observational Studies*, *4*(1), 217–249. DOI: 10.1353/obs.2018.0012

Vogel, B., Džuverović, N., Tripathi, S., Kušić, K., Zapata, M. L., Ramachandran, S., Dhungana, N., & Taithe, B. (2024). Upholding Hierarchies of Knowledge Production: Mundane Obstacles to Global International Relations. *International Studies Perspectives*, •••, ekae025. DOI: 10.1093/isp/ekae025

Voigt, P., & Von dem Bussche, A. (2017). The eu general data protection regulation (gdpr). *A practical guide, 1st ed., Cham: Springer International Publishing, 10*(3152676), 10-5555.

Von Ahn, L., & Hacker, S. (2020). Building a Billion-User Product Without Selling Your Soul. *Harvard Business Review*, *98*(6), 80–89.

Vygotsky, L. S. (1978). *Mind in society: The development of higher psychological processes*. Harvard University Press.

Wahyuni, S., Indrawati, I., Sudarti, S., & Suana, W. (2017). Developing science process skills and problemsolving abilities based on outdoor learning in junior high school. *Jurnal Pendidikan IPA Indonesia*, *6*(1), 158–162. DOI: 10.15294/jpii.v6i1.6849

Walker, H., Miemczyk, J., Johnsen, T., & Spencer, R. (2012). Sustainable procurement: Past, present and future. *Journal of Purchasing and Supply Management*, *18*(4), 201–206. DOI: 10.1016/j.pursup.2012.11.003

Wang, D., Han, H., Zhan, Z., Xu, J., Liu, Q., & Ren, G. (2015). A problem solving oriented intelligent tutoring system to improve students' acquisition of basic computer skills. *Computers & Education*, *81*, 102–112. DOI: 10.1016/j.compedu.2014.10.003

Wang, H., Long, Z., Chen, J., Guo, Y., & Wang, A. (2023). Collaborative decision-making in supply chain management: A review and bibliometric analysis. *Cogent Engineering*, *10*(1), 2196823. DOI: 10.1080/23311916.2023.2196823

Wang, Q., Zhao, N., Wu, J., & Zhu, Q. (2019). Optimal pricing and inventory policies with reference price effect and loss-averse customers. *Omega*, *99*, 102174. DOI: 10.1016/j.omega.2019.102174

Watson, R. A., Hornby, G. S., & Pollack, J. B. (1998, September). Modeling building-block interdependency. In *International Conference on Parallel Problem Solving from Nature* (pp. 97-106). Berlin, Heidelberg: Springer Berlin Heidelberg.

Wawak, S. (2024). Enhancing project quality through effective team management. *International Journal of Information Systems and Project Management*, *12*(2), 50–67. DOI: 10.12821/ijispm120203

Weiss, R. L., & Heyman, R. E. (2004). Couples observational research: An impertinent, critical overview. *Couple observational coding systems*, 11-25.

Weisz, E., Herold, D. M., Ostern, N. K., Payne, R., & Kummer, S. (2024). Artificial intelligence (AI) for supply chain collaboration: Implications on information sharing and trust. *Online Information Review*, *49*(1), 164–181. DOI: 10.1108/OIR-02-2024-0083

Whang, J. B., Song, J. H., Choi, B., & Lee, J. H. (2021). The effect of Augmented Reality on purchase intention of beauty products: The roles of consumers' control. *Journal of Business Research*, *133*, 275–284.

Wigfield, A., & Eccles, J. S. (2002). The development of competence beliefs, expectancies for success and achievement values from childhood through adolescence. In Wigfield, A., & Eccles, J. S. (Eds.), *Development of Achievement Motivation* (pp. 91–120). Academic Press., DOI: 10.1016/B978-012750053-9/50006-1

Wilczenski, F. L., Bontrager, T., Ventrone, P., & Correia, M. (2001). Observing collaborative problem-solving processes and outcomes. *Psychology in the Schools, 38*(3), 269–281. DOI: 10.1002/pits.1017

Wilkinson, M. D., Dumontier, M., Aalbersberg, I. J., Appleton, G., Axton, M., Baak, A., Blomberg, N., Boiten, J.-W., da Silva Santos, L. B., Bourne, P. E., Bouwman, J., Brookes, A. J., Clark, T., Crosas, M., Dillo, I., Dumon, O., Edmunds, S., Evelo, C. T., Finkers, R., & Mons, B. (2016). The FAIR Guiding Principles for scientific data management and stewardship. *Scientific Data, 3*(1), 160018. DOI: 10.1038/sdata.2016.18 PMID: 26978244

Willis, G. B. (2005). *Cognitive interviewing: A tool for improving questionnaire design*. SAGE Publications. DOI: 10.4135/9781412983655

Wilson, F., & McCarthy, J. (2010). The Freemium Model in Mobile Apps. *Mobile Business Review, 12*(3), 89–103.

Wilson, M., & Goffnett, S. (2022). Reverse logistics: Understanding end-of-life product management. *Business Horizons, 65*(5), 643–655. DOI: 10.1016/j.bushor.2021.10.005

Witten, I. H., Frank, E., & Hall, M. A. (2016). *Data mining: Practical machine learning tools and techniques* (4th ed.). Morgan Kaufmann.

Wong, C. W., Sancha, C., & Thomsen, C. G. (2017). A national culture perspective in the efficacy of supply chain integration practices. *International Journal of Production Economics, 193*, 554–565. DOI: 10.1016/j.ijpe.2017.08.015

Wood-Harper, T. (2021). Emerging EdTechs amidst the COVID-19 pandemic: Cases in higher education institutions. In *Fostering communication and learning with underutilized technologies in higher education* (pp. 93–107). IGI Global. DOI: 10.4018/978-1-7998-4846-2.ch007

Wu, J., & Or, C. K. (2025). Position Paper: Towards Open Complex Human-AI Agents Collaboration System for Problem-Solving and Knowledge Management. arXiv preprint arXiv:2505.00018.

Xia, J., Li, H., & He, Z. (2023). The effect of blockchain technology on supply chain collaboration: A case study of Lenovo. *Systems, 11*(6), 299. DOI: 10.3390/systems11060299

Yang, Z., Liu, Z., Zhang, J., Lu, C., Tai, J., Zhong, T., . . . Liu, T. (2024). Analyzing nobel prize literature with large language models. arXiv preprint arXiv:2410.18142.

Yazo-Cabuya, E. J., Ibeas, A., & Herrera-Cuartas, J. A. (2024). Integration of sustainability into risk management and operational excellence using the VIKOR method, considering comparisons between multi-criteria decision-making methods. *Sustainability (Basel)*, *16*(11), 4585. DOI: 10.3390/su16114585

Yildiz Çankaya, S., & Sezen, B. (2019). Effects of green supply chain management practices on sustainability performance. *Journal of Manufacturing Technology Management*, *30*(1), 98–121. DOI: 10.1108/JMTM-03-2018-0099

Yin, R. K. (2014). *Case study research: Design and methods* (5th ed.). SAGE Publications.

Yin, R. K. (2017). *Case study research and applications: Design and methods* (6th ed.). SAGE Publications.

Zarrabeitia-Bilbao, E., Jaca-Madariaga, M., Rio-Belver, R.-M., & Alvarez-Meaza, I. (2023). From the Sustainable Development Goals to Industry, Innovation and Sustainable Infrastructure: Perspectives from the Digital Sphere. *Environment, Development and Sustainability*, *27*(4), 9407–9425. DOI: 10.1007/s10668-023-04288-5

Zeithaml, V. A. (1988). Consumer perceptions of price, quality, and value: A means-end model and synthesis of evidence. *Journal of Marketing*, *52*(3), 2–22.

Zhang, A. G., Tang, X., Oney, S., & Chen, Y. (2024). CFlow: Supporting semantic flow analysis of students' code in programming problems at scale. *arXiv*. https://doi.org//arXiv.2404.10089DOI: 10.1145/3657604.3662025

Zhang, W., Li, Q., Dai, X., Chen, J., Du, K., Zhang, W., Liu, W., Wang, Y., Tang, R., & Yu, Y. (2025). NL-Debugging: Exploiting natural language as an intermediate representation for code debugging. *arXiv preprint arXiv:2505.15356*. https://doi.org//arXiv.2505.15356DOI: 10.18653/v1/2025.emnlp-main.80

Zhang, R., Cao, L., Wang, L., Wang, L., Wang, J., Xu, N., & Luo, J. (2024). Assessing the relationship between urban park spatial features and physical activity levels in Residents: A spatial analysis Utilizing drone remote sensing. *Ecological Indicators*, *166*, 112520. DOI: 10.1016/j.ecolind.2024.112520

Zhang, W., Liu, Y., Dong, Y., He, W., Yao, S., Xu, Z., & Mu, Y. (2023). How we learn social norms: A three-stage model for social norm learning. *Frontiers in Psychology*, *14*, 1153809. DOI: 10.3389/fpsyg.2023.1153809 PMID: 37333598

Zhang, Y. (2024). Application of Algorithm Visualization Techniques in Teaching Computer Data Structure Course. *Applied Mathematics and Nonlinear Sciences*, *9*(1), 20240788. Advance online publication. DOI: 10.2478/amns-2024-0788

Zhang, Y. (2024). Cultivating a culture of innovation: The impact of leadership style on employee well-being and organizational creativity. *International Journal of Global Economics and Management*, *2*(1), 202–210. DOI: 10.62051/ijgem.v2n1.26

Zhao, Z. (2024). Theoretical and practical exploration of work-based learning curriculum with a case study. Vocation, Technology & Education, 1(1).

Zhao, B., Rubinstein, B. I., Gemmell, J., & Han, J. (2012). A Bayesian approach to discovering truth from conflicting sources for data integration. *Proceedings of the VLDB Endowment International Conference on Very Large Data Bases*, *5*(6), 550–561. DOI: 10.14778/2168651.2168656

Zhao, X., Salako, K., Strigini, L., Robu, V., & Flynn, D. (2020). Assessing safety-critical systems from operational testing: A study on autonomous vehicles. *Information and Software Technology*, *128*, 106393. DOI: 10.1016/j.infsof.2020.106393

Zheng, A., Casari, A., & Fawcett, T. (2018). *Feature engineering for machine learning: Principles and techniques for data scientists*. O'Reilly Media.

Zimmerman, B. J. (2002). Becoming a self-regulated learner: An overview. *Theory into Practice*, *41*(2), 64–70. DOI: 10.1207/s15430421tip4102_2

Zingales, F. G., & Hockerts, K. (2003). Balanced scorecard and sustainability: Examples from literature and practice. Working paper: Center for Management and Environmental Resources, Fontainebleau: INSEAD, 1-15.

Zook, M., Graham, M., Shelton, T., & Gorman, S. (2010). Volunteered geographic information and crowdsourcing disaster relief: A crowdsourced mapping example with OpenStreetMap, Haiti earthquake. *Geomatica*, *64*(1), 69–88.

Zubari, H., & Sherman, S. (2024, May). Unlocking Innovation Potential: A Pragmatic Approach to Overcoming Barriers and Fostering Collaboration. In SPE Gas & Oil Technology Showcase and Conference (p. D021S017R001). SPE. DOI: 10.2118/219106-MS

About the Contributors

Shalin Hai-Jew works for county government. Prior, she has worked in higher education in the U.S. and stateside for decades. She has worked as tenured faculty, newspaper advisor, course developer and instructional designer, grant writer, and researcher. She has B.A.s in English and psychology, an MA in English (from the University of Washington in Seattle), and an Ed.D. in Educational Leadership with a focus on public administration and online learning (from Seattle University). She has received several scholarships from multiple institutions of higher education. She has edited over 25 nonfiction educational books and authored a dozen.

***

Nitika Malik is a dedicated academic and researcher with a keen interest in emerging technologies, sustainable innovation, and interdisciplinary education. Her work focuses on the transformative role of artificial intelligence, digital systems, and responsible business practices in reshaping contemporary industries and societal frameworks. Nitika has contributed to numerous scholarly publications and book chapters that explore themes such as energy storage technologies, AI-driven strategic planning, and the integration of ethical leadership in modern enterprises. Her research reflects a commitment to bridging the gap between technological advancement and human-centered development. With a background in science and innovation management, she combines technical expertise with critical analysis to address pressing global challenges. Nitika is passionate about fostering knowledge that empowers educators, policymakers, and professionals to make informed, ethical, and sustainable decisions. She continues to collaborate with academic institutions and industry experts to advance impactful research and thought leadership in her field.

Rishi Chaudhry is a respected academic and researcher known for his expertise in management, strategic leadership, and organizational development. As a faculty member at Maharshi Dayanand University, he has played a vital role in advancing interdisciplinary research and innovative teaching methodologies. His academic contributions span areas such as corporate strategy, entrepreneurship, business ethics, and digital transformation in management practices. Prof. Chaudhry has authored and co-authored several research papers and book chapters, contributing valuable insights into how organizations can adapt to emerging global challenges through ethical leadership and data-driven strategies. In addition to his scholarly work, he is deeply committed to academic mentorship, guiding numerous postgraduate and doctoral students toward impactful research outcomes. Known for his analytical depth and practical orientation, Prof. Rishi Chaudhry remains actively engaged in academic collaborations, curriculum development, and institutional capacity building. His work continues to influence both academic and professional circles within the field of business and management.

Ashraf Alam currently holds the position of Research Faculty at the Centre of Excellence in Public Policy, Sustainability and ESG Research, housed within the Faculty of Law and Policy Studies at Alliance University, Bangalore. Renowned for his transdisciplinary acumen spanning education, technology, and policy studies, Dr. Alam has been distinguished as one of the World's Top 2% Scientists by Stanford University and Elsevier, an accolade that highlights the breadth and depth of his scholarly impact. His prolific academic output includes over fifty SCOPUS-indexed publications and more than one hundred conference presentations at esteemed national and international academic forums. His educational trajectory reflects both depth and versatility: a Ph.D. in Education from the Indian Institute of Technology (IIT) Kharagpur, an M.Ed. with a concentration in Mathematics Education, and a B.S. in Computer Science from the University of Delhi. He also holds postgraduate degrees in Public Administration (M.A.) and Mathematics (M.Sc.), supplemented by a suite of postgraduate diplomas in Higher Education, Guidance and Counselling, Educational Technology, Criminology and Police Administration, and Value Education. Dr. Alam is an active participant in global scholarly discourse. As Associate Editor of Frontiers in Education, he plays a pivotal role in curating and guiding intellectual contributions across the Educational, Pedagogical, and Learning Sciences. Concurrently, he serves as Founder and Director of Academic Chronicles Private Limited, where he orchestrates editorial board formation and develops strategic frameworks for peer-reviewed publishing in the Social, Behavioural, and Humanistic Sciences. His research has been disseminated through elite academic platforms, including Elsevier, Springer, Taylor & Francis, Wiley, Routledge, Sage, Emerald, and IEEE, and addresses a remarkably diverse array of topics such as pedagogical theories, educational administration, educational psychology, educational sociology, educational policy, technology-integrated learning, mathematics education, educational philosophy, educational technology, teacher education, and AI/ML in learning environments. Dr. Alam's scholarly rigor is further demonstrated by his success in qualifying multiple prestigious examinations including UGC-NET-JRF in both Education and Adult and Continuing Education, UGC- NET in Public Administration, and GATE in Humanities and Social Sciences. At the heart of Dr. Alam's intellectual ethos lies a steadfast belief in education as a catalytic and emancipatory force capable of engendering social justice, human flourishing, societal progress, and sustainable transformation. His recent explorations into 'Happiness Engineering' and holistic well- being in school ecosystems articulate a vision of education that transcends instrumentalist paradigms, prioritizing emotional intelligence, global consciousness, empathy, and psychosocial resilience among learners. His research agenda seeks to conceive educational praxis through the affordances of inclusive digital learning, gamified instructional design, and artificial intelligence (AIEd), thereby constructing robust, ethically grounded frameworks for 21st century education. At Alliance University, Dr. Alam remains committed to architecting pedagogical models that not only cultivate intellectual dexterity and cognitive excellence but also prepare learners for morally responsive leadership, intellectual nimbleness, and responsible global citizenship in an increasingly volatile, uncertain, complex, and ambiguous (VUCA) world.

Juan Manuel Castro is a full professor at Universidad Pontificia de Salamanca, Spain, specializing in language education, instructional innovation, and internationalization of higher education.

Alfred L. Guiffrida is an Associate Professor Emeritus of Management and Information Systems in the Department of Information Systems and Business Analytics at Kent State University and teaches in the areas of Operations and Supply Chain Management. He holds his Ph.D., M.S. and B.S. in Industrial Engineering from the State University of New York at Buffalo. His papers have been published in Applied Mathematical Modelling, The Engineering Economist, European Journal of Operational Research, Information Systems and Operational Research, International Journal of Integrated Supply Management, International Journal of Production Economics, International Journal of Production Research, and International Transactions in Operations Research.

Keshav Gupta is currently serving as a faculty member in the field of Computer Science and Engineering. He earned his Ph.D. from Delhi Technological University,

New Delhi, in 2020, with prior qualifications including an M.Tech. in Software Engineering from the same university and a B.Tech. from UIET, Kurukshetra University. His research interests include biometric systems, pattern recognition, image processing, and machine learning. Dr. Gupta has over five years of academic and research experience and has published extensively in reputed SCI-indexed international journals and conferences. He is also a contributor to book chapters and has a strong academic footprint in the domain of intelligent systems and secure biometrics.

Syed Tabrez Hassan is currently Associate Professor at School of Business, Adamas University, Kolkata, India. His research & teaching interest areas are Strategic Management, Business Analytics using R, Technology Strategy, Merger & Acquisitions, Gamification in Business, Business models of Sports & Entertainment, E-commerce and Sports Analytics. In his career spanning over 12 years, he has served at ICICI Lombard as Sales Manager in Hyderabad before joining the teaching assignment. He has attended 8 relevant courses for continuous learning including workshop arranged by Harvard Business School in India. He has also acted as resource person in Faculty Development Programs conducted by the University. He has keen interest in case-based learning and has authored the book titled as "Short Cases for Business Studies (ISBN 9781545702963). He is currently working on the book "Technology Strategy for Managers" for the MBA students.

Raj Kumar is a distinguished academic and seasoned researcher at Maharshi Dayanand University, with extensive experience in higher education, policy analysis, and interdisciplinary research. His scholarly interests span a broad range of subjects, including public administration, governance, education reform, and sustainable development. With a career dedicated to academic excellence and institutional growth, Prof. Kumar has published widely in national and international journals, contributing critical insights into the evolving dynamics of policy, ethics, and leadership in public systems. He is known for his mentorship, administrative acumen, and commitment to nurturing future scholars and professionals. At Maharshi Dayanand University, he plays a pivotal role in curriculum development, research supervision, and academic policy formation. Prof. Kumar's work consistently reflects a balance between theoretical rigor and practical relevance, aiming to drive meaningful change in academia and society. His contributions continue to shape scholarly discourse and inspire a new generation of researchers and educators.

Archan Mitra Dedicated and accomplished media and communication specialist with over 12 years of experience in academia, research, and industry. Expertise in teaching, research, and curriculum development, with significant contributions to the fields of journalism, mass communication, and environmental sustainability. Proven ability to lead interdisciplinary 4+ projects, such as the development of the GREEN MBA initiative for IIM Kashipur and World Bank and other digital education programs, showcasing a commitment to innovative pedagogy and sustainable practices. Published extensively, including 35+ Scopus-indexed articles and 10+ authored books on emerging topics such as artificial intelligence and media, New Media and digital transformation, Science Communication, and Environmental communication. Recognized for peer-review excellence with over 80+ journal reviews. Adept at leveraging advanced tools and technologies, including Adobe Creative Suite, SPSS, and multimedia platforms, to deliver impactful research and teaching outcomes. With specializing in NVIVO analysis. Strong academic leadership skills demonstrated through roles such as Research Coordinator and Media Centre In-Charge, enhancing institutional outreach, accreditation, and student success. Passionate about bridging traditional and digital media paradigms, fostering inclusive learning environments, and contributing to sustainable development through scholarly work.

Hitesh Mohapatra received the B.E. degree in Information Technology from Biju Patnaik University of Technology (BPUT), Odisha in 2006, and the MTech. Degree in CSE from Odisha University of Technology and Research (OUTR) University, Odisha in 2009. He received his Ph.D. in Computer Science & Engineering in 2021 from Veer Surendra Sai University of Technology (VSSUT), Burla, India. He has contributed 50+ SCI and Scopus indexed research articles. He has authored two books on Software Engineering and C Programming respectively. He has 15 years of teaching experience both in industry and academia. He has served the research community with various capacities like session chair, technical chair, keynote speaker etc. His research interests include wireless sensor network, smart city, smart grid and smart water. Currently he is working as Associate Professor at School of Computer Engineering, KIIT (Deemed to be) University, Bhubaneswar, Odisha, India

Ravi Shankar Poddar is a B.Tech Computer Science student at Sharda University. With experience in software and IoT development through internships, he has worked on diverse projects in web technologies and AI. Ravi is enthusiastic about software engineering and aims to contribute to meaningful technological advancements.

Carol Putman has been a faculty member at Penn State Behrend for 20 years. Prior to that, she worked for 10 years in the paper industry in process engineering and product development. At the start of her professional career, she earned her

MBA from Penn State. Her teaching areas include strategic product development, project management, statistics, and supply chain management. She also has an administrative role as the department chair for management and interdisciplinary programs in the Black School of Business at Penn State Behrend.

Franz Rodríguez Franky Professional with more than 15 years of experience, with more than 8 years in University Teaching. Research professor recognized by Minciencias. Master's Degree in Environmental Management and Auditing, Specialist in Administration and Management of Quality Systems from the University of Santo Tomas in agreement with ICONTEC, and Agricultural Engineer. Professional with the ability to integrate technical, administrative, economic and human resources of the field, educational, virtual LMS, Moodle and others. Knowledge of ISO, 9001, 14001 and 45001 Standards.

Ruma Roy is a dynamic media professional with a strong academic foundation in Mass Communication and Journalism, having earned her postgraduate degree from Visva Bharati University and a gold medal in her undergraduate studies. She brings a diverse portfolio of experiences, including roles as a content moderator at ByteDance and a social media expert at Immigration Ultimate. With hands-on expertise in SEO, content moderation, social media management, and customer service, she is also proficient in tools like Adobe Premiere Pro, Photoshop, Canva, and MS Office Suite. Ruma is a dedicated team player, known for her discipline, adaptability, and relentless drive to acquire new skills across domains. Outside her professional pursuits, she is an accomplished classical dancer and award-winning painter with accolades from institutions like Pracheen Kala Kendra. Ruma blends creativity with strategic communication, making her a valuable asset in any multidisciplinary team.

Mohit Sharma is an emerging scholar and academic writer specializing in the intersection of technology, ethics, and organizational transformation. With a strong foundation in business management and legal studies, he focuses on how artificial intelligence, corporate responsibility, and digital innovation shape modern professional landscapes. His recent work explores the integration of AI in legal education, socially responsible entrepreneurship, and the role of ethical leadership in sustainable development. Passionate about academic research and interdisciplinary inquiry, Mohit brings a nuanced perspective to the evolving challenges of the digital era. He has contributed to various book chapters and research projects that examine future-ready strategies in business, law, and education. Through his writing, Mohit seeks to bridge theory and practice, offering insights that are both intellectually rigorous and socially relevant. He continues to collaborate with thought leaders and academic institutions to advance knowledge that informs ethical, inclusive, and technology-driven transformation.

Shubham Sharma is currently pursuing a Bachelor of Technology in Computer Science and Engineering from Sharda University. He has completed internships in software and embedded systems development and has worked on various projects involving IoT, full-stack web development, and AI. He is passionate about problem-solving, software engineering, and contributing to innovative technology solutions. Shubham aspires to become a software engineer and is continuously learning to grow in the field.

Satya Subrahmanyam is a distinguished academic leader, researcher, and institutional strategist with over 27 years of experience in higher education, leadership, and research management. He holds two PhDs and a Postdoctoral qualification from the Polytechnic Institute of Leiria, Portugal. Currently serving as Professor and Dean (Research) at Holy Spirit University of Kaslik (USEK), Lebanon, he spearheads research initiatives that enhance academic excellence and institutional reputation. He played a pivotal role in the development of the Catholic University in Erbil, Kurdistan, where he established new departments, led research programs, and collaborated on international educational projects. As a founding member and Managing Partner of Vignan Institute of Technology and Management, India, he contributed to its transformation into a premier institution. With expertise in AI-driven business strategies, HR analytics, and leadership in technology adoption, he has published extensively, guided PhD research, and led training programs in corporate and academic settings.

Ionut R. Vlad is a second-year Business PhD student at Indiana University of Pennsylvania Eberly College of Business. He received a bachelor's degree in Supply Chain and Information Systems from Penn State University and a master's degree in Industrial Engineering from Clemson University. He has 15 years of practitioner experience in various supply chain roles, including his current role as a Senior Supply Chain Analyst for Kennametal Inc.

Index

Symbols

A

B

C

D

R

S

T

W

www.ingramcontent.com/pod-product-compliance
Lightning Source LLC
LaVergne TN
LVHW081320300926
849161LV00008B/1824
* 9 7 9 8 3 3 7 3 3 3 0 1 4 *